THE
PLAYWRIGHT'S
COMPANION
1999

THE PLAYWRIGHT'S COMPANION 1999

A Practical Guide to Script Opportunities in the U.S.A.

Compiled and introduced

by

Mollie Ann Meserve

Feedback Theatrebooks

Copyright © 1999 by Feedback Theatrebooks

Manufactured in the United States of America.

Feedback Theatrebooks
305 Madison Avenue, Suite 1146
New York, NY 10165

Order Department
Feedback Theatrebooks
P.O. Box 220, Naskeag Point
Brooklin, ME 04616

Phone: 207/359-2781
FAX: 207/359-5532
E-mail: feedback@hypernet.com

ISSN   0887-1507
ISBN   0-937657-47-6

Contents

The Playwright's Companion 1999

Here is the fifteenth annual edition of *The Playwright's Companion!* In its pages you'll find the most comprehensive and up-to-date information on opportunities for America's dramatic writers available today.

Each year, we survey nearly two thousand play producers and theatre companies from Broadway to regional repertories, from community theatres to college and university programs-- along with publishers, contest sponsors, literary agents, membership and support groups, organizations awarding grants and residencies and loans, new play workshops, script and career development programs, artists' colonies, new play festivals, and many more--to bring you as many choices as possible for your scripts and for your professional advancement.

You've already noticed that this 15th annual edition of *The Playwright's Companion* is also the 1999 edition. As the 20th Century draws to a close, this seems like a good time to reflect on the changes which have taken place since *The Playwright's Companion* first appeared in 1985.

Back then, we were the "new kid on the block" in the field of providing information for America's dramatic writers. *The Playwright's Companion 1985* was typed (tediously) on an ancient Olympus, photocopied and comb-bound at a little print-shop around the corner. That first *Playwright's Companion* was 170 pages long and listed 315 theatres and fewer than 100 contests. And that was it. Still, looking through that old edition, we can't help feeling a surge of pride--perhaps because we now know where that early effort would lead.

Today, we include approximately eight hundred theatres and producers and more than a thousand other opportunities-- awards, prizes, publications, grants, fellowships, workshops, festivals, support groups, service organizations, retreats, residencies, agency representation, and career training and development. Our page count is now in the neighborhood of 400. Despite the growth in size and content of *The Playwright's Companion*, the increase in paper and printing costs, and the costs of our four computer systems, we have increased the price of this book only once in our fifteen editions--and then by only $2.00!

In 1985, we sold fewer than 200 copies; the following year, 300 plus. Today, *The Playwright's Companion* is known around the world, and eagerly anticipated each December by loyal readers numbering in the thousands. With every new edition, we receive many kind comments from those readers, and over the years their support and encouragement have made our task of collecting and up-dating reams of data worthwhile.

Upon reflection, it seems that *The Playwright's Companion* has come of age during these last years of the century. As the century closes, we owe a sincere "Thank You!" to everyone who has so graciously responded to our surveys year after year, as well as to the readers who have made invaluable contributions in helping us keep *The Playwright's Companion* up to date.

Even with the approach of the New Millennium, some things do not change--"Submission Etiquette," for example. If you are a regular reader of *The Playwright's Companion* or an old hand at submissions, you're undoubtedly aware of the rules, but it never hurts to review them.

The Cardinal Rule: If you want your materials returned to you, enclose a self-addressed mailer--with adequate postage! And here are some other frequently repeated admonitions from those who will be deciding the fate of your plays:

"Use *Professional Playscript Format* only!"
"Type your play on only one side of the paper!"
"Send a clean, new photocopy--not the original."
"Bind your play in a clean folder!"
"Heed our guidelines and regulations!"
"Include character and technical breakdowns in your
    synopsis!"
"Include your contact information with your submission!"
"Include SASE or SASP for our response!"
"Give us time to read your script before you follow up!"

And here are our tips to help you use *The Playwright's Companion 1999*:

The Playwright's Companion comprises seven main sections of entries, a cross reference, a deadline calendar, a bibliography, a submission record, and an index to the listings.

The major sections are Theatres and Production Companies, Contests, Special Programs, Publishers, Agents, College and University Playwriting Programs, and State Arts Councils.

Each major section is arranged in alphabetical order, using the first letter of the organization's name or title. Articles (a, an, the) are not used in alphabetizing unless they are a vital part of the name. When an organization bears the name of a person, it is alphabetized under the person's first name.

"Submission policy" or "Procedure" tells you what materials will be accepted. When more than one type of submission is welcome (i.e., query/synopsis; professional recommendation), you may choose whichever method you prefer. Types of submissions are separated by semi-colons. Materials to be sent together are separated by commas. "Best time" refers to the time of year when submissions are encouraged. If this heading does not appear, you may assume that submissions are welcome year-round.

"Deadline," unless followed by the word "postmark," indicates the date by which materials must be received. You should request all guidelines well in advance, as dates and other details may be changed without notice. Before entering into an agreement with a producer or publisher, be sure you understand the terms of "Remuneration" (any payment you receive) and "Future commitment" (options, percentages of future royalties, future program credit and other requirements placed upon you after your work is produced or published). When both remuneration and commitment are negotiable, we refer to them as "Terms."

In the Cross-Reference to Special Interests, you'll find a number of topics on which many of the theatres and organizations place particular emphasis. (For information on our expanded cross-reference, see the description of *Etcetera, Etcetera, Etcetera!* in the back of this book.) The Deadline Calendar provides specific, announced deadlines for the 1999 calendar year.

We hope that this new edition of *The Playwright's Companion* will serve you well and that your career as a writer for the theatre will bring you many rewarding experiences in 1999 and beyond.

M.A.M.

✓   The Playwright's Checklist   ✓
of Submission Methods and Materials

☐ *Agent Submission.* A referral or submission on behalf of a playwright whom the agent has agreed to represent professionally.

☐ *Bio.* An informal statement giving details of the playwright's professional activities, achievements, and education, including mention of productions, publications and awards.

☐ *Character Breakdown.* That part of the synopsis which lists the characters and indicates their gender, ages, relationships with each other, special skills required of the actors, and, if required by the play, physical characteristics.

☐ *Dialogue Sample.* A brief (5-10 pages unless otherwise specified), carefully selected excerpt which best reveals the central conflict, pace, dialogue, characterization, and mood of the play. (Tip: Opening scenes are not usually the best samples, but they should be sent if requested.)

☐ *Professional Playscript Format.* The standard format in which plays intended for the stage are typed and presented to potential producers, publishers, and other organizations. (For information on obtaining *Professional Playscript Format Guidelines*, see the back of this book.)

☐ *Professional Recommendation.* A letter of recommendation accompanied by a query/synopsis or script with the playwright's resume or bio, or an informal referral from a theatre professional (director, artistic director, literary manager or playwriting teacher) to a producer or other organization on behalf of a playwright or a particular play.

☐ *Query.* A brief, polite and business-like letter, addressed to an individual by name, introducing the play by title, explaining why the play might be appropriate for this particular theatre or organization, and indicating a willingness to provide the full script upon request.

(Tip: Compose your own query letters, rather than use a form letter. Writing an individual letter to a person and showing a knowledge of the recipient's specific interests and policies will make a good first impression.)

☐ *Query/Synopsis.* A query letter accompanied by a synopsis of the play (see below).

☐ *Resume.* A comprehensive, formal listing, usually in outline form, detailing professional activities and achievements, beginning with the present and working backward chronologically. The resume should include information on education (school, dates, degrees earned), employment (employer, job title or brief desciption of duties, dates), and theatrical experience including plays produced or published and awards received.

☐ *SASE.* 1.) A #10 business envelope, addressed to the playwright and bearing first class postage (not metered postage, loose stamps, or coins), which is sent along with submitted materials in order for the recipient to respond. (Tip: Even if an organization does not state that the SASE is a requirement, it is a good idea to include one.)

2.) A sturdy mailer, large enough to accommodate any materials to be returned (script, cassette tape, videotape, etc.) and bearing sufficient stamps (not metered postage, loose stamps, or money). This SASE must accompany all materials which the playwright wants returned but should not be sent to organizations which state that they do not return materials.

☐ *SASP.* A stamped postcard, addressed to the playwright, which is sent with submitted material for one of two purposes: to be returned in confirmation that a submission has been received; or, to be returned with the recipient's response.

☐ *Synopsis.* A brief and comprehensive description of the play, including character and technical breakdowns and a concise, scene-by-scene summary of the action. (Tip: Don't be mysterious about the ending in an attempt to make the reader want to read the play. It is the ending which gives the play its meaning, and the reader will want to know this in order to make a knowledgeable decision.)

☐ *Technical Breakdown.* That part of the synopsis which indicates the number of acts and scenes, briefly describes all locales and set changes, and provides details of any unusual technical requirements (special lighting and/or sound effects, period costumes, extraordinary props and set pieces).

• **Tip: All submitted materials should be typed on one side only of high quality 8.5"x11" white paper.**

-- NOTE --

The U.S. Copyright Office has announced that the filing fee for registering a work for copyright (currently $20) may change as of July 1, 1999. For information on copyright, or to request Form PA for registering a dramatic work, write to Register of Copyrights, Library of Congress, Washington, D.C. 20559; or phone (202) 707-3000 for information, or (202) 707-9100 for forms. Information and forms are also available through the Library of Congress's web page at <www.loc.gov>.

Key To Quick Reference Symbols

ℵ   A New listing in *The Playwright's Companion*.

ℜ   An organization previously closed to submissions, newly restored to *The Playwright's Companion*.

F-l   Full-length plays

1-   One-act plays and/or short plays

Tr   Translations

Ad   Adaptations

♪   Musicals

CY   Children's plays

12+   Teen issues, teenaged actors

Rv   Revues

1p   One-person shows

P   Premieres

2d   Second productions (works which have been produced elsewhere)

C   Contemporary, social, political issues

x   Experimental, avant garde, innovative, non-traditional works

mm   Multimedia, multidisciplinary works

Rg   Regional or local playwrights and/or themes

cm   Comedies, farces, satires

dr   Dramas

my   Mysteries, suspense, thrillers

po   Poetry, verse dramas

L   Language

Am   American playwrights and/or themes

B   Biographies

H   Historical topics

Cl   Classical material

V   Variety shows (vaudeville, skits, clowns, mime, puppets)

†   Christian/religious themes

❄   Holiday and seasonal themes

Sp	Spiritual themes; works which lift or celebrate the human spirit
J	Jewish playwrights and/or themes
W	Women playwrights, women's issues, roles for women
Œ	European (including UK) culture and themes, residency in Europe
Sn	Works for older actors and/or audiences
Y	Young playwrights
Fm	Works suitable for family and/or conservative audiences
🚚	Some shows (in some cases all shows) tour
h/d	Health/disability
M	Multicultural and/or minority playwrights, themes, casts
NA	Native American playwrights and/or themes
Af	African-American playwrights and/or themes
As	Asian or Asian-American playwrights, themes, casts
Hi	Hispanic/Latino playwrights and/or themes
Esp	Works written in Spanish, residency in Spanish-speaking country
Fr	Works written in French, residency in French-speaking country
g/l	Gay and/or lesbian playwrights and/or themes
D	Works for development, developmental theatre or program
Lc	Large casts (25 or more)
Pl	Stage plays and playwrights (in addition to other genres/writers)
S	Screenplays
Tv	Teleplays
Rd	Radio plays
F	Festival, convention, or conference presenting new works
Rs	Residency or artists' colony
g/f	Grant, fellowship, or other financial support
Mb	Membership organization
Sv	Service organization
i	Information service
ws	Writer's work space
G	An agent with general interests
$	An organization which charges a submission or application fee

Theatres

and

Production Companies

Mini-Checklist

What to Send to

Theatres and Production Companies

With a query/synopsis:
- ☐ A cover letter.
- ☐ A play synopsis, including character and technical breakdowns and a summary of the play's action.
- ☐ A script history: previous productions, workshops, readings, publications, awards. Include favorable reviews.
- ☐ A dialogue sample.
- ☐ Your resume or bio.
- ☐ Your SASP or #10 SASE for response.

With an unsolicited script:
- ☐ A cover letter.
- ☐ A new copy of the script, typed in *Professional Playscript Format* and securely bound in a sturdy folder.
- ☐ A cassette tape of original music used in the play.
- ☐ A succinct play synopsis.
- ☐ A script history: previous productions, workshops, readings, publications, awards. Include favorable reviews.
- ☐ Your resume or bio.
- ☐ Your SASP or #10 SASE for response.
- ☐ Your SASE for all materials you want returned.
- ☐ Any additional materials requested.

With a solicited script:
- ☐ A cover letter (politely reminding the reader that he or she requested the play).
- ☐ A new copy of the script, typed in *Professional Playscript Format* and securely bound in a sturdy folder.
- ☐ A cassette tape of original music used in the play.
- ☐ A succinct play synopsis.
- ☐ A script history: previous productions, workshops, readings, publications, awards. Include favorable reviews.
- ☐ Your resume or bio.
- ☐ Your SASP or #10 SASE for response.
- ☐ Your SASE for all materials you want returned.
- ☐ Any additional materials requested.

Theatres and
Production Companies

A CONTEMPORARY   F-l Tr Ad ♪ 2d Rg C L M Rs
THEATRE 700 Union St., Seattle, WA 98101-2330 (206) 292-7660
FAX (206) 292-7670 **Contact:** Liz Engelman, Literary Mgr. **Theatre:** professional **Works:** full-length plays, translations, adaptations, musicals **2nd productions:** yes **Special interests:** "Pacific Northwest playwrights only; contemporary issues, theatrical imagination, vibrant language, diverse voices, no 'kitchen sink' drama." **Stages:** thrust, 390 seats; arena, 390 seats; cabaret, 150 seats **Submission policy:** professional recommendation; agent submission; query/1-page synopsis with 10-page dialogue sample and resume **Best time:** Sept.-Apr. **Response:** 1 month query; 6-8 months solicited script **Your chances:** 500 new scripts read annually/usually 1 produced **Remuneration:** royalties, possible residency **Programs:** script development, Young ACT Co., children's workshops; First ACT (see Special Programs)

A NOISE WITHIN   Tr Ad Cl 2d
234 S. Brand Blvd., Glendale, CA 91204 (818) 546-1449 FAX (818) 240-3004 **Contact:** Art Manke, Artistic Co-Director **Theatre:** professional **Works:** translations, adaptations **2nd productions:** yes **Exclusive interest:** classics **Stage:** thrust, 144 seats **Submission policy:** unsolicited script; query/synopsis **Best time:** fall **Response:** 6-8 months

A.D. PLAYERS   F-l 1- Tr Ad ♪ CY 2d † ⊐
2710 W. Alabama, Houston, TX 77098 (713) 439-0181 **e-mail** adplayers@hotmail.com **Contact:** Bill Shryock, Director, Special Projects **Theatre:** professional **Works:** full-length plays, one-acts, translations, adaptations, musicals, children's plays **2nd productions:** yes **Exclusive interest:** "Christian world view." **Specifications:** maximum cast: 20, 10 or fewer preferred; no fly space; low ceiling **Tours:** yes **Stages:** proscenium, 220 seats; rotunda, 200 seats **Casting:** Equity, non-Equity **Audience:** "Conservative." **Submission policy:** unsolicited script; query/synopsis **Best time:** early fall **Response:** 6-8 months query; 8-10 months script **Your chances:** 100 new scripts read annually/usually 1-2 produced **Remuneration:** negotiable **Future commitment:** credit **Programs:** staged readings, classes

ABINGDON THEATRE COMPANY   D Mb F-l cm dr
P.O. Box 110 Radio City Station, New York, NY 10101-0110 (212) 802-8383 **Contact:** Ray Atherton, Literary Mgr. **Theatre:** professional, membership **Works:** full-length plays, works-in-progress **Special interests:** "Work that portrays people grappling with crises, tragic or comic; plays told truthfully, with great energy and fully developed characters and relationships." **Submission policy:** unsolicited script; professional recommendation; agent submission **Response:** 6 months **Programs:** Actors Workshops (playwrights and directors welcome;

inquire for time and place); Abingdon Theatre Co. Bi-Weekly Readings and Staged Readings (see Special Programs) **Advice:** "Projects with appeal to and enrichment of a broad audience. We are open to all forms and styles." **Comment:** Members pay no dues or fees but are expected to devote time and energy to the company and its productions.

♫ ABOUT FACE THEATRE   D F-l 1- Tr Ad 2d g/l ⌧
3212 N. Broadway, Chicago, IL 60657 (773) 549-7943 FAX (773) 935-4483 e-mail faceline1@aol.com **Contact:** Carl Hippensteel, Literary Mgr. **Theatre:** professional, developmental **Works:** full-length plays, one-acts, shorts, translations, adaptations, musicals **Exclusive interests:** "Gay/lesbian and bisexual writers and themes, especially lesbian plays." **Stage:** flexible thrust, 99 seats **Tours:** "Occasionally." **Submission policy:** query/synopsis, cast list, 1st 10 pages of dialogue, resume; agent submission encouraged **Response:** 1 month query; 3 months solicited script **Programs:** Playreading Series (inquire); Face to Face Workshop Series (see Special Programs)

ABRAHAM LINCOLN CABIN THEATRE/   F-l 1- 2d H Am
GROVES THEATRE AMERICANA   8768 Desert Willow,
Morongo Valley, CA 92256 (760) 363-6126 **Contact:** Joy Groves, Producer **Theatre:** professional **Works:** full-length plays, one-acts (1 hour±) **2nd productions:** yes **Special interests:** "Historical subjects, mainly 19th-century America." **Submission policy:** unsolicited script **Response:** 2 months

ACACIA THEATRE   Milwaukee, WI   This theatre is no longer open to submissions.

THE ACADEMY PLAYHOUSE   F-l Tr Ad ♪ CY 2d
P.O. Box 1843, 120 Main St., Orleans, MA 02653 (508) 255-3075 FAX (508) 255-5509 e-mail apa@capecod.net **Contact:** Peter Earle, Interim Art. Director **Theatre:** community **Works:** full-length plays, translations, adaptations, musicals, children's plays **2nd productions:** "Possibly." **Specifications:** maximum cast: 15; no more than 2 sets, unit set preferred; no wing/fly space **Stage:** 3/4 thrust, 162 seats **Casting:** Equity, non-Equity **Submission policy:** query/synopsis, dialogue sample; commission **Best time:** late fall-early winter **Response:** 3 weeks query; 3 months solicited script **Your chances:** 30 new scripts read annually/usually 1-2 produced **Remuneration:** negotiable **Programs:** readings, staged readings, worskhops **Advice:** "Work like you were living in the early days of a better nation." **Comment:** Submissions are not returned.

ACADEMY THEATRE   F-l 1- C Rg $
501 Means St. NW, Atlanta, GA 30318 (404) 525-4111 FAX (404) 525-3659 e-mail academytheatre@mindspring.com **Contact:** Frank Wittow, Artistic Director **Theatre:** professional **Works:** full-length plays, one-

acts **Special interests:** plays-in-progress; issues; Southeastern writers **Submission policy:** unsolicited script, bio, fee (full-length: $20; 20 minutes: $10), SASP; query/synopsis **Response:** 3 months

ACT I PRESENTATIONS Leonia, NJ This company is no longer open to submissions.

THE ACTING COMPANY F-l 1- Tr Ad ♪ Cl po L ⊐
P.O. Box 898 Times Square Station, New York, NY 10108 (212) 564-3510 FAX (212) 714-2643 e-mail mail@theactingcompany.org **Contact:** Margot Harley, Producing Director **Theatre:** professional **Works:** full-length plays, one-acts, translations, adaptations, musicals **Special interests:** "Classics; new works for ensemble of 8 men, 3 women, 24-45; poetic dimension, heightened language." **Specifications:** simple demands; set must tour **Submission policy:** professional recommendation **Best time:** Nov.-Jan. **Response:** 3 months

ACTHEATER Anniston, AL Mail addressed to this theatre has been returned as undeliverable; the phone has been disconnected.

ACTORS ALL EY F-l 1- Tr Ad CY 2d Rg
5269 Lankershim Blvd., N. Hollywood, CA 91601 (818) 508-4200 FAX (818) 508-5113 **Contact:** Jeremiah Morris, Art. Director **Theatre:** professional **Works:** full-length plays, one-acts, translations, adaptations, children's plays **2nd productions:** yes **Special interests:** "New plays, West Coast premieres; area writers; small cast for StoreFront." **Casting:** Equity, non-Equity **Stages:** proscenium/thrust, 350 seats; flexible, 99 seats; StoreFront, 42 seats **Submission policy:** unsolicited script with synopsis **Best time:** Nov. **Response:** 1 year **Your chances:** 250 new scripts read annually/usually 2-4 produced **Remuneration:** $500-$600 **Program:** Actors Alley Reading Series (see Special Programs)

ACTORS ALLIANCE THEATRE CO. F-l Ad CY 2d C x ⊐
P.O. Box 1579, Royal Oak, MI 48068-1579 (248) 559-4100 FAX (248) 552-1225 **Contact:** Jeffrey Nahan, Founding Artistic Director **Theatre:** professional **Works:** full-length plays, adaptations, children's plays **2nd productions:** yes **Special interests:** issues; new forms **Specifications:** single or unit set; no fly or wing space **Tours:** yes **Stages:** thrust, 499 seats; flexible, 49 seats **Audience:** "Upper middle class." **Submission policy:** query/synopsis; professional recommendation **Best time:** Oct.-Feb. **Response:** 1-6 months **Your chances:** 30-60 new scripts read annually/usually 1 produced **Remuneration:** royalty

ACTORS & PLAYWRIGHTS' INITIATIVE F-l 1- Ad 2d Rg C
API Theatre, P.O. Box 50051, Kalamazoo, MI 49005-0051 (616) 343-8090 FAX (616) 343-8310 **Contact:** Robert C. Walker, Artistic Director **Theatre:** professional **Works:** full-length plays, one-acts, adaptations **2nd productions:** yes **Exclusive interest:** writers residing in IL, IN,

MI, OH, WI, Ontario **Specifications:** maximum cast: 8; single set **Stage:** thrust, 75 seats **Casting:** non-Equity **Audience:** "Academic, liberal, professional." **Submission policy:** query/synopsis, videotape, resume; professional recommendation **Best time:** Oct.-May **Response:** 90 days **Your chances:** 30+ new scripts read annually/usually 4 produced **Remuneration:** negotiable **Programs:** staged readings, development **Advice:** "Keep it simple. Don't avoid provocation, political/social subjects."

ACTORS ART THEATRE ENSEMBLE   1-
AAT, 6128 Wilshire Blvd. #110, Los Angeles, CA 90048 **Contact:** Literary Mgr. **Theatre:** professional **Works:** one-acts (20 minutes maximum), excerpts **Special interests:** themes change; inquire **Specifications:** maximum cast: 6; 2 (ages 28-45) preferred **Stage:** black box, 32 seats **Casting:** Equity **Submission policy:** query/dialogue sample **Response:** 3 weeks

ACTOR'S COMPANY OF PENNSYLVANIA   F-l ♪ 2d C
P.O. Box 1865, Lancaster, PA 17608-1865 (717) 394-7133 FAX (717) 397-3780 **Contact:** Artistic Director **Theatre:** professional **Works:** full-length plays, musicals **2nd productions:** yes **Special interest:** contemporary themes **Specifications:** maximum cast: 10; unit set **Stage:** proscenium, 684 seats **Submission policy:** query/synopsis; professional recommendation; agent submission **Response:** 3 weeks query; 4 months solicited script **Your chances:** 200-300 new scripts read annually/ usually 1 produced

THE ACTOR'S EXPRESS   F-l Tr Ad ♪
King Plow Arts Center Suite J-107, 887 W. Marietta St. NW, Atlanta, GA 30318 (404) 875-1606 FAX (404) 875-2791 **Contact:** Literary Mgr. **Theatre:** professional **Works:** full-length plays, translations, adaptations, musicals **Specifications:** small cast; minimal set changes; no fly space **Stage:** black box, 150 seats **Casting:** non-Equity **Submission policy:** query/synopsis; professional recommendation **Best time:** Nov.-Jan. **Response:** 1 month query; 4-6 months solicited script

ACTORS FORUM THEATRE   F-l 1- ♪ 2d cm dr C my
10655 Magnolia Blvd., N. Hollywood, CA 91601 (818) 506-0600 FAX (213) 465-6898 e-mail audsin@aol.com **Contact:** Audrey Marlyn Singer, Artistic Director **Theatre:** professional **Works:** full-length plays, one-acts, musicals **2nd productions:** yes **Special interests:** "Comedy; socially relevant drama; mystery." **Casting:** Equity, non-Equity **Submission policy:** unsolicited script **Remuneration:** no **Program:** Actors Forum Theatre Workshop (see Special Programs)

♫ ACTORS' GANG THEATER   F-l CY C x
6201 Santa Monica Blvd., Hollywood, CA 90038 (213) 465-0566 FAX (213) 467-1246 e-mail actorsgng1@aol.com   **Contact:** Steve Porter, Submissions Coord. **Theatre:** professional **Works:** full-length plays,

children's plays **Special interests:** political themes, avant-garde works, theatricality **Stages:** 2 flexible spaces, 99, 40 seats **Procedure:** professional recommendation; agent submission **Response:** 2 months

ACTORS' PLAYHOUSE
F-l Tr Ad ♪ CY 2d C cm

280 Miracle Mile, Coral Gables, FL 33134 (305) 444-9293 FAX (305) 444-4181 Contact: George Contini (full-length plays); Earl Maulding (children's shows) **Theatre:** professional **Works:** full-length plays, translations, adaptations, musicals, children's musicals **2nd productions:** yes **Special interests:** "Mainstream, contemporary comedies and musicals; children's musicals." **Stages:** proscenium, 600 seats; flexible, 300 seats **Casting:** Equity, non-Equity **Submission policy:** unsolicited script, synopsis, letter of professional recommendation **Best time:** May-Sept. **Response:** 6 months **Future commitment:** negotiable **Programs:** National Children's Theatre Festival (see Contests); Actors' Playhouse Playreading Series (see Special Programs)

ACTORS THEATRE
F-l 1- Tr Ad ♪ CY 2d Cl Fm ▭

P.O. Box 780, Talent, OR 97540-0780 (541) 535-5250 Theatre: community/professional **Contact:** Peter Alzado, Artistic Director **Works:** full-length plays, one-acts, translations, adaptations, musicals, children's plays **2nd productions:** yes **Special interest:** "Adaptations of classics and children's books." **Specifications:** maximum cast: 16; unit set preferred **Tours:** "Yes, especially ." **Stage:** thrust, 108 seats **Casting:** 1 Equity Guest Artist per season, non-Equity, students **Audience:** "Love the new, the bizarre, the challenging; also a strong family audience-- community, socially, environmentally conscious." **Submission policy:** query/synopsis, 10-page dialogue sample, resume **Response:** 3 months query; 4 months solicited script **Your chances:** 75 new scripts read annually/usually 1 produced; 2 receive readings **Remuneration:** $50 for reading; $50/$25 royalty for production **Future commitment:** "1% for 5 years." **Programs:** script development **Advice:** "Be willing to rewrite."

ACTORS THEATRE OF LOUISVILLE
F-l 1- Tr Ad 2d L x cm

316 W. Main St., Louisville, KY 40402-4218 (502) 584-1265 Contact: Michael Bigelow Dixon, Literary Mgr. **Theatre:** professional **Works:** full-length plays, one-acts, translations, adaptations **2nd productions:** yes **Special interests:** ideas, language, experimentation, humor **Maximum cast:** 15 **Stages:** thrust, 637 seats; arena, 310 seats; 3/4 arena, 159 seats **Audience:** "Louisville community." **Submission policy:** professional recommendation **Best time:** Mar.-Oct. **Response:** 6+ months; most scripts returned in fall **Your chances:** 2500 new scripts read annually/usually 30 produced **Remuneration:** "Dramatists Guild contracts." **Future commitment:** negotiable **Programs:** National Ten-Minute Play Contest (see Contests); Flying Solo and Friends, Humana Festival (see Actors Theatre of Louisville Programs in Special Programs)

ACTORS' THEATRE OF WASHINGTON F-l 1- Tr Ad ♪ 1p 2d C x $
c/o 1625 Q St. NW #106, Washington, DC 20009 e-mail safford@aol.com **Contact:** Paul MacWhorter, Mng./Literary Director **Theatre:** professional **Works:** full-length plays, one-acts, translations, adaptations, musicals, monologues **2nd productions:** yes **Special interests:** "Social/cultural issues; unconventional work." **Stage:** proscenium, 125 seats **Casting:** non-Equity **Audience:** "Sophisticated, 18-50." **Submission policy:** unsolicited script, $5 fee; query/synopsis, dialogue sample; professional recommendation; agent submission; resume, script history with all material **Remuneration:** fee **Future commitment:** for world premiere **Programs:** readings, workshops; Act Out (see Contests)

THE ACTORS THEATRE WORKSHOP F-l 1- 2d
145 W. 28th St., New York, NY 10001 (212) 947-1386 FAX (212) 947-0642 Contact: Jeanne T. Korn, Literary Mgr. **Theatre:** professional **Works:** full-length plays, one-acts **2nd productions:** yes **Submission policy:** unsolicited script **Response:** 3-6 months

ADOBE THEATRE COMPANY F-l 1- Ad 2d x cm
453 W. 16th St., New York, NY 10011 (212) 352-0441 FAX same, call first **Contact:** Jordan Schildcrout, Literary Mgr. **Theatre:** professional **Works:** full-length plays, one-acts, adaptations **2nd productions:** yes **Special interest:** unconventional comedies **Stage:** flexible, 75 seats **Submission policy:** query/synopsis, dialogue sample **Response:** 4 months

ADVENTURE THEATRE CY Ad 2d Cl
7300 MacArthur Blvd., Glen Echo, MD 20812 (301) 320-5331 FAX (301) 320-3268 Contact: Carol Leahy, President **Theatre:** children's, theatre **2nd productions:** yes **Special interest:** "Must be appropriate for children, nice if there is a lesson taught." **Specifications:** maximum cast: 10-12; no more than 2 sets; limited wing space, no fly space **Tours:** yes **Stage:** proscenium, 193 seats **Casting:** non-Equity, students, children **Audience:** "Prefers classical literature; developing audience for more contemporary plays." **Submission policy:** query/synopsis **Best time:** spring **Response:** 2 months **Your chances:** 12-24 new scripts read annually; usually 1-2 produced, latest in Apr. 1998 **Remuneration:** "Royalties, from $15 per performance." **Program:** staged readings

AFRICA ARTS THEATER CO. F-l 1- 2d Af
660 Riverside Dr., New York, NY 10031 (212) 281-4880 FAX same, call first **Contact:** Adusah Boakye, Art. Dir. **Theatre:** off off Broadway **Works:** full-length plays, one-acts **2nd productions:** yes **Exclusive interests:** African, African-American writers, themes **Casting:** Equity, non-Equity **Submission policy:** query/synopsis **Response:** 2 months

AFRICAN GLOBE THEATREWORKS F-l 2d Af
1028 Broad St., Newark, NJ 07102 (973) 624-1584 FAX (973) 624-6333 Theatre: professional **Works:** full-length plays **2nd productions:**

yes **Exclusive interests:** African and African-American playwrights and themes **Maximum cast:** 10 **Submission policy:** unsolicited script **Best time:** summer-fall **Response:** 3 months **Program:** workshops

ALABAMA SHAKESPEARE FESTIVAL · F-l Tr Ad Rg

1 Festival Dr., Montgomery, AL 36117-4605 (334) 271-5300 FAX (334) 271-5342 e-mail Pr4bard@wsnet.com **Contact:** Jennifer Hebblethwaite, Literary Assoc. **Theatre:** professional **Works:** full-length plays, translations, adaptations **2nd productions:** yes **Special interests:** Southern writers, Southern issues **Specifications:** maximum cast: 20; no more than 3-4 sets **Stages:** modified thrust, 750 seats; flexible, 225 seats **Casting:** Equity **Submission policy:** query/synopsis, 3-5 page dialogue sample **Response:** 6 weeks query; 9-12 months solicited script **Your chances:** 500 new scripts read annually/2 produced **Remuneration:** royalty **Programs:** staged readings, development **Advice:** "Southern Writers' Project is the main arm of our new play program."

ALBERT POLAND, PRODUCER · F-l ♪

311 W. 43rd St., New York, NY 10036 (212) 956-7050 FAX (212) 956-0097 **Production company:** professional **Works:** full-length plays, musicals **Submission policy:** unsolicited script; query/synopsis; professional recommendation; agent submission

ALCAZAR THEATRE · F-l Tr Ad ♪ CY Rv C

650 Geary St., San Francisco, CA 94102 (415) 441-6655 FAX (415) 441-9567 **Contact:** Alan Ramos, Mng. Director **Theatre:** off Broadway **Works:** full-length plays, translations, adaptations, musicals, children's plays, revues **Special interests:** political work, musicals **Maximum cast:** 16 **Stages:** black box, 75 seats; proscenium, 500 seats; cabaret, 500 seats **Audience:** "All ethnic groups, 25-60." **Submission policy:** unsolicited script; query/synopsis, dialogue sample; professional recommendation; agent submission **Response:** 1 month query; 6-8 months script **Your chances:** 400 new scripts read annually/usually 2 produced **Remuneration:** "4-6%." **Future commitment:** 12-month option **Program:** Alcazar Staged Readings (see Special Programs)

ALLENBERRY PLAYHOUSE · ♪

P.O. Box 7, Boiling Springs, PA 17007 (717) 258-3211 **Contact:** Richard Frost, Artistic Director **Theatre:** professional Equity stock **Works:** musicals **2nd productions:** yes **Maximum cast:** 8 **Submission policy:** query/1-page synopsis, cassette tape **Best time:** winter

ALLEY THEATRE · F-l Tr Ad ♪ 2d Cl

615 Texas Ave., Houston, TX 77002 (713) 228-9341 **Contact:** Gregory Boyd, Artistic Director **Theatre:** professional **Works:** full-length plays, translations, adaptations, musicals **2nd productions:** yes **Special interests:** "Classics." **Casting:** Equity **Stages:** thrust, 800 seats; arena, 300 seats **Submission policy:** professional recommendation; agent submission

ALLIANCE REPERTORY COMPANY   F-l 1- Tr Ad 2d x Rs
3204 W. Magnolia Blvd., Burbank, CA 91505 (818) 566-7935 FAX
(213) 876-4673 Contact: Steve Liska, Dramaturge Theatre: professional
Works: full-length plays, one-acts, translations, adaptations 2nd productions: if CA, West Coast premieres Special interests: experimental
works Specifications: unit set, small budget Casting: Equity, non-
Equity Stage: flexible, 50 seats Submission policy: unsolicited script;
query/synopsis, 10-page dialogue sample; professional recommendation;
agent submission; script history, resume with all material Response: 2-
10 weeks Your chances: 350 new scripts read annually/usually 15 produced Remuneration: negotiable; travel, housing, per diem for residency
Program: The Alliance Writer's Project (see Special Programs)

ALLIANCE THEATRE COMPANY   F-l Ad ♪ CY 2d M
1280 Peachtree St. NE, Atlanta, GA 30309 (404) 733-4650 FAX (404)
733-4625 e-mail shumeg@woodruff-arts.org Contact: Megan Shultz,
Literary Asst. Theatre: professional Works: full-length plays, adaptations, musicals, children's plays 2nd productions: yes Special interests: "Works that speak to a culturally diverse community; compelling
stories, engaging characters." Stages: proscenium, 864 seats; flexible, 200
seats Submission policy: query/synopsis, dialogue sample; professional
recommendation Best time: Mar.-Sept. Response:1-3 months Your
chances: 200 new scripts read annually/usually 0-1 produced, latest in
Feb. 1998 Future commitment: negotiable Program: staged readings

♫ ALPHA-OMEGA THEATRE PROJECT   F-l ♪ 2d
4400 Holly, Kansas City, MO 64111 (816) 931-1189 Contact: Jamie
Rich, Producer Theatre: professional Works: full-length plays, musicals
2nd productions: yes Maximum cast: 6 Submission policy: unsolicited script Response: 2 months Program: workshops

AMAS MUSICAL THEATRE   ♪ 2d M
450 W. 42nd St.Suite 2J, New York, NY 10036 (212) 563-2565 FAX
(212) 268-5501 Contact: Donna Trinkoff, Producing Director Theatre:
professional Works: musicals 2nd productions: yes Special interest:
"Original works; multiracial casts." Maximum cast: 15 Stages: 74-99
seats Casting: Equity, non-Equity Submission policy: unsolicited
script, resume, script history; videotape; agent submission; commission
Best time: summer, winter Response: 6 months Your chances: usually
2 new works produced annually; 10 receive staged readings Remuneration: negotiable Future commitment: 1% Program: The Six
O'Clock Musical Theatre Lab (see Special Programs)

AMERICAN CABARET THEATRE   Rv Am P
401 E. Michigan St., Indianapolis, IN 46204 (317) 631-0334 FAX
(317) 686-5443 Contact: Mary Lou Szczesiul, Assoc. Director Theatre:
professional Works: cabaret/revues Special interests: "Original
revues on American themes; revues which accentuate and investigate the

origins of cabaret." **Specifications:** cast size: 6-12; limited fly and wing space **Stages:** 2 prosceniums 400, 150 seats **Submission policy:** professional recommedation preferred; query/synopsis **Best time:** Jul.-Sept. **Response:** 1-2 months query; 2-3 months solicited script

AMERICAN CONSERVATORY THEATER   F-l Tr Ad
30 Grant Ave. 6th Floor, San Francisco, CA 94108-5800 (415) 439-2445 FAX (415) 834-3360 Contact: Paul Walsh, Literary Mgr. **Theatre:** professional **Works:** full-length plays, translations, adaptations **Stage:** proscenium, 1000 seats **Casting:** Equity **Submission policy:** query/synopsis, 10-page dialogue sample from theatre professional or agent **Response:** 3 months query; 6 months solicited script

AMERICAN JEWISH THEATRE   F-l Tr Ad ♪ 2d J
307 W. 26th St., New York, NY 10001 (212) 633-9797 Contact: Ned Levinson, Literary Mgr. **Theatre:** professional **Works:** full-length plays, translations, adaptations, musicals **2nd productions:** yes **Exclusive interest:** Jewish themes **Maximum cast:** 8 **Stage:** black box, 150 seats **Submission policy:** unsolicited script; professional recommendation **Response:** 3 months **Your chances:** 150 new scripts read annually/usually 4-5 produced **Future commitment:** yes

AMERICAN LIVING HISTORY THEATER   1- 1p 2d H Am
P.O. Box 752, Greybull, WY 82426 (307) 765-9449 Contact: Dorene Ludwig, Artistic Director **Theatre:** professional **Works:** one-acts, 1-person plays **2nd productions:** yes **Exclusive interests:** "American historical and literary characters and events; primary source material only." **Specifications:** cast size: 1-2 preferred; 35-60 minutes; no set, few props **Stage:** "Any location--from classroom or living room to amphitheater." **Audience:** "Junior high-adult, all ethnic groups and educational levels." **Submission policy:** query/synopsis, SASP **Response:** 6 months **Your chances:** 20-35 new scripts read annually/"rarely produce outside work" **Terms:** negotiable

AMERICAN MUSIC THEATRE FESTIVAL   ♪ 2d x cm dr
123 S. Broad St. 18th Floor, Philadelphia, PA 19109 (215) 893-1570 FAX (215) 893-1233 Contact: Ben Levit, Artistic Director **Theatre:** professional **Works:** "Song-driven music-theatre works." **2nd productions:** "Yes; prefer new or developing works." **Special interests:** "Popular and experimental forms; comedies; dramas." **Stage:** proscenium, 450 seats **Submission policy:** cassette tape of at least 3 songs, synopsis; no score; agent submission **Response:** 6 months **Future commitment:** yes

AMERICAN MUSICAL THEATRE OF SAN JOSE   ♪ 2d Lc
1717 Technology Dr., San Jose, CA 95110 (408) 453-7100 Ext. 145 FAX (408) 453-7123 e-mail amtsj@amtsj.org **Contact:** Marc Jacobs, Assoc. Artistic Director **Theatre:** professional **Works:** musicals **2nd productions:** yes **Special interest:** "Commercial potential." **Maximum**

cast: 30-40 **Tours:** "Not yet but possibly." **Stage:** proscenium, 2615 seats **Casting:** Equity, non-Equity **Submission policy:** agent submission **Response:** 6 months **Your chances:** 100-150 new scripts read annually **Terms:** "Commission or royalties."

THE AMERICAN PLACE   F-l Ad 2d Am x L W M
THEATRE   111 W. 46th St., New York, NY 10036 (212) 840-2960
Contact: Literary Dept. **Theatre:** off Broadway **Works:** full-length plays, adaptations **2nd productions:** "If not produced professionally in New York." **Special interests:** "American material only; innovative structure, language, theme; ethnic and women writers." **Specifications:** maximum cast: 8-10, moderate production demands preferred **Stages:** 3 flexible spaces, 180-299, 75, 75 seats **Casting:** Equity **Submission policy:** agent submission **Best time:** Sept.-Jun. **Response:** 2 weeks query; 3-4 months solicited script **Your chances:** 1500 new scripts read annually/usually 3-4 produced **Terms:** negotiable **Program:** The Humor Hatchery (see Special Programs)

AMERICAN RENEGADE THEATRE CO.   F-l 1- Am
11136 Magnolia Blvd., North Hollywood, CA 91601 (818) 763-4430
FAX (818) 763-8082 Contact: Barry Thompson, Dramaturg **Works:** full-length plays, one-acts **2nd productions:** no **Exclusive interest:** "Works by residents of North America." **Stages:** 2 black boxes, 99, 49 seats **Submission policy:** query letter preferred; unsolicited script **Response:** 3-6 months

AMERICAN REPERTORY THEATRE   F-l Tr Ad ♪ Rv po
64 Brattle St., Cambridge, MA 02138 (617) 495-2668 Contact: Scott Zigler, Artistic Assoc. **Theatre:** professional **Works:** full-length plays, translations, adaptations, musicals, revues **2nd productions:** "Seldom." **Special interest:** "Poetic use of the stage." **Maximum cast:** 15 **Stages:** flexible, 556 seats; proscenium, 350 seats; black box, 200 seats **Submission policy:** agent submission **Best time:** Sept.-Jun. **Response:** 5 months

AMERICAN STAGE   F-l Ad CY 2d Am Fm
P.O. Box 1560, 211 3rd St. S, St. Petersburg, FL 33731 (813) 823-1600
FAX (813) 823-7529 Contact: Kenneth Mitchell, Artistic Director; Lee Manwaring Lowry, Mng. Director **Theatre:** professional **Works:** full-length plays, adaptations, children's plays **2nd productions:** yes **Special interests:** "Recent works by American playwrights; plays for families, young audiences." **Specification:** maximum cast: 6; 1 set **Stage:** flexible, 130 seats **Casting:** Equity, non-Equity **Submission policy:** query/synopsis; professional recommendation **Response:** 1 year

AMERICAN STAGE COMPANY   F-l ♪ 2d Am ▭
P.O. Box 336, Teaneck, NJ 07666 Contact: James N. Vagias, Exec. Producer **Theatre:** professional **Works:** full-length plays, musicals **2nd productions:** yes **Special interest:** American playwrights and themes

Specifications: maximum cast: 15; single set; low proscenium **Tours:** yes **Stage:** proscenium, 290 seats **Submission policy:** professional recommendation; agent submission **Response:** 6 months **Your chances:** 200-300 new scripts read annually/usually 1 produced **Remuneration:** no **Future commitment:** yes **Program:** workshops

AMERICAN STAGE FESTIVAL F-l ♪ CY 2d Fm

14 Court St., Nashua, NH 03060 (603) 889-2336 **FAX** same, call first **Contact:** ATTN: New Scripts, EARLY STAGES **Theatre:** professional **Works:** full-length plays, musicals, children's plays **2nd productions:** yes **Special interests:** "Plays and musicals for young audiences; family material." **Specifications:** maximum cast: 10 plus 5 musicians; no fly system **Stage:** proscenium, 497 seats **Audience:** "Traditional, conservative." **Submission policy:** agent submission preferred; query/synopsis, 10-page dialogue sample, cassette tape of 2-3 songs for musical, resume **Best time:** Sept.-Dec. **Response:** 2-3 months query; 4-6 months solicited script **Your chances:** 300 new scripts read annually/usually 0-2 produced **Terms:** negotiable **Program:** EARLY STAGES (see Special Programs)

♫ THE AMERICAN THEATER CO. F-l Tr Ad ♪ L cm

1909 W. Byron St., Chicago, IL 60613 (773) 929-5009 **FAX** (773) 929-5171 **e-mail** atcdir@aol.com **Contact:** Brian Russell, Artistic Director **Theatre:** professional **Works:** full-length plays, translations, adaptations, musicals **Special interests:** "Language, heightened reality; musicals; comedies of substance." **Specifications:** maximum cast: 15; modest technical demands **Stage:** modified thrust, 137 seats **Submission policy:** query/synopsis **Response:** 3 months query; 6-12 months solicited script

AMERICAN THEATRE OF ACTORS F-l dr ▭

314 W. 54th St., New York, NY 10019 (212) 581-3044 **Contact:** James Jennings, Artistic Director **Theatre:** off off Broadway **Works:** full-length plays **2nd productions:** "If New York City premieres." **Special interest:** "Dramas, naturalistic or realistic only." **Specifications:** maximum cast: 8-10; no musicals, historical works, or avant garde plays **Tours:** yes **Stages:** 2 prosceniums, 140, 65 seats; arena, 35+ seats **Casting:** Equity, non-Equity **Submission policy:** unsolicited script **Response:** 2 weeks **Your chances:** 500 new scripts read annually/usually 25 produced **Remuneration:** no **Future commitment:** "Not usually." **Programs:** staged readings, workshop productions

AMERICAN THEATRE WORKS/ F-l Ad ♪ Fm Rs
DORSET THEATRE FESTIVAL P.O. Box 510, Dorset, VT 05251

(802) 867-2223 **FAX** (802) 867-0144 **e-mail** theatre@sover.net **Contact:** Jill Charles, Artistic Director **Theatre:** professional **Works:** full-length plays, adaptations, musicals **Special interest:** plays which have not had off Broadway or 1st-class productions **Maximum cast:** 8 preferred **Stage:** proscenium, 220 seats **Casting:** Equity **Audience:** "Sophisticat-

ed; conservative in language." **Submission policy:** query/synopsis, 10-page dialogue sample, resume, script history, SASP; professional recommendation; agent submission **Best time:** Sept.-Dec. **Response:** 4 months **Your chances:** 150 new scripts read annually/usually 1 produced **Remuneration:** negotiable royalty; transportation, expenses for required 3-week residency **Future commitment:** "Varies."

AMIL TELLERS OF DRAMATICS   F-l ♪ CY 2d Lc cm Fm

ENCORE THEATRE 991 North Shore Dr., Lima, OH 45801 (419) 223-8866 **Contact:** George Dunster, President **Theatre:** community **Works:** full-length plays, musicals, children's plays **2nd productions:** yes **Specifications:** maximum cast: 25; easy set changes; no fly space **Stage:** thrust, 289 seats **Casting:** amateur actors, students **Audience:** "Likes comedies, musicals; no 4-letter words." **Submission policy:** query/synopsis **Best time:** late fall **Response:** 6-9 months **Your chances:** 10 scripts read annually/none produced to date **Remuneration:** negotiable **Advice:** "Be available to attend rehearsals."

AN CLAIDHEAMH SOLUIS   F-l 2d M ₵

Celtic Arts Center, P.O. Box 861778, Los Angeles, CA 90086-1778 (213) 462-6844 **FAX** (213) 482-2023 **Contact:** Sean Fallon Walsh, Exec. Director **Theatre:** professional **Works:** full-length plays **2nd productions:** yes **Exclusive interests:** "Plays by writers of Irish descent, Gaelic/Celtic themes or themes of ethnic survival." **Casting:** Equity **Submission policy:** unsolicited script; query/synopsis **Response:** 3 months **Program:** developmental workshops

THE ANGELS COMPANY   F-l 1- Ad 2d W

2001 Sewell St., Lincoln, NE 68502 (402) 474-2206 **Contact:** Judy Hart, Mgr. **Theatre:** professional **Works:** full-length plays, one-acts, adaptations **2nd productions:** yes **Special interests:** "Any form or subject matter; company is about 70% women." **Specifications:** "Less tech (setwise); projection screens/light are more important." **Stage:** flexible, 99-125 seats **Casting:** Equity, non-Equity **Audience:** "Enjoys a challenge." **Submission policy:** unsolicited script, query/synopsis; professional recommendation **Terms:** negotiable **Programs:** readings, staged readings **Advice:** "We are a new theatre company consisting primarily of Equity members living in Lincoln, with no Equity company around. We produce plays that serve our limited company of 15."

ANGEL'S TOUCH PRODUCTIONS   S Tv

22906 Calabash St., Woodland Hills, CA 91364 **Contact:** Phil Nemy, Director of Development **Production company:** professional **Works:** teleplays, screenplays **Submission policy:** unsolicited script; query/synopsis; agent submission **Response:** 6 months **Your chances:** 400 new scripts read annually/usually 5 produced **Remuneration:** negotiable **Advice:** "No phone calls."

APPLE TREE THEATRE
F-l Ad ♪ CY

595 Elm Pl. Suite 210, Highland Park, IL 60035 (847) 432-8223 FAX (847) 432-5214 **Contact:** Ligia Popescu, Literary Mgr. **Theatre:** professional **Works:** full-length plays, adaptations, musicals, children's plays **Specifications:** maximum cast: 9; unit set **Stage:** modified thrust, 171 seats **Submission policy:** query/synopsis, cassette tape for musical **Response:** 1 month query; 4 months solicited script **Program:** staged readings

ARDEN THEATRE COMPANY
F-l Tr Ad ♪ 2d

40 N. 2nd St., Philadelphia, PA 19106 (215) 922-8900 **Contact:** Terrence J. Nolen, Producing Art. Director **Theatre:** professional **Works:** full-length plays, translations, adaptations, musicals **2nd productions:** yes **Special interest:** "New adaptations of literature." **Maximum cast:** 15± **Stages:** 2 flexible spaces: 400, 175 seats **Audience:** "Literate." **Submission policy:** query/synopsis; professional recommendation; agent submission **Response:** 3-6 months **Your chances:** 150 new scripts read annually/usually 1 produced **Remuneration:** negotiable

AREA STAGE COMPANY
F-l 2d

645 Lincoln Rd., Miami Beach, FL 33139 (305) 673-8002 **Contact:** John Rodaz, Artistic Director **Theatre:** professional **Works:** full-length plays **2nd productions:** yes **Maximum cast:** 3 **Casting:** Equity **Stage:** black box **Submission policy:** unsolicited script **Response:** 1 year **Future commitment:** yes **Program:** developmental workshops

ARENA PLAYERS REPERTORY COMPANY
F-l ♪ C Rs

OF LONG ISLAND   296 Route 109, East Farmingdale, NY 11735 (516) 293-0674 **Contact:** Audrey Perry, Literary Mgr. **Theatre:** professional **Works:** full-length plays, musicals **2nd productions:** no **Special interest:** "Significant contemporary subjects." **Specifications:** maximum cast: 10; single or unit set **Stages:** 2 arenas, 240, 100 seats **Submission policy:** unsolicited script; query/synopsis; professional recommendation; resume with all material **Response:** 6 months **Your chances:** 560 new scripts read annually/usually 3 produced **Remuneration:** $600 **Future commitment:** no **Programs:** script development, residencies

ARENA STAGE
F-l Tr Ad 2d Am W M

1101 6th St. SW, Washington, DC 20024 (202) 554-9066 **Contact:** Cathy Madison, Literary Mgr. **Theatre:** professional **Works:** full-length plays, translations, adaptations **2nd productions:** yes **Special interests:** American themes; women and minority writers, multiracial casts **Casting:** Equity **Stages:** modified thrust, 514 seats; arena, 827 seats; cabaret, 110 seats **Submission policy:** videotape; query/synopsis, resume; professional recommendation; agent submission **Best time:** late summer-early fall **Response:** 6 months-1 year solicited script **Your chances:** 300+ new scripts read annually/usually 1-5 receive staged readings/workshops

ARIZONA THEATRE COMPANY   F-l Tr Ad ♪ Rv 2d Rg
P.O. Box 1631, Tucson, AZ 85702 (520) 884-8210 FAX (520) 628-9129
Contact: Samantha Wyer, Asst. Artistic Director **Theatre:** professional
Works: full-length plays, translations, adaptations, musicals, musical
revues **2nd productions:** yes **Stages:** proscenium, 800 seats (Phoenix);
proscenium, 600 seats (Tucson) **Submission policy:** unsolicited script
from AZ writer; query/synopsis, 10-page dialogue sample, resume from
other writer; agent submission **Best time:** spring-summer **Response:** 1-3
months query; 4-6 months script   **Future commitment:** negotiable
Programs: GENESIS: New Play Development Program (inquire);
National Hispanic Playwriting Award (see Contests)

THE ARKANSAS ARTS CENTER F-l 1- Ad CY Cl C Fm ⊡
CHILDREN'S THEATRE **P.O. Box 2137, Little Rock, AR 72203**
(501) 372-4000   **Contact:** Bradley D. Anderson, Artistic Director
Theatre: professional **Works:** full-length plays, one-acts, adaptations,
children's plays **Special interests:** works for family audiences; adaptations of classics and contemporary literature **Tours:** yes **Stage:** proscenium, 389 seats **Submission policy:** query/synopsis preferred;
unsolicited script **Response:** 6-8 weeks query; 6 months script

ARKANSAS REPERTORY   F-l Tr Ad ♪ Rv 2d Rg C M ⊡
THEATRE **P.O. Box 110, Little Rock, AR 72203-0110** **(501) 378-**
0445 FAX (501) 378-0012 Contact: Brad Mooy, Literary Mgr. **Theatre:**
professional **Works:** full-length plays, translations, adaptations, musicals, revues **2nd productions:** yes **Special interests:** Southern, regional,
national, multiracial issues **Specifications:** maximum cast: 10; no more
than 2 sets **Tours:** yes **Stages:** proscenium, 354 seats; black box, 99 seats
Submission policy: query/synopsis, 10-page dialogue sample; professional recommendation; agent submission **Response:** 3 months query; 6
months solicited script **Your chances:** 200 new scripts read annually/
usually 1 produced **Remuneration:** varies **Future commitment:** for
premiere **Program:** Arkansas Rep New Play Reading Series (see Special
Programs) **Advice:** "We rarely produce historical dramas."

ARROW ROCK LYCEUM   F-l Tr Ad ♪ 2d Am cm ⊡
THEATRE   High St., Arrow Rock, MO 65320 (660) 837-3311 FAX
(573) 443-7414 Contact: Michael Bollinger, Producing Dir. **Theatre:** professional **Works:** full-length plays, translations, adaptations, musicals
2nd productions: if not professionally produced **Special interests:**
"Small-town America, American Dream, comedy." **Specifications:** maximum cast: 12; single set **Tours:** yes **Stage:** thrust, 410 seats **Submission
policy:** professional recommendation; agent submission **Terms:** negotiable

ART STATION   F-l Ad ♪ 2d C Rg
P.O. Box 1998, Stone Mountain, GA 30083 (770) 469-1105 FAX (770)
469-0355 e-mail artstation@mindspring.com **Contact:** Jon Goldstein,
Literary Mgr. **Theatre:** professional **Works:** full-length plays, adapta-

tions, musicals **2nd productions:** yes **Special interest:** "Work relating to the contemporary Southern experience." **Specifications:** maximum cast: 6, single set **Stage:** proscenium/thrust, 100 seats **Casting:** Equity, non-Equity **Submission policy:** unsolicited script; query/synopsis; professional recommendation; agent submission; resume, script history with all material **Best time:** summer **Response:** 3-6 months **Future commitment:** yes **Programs:** staged readings, script development

ARTGROUP/THE MURRAY HILL PLAYERS/THE PLAYWRIGHTS' CORNER
F-l 1- 2d Rg Fm
P.O. Box 1751

Murray Hill Station, New York, NY 10156-1751 (212) 229-7533 e-mail AnARTGroup@aol.com **Contact:** Mike Schwartz **Theatre** community **Works:** full-length plays, one-acts **2nd productions:** "Sometimes." **Special interest:** "NY, NJ, CT playwrights who want to become part of an ongoing company with a holistic approach." **Specifications:** "No nudity; minimal profanity, which if used, must serve a valid artistic purpose rather than act as a substitute for character development." **Submission policy:** 1st 10 pages of script, synopsis of the remainder of the play; no query or full script **Program:** staged readings

ARTHUR CANTOR PRODUCTIONS
F-l 2d cm ▭

1501 Broadway Suite 403, New York, NY 10036 (212) 391-2650 FAX (212) 391-2677 Contact: Arthur Cantor **Production company:** Broadway, off Broadway **Works:** full-length plays **2nd productions:** exclusively **Specifications:** maximum cast: 8; no more than 2 sets **Tours:** yes **Submission policy:** professional recommendation; agent submission **Best time:** summer **Response:** 3-4 weeks **Your chances:** 200 scripts read annually/1 produced every 2-3 years **Terms:** "Standard." **Advice:** "The 'well-made play'. Comedy."

ARTHUR RUBIN, PRODUCER
F-l ♪

29 W. 57th St., New York, NY 10019 (212) 750-3800 FAX (212) 750-5777 Production company: professional **Works:** full-length plays, musicals **Submission policy:** query/brief synopsis; agent submission; professional recommendation

ARTISTS REPERTORY THEATRE
F-l Tr Ad 2d Rs

1516 SW Alder St., Portland, OR 97205 (503) 241-9807 FAX (503) 241-8268 e-mail allen@artistsrep.org **Contact:** Allen Nause, Artistic Director **Theatre:** professional **Works:** full-length plays, translations, adaptations **2nd productions:** yes **Special interests:** "Northwest premieres; new plays." **Specifications:** maximum cast: 10; single or unit set **Stage:** flexible, 150-170 seats **Casting:** Equity, non-Equity **Audience:** "Educated." **Submission policy:** query/synopsis, resume, script history; videotape; agent submission **Best time:** fall **Response:** 6 months-1 year **Your chances:** 300 new scripts read annually/usually 2 produced **Remuneration:** negotiable; negotiable expenses for residency **Future commitment:** credit **Program:** Play Lab (see Special Programs)

ARTREACH TOURING THEATRE   CY 2d C H Rg ⊐
3567 Edwards Rd. #5, Cincinnati, OH 45208 (513) 871-2300 FAX
(513) 533-1295 Contact: Kelly Germain, Artistic Director Theatre: professional Works: children's plays (50-60 minutes) 2nd productions: yes
Special interests: "Intelligent works on serious themes; literature;
history; social issues." Specifications: cast size: 3-5; single set; "set must
fit into stretch van" Stages: flexible, schools Casting: non-Equity
Audience: young audiences, families Submission policy: unsolicited
script; query/synopsis, dialogue sample; professional recommendation;
resume with all material Response: 6 weeks query; 3 months script
Your chances: 50 new scripts read annually/usually 1 produced
Remuneration: "Usually $10 per performance for about 200 perform-
ances." Advice: "No trite, holiday or animal stories."

THE ARTS AT ST. ANN'S   F-l ♪
157 Montague St., Brooklyn, NY 11201 (718) 834-8794 FAX (718)
522-2470 Contact: Susan Feldman, Artistic Director Theatre: professional Works: full-length plays, musicals Special interests: "New musical works; collaborative efforts." Specifications: simple demands Stages:
2 flexible spaces, 100, 652 seats Submission policy: query/synopsis,
cassette tape of music Response: 2 months query; 3 months solicited
script Your chances: 6-10 scripts read annually/"we produce 3-4 new
works in their early stages each season" Remuneration: $500-$2000

ARTSPOWER NATIONAL   CY F-l 1- ♪ 2d Fm ⊐
TOURING THEATRE   39 S. Fullerton Ave., Montclair, NJ 07042-
3354 FAX (201) 744-3609 Contact: Gail P. Stone, Director of Education
Theatre: professional children's theatre Works: full-length plays, one-
acts, musicals 2nd productions: yes Exclusive interest: plays for
national tours for family and young audiences Specifications: maximum
cast: 5; set must tour in van Submission policy: query/synopsis, score
and cassette tape for musical Future commitment: yes

ARVADA CENTER FOR THE ARTS &   1- 2d 12+ Lc
HUMANITIES   6901 Wadsworth Blvd., Arvada, CO 80003 (303)
431-3080 FAX (303) 431-3083 Contact: Lisa Leafgreen, Education Coordinator Theatre: professional Works: one-acts 2nd productions:
yes Special interest: "Works for teens." Specifications: "Maximum
cast: 30; minimal sets and costumes." Stage: thrust, 500 seats
Submission policy: unsolicited script, resume Best time: winter Your
chances: 10-12 new scripts read annually Remuneration: $25

ASIAN AMERICAN THEATER CO.   F-l 1- Ad CY 2d As Rs
1840 Sutter St. #207, San Francisco, CA 94115 (415) 440-5545 FAX
(415) 440-5597 e-mail aatc@wenet.net Contact: Pamela A. Wu, Producing Director Theatre: professional Works: full-length plays, one-acts,
adaptations, children's plays 2nd productions: yes Special interest:

"Plays by and about Asian Pacific Islander Americans." **Casting:** Equity, non-Equity **Submission policy:** unsolicited script or videotape with synopsis, SASP; professional recommendation; agent submission **Response:** 3-6 months **Your chances:** 30-40 new scripts read annually/ usually 3-4 produced **Remuneration:** negotiable; travel for 1-week residency **Future commitment:** credit; 5%-6% for 3 years **Programs:** staged readings, workshops, classes; Asian American Theater Co. New Plays & Playwrights Development Program (see Special Programs)

A.S.K. THEATER PROJECTS   D F-l
11845 W. Olympic Blvd. Suite 1250 West, Los Angeles, CA 90064 (310) 478-3200 FAX (310) 478-5300 e-mail askplay@primenet.com **Contact:** Mead Hunter, Director of Literary Programs **Theatre:** professional **Works:** full-length plays **2nd productions:** no **Special interest:** "New plays for workshop productions or staged readings presented for the purpose of developing works-in-progress." **Casting:** Equity **Submission policy:** query/synopsis, dialogue sample; professional recommendation; agent submission **Response:** 1-2 months query; 3-6 months solicited script **Your chances:** 600 new scripts read annually/usually 20 receive workshops or staged readings **Remuneration:** "$150 for reading, $1000 for workshop." **Future commitment:** no **Programs:** A.S.K. Theater Projects Programs (see Special Programs) **Advice:** "We are interested in recent scripts that have not had full production or a great deal of development."

ASOLO THEATRE COMPANY   F-l Tr Ad 2d
Asolo Center for the Performing Arts, 5555 N. Tamiami Trail, Sarasota, FL 34243 (941) 351-9010 FAX (941) 351-5796 e-mail brodger @home.com **Contact:** Bruce E. Rodgers, Assoc. Art. Director **Theatre:** professional **Works:** full-length plays, translations, adaptations **2nd productions:** yes **Special interest:** "Literary adaptations." **Stages:** 2 prosceniums, 499, 161 seats **Submission policy:** query/1-page synopsis **Best time:** Jun.-Aug. **Response:** 2 months query **Your chances:** 500 new scripts read annually/new plays rarely produced

ATLANTIC THEATER COMPANY   F-l 1- Ad
336 W. 20th St., New York, NY 10011 (212) 645-8015 FAX (212) 645-8755 Contact: Toni Amicarella, Literary Mgr. **Theatre:** professional **Works:** full-length plays, one-acts, adaptations **Stage:** proscenium, 150 seats **Casting:** Equity **Submission policy:** agent submission **Program:** Fast Forward Play Readings

AT THE GROVE PRODUCTIONS   F-l ♪ 2d Lc
P.O. Box 1282, Upland, CA 91785 (909) 920-4343 FAX (909) 920-4342 Contact: David Masterson, Art. Director **Theatre:** professional **Works:** full-length plays, musicals **2nd productions:** yes **Specifications:** maximum cast: 40; minimal or flexible set **Stage:** thrust, 400 seats **Submission policy:** unsolicited script, score for musical **Response:** 1 month

ATTIC THEATRE   Detroit, MI   Mail addressed to this theatre has been returned as undeliverable; the phone has been disconnected.

ATTIC THEATRE CENTRE   F-l 1- 2d
6562 1/2 Santa Monica Blvd., Los Angeles, CA 90038 (213) 469-3786 FAX (213) 463-9571 **Contact:** James Carey, Producing Art. Director **Works:** full-length plays, one-acts **2nd productions:** yes **Specifications:** small cast, single set; no fly/wing space **Stages:** 2 flexible spaces, 53, 43 seats **Casting:** 30-50 members ensemble **Audience:** "21-70, varied interests." **Submission policy:** query/synopsis, dialogue sample, resume; agent submission **Response:** no guaranteed response to query; 4-6 months solicited script **Your chances:** 100 new scripts read annually/usually 1 produced **Remuneration:** varies **Future commitment:** "Usually 1st production rights for full-length play." **Programs:** reading series, workshops; Attic Theatre Centre One-Act Marathon (see Contests)

THE AUDREY SKIRBALL-KENIS THEATRE   See A.S.K. Theatre Projects in this section.

THE AULIS COLLECTIVE FOR THEATRE   F-l 1- Ad ♪ 2d
AND MEDIA, INC.   P.O. Box 673 Prince St. Station, New York, NY 10012 **Contact:** Literary Mgr. **Theatre:** off off Broadway **works:** full-length plays, one-acts, adaptations, plays with music **2nd productions:** yes **Special interests:** "The connection between domestic violence against children and global violence; use of music within plays very important." **Stages:** black box, under 99 seats **Casting:** Equity, non-Equity **Submission policy:** query/synopsis with SASE **Response:** 3-6 months query; 6-12 months solicited script **Program:** script development

AXIS CO.   New York, NY   Mail addressed to this theatre has been returned as undeliverable; no phone number is listed.

THE B STREET THEATRE   F-l 2d
2711 B Street, Sacramento, CA 95816 (916) 443-5391 **Contact:** Buck Busfield, Producing Director **Theatre:** professional **Works:** full-length plays **2nd productions:** yes **Specifications:** maximum cast: 6; simple set **Stage:** black box, 150 seats **Casting:** Equity, non-Equity **Submission policy:** agent submission **Response:** 3-6 months solicited script **Your chances:** 50 new scripts read annually **Remuneration:** royalty **Future commitment:** credit, percentage **Programs:** workshops

BACKROADS THEATER   New York, NY   Mail addressed to this theatre has been returned as undeliverable; no phone number is listed.

BAILIWICK REPERTORY   F-l Tr Ad ♪ 2d x
1229 W. Belmont, Chicago, IL 60657-2305 (312) 883-1090 FAX (312) 525-3254 **e-mail** BailiwicR@aol.com **Contact:** David Zak, Artistic Director **Theatre:** professional **Works:** full-length plays, translations, adaptations, musicals **2nd productions:** yes **Special interests:** "Innova-

tion, translations, adaptations." **Stages:** thrust, 150 seats; studio, 90 seats; loft, 49 seats **Submission policy:** send SASE for submission guidelines **Response:** 4 months **Your chances:** 500 new scripts read annually/usually 1 produced **Remuneration:** royalty **Programs:** Bailiwick Repertory Programs (see Special Programs)

BAINBRIDGE PERFORMING ARTS 200 Madison Ave. N, Bainbridge Island, WA 98110 This theatre is closed to submissions.

BALL STATE THEATRE F-l ♪ Rs
Theatre & Dance, Ball State Univ., Muncie, IN 47306 (765) 285-8740 FAX (765) 285-3790 **e-mail** dlacasse@wp.bsu.edu **Contact:** Don La Casse, Chairperson **Theatre:** university **Works:** full-length plays, musicals **Stages:** proscenium, 410 seats; flexible, 110 seats **Casting:** students, amateur actors **Submission policy:** unsolicited script; query/ synopsis; resume, script history, SASP with all material **Best time:** fall **Response:** 5 months **Remuneration:** negotiable royalties; travel, housing for 1-2 week requested residency

BARKSDALE THEATRE F-l 1- Tr Ad ♪ CY Rv
1601 Willow Lawn Dr. #301E, Richmond, VA 23230 (804) 282-9440 FAX (804) 288-6470 **Contact:** Randy Strawderman, Art. Director **Theatre:** professional **Works:** full-length plays, one-acts, translations, adaptations, musicals, children's plays, revues **Specifications:** small cast; simple set **Stage:** arena, 214 seats **Submission policy:** query/synopsis **Best time:** summer **Response:** 2-6 months **Your chances:** 40 new scripts read annually/usually 1 produced **Remuneration:** royalties

THE BARROW GROUP F-l Tr Ad
P.O. Box 5112, New York, NY 10185 (212) 522-1421 FAX (212) 522-1402 **Contact:** Nicole Foster, Asst. Literary Mgr. **Theatre:** professional **Works:** full-length plays, translations, adaptations **Specifications:** maximum cast: 12; minimal set **Stages:** various spaces **Submission policy:** professional recommendation **Response:** 1-6 months

BARTER THEATRE F-l Tr Ad ♪ CY 2d ⌷
P.O. Box 867, Abingdon, VA 24212-0867 (540) 628-2281 FAX (540) 628-4551 **e-mail** barter@naxs.com **Contact:** Early Stages **Theatre:** professional **Works:** full-length plays, translations, adaptations, musicals, children's plays **2nd productions:** yes **Special interest:** "Non-urban or highly theatrical plays." **Cast size:** 4-12 **Tours:** children's plays **Stages:** proscenium, 500 seats; thrust, 150 seats **Casting:** Equity, non-Equity **Submission policy:** query/synopsis, dialogue sample, #10 SASE; agent submission; commission **Best time:** Mar., Sept. **Response:** 6 months query; 9 months solicited script **Your chances:** 100-150 new scripts read annually/usually 6-8 produced **Remuneration:** "Percentage or fee." **Future commitment:** "Standard participation." **Program:** Early Stages: script development (no one-acts or children's plays)

THE BASIC THEATRE F-l 1- x po Cl
P.O. Box 434 Radio City Station, New York, NY 10101 (212) 397-1511
FAX same Contact: Jared Hammond, Art. Director Theatre: professional
Works: full-length plays, one-acts Special interests: "Juxtaposition of
past/present; nonnaturalistic style; poetic language; reworked classics."
Specifications: minimal set Casting: Equity Submission policy: query/
synopsis, dialogue sample Best time: summer Response: 6 months

BAY STREET THEATRE F-l ♪ 2d Sp
P.O. Box 810, Sag Harbor, NY 11963 (516) 725-0818 FAX (516) 725-
0906 Contact: Mia Emlen Grosjean, Literary Mgr. Theatre: professional Works: full-length plays, small-scale musicals 2nd productions: if
not previously produced in NYC Special interest: "Works which challenge, entertain, and champion the human spirit." Specifications: maximum cast: 8-9; unit set preferred; no wing or fly space Stage: thrust, 299
seats Casting: Equity, non-Equity Submission policy: agent submission Response: 3-6 months Your chances: 100 new scripts read annually Program: Bay Street Theatre Reading Series (see Special Programs)

THE BELMONT ITALIAN-AMERICAN PLAYHOUSE F-l 1- ℭ
2385 Arthur Ave., Bronx, NY 10458 (718) 364-4348 FAX (718) 563-
5053 Contact: Dante Albertie, Artistic Director Theatre: professional
Works: full-length plays, one-acts 2nd productions: no Special interest:
"Italian-American writers and themes, but not exclusively." Maximum
cast: 10 Stage: black box, 80 seats Submission policy: unsolicited
script Best time: summer for one-act Response: 3 months

BEN SPRECHER, PRODUCER F-l ♪
Lucille Lortel Theatre, 121 Christopher St., New York, NY 10014
(212) 924-2817 FAX (212) 989-0036 Production company: professional Works: full-length plays, musicals Submission policy: query/
synopsis; agent submission

BENJAMIN MORDECAI, PRODUCER F-l ♪
226 W. 47th St., New York, NY 10036 (212) 921-9040 FAX (212) 768-
2711 Production company: professional Works: full-length plays,
musicals Submission policy: query/brief synopsis; agent submission;
professional recommendation

BERKELEY REPERTORY THEATRE F-l Tr Ad 2d ⤳
2025 Addison St., Berkeley, CA 94704 (510) 204-8901 FAX (510) 841-
7711 e-mail litman@berkleyrep.org Contact: Tony Kelly, Literary Mgr.
Theatre: professional Works: full-length plays, translations, adaptations 2nd productions: yes Specifications: no fly space Tours: educational shows Stage: thrust, 400 seats Submission policy: professional
recommendation; agent submission Best time: Sept.-May Response: 2
months Your chances: 500 new scripts read annually/usually 1-2 produced in Parallel Season Remuneration: varies Program: readings

BERKSHIRE THEATRE FESTIVAL   F-1 ♪ 2d
P.O. Box 797, Stockbridge, MA 01262 (413) 298-5536 FAX (413) 298-3368 e-mail info@berkshiretheatre.org Contact: Kate Maguire, Producing Director Theatre: professional Works: full-length plays, musicals 2nd productions: yes Special interests: "Thought-provoking, entertaining works." Specifications: maximum cast: 8; small orchestra; simple set Stages: proscenium, 413 seats; thrust, 124 seats Casting: Equity Audience: "Vacationers." Submission policy: agent submission Best time: Oct.-Dec. Response: 3 months Terms: negotiable Program: readings

THE BILINGUAL FOUNDATION   F-1 Tr Ad CY 2d Hi Esp ⌫
OF THE ARTS   421 N. Ave. 19, Los Angeles, CA 90031 (213) 225-4044 FAX (213) 225-1250 Contact: Agustin Coppola, Literary Mgr. Theatre: professional Works: full-length plays, translations, adaptations, children's plays 2nd productions: yes Exclusive interest: "Hispanic playwrights, issues, cultural interests." Specifications: maximum cast: 10; simple set Tours: children's plays Stages: thrust, 99 seats; rented spaces Casting: Equity, non-Equity Audience: "Likes traditional, well written plays." Submission policy: unsolicited script; query/synopsis; agent submission Response: 2-3 weeks query; 3-6 months script Your chances: 100+ new scripts read annually/usually 1-2 produced; 9 receive readings Terms: negotiable Program: workshops Advice: "Abstract theatre without conflict and resolution won't do well here."

BIRMINGHAM CHILDREN'S THEATRE   CY Ad Cl 12+ ⌫
P.O. Box 1362, Birmingham, AL 35201 (205) 458-8181 FAX (205) 458-8895 e-mail drama2sell@mindspring.com Contact: Joe Zellner, Assoc. Artistic Director Theatre: professional Works: full-length children's plays Special interest: "3 series: Wee Folks (preschool-1st grade), Children (K-6th), Young Adult (4th-12th)." Specifications: cast of 5-10 preferred Tours: yes Stages: thrust, 1073 seats; lab space, 250 seats Casting: non-Equity Audience: "Likes original adaptations of classic children's stories." Submission policy: query/synopsis Best time: Sept.-Dec. Response: 6 weeks query; several months solicited script Future commitment: credit

THE BLACK SWAN   F-1 1- ♪ 2d W x ⌫
P.O. Box 2864, Asheville, NC 28802 (704) 254-6057 e-mail Swanthtre @aol.com Contact: David Hopes, Ellen Pfirrmann, Directors Theatre: community Works: full-length plays, one-acts, musicals 2nd productions: "Occasionally." Special interests: "New plays; highly imaginative, experimental, literary plays; at least 1 project a year with a strong feminist slant." Tours: yes Stages: proscenium, 600 seats; half-thrust, 300 seats; coffeehouse Casting: non-Equity Submission policy: unsolicited script Response: 4 weeks Your chances: 200+ new scripts read annually; latest produced in Sept. 1997 Remuneration: percentage Future commitment: credit Advice: "Take risks. Send the 'well-made play' and the glib crowd pleaser elsewhere."

BLOOMINGTON PLAYWRIGHTS PROJECT F-l 1-

308 S. Washington St., Bloomington, IN 47401 (812) 334-1188 Contact: John Edward Kinzer, Artistic Director Theatre: community Works: full-length plays, one-acts Special interest: 10-minute plays Specifications: maximum cast: 15; minimal demands Casting: amateur Audience: middle class Submission policy: unsolicited script Response: 4 months Program: Reva Shiner Play Contest (see Contests)

BLOOMSBURG THEATRE ENSEMBLE Tr Ad 2d Cl

P.O. Box 66, Bloomsburg, PA 17815 (717) 784-5530 FAX (717) 784-4912 Contact: Tom Byrn, Play Selection Chair Theatre: professional Works: translations, adaptations 2nd productions: yes Special interests: "Translations of classics; plays for small ensemble." Specifications: maximum cast: 9-12; single or unit set Stage: proscenium, 369 seats Casting: non-Equity Audience: "Professional, conservative." Submission policy: professional recommendation with query/synopsis and dialogue sample Best time: summer Response: 3 months query; 6 months solicited script Your chances: 150-200 queries read annually/ usually none produced Remuneration: negotiable Future commitment: no Program: workshops

BLOWING ROCK STAGE COMPANY F-l ♪ Rv 2d cm Sp

P.O. Box 2170, Blowing Rock, NC 28605 (828) 295-9168 FAX (828) 295-9104 e-mail theatre@blowingrock.com Contact: Robert Warren, Producer Theatre: professional Works: full-length plays, small-scale musicals, revues 2nd productions: yes Special interests: "Popular appeal: comedies, musicals." Maximum cast: 10 Casting: Equity Audience: "Want to feel uplifted, to laugh, to feel hope, to celebrate, to be entertained." Submission policy: query/synopsis Best time: Oct.-Jan. Response: 1 year Your chances: 50+ new scripts read annually Remuneration: negotiable

BLUE HERON THEATRE New York, NY Mail addressed to this

theatre has been returned as undeliverable; no phone number is listed.

BOARSHEAD: MICHIGAN PUBLIC F-l CY 2d cm x C

THEATER 425 S. Grand Ave., Lansing, MI 48933 (517) 484-7800 FAX (517) 484-2564 Contact: John Peakes, Art. Director Theatre: professional Works: full-length plays, children's plays 2nd productions: yes Special interests: comedies; new forms; issues Specifications: maximum cast: 10; if realistic, single set Stage: thrust, 249 seats Casting: Equity, non-Equity Submission policy: query/synopsis, 5-10 page dialogue sample, SASP; no SASE necessary Response: 1-2 months query; 6 months solicited script Your chances: 700 new scripts read annually/ usually 1 produced Remuneration: royalty Future commitment: credit Program: BoarsHead Staged Readings (see Special Programs) Advice: "Good scripts. They'll get read."

BOND STREET THEATRE F-l Tr Ad ♪ CY C x Fm ⌐⊃
2 Bond St., New York, NY 10012 (212) 254-4614 FAX (212) 254-4614
e-mail Bondst@webspan.net Contact: Joanna M. Sherman, Art. Director
Theatre: professional Works: full-length plays, translations, adaptations, experimental musicals, children's plays 2nd productions: "Rarely."
Special interests: "Global political/social significance; surreal, nonlinear scripts." Specifications: maximum cast: 8-10 Tours: yes Casting:
"Equity, non-Equity; interns." Audience: "From family to avant garde."
Submission policy: query/synopsis, 10-page dialogue sample, resume;
professional recommendation Best time: fall-spring; not summer Response: 1-3 months query; 3-6 months solicited script Your chances: 50
new scripts read annually/usually 0-1 produced Remuneration: $500-
$2000 Future commitment: varies Programs: readings, workshops

BORDERLANDS THEATER F-l Tr Ad 2d Rg M C
P.O. Box 2791, Tucson, AZ 85702-2791 (520) 882-8607 FAX (520)
882-7406, call first e-mail bltheater@aol.com Contact: Barclay Goldsmith, Producing Director Theatre: professional Works: full-length plays,
translations, adaptations 2nd productions: yes Special interest:
"Border issues; cultural diversity; border as metaphor." Specifications:
maximum cast: 12; minimal set Stages: proscenium, 400 seats; black box,
160 seats Submission policy: query/synopsis Response: 1 month
query; 3-6 months solicited script Your chances: 40 new scripts read
annually/usually 5 produced Remuneration: negotiable Future
commitment: no Programs: Border Playwrights Project (see Contests)

BOSTON PLAYWRIGHTS' THEATRE F-l 1- Tr Ad ♪ Rg
949 Commonwealth Ave., Boston, MA 02215 (617) 353-5899 FAX
(617) 353-6196 Contact: Kate Snodgrass, Producing Director Theatre:
professional Works: full-length plays, one-acts, translations, adaptations, musicals 2nd productions: no Exclusive interest: works by
Boston U. students/alumni Casting: Equity Submission policy: query/
synopsis Best time: summer Response: 6 months Program: workshops

BRAVE NEW WORKSHOP V ♪ cm C
2605 Hennepin Ave. S, Minneapolis, MN 55408-1150 (612) 377-
8445 FAX (612) 377-8472 Contact: Mark Bergren, Co-Producer Theatre:
professional Works: sketches, songs Exclusive interest: "Satire on current events." Specifications: maximum cast: 10; minimal demands Stage:
modified thrust, 230 seats Submission policy: unsolicited script,
available reviews Response: 1 month Comment: "Founded by Dudley
Riggs in 1958, this is America's oldest satirical comedy theatre."

BRAVO THEATRE PRODUCTIONS F-l 1- ♪ Rv CY 2d cm
71 Ridge Rd., Nutley, NJ 07110 (212) 724-2800 Contact: Donna
Castellano, Artistic Director Theatre: off off Broadway Works: full-
length plays, one-acts, 10-minute plays, musical revues, children's plays
2nd productions: yes Special interests: "Full-length and one-act

comedies." **Maximum cast:** 2-5 **Casting:** Equity **Submission policy:** query/synopsis, 10-15 page dialogue sample; one-act: unsolicited script **Best time:** summer-fall **Response:** 1-6 months **Program:** workshops

BREAK A LEG PRODUCTIONS   1- cm
680 West End Ave. #11E, New York, NY 10025 **Contact:** E. London, Literary Mgr. **Theatre:** professional **Works:** one-acts **Exclusive interest:** comedies **Maximum cast:** 8 **Casting:** Equity, ages 20-70 **Submission policy:** unsolicited script **Response:** 6-9 months

BRENT PEEK PRODUCTIONS   F-l ♪
234 W. 44th St. Suite 1003, New York, NY 10036 (212) 764-7946 FAX (212) 764-7962 **Contact:** Kelly Truitt, Associate **Production company:** professional **Works:** full-length plays, musicals **Submission policy:** query/synopsis; agent submission; professional recommendation

BRIDGE THEATRE CO.   F-l 1- ♪ CY Rv 2d Sn Rs ⌂
c/o Bryan Wade, 250 Ft. Washington Ave. #4F, New York, NY 10032 (212) 714-7186 FAX (212) 740-5024 e-mail wdotson890@aol.com **Contact:** Bryan Wade **Theatre:** off off Broadway **Works:** full-length plays, one-acts, musicals, children's plays, revues **2nd productions:** yes **Specifications:** maximum cast: 15; no more than 3 sets **Tours:** schools, senior citizens' organizations **Casting:** Equity, non-Equity **Submission policy:** no submissions accepted until Aug. 1999; inquire for plans **Response:** 2 months query; 3-6 months solicited script **Your chances:** 40 new plays read annually/usually 10 produced **Terms:** negotiable **Programs:** staged readings, workshops, residencies, festivals

BCC THEATRE Fall River, MA This theatre is closed to submissions.

BRISTOL RIVERSIDE THEATRE   F-l 1- Tr Ad ♪ 2d x ⌂
P.O. Box 1250, Bristol, PA 19007 (215) 785-6664 FAX (215) 785-2762 **Contact:** David J. Abers, Asst. to Artistic Director **Theatre:** professional **Works:** full-length plays, one-acts, translations, adaptations, musicals **2nd productions:** yes **Special interest:** experimental works **Specifications:** maximum cast: 10, 18 for musical, 9 for orchestra; 1 set; simple demands **Tours:** yes **Stage:** flexible, 302 seats **Audience:** "Affluent to blue collar." **Submission policy:** unsolicited script; query/synopsis, dialogue sample **Best time:** Jan. **Response:** 6-8 months **Your chances:** 250 new scripts read annually/usually 0-1 produced **Terms:** percentages

BROADSIDE PRODUCTIONS   1- 2d po ♪ W cm
Johnson County Community College, 12345 College Blvd., Box 14, Overland Park, KS 66210 (913) 469-2535 FAX (913) 469-2566 e-mail jwilkers@johnco.cc.ks.us **Contact:** Jeannie Wilkerson, Director of Operations **Production company:** professional **Works:** 10-15 minute plays, poetry, pieces with music **2nd productions:** yes **Exclusive interest:** "Humorous and satirical approaches to women's issues."

Casting: Equity, non-Equity **Audience:** "80% women from college age to 80s." **Submission policy:** unsolicited script **Your chances:** 90 new scripts read annually/1 evening's entertainment including 7± plays produced every other year in Mar. **Advice:** "Keep it funny."

BROADWAY ARTS   **49 Broadway, Asheville, NC 28801 (704) 258-9206 FAX (704) 281-4926 e-mail** dbhobbs@buncombe.main.nc.us **Contact:** Bonnie Hobbs, Director **Theatre:** professional **Program:** New Play Festival   This theatre is not accepting submissions until further notice; see *The Playwright's Companion 2000* or inquire for future plans.

BROKEN ARROW COMMUNITY   F-l 1- ♪ CY Fm Lc **PLAYHOUSE**   **P.O. Box 452, Broken Arrow, OK 74013 (918) 258-0077 e-mail** BACPMail@aol.com **Contact:** Linda Tabberer, Office Mgr. **Theatre:** community **Works:** full-length plays, one-acts, musicals, children's plays **2nd productions:** no **Maximum cast:** 35 **Stage:** thrust, 285 seats **Audience:** "White collar, family." **Submission policy:** unsolicited script **Response:** 1 month **Your chances:** 5 new scripts read annually/none produced to date

BROWN GRAND THEATRE   F-l Tr Ad ♪ CY 2d Rg **310 W. 6th St., Concordia, KS 66901 (913) 243-2553 Contact:** Susan L. Sutton, President **Theatre:** community **Works:** full-length plays, translations, adaptations, musicals, children's plays **2nd productions:** "Possibly." **Special interest:** regional themes **Specifications:** moderate cast size and sets **Stage:** proscenium, 650 seats **Submission policy:** unsolicited script; query/synopsis **Best time:** fall-winter **Response:** 6 weeks

B T MEDIA, INC.   F-l J Sp ⟳ **50 E. Palisade Ave., Englewood, NJ 07631 (201) 567-6664 FAX (201) 567-6622 e-mail** EntBTMEDIA@aol.com **Contact:** Michael Gurin, Dramaturg **Theatre:** off Broadway, touring **Works:** full-length plays **2nd productions:** no **Exclusive interest:** "Jewish and spiritual themes for mainstream audiences." **Casting:** Equity, non-Equity **Submission policy:** query/synopsis, SASP; agent submission **Response:** 2 months query; 4-6 months solicited script **Your chances:** 200 new scripts read annually/usually 2 produced **Terms:** negotiable

BUFFALO NIGHTS THEATRE CO.   F-l Tr Ad ♪ 2d cm **8332 1/2 Melose Ave., Los Angeles, CA 90069 (323) 969-4744 FAX (310) 385-7845 e-mail** submissions@buffalonights.org **Contact:** Artistic Committee **Theatre:** professional **Works:** full-length plays, one-acts ("rarely"), translations, adaptations, musicals **2nd productions:** yes **Special interests:** "Realism, off-kilter realism, dark comedy, works with an edge." **Specifications:** maximum cast: 20, ages 25-40 preferred: unit set preferred **Stages:** "Various spaces." **Casting:** Equity **Audience:** "20s-30s; adventurous; likes a challenge." **Submission policy:** query/ synopsis, 2-3 page dialogue sample; professional recommendation; agent submission **Response:** 4-6 months **Your chances:** 30-40 new scripts read annually/usually 3 produced **Terms:** negotiable **Program:** workshop productions **Advice:** "Send us plays which will take the audience on a journey and will inspire new perspectives."

CALDWELL THEATRE COMPANY F-l ♪ 2d cm dr Sn
7873 N. Federal Hwy., Boca Raton, FL 33487 (561) 241-7432 **Contact:** Kenneth Kay, Director of Outreach Programs **Theatre:** professional **Works:** full-length plays, musicals **2nd productions:** yes **Special interest:** "Comedies, dramas and musicals; works which will appeal to an older audience." **Specifications:** maximum cast: 8-9; single or unit set **Stage:** proscenium, 305 seats **Submission policy:** query/synopsis, SASP; professional recommendation; agent submission **Response:** 3-4 months **Future commitment:** yes **Program:** workshops

CALIFORNIA REPERTORY COMPANY F-l Tr Ad 2d ▭
1250 Bellflower Blvd., Long Beach, CA 90840 (562) 985-5243 FAX (562) 985-2263 **Contact:** Paul Stuart Graham, Mng. Director **Theatre:** professional **Works:** full-length plays, translations, adaptations **2nd productions:** yes **Special interests:** new works; adaptations of international material **Specifications:** cast size: 8-18; small space **Tours:** yes **Stages:** 2 prosceniums, 90, 400 seats; 2 flexible, 99, 225 seats; **Casting:** Equity **Submission policy:** professional recommendation, agent submission **Best time:** May-Jul. **Response:** 3 months **Your chances:** 100-200 new scripts read annually/usually 1-3 produced

CALIFORNIA THEATRE CY Ad ♪ 2d Cl cm C H ▭
CENTER P.O. Box 2007, Sunnyvale, CA 94087 (408) 245-2979 **FAX (408) 245-0235 Contact:** Will Huddleston, Literary Mgr. **Theatre:** professional **Works:** children's plays, small-scale children's musicals **2nd productions:** yes **Special interests:** adaptations of classics, comedies, issues, historical subjects, plays for K-4th grade **Specifications:** maximum cast: 8 for mainstage; cast of 20 (minimum)-25 for student conservatory productions; works tour; 1 hour maximum **Stages:** prosceniums, 300-1500 seats **Casting:** main season: professionals; conservatory: children **Submission policy:** query/synopsis preferred; unsolicited script; agent submission **Best time:** fall **Response:** 3 months query; 4-6 months script **Your chances:** 50 new scripts read annually/ usually 2 produced **Remuneration:** royalty

CAMERON MACKINTOSH 1650 Broadway, New York, NY
10019 (212) 921-9290 This producer is not open to submissions.

CAPITAL REPERTORY THEATRE F-l Tr Ad ♪ 2d
111 N. Pearl St., Albany, NY 12207 (518) 462-4531 Ext. 293 FAX (518) 465-0213 **e-mail** submissions@capitalrep.org **Contact:** Maggie Mancinelli-Cahill, Producing Artistic Director **Theatre:** professional **Works:** full-length plays, translations, adaptations, small-scale musicals

2nd productions: yes **Maximum cast:** 10 **Stage:** 3/4 thrust, 286 seats **Audience:** "Middle aged; middle class; college." **Casting:** Equity, non-Equity **Submission policy:** agent submission **Best time:** May-Aug. **Response:** 6 months **Your chances:** 200 new scripts read annually/1 produced **Remuneration:** royalties **Program:** Capital Repertory Theatre Author's Theatre (see Special Programs)

CAROLE SHORENSTEIN HAYS, PRODUCER   See Shorenstein Hays/Nederlander Productions in this section.

CARMEL PERFORMING ARTS FESTIVAL   F-l 1- Tr Ad CY
P.O. Box 221473, Carmel, CA 93922 (831) 644-8383 FAX (831) 622-7631 **Contact:** Robin McKee, Producing Artistic Director **Theatre:** professional **Works:** full-length plays, one-acts, translations, adaptations, children's plays **Stages:** 2 prosceniums, 305, 48 seats; 3/4 thrust, 99 seats **Submission policy:** professional recommendation **Best time:** Mar.-Apr. **Response:** 5 months **Program:** CPAF Reading Series (see Special Programs)

CASA MAÑANA THEATRE   F-l ♪ CY 2d
3101 W. Lancaster, Fort Worth, TX 76107 (817) 332-9319 **Contact:** Denton Yockey, Exec. Producer; Joel Ferrell, Artistic Director **Theatre:** professional **Works:** full-length plays, musicals, children's plays **2nd productions:** yes **Special interests:** new musicals; traditional, commercial works; previously produced works **Maximum cast:** 2-10 **Stages:** arena, 1800 seats; proscenium, 700 seats **Casting:** Equity **Submission policy:** unsolicited script **Future commitment:** negotiable

THE CAST THEATRE   F-l
804 N. El Centro Ave., Hollywood, CA 90038 (213) 462-0265 **Contact:** Lit. Mgr. **Theatre:** professional **Works:** full-length plays **Special interest:** premieres **Stages:** 2 prosceniums, 99, 65 seats **Submission policy:** unsolicited script **Response:** 6 months **Future commitment:** yes

CASTILLO THEATRE   D F-l 1- C M
500 Greenwich St. Suite 201, New York, NY 10013 (212) 941-5800 FAX (212) 941-8340 **e-mail** castilloth@aol.com **Contact:** Fred Newman, Art. Director **Theatre:** professional **Works:** full-length plays, one-acts **Special interests:** issues; multiracial casts **Stage:** thrust, 71 seats **Casting:** non-Equity **Submission policy:** query/synopsis, dialogue sample **Response:** 2-6 months **Terms:** negotiable **Program:** Castillo Playwriting Workshop (see Special Programs)

CATAWBA COLLEGE THEATRE   F-l ♪
Theatre Arts Dept., 2300 W. Innes St., Salisbury, NC 28144 (704) 637-4440 **e-mail** jepperso@catawba.edu **Contact:** Jim Epperson, Chair **Theatre:** college **Works:** full-length plays, musicals **2nd productions:** no **Casting:** non-Equity, students **Audience:** college, community **Sub-**

mission policy: unsolicited script, cassette tape for musical **Best time:** spring **Response:** 3 months **Programs:** workshops; Peterson Emerging Playwright Competition (see Contests)

℟ CELEBRATION THEATRE F-l Ad ♪ Rv g/l
7985 Santa Monica Bl. #109-1, W. Hollywood, CA 90046 (213) 957-1884 FAX (310) 271-8870 **Contact:** Tom Jacobson, Lit. Mgr. **Theatre:** professional **Works:** full-length plays, adaptations, musicals, revues **2nd productions:** no **Exclusive interest:** gay/lesbian issues **Specifications:** small cast; simple demands **Stage:** thrust, 65 seats **Submission policy:** unsolicited script **Response:** 6 months

CENTER FOR PUPPETRY ARTS F-l 1- Tr Ad ♪ CY V ⌐
1404 Spring St. NW, Atlanta, GA 30309 (404) 873-3089 FAX (404) 873-9907 e-mail puppet@mindspring.com **Contact:** Bobby Box, Producer **Theatre:** professional **Works:** full-length plays, one-acts, translations, adaptations, musicals, children's plays **Specifications:** "Puppets or combination of puppets/actors." **Tours:** yes **Stages:** proscenium, 332 seats; flexible, 121 seats **Audience:** 2 series: adults, children **Submission policy:** unsolicited script **Response:** 8 weeks **Your chances:** 10-12 new scripts read annually/none produced to date **Remuneration:** royalties **Program:** Experimental Puppetry Theatre (see Special Programs)

CENTER STAGE F-l Tr Ad ♪ 2d P
700 N. Calvert St., Baltimore, MD 21202 (410) 685-3200 FAX (410) 539-3912 **Contact:** James Magruder, Resident Dramaturg **Theatre:** professional **Works:** full-length plays, translations, adaptations, music theatre pieces **2nd productions:** yes **Special interests:** plays which have not received a mainstage production **Stages:** modified thrust, 541 seats; flexible, 100-400 seats **Casting:** Equity **Submission policy:** query/synopsis, dialogue sample, script history, resume; professional recommendation; agent submission **Best time:** summer **Response:** 7 weeks query; 6 months solicited script **Your chances:** 350 new scripts read annually/usually 2 produced **Terms:** negotiable **Advice:** "No mystery, sci-fi, backstage settings, spoofs, or Biblical plays; inquire for other limitations."

CENTER STAGE THEATRE F-l 1- Tr Ad ♪ CY Rv 2d J cm C dr
JCC, 3600 Dutchmans Ln., Louisville, KY 40205 (502) 459-0660 FAX (502) 459-6885 **Contact:** Cultural Arts Director **Theatre:** community **Works:** full-length plays, one-acts, translations, adaptations, musicals, children's plays, revues **2nd productions:** yes **Special interests:** Jewish writers/themes **Specifications:** maximum cast: 8, no more than 2 sets; 2 hours maximum **Stage:** proscenium, 250 seats **Audience:** "Prefers comedies with underlying issues, off Broadway dramas." **Submission policy:** query/synopsis, dialogue sample, resume **Best time:** Sept.-Nov. **Remuneration:** negotiable **Comment:** Formerly Heritage Theatre.

CENTER THEATER ENSEMBLE   F-l Tr Ad ♪ 2d L cm dr
1346 W. Devon, Chicago, IL 60660 (773) 508-0200   Contact: Jay
Skelton, Producing Artistic Director **Theatre**: professional **Works**: full-
length plays, translations, adaptations, musicals **2nd productions**: "Yes,
but not musicals." **Special interests**: "Language, comedy, dramas of substance." **Specifications**: maximum cast: 12±; limited space **Stages**: modified thrust, 75 seats; black box, 35 seats **Submission policy**: query/
synopsis, resume; agent submission **Response**: 3 months **Your chances**:
500 new scripts read annually/usually 1 produced **Remuneration**:
royalties **Program**: Center Theater International Contest (see Contests)
Advice: "Only finished work in *Professional Playscript Format!*"

CENTRE STAGE–SOUTH   F-l 1- ♪ CY Rv Sn M
CAROLINA!   P.O. Box 8451, Greenville, SC 29604-8451 (864) 233-
6733 FAX (864) 233-3901 e-mail cbla@infoave.net **Contact**: Claude
W. Blakely, Administrative Director **Theatre**: professional **Works**:
full-length plays, one-acts, musicals, children's plays, revues **Special
interests**: musical revues, issues of interest to senior citizens; minority
issues; children's plays **Specifications**: no more than 2 sets; limited
wing and no fly space **Stage**: thrust, 292 seats **Submission policy**:
unsolicited script **Response**: 2 months **Program**: Sunday Evening
Readers Theatre (see Special Programs)

CENTURY CENTER FOR THE PERFORMING   F-l ♪ 2d dr
ARTS   111 E. 15th St., New York, NY 10001 **Contact**: Lee Gunder-
sheimer, Producing Dir. **Theatre**: off Broadway **Works**: full-length plays,
musicals **2nd productions**: yes **Special interests**: dramas **Maximum
cast**: 9 **Casting**: Equity **Submission policy**: agent submission only

CHAMBER THEATRE PRODUCTIONS, INC.   F-l
2 Park Plaza, Boston, MA 02116 (617) 542-9155 FAX (617) 542-0341
Production company: professional **Works**: full-length plays **Submission policy**: query/brief synopsis; agent submission; professional recommendation

THE CHANGING SCENE   F-l 1- x
1527 1/2 Champa St., Denver, CO 80202 (303) 893-5775 **Contact**:
Alfred Brooks, President **Theatre**: professional **Works**: full-length
plays **2nd productions**: no **Special interest**: non-naturalistic works;
10-minute plays for annual Colorado Quickies **Specifications**: small
cast, simple set **Stage**: flexible, 76 seats **Submission policy**: unsolicited
script **Response**: 6 months **Your chances**: 100 new scripts read annual-
ly/usually 6 produced **Program**: SummerPlay (see Special Programs)

CHARLES HOLLERITH, JR. PRODUCTIONS   F-l
435 E. 57th St. #14A, New York, NY 10022 **Contact**: Charles
Hollerith, Jr., Producer **Production company**: professional **Works**:
full-length plays **Submission policy**: agent submission

CHARLOTTE REPERTORY THEATRE   F-l Tr Ad ♪ Rv 2d
129 W. Trade St., Charlotte, NC 28202 (704) 375-4796 Ext. 106 FAX (704) 375-9462 Contact: Claudia Carter Covington, Lit. Mgr. **Theatre:** professional **Works:** full-length plays, translations, adaptations, revues **2nd productions:** if not professionally produced **Stage:** flexible, 450 seats **Casting:** Equity **Submission policy:** unsolicited script; query/ synopsis; cassette tape for musical **Response:** 3 weeks query, 3 months script **Your chances:** 500 new scripts read annually/usually 4 produced **Program:** Charlotte Festival (see Contests)

CHELSEA REPERTORY CO. LAB   F-l 1- Tr Ad ♪ 2d x C 12+
29 E. 19th St. 4th Floor, New York, NY 10003 (212) 228-2700 Contact: Joe Bascetta, Studio Admin. **Theatre:** off off Broadway **Works:** full-length plays, one-acts, 10-minute plays, translations, adaptations, musicals **2nd productions:** yes **Special interests:** experimental works; issues **Specifications:** cast in late teens--mid-30s **Stage:** flexible, 75 seats **Submission policy:** unsolicited script; query/synopsis, dialogue sample; professional recommendation; agent submission **Best time:** Jun.-Aug. **Response:** 3 months query; 6 months script **Your chances:** 300 new scripts read annually/usually 3 produced **Remuneration/commitment:** no **Programs:** staged readings, workshops, festivals (inquire)

CHELTENHAM CENTER FOR THE ARTS   F-l Tr Ad 2d
439 Ashbourne Rd., Cheltenham, PA 19012 (215) 379-4660 FAX (215) 663-1946 Theatre: professional **Works:** full-length plays, translations, adaptations **2nd productions:** yes **Maximum cast:** 10 **Stage:** proscenium, 140 seats **Casting:** Equity **Audience:** "Educated." **Submission policy:** query/synopsis; professional recommendation; agent submission **Best time:** Jul.-Feb. **Response:** 1-6 months **Your chances:** usually 1 new play produced each year **Remuneration:** negotiable

THE CHILDREN'S THEATRE CO.   CY Ad ♪ 2d Cl C Lc ⌐
2400 Third Ave. S, Minneapolis, MN 55404 (612) 874-0500 FAX (612) 874-8119 Contact: Peter C. Brosius, Artistic Director **Theatre:** professional **Works:** children's plays, adaptations, musicals **2nd productions:** yes **Special interests:** "Adaptations: classics, contemporary works; ballet; opera." **Specifications:** maximum cast: 50 **Tours:** yes **Stages:** proscenium, 745 seats; studio, 100 seats **Audience:** "65% adults." **Submission policy:** query/synopsis, resume; agent submission **Best time:** Oct.-Apr. **Response:** 1-6 months **Terms:** negotiable **Program:** workshops

CHILDSPLAY, INC.   CY 2d Fm ⌐
P.O. Box 517, Tempe, AZ 85280 (602) 350-8101 e-mail childsplayaz @juno.com **Contact:** David Saar, Artistic Director **Theatre:** professional **Works:** children's plays **2nd productions:** yes **Stages:** proscenium, 800 seats; courtyard theatre, 320 seats; black box, 100 seats **Casting:** non-Equity **Audience:** "Tours: grades K-8; season: families." **Submission policy:** query/synopsis, dialogue sample; professional recommenda-

tion; commission **Best time:** Jun.-Aug. **Response:** 2 months query; 6 months script **Your chances:** 50 new scripts read annually/usually 2-3 produced **Remuneration:** negotiable **Future commitment:** for commission **Programs:** staged readings, workshops, development

CHILD'S PLAY TOURING THEATRE   CY Ad ♪ po Y Fm ⌐
2518 W. Armitage, Chicago, IL 60647 (773) 235-8911 FAX (773) 235-5478 e-mail cptt@sprynet.com **Contact:** June Podagrosi, Exec. Director **Theatre:** professional **Works:** children's plays and musicals, poems, stories **2nd productions:** no **Exclusive interest:** "We perform plays adapted from writings of children." **Maximum cast:** 4 **Tours:** all shows **Casting:** non-Equity **Audience:** "Grades K-8, family members." **Submission policy:** unsolicited script **Response:** 2-4 weeks **Remuneration:** no

CINCINNATI PLAYHOUSE IN THE PARK   F-l Tr Ad ♪ 2d
P.O. Box 6537, Cincinnati, OH 45206-0537 (513) 345-3342 FAX (513) 345-2254 Contact: Assoc. Artistic Director **Theatre:** professional **Works:** full-length plays, translations, adaptations, musicals **2nd productions:** yes **Maximum cast:** play: 10-12, musical: 15-18 **Stages:** 2 modified thrusts, 629, 225 seats **Casting:** Equity **Submission policy:** agent submission **Response:** 2-6 months **Your chances:** 400 new scripts read annually/usually 1-2 produced **Remuneration:** royalties, expenses **Future commitment:** negotiable **Program:** Lois & Richard Rosenthal New Play Prize (see Contests)

CIRCLE IN THE SQUARE THEATRE   1633 Broadway, New York, NY 10019-6795 (212) 307-2700 **Theatre:** Broadway This theatre now solicits scripts and is no longer open to submissions from playwrights, professionals or agents.

CIRCLE THEATRE   F-l 1- Ad ♪ Rv 2d
7300 W. Madison, Forest Park, IL 60130 (708) 771-0700 Contact: James C. Wall, Literary Mgr. **Theatre:** professional **Works:** full-length plays, one-acts (full evening), adaptations, musicals, revues **2nd productions:** yes **Specifications:** maximum cast: 12, 3-7 preferred; single set; minimal orchestration; minimal wing space, no fly space; modest demands **Stages:** proscenium, 45 seats; black box, 70 seats **Submission policy:** send SASE for guidelines **Best time:** summer **Response:** 9-12 months **Your changes:** 2-4 new plays produced each year **Remuneration:** yes **Future commitment:** credit

CIRCLE THEATRE   F-l 1- Ad ♪ Rg
2015 S. 60th St., Omaha, NE 68106-2154 (402) 553-4715 FAX same **e-mail** demarr1523@aol.com **Contact:** Doug Marr, Art. Director **Theatre:** professional **Works:** full-length plays, one-acts, adaptations, musicals **2nd productions:** no **Exclusive interest:** NE and regional writers **Specifications:** maximum cast: 10; no more than 2 sets **Stage:** flexible, 80 seats **Casting:** non-Equity **Submission policy:** unsolicited script, re-

sume; query/synopsis **Response:** 4 months **Your chances:** 45 new
scripts read annually/usually 1-2 produced; 1-2 receive staged readings
Remuneration: $20 per performance **Future commitment:** no

CITY LIT THEATRE COMPANY   Ad 2d po cm ⊏►
410 S. Michigan Ave. Penthouse, Chicago, IL 60605 (312) 913-9446
FAX (312) 913-9472 e-mail metapage@aol.com **Contact:** Mark Richard,
Art. Director **Theatre:** professional **Works:** adaptations **2nd productions:** "Possibly." **Exclusive interests:** adaptations: fiction, poetry; comedy **Specifications:** maximum cast: 12; single set **Stage:** black box, 100
seats **Casting:** non-Equity **Submission policy:** query/synopsis, dialogue
sample, resume; professional recommendation; agent submission **Best
time:** late spring-summer **Response:** 6 weeks query; 9 months solicited
script **Your chances:** 12-15 new scripts read annually **Remuneration:**
royalty or fee **Advice:** "We work with a small group of Chicago artists."

CITY THEATRE   1- 2d
P.O. Box 248268, Coral Gables, FL 33124 (305) 284-3605 FAX (305)
365-9623 **Contact:** Stephanie Norman, Producer **Theatre:** professional
Works: 10-minute plays **2nd productions:** yes **Submission policy:** un-
solicited script **Best time:** fall **Response:** Mar. **Programs:** workshops;
Summer Shorts Festival (see Contests)

CITY THEATRE COMPANY   F-l 2d Am cm
57 S. 13th St., Pittsburgh, PA 15203 (412) 431-4400   FAX (412) 431-
5535 **Contact:** Literary Dept. **Theatre:** professional **Works:** full-length
plays **2nd productions:** yes **Special interests:** "American themes, strong
story lines, comedies of substance." **Specifications:** maximum cast: 10; no
fly space; no multiple realistic sets **Stages:** proscenium-thrust, 250 seats;
black box, 99 seats **Audience:** "Sophisticated professionals." **Submission policy:** agent submission **Response:** 2-6 months **Your chances:** 250
new scripts read annually/usually 1-2 produced **Remuneration:** percentage **Future commitment:** no

THE CLARENCE BROWN COMPANY   F-l 2d C Am
206 McClung Tower, Knoxville, TN 37996 (423) 974-6011 FAX 974-
4867 **Contact:** Thomas P. Cooke, Producing Art. Director **Theatre:** professional **Works:** full-length plays **2nd productions:** yes **Special
interest:** contemporary American works **Specifications:** small cast,
limited sets **Stages:** proscenium, 600 seats; arena, 250 seats **Casting:**
Equity **Submission policy:** query/synopsis, 2 page dialogue sample

CLASSIC STAGE CO.   Tr Ad Cl 2d
136 E. 13th St., New York, NY 10003 (212) 677-4210 FAX (212) 477-
7504 **Contact:** Barry Edelstein, Artistic Director **Theatre:** professional
Works: full-length translations and adaptations of classics; adaptations
of classic works from non-dramatic genres **2nd productions:** yes **Maximum cast:** 10 **Stage:** flexible, 180 seats **Casting:** Equity **Submission**

policy: query/synopsis, dialogue sample; professional recommendation; agent submission; commission **Response:** 1 month query; 3 months solicited script **Your chances:** 200 new scripts read annually **Programs:** readings, workshops **Comment:** Formerly CSC Repertory Ltd.

THE CLEVELAND PLAY HOUSE   F-l Ad ♪ 2d

8500 Euclid Ave., Cleveland, OH 44106-0189 (216) 795-7010 FAX (216) 795-7005 Contact: Scott Kanoff, Lit. Mgr. **Theatre:** professional **Works:** full-length plays, adaptations, musicals **2nd productions:** yes **Stages:** 2 prosceniums, 612, 501 seats **Submission policy:** query/synopsis, 5-10 page dialogue sample; agent submission **Best time:** Sept.-Dec. **Response:** 1-2 months query; 1-3 months solicited script **Your chances:** 600 new scripts read annually/usually 1-2 produced **Terms:** negotiable **Program:** The Next Stage (see Special Programs)

CLEVELAND PUBLIC   F-l 1- Tr Ad ♪ CY Rv 2d C Sp

THEATRE   6415 Detroit Ave., Cleveland, OH 44102 (216) 631-2727 FAX (216) 631-2575 e-mail cpt@en.com **Contact:** James A. Levin, Artistic Director **Theatre:** professional **Works:** full-length plays, one-acts, translations, adaptations, musicals, children's plays, revues **2nd productions:** yes **Exclusive interests:** "Challenging, political works; work that reflects the triumph of the human spirit." **Specifications:** maximum cast: 10; simple set, small budget **Stage:** arena-proscenium, 150-175 seats **Submission policy:** query/synopsis, dialogue sample **Best time:** Nov.-Jan. **Response:** 6 weeks query; 6 months solicited script **Your chances:** 350 new scripts read annually/usually 2 produced **Remuneration:** "Nominal." **Future commitment:** percentage, credit **Program:** Cleveland Public Theatre Festival (see Contests)

CLEVELAND SIGNSTAGE   F-l 1- Tr Ad ♪ CY 2d h/d ⌯

8500 Euclid Ave., Cleveland, OH 44106 (216) 229-2838 Contact: Aaron Weir, Artistic Director **Theatre:** professional **Works:** full-length plays, one-acts, translations, adaptations, musicals, children's plays **2nd productions:** yes **Specifications:** maximum cast: 8; no more than 2 sets **Tours:** yes **Casting:** non-Equity **Audience:** "Deaf and hearing; all productions are in sign language and spoken English." **Submission policy:** unsolicited script; query/synopsis, dialogue sample, resume; professional recommendation; agent submission **Best time:** Jan-Aug. **Your chances:** 50 new scripts read annually/usually 0-1 produced **Remuneration:** negotiable

COCHRAN PRODUCTIONS, LTD.   F-l ♪

1501 Broadway #1800, New York, NY 10036 (212) 719-5640 Contact: Richard C. Norton **Production company:** professional **Works:** full-length plays, musicals **Special interest:** new plays **Submission policy:** agent submission **Response:** responds only if interested

COCONUT GROVE PLAYHOUSE   F-l ♪ Rv 2d cm dr my
3500 Main Hwy., Miami, FL 33133 (305) 442-2662 FAX (305) 444-6437 **Contact:** Arnold Mittelman, Producing Art. **Director Theatre:** professional **Works:** full-length plays, musicals, revues **2nd productions:** yes **Special interests:** musicals, comedy, drama, mystery **Stages:** proscenium, 1100 seats; cabaret, 150 seats **Submission policy:** query/synopsis; agent submission **Response:** 1 week query; 2 months solicited script

COLLABORATIVE ARTS PROJECT 21 INC.   D F-l ♪
(CAP 21)   18 W. 18th St., New York, NY 10011 (212) 807-0202 FAX (212) 807-0166 **Contact:** Jennifer Camp, Literary Mgr. **Theatre:** developmental **Works:** full-length plays, musicals **2nd productions:** no **Submission policy:** unsolicited script, cassette tape for musical **Response:** 4-6 months **Programs:** Blackjacks Festival and Monday Night Reading Series (see CAP 21 Programs in Special Programs)

THE COLONY STUDIO THEATRE   F-l Ad
1944 Riverside Dr., Los Angeles, CA 90039 **Contact:** Barbara Beckley, Producing Director **Theatre:** professional **Works:** full-length plays, adaptations **Specifications:** cast size: 10+ **Stage:** thrust, 99 seats **Casting:** Equity, non-Equity **Submission policy:** "Agent submissions and referrals by people known to this theatre only." **Response:** up to 1 year **Your chances:** 50 new scripts read annually/usually 0-1 produced, latest in summer 1997 **Remuneration:** royalties **Future commitment:** negotiable **Advice:** "Do not phone." **Comment:** "We plan to move to a 250-seat Equity house by Aug. 2001; write for new address."

COMMONWEAL THEATRE CO.   F-l Tr Ad
P.O. Box 15, Lanesboro, MN 55949 (507) 467-2525 FAX (507) 467-2468 **e-mail** cmmnweal@means.net **Contact:** Hal Cropp **Theatre:** professional **Works:** full-length plays, translations, adaptations **Specifications:** maximum cast: 9 preferred; single set; no wing space **Stage:** proscenium, 126 seats **Submission policy:** professional recommendation **Best time:** Oct.-Dec. **Response:** 4 weeks **Program:** Commonweal New Plays Workship (see Special Programs)

CONEJO PLAYERS, INC.   F-l ♪ 2d
P.O. Box 1695, Thousand Oaks, CA 91358 (805) 495-3715 FAX (805) 498-8065 **Contact:** Dick Johnson, Exec. Director **Theatre:** professional **Works:** full-length plays, musicals **2nd productions:** yes **Submission policy:** unsolicited script; query/synopsis; cassette tape for musical **Best time:** Nov.-Apr. **Response:** 3 months **Program:** workshops

CONEY ISLAND, USA/SIDESHOWS BY THE   V ♪ Am
SEASHORE   1208 Surf Ave., Brooklyn, NY 11224 (718) 372-5159 FAX (718) 372-5101 **e-mail** dzigun@echonyc.com **Contact:** Dick D. Zigun, Artistic Director **Theatre:** professional **Works:** already mounted productions: vaudeville, pop music, performance/popular culture pieces

Special interest: "Old-new vaudeville; American bizarro." **Stages:** arena, 150 seats; streets, boardwalk, beach **Submission policy:** query/ synopsis, resume, reviews of prior work **Response:** 1 month query; 6 months solicited script

CONTEMPORARY AMERICAN THEATRE FESTIVAL
F-l Tr Ad 2d Am C

Shepherd College, P.O. Box 429, Shepherdstown, WV 25443 (304) 876-3473 FAX (304) 876-0955 **Contact:** Ed Herendeen, Producing Director **Theatre:** professional **Works:** full-length plays, translations, adaptations **2nd productions:** yes **Special interests:** American playwrights, contemporary issues **Stages:** proscenium, 350 seats; black box, 99 seats **Casting:** Equity **Submission policy:** query/synopsis, resume; agent submission **Best time:** fall **Response:** 1 month query; 3-6 months solicited script **Program:** Summer Tues. Night Staged Readings

CONTEMPORARY THEATRE OF SYRACUSE
F-l 1- Rg

P.O. Box 6427, Syracuse, NY 13217 (315) 425-0405 **Contact:** Director, New Plays Program **Theatre:** semi-professional **Works:** full-length plays, one-acts **2nd productions:** "Rarely." **Special interest:** "Area writers and settings." **Maximum cast:** 10 **Stage:** coffee house, 50-80 seats **Casting:** Equity, non-Equity **Audience:** "Educated; professionals, students." **Submission policy:** query/synopsis; professional recommendation; "referral by local theatre people" **Best time:** late spring **Response:** 1 month query; 1-6 months solicited script **Your chances:** 30 new scripts read annually/usually 8-9 receive readings; "we try to include in mainstage season 1 play which has been presented as a reading" **Remuneration:** $50 for full-length reading; varies for one-act **Future commitment:** no

CORNERSTONE THEATER COMPANY
F-l Ad 2d D Rg

1653 18th St. #6, Santa Monica, CA 90404 (310) 449-1700 FAX (310) 453-4347 **e-mail** cornerstn@aol.com **Contact:** Daniel Forcey, Program Assoc. **Theatre:** professional **Works:** full-length plays, adaptations **2nd productions:** yes **Special interests:** "Special commissioned community collaborations performed with and about the community." **Casting:** Equity, non-Equity **Submission policy:** query/synopsis, resume; professional recommendation; agent submission **Response:** 2 months

COSSETTE PRODUCTIONS, INC.
F-l ♪

8899 Beverly Blvd., Los Angeles, CA 90048 (310) 278-3366 **Contact:** Pierre Cossette **Production company:** Broadway **Works:** full-length plays, musicals **Submission policy:** query/synopsis

THE COTERIE, INC.
1- Ad ♪ CY 2d M Y ▭

2450 Grand Ave. Suite 144, Kansas City, MO 64108 (816) 474-6785 FAX (816) 474-7112 **Contact:** Jeff Church, Producing Artistic Director **Theatre:** professional **Works:** one-acts: adaptations, musicals, children's plays **2nd productions:** yes **Special interest:** "Young minority protagonists; no fairy tales." **Specifications:** maximum cast: 12, 5-9 preferred; no fly or wing space **Tours:** yes **Stage:** flexible, 243 seats **Casting:** Equity, non-Equity **Audience:** "Families, minorities." **Submission policy:** send SASE for information sheet **Response:** 8 months **Your chances:** 80 new scripts read annually/usually 1 produced **Remuneration:** royalty **Future commitment:** "For commission, 15% for 1-2 years." **Programs:** staged readings, Young Playwrights Roundtable

COURT THEATRE   Tr Ad 2d Cl

5535 S. Ellis Ave., Chicago, IL 60637 (773) 702-7005 FAX (773) 834-1897 Contact: Resident Dramaturg **Theatre:** professional **Works:** translations, adaptations **2nd productions:** yes **Exclusive interests:** "Classics; new works inspired by classical elements." **Specifications:** maximum cast: 6-8; no more than 2 sets; limited fly space **Stage:** thrust, 253 seats **Submission policy:** query/synopsis preferred; unsolicited script **Best time:** fall **Response:** 1 month query (if interested); 2-6 months solicited script **Program:** workshops

COVINA VALLEY PLAYHOUSE   F-l 1- ♪

104 N. Citrus Ave., Covina, CA 91744 (626) 339-5135 Contact: Artistic Director **Theatre:** community **Works:** full-length plays, one-acts, musicals **2nd productions:** no **Submission policy:** unsolicited script; videotape; query/synopsis; professional recommendation; agent submission; resume with all material **Response:** 8-12 months **Your chances:** 45 new scripts read annually **Programs:** workshops, internships, contests (inquire) **Comment:** Submitted materials are not returned.

THE COYOTE THEATRE   F-l 1- Tr Ad 2d C x

P.O. Box 403 Back Bay Annex, Boston, MA 02117 (617) 695-0659 FAX (617) 695-6775, call first **Contact:** Joshua White, Lit. Mgr. **Theatre:** professional **Works:** full-length plays, one-acts, translations, adaptations **2nd productions:** yes **Special interests:** "Social relevance; innovative works." **Maximum cast:** 5 **Stages:** black box or modified thrust, 80-140 seats **Casting:** Equity, non-Equity **Audience:** "Young, urban, sophisticated theatregoers." **Submission policy:** query/synopsis, 10-15 page dialogue sample, script history, SASP **Response:** 3-4 months query; 6-8 months solicited script **Terms:** negotiable **Program:** Coyote Theatre Festival of Ten-Minute Plays (see Special Programs)

CREATIVE ARTS TEAM   CY 2d 12+ ⌑

411 Lafayette St. 4th Floor, New York, NY 10003 (212) 992-9807 Contact: Anna Wong **Theatre:** professional **Works:** young people's plays **2nd productions:** yes **Exclusive interest:** "Inner-city youth." **Specifications:** maximum cast: 6; 1 tourable set **Stages:** "Auditoria, arena, up to 300 seats; non-theatre spaces, 30-100 seats." **Casting:** Equity, non-Equity **Audience:** "Teens; through school system." **Submission policy:** videotape or query/synopsis, resume, SASP; commission

Best time: late fall **Response:** 4 weeks query; 3 months solicited script **Your chances:** 12 new scripts read annually/usually 1 produced, latest in spring 1998 **Remuneration:** negotiable **Future commitment:** varies

CREATIVE PRODUCTIONS ♪ 2d Fm h/d

2 Beaver Pl., Aberdeen, NJ 07747-2303 (908) 566-6985 e-mail wlbtoc @aol.com **Contact:** W. L. Born, Artistic Director, CEO **Theatre:** professional **Works:** musicals **2nd productions:** yes **Special interests:** "No 'blue' material; 90-minutes maximum." **Specifications:** maximum cast: 10; no more than 2 sets; "no flying parts" **Stage:** proscenium, 300 seats **Casting:** "Folks with disabilities integrated with non-disabled." **Audience:** "Likes family-type musicals." **Submission policy:** unsolicited script; query/synopsis, 6-page dialogue sample, SASP; commission; send #10 SASE for "Submission Procedures" **Best time:** summer **Response:** 30 days **Your chances:** 12 new scripts read annually/usually 2 produced, 2 receive staged readings **Remuneration:** negotiable **Future commitment:** credit **Programs:** occasional workshops (inquire)

CREEDE REPERTORY THEATRE F-l ♪ CY 12+ 2d Rg NA Hi H Fm ▭

P.O. Box 269, Creede, CO 81130 (719) 658-2541 FAX (719) 658-2343 e-mail crt@creederep.com **Contact:** Richard Baxter, Literary Mgr. **Theatre:** professional **Works:** full-length plays, musicals, children's plays **2nd productions:** yes **Special interests:** "Western, mining themes; Native American, Hispanic folklore." **Specifications:** maximum cast: 10; no more than 2 sets; no fly space **Tours:** "Young audience program: 60 minute maximum, for children/young adults." **Stages:** proscenium, 243 seats; black box, 79 **Casting:** non-Equity **Audience:** "Conservative, educated; family material." **Submission policy:** request release form **Best time:** Oct.-Feb. **Response:** 2 months **Remuneration:** yes **Advice:** "We look for a good working relationship with the playwright."

THE CROSSLEY THEATRE F-l 1- Tr Ad ♪ CY Rv 2d Fm Sp

1760 N. Gower St., Hollywood, CA 90028 (213) 462-8460 FAX (213) 462-3199 **Contact:** Cynthia Sanders, New Play Coordinator **Theatre:** professional **Works:** full-length plays, one-acts, translations, adaptations, musicals, children's plays, revues **2nd productions:** yes **Special interests:** "Large themes that uplift the human spirit. We are located on church grounds; there are language and moral restrictions." **Specifications:** cast of 12 or fewer preferred; minimal set **Stage:** flexible proscenium, 99 seats **Casting:** Equity, non-Equity **Audience:** "Entertainment professionals; general." **Submission policy:** unsolicited script; query/ synopsis, dialogue sample; agent submission; synopsis, resume, script history with all material **Response:** 4 weeks query; 12 weeks script **Your chances:** 100 new scripts read annually/2 produced to date **Terms:** negotiable **Advice:** "No abuse stories unless a moral dilemma is investigated. No family dramas unless conflict transcends mere venting of hurt feelings."

CROSSROADS THEATRE CO.   F-l 1- Tr Ad ♪ Rv 2d M C x
7 Livingston Ave., New Brunswick, NJ 08901 (732) 249-5581 FAX
(732) 249-1861 Contact: Lenora Inez Brown, Literary Mgr. Theatre:
professional Works: full-length plays, one-acts, translations, adaptations, musicals, revues 2nd productions: yes Special interests: "African-American, West Indian, Native American, Asian American experience; issue-oriented, experimental plays." Stage: thrust, 264 seats Submission policy: query/synopsis, dialogue sample; agent submission; commission Response: 1 month query; 1 year solicited script Your chances: 150 new scripts read annually/usually 5 produced Terms: negotiable Program: The Genesis Festival (see Special Programs)

CSC: REPERTORY LTD.   See Classic Stage Co. in this section.

CUMBERLAND COUNTY   F-l Ad ♪ CY 2d Rg Fm
PLAYHOUSE   P.O. Box 830, Crossville, TN 38557 (931) 484-4324
FAX (931) 484-6299 Contact: Jim Crabtree, Producing Director Theatre:
professional Works: full-length plays, adaptations, musicals, children's plays 2nd productions: yes Special interests: "Plays for family audiences; TN history, culture; Southern/rural themes." Stages: proscenium, 490 seats; outdoor arena, 200 seats; flexible, 180-220 seats Submission policy: query/synopsis Best time: Aug.-Dec. Response: 2 weeks query (if interested); 6-12 months solicited script Your chances: 100 new scripts read annually/usually 1 produced Remuneration: royalties

CURRICAN/PLAYFUL REP   F-l cm dr
154 W. 29th St., New York, NY 10001 (212) 736-2533 Contact:
Andrew Miller, Artistic Director Works: full-length plays 2nd productions: no Special interests: comedies, dramas Specifications: maximum cast: 6; simple set; unpublished plays only Stage: black box Casting: Equity Submission policy: query/synopsis, 1st 10 pages of dialogue Response: 4 months Your chances: 4 plays produced each season

CURTAIN TIME PLAYERS   1- Sn Fm cm ▭
P.O. Box 256, Ada, MI 49301 (616) 676-1583 Contact: Robert Redd
Theatre: community Works: short plays (5-10 minutes) Exclusive interest: "Light, upbeat entertainment for senior actors and audiences; clean humor; no sex, romance, or obscenity." Specifications: maximum cast: 5; plays must tour Stages: "Common rooms, church stages, etc." Casting: volunteers Audience: "Retirement homes, church groups, clubs, condo associations, business groups, community events." Submission policy: unsolicited script Response: 2 weeks Remuneration: "Small fee." Future commitment: "Publication rights for Thornapple Publishing Co." Advice: "Comic domestic issues, with conflict and resolution."

CYPRESS CIVIC THEATRE GUILD   F-l ♪ CY 2d
P.O. Box 2212, Cypress, CA 90630 (714) 229-6796 Contact: Jewell
Tolkin, President Theatre: community Works: full-length plays,

musicals, children's plays **2nd productions:** yes **Maximum cast:** 10 **Casting:** adults (18 and over) **Submission policy:** unsolicited script; query/synopsis; score for musical **Best time:** May **Response:** 2 months

DALLAS CHILDREN'S THEATRE   F-l Ad CY 2d Fm ⌐⎤
2215 Cedar Springs, Dallas, TX 75201 (214) 978-0110 FAX (214) 978-0118 **Contact:** Robyn Flatt, Artistic Director **Theatre:** professional **Works:** full-length plays, adaptations, children's plays **2nd productions:** yes **Special interests:** "Works appropriate for a family audience: adaptations of popular literature, known titles, mythology, folk tales." **Maximum cast:** 12 **Tours:** yes **Stages:** proscenium, 500 seats; flexible, 180 seats **Casting:** Equity, non-Equity, students, ensemble **Submission policy:** unsolicited script with synopsis; query/synopsis **Response:** 6 months query; "lengthy" for script **Your chances:** 100 new plays read annually/usually 3 produced **Terms:** negotiable

DALLAS THEATRE CENTER   F-l Tr Ad 2d Af Hi
3636 Turtle Creek Blvd., Dallas, TX 75219 (214) 526-8210 FAX (214) 521-7666 **Contact:** Alice Levieux-Donohoe, Artistic Ofc. **Theatre:** professional **Works:** full-length plays, translations, adaptations **2nd productions:** yes **Special interest:** African-American/Hispanic works **Stages:** thrust, 466 seats; flexible, 530 seats **Submission policy:** professional recommendation **Response:** 1 year **Terms:** negotiable

DARK HORSE THEATER GROUP LTD. 230 West End Ave. #2A,
New York, NY 10023 (212) 714-8127 **Contact:** Cindy Sandmann, Artistic Director   This theatre is closed to submissions in 1999; see *The Playwright's Companion 2000* or inquire for future plans.

DEAF WEST THEATRE COMPANY   F-l 1- 2d h/d
5112 Lankershim Blvd., North Hollywood CA 91601 (818) 762-2998 TTY (818) 762-2782 FAX (818) 762-2981 **Contact:** Ed Waterstreet, Artistic Director **Theatre:** professional **Works:** full-length plays, one-acts **2nd productions:** yes **Exclusive interest:** "Works prominently presenting deaf characters, especially those who use sign language." **Maximum cast:** 10-12; simple demands **Submission policy:** unsolicited script **Response:** 6 months **Future commitment:** "If we develop the work."

DELAWARE THEATRE COMPANY   F-l Tr Ad 2d ⌐⎤
200 Water St., Wilmington, DE 19801-5030 (302) 594-1104 FAX (302) 594-1107 **Contact:** Fontaine Syer, Artistic Director **Theatre:** professional **Works:** full-length plays, translations, adaptations **2nd productions:** yes **Specifications:** maximum cast: 10; single or unit set preferred **Tours:** yes **Stage:** thrust, 400 seats **Casting:** "NY, DC, local." **Audience:** "Educated, professional, middle-aged." **Submission policy:** agent submission; commission **Best time:** Feb.-May **Response:** 6 months **Your chances:** 350 new scripts read annually/usually 0-1 produced **Terms:** negotiable **Advice:** "Scripts must be close to completion."

DELL'ARTE PLAYERS CO.   D F-l Tr Ad CY C cm V ☙ ▭

P.O. Box 816, Blue Lake, CA 95525   (707) 668-5663 Contact: Michael Fields, Managing Director Theatre: professional Works: full-length plays, translations, adaptations, children's plays 2nd productions: seldom Special interests: "Comedy/satire; new vaudeville; Christmas plays for young audiences; issues." Specifications: cast size: 3-4; works must tour Stage: flexible, 100 seats Casting: Equity, non-Equity, ensemble Audience: "Loyal." Submission policy: query/synopsis Best time: Jan.-Mar. Response: 3 weeks query; 6 weeks solicited script Your chances: 3-4 new scripts read annually Advice: "We usually create our own works; collaboration is a possibility."

THE DELRAY BEACH PLAYHOUSE   F-l ♪ 2d Fm

P.O. Box 1056, Delray Beach, FL 33447-1056 (561) 278-3523 FAX same Contact: Randolph DelLago, Director Theatre: community Works: full-length plays, musicals 2nd productions: yes Specifications: simple sets; limited effects Stage: proscenium, 238 seats Audience: "Conservative." Submission policy: query/synopsis; professional recommendation Best time: winter Your chances: 20 new scripts read annually/ usually 1 produced Program: possible Monday night readings

DENNIS GRIMALDI PRODUCTIONS   F-l ♪

250 W. 57th St. Suite 1818, New York, NY 10107 (212) 581-9450 FAX (212) 581-9373 Production company: professional Works: full-length plays, musicals Submission policy: query/brief synopsis; agent submission; professional recommendation

DENVER CENTER THEATRE COMPANY   D F-l P

1050 13th St., Denver, CO 80204 (303) 893-4000 FAX (303) 825-2117 e-mail bsevy@star.dcpa.org Contact: Bruce Sevy, Assoc. Art. Director Theatre: professional Works: full-length plays 2nd productions: if not professionally produced Stages: 2 thrusts, 200, 642 seats; arena, 450 seats; proscenium, 250 seats Casting: Equity Submission policy: query/ synopsis, dialogue sample, resume; agent submission; Rocky Mountain writer: unsolicited script Response: 6 week-6 months Remuneration: royalties Programs: staged readings, workshops; Francesca Primus Prize (see Contests); U S West TheatreFest (see Special Programs)

DETROIT REPERTORY THEATRE   F-l 2d C

13103 Woodrow Wilson Ave., Detroit, MI 48238 (313) 868-1347 FAX (313) 868-1705 Contact: Barbara Busby, Literary Mgr. Theatre: professional Works: full-length plays 2nd productions: "Yes; unproduced plays preferred." Special interest: issues Maximum cast: 8 preferred Stage: proscenium, 194 seats Casting: "Equity; without regard to color and, often, gender." Audience: "70% black." Submission policy: unsolicited script; agent submission Best time: Sept.-Feb. Response: 3-6 months Your chances: 200 new scripts read annually/usually 1-3 produced Remuneration: royalties Future commitment: no

DIAMOND HEAD THEATRE

F-l 1- Ad CY 2d

520 Makapuu Ave., Honolulu, HI 96816 (808) 734-8763 FAX (808) 735-1250 Contact: John Rampage, Art. Director Theatre: professional Works: full-length plays, one-acts, adaptations, children's plays 2nd productions: yes Stage: proscenium, 492 seats Audience: "All races, 25-85." Submission policy: query/synopsis Your chances: 1 new play produced every 2 years Remuneration: yes Programs: readings, staged readings; Originals Playwrights Workshop (see Special Programs)

THE DIRECTORS COMPANY

F-l ♪ 2d

311 W. 43rd St. Suite 307, New York, NY 10036 (212) 246-5877 Contact: Sarah Orth, General Mgr. Theatre: professional Works: full-length plays, small-scale musicals 2nd productions: if NY premieres Special interest: "Strong stories." Specifications: small cast; small set; simple demands Submission policy: professional recommendation; agent submission Response: 3 months Terms: negotiable Programs: readings, workshops Comment: "3 divisions: Mainstage; Harold Prince Musical Theatre Program [see Special Programs], the Directors Studio Division."

♫ DILLON STREET PLAYERS

F-l 2d

802 N. Dillon St., Los Angeles, CA 90026 (213) 663-1664 FAX same Contact: Scott Crawford Theatre: professional Works: full-length plays 2nd productions: if L.A. premieres Maximum cast: 20, aged 40+ Casting: Equity Submission policy: unsolicited script Response: 3 months

DISNEY THEATRICAL PRODUCTIONS

F-l ♪

1546 Broadway, 29th Floor, New York, NY 10036 (212) 827-5400 FAX (212) 827-5454 Production company: professional Works: full-length plays, musicals Submission policy: query/brief synopsis; agent submission; professional recommendation

DLT ENTERTAINMENT LTD.

F-l ♪

31 W. 56th St., New York, NY 10019 (212) 245-4680 FAX (212) 315-1132 Production company: professional Works: full-length plays, musicals Submission policy: query/brief synopsis; agent submission; professional recommendation

DIXON PLACE

F-l 1- ♪ x W M Rg

258 Bowery, New York, NY 10012 (212) 219-3088 FAX (212) 274-9114 Contact: Andrew J. Mellen, Reading Series Theatre: professional Works: full-length plays, one-acts, musicals, works-in-progress Special interests: "Experimental, original work; collaborations; women; writers of color." Specifications: readings only; small stage, no sets, minimal lighting Stage: 3/4 thrust, 50 seats Casting: Equity, non-Equity Audience: "Arts community." Submission policy: NYC-area writer only: query/10-page dialogue sample Response: 6 months Your chances: 100's of new scripts read annually/usually 28 receive readings Remuneration: fee Future commitment: no

DO GOODER PRODUCTIONS, INC.   F-l 1-
359 W. 54th St. Suite 4FS, New York, NY 10019 **Contact:** Mark Robert Gordon, Founding Artistic Director **Theatre:** professional **Works:** full-length plays, one-acts **Stages:** various spaces, 99-150 seats **Submission policy:** agent submission **Response:** 4 months **Program:** DGP New Playwright Award (see Contests)

DOBAMA THEATRE   F-l C M
1846 Coventry Rd., Cleveland Hts., OH 44118 (216) 932-6838 FAX (216) 932-3259 **Theatre:** professional **Works:** full-length plays **Special interests:** issues; diverse casting **Specifications:** maximum cast: 9; simple demands **Stage:** thrust, 200 seats **Submission policy:** query/synopsis, dialogue sample; OH writer: unsolicited script **Response:** 9 months **Programs:** see listing in Contests; Owen Kelly Adopt-a-Playwright Program (see Special Programs)

DODGER PRODUCTIONS   F-l ♪
1501 Broadway Suite 1904, New York, NY 10036 (212) 575-9710 FAX (212) 398-1723 **Production company:** professional **Works:** full-length plays, musicals **Submission policy:** query/synopsis; agent submission; professional recommendation

DOWNTOWN PLAYHOUSE   929 E. 2nd St. #105, Los Angeles, CA 90012 (213) 626-6906 FAX (213) 626-0272 **Contact:** Michael Beubis, Art. Director   This theatre is closed to submissions in 1999; see *The Playwright's Companion 2000* for future plans.

DRAMA COMMITTEE REPERTORY THEATRE   Ad Am Cl
118 W. 79th St., New York, NY 10024 (212) 595-1733 **Contact:** Arthur Reel, Art. Director **Theatre:** professional **Works:** "Old American classics." **2nd productions:** no **Specifications:** maximum cast: 10; moveable sets **Submission policy:** query/synopsis, 1st act **Response:** 2 months

DREAM DRAMA COMPANY   F-l 1- ♪ CY 12+ 2d $
8 Arbutus Rd., Swampscott, MA 01907 (781) 599-7793 FAX same **Contact:** Mary Valentine King, Artistic Director **Theatre:** professional **Works:** full-length plays, one-acts, musicals **2nd productions:** yes **Special interests:** "Audience-participation pieces for teen actors, young audiences; unproduced works." **Maximum cast:** 12 **Submission policy:** query/synopsis, $10 fee **Best time:** summer **Response:** 3 months

DREAMCATCHER REPERTORY THEATRE   F-l 1- ♪ 2d W
52 Highwood Terrace, Weehawken, NJ 07087 (201) 223-5905 FAX (201) 223-5902 e-mail lekstrand@aol.com **Contact:** Janet Sales, Producing Director **Theatre:** professional **Works:** full-length plays, one-acts, musicals **2nd productions:** yes **Special interest:** women's roles **Maximum cast:** 10 **Submission policy:** unsolicited script, cassette tape for musical **Best time:** fall-winter **Response:** 6 months

EAST WEST PLAYERS   F-l Tr Ad ♪ CY 2d As ⊑⬐
244 S. San Pedro St. Suite 301, Los Angeles, CA 90012 (213) 625-7000 FAX (213) 625-7111 Contact: Ken Narasaki, Literary Mgr. Theatre: professional Works: full-length plays, translations, adaptations, musicals, children's plays 2nd productions: yes Exclusive interest: "Asian-Pacific/Asian-American authors, casts, themes." Specifications: minimal demands Tours: children's plays Stage: proscenium, 265 seats Casting: Equity, non-Equity Submission policy: query/synopsis, dialogue sample, resume preferred; unsolicited script; professional recommendation; agent submission Response: 3-8 months Your chances: 100-120 new scripts read annually/usually 2-3 produced Terms: negotiable Programs readings; EWP New Voices (see Contests); David Henry Hwang Writer's Institute (see Special Programs)

ECLIPSE THEATRE COMPANY   F-l Tr 2d
2074 N. Leavitt St., Chicago, IL 60647 (773) 862-7415 Contact: Artistic Director Theatre: professonal Works: full-length plays; translations 2nd productions: yes Casting: non-Equity Submission policy: inquire Comment: This theatre was damaged by fire in 1998; inquire for future plans.

EDGAR LANSBURY, PRODUCER   F-l ♪
630 Ninth Ave. Suite 214, New York, NY 10036 (212) 489-9202 FAX (212) 489-9471 Production company: professional Works: full-length plays, musicals Submission policy: query/synopsis; agent submission; professional recommendation

♫ **EDYVEAN REPERTORY THEATRE**   F-l 1- Tr Ad ♪ CY Rv
1400 East Hanna Ave., Indianapolis, IN 46227 (317) 927-8052 FAX (317) 927-8059 e-mail ert@indy.net Contact: Karla Ries, Marketing Sales Director Theatre: professional Works: full-length plays, one-acts, translations, adaptations, musicals, children's plays, revues Stages: thrust, 425 seats; flexible, 400 seats Submission policy: unsolicited script Response: 6 months

EL TEATRO CAMPESINO   F-l 1- Tr Ad ♪ CY Rv C Cl M
P.O. Box 1240, San Juan Bautista, CA 95045 (408) 623-2444 FAX (408) 623-4127 Theatre: professional Works: full-length plays, one-acts, translations, adaptations, musicals, children's plays, cabarets Special interests: "Adaptations of classics; issues; multiethnic themes." Stage: flexible, 150 seats Submission policy: query/synopsis, resume Best time: Jan.-Apr. Response: 6 months query; 1 year solicited script

ELIZABETH I. McCANN, PRODUCER   F-l ♪
1501 Broadway Suit 1514, New York, NY 10036 (212) 730-1022 FAX (212) 730-1262 Production company: professional Works: full-length plays, musicals Submission policy: query/brief synopsis; agent submission; professional recommendation

ELLIOT MARTIN, PRODUCER   F-l Tr Ad ♪ Rv

152 W. 58th St., New York, NY 10019 (212) 245-4176 **Contact:** Elliot Martin, Producer **Production company:** professional **Works:** full-length plays, musicals, translations, adaptations, revues **Special interest:** "New playwrights." **Submission policy:** agent submission **Advice:** "Highly recommended works only."

EMANUEL AZENBERG PRODUCTIONS   cm

250 W. 52nd St. 4th Floor, New York, NY 10019 (212) 489-9140 **Contact:** Emanuel Azenberg **Production company:** Broadway **Special interest:** comedy **Submission policy:** "Agent submission <u>only</u>!"

THE EMELIN THEATRE FOR THE   F-l ♪ Rv 2d
PERFORMING ARTS   Library Ln., Mamaroneck, NY 10543 (914) 698-3045 **Contact:** John Raymond, General Mgr. **Theatre:** professional **Works:** full-length plays, chamber musicals, revues **2nd productions:** yes **Specifications:** small cast; no fly space **Stage:** proscenium, 280 seats **Submission policy:** unsolicited script with professional recommendation; agent submission **Response:** 2 months **Your chances:** usually 0-1 new plays produced each year

THE EMPTY SPACE THEATRE   F-l 1- Tr Ad ♪ 2d

3509 Fremont Ave. N, Seattle, WA 98103-8813 (206) 547-7633 **FAX** (206) 547-7635 **Contact:** Eddie Levi Lee, Artistic Director **Theatre:** professional **Works:** full-length plays, one-acts, translations, adaptations, musicals **2nd productions:** yes **Specifications:** small cast preferred **Stage:** endstage, 150 seats **Audience:** "Middle class." **Submission policy:** query/synopsis, resume, dialogue sample; professional recommendation; agent submission **Response:** 6 months

EN GARDE ARTS, INC.   F-l Ad ♪ 2d x ▭

259 W. 30th St. 14th Floor, New York, NY 10001 (212) 279-1461 **FAX** (212) 279-1492 **e-mail** EnGardeArt@aol.com **Contact:** Andrea Berloff, Assoc. Producer **Theatre:** professional **Works:** full-length plays, adaptations, musicals **2nd productions:** "Occasionally." **Special interests:** "Experimental, site-specific new works; non-traditional spaces." **Submission policy:** professional recommendation **Best time:** Aug. **Response:** 6-8 months **Remuneration:** fee

ENSEMBLE STUDIO THEATRE   F-l 1- 2d

549 W. 52nd St., New York, NY 10019 (212) 247-4982 **FAX** (212) 664-0041 **Contact:** Curt Dempster, Artistic Director **Theatre:** professional **Works:** full-length plays, one-acts **2nd productions:** if New York City premieres **Stages:** black box, 99 seats; proscenium, 60 seats **Casting:** "Members, agents, files." **Submission policy:** unsolicited script; agent submission; no query/synopsis **Response:** 6 months **Your chances:** 2000 new scripts read annually **Programs:** Marathon of One-Act Plays, First Look readings, workshops (inquire)

THE ENSEMBLE THEATRE   F-l Ad ♪ CY Af
3535 Main St., Houston, TX 77002-9529 (713) 520-0055 Contact:
Eileen J. Morris, Artistic Director **Theatre:** professional **Works:** full-
length plays, adaptations, musicals, children's plays **Special interest:**
African-American themes **Specifications:** maximum cast: 10; no more
than 2 sets **Stages:** proscenium, 199 seats; black box, 80 seats **Submission policy:** unsolicited script **Best time:** Aug. **Response:** 5 months
Program: George Hawkins Playwriting Contest (see Contests)

ENSEMBLE THEATRE COMPANY   CY 2d
P.O. Box 2307, Santa Barbara, CA 93120 (805) 965-6252 FAX (805)
965-5322 **Contact:** Robert G. Weiss, Artistic Director **Theatre:** professional **Works:** children's plays **2nd productions:** yes **Maximum
cast:** 7 **Casting:** Equity **Submission policy:** agent submission

ENSEMBLE THEATRE OF CINCINNATI   F -l Ad CY P
1127 Vine St., Cincinnati, OH 45210 (513) 421-3556 FAX (513) 421-
8002 **Contact:** D. Lynn Meyers, Producing Art. Director **Theatre:** professional **Works:** full-length plays, adaptations, children's plays **Special
interest:** "U.S., world premieres." **Specifications:** maximum cast 6; simple
set **Tours:** "Possibly." **Stage:** 3/4 arena, 202 seats **Submission policy:**
query/synopsis, dialogue sample, resume; professional recommendation;
agent submission; commission **Best time:** Sept. **Response:** 6 weeks query;
6 months solicited script **Your chances:** 500 new scripts read annually/
usually 6 produced **Terms:** fee, expenses; 3% subsidiary rights

EQUITY LIBRARY THEATRE CHICAGO   F-l 1- Tr Ad ♪ CY 2d
345 W. Dickens, Chicago, IL 60614 (773) 743-0266 FAX (847) 677-
0062 **e-mail** sirtoby@aol.com **Contact:** President **Theatre:** professional
Works: full-length plays, one-acts, translations, adaptations, musicals,
children's plays **2nd productions:** yes **Submission policy:** unsolicited
script, cassette tape for musical **Response:** 6-12 months **Program:**
workshops **Comment:** Scripts are not returned.

ERIC KREBS PRODUCTION MANAGEMENT   F-l 1- ♪
450 W. 42nd St. Suite 2B, New York, NY 10036 (212) 967-7079 FAX
(212) 868-5501 **Contact:** Susan Minoff **Production company:** professional **Works:** full-length plays, musicals **Submission policy:** query/
brief synopsis; agent submission; professional recommendation
Program: Chutzpah Fest of One-Act Plays (inquire)

EUREKA THEATRE CO.   F-l 1- Tr Ad 2d C dr cm mm
330 Townsend St. Ste. 210, San Francisco, CA 94107 (415) 243-9899
FAX (415) 243-0789 **Contact:** Joe DeGuglielmo, Art. Director **Theatre:**
professional **Works:** full-length plays, one-acts, translations, adaptations **2nd productions:** yes **Special interests:** "Drama, comedy; music/
dance/dialogue; contemporary works." **Maximum cast:** 8 **Casting:**
Equity, non-Equity **Stage:** flexible, 300 seats **Submission policy:** query/

synopsis, resume, 1st 15 pages; unsolicited script, synopsis **Response:** 2-6 months **Your chances:** 200-300 new scripts read annually **Remuneration:** royalties **Program:** Discovery Series (see Special Programs)

FAIRBANKS DRAMA ASSN. & FAIRBANKS CHILDREN'S THEATRE, INC.
F-l 1- ♪ CY 2d ▭

P.O. Box 73610, Fairbanks, AK 99707-3610 (907) 456-7529 **Contact:** B. J. Ryder, Bus. Mgr. **Theatre:** community **Works:** full-length plays, one-acts, musicals, children's plays **2nd productions:** yes **Specifications:** maximum cast: 12-14; minimal set **Tours:** children's plays **Stage:** proscenium, 400 seats **Submission policy:** unsolicited script; query/synopsis, dialogue sample; professional recommendation **Best time:** Feb.-Mar. **Response:** spring **Remuneration:** no **Your chances:** 5-6 new scripts read annually/ usually 0-1 produced **Advice:** "Not too far off the wall."

FAIRBANKS LIGHT OPERA THEATRE (FLOT)
♪ Lc Fm ▭

P.O. Box 72787, Fairbanks, AK 99707 (907) 456-3568 FAX (907) 456-3662 **e-mail** flot@polarnet.com **Contact:** Susan Burroughs, Operations Secretary **Theatre:** community **Works:** musicals, operas, light operas **2nd productions:** no **Specifications:** simple set **Tours:** yes **Stages:** proscenium, 903 seats; small arena **Casting:** "Large chorus." **Audience:** "Families." **Submission policy:** query/synopsis **Response:** 2 months **Your chances:** "We receive about 12 new scripts each year and hope to receive more." **Remuneration:** "Possibly."

FALSTAFF PRESENTS
F-l Tr Ad 2d W

116 N. Robertson Blvd. Suite 905, Los Angeles, CA 90048 (310) 652-8844 FAX (310) 652-5595 **Contact:** Michael Winter, Producer **Production company:** professional **Works:** full-length plays, translations, adaptations **2nd productions:** yes **Special interests:** "Strong roles for mature women." **Casting:** Equity **Submission policy:** query/synopsis, resume **Response:** 1 month query; 3-6 months solicited script **Program:** workshops

FERNDALE REPERTORY THEATRE
F-l ♪ C

P.O. Box 892, Ferndale, CA 95536-0892 (707) 786-5486 **Contact:** Artistic Director **Theatre:** semi-professional **Works:** full-length plays, musicals **2nd productions:** "Rarely." **Special interest:** "Contemporary themes." **Specifications:** small cast; simple demands **Stage:** proscenium, 267 seats **Audience:** "Educated, 35-65." **Submission policy:** unsolicited script; query/synopsis **Best time:** spring-summer **Response:** 1 month query; 6-12 months script **Your chances:** 125 new scripts read annually/ usually 1 produced **Remuneration:** royalty

FIRST STAGE MILWAUKEE
CY 1- Tr Ad ♪ 2d Fm

929 N. Water St., Milwaukee, WI 53202 (414) 273-7121 FAX (414) 273-5480 **e-mail** firststage@aol.com **Contact:** Rob Goodman, Producer **Theatre:** professional **Works:** children's plays: one-acts, translations,

adaptations, musicals **2nd productions:** yes **Stage:** thrust, 500 seats **Casting:** Equity, non-Equity, students **Audience:** schools, families **Submission policy:** query/synopsis, resume **Best time:** spring-summer **Response:** 1 month query; 3 months solicited script **Your chances:** 50 new scripts read annually/usually 2 produced **Remuneration:** commission or royalty--5% **Future commitment:** percentage, credit **Programs:** staged readings, workshops **Advice:** "Be patient and keep writing."

FLEETWOOD STAGE   F-l
44 Wildcliff Dr., New Rochelle, NY 10805 (914) 654-8533 FAX (914) 699-1536 Contact: Bruce Post, Literary Mgr. **Theatre:** professional **Works:** full-length plays **2nd productions:** no **Specifications:** maximum cast: 8; small, flexible unit set **Stage:** proscenium, 100 seats **Casting:** Equity, non-Equity **Submission policy:** professional recommendation preferred; unsolicited script **Response:** 6-9 months **Program:** Fleetwood Stage Playwrights Forum (see Special Programs)

FLORIDA STUDIO THEATRE   F-l Tr Ad ♪ Rv 2d ▭
1241 N. Palm Ave., Sarasota, FL 34236 (813) 366-9017 FAX (813) 955-4137 Contact: Chris Angermann, Assoc. Director **Theatre:** professional **Works:** full-length plays, translations, adaptations, musicals, cabarets **2nd productions:** yes **Special interest:** universal themes **Tours:** yes **Stages:** proscenium, 173 seats; cabaret, 105 seats **Audience:** "Older." **Submission policy:** unsolicited script; query/synopsis **Best time:** Mar.-Nov. **Response:** 1-2 months query; 3-6 months script **Your chances:** 1000 new scripts read annually/usually 2-3 produced **Terms:** negotiable **Programs:** staged readings, workshop productions; Florida Studio Theatre Contests (see Contests)

FOLKSBIENE THEATER   F-l Tr 2d J
123 E. 55th St., New York, NY 10022 (212) 663-2125 **Contact:** Elyse Frymer, Mng. Director **Theatre:** off Broadway **Works:** full-length plays, translations **2nd productions:** yes **Exclusive interest:** Jewish themes **Maximum cast:** 10-12 **Audience:** "Yiddish-speaking and diversified." **Submission policy:** inquire **Advice:** "May be literary but must also entertain." **Comment:** Plays written in English will be translated and performed in Yiddish; simultaneous English and Russian translations are available. Theatre was recently damaged by fire; inquire for plans.

FOOTHILL THEATRE CO.   F-l 1- Tr Ad ♪ CY 2d Rg
P.O. Box 1812, Nevada City, CA 95959 (530) 265-9320 Contact: Philip Charles Sneed, Artistic Director **Theatre:** professional **Works:** full-length plays, one-acts, translations, adaptations, musicals, children's plays **2nd productions:** yes **Special interest:** "Local themes." **Specifications:** maximum cast: 15; no more than 4 sets; no fly, little wing space **Stages:** proscenium, 247 seats; flexible, 75 seats **Casting:** Equity, non-Equity **Submission policy:** unsolicited script; query/synopsis, dialogue sample; professional recommendation; agent submission **Your chances:**

150 new scripts read annually/0 produced to date **Remuneration:** negotiable **Future commitment:** no **Program:** staged readings **Advice:** "Sarcasm, glibness, etc., will not play here."

force. P.O. Box 8033, New York, NY 10150 (212) 757-3905

Contact: Steven Packard, Art. Director   This theatre is closed to submissions in 1999; see *The Playwright's Companion 2000* for future plans.

FORD'S THEATRE   F-l ♪ 2d Af

511 Tenth St. NW, Washington, DC 20004 (202) 638-2941 FAX (202) 347-6269 **Contact:** John Rogers, Literary Assoc. **Theatre:** professional **Works:** full-length plays, small-scale musicals **2nd productions:** yes **Special interest:** "African American issues." **Maximum cast:** 12 **Stage:** proscenium-thrust, 699 seats **Casting:** Equity **Submission policy:** query/synopsis, dialogue sample preferred; unsolicited script **Best time:** summer **Response:** 4+ week- 4+ months **Future commitment:** yes

FOUNDATION THEATRE   F-l Tr Ad ♪ CY 2d Rg Cl

Burlington County College, Rte. 530, Pemberton, NJ 08068 (609) 894-2138 **Contact:** Producing Director **Theatre:** professional **Works:** full-length plays, translations, adaptations, musicals, children's plays **2nd productions:** yes **Special interests:** NJ writers; adaptations of classics **Specifications:** simple demands **Casting:** Equity, non-Equity **Submission policy:** query/synopsis **Best time:** Sept. **Response:** 8 weeks query; 8 months script **Remuneration/commitment:** yes **Programs:** readings, staged readings

FOUNTAIN THEATRE CO.   F-l Tr Ad ♪ 2d po mm cm Am

5060 Fountain Ave., Los Angeles, CA 90029 (213) 663-2235 FAX (213) 663-1629 **Contact:** Simon Levy, Producing Director **Theatre:** professional **Works:** full-length plays, translations, adaptations, musicals **2nd productions:** yes **Special interests:** "Poetic works with dance, music; contemporary comedy; adaptations of American literature." **Specifications:** maximum cast: 12; 1 set/open staging **Stage:** thrust, 78 seats **Casting:** Equity **Audience:** "Issue-specific." **Submission policy:** agent submission preferred; query/synopsis, dialogue sample, SASP **Best time:** Feb.-Jul. **Response:** 6 months **Your chances:** 200 new scripts read annually/1-3 produced **Terms:** negotiable

FOURTH WALL PRODUCTIONS   F-l 1- Tr Ad 2d

4300 N. Narragansett, Chicago, IL 60634 (773) 481-8535 **Contact:** Stephen A. Donart, Artistic Director **Theatre:** professional **Works:** full-length plays, one-acts, translations, adaptations **2nd productions:** yes **Maximum cast:** 15 **Stage:** proscenium, 201 seats **Casting:** non-Equity **Submission policy:** unsolicited script; videotape **Response:** 6 months **Your chances:** 50 new scripts read annually/usually 1 produced **Remuneration:** "10% of box office." **Future commitment:** no **Programs:** readings, staged readings

FRANCINE LE FRAK, PRODUCER   F-l ♪

40 W. 57th St., New York, NY 10019 (212) 541-9444 FAX (212) 974-8205 **Production company:** professional **Works:** full-length plays, musicals **Submission policy:** query/synopsis; agent submission; professional recommendation

FREE STREET PROGRAMS F-l 1- ♪ 2d 12+ Sn h/d mm V Rg ▭

1419 W. **Blackhawk St.**, Chicago, IL 60622 (773) 772-7248 FAX same e-mail freest@mcs.net **Contact:** David Schein, Exec. Director **Theatre:** professional **Works:** full-length plays, one-acts, musicals **2nd productions:** yes **Special interests:** "Inner city--teens, seniors, the disabled; literacy; music, dance; Chicago-area writers." **Specifications:** simple demands **Tours:** all shows **Stage:** mobile outdoor **Casting:** non-Equity **Submission policy:** videotape; idea for outreach program **Response:** 2 months **Your chances:** 10 new scripts read annually/usually none produced **Terms:** negotiable **Program:** workshops

FREED-HARDEMAN UNIV. THEATRE F-l 1- ♪ 2d † W ▭

Henderson, TN 38340 (901) 989-6780 **e-mail** cthompson@fhu.edu **Contact:** R. Cliff Thompson **Theatre:** university **Works:** full-length plays, one-acts, musicals **2nd productions:** yes **Special interests:** "Christian world view; strong women's roles." **Specifications:** limited demands **Tours:** yes **Stage:** proscenium, 650 seats **Submission policy:** query/synopsis **Best time:** fall **Response:** 3-4 months **Your chances:** 10 new plays read annually/usually 1 produced

FREEDOM THEATRE   F-l ♪ Rv C Af Rs

1346 N. **Broad St.**, Philadelphia, PA 19121 (215) 765-2793 FAX (215) 765-4191 **Contact:** Walter Dallas, Artistic Director **Theatre:** professional **Works:** full-length plays, musicals, revues **Special interest:** contemporary plays on African-American themes **Stages:** proscenium, 298 seats; cabaret, 120 seats **Submission policy:** query/synopsis, resume; professional recommendation; commission **Response:** 6-12 weeks **Programs:** staged readings, residencies (programs by invitation only)

FRONTERA @ HYDE PARK   F-l Tr Ad ♪ Rg x

THEATRE 511 W. **43rd St.**, Austin, TX 78751 (512) 419-7408 FAX (512) 419-7408 **Contact:** Megan Monaghan, Literary Mgr. **Theatre:** professional **Works:** full-length plays, translations, adaptations, musicals **Special interests:** "Nonnaturalistic works; border issues, literal or metaphorical." **Stage:** flexible, 90 seats **Submission policy:** unsolicited script **Response:** 6-12 months

GALA HISPANIC THEATRE   F-l Hi Esp po

P.O. Box 43209, Washington, DC 20010 (202) 234-7174 FAX (202) 332-1247 **e-mail** galadc@aol.com **Contact:** Hugo J. Medrano, Producing Art. Director **Theatre:** professional **Works:** full-length plays **Exclusive**

interests: Hispanic writers, themes; plays in Spanish with English translation preferred **Specifications:** cast size: 6-8 **Stage:** proscenium, 200 seats **Submission policy:** query/synopsis preferred; unsolicited script **Best time:** Apr.-May **Response:** 1 month query; 1 year script **Program:** Poetry Onstage (inquire)

GARY YOUNG MIME THEATRE 23724 Park Madrid, Calabasas, CA 91302 (818) 222-5554 **Contact:** Gary Young, Artistic Director This theatre is in operation but not open to submissions in 1999; inquire, or see *The Playwright's Companion 2000* for future plans.

♫ **GEFFEN PLAYHOUSE** F-l Ad ♪
10886 LeConte Ave., Los Angeles, CA 90024 (310) 208-6500 FAX (310) 208-0341 **Contact:** Ethan Lipton, Literary Assoc. **Theatre:** professional **Works:** full-length plays, adaptations, musicals **Stage:** proscenium, 498 seats **Submission policy:** agent submission **Response:** 6 months

GENE FRANKEL THEATRE F-l 1- ♪ 2d Lc ⌂
24 Bond St., New York, NY 10012 (212) 777-1767 **Contact:** Gene Frankel, Artistic Director **Theatre:** off off Broadway **Works:** full-length plays, one-acts, musicals **2nd productions:** yes **Specifications:** maximum cast: 25; limited sets; no fly space **Tours:** yes **Stage:** flexible, up to 70 seats **Audience:** "From agents and critics to 1st-time theatregoers." **Submission policy:** unsolicited script; query/synopsis; professional recommendation; agent submission **Best time:** "Now!" **Response:** 1-4 months **Your chances:** 100 new scripts read annually **Terms:** negotiable

GENERIC THEATER F-l 1- Tr Ad 2d
P.O. Box 11071, Norfolk, VA 23517 (804) 441-2160 e-mail generic@generictheater.org **Contact:** Steven Harders, Artistic Director **Theatre:** semi-professional **Works:** full-length plays, one-acts, translations, adaptations **2nd productions:** "Considered." **Specifications:** maximum cast: 7; simple sets **Stage:** semi-flexible, 80 seats **Audience:** "Adventurous." **Submission policy:** unsolicited script, synopsis, script history, resume, SASP **Response:** 2 weeks query; 1 year script **Your chances:** 30+ new scripts read annually/usually 0-1 produced **Remuneration:** negotiable **Future commitment:** credit **Program:** New Plays for Dog Days Festival (see Contests)

GENESEE COMMUNITY F-l Tr Ad CY 2d Am W M
COLLEGE THEATRE 1 College Rd., Batavia, NY 14020 (716) 343-0055 Ext. 6439 e-mail marciam@sgccvb.sunygenessee.cc.ny.us **Contact:** Marcia K. Morrison, Director **Works:** full-length plays, translations, adaptations, children's plays **2nd productions:** yes **Special interests:** rural America; women and minority writers **Specifications:** small cast, small budget **Casting:** students **Submission policy:** unsolicited script **Best time:** spring **Response:** 1-2 months **Program:** workshops

♬ THE GENESIUS GUILD   D F-l ♪

P.O. Box 2273, New York, NY 10108 (212) 946-5625 **Contact:** Thomas Morrissey, Artistic Director **Theatre:** off off Broadway **Works:** full-length plays, musicals **Stage:** proscenium, 99 seats **Submission policy:** query/synopsis **Your chances:** 50 new scripts read annually **Future commitment:** credit **Programs:** staged readings; The Genesius Guild Developmental Workshop (see Special Programs)

GEORGE STREET PLAYHOUSE   F-l ♪ CY 2d M W

9 Livingston Ave., New Brunswick, NJ 08901 (908) 846-2895 **Contact:** Maxine Kern, Literary Mgr. **Theatre:** professional **Works:** full-length plays, musicals, children's one-acts **2nd productions:** yes **Special interests:** multicultural and women's issues; women playwrights **Maximum cast:** 8, 12 for musical **Stage:** proscenium-thrust, 380 seats **Submission policy:** professional recommendation **Response:** 6-8 months **Future commitment:** varies **Program:** 2-week new play workshop series

GEORGIA ENSEMBLE THEATRE

P.O. Box 607, Roswell, GA 30077-0607 (770) 641-1260 FAX (770) 641-1360 **Contact:** Robert J. Farley, Artistic Director **Theatre:** professional This theatre is not currently open to submissions.

GEORGIA REPERTORY THEATRE   F-l

Univ. of Georgia Drama Dept., Athens, GA 30602-3154 (706) 542-2836 FAX (706) 542-2080 **e-mail** longman@uga.cc.uga.edu **Contact:** Stanley Longman, Dramaturg **Theatre:** professional **Works:** full-length plays **Special interest:** unproduced plays **Specifications:** maximum cast: 8; minimal set **Stages:** 2 prosceniums, 750, 100 seats **Submission policy:** unsolicited script **Best time:** late spring **Response:** 3-6 months

GERMINAL STAGE DENVER   F-l Tr Ad

2450 W. 44th Ave., Denver, CO 80211 (303) 455-7108 **e-mail** gsden@ privatei.com **Contact:** Edward Baierlein, Director/Mgr. **Theatre:** professional **Works:** full-length plays, translations, adaptations **Special interest:** "Adaptations using dialogue and narration." **Specifications:** maximum cast: 10; minimal demands **Stage:** thrust, 100 seats **Submission policy:** query/synopsis, 5-page dialogue sample, SASP **Response:** 2 weeks query; 6 months solicited script

GEVA THEATRE   F-l Tr Ad

75 Woodbury Blvd., Rochester, NY 14607 (716) 232-1366 FAX (716) 232-4031 **Contact:** Jean Ryon, New Plays Coordinator **Theatre:** professional **Works:** full-length plays, translations, adaptations **Stages:** modified thrust, 552 seats; flexible, 175 seats **Casting:** Equity **Submission policy:** query/synopsis, dialogue sample (5 pages maximum), script history, resume **Program:** See GeVa Theatre in Special Programs,

GINDI THEATRICAL MANAGEMENT, INC. F-l ♪

311 W. 43rd St., New York, NY 10036 (212) 489-7050 FAX (212) 489-7062 e-mail RaGTM@aol.com Production company: professional Works: full-length plays, musicals Submission policy: query/synopsis; agent submission; professional recommendation

GLADYS NEDERLANDER PRODUCTIONS See Nederlander Productions in this section.

THE GLINES F-l Tr Ad ♪ 2d g/l

240 W. 44th St., New York, NY 10036 (212) 354-8899 e-mail theglines@aol.com Contact: John Glines, Artistic Director Theatre: professional Works: full-length plays, translations, adaptations, musicals 2nd productions: if New York City premieres Exclusive interest: "The gay experience." Specifications: maximum cast: 10; simple sets Submission policy: unsolicited script; professional recommendation Response: 2 months Your chances: 300 new scripts read annually/usually 2-3 produced Response: 2 months Remuneration: fee or royalty Future commitment: percentage, credit

GOLDEN SQUIRREL THEATRE F-l 2d C Sp

230 Riverside Dr. #14D, New York, NY 10025 (212) 663-5787 FAX same Contact: Steven Somkin, Artistic Director Theatre: professional Works: full-length plays 2nd productions: "If not previously produced in New York City" Special interest: "Contemporary themes that celebrate the human spirit; no performance art, children's plays, musicals." Stages: rental spaces Casting: Equity, non-Equity Submission policy: unsolicited script, synopsis; agent submission Response: 6-8 weeks Your chances: 200 new scripts read annually/usually 4 produced, latest in May 1998 Remuneration: negotiable for production Future commitment: no Response: 6-8 weeks Program: staged readings Advice: "Send script!"

THE GOODMAN THEATRE F-l Tr ♪ 2d C

200 S. Columbus Dr., Chicago, IL 60603-6491 (312) 443-3811 FAX (312) 263-6004 e-mail staff@goodmantheatre.org Contact: Susan V. Booth, Director, New Play Dev.Theatre: professional Works: full-length plays, translations, musicals 2nd productions: yes; premieres preferred Maximum cast: 20 Special interest: social/political themes Stages: 2 prosceniums, 135, 683 seats Casting: Equity, non-Equity; Submission policy: query/synopsis, dialogue sample; agent submission Response: 8 months Your chances: 400 new scripts read annually Terms: negotiable

GOODSPEED OPERA HOUSE ♪

P.O. Box A, E. Haddam, CT 06423 (860) 873-8664 FAX (860) 873-2329 Contact: Sue Frost, Assoc. Producer Theatre: professional Works: original musicals Stages: proscenium, 400 seats; flexible proscenium, 200 seats Submission policy: query/synopsis only Best time: Jan.-

Mar. **Response:** 3 months query; 1 year solicited script **Your chances:** 300 new scripts read annually/usually 3 produced **Remuneration:** yes **Future commitment:** yes

GOSHEN COLLEGE THEATRE   See Peace Play Contest.

GREASY JOAN AND COMPANY   Tr Ad 2d Cl
P.O. Box 267995, Chicago, IL 60626 (773) 761-8284 FAX (773) 472-4923 **Theatre:** professional **Works:** full-length translations, adaptations **2nd productions:** yes **Exclusive interest:** "Classically-based material." **Maximum cast:** 5-8 **Casting:** Equity **Submission policy:** query/synopsis, dialogue sample preferred; unsolicited script **Response:** 3 months

GREAT AMERICAN HISTORY THEATRE
30 E. 10th St., St. Paul, MN 55101 (651) 292-4323 FAX (651) 292-4322 **Contact:** Ron Peluso, Artistic Director **Theatre:** professional   This theatre is not open to submissions in 1999; see *The Playwright's Companion 2000* or inquire for future plans.

THE GREAT AMERICAN MELODRAMA   F-l Rv 2d cm V
1827 Pacific Blvd., Oceano, CA 93445 (805) 489-2499 FAX (805) 489-5539 **Contact:** Art. Director **Works:** 75-minute plays **2nd productions:** yes **Special interests:** "Melodramas, comedy routines, revues for all ages." **Submission policy:** query/synopsis **Response:** 3-12 months

GREAT LAKES THEATER FESTIVAL   1501 Euclid Ave. # 423,
Cleveland, OH 44115   This theatre commissions scripts and is not open to submissions from playwrights.

GRETNA THEATRE   F-l ♪ 2d cm Fm
P.O. Box 578, Mt. Gretna, PA 17064-0578 (717) 964-3322 FAX (717) 964-2189 **Contact:** Pat Julian, Exec. Director **Theatre:** professional **Works:** full-length plays, small-cast musicals **2nd productions:** yes **Special interest:** comedy **Maximum cast:** 20 **Stage:** open-air proscenium, 700 seats **Casting:** Equity **Audience:** "Educated, conservative, mature." **Submission policy:** query/synopsis, 5-page dialogue sample, script history, resume **Best time:** Aug.-Apr. **Response:** 1 month query; 3 months solicited script **Your chances:** 60-75 new scripts read annually/ 2-5 produced **Terms:** negotiable **Comment:** Materials are not returned.

GROUP PRODUCTIONS   71 Harrington Ave., Westwood, NJ
07675 (201) 664-4636   This theatre is closed to submissions in 1999; see *The Playwright's Companion 2000* for future plans.

THE GROUP THEATRE   F-l Tr Ad ♪ CY 2d C M dr cm ▭
305 Harrison St., Seattle, WA 98109 (206) 441-9480 FAX (206) 441-9839 **Contact:** Lit. Dept. **Theatre:** professional **Works:** full-length plays, translations, adaptations, musicals, children's plays **2nd productions:** yes **Special interests:** multicultural issues/casting; satire, comedy

Specifications: maximum cast: 7; simple set preferred **Tours:** yes **Stage:** modified thrust, 192 seats **Submission policy:** query/synopsis, dialogue sample, resume **Best time:** Aug.-Nov. **Response:** 6 months

THE GROWING STAGE THEATRE   CY 2d ▱

P.O. Box 36, Netcong, NJ 07857 (973) 347-4946 FAX (973) 691-7069 **Contact:** Stephen L. Fredericks, Exec. Director **Theatre:** professional **Works:** children's plays **2nd productions:** yes **Specifications:** maximum cast: 8; no more than 3 sets **Tours:** yes **Stage:** proscenium **Casting:** Equity, non-Equity **Submission policy:** query/synopsis; videotape **Best time:** Jan.-Jun. **Response:** 1 month query; 2-3 months solicited script **Your chances:** 50 new scripts read annually/usually 1 produced **Remuneration:** negotiable **Future commitment:** no

THE GUTHRIE THEATER   F-l Tr Ad

725 Vineland Pl., Minneapolis, MN 55403 (612) 347-1100 **Contact:** Jo Holcomb, Librarian/Literary Specialist **Theatre:** professional **Works:** full-length plays, translations, adaptations **Stage:** thrust, 1309 seats **Submission policy:** query/synopsis, 10-page dialogue sample; professional recommendation; agent submission **Response:** 4-5 weeks query; 4 months solicited script

HAIDEE AND ALLEN WILD   F-l 2d W cm dr my C Fm
CENTER FOR THE ARTS **Cottey College, 1000 W. Austin, Nevada, MO 64772** (417) 667-8181 FAX (417) 667-8103 e-mail afenske@cottey.edu **Contact:** Dr. Rusalyn Andrews **Theatre:** college **Works:** full-length plays **2nd productions:** yes **Special interests:** "Plays for women or with predominately female casts; comedies, dramas, thrillers; issues." **Specifications:** maximum cast: 15, no more than 2 males; no more than 2 sets, single interior preferred **Stage:** proscenium, 495 seats **Casting:** students **Audience:** "College, community." **Submission policy:** unsolicited script; query/synopsis **Best time:** May-Jul. **Response:** 3 months query; 3-6 months script **Your chances:** 6-12 new scripts read annually/usually 1-2 produced **Remuneration:** royalty **Future commitment:** credit **Advice:** "Realism preferred. Subject matter may be current but not too controversial or profane."

THE HARBOR THEATRE   D F-l ♪ 2d Rg

160 W. 71st St. PHA, New York, NY 10023 (212) 787-1945 FAX (212) 712-2378 **Contact:** Stuart Warmflash, Artistic Director **Theatre:** professional **Works:** full-length plays, musicals, excerpts **2nd productions:** yes **Special interests:** "All genres; writers with a unique theatrical voice." **Stages:** rental spaces, usually 99 seats **Casting:** repertory company **Audience:** New York City, off and off-off Broadway **Submission policy:** "Must be a member of the Harbor Theatre Lab" (see Special Programs) **Best time:** Dec.-Jun. **Response:** 2-3 months **Remuneration:** "Dramatists Guild contract." **Future commitment:** varies **Advice:** "Must firmly believe in rewrites."

HARLEQUIN PRODUCTIONS　　　　F-l 1- Tr Ad 2d C
**Cayuga County CC, 197 Franklin St., Auburn, NY 13021-3099 (315)
255-1743 Ext. 340 FAX (315) 255-2117 e-mail** framer@admin.cayuga-
cc.edu **Contact:** Robert M. Frame, Director **Theatre:** community **Works:**
full-length plays, one-acts, translations, adaptations **2nd productions:**
yes **Special interest:** contemporary plays **Cast size:** 5-10 **Stages:** proscenium, 525 seats; flexible, 95 seats **Casting:** non-Equity **Submission
policy:** unsolicited script **Best time:** late spring-summer **Response:** 9
weeks (if interested) **Your chances:** 20 new scripts read annually/
usually 1-2 produced, latest in Mar. 1998 **Remuneration:** negotiable
Future commitment: credit

HAROLD PRINCE　　　10 Rockefeller Plaza #1009, New York, NY
10020　Harold Prince is not currently producing plays.

HARRIS PRODUCTION SERVICES　　　　F-l Ad ♪ ▭
**630 Ninth Ave., New York, NY 10036 (212) 589-5400 FAX (212) 869-
7714 e-mail** JGelick@PRG.com **Contact:** Jennifer Gelick **Production
company:** Broadway, off Broadway **Works:** full-length plays, adaptations, musicals **2nd productions:** "Yes, 1st produced in London." **Casting:** Equity **Submission policy:** query/synopsis; agent submission; professional recommendation

HARTFORD STAGE COMPANY　　　　F-l Tr Ad 2d
**50 Church St., Hartford, CT 06103 (860) 525-5601 FAX (860) 525-
4420 Contact:** Shawn René Graham, Literary Assoc. **Theatre:** professional **Works:** full-length plays, translations, adaptations **2nd productions:** yes **Stage:** thrust, 489 seats **Submission policy:** query/synopsis,
dialogue sample; professional recommendation; agent submission **Response:** 1 month query; 9 months solicited script **Your chances:** 600
new scripts read annually/usually 0-1 produced

HART-SHARPE ENTERTAINMENT　　　　　　F-l ♪
**380 Lafayette St. 3rd Floor, New York, NY 10003 (212) 475-7555
Contact:** Peter Burns **Company:** professional **Works:** full-length plays,
musicals **Submission policy:** query/synopsis; agent submission;
professional recommendation

HARVE BROSTEN PRODUCTIONS　　　　　　　♪
240 W. 44rd St., New York, NY 10036 (212) 302-3585 Contact:
Harve Brosten, Producer **Production company:** professional **Works:**
musicals **Special interest:** "Strong books, intelligent lyrics." **Submission policy:** query/synopsis

♫ **THE HASTY PUDDING THEATRE**　　F-l Tr Ad ♪ CY Rv
**12 Holyoke St., Cambridge, MA 02138 (617) 496-6757 FAX (617) 495-
5205 Contact:** Michael McClung, Exec. Director **Theatre:** professional
Works: full-length plays, translations, adaptations, musicals, children's

plays, revues **Special interest:** "Gender issues." **Stage:** proscenium, 360 seats **Submission policy:** unsolicited script **Response:** 2-3 months **Program:** monthly reading series

HEARTLAND THEATRE COMPANY   Bloomington, IL 61702
This theatre is no longer open to submissions.

HEARTLANDE THEATRE   **F-l Rg**
P.O. Box 2014, **Birmingham, MI 48012 Theatre:** professional **Works:** full-length plays **Exclusive interest:** Midwest playwrights **Specifications:** small cast, single or unit set **Submission procedure:** query/1-page synopsis, 15-page dialogue sample, resume **Program:** Playscape Festival (see Special Programs)

HEDGEROW THEATRE   **F-l CY 2d Rg my cm Cl** ⌐
146 W. Rose Valley Rd., Rose Valley, PA 19065   (610) 565-4211
Contact: Walt Vail, Lit. Director **Theatre:** professional **Works:** full-length plays, children's plays **2nd productions:** yes **Special interests:** "DE, NJ, PA playwrights; mysteries, comedies." **Tours:** children's plays **Stage:** flexible, 144 seats **Casting:** non-Equity **Submission policy:** unsolicited script, resume; query/synopsis, dialogue sample **Response:** 3 weeks-5 months **Program:** Hedgerow Horizons (see Special Programs)

HERE THEATRE AND ART CENTER   **F-l Ad ♪ Rv mm x V**
145 Avenue of the Americas, New York, NY 10013 (212) 647-0202
Contact: Tim Maner, Director of Communications **Theatre:** professional **Works:** full-length plays, adaptations, musicals, revues, multidisciplinary works **Exclusive interests:** experimental work; puppetry; NYC premieres **Stages:** flexible, 99 seats; proscenium, 74 seats; cabaret, 74 seats **Submission policy:** query/synopsis, resume, dialogue sample; professional recommendation; agent submission; NYC writer: unsolicited script **Response:** 3-5 months **Your chances:** 300 new scripts read annually/usually 0-1 produced **Comment:** Formerly Home for Contemporary Theatre and Art.

HERITAGE THEATRE   See Center Stage Theatre in this section.

HIP POCKET THEATRE   **F-l Ad ♪ mm 2d V po**
7344 Love Circle, Ft. Worth, TX 76135 (817) 237-5977 FAX (817) 272-2697 **Contact:** Johnny Simons, Artistic Director **Theatre:** professional **Works:** full-length plays, adaptations, musicals, multimedia works **2nd productions:** yes **Special interests:** "Folklore; Commedia; mime; poetic, mythic works." **Specifications:** maximum cast: 10-15 preferred; simple set **Stages:** outdoor amphitheatre, 175 seats **Casting:** non-Equity **Audience:** "Slightly off mainstream." **Submission policy:** unsolicited script, cassette tape for musical **Best time:** Oct.-Mar. **Response:** 6 weeks **Your chances:** 150 new scripts read annually/usually 2 produced **Remuneration:** negotiable **Program:** workshops

THE HIPPODROME STATE THEATRE   F-l Tr Ad 1- 2d ⌐⊐
25 SE 2nd Pl., Gainesville, FL 32601-6596   (352) 373-5968   FAX (352)
371-9130   e-mail hipp@afn.org   Contact: Tamerin Dygert, Dramaturg
Theatre: professional   Works: full-length plays, translations, adaptations; one-acts for 2nd stage series 2nd productions: yes Specifications: maximum cast: 8, unit set preferred Tours: yes Stages: thrust, 266
seats; flexible, 87 seats Casting: Equity, non-Equity Audience: "Professionals, artists, writers, students." Submission policy: query/synopsis,
dialogue sample, resume; professional recommendation; agent submission
Best time: Apr.-Jul. Response: 2 months query; 4 months solicited script
Your chances: 30-70+ new scripts read annually/usually 1 produced
Remuneration: royalties Future commitment: credit Programs:
staged readings; contests/festivals (inquire)

HOFSTRA U.S.A. PRODUCTIONS   F-l 1- Tr Ad ♪ Rv 2d
Hofstra Cultural Center, 107 Hofstra Univ., Hempstead, NY 11549
(516) 463-5669 Contact: Bob Spiotto, Artistic Director Theatre: non-
professional Works: full-length plays, one-acts, translations, adaptations, musicals, revues 2nd productions: yes Special interests: topics
appropriate to conference themes (inquire) Specifications: maximum
cast: 15; no more than 2 sets Stages: proscenium, 1134 seats; thrust, 400
seats; flexible, 100 seats Casting: "Students, community." Submission
policy: query/synopsis, resume Response: 2-3 weeks Your chances:
20 new scripts read annually Remuneration: negotiable

♫ **HOLLYWOOD BOULEVARD**   F-l 1- Tr Ad k CY Rv
THEATRE   1938 Hollywood Blvd., Hollywood, FL 33020 (954) 929-
5400 (954) 929-0111 Theatre: professional Works: full-length plays,
one-acts, translations, adaptations, musicals, children's plays, revues
2nd productions: preferred Specifications: maximum cast: 4; minimal
or unit set Stage: arena, 85 seats Casting: Equity, non-Equity Audience: 35-60, professionals Submission policy: unsolicited script Response: 1 month Your chances: 60 new scripts read annually/usually
0-1 produced Remuneration: stipend Future commitments: option

HOME FOR CONTEMPORARY THEATRE AND ART
See Here Theatre and Art Center in this section.

HONOLULU THEATRE FOR YOUTH   CY 1- Ad Rg 12+ C
2846 Ualena St., Honolulu, HI 96819 (808) 839-9885 FAX (808) 839-
7018 e-mail hnlty@aol.com Contact: Jane Campbell, Producing Director
Theatre: professional Works: children's plays, one-acts, adaptations
Special interests: "Contemporary themes; Pacific Rim cultures; adaptations of literary classics." Maximum cast: 6 Stages: proscenium, 650
seats; flexible, 300 Audience: "Young audiences to high school." Submission policy: query/synopsis/resume Response: 1 month query; 6
months solicited script

HORIZON THEATRE CO.   F-l Tr Ad ♪ 2d C W Rg cm 12+ Sn
P.O. Box 5376 Station E, Atlanta, GA 30307 (404) 523-1477 FAX (404) 584-8815 **e-mail** horizonco@mindspring.com **Contact:** Sarah Baskin, Literary Mgr. **Theatre:** professional **Works:** full-length plays, one-acts (for teen and senior citizens ensembles) translations, adaptations, musicals **2nd productions:** yes **Special interests:** "Contemporary issues; women writers; Southern-urban themes; comedies." **Maximum cast:** 12 **Stage:** flexible, 170-200 seats **Casting:** Equity, non-Equity **Submission policy:** query/synopsis, dialogue sample, resume; professional recommendation; agent submission; GA writer: unsolicited script **Best time:** May-Jun. **Response:** 6-12 months **Your chances:** 200 new scripts read annually/usually 1-3 produced **Remuneration:** percentage

HORSE CAVE THEATRE   F-l Rg
P.O. Box 215, Horse Cave, KY 42749 (502) 786-1200 FAX (502) 786-5298 **Contact:** Warren Hammack, Director **Theatre:** professional **Works:** full-length plays **2nd productions:** no **Exclusive interest:** "Plays by and about Kentuckians." **Specifications:** maximum cast: 10; single set **Stage:** thrust, 345 seats **Submission policy:** professional recommendation **Best time:** Oct.-Apr. **Response:** several weeks **Your chances:** 30-50 new scripts read annually/usually 0-2 produced **Terms:** negotiable

HUDSON THEATRE   F-l 1- Tr Ad ♪ CY Rv 2d Am
6539 Santa Monica Blvd., Hollywood, CA 90038 (213) 856-4249 FAX (213) 856-4252 **Contact:** Elizabeth Reilly, Artistic Director **Theatre:** professional **Works:** full-length plays, one-acts, translations, adaptations, musicals, children's plays, revues **2nd productions:** yes **Special interest:** "New American plays, but not exclusively." **Stages:** modified thrust, 99 seats; 2 raised stages, 75, 35 seats; modular, 99 seats **Casting:** Equity **Submission policy:** unsolicited script; query/synopsis; professional recommendation; agent submission; synopsis, dialogue sample, script history with all material **Response:** 3-6 months **Your chances:** 1000 new scripts read annually/usually 1-5 produced **Remuneration:** "Percentage or royalties." **Future commitment:** credit; percentage of future royalties **Programs:** readings, staged readings

THE HUMAN RACE THEATRE CO.   F-l 1- CY Rg 12+ C ⌑
126 N. Main St. Suite 300, Dayton, OH 45402 (937) 461-3823 FAX (937) 461-7223 **e-mail** hrtheatre@aol.com **Contact:** Tony Dallas, Playwright in Residence **Theatre:** professional **Works:** full-length plays, one-acts, plays for young audiences **Special interests:** "OH writers; 40-minute plays for junior-senior high audiences; contemporary issues." **Specifications:** small cast, no fly space; youth plays tour **Stage:** thrust, 219 seats **Casting:** Equity, non-Equity **Submission policy:** query/synopsis, dialogue sample; professional recommendation; agent submission **Response:** 6 months **Your chances:** 150 new scripts read annually/1 play receives staged reading

HUNTINGTON THEATRE COMPANY   F-l Tr Ad 2d Rg
**264 Huntington Ave., Boston, MA 02115 (617) 266-7900 FAX (617)
353-8300 Contact:** Scott Edmiston, Lit. Assoc. **Theatre:** professional
Works: full-length plays, translations, adaptations **2nd productions:**
yes **Special interests:** New England authors, themes, adaptations of
literature **Stage:** proscenium, 850 seats **Submission policy:** query/synopsis; professional recommendation **Best time:** May-Sept. **Response:**
3 months query; 6 months solicited script

IDAHO THEATER FOR YOUTH   CY 1- Ad Tr ♪ x ▭
**P.O. Box 7926, Boise, ID 83707 (208) 345-0060   FAX (208) 345-6433
e-mail** ity@cyberhighway.net **Contact:** Pam Sterling, Artistic Director
Theatre: professional **Works:** children's plays, one-acts, adaptations
and musicals **2nd productions:** mainstage **Special interest:** "Innovative,
simple theatricality from a young person's perspective." **Specifications:**
maximum cast: 4; minimal set **Tours:** "Extensively." **Casting:** non-Equity
Submission policy: query/synopsis, dialogue sample, resume, script
history, SASP; professional recommendation; agent submission; commission **Your chances:** 25 new scripts read annually/usually 2-4
produced **Remuneration:** "Commission fee." **Future commitment:**
credit **Programs:** readings, staged readings, development

ILLINOIS THEATRE CENTER   F-l ♪ 2d
400A Lakewood Blvd., Park Forest, IL 60466 (708) 481-3510 e-mail
itcbillig@juno.com **Contact:** Etel Billig, Producing Director **Theatre:** professional **Works:** full-length plays, musicals **2nd productions:** yes
Maximum cast: 9 for play, 14 for musical **Stage:** proscenium, 200 seats
Submission policy: query/synopsis, dialogue sample **Response:** 1-2
months **Remuneration:** royalty **Future commitment:** negotiable

ILLUSION THEATER   D F-l 1- Tr Ad ♪ 2d W g/l M
**528 Hennepin Ave. Suite 704, Minneapolis, MN 55403 (612) 339-
4944 FAX (612) 337-8042   Contact:** Michael Robins, Exec. Director
Theatre: professional **Works:** full-length plays, one-acts, translations,
adaptations, musicals **2nd productions:** yes **Special interests:** "New
collaborative projects; women, lesbian, gay, minority writers." **Maximum cast:** 12 **Stage:** thrust, 250 seats **Submission policy:** unsolicited
script; query/proposal **Best time:** Jul.-Nov. **Response:** 6-12 months
Remuneration: negotiable **Program:** Fresh Ink (see Special Programs)

IMMIGRANTS' THEATRE   F-l 1- Tr Ad V 2d M x ▭
**PROJECT, INC.   44 Douglas St., Brooklyn, NY 11231-4714 (718)
237-4545 FAX (718)** same **Contact:** Marcy Arlin, Artistic Director
Theatre: off off Broadway **Works:** full-length plays, one-acts, translations, adaptations, puppets **2nd productions:** yes **Special interests:**
"Immigrant playwrights and themes; works suitable for readings." **Specifications:** maximum cast: 11-15; simple set **Tours:** yes **Stage:**"Depends on
venue; nothing too extravagant." **Casting:** Equity, non-Equity, ensemble,

pool **Audience:** "Likes experimental works and/or good stories; ethnically focused, reflecting newcomer population." **Submission policy:** unsolicited script, resume; professional recommendation; agent submission **Response:** "Quite a while." **Your chances:** 25 new scripts read annually/usually 4-6 produced **Remuneration:** "$50 for a reading (if paid/hired); share of box office, fee if showcased." **Future commitment:** credit, possible option **Programs:** staged readings, workshops; New Immigrant Play Festival (see Special Programs); Library Shows (short plays, ethnically focused) **Advice:** "Be careful with stereotypes."

IMPULSE DRAMATISTS   D F-l 1- Ad ♪ 2d cm dr my
3131 S.W. Sherwood Pl., Portland, OR 97201-2254 (503) 228-8877 e-mail idedu@teleport.com **Contact:** Ed Udovick, Exec. Director **Production company:** professional **Works:** full-length plays, one-acts, adaptations, musicals **Special interests:** previously produced works; comedies, musicals, mysteries, dramas, collaborations **Specifications:** "Musical works must be on tape; no TV/film scripts." **Submission policy:** unsolicited script **Response:** 10 months **Advice:**"Im.pulse--noun, something that rouses the mind or spirit or impels to activity."

INDIANA REPERTORY THEATRE   F-l Tr Ad 2d Cl Rg M
140 W. Washington, Indianapolis, IN 46204 (317) 635-5277 FAX (317) 236-0767 e-mail irt@iquest.net **Contact:** Literary Mgr. **Theatre:** professional **Works:** full-length plays, translations, adaptations **2nd productions:** yes **Special interests:** "Classics; Midwestern voices; diversity." **Maximum cast:** 6-8 **Stages:** proscenium, 600 seats; thrust, 300 seats **Submission policy:** query/synopsis, dialogue sample **Response:** 3-6 months **Program:** The Discovery Series (see Special Programs)

INGRAM PRODUCTIONS   F-l ♪
1500 Broadway Suite 1107, New York, NY 10036 (212) 303-2481 Contact: Jeff Ash **Production company:** off Broadway **Works:** full-length plays, small-scale musicals **Submission policy:** professional recommendation; agent submission

INTAR   F-l 1- Tr Ad ♪ Hi Esp
P.O. Box 788, New York, NY 10108 (212) 695-6135 Ext. 17 FAX (212) 268-0102 Contact: Lorenzo Mans, Literary Mgr. **Theatre:** professional **Works:** full-length plays, one-acts, translations, adaptations, musicals **Exclusive interest:** Hispanic issues, writers **Maximum cast:** 8 **Stages:** 2 prosceniums, 75, 99 seats **Submission policy:** unsolicited script **Response:** 3-6 months **Program:** INTAR Lab (see Special Programs)

INTERACT THEATRE COMPANY   F-l 2d C M
The Adrienne, 2030 Sansom St., Philadelphia, PA 19103 (215) 568-8077 (FAX) 568-8095 Contact: Seth Rozin, Producing Artistic Director **Theatre:** professional **Works:** full-length plays **2nd productions:** yes **Exclusive interests:** cultural conflict; social relevance **Specifications:**

maximum cast: 10; no more than 2 sets **Stage:** proscenium, 106 seats **Submission policy:** query/synopsis **Response:** 1 month query; 4 months solicited script **Programs:** readings, Showcase of New Plays

INTERBOROUGH   F-l 1- Tr Ad ♪ Rv 2d g/l h/d Rg
REPERTORY THEATRE (IRT)   154 Christopher St. #3B, New York, NY 10014 (212) 206-6875 **Contact:** Luane Davis, Artistic Director **Theatre:** professional **Works:** full-length plays, one-acts, translations, adaptations, musicals, revues **2nd productions:** yes **Special interests:** "Gay themes, hearing-impaired characters, American Sign Language." **Maximum cast:** 9 **Casting:** Equity, non-Equity **Submission policy:** NY playwright: query/synopsis **Best time:** summer **Response:** 2-3 months **Your chances:** 50 new scripts read annually/usually 1 produced **Terms:** percentages **Programs:** workshops; New Directions Theater Contest (see Contests)

INTERNATIONAL CITY THEATRE   F-l 1-
4901 E. Carson St., Long Beach, CA 90808 (562) 938-4051 **Contact:** Caryn Morse Desai, General Mgr. **Works:** full-length plays, one-acts **Special interests:** "New voices, new works." **Submission policy:** unsolicited script; query/synopsis

INTERNATIONAL PERFORMANCE   F-l Tr Ad x mm ⊐
STUDIO   1517 W. Fullerton Ave., Chicago, IL 60614 (773) 281-9075 **FAX** (773) 929-5437 **Contact:** Nicole Dreiske, Artistic Director **Theatre:** professional **Works:** full-length plays, translations, adaptations **2nd productions:** no **Special interests:** "Non-linear, choral scripts with movement; multimedia works." **Maximum cast:** 15 **Tours:** yes **Stages:** all-purpose room, 159 seats; arena/thrust, 90 seats **Audience:** "Tours: international festivals, conventions, universities." **Submission policy:** query/synopsis, dialogue sample; professional recommendation **Response:** 8 weeks **Your chances:** 30 new scripts read annually/usually 1 produced **Terms:** negotiable

INTIMAN THEATRE COMPANY   F-l Tr Ad 2d
P.O. Box 19760, Seattle, WA 98109 (206) 269-1901 **FAX** (206) 269-1928 **e-mail** intiman@scn.org **Contact:** Liz Engelman, Lit. Mgr. **Theatre:** professional **Works:** full-length plays, translations, adaptations **2nd productions:** yes **Stage:** thrust, 480 seats **Casting:** Equity, non-Equity **Submission policy:** professional recommendation; agent submission **Best time:** Jan.-Jun. **Your chances:** 400 new scripts read annually/ usually 4 produced **Response:** 6 months **Remuneration:** royalties, travel, housing **Future commitment:** negotiable **Program:** development

INVISIBLE THEATRE   F-l 1- ♪ 2d W C
1400 N. First Ave., Tucson, AZ 85719 (520) 882-9721 **FAX** (520) 884-0672, call first **Contact:** Susan Claassen, Art. Director **Theatre:** professional **Works:** full-length plays, one-acts, small-cast musicals **2nd pro-**

ductions: yes **Special interests:** female roles; social issues; contemporary settings **Specifications:** maximum cast: 8-10; single set; simple demands **Stage:** black box, 78 seats **Submission policy:** professional recommendation **Best time:** Jul.-Dec. **Response:** 6-12 months **Your chances:** 25 new scripts read annually/usually 1 produced **Terms:** negotiable

IRISH ARTS CENTER F-l 1- ♪ 2d ℰ
553 W. 51st St., New York, NY 10019 (212) 757-3318 **Contact:** Nye Heron, Artistic Director **Theatre:** professional **Works:** full-length plays, one-acts, musicals **2nd productions:** yes **Exclusive interest:** "Irish and Irish-American issues." **Maximum cast:** 8 **Submission policy:** agent submission **Response:** 1 month

IRONDALE ENSEMBLE PROJECT D F-l Ad ♪ 2d x C
P.O. Box 1314 Old Chelsea Station, New York, NY 10011-1314 (212) 633-1292 FAX (212) 633-2078 **e-mail** irondalert@aol.com **Contact:** Jim Niesen, Artistic Director **Theatre:** professional, experimental theatre **Works:** full-length plays, adaptations, plays with music **2nd productions:** yes **Special interest:** social/political relevance **Specifications:** maximum cast: 10-12; unit set **Stages:** various spaces **Submission policy:** query/1-page synopsis or project description **Best time:** Sept.-Jun. **Response:** 10 weeks **Future commitment:** yes **Advice:** "All plays are developed in our workshops; be willing to participate."

IRVING SIDERS F-l ♪
250 W. 52nd St., New York, NY 10019 (212) 975-0293 FAX (212) 489-1372 **Production company:** professional **Works:** full-length plays, musicals **Submission policy:** query/synopsis; agent submission; professional recommendation

ISOBEL ROBINS, PRODUCER F-l ♪
248 E. 68th St., New York, NY 10021 (212) 744-6003 FAX (212) 744-6838 **Production company:** professional **Works:** full-length plays, musicals **Submission policy:** query/synopsis; agent submission; professional recommendation

JAMES B. FREYDBERG F-l Tr Ad ♪ CY dr cm
PRODUCTIONS Pachyderm Entertainment, 1560 Broadway Suite 400, New York, NY 10036 (212) 840-8400, -1124 **Contact:** James B. Freydberg **Production company:** professional **Works:** full-length plays, translations, adaptations, musicals, children's plays **Special interests:** drama, comedy, musicals **Submission policy:** agent submission

JANE DOE THEATRE-NORTHWEST PLAYWRIGHTS GUILD
P.O. Box 95259, Seattle, WA 98145-2259 (206) 298-9361 This theatre is currently closed to submissions; inquire, or see *The Playwright's Companion 2000* for future plans.

JANE HARMON ASSOCIATES   F-l C
One Lincoln Plaza Suite 28-0, New York, NY 10023 (212) 362-6836
Contact: Jane Harmon, Nina Keneally, Producers **Production company:**
Broadway, off Broadway **Works:** full-length plays **Special interests:**
new plays; unique voices; issues **Submission policy:** query/synopsis;
agent submission **Response:** 6-8 weeks

JAN McART'S ROYAL PALM DINNER   F-l 1- ♪ 2d ⌑
THEATRE   **315 SE Mizner Blvd.**, Boca Raton, FL 33432 (561) 392-
8066, -3755 FAX (407) 392-1443 Contact: Jan McArt **Theatre:** dinner
Works: full-length plays, one-acts, musicals **2nd productions:** yes
Special interest: "New works." **Tours:** yes **Stages:** arena, 283 seats;
cabaret, 100 seats **Audience:** "Tour groups, subscribers." **Submission
policy:** query/synopsis, resume **Best time:** May-Sept. **Your chances:**
100's of new scripts read annually/usually 1 produced **Remuneration:** "Sometimes." **Future commitment:** no

JAY S. HARRIS, PRODUCER   F-l C
**Weissberger Theater Group, 909 Third Ave. 27th Floor, New York,
NY 10022 (212) 339-5529 FAX (212) 486-8996** Contact: Jay S. Harris,
Producer **Theatre:** professional **Works:** full-length plays **Special in-
terests:** "Small-cast plays with a clear plotline; contemporary issues."
Submission policy: query/synopsis **Response:** 1-2 months

JEAN DOUMANIAN, PRODUCER   F-l ♪
**595 Madison Ave. Suite 2200, New York, NY 10022 (212) 486-6981
FAX (212) 688-6236** **Production company:** professional **Works:** full-
length plays, musicals **Submission policy:** query/brief synopsis; agent
submission; professional recommendation

JEFF GOTTESFELD PRODUCTIONS   F-l J 12+ S
**P.O. Box 150326, Nashville, TN 37215 (615) 354-0950 FAX (615)
354-0951** Contact: Jeff Gottesfeld, Esq. **Company:** regional, New York
Works: full-length plays **Special interests:** "Jewish issues; plays about
teens." **Submission policy:** query/synopsis, resume; agent submission
Your chances: 1-2 new works produced each year **Future commitment:** "Option produced works for film." **Advice:** "No cold phone calls."

℟ JEFFERSON STREET THEATRE   F-l 1- Tr Ad ♪ CY Rv 2d cm
8919 Shady Pine Rd., Klamath Falls, OR 97601 (541) 882-3300 FAX
same, call first **e-mail** warshauerp@aol.com Contact: Paul Warshauer,
President **Theatre:** community **Works:** full-length plays, one-acts, translations, adaptations, musicals, revues, children's plays **2nd productions:** yes **Special interest:** children's plays **Stages:** 2 prosceniums,
790, 200 seats; outdoor stage, 350 seats **Casting:** Equity, non-Equity
Audience: "Rural, middle class; likes comedies, musicals." **Submission
policy;** query/synopsis, dialogue sample, resume; professional recom-

mendation; agent submission; no e-mail submission **Best time:** Dec.-Mar. **Response:** 2 weeks query; 1 month solicited script **Your chances:** 25-50 new scripts read annually **Terms:** negotiable **Program:** Jefferson Street Theatre Children's Musical Contest (see Contests) **Advice:** "Query should tell as much as possible about the relevance of your work."

JET THEATRE--JEWISH ENSEMBLE   F-l 1- Tr Ad CY 2d J
THEATRE 6600 W. Maple Rd, W. Bloomfield, MI 48322-3002 (810) 788-2900 FAX (810) 661-3680 **Contact:** Evelyn Orbach, Art. Director **Theatre:** professional **Works:** full-length plays, one-acts, translations, adaptations, children's plays **2nd productions:** yes **Special interests:** "Jewish writers/themes--<u>not</u> exclusively; plays which have not been professionally produced." **Specifications:** maximum cast: 10; limited demands **Stage:** modified thrust, 193 seats **Casting:** Equity, non-Equity **Submission policy:** unsolicited script; query/synopsis **Response:** 6 months **Terms:** negotiable **Program:** JET Theatre Festival (see Special Programs)

JEWISH REPERTORY THEATRE   F-l ♪ 2d J
c/o 92nd Street Y, 1395 Lexington Ave., New York, NY 10128 (212) 415-5550 FAX (212) 415-5575 e-mail jrep@echonyc.com **Contact:** Ran Avni, Art. Director **Theatre:** professional **Works:** full-length plays, musicals **2nd productions:** "If not reviewed in NYC during past 5 years." **Exclusive interests:** Jewish themes; plays written in English **Maximum cast:** 5-8 **Stage:** thrust, 299 seats **Submission policy:** unsolicited script **Best time:** Sept.-May **Response:** 4 weeks **Remuneration:** royalties **Program:** Lee Guber Playwrights' Lab (see Special Programs)

THE JEWISH WOMEN'S   F-l 1- Tr Ad ♪ 2d J W 1p C ⊡
THEATRE PROJECT 1511 Sawtelle Blvd. Suite 286, Los Angeles, CA 90025 (310) 398-7117 e-mail jwtpsite@aol.com **Contact:** Jan Lewis, Artistic Director **Theatre:** professional **Works:** full-length plays, one-acts, translations, adaptations, musicals **2nd productions:** yes **Special interests:** "Jewish women; plays which challenge preconceptions and explore the enduring questions of Jewish identity." **Maximum cast:** 1-12 **Tours:** yes **Stages:** various spaces **Casting:** Equity **Audience:** "20-80; upper middle class, college educated." **Submission policy:** query/synopsis, dialogue sample, resume **Response:** 2 weeks query; 4 months solicited script **Your chances:** 50 new plays read annually/usually 4 produced **Terms:** negotiable **Programs:** staged readings, workshops, internships; classes **Advice:** "Open to all kinds of ideas and forms."

J. MICHAELS AND THE MILLION   F-l 1- Ad ♪ CY Rv 2d C
STORIES   425 E. 76th St. Suite 6B, New York, NY 10021 (212) 861-4998 Ext. 2 FAX same **e-mail** million01@aol.com **Contact:** J. Michaels **Production company:** professional **Works:** full-length plays, one-acts, adaptations, musicals, children's plays, revues **2nd productions:** yes **Special interest:** "Contemporary stories about the common man." **Specifications:** maximum cast: 10 for play, 15-20 for musical; no more than 2

sets for play   **Stages:** thrust, 300 seats; flexible, 99 seats   **Casting:** Equity, non-Equity **Submission policy:** unsolicited script; query/synopsis **Best time:** May-Aug.   **Response:** varies   **Your chances:** 150 new scripts read annually/usually 10-20 produced   **Terms:** negotiable **Programs:** staged readings, workshops, internships, classes; New Play Festivals (inquire)   **Advice:** "We are looking for allies--not employees."

JOAN CULLMAN, PRODUCER   F-l ♪
1501 Broadway, New York, NY 10036 (212) 719-5640   FAX (212) 719-5668   Production company: professional   **Works:** full-length plays, musicals **Submission policy:** query/brief synopsis; agent submission; professional recommendation

JOAN STEIN, PRODUCER   F-l ♪
205 N. Cannon Dr., Beverly Hills, CA 90210 (310) 859-8001   FAX (310) 859-8024   Production company: professional   **Works:** full-length plays, musicals   **Submission policy:** query/brief synopsis; agent submission; professional recommendation

JOHN A. McQUIGGAN PROD.   NYC, NY   Mail addressed to this company has been returned as undeliverable; no phone number is listed.

JOHN DREW THEATRE   F-l 2d cm C
158 Main St., East Hampton, NY 11937   (516) 324-0806   FAX (516) 324-2722   Contact: Leonard Ziemkiewicz, General Mgr.   **Theatre:** professional **Works:** full-length plays **2nd productions:** yes **Special interests:** comedies, contemporary settings   **Specifications:** maximum cast: 4; unit set; simple demands **Stage:** proscenium, 386 seats **Casting:** Equity **Submission policy:** phone call preferred; query/1-page synopsis **Response:** 3 months   **Remuneration:** negotiable **Program:** workshops

JOHNSON COUNTY COMMUNITY COLLEGE   1- CY 2d
THEATRE   Theatre Dept., 12345 College Blvd., Overland Park, KS 66210 (913) 469-8500   Ext. 3132 FAX (913) 469-2585   e-mail sphilip @johnco.cc.ks.us **Contact:** Sheilah Philip-Bradfield, Chair   **Theatre:** college **Works:** one-acts, 10-minute plays, children's plays **2nd productions:** yes **Special interests:** "Thought-provoking works; pairs or trios of related one-acts." **Specifications:** maximum cast: 12; no more than 2 sets, 1 preferred   **Stages:** flexible, 100 seats; modified thrust, 400 seats **Casting:** non-Equity, students **Audience:** college, community **Submission policy:** unsolicited script; query/10-page dialogue sample   **Best time:** Nov.-Dec. **Response:** 2-3 months query **Your chances:** 40 new scripts read annually/usually 2-3 produced   **Remuneration:** royalties

JOMANDI PRODUCTIONS, INC.   F-l Ad ♪ CY 2d Af ➪
1444 Mayson St. NE, Atlanta, GA 30324   (404) 876-6346   FAX (404) 872-5764   Contact: Literary Mgr.   **Theatre:** professional   **Works:** full-length plays, adaptations, musicals, children's plays **2nd productions:**

yes **Special interests:** "African-American characters, themes; adaptations of African literature." **Specifications:** average cast: 7; unit set; no fly space **Tours:** yes **Stage:** proscenium-thrust, 370 seats **Audience:** "Mostly African-American, 30-50." **Submission policy:** query/synopsis, dialogue sample, resume **Best time:** spring-summer **Response:** 1 month query; 4-6 months solicited script **Your chances:** 15-20 new scripts read annually/usually 12 produced **Remuneration:** "$750± for new play; percentage for previously produced play." **Future commitment:** "1st presenter royalty, option."

JOSEPH PAPP PUBLIC THEATER/ F-l Tr Ad ♪ 2d C M Rs
NEW YORK SHAKESPEARE FESTIVAL 425 Lafayette St., New York, NY 10003 (212) 539-8500 FAX (212) 598-8505 **Contact:** Mervin P. Antonio, Shirley Fishman, Literary Mgrs. **Theatre:** professional **Works:** full-length plays, translations, adaptations, musicals **2nd productions:** "Occasionally." **Special interests:** "Social impact, diversity of culture, style." **Stages:** 2 prosceniums, 200, 299 seats; thrust, 275 seats; 2 flexible spaces, 150, 100 seats **Casting:** Equity **Submission policy:** query/synopsis, 10-page dialogue sample, resume, cassette tape of 3-5 songs (address musical/opera to Wiley Hausam, Assoc. Producer); agent submission **Response:** 1 month query; 6 months solicited script **Your chances:** 600 new scripts read annually/usually 8 produced **Terms:** negotiable **Programs:** readings, staged readings, workshop productions, internships, residencies; New Works Now Festival (inquire)

JUJAMCYN PRODUCTIONS F-l C
246 W. 44th St., New York, NY 10036 (212) 840-8181 **Contact:** Jack Viertel, Creative Director **Production company:** Broadway **Special interest:** contemporary social issues **Submission policy:** agent query

JULES FISHER, PRODUCER F-l ♪
126 Fifth Ave. 4th Floor, New York, NY 10011 (212) 691-3020 FAX (212) 633-1644 **Production company:** professional **Works:** full-length plays, musicals **Submission policy:** query/synopsis; agent submission; professional recommendation

JULIAN SCHLOSSBERG, PRODUCER F-l ♪
1414 Avenue of the Americas, New York, NY 10019 (212) 888-0080 FAX (212) 644-0956 **Production company:** professional **Works:** full-length plays, musicals **Submission policy:** agent or legal submission; professional recommendation

JUNGLE THEATER F-l P
709 W. Lake St., Minneapolis, MN 55408 (612) 822-7063 FAX (612) 822-9408 **e-mail** bain@jungletheater.com **Contact:** Bain Boehlke, Art. Director **Theatre:** professional **Works:** full-length plays **Stage:** proscenium, 140 seats **Submission policy:** query/synopsis, dialogue sample, resume **Response:** 1-3 months **Advice:** "We welcome new playwrights."

KARAMU HOUSE PERFORMING ARTS F-l 1- ♪ CY Rv M Af
THEATRE 2355 E. 89th St., Cleveland, OH 44106 (216) 795-7070
Contact: Gerry McClamy, Interim Exec. Director **Theatre:** professional
Works: full-length plays, one-acts, musicals, children's plays, revues
Special interest: multiethnic/African American themes **Maximum cast:**
10 **Stages:** proscenium, 223 seats; 2 flexible, 100 seats each **Submission policy:** query/synopsis, dialogue sample **Best time:** by Jan. 1 **Response:** 4 week-4 months **Your chances:** 6-8 new plays receive staged
readings **Terms:** negotiable **Program:** ArenaFest (see Special Programs)

KATHLEEN RAITT, PRODUCER F-l ♪
810 7th Ave., New York, NY 10019 (212) 262-2400 FAX (212) 262-
5558 **Production company:** professional **Works:** full-length plays, musicals **Submission policy:** agent submission; professional recommendation

KINCAID REGIONAL THEATRE F-l ♪ cm cm-dr
Box 208, Falmouth, KY 41040 (606) 654-2117, -2636 FAX (606) 654-
4309 **Contact:** Charles Kondek, Producing Art. Director **Theatre:** professional **Special interests:** musicals, comedies, comedy/drama **Stage:**
thrust, 300 seats **Casting:** Equity, non-Equity **Submission policy:** unsolicited script; query/synopsis; professional recommendation; agent
submission; commission **Response:** 1-2 months

KRACKERJACK THEATRE COMPANY CY Cl ⌷
85 Watson Mill Rd, Saco, ME 04072 (207) 284-4063, (800) 456-0280
Contact: Mark A. Bedell, Artistic Director **Theatre:** professional touring **Special interests:** "Adaptations of classic literature for young
people; folk tales." **Specifications:** cast of 1 man, 1 woman, with doubling; single changeable set; 45 minutes maximum **Casting:** "Husbandwife team." **Audience:** elementary schools **Submission policy:** query/
synopsis **Response:** 6 months **Your chances:** 1-2 new scripts read
annually/usually none produced **Remuneration:** negotiable **Advice:**
"Please don't submit a script until we ask you to send it!"

L. A. THEATRE WORKS F-l 1- Tr Ad Rd
681 Venice Blvd., Venice, CA 90291 (310) 827-0808 FAX (310) 827-
4949 **e-mail** latworks@aol.com **Contact:** Kirsten Dahl, Literary Mgr.
Theatre: professional **Works:** full-length plays, one-acts, translations,
adaptations, radio plays **2nd productions:** yes **Special interests:** "Stage
plays by established writers that can be adapted for radio." **Specifications:** maximum cast: 7-10 **Casting:** Equity **Audience:** "Serious theatregoers." **Submission policy:** agent submission **Remuneration:** royalty
Program: L. A. Theatre Works Radio Theatre (see Special Programs)

LA JOLLA PLAYHOUSE F-l Tr ♪ cm dr C Am x
P.O. Box 12039, La Jolla, CA 92039 (619) 550-1070 **e-mail** ljplayhouse
@ucsd.edu **Contact:** Elizabeth Bennett, Literary Mgr. **Theatre:** professional **Works:** full-length plays, translations, musicals **2nd produc-**

tions: no **Special interests:** "Serious handling of current American themes in comedies, dramas, musicals; innovative works." **Maximum cast:** 15 **Stages:** proscenium, 500 seats; thrust, 400 seats **Casting:** Equity **Submission policy:** query/synopsis, 10-page dialogue sample; professional recommendation **Response:** 6 months

LA MAMA EXPERIMENTAL THEATER   F-l 1- ♪ M mm x

74A E. 4th St., New York, NY 10003 (212) 254-6468 FAX (212) 254-7597 **Contact:** Beverly Petty, Assoc. Dir. **Theatre:** off off Broadway **Works:** full-length plays, one-acts, musicals **Special interest:** multiethnic, multimedia work not reliant on language **Stages:** flexible, 299 seats; 2 black boxes **Submission policy:** videotape, query/synopsis **Response:** 6 months **Programs:** See listing in Special Programs.

℞ LAGUNA PLAYHOUSE   F-l ♪ CY

606 Laguna Canyon Rd., Laguna Beach, CA 92651 (714) 494-8022 FAX (714) 497-6948 **Contact:** Andrew Barnicle, Artistic Director **Theatre:** professional **Works:** full-length plays, musicals, children's plays **Stage:** proscenium, 418 seats **Submission policy:** professional recommendation; agent submission **Response:** only if interested

LAKE GEORGE DINNER THEATRE   F-l cm

P.O. Box 266, Lake George, NY 12845 (518) 668-2198 FAX (518) 668-2198 **Contact:** Victoria Eastwood, Producer **Theatre:** dinner **Works:** full-length plays **Special interest:** comedy **Specifications:** maximum cast: 6; single set **Stage:** 160-170 seats **Casting:** Equity, non-Equity **Submission policy:** unsolicited script; query/synopsis; professional recommendation **Best time:** Nov.-Feb. **Your chances:** 10 new scripts read annually/none produced recently **Remuneration:** negotiable

LAMB'S PLAYERS THEATRE   F-l Tr Ad ♪ CY Rv 2d ▭

P.O. Box 182229, Coronado, CA 92178 (619) 437-6050 FAX (619) 437-6053 **e-mail** LPTJeff@aol.com **Contact:** Jeff Miller, Director of Education **Theatre:** professional **Works:** full-length plays, translations, adaptations, musicals, children's plays, revues **2nd productions:** yes **Tours:** shows with cast of 4 **Stages:** arena, 180 seats; modified thrust, 347 seats **Submission policy:** professional recommendation **Response:** 6 months **Your chances:** 50 new scripts read annually/usually 1 produced **Remuneration:** royalty **Future commitment:** credit **Program:** Writers/Directors Workshop, by invitation

THE LAMB'S THEATRE COMPANY   F-l ♪ Fm ▭

130 W. 44th St., New York, NY 10036 (212) 575-0300 FAX (212) 768 1380 **Contact:** Larry Belew **Theatre:** off Broadway **Works:** full-length plays, musicals **2nd productions:** "Rarely." **Special interest:** "Family-oriented works." **Specifications:** maxmum cast: 10, 8 preferred; 1 set preferred; no nudity or obscenity **Tours:** yes **Stages:** proscenium, 350 seats; flexible, 116 seats **Submission policy:** query/synopsis, dialogue

sample, SASP; professional recommendation; agent submission **Response:** 1 month query; 3-6 months solicited script **Your chances:** 150 new scripts read annually/usually 3 produced **Remuneration:** $1000-$1500 **Future commitment:** yes

THE LARK THEATRE D F-l 1- Tr Ad ♪ 2d L M $ Rs
COMPANY **939 Eighth Ave. Suite 301, New York, NY 10019 (212) 246-2676 FAX (212) 246-2609 e-mail** LarkCo@aol.com **Contact:** Miles Lott, Literary Mgr. **Theatre:** professional **Works:** full-length plays, one-acts, translations, adaptations, musicals **2nd productions:** yes **Special interests:** "Language; variety of cultural perspectives." **Stage:** large studio space **Casting:** Equity, non-Equity **Submission policy:** unsolicited script; agent submission; 1 script per submission per author; $15 fee **Best time:** Jul.-Nov. **Response:** 6 months **Your chances:** 400 new scripts read annually/usually 3-5 produced **Terms:** negotiable **Programs:** staged readings, Barebones workshop productions, Translation & Adaptation Project, internships, residencies, classes; Playwrights Week (see Contests) **Advice:** "We work with writers through an ongoing development process."

LATIN AMERICAN THEATRE ENSEMBLE F-l 1- Hi Esp
P.O. Box 18, New York, NY 10101 (212) 397-3262 Contact: Margarita Toirac, Exec. Director **Theatre:** professional **Works:** full-length plays, one acts **2nd productions:** yes **Maximum cast:** 3 **Exclusive interest:** Latino writers and themes **Submission policy:** unsolicited script

LAWRENCE WELK RESORT THEATRE ♪ 2d Fm Sn
8860 Lawrence Welk Dr., Escondido, CA 92026 (760) 749-3448 FAX (760) 749-6182 Contact: Sean Coogan, Producer **Theatre:** dinner **Works:** musicals **2nd productions:** yes **Specifications:** maximum cast: 15; no obscenity **Casting:** Equity, non-Equity **Audience:** "Seniors." **Submission policy:** unsolicited script **Your chances:** 12 new scripts read annually **Remuneration:** yes **Future commitment:** no

LE PETIT THEATRE DE VIEUX CARRE F-l Tr Ad ♪ CY
616 St. Peter St., New Orleans, LA 70116 (504) 522-9958 (504) 524-9027 Contact: Sonny Borey, Exec. Director **Theatre:** community **Works:** full-length plays, translations, adaptations, musicals, children's plays **2nd productions:** no **Stages:** proscenium, 450 seats; arena, 150 seats **Submission policy:** unsolicited script; professional recommendation **Best time:** summer **Response:** 1 year **Your chances:** 30 new scripts read annually **Remuneration:** no **Advice:** "Send reviews of other work."

LEMA PRODUCTIONS F-l 2d cm my
226 W. 47th St., New York, NY 10036 (212) 354-3729 FAX (212) 768-7308 Contact: Jessica Levy, Producer **Production company:** professional **Works:** full-length plays **2nd productions:** "Possibly." **Special interests:** "Comedy, suspense, good writing." **Stage:** proscenium

Submission policy: query/synopsis, dialogue sample, resume; professional recommendation; agent submission **Response:** immediate query; 2 months solicited script

LEONARD SOLOWAY, PRODUCER F-l 1- ♪
1776 Broadway 11th Floor, New York, NY 10019 (212) 459-3000 Production company: professional **Works:** full-length plays, one-acts, musicals **Submission policy:** query/brief synopsis; agent submission; professional recommendation

LESLEY SAVAGE, PRODUCER 910 Fifth Ave., New York, NY
10021 (212) 988-0100 This company is closed to submissions in 1999; see *The Playwright's Companion 2000* or inquire for future plans.

LEWIS ALLEN PRODUCTIONS, INC. F-l dr
1501 Broadway, New York, NY 10036 (212) 768-4610 FAX (212) 768-4614 e-mail laprods@aol.com **Contact:** Lewis Allen, President; Sharon Fallon **Production company:** professional **Works:** full-length plays **Special interests:** "Straight plays, dramas." **Submission policy:** agent submission

LEXINGTON CHILDREN'S THEATRE CY 2d M Rg Lc ⊏⃗
161 N. Mill St., Lexington, KY 40507-1125 (606) 254-4546 FAX (606) 254-9512 e-mail lct@mis.net **Theatre:** professional **Works:** children's plays **2nd productions:** yes **Special interests:** "Diversity; regional, local authors." **Specifications:** maximum cast: 40; no more than 3 sets; modest demands **Tours:** yes **Stage:** proscenium, 1000 seats; flexible, 150 seats **Submission policy:** unsolicited script; query/synopsis; professional recommendation; commission **Best time:** fall-winter **Response:** 4 months **Your chances:** 10-15 new scripts read annually/usually 1 produced **Terms:** negotiable **Advice:** "Small-cast touring productions."

♫ LIFELINE THEATRE Ad
6912 N. Glenwood Ave., Chicago, IL 60626 (773) 761-0667 FAX (773) 761-4582 e-mail lifeline@suba.com **Contact:** Meryl Friedman, Producing Director **Theatre:** professional **Works:** adaptations **Stage:** proscenium, 100 seats **Submission policy:** query/synopsis **Response:** 1 month query; 6 months solicited script

LINCOLN CENTER THEATER F-l 1- Tr Ad ♪
150 W. 65th St., New York, NY 10023 (212) 362-7600 **Contact:** Anne Cattaneo, Dramaturg **Theatre:** professional **Works:** full length plays, one-acts, translations, adaptations, musicals **Stages:** 2 thrusts, 300, 1000 seats **Submission policy:** agent submission **Response:** 2-4 months

LINCOLN COMMUNITY PLAYHOUSE F-l 1- Ad CY Rv Rs
2500 S. 56th St., Lincoln, NE 68506 (402) 489-4527 FAX (402) 489-1035 **Contact:** Rhonda Lake, Literary Mgr. **Theatre:** community **Works:** full-length plays, one-acts, adaptations, children's plays, revues

2nd productions: yes Specifications: maximum cast: 10; no more than 3 sets Stages: thrust, 300 seats; arena, 280 seats; black box, 75-100 seats Casting: Equity, non-Equity Submission policy: unsolicited script, resume; videotape; query/synopsis Best time: Apr.-Aug. Response: 1 month query; 2-6 months script Your chances: 5 new plays read annually/usually 1-2 produced, latest in Aug. 1998 Remuneration: fee- -$50-$150 Programs: staged readings, workshops, development, residencies, classes; New Plays Series (inquire)

LIVE BAIT THEATRICAL CO.   F-l Tr Ad Rg po mm x
3914 N. Clark St., Chicago, IL 60613 (773) 871-1212 FAX (773) 871-3191 Contact: Ryan C. LaFleur, Mng. Director Theatre: professional Works: full-length plays, translations, adaptations Special interests: "Chicago-area writers only; the visual; performance poetry; multimedia, non-realistic plays." Specifications: maximum cast: 9 preferred; single set; no fly or wing space Stage: black box, 70 seats Casting: non-Equity Submission policy: query/synopsis, resume, dialogue sample Response: 6 weeks query; 6 months solicited script Your chances: 30-40 new scripts read annually/usually 1-2 produced Remuneration: yes Future commitment: no

LIVE OAK THEATRE   F-l Tr Ad ♪ 2d
719 Congress Ave., Austin, TX 78701 (512) 472-5143 FAX (512) 472-7199 Theatre: professional Works: full-length plays, translations, adaptations, musicals 2nd productions: yes Casting: Equity, non-Equity Audience: "Mainstream." Stage: proscenium, 400 seats Submission policy: agent submission

THE LIVING THEATRE   F-l Tr Ad V 2d x ▭
800 West End Ave. #5A, New York, NY 10025 (212) 865-3957 FAX (212) 865-3234 Contact: Craig Peritz, Admin. Asst. Theatre: profession-al, touring Works: full-length plays, translations, adaptations, street theatre 2nd productions: yes Special interests: "Experimental, partici-patory works; site/actor-specific works; literary adaptations." Maxi-mum cast: 12 Casting: Equity, non-Equity Submission policy: query/synopsis, resume Response: 2-6 months Terms: negotiable

LOFT PRODUCTION CO.   Tampa, FL   Mail addressed to this
theatre has been returned as undeliverable; no phone number is listed.

LOIS DEUTCHMAN PRODUCTIONS   F-l ♪
23 E. 10th St., New York, NY 10003 Contact: Lois Deutchman, Producer Production company: professional Works: full-length plays, musicals Special interests: original plays, musicals Submission policy: agent submission

LONG WHARF THEATRE   F-l Tr Ad dr cm C
222 Sargent Dr., New Haven, CT 06511 (203) 787-4284 FAX (203) 776-2287 Contact: Literary Assoc. Theatre: professional Works: full-

length plays, translations, adaptations **Special interests:** "Dramatic plays and comedies about human relationships, social concerns, ethical and moral dilemmas." **Stages:** thrust, 484 seats; proscenium, 199 seats **Submission policy:** query/synopsis with dialogue sample, resume, and professional recommendation; agent submission **Response:** 1 month query; 6 months script **Your chances:** 1000-1500 new scripts read annually/usually 1-2 produced, 4 receive workshops **Remuneration/commitment:** yes **Programs:** inquire for future plans

LORRAINE HANSBERRY THEATRE   F-l 1- Tr Ad ♪ 2d Af
414 Mason St. Suite 401, San Francisco, CA 94102   (415) 288-0320 FAX (415) 288-0326 **Contact:** Stanley Williams, Artistic Director **Theatre:** professional **Works:** full-length plays, one-acts, translations, adaptations, musicals **2nd productions:** yes **Special interest:** "Black writers, themes." **Stage:** proscenium, 300 seats **Submission policy:** unsolicited script, resume; query/synopsis, dialogue sample; professional recommendation; agent submission **Response:** 2 months

LOS ANGELES DESIGNERS'   F-l 1- Tr Ad ♪ Rv 2d Sp C Lc Rs
THEATRE   P.O. Box 1883, Studio City, CA 91614-0883 (323) 650-9600, (323) 654-2700 TDD and ISDN FAX (323) 654-3260   e-mail ladesigners@juno.com **Contact:** Richard Niederberg, Artistic Director **Theatre:** professional **Works:** full-length plays, evenings of one-acts, translations, adaptations, musicals, revues **2nd productions:** "After rewrites, if no strings are attached." **Special interests:** "Controversial works; nudity, street language accepted, not required; religious, political, social themes." **Specifications:** large cast preferred; quick set changes **Tours:** "Sometimes." **Casting:** Equity, non-Equity **Audience:** "Very 'jaded' entertainment industry types who 'have seen it all' yet want to 'discover' a show that they can make money on by filming or taping." **Submission policy:** non-returnable proposal preferred; unsolicited script, videotape or query/synopsis, resume; professional recommendation; agent submission **Response:** 120+ days **Your chances:** 1200+ new scripts read annually/usually 35-40 produced **Remuneration:** negotiable **Future commitment:** "2%, credit, 1st refusal." **Programs:** internships, residencies, L.A.D.T. Play Commissioning Project (see Contests) **Advice:** "Make it commercial, easy to film or tape." **Comment:** Theatre was founded in 1970, has produced 5000+ performances of 400+ plays.

LOVE CREEK PRODUCTIONS   F-l 1- 2d W g/l Sp
c/o Granville, 162 Nesbit St., Weehawken, NJ 07087   e-mail Creekread@aol.com **Contact:** Cynthia Granville-Callahan, Literary Mgr. **Theatre:** off off Broadway **Works:** full-length plays, one-acts **2nd productions:** "If not produced in New York City in the previous year." **Special interests:** "Scripts featuring women; scripts on various themes, such as gay/lesbian, Fear of God." **Specifications:** no fly space **Stages:** proscenium; black box; 45-99 seats **Casting:** Equity, non-Equity **Submission policy:** send SASE for guidelines **Response:** up to 6 months for

one-act; up to 1 year full-length play **Your chances:** 700 new scripts read annually/usually 100 produced **Future commitment:** credit **Programs:** Love Creek Annual Short Play Festival and Off-Off Broadway Original Short Play Festival (see Contests) **Advice:** "Please do not submit without first obtaining our guidelines; submissions not following our procedures are rejected--returned/recycled."

LUCILLE LORTEL, PRODUCER F-1 ♪
Lucille Lortel Theatre, 121 Christopher St., New York, NY 10014 (212) 355-2800 FAX (212) 989-0036 **Production company:** professional **Works:** full-length plays, musicals **Submission policy:** query/ brief synopsis; agent submission; professional recommendation

MABOU MINES F-1 1- Tr Ad C
150 1st Ave., New York, NY 10009 (212) 473-0559 FAX (212) 473-2410 **Contact:** Martha Elliot, Company Mgr. **Theatre:** professional **Works:** full-length plays, one-acts, translations, adaptations **Special interest:** contemporary issues **Stage:** flexible, 60 seats **Submission policy:** professional recommendation **Response:** 6 months

MADISON REPERTORY THEATRE F-1 Tr Ad ♪ 2d Rs
122 State St. Suite 201, Madison, WI 53703-2500 (608) 256-0029 FAX (608) 256-7433 **e-mail** madisonrep@aol.com **Contact:** D. Scott Glasser, Artistic Director **Theatre:** professional **Works:** full-length plays, translations, adaptations, musicals **2nd productions:** yes **Specifications:** maximum cast: 15; no fly space **Stage:** thrust, 335 seats **Casting:** Equity, non-Equity **Submission policy:** query/synopsis, dialogue sample, SASP **Response:** 3-4 months **Your chances:** 100 new scripts read annually/ usually none produced **Terms:** negotiable; housing for 1-2 day residency **Program:** Madison Repertory Reading Series (see Special Programs)

MAGIC THEATRE F-1 2d C x
Ft. Mason Center, Bldg. D, San Francisco, CA 94123 (415) 441-8001 **e-mail** magicthtre@aol.com **Contact:** Kent Nicholson, Literary Mgr. **Theatre:** professional **Works:** full-length plays **2nd productions:** yes **Special interests:** "Political, innovative, non-linear, plays." **Maximum cast:** 6 **Stages:** proscenium, 170 seats; thrust, 155 seats **Casting:** Equity, non-Equity **Audience:** "Well educated, adventurous." **Submission policy:** query/synopsis, 1st 10 pages of dialogue, resume; professional recommendation; agent submission **Best time:** Sept.-May **Response:** 6 weeks query; 6-8 months solicited script **Your chances:** 600 new scripts read annually/usually 3 produced **Remuneration:** "Fee and royalties." **Future commitment:** percentage, credit

MAGNET THEATRE COMPANY, INC. F-1 2d dr cm
318 Elmer Street, Trenton, NJ 08611-1513 (609) 392-5589 **Contact:** Charles Hayman, Artistic Director **Theatre:** professional **Works:** full-length plays **2nd productions:** yes **Special interests:** drama, comedy

Specifications: maximum cast: 7; single set **Stage:** thrust **Casting:** Equity, non-Equity **Submission policy:** unsolicited script; query/synopsis **Best time:** summer-fall **Your chances:** 25 new scripts read annually/none produced to date **Remuneration:** TBD

♫ MAIN STREET ARTS   F-l 1-
94 Main St., Nyack, NY 10960 (914) 358-7701 FAX same **e-mail** msapaul@juno.com **Contact:** Literary Mgr. **Theatre:** professional **Works:** full-length plays, one-acts **Maximum cast:** 6 for full-length, 4 for one-act **Stage:** black box, 65 seats **Submission policy:** query/synopsis, dialogue sample **Response:** 3 weeks (if interested); 6 weeks solicited script **Programs:** See listing in Special Programs.

MAIN STREET THEATER   F-l 1- Tr Ad ♪ CY 12+ 2d L
2540 Times Blvd., Houston, TX 77005 (713) 524-3622 **Contact:** Rebecca Greene Udden, Artistic Director **Theatre:** non-Equity, professional **Works:** full-length plays, one-acts, translations, adaptations, musicals, plays for youth **Special interests:** "2nd productions, language." **Maximum cast:** 15 **Stages:** 2 thrusts, 91, 185 seats **Audience:** "Educated." **Submission policy:** query/synopsis, dialogue sample, cassette tape for musical **Response:** 1 year **Your chances:** 300 new scripts read annually/usually 1-2 produced **Remuneration:** royalty

MAIN STREET THEATRE & DANCE   F-l Tr Ad ♪ CY 2d
ALLIANCE   548 Main St., New York, NY 10044 (212) 371-4449 **Contact:** Worth Howe, Artistic Director **Theatre:** off off Broadway **Works:** full-length plays, translations, adaptations, musicals, children's plays **2nd productions:** if not produced in New York **Specifications:** maximum cast: 12-14; no 2-story sets **Stages:** proscenium; flexible **Audience:** "Upscale; theatre professionals." **Submission policy:** unsolicited script; query/synopsis, dialogue sample; professional recommendation; agent submission **Best time:** early summer **Response:** 4 weeks query; 8 weeks script **Your chances:** 250 new scripts read annually/usually 2 produced **Remuneration/commitment:** no

MANHATTAN CLASS CO.   See MCC Theater in this section.

MANHATTAN PLAYHOUSE   F-l 1- ♪ CY cm 2d
460 W. 49th St., New York, NY 10019 (212) 245-7798 **Contact:** Diana Walker, Producing Director **Theatre:** professional **Works:** full-length plays, one-acts, musicals, children's plays **Special interests:** comedies, musicals **2nd productions:** if not produced in New York **Maximum cast:** 6-12 **Submission policy;** query/synopsis, cassette tape for musical **Response:** 2 months **Program:** workshops

THE MANHATTAN PROJECT   C cm
1775 Broadway Suite 410, New York, NY 10019 (212) 258-2541 FAX
(212) 258-2546 Contact: David Brown, Producer Production company: Broadway Special interests: new plays, contemporary comedies,
universal themes Submission policy: agent submission; recommendation
by other producers

MANHATTAN THEATRE CLUB   F-l Tr Ad ♪ Rv 2d
311 W. 43rd St. 8th Floor, New York, NY 10036 (212) 399-3000 FAX
(212) 399-4329 e-mail 76735.3316@compuserve.com Contact: Kate
Loewald, Play Development; Clifford Lee Johnson III, Musical Theatre
Theatre: off Broadway Works: full-length plays, translations, adaptations, musicals, revues 2nd productions: yes Specifications: maximum
cast: 12; single set preferred Stages: proscenium, 299 seats; thrust, 150
seats Casting: Equity Submission policy: play: agent submission; musical: query/synopsis, cassette tape Response: 4 months Your chances:
1000 new scripts read annually/usually 8 produced Terms: negotiable
Program: Manhattan Theatre Club Fellowship (see Special Programs)

MANNY KLADITIS, PRODUCER   F-l ♪
234 W. 44th St., New York, NY 10036 (212) 382-3410 FAX (212) 382-
3548 Production company: professional Works: full-length plays,
musicals Submission policy: query/brief synopsis; agent submission;
professional recommendation

MARGO LION, LTD.   F-l ♪ C dr
246 W. 44th St., New York, NY 10036 (212) 869-1112 FAX (212) 730-
0381 Contact: Margo Lion Production company: Broadway Works:
full-length plays, musicals Special interest: "Contemporary dramas."
Submission policy: query/synopsis with 10-page dialogue sample

MARIA DI DIA   165 W. 46th St., New York, NY 10036 (212) 354-
5040   This producer is no longer accepting submissions.

MARIN THEATRE COMPANY   F-l Tr Ad CY 2d
397 Miller Ave., Mill Valley, CA 94941 (415) 388-5200 FAX (415) 388-
0768 Contact: Lee Sankowich, Artistic Director Theatre: professional
Works: full-length plays, translations, adaptations, children's plays
2nd productions: yes Maximum cast: 15 Stages: proscenium, 250
seats; black box, 109 seats Audience: "Older, white, upper class."
Submission policy: professional recommendation Best time: Jun.-Aug.
Response: 6 months Terms: negotiable

MARJORIE LYONS PLAYHOUSE   F-l ♪ dr 2d
Centenary College, 2911 Centenary Blvd., Shreveport, LA 71134-
1188 (318) 869-5074 FAX (318) 869-5760 e-mail rbuseick@beta.
centenary.edu Contact: Robert Buseick, Chairman, Theatre Dept.
Theatre: college Works: full-length plays, musicals Special interest:
dramas 2nd productions: yes Stage: proscenium, 250 seats Casting:

non-Equity, students **Submission policy:** query/synopsis **Best time:** fall **Response:** 2-6 months **Future commitment:** no

MARKET HOUSE THEATRE 1- CY 2d Lc Fm ⌐•
141 Kentucky Ave., Paducah, KY 42003 (502) 444-6828 FAX (502) 575-9321 **Contact:** Michael Cochran, Exec. Director **Theatre:** community **Works:** one-acts, children's plays **2nd productions:** children's plays **Special interests:** "Small cast, tourable children's plays, 40-50 minutes; large-cast family shows with young actors." **Specifications:** few set changes **Stage:** proscenium, 250 seats **Audience:** "Conservative." **Submission policy:** send SASE for guidelines **Remuneration:** negotiable **Program:** Market House Theatre Bi-Annual National One-Act Playwriting Competition (see Contests) **Advice:** "Good one-acts and children's plays with audience participation."

THE MARK TAPER FORUM F-l 1- Tr Ad ♪ CY Rv x
135 N. Grand Ave., Los Angeles, CA 90012 (213) 972-7574 **Contact:** Pier Carlo Talenti, Literary Assoc. **Theatre:** professional **Works:** full-length plays, one-acts, translations, adaptations, musicals, plays for young audiences **2nd productions:** yes **Stages:** thrust, 742 seats **Submission policy:** query/description (not synopsis) of play, 5-10 page dialogue sample; agent submission **Response:** 4-6 weeks query; 8-10 weeks solicited script **Programs:** See Mark Taper Forum in Special Programs

♬ **MARQUETTE UNIV. THEATRE** F-l 1- Tr Ad ♪ CY
Dept. of Performing Arts, P.O. Box 1881, Milwaukee, WI 53210-1881 (414) 288-7149 **Works:** full-length plays, one-acts, translations, adaptations, musicals, children's plays **Exclusive interest:** small-cast plays for college-age actors **Stages:** mainstage, 226 seats; studio, 75 seats **Submission policy:** query/synopsis **Program:** workshop productions

MARSHALL UNIV. THEATRE PLAYWORKS F 1- 2d
400 Hal Greer Blvd., Huntington, WV 25755-2242 e-mail elwell @marshall.edu **Contact:** Jeffery S. Elwell, Chair **Works:** one-acts (60 pages maximum) **2nd productions:** yes **Stages:** proscenium, 543 seats; black box, 251 seats; rehearsal room, 50 seats **Specifications:** single set **Casting:** Equity, non-Equity **Submission policy:** unsolicited script **Best time:** after Jun. 1, 1999 only **Response:** 4 months **Your chances:** 160 new scripts read annually/usually 5 produced **Remuneration:** negotiable royalties

MARTIN MARKINSEN, PRODUCER F-l ♪
240 W. 44th St., New York, NY 10036 (212) 944-9457 FAX (212) 302-3584 **Production company:** professional **Works:** full-length plays, musicals **Submission policy:** query/synopsis; agent submission; professional recommendation

MARVIN A. KRAUSS, PRODUCER F-l ♪

234 W. 44th St., New York, NY 10036 (212) 382-3410 FAX (212) 382-3548 Production company: professional **Works:** full-length plays, musicals **Submission policy:** query/synopsis; agent submission; professional recommendation

MARY BALDWIN COLLEGE THEATRE F-l 1- Tr ♪ 2d W

Theatre Dept., Staunton, VA 24401 (540) 887-7189 Contact: Terry Southerington **Theatre:** college **Works:** full-length plays, one-acts, translations, musicals **2nd productions:** yes **Stages:** thrust, 230 seats; flexible, 130 seats **Casting:** amateur actors, students **Audience:** "Students; conservative, educated professionals." **Submission policy:** unsolicited script; query/synopsis **Best time:** May-Jul. **Response:** 1 month query; 1 year script **Your chances:** 50 new scripts read annually **Remuneration:** royalties **Future commitment:** no **Advice:** "Women's issues, roles."

MASTER ARTS THEATRE F-l 1- Ad ♪ CY † ⌓

3540 Fairlanes Ave. SW, Grandville, MI 49418-1536 (616) 531-5020 FAX (616) 249-9525 Contact: Priscilla McDonald, Exec. Director **Theatre:** community **Works:** full-length plays, one-acts, adaptations, musicals, children's plays **Special interests:** "A variety of work from a Christian world view." **Tours:** yes **Stage:** black box, 150 seats **Casting:** non-Equity **Submission policy:** unsolicited script, synopsis **Your chances:** 5-10 new scripts read annually/usually 0-1 produced **Remuneration:** royalty **Future commitment:** no

MAX WEITZENHOFFER PRODUCTIONS F-l ♪

350 Park Ave., New York, NY 10022 (212) 759-0972 Contact: Max Weitzenhoffer, Producer **Production company:** Broadway **Works:** full-length plays, musicals **Submission policy:** agent submission

MCC THEATER F-l 1- Tr Ad ♪ 2d po

120 W. 28th St., New York, NY 10001 (212) 727-7722 FAX (212) 727-7780 Contact: Stephen Willems, Literary Mgr. **Theatre:** off off Broadway **Works:** full-length plays, one-acts, translations, adaptations, musicals **2nd productions:** if New York City premieres **Special interest:** "Poetic realism." **Maximum cast:** 10 **Stage:** black box, 99 seats **Casting:** Equity **Submission policy:** query/synopsis, SASP; professional recommendation; agent submission **Response:** 2 weeks query; 2 months solicited script **Your chances:** 1000 new scripts read annually/ usually 3 full-length plays and 6 workshops produced **Remuneration:** fee **Future commitment:** credit **Program:** workshops **Comment:** Formerly Manhattan Class Co.

McCARTER THEATRE F-l Tr Ad ♪ 2d

91 University Pl., Princeton, NJ 08540 (609) 683-9100 FAX (609) 497-0369 Contact: Charles McNulty, Literary Mgr. **Theatre:** professional **Works:** full-length plays, translations, adaptations, musicals **2nd**

productions: yes **Specifications:** maximum cast: 12 preferred; single or unit set **Stage:** proscenium, 1067 seats **Submission policy:** agent submission **Your chances:** 600 new scripts read annually/usually 1-2 produced **Remuneration:** negotiable

MEADOW BROOK THEATRE F-l Tr Ad 2d cm my Rg C ⌂ Oakland Univ., Rochester, MI 48309-4401 (248) 370-3310 FAX (248) 370-3108 **e-mail** mbrkthea@oakland.edu **Contact:** Karim Alrawi, Literary Mgr. **Theatre:** professional **Works:** full-length plays, translations, adaptations **2nd productions:** yes **Special interest:** "Comedies and thrillers with local interest and some social relevance." **Specifications:** maximum cast: 12, fewer preferred; simple sets **Stage:** proscenium, 608 seats **Casting:** Equity **Audience:** "Middle America." **Submission policy:** query/1-page synopsis, 10-page dialogue sample **Response:** 3 months **Remuneration:** negotiable percentage **Programs:** outreach, workshops, state-wide touring **Advice:** "Entertain and broaden our audience's horizons."

♫ **MELANEC'S WHEELHOUSE DINNER** F-l 1- ♪ my **THEATRE** 2178 N. Riverboat Rd., Milwaukee, WI 53212 (414) 264-6060 **Works:** full-length plays, one-acts, musicals **Special interest:** mysteries **Specifications:** small cast; unit set **Stages:** 2 stages, 110, 75 seats **Casting:** non-Equity **Submission policy:** query/synopsis

MERRIMACK REPERTORY F-l Tr Ad ♪ CY 2d po Am M Rs **THEATRE** 50 E. Merrimack St., Lowell, MA 01852 (508) 454-6324 FAX (508) 934-0166 **e-mail** mrtlowell@aol.com **Contact:** David G. Kent, Producing Art. Director **Theatre:** professional **Works:** full-length plays, translations, adaptations, musicals, children's plays **2nd productions:** yes **Special interests:** "Poetic dimensions; American, ethnic themes." **Specifications:** maximum cast: 14; simple set **Stage:** thrust, 372 seats **Casting:** Equity, non-Equity **Submission policy:** query/synopsis, SASP; professional recommendation **Best time:** spring-Sept. **Response:** 1 month query (if interested); 6-8 months solicited script **Your chances:** 300 new scripts read annually/2 receive staged readings **Remuneration:** royalties; travel, housing for residency; possible advance on commission **Future commitment:** credit, percentage, subsidiary rights

MERRY-GO-ROUND PLAYHOUSE F-l Tr Ad ♪ CY 12+ 2d ⌂ P.O. Box 506, Auburn, NY 13021 (315) 255-1305 FAX (315) 252-3815 **Contact:** Emily Mattina, Literary Mgr. **Theatre:** professional, touring **Works:** full-length plays, translations, adaptations, musicals, children's plays **2nd productions:** yes **Special interest:** " Audience participation, grades K-12." **Specifications:** cast size: 3-5 **Stage:** flexible, 100-325 seats **Audience:** "Musicals: all ages." **Submission policy:** unsolicited script **Best time:** Jan.-Feb. **Response:** 2 months **Terms:** "By contract."

MESA STATE COLLEGE THEATRE See listing in Contests.

METRO THEATER COMPANY   D 1- CY ⮑
8308 Olive Blvd., St. Louis, MO 63132-2814 (314) 997-6777 FAX
(314) 997-1811 e-mail BravoMTC@aol.com Contact: Carol North, Producing Director Theatre: professional Works: plays for young audiences and adults 2nd productions: "Seldom." Special interest: "Music
is integral, but we do not do 'musicals.'" Specifications: 5-member ensemble tours; 60 minutes maximum Casting: non-Equity Submission
policy: query/synopsis, dialogue sample; professional recommendation;
commission Best time: summer Response: 2 months query; 3-4 months
solicited script Your chances: 50 new scripts read annually/none
produced to date Remuneration: "Commission fee, royalties." Future
commitment: percentage for commissioned works Advice: "The more
open-ended, the better. MTC develops material."

THE METROPOLITAN PLAYHOUSE   F-l Tr Ad 2d H Am
70 Greenwich Ave. #370, New York, NY 10011 (212) 532-2841
Theatre: off off Broadway Works: full-length plays, translations, adaptations 2nd productions: yes Special interests: "New plays and
adaptations dealing with pre-WWI America." Specifications: maximum
cast: 15; open staging preferred Stage: flexible, 90 seats Casting: Equity
Audience: "From sophisticated theatregoers to inner city students; our
plays must serve both." Submission policy: query/synopsis, dialogue
sample, resume Best time: Sept. 1-Jun. 1 only Response: 6 weeks query;
10 weeks solicited script Your chances: 50-100 new scripts read
annually/usually 1 produced Terms: negotiable Program: workshops

METROSTAGE   F-l 1- ♪ Rv 2d
P.O. Box 329, Alexandria, VA 22313 (703) 548-9044 FAX (703) 548-
9089 Contact: Carolyn Griffin, Producing Artistic Director Theatre:
professional Works: full-length plays, one-acts, small musicals, revues
2nd productions: yes Special interests: "Works developed or show-
cased elsewhere; strong characterization." Specifications: maximum
cast: 8, 4-6 preferred Stage: thrust, 150 seats Casting: Equity, non-
Equity Submission policy: unsolicited script; query/synopsis, 10-page
dialogue sample, script history, SASP; professional recomendation Best
time: Mar.-Apr. Response: 1 month Your chances: 300 new scripts
read annually/usually 1 produced; 5 receive staged readings Remuneration: royalties Future commitment: percentage, credit

METTAWEE RIVER COMPANY   D mm ⮑
463 West St. #D405, New York, NY 10014 (212) 929-4777 Contact:
Ralph Lee, Artistic Director Theatre: professional, touring Works:
multimedia pieces Special interests: "Collaboration with writer; visual
elements; myth, legend." Stages: outdoor (summer), indoor Casting:
company of 6 Submission policy: query/synopsis, dialogue sample
Response: 4 weeks query; 8 weeks solicited script Comment: Address
Jun.-Aug.: R.D. 3, Salem, NY 12865 (518) 854-9357.

MILL MOUNTAIN THEATRE   F-l 1- ♪ 2d M W

1 Market Sq. SE 2nd Floor, Roanoke, VA 24011 (540) 342-5730 FAX (540) 342-5745 e-mail mmtmail@intrlink.com Contact: Jack Parrish, Literary Mgr. Theatre: professional regional Works: full-length plays, one-acts, musicals 2nd productions: yes Special interests: "Mixed casts; one-acts (25-35 minutes) for Centerpieces." Maximum cast: 15, 24 for musical Casting: Equity, non-Equity Stages: proscenium, 400+ seats; flexible, 125 seats Audience: "Conservative, becoming more flexible." Submission policy: full-length play: query/synopsis, resume, dialogue sample; agent submission; one-act: unsolicited script Response: immediate if interested in query; 6 months script Your chances: 500 new scripts read annually/2 produced in festival, 10 in Centerpieces (lunchtime shows) Terms: negotiable Programs: Mill Mountain Theatre New Play Competition (see Contests); The Reading Room: plays by women

MILLS COLLEGE THEATRE   F-l 1- Ad ♪ Rv 2d W M ⊏▸

5000 MacArthur Blvd., Oakland, CA 94613-1301 (510) 430-2327 FAX (510) 430-3314 e-mail strlght@mills.edu Contact: James C. Wright, Head, Dept. of Dramatic Arts & Communication Theatre: women's college Works: full-length plays, one-acts, adaptations, musicals, cabarets 2nd productions: yes Special interests: "Female roles; women of color." Maximum cast: 15 Tours: yes Stages: thrust, 187 seats; proscenium, 65 seats Casting: non-Equity, students Audience: "Likes classical and contemporary plays." Submission policy: query/synopsis; agent submission Best time: spring Response: 2-3 weeks query; 2 months solicited script Your chances: 5 new scripts read annually/ usually 0-1 produced Remuneration: royalty Future commitment: no

MILWAUKEE CHAMBER THEATRE   F-l 1- Tr Ad 2d ⊏▸

158 N. Broadway, Milwaukee, WI 53202 (414) 276-8842 FAX (414) 277-4477 e-mail montydavis@chambertheatre.com Contact: Montgomery Davis, Artistic Director Theatre: professional Works: full-length plays, one-acts, translations, adaptations 2nd productions: yes Special interest: literary merit Specifications: maximum cast: 10; single or unit set Tours: small shows Stages: proscenium, 358 seats; black box, 96 seats Audience: "The older, well-read couple." Submission policy: query/ synopsis, resume; professional recommendation; agent submission Best time: Jul.-Aug. Response: 2-3 months Your chances: 200 new scripts considered annually/"1 new play considered each season."

MILWAUKEE   F-l 1- Tr Ad CY Rv V 2d Fm h/d Rg C mm ⊏▸

PUBLIC THEATRE   626 E. Kilbourn Ave. #802, Milwaukee, WI 53202-3237 (414) 347-1685 FAX same Contact: Barbara Leigh, Art./ Producing Director Theatre: professional Works: full-length plays, one-acts, translations, adaptations, children's plays, revues, clown/vaudeville 2nd productions: yes Special interests: "Plays for family audiences, disability, regional/local or social issues, interarts, political satire, casts of 1-3 with multiple roles, new clown/vaudeville shows."

Tours: all works **Stages:** outdoor spaces, parks **Submission policy:** query/synopsis; commission **Best time:** anytime for works on disabilities; Sept. only for other works **Response:** 6 months query; 1 year solicited script **Your chances:** 100-180 new scripts read annually/ usually 0-1 produced **Terms:** negotiable

MILWAUKEE REPERTORY THEATER F-l Tr Ad Rv 2d
108 E. Wells St., Milwaukee, WI 53202 (414) 224-1761 **Contact:** Joseph Hanreddy, Artistic Director **Theatre:** professional **Works:** full-length plays, translations, adaptations, revues **2nd productions:** yes **Special interest:** "Cabaret with music." **Specifications:** 80-minutes maximum for cabaret **Stages:** thrust, 720 seats; flexible, 200 seats; cabaret, 100 seats **Casting:** Equity **Submission policy:** query/synopsis; agent submission **Response:** 2-3 months **Remuneration:** royalty

MINT THEATRE CO. 311 W. 43rd St. 5th Floor, New York, NY
10036 (212) 315-9434 This theatre is not producing new plays in 1999; see *The Playwright's Companion 2000* for future plans.

MIRANDA THEATRE COMPANY F-l 1- C x
259 W. 30th St., New York, NY 10001 (212) 268-9829 **Contact:** Valentina Fratti, Art. Director **Theatre:** professional **Works:** full-length plays, one-acts **2nd productions:** no **Special interests:** "Social relevance; new forms." **Submission policy:** query/synopsis, resume **Response:** 2 months **Future commitment:** yes **Advice:** "No phone calls."

MIRVISH PRODUCTIONS 266 King St. W, Toronto, Ontario,
Canada M5V 1H9 (416) 593-0351 FAX (416) 593-9221 **Contact:** Kelly Robinson **Submission policy:** agent submission

MISSOURI REPERTORY THEATRE 4949 Cherry St., Kansas
City, MO 64110-2499 (816) 235-2727 FAX (816) 235-5367 **e-mail** reecek@umkc.edu **Contact:** George Keathley, Artistic Director (until Jun. 2000) **Theatre:** professional This theatre is closed to submissions until further notice; inquire after Jun. 2000.

MITCHELL MAXWELL, PRODUCER F-l ♪
12 W. 27th St., New York, NY 10001 (212) 683-5666 FAX (212) 686-6755 **Production company:** professional **Works:** full-length plays, musicals **Submission policy:** query/synopsis; agent submission; professional recommendation

MIXED BLOOD THEATRE COMPANY F-l ♪ Rv 2d cm
1501 S. 4th St., Minneapolis, MN 55454 (612) 338-0937 **e-mail** hkc@ pconline.com (queries only) **Contact:** David Kunz, Script Czar **Theatre:** professional **Works:** full-length plays, musicals, revues **2nd productions:** yes **Special interests:** "Comedies and satires are always welcome." **Maximum cast:** 10 preferred **Stage:** flexible, 200 seats **Submis-**

sion policy: query/synopsis **Response:** 1-2 months query; 2-6 months solicited script **Your chances:** 350 new scripts read annually **Program:** Mixed Blood's "We Don't Need No Stinkin' Dramas" (Comedy) Playwriting Contest (see Contests) **Advice:** "Best means: via contest."

MONTANA REPERTORY THEATRE   F-l 1- ♪ ▭

Drama & Dance Dept., Univ. of Montana, Missoula, MT 59812-1582 (406) 243-6809 FAX (406) 243-5726 Contact: Greg Johnson, Artistic Director **Theatre:** professional **Works:** full-length plays, one-acts, small-scale musicals **Maximum cast:** 8 **Tours:** all plays **Casting:** Equity guest artists, students **Submission policy:** query/synopsis, resume **Best time:** summer **Response:** 3 months query; 6 months solicited script **Future commitment:** negotiable **Program:** workshops

MOUNT VERNON COMMUNITY   CY Ad 2d Lc 12+
CHILDREN'S THEATRE 1900 Elkin St. Suite 270, Alexandria, VA 22308 (703) 360-0686 Contact: Susan Lynskey, Education Director

Theatre: community **Works:** children's plays **2nd productions:** yes **Specifications:** maximum cast: 50; no more than 3 sets **Stage:** 500 seats **Casting:** children **Audience:** "Ages 4-high school." **Submission policy:** unsolicited script, videotape or query/synopsis, SASP **Best time:** spring **Response:** 2 months query **Advice:** "Adaptations of known stories with large (25-50), flexible casts and good music--easy for kids to sing."

MOVING ARTS   F-l 1- Tr Ad 2d

1822 Hyperion Ave., Los Angeles, CA 90027 (213) 665-8961 FAX (213) 665-1816 e-mail treynich@aol.com **Contact:** Trey Nichols, Literary Director **Theatre:** professional **Works:** full-length plays, one-acts (for competition), translations, adaptations **2nd productions:** if L.A. premieres **Specifications:** maximum cast: 6; no wing or fly space; simple set, small budget **Stage:** black box, 36 seats **Casting:** Equity, non-Equity **Submission policy:** query/synopsis, dialogue sample, resume **Response:** 1-3 months query; 6-8 months solicited script **Your chances:** 300 new scripts read annually/usually 6 produced **Remuneration:** negotiable **Future commitment:** "5% for 5 years." **Programs:** Premiere One-Act Competition (see Contests); Words That Speak (see Special Programs)

THE MUNY 1ST STAGE St. Louis This theatre is permanently closed.

MUSIC THEATRE FOUNDATION Chicago Mail addressed to this theatre has been returned as undeliverable; no phone number is listed.

MUSIC-THEATRE GROUP   ♪ Rv x mm

30 W. 26th St. #1001, New York, NY 10010 (212) 366-5260 Ext. 22 FAX (212) 366-5265 Contact: Lyn Austin, Producing Director **Theatre:** professional **Works:** musicals, operas, cabarets **Special interests:** "Experimental works incorporating dance, visual arts; works not professionally produced only." **Stages:** various spaces **Submission policy:** agent submission

MUSIC THEATRE OF CONNECTICUT   ♪ Ad 2d
P.O. Box 344, Westport, CT 06881-0344 (203) 454-3883 **FAX** (203) 227-8818 **Contact:** Kevin Connors, Producing Art. Director **Theatre:** professional **2nd productions:** yes **Works:** musicals, musical adaptations **Special interest:** world premieres **Maximum cast:** 7 **Stage:** proscenium, 700 seats **Casting:** Equity **Submission policy:** query/synopsis, dialogue sample, cassette tape **Best time:** summer **Response:** 1 year **Programs:** workshops, classes; Music Theatre of Connecticut Staged Reading Program (see Special Programs)

MUSICAL THEATRE WORKS   D ♪ 2d
440 Lafayette St., New York, NY 10003 (212) 677-0040 **FAX** (212) 598-0105 **Contact:** Lonny Price, Artistic Director **Theatre:** professional, developmental **Works:** full-length musicals **2nd productions:** "For development." **Specifications:** simple technical demands **Stages:** flexible, 90 seats; small black box **Casting:** Equity **Submission policy:** query/synopsis, cassette tape or part of score, resume; agent submission; commission **Response:** 6 months **Your chances:** 200+ new scripts read annually/usually 1 produced, 10-20 receive readings, 3-7 workshop productions **Remuneration:** no **Future commitment:** credit for reading, percentage for workshop production **Advice:** "No phone calls."

MUTT REP   F-l Tr Ad 2d x M
446 W. 50th St. #1W, New York, NY 10019 (212) 262-7250 **Theatre:** professional **Works:** full-length plays **2nd productions:** yes **Exclusive interest:** "Non-traditional plays for multicultural theatre." **Submission policy:** query/synopsis **Response:** 4-6 months **Program:** workshops

THE NATIONAL THEATRE   F-l 1- Tr Ad CY 2d h/d M ⌐⊃
OF THE DEAF   P.O. Box 659, Chester, CT 06412 (860) 526-4971, **TTY** (860) 526-4974 **FAX** (860) 526-0066 **e-mail** bookntd@aol.com **Contact:** Camille Jeter, Will Rhys, Art. Directors **Theatre:** professional, touring **Works:** full-length plays, one-acts, translations, adaptations, children's plays **2nd productions:** if not professionally produced **Special interests:** "Deaf issues; diversity." **Maximum cast:** 10 **Submission policy:** query/synopsis, dialogue sample, resume; commission **Response:** 1 month-6 months **Your chances:** 6-8 new scripts read annually

NATIVE AMERICANS IN THE ARTS   F-l 1- 2d NA ⌐⊃
American Indian Community House, 780 Broadway 8th Floor, New York, NY 10003 (212) 598-0100 **FAX** (212) 598-4909 **Contact:** Jim Cyrus, Director of Theatre **Works:** full-length plays, one-acts **2nd productions:** yes **Exclusive interest:** Native American writers, themes **Maximum cast:** 10 **Tours:** yes **Submission policy:** professional recommendation **Best time:** fall **Response:** 2 weeks query; 2 months script **Your chances:** 5-10 new scripts read annually/usually 1-2 produced **Remuneration:** "Possibly." **Programs:** readings, workshops, showcases

N. C. BLACK REPERTORY CO.   F-l 1- Tr Ad ♪ C Y 2d Af ⌑

610 Coliseum Dr., Winston-Salem, NC 27106 (336) 723-7907 FAX (336) 723-2223 **Contact:** Larry Leon Hamlin, Exec. Director **Theatre:** professional **Works:** full-length plays, related one-acts, translations, adaptations, musicals, children's plays **2nd productions:** yes **Special interest:** African-American issues **Maximum cast:** 3-5 **Tours:** yes **Stages:** proscenium; thrust **Submission policy:** unsolicited script, synopsis, resume; query/synopsis, resume; cassette tape of music **Response:** 3-6 months **Terms:** negotiable **Program:** National Black Theatre Festival (see Special Programs)

NEBRASKA REPERTORY THEATRE   215 Temple Bldg., 12th & R Streets, Lincoln, NE 68588-0201 (402) 472-2072 FAX (402) 472-9055 **e-mail:** jeh@unlgrad1.unl.edu **Contact:** Julie Hagemeier, Mng. Director **Theatre:** professional This theatre is closed to submissions in 1999; see *The Playwright's Companion 2000* or inquire for future plans.

NEBRASKA THEATRE CARAVAN   CY F-l Ad ♪ 2d ⌑

6915 Cass St., Omaha, NE 68132 (402) 553-4890 FAX (402) 553-6288 **e-mail** necaravan@aol.com **Contact:** Marya Lucca-Thyberg **Theatre:** professional, touring **Works:** full-length children's plays, adaptations and musicals **2nd productions:** yes **Special interest:** "Full-length family musicals." **Specifications:** maximum cast: 10; flexible set **Submission policy:** query/synopsis; agent submission **Response:** 1 month query; 3 months solicited script

NEDERLANDER PRODUCTIONS   F-l ♪ 2d ⌑

810 Seventh Ave., New York, NY 10019 (212) 262-2400 FAX (212) 262-5558 **Contact:** James M. Nederlander **Production company:** Broadway and 1st class tours **Works:** full-length plays, musicals **2nd productions:** yes **Submission policy:** agent submission only

NEGRO ENSEMBLE CO.   F-l 1- Tr Ad Af ⌑

1600 Broadway Suite 611, New York, NY 10019 (212) 582-5860 **Contact:** Susan Watson Turner, Artistic Director **Theatre:** professional **Works:** full-length plays, one-acts, translations, adaptations **2nd productions:** no **Exclusive interest:** "The black experience." **Tours:** yes **Stage:** proscenium, 99-199 seats **Submission policy:** unsolicited script; query/synopsis; professional recommendation **Response:** 6-10 months **Your chances:** 100 new scripts read annually/usually 4 produced **Remuneration:** royalties **Programs:** staged readings, classes, workshops

NEW AMERICAN THEATER   F-l Ad Rv 2d cm dr

118 N. Main St., Rockford, IL 61101 (815) 963-9454 FAX (815) 963-7215 **Contact:** William Gregg, Producing Art. Director **Theatre:** professional **Works:** full-length plays, adaptations, revues **2nd productions:** yes **Special interests:** comedy; drama **Specifications:** moderate cast

size; single or unit set; simple demands **Stages:** thrust, 282 seats; flexible, 90 seats **Casting:** Equity, non-Equity **Submission policy:** agent submission; commission **Best time:** fall **Response:** 3 months **Terms:** negotiable **Program:** workshops

NEW ARTS THEATRE   F-l 1- Tr Ad ♪ CY C Cl ⌐
P.O. Box 81, Bristol, TN 37621 e-main newartstheatreco@hotmail.com
Contact: Cody Miller, Artistic Director **Theatre:** professional **Works:** full-length plays, one-acts, translations, adaptations, musicals, children's plays **Special interests:** "Current issues; unproduced full-length plays and musicals for adult audiences; small-cast children's plays, including musicals and adaptations of classics." **Specifications:** maximum cast: 15, doubling okay; single or unit set **Tours:** "Children's plays tour under the banner Dreamworks Theatre for Youth." **Submission policy:** unsolicited script, score for musical **Response:** 2-3 months **Program:** New Arts Theatre New Play Readings (see Special Programs)

NEW CITY THEATER & ART CENTER   F-l 1- Tr Ad Rv x C
1703 13th Ave., Seattle, WA 98122 (206) 328-4683 **Contact:** John Kazanjian, Art. Director; Karen Uffelman, Mng. Director **Theatre:** professional **Works:** full-length plays, one-acts, translations, adaptations, revues **2nd productions:** no **Special interest:** non-naturalistic contemporary works **Specifications:** limited demands; low ceiling **Stage:** flexible, 100 seats **Casting:** Equity, non-Equity **Submission policy:** professional recommendation; agent submission **Response:** 5 months **Future commitment:** credit **Programs:** staged readings, workshops

THE NEW CONSERVATORY   F-l Ad CY 2d C g/l Fm
THEATRE CENTER 25 Van Ness, San Francisco, CA 94102-6033 (415) 861-4914 FAX (415) 861-6988 **Contact:** Ed Decker, Artistic Director **Theatre:** professional **Works:** full-length plays, adaptations, children's plays **2nd productions:** yes **Special interest:** "Socially relevant work for young audiences; new work; gay/lesbian themes." **Maximum cast:** 5 **Tours:** "Possibly." **Stages:** proscenium, 130 seats; flexible, 60 seats; flexible, 50 seats **Casting:** non-Equity, students **Audience:** "Family; gay/lesbian." **Submission policy:** "Letter of inquiry prior to submission." **Response:** up to 1-year **Your chances:** "Young Audience series produces 3-5 scripts; Gay/Lesbian Pride Season produces 6-8 scripts." **Remuneration:** royalty **Program:** workshops

NEW ENSEMBLE ACTORS F-l 1- CY po 2d ⌐ M V x $ M b Rs
THEATRE OF SALT & PEPPER MIME   320 E. 90th St. Suite 1B,
New York, NY 10128-4424 (212) 262-4989 FAX (212) 722-4782
Contact: Scottie Davis, Producing Director **Theatre:** off off Broadway **Works:** children's plays, one-acts, poetry/narratives **2nd productions:** yes **Special interest:** "Non-traditional casting; surreal, mimetic, psychologically challenging works." **Specifications:** maximum cast: 5; single set

Tours: yes Stages: proscenium, 200 seats; flexible, 20 seats Casting: Equity, non-Equity, ensemble Audience: "Professionals, artists, working class, youth, people of color." Submission policy: unsolicited script or query/synopsis, resume, $5 fee Best time: summer-fall Response: 1 month query; 3 months script Your chances: 8 new scripts read annually/usually 2 produced, latest in Sept. 1998 Remuneration: "Homebased, none; tours, percentage; commission if produced in larger venue." Future commitment: credit, options Programs: readings, staged readings, workshop productions, residencies Advice: "Small grass-roots theatre with limited memberships for creative artists as guest residents-- guaranteed development of work."

NEW FEDERAL THEATRE   F-l C M W
292 Henry St., New York, NY 10002 (212) 353-1176 FAX (212) 353- 1088 Contact: Ms. Pat White, Co. Mgr. Theatre: off off Broadway Works: full-length plays 2nd productions: no Special interest: minority and women's issues Specifications: maximum cast: 10; no more than 2 sets Stages: proscenium, 300+ seats; arena, 100 seats; endstage, 100 seats Casting: Equity Submission policy: unsolicited script; professional recommendation; agent submission Response: 5-6 months Remuneration: "$250-$500 option for 6 months." Future commitment: yes

NEW GEORGES   D F-l 1- W
90 Hudson St. #2E, New York, NY 10013 (212) 334-9239 FAX same e-mail newgeorges@aol.com Contact: Susan Bernfield, Artistic Director Theatre: professional Works: full-length plays, one-acts, 10-minute plays 2nd productions: no Exclusive interest: women playwrights Submission policy: unsolicited script or work-in-progress, cover letter, resume Response: 6 months Program: workshops

THE NEW GROUP   F-l Tr Ad ♪ C
85 Fifth Ave. 5th Fl., New York, NY 10003 (212) 647-0752 Contact: Kevin Scott, Literary Mgr. Theatre: off Broadway Works: full-length plays, translations, adaptations, musicals 2nd productions: no Special interests: "Plays which reflect common human truths, the current spirit of our times, and tell their story with immediacy, fearlessness, discipline." Stages: prosceniums, 99-300 seats Casting: Equity, non-Equity Submission policy: unsolicited script Response: 6 months Your chances: 800 new scripts read annually/usually 3-4 produced Terms: negotiable Program: New Group Playwrights Unit (see Special Programs)

NEW HAMPSHIRE THEATRE PROJECT   CY 12+ Ad 2d Fm ⌑
P.O. Box 6507, Portsmouth, NH 03802-6507 (603) 431-6644 FAX (603) 433-3996 Contact: Genevieve Aichele, Artistic Director Theatre: professional Works: children's plays and adaptations 2nd productions: "Occasionally." Special interests: "High quality works for children, youth, families; particular interest in adaptations of children's liter-

ature." **Specifications:** maximum cast: 3-8; all shows tour **Stages:** 2 proseceniums, 40, 800 seats; thrust, 100 seats; "we premiere locally before touring" **Casting:** Equity, non-Equity **Audience:** "Families, grades K-12; some special needs." **Submission policy:** query/synopsis, resume, dialogue sample, SASP **Best time:** Jan.-May **Response:** 2-4 weeks query; 6-8 weeks solicited script **Your chances:** "Very few new scripts received annually--we would like more!" **Remuneration:** royalties **Programs:** readings, staged readings **Advice:** "We adapt or create most of our material but are open to new work.."

♫ NEW JERSEY REPERTORY COMPANY   F-l ♪
P.O. Box 138, Oakhurst, NJ 07755 (732) 571-1298 Contact: Suzanne Barabas, Artistic Director **Works:** full-length plays, musicals **2nd productions:** no **Casting:** non-Equity **Submission policy:** unsolicited script; query/synopsis **Response:** 3-6 months

NEW JERSEY SHAKESPEARE FESTIVAL   F-l Tr Ad Cl Rs
36 Madison Ave., Madison, NJ 07940 (201) 408-3278 FAX (201) 408-3361 e-mail njsf@njshakespeare.org **Contact:** Bonnie J. Monte, Artistic Director **Theatre:** professional **Works:** full-length plays, translations, adaptations **Special interests:** translations and adaptations of classics **Stage:** proscenium, 308 seats **Casting:** Equity, non-Equity, students **Submission policy:** query/synopsis; agent submission **Best time:** early fall **Response:** 2 months query; 1 month solicited script **Remuneration:** negotiable **Future commitment:** percentage, credit **Your chances:** 25 new scripts read annually/"we seldom produce new work" **Programs:** script development, internships, residencies, classes

♫ NEW LINE THEATRE   ♪ C
3649 Dunnica Ave. #2E, St. Louis, MO 63116 (314) 773-6526 Contact: Scott Miller, Artistic Director **Theatre:** professional **Works:** full-length musicals **Special interest:** "Social or political issues." **Submission policy:** unsolicited script **Program:** readings

NEW PERSPECTIVES THEATRE CO.   F-l 1- M
750 Eighth Ave. #601, New York, NY 10036 (212) 730-2030 Theatre: professional **Works:** full-length plays **2nd productions:** no **Exclusive interest:** "Multiracial/nontraditional casting." **Casting:** Equity **Submission policy:** query/1-page synopsis, 15-page dialogue sample preferred; unsolicited script **Response:** 3-4 months **Program:** workshops

NEW REPERTORY THEATRE   F-l Tr Ad dr
P.O. Box 418, Newton Highlands, MA 02161 (617) 332-7058 e-mail NewRepThtr.@aol.com **Contact:** Rick Lombardo, Producing Artistic Director **Theatre:** professional **Works:** full-length plays, translations, adaptations **Special interest:** "Small-cast, idea-driven dramas." **Stage:** thrust, 160 seats **Submission policy:** solicited script

NEW STAGE THEATRE   F-l 1-

P.O. Box 4792, Jackson, MS 39296 (601) 948-0143 FAX (601) 948-3538 **Contact:** John Maxwell, Artistic Director **Theatre:** professional **Works:** full-length plays, one-acts **Cast size:** 3-8 **Stage:** proscenium, 364 seats **Submission policy:** query/synopsis **Best time:** summer-fall **Response:** 4 weeks query; 5 months solicited script **Remuneration:** royalties **Program:** Eudora Welty New Plays Series (see Special Programs)

NEW THEATRE   F-l Tr Ad 2d x dr L

65 Almeria Ave., Coral Gables, FL 33134 (305) 443-5373, -5909 FAX (305) 443-5373 **Contact:** Rafael DeAcha, Artistic Director **Theatre:** professional **Works:** full-length plays, translations, adaptations **2nd productions:** yes **Special interests:** "Non-realistic drama; language." **Maximum cast:** 6 **Stage:** endstage, 70 seats **Casting:** Equity, non-Equity **Submission policy:** unsolicited script; videotape; query/synopsis **Response:** 1 month query; 1-2 months script **Your chances:** 50 new scripts read annually **Terms:** negotiable

NEW THEATRE--ST. LOUIS   634 N. Grand Blvd. Suite 10-C,

St. Louis, MO 63103 This theatre is closed to submissions in 1999; inquire, or see *The Playwright's Companion 2000* for future plans.

NEW TUNERS THEATRE   ♪ F

1225 W. Belmont, Chicago, IL 60657 (312) 929-7367 Ext. 10 FAX (312) 327-1404 **e-mail** Hotuners@aol.com **Contact:** Warner Crocker **Theatre:** professional **Works:** full-length musicals, musical adaptations **Special interest:** "New musicals for annual festival." **Stage:** flexible, 148 seats **Casting:** non-Equity **Audience:** "City, suburban." **Submission policy:** query/synopsis, resume, work sample, cassette tape **Best time:** Jan. **Response:** 2 weeks **Your chances:** 120 new scripts read annually/usually 8-12 produced **Terms:** option fee; royalties; negotiable future commitment **Program:** New Tuners Workshop (see Special Programs)

NEW VILLAGE PRODUCTIONS   D F-l 1- Rv

145 E. 27th St. Suite 1A, New York, NY 10016 (212) 779-3051 **Contact:** Gale Albahae, Program Director **Theatre:** off off Broadway **Works:** full-length plays, one-acts, revues **2nd productions:** no **Exclusive interest:** "Scripts for development." **Specifications:** maximum cast: 6; single set preferred **Stages:** various spaces, 65-100 seats **Submission policy:** professional recommendation; agent submission; commission **Remuneration:** negotiable **Future commitment:** "Not usually." **Programs:** readings, workshops, classes; New Village Productions Playwrights Wing (see Special Programs) **Advice:** "Break stereotypes."

NEW YORK STAGE AND FILM   F-l ♪ cm dr

151 W. 30th St. Suite 902, New York, NY 10001 (212) 750-6703 FAX (212) 750-6784 **Contact:** Peter Manning, Producer **Theatre:** professional **Works:** full-length plays, musicals **2nd productions:** no **Special**

interests: comedy; drama **Stages:** proscenium, 135 seats; black box, 100 seats **Submission policy:** unsolicited script; query/synopsis **Best time:** Sept 1-Oct. 31 only **Response:** 3-6 months **Future commitment:** no

NEW YORK STATE THEATRE   F-l Tr Ad ♪ CY 2d Fm ▭
INSTITUTE **155 River St., Troy, NY 12180 (518) 274-3200 FAX (518) 274-3815 e-mail** nysti@crisny.org **Contact:** Patricia B. Snyder, Producing Director **Theatre:** professional **Works:** full-length plays, translations, adaptations, musicals, children's plays **2nd productions:** yes **Special interests:** "Unproduced plays; works for family audiences with strong values, educational potential." **Maximum cast:** 6-13 **Tours:** yes **Stage:** proscenium, 900 seats **Casting:** Equity, non-Equity **Submission policy:** query/synopsis, dialogue sample, resume, SASP; agent submission **Best time:** Apr.-Sept. **Response:** 1-2 months query; 3-4 months script **Your chances:** 300 new scripts read annually/usually 1-2 produced **Terms:** negotiable **Advice:** "No works exclusively for 'mature' audiences."

NEW YORK THEATRE   D F-l 1- Tr ♪ 2d C x L
WORKSHOP **79 E. 4th St., New York, NY 10003 (212) 780-9037 FAX (212) 460-8996 Contact:** Mandy Mishell Hackett, Literary Mgr. **Theatre:** off Broadway **Works:** full-length plays, one-acts, translations, musicals, performance pieces **2nd productions:** yes **Special interests:** "Large issues; innovative form, language." **Stage:** proscenium, 150 seats **Casting:** Equity **Submission policy:** query/synopsis, 10-page dialogue sample, resume; performance piece proposal; professional recommendation; agent submission **Response:** 6 months **Your chances:** 1000 new scripts read annually **Remuneration:** fee **Future commitment:** yes **Program:** Van Lier Fellowships (see Contests) **Advice:** "Interested in long-term collaborative relationships."

NEWBERRY COLLEGE THEATRE   F-l 1- Ad ♪ 2d
2100 College St., Newberry, SC 29108 (803) 321-5620 Contact: Patrick Gagliano, Director of Theatre **Theatre:** college **Works:** full-length plays, one-acts, adaptations, musicals **2nd productions:** yes **Maximum cast:** 15 **Stages:** proscenium, 175 seats; arena, 130 seats **Submission policy:** unsolicited script **Best time:** May-Aug. **Response:** 3 months **Your chances:** 10 new scripts read annually/usually 0-1 produced **Remuneration:** no

NEXT ACT THEATRE   F-l Tr Ad 2d
P.O. Box 394, Milwaukee, WI 53201 (414) 278-7780 FAX (414) 278-5930 Contact: David Cecsarini, Producing Director **Theatre:** professional **Works:** full-length plays, translations, adaptations **2nd productions:** "Almost always." **Specifications:** maximum cast: 8, fewer preferred; flexible unit set; small budget **Stage:** flexible, 150-200 seats **Casting:** Equity, non-Equity **Submission policy:** query/synopsis, resume,

dialogue sample; professional recommendation **Response:** 6-12 months query; 18 months solicited script **Your chances:** 50 new scripts read annually **Remuneration:** negotiable **Future commitment:** options

THE NEXT THEATRE COMPANY F-l Tr Ad 2d
927 Noyes, Evanston, IL 60201 (847) 475-6763 FAX (847) 475-6767 e-mail sarah@lightoperaworks.org **Contact:** Sarah Tucker, Assoc. Art. Director **Theatre:** professional **Works:** full-length plays, translations, adaptations **2nd productions:** yes **Specification:** simple demands **Stage:** proscenium, 175 seats **Casting:** Equity, non-Equity **Submission policy:** query/synopsis, dialogue sample **Response:** 6 weeks-3 months

NICHOLAS NEUBAUER New York, NY Mail addressed to this producer has been returned as undeliverable; no phone number is listed.

NIKO ASSOCIATES 234 W. 44th St. #902, New York, NY 10036 See Manny Kladitis and Marvin A. Krauss in this section.

NONE OF THE ABOVE THEATRE CO. F-l 1- 2d Rg ⊏⊐
2161 Coney Island Ave., Brooklyn, NY 11223 (718) 782-8317 Contact: Robert Liebowitz, Art. Dir. **Theatre:** professional **Works:** full-length plays, one-acts **2nd productions:** yes **Special interest:** "Life in NYC." **Specifications:** maximum cast: 10; simple demands **Tours:** yes **Stage:** black box, 75 seats **Casting:** Equity, non-Equity **Audience:** "Eclectic." **Submission policy:** unsolicited script; query/synopsis **Response:** 2-8 weeks **Your chances:** 150 new scripts read annually/usually 10-20 produced **Terms:** negotiable **Programs:** workshops, one-act festivals

NORTH CAROLINA SHAKESPEARE F-l Tr Ad Rg Cl
FESTIVAL P.O. Box 6066, High Point, NC 27262-6066 (336) 841-2273 FAX (336) 841-8627 Contact: Louis Rackoff, Artistic Director **Theatre:** professional **Works:** full-length plays, translations, adaptations **Special interests:** NC writers; adaptations of classics **Specifications:** maximum cast: 15, simple set **Stage:** proscenium, 620 seats **Submission policy:** query/synopsis **Best time:** fall-winter **Response:** 3 weeks query; 4 months solicited script

NORTH COAST REPERTORY THEATRE F-l 2d
987 D Lomas Santa Fe Dr., Solana Beach,CA 92075 (619) 481-2155 FAX (619) 481-1527 Contact: Sean Murray, Artistic Director **Theatre:** professional **Works:** full-length plays **2nd productions:** yes **Maximum cast:** 10 **Submission policy:** query/synopsis; agent submission **Best time:** Sept.-Jan.

NORTH SHORE MUSIC THEATRE ♪ 2d Lc
P.O. Box 62, Dunham Rd., Beverly, MA 01915 (978) 922-8500 FAX (978) 921-0793 e-mail nsmt@aol **Contact:** Kevin P. Hale, Asst. to Producer **Theatre:** professional **Works:** musicals **2nd productions:** yes **Maximum cast:** 25 **Stages:** arena, 1800 seats; flexible, 100 seats **Sub-**

mission policy: query/synopsis, dialogue sample, 2-3 songs **Response:** 6-9 months **Future commitment:** yes **Program:** North Shore Music Theatre New Works Development Program (see Special Programs)

NORTHEASTERN UNIV. NU PLAY/   F-l 2d dr Rg
PROJECT   360 Huntington Ave., Boston, MA 02115 (617) 373-4476
FAX (617) 373-4488 **Contact:** Ed Bullins, Artistic Director **Works:** full-length plays **2nd productions:** yes **Exclusive interests:** "Dramas; Boston-area playwrights." **Submission policy:** unsolicited script; query/1-page synopsis **Best time:** fall **Response:** 6 months

NORTHLIGHT THEATRE   F-l Tr Ad ♪ 2d C cm
9501 Skokie Blvd., Skokie, IL 60076 (847) 679-9501 Ext. 3303 FAX (847) 679-1879 **Contact:** Cecilie Keenan, Asst. Art. Director **Theatre:** professional **Works:** full-length plays, translations, adaptations, musicals **2nd productions:** yes **Special interests:** "Translations, adaptations of 'lost' plays; issues; comedies; no domestic realism." **Stage:** thrust, 345 seats **Casting:** "Non-traditional." **Audience:** "Middle class." **Submission policy:** query/synopsis, resume; agent submission **Best time:** Sept.-Feb. **Response:** 1 month query; 4 months solicited script **Your chances:** 300+ new scripts read annually/usually 2 produced

NORTHSIDE THEATRE CO.   F-l 1- 2d Fm ⌐
OF SAN JOSE   848 E. William St., San Jose, CA 95116 (408) 288-7820 **e-mail** northside8@hotmail.com **Contact:** Richard T. Orlando, Artistic Director **Theatre:** community **Works:** full-length plays, one-acts **2nd productions:** yes **Special interest:** "Thoughtful, imaginative works for family audiences." **Specifications:** maximum cast: 15, "some core roles for young adults"; unit set preferred **Stages:** proscenium, under 100 seats; touring wagon **Casting:** non-Equity **Submission policy:** unsolicited script, resume; query/synopsis, dialogue sample, resume **Best time:** Oct.-Jan. **Response:** 2 months **Your chances:** 35 new scripts read annually/usually 1-2 produced **Remuneration:** honorarium; videotape **Future commitment:** negotiable **Program:** staged readings

NORTHWESTERN UNIV. THEATRE   Evanston, IL
This theatre is no longer open to submissions.

NOVEL STAGES   Mail addressed to this theatre has been returned as undeliverable; no phone number is listed.

OAK RIDGE   F-l 1- Tr Ad ♪ CY Rv 2d Rd Lc
COMMUNITY PLAYHOUSE   P.O. Box 5705, Oak Ridge, TN 37831-5705 (423) 482-9999 FAX (423) 482-0945 **Contact:** Beverly Broyles, General Mgr. **Works:** full-length plays, one-acts, translations, adaptations, musicals, children's plays, revues, radio plays **2nd productions:** yes **Specifications:** maximum cast: 50; no more than 2 sets; no fly space **Stage:** small proscenium, 344 seats **Casting:** non-Equity

Submission policy: unsolicited script **Best time:** early Jan. **Response:** 6 months **Your chances:** 20 new scripts read annually/usually 2-5 produced **Remuneration:** "Limited." **Programs:** Oak Ridge Community Playhouse Programs (see Special Programs)

OAKLAND ENSEMBLE THEATRE   **F-l ♪ Rv 2d Af**
1428 Alice St. #306, Oakland, CA 94612 (510) 763-7774 FAX (510) 763-7536 Contact: Helena J. Wright, Producing Art. Director **Theatre:** professional **Works:** full-length plays, musicals, revues **2nd productions:** yes **Exclusive interests:** "African-American perspectives." **Maximum cast:** 16 **Stage:** flexible, 400 seats **Audience:** "75% African-American." **Submission policy:** query/synopsis; professional recommendation; agent submission **Response:** 10 months **Terms:** negotiable

ODYSSEY THEATRE ENSEMBLE   **F-l Tr Ad ♪ 2d x ▭**
2055 S. Sepulveda Blvd., Los Angeles, CA 90025 (310) 477-2055 FAX (310) 444-0455 Contact: Sally Essex-Lopresti, Literary Mgr. **Theatre:** professional **Works:** full-length plays, translations, adaptations, musicals **2nd productions:** yes **Special interests:** "Provocative subject matter; innovative form." **Maximum cast:** 12 **Tours:** yes **Stages:** thrust, endstage, proscenium; 99 seats **Audience:** "Educated, upper-middle class, interested in being challenged, surprised, entertained." **Submission policy:** query/synopsis, dialogue sample, script history, resume; agent submission **Response:** 2 weeks query; 6 months solicited script **Your chances:** 300 new scripts read annually/usually 1-2 produced **Terms:** negotiable **Programs:** staged readings, development, internships

OFF BROADWAY THEATRE   **F-l ♪ 2d**
1444 NE 26th St., Fort Lauderdale, FL 33305-1322 (954) 566-0554 FAX (954) 566-6605 Contact: Brian C. Smith, Producer **Theatre:** professional **Works:** full-length plays, musicals **2nd productions:** yes **Maximum cast:** 12 **Stage:** proscenium, 300 seats **Casting:** Equity, non-Equity **Submission policy:** query/synopsis, resume **Best time:** Oct.-May **Response:** 2 weeks **Your chances:** 300 new scripts read annually **Remuneration:** negotiable

OFFSTAGE THEATRE   **1- 2d ▭**
P.O. Box 131, Charlottesville, VA 22902 Contact: Steve Tharp **Theatre:** semi-professional **Works:** one-acts **2nd productions:** yes **Special interest:** "Orignial short plays; monologues; plays set in bars, galleries, fitness centers, libraries, etc., for site-specific staging." **Specifications:** maximum cast: 10; single set; simple demands **Tours:** "Site-specific locations." **Stages:** "Indoor, outdoor, 50-100 seats." **Casting:** non-Equity **Audience:** "Adults, families." **Submission policy:** unsolicited script; query/synopsis **Response:** 1-6 months **Your chances:** 200 new scripts read annually/usually 5 produced **Remuneration:** varies **Future commitment:** no **Advice:** "Keep it simple, honest, light."

OLD GLOBE THEATRE　　　　　　　　　　　**F-l Tr Ad 2d**
P.O. Box 2171, San Diego, CA 92112-2171 (619) 231-1941 Contact: Raúl Moncada, Literary Mgr. **Theatre:** professional **Works:** full-length plays, translations, adaptations **2nd productions:** yes **Maximum cast:** 10 **Stages:** thrust, 581 seats; arena, 225 seats; outdoor, 620 seats **Audience:** "Sophisticated, conservative." **Submission policy:** query/synopsis; agent submission **Response:** 3 weeks query; 10 months solicited script **Your chances:** 150 new scripts read annually **Terms:** negotiable

OLD LOG THEATER　　　　　　　　　　**F-l Ad 2d cm**
P.O. Box 250, Excelsior, MN 55331 (612) 474-5951 FAX (612) 474-1290 **Contact:** Don Stolz, Producing Artistic Director **Theatre:** professional **Works:** full-length plays, adaptations **2nd productions:** yes **Special interest:** "Small-cast comedies." **Stage:** proscenium, 655 seats **Audience:** "All ages." **Submission policy:** unsolicited script; query/synopsis **Response:** 1 month query; 6 months script **Your chances:** 200 new scripts read annually **Remuneration:** negotiable

OLDCASTLE THEATRE COMPANY　　　　　　**F-l 2d Rg**
P.O. Box 1555, Bennington, VT 05201 (802) 447-0564 **e-mail** Oldcast @sover.net **Contact:** Eric Peterson, Producing Director **Theatre:** professional **Works:** full-length plays **2nd productions:** yes **Special interest:** "New England themes." **Casting:** Equity **Submission policy:** query/synopsis, 15-20 page dialogue sample preferred; unsolicited script; agent submission **Best time:** winter **Response:** 6 months **Your chances:** usually 1-2 new plays produced each year **Remuneration:** royalty **Future commitment:** negotiable **Programs:** staged readings, workshops

OLNEY THEATRE CENTER　　　　　　　　**F-l Tr Ad 2d**
2001 Olney-Sandy Spring Rd., Olney, MD 20832 (301) 924-4485 FAX (301) 924-2654 **Contact:** David Jackson, Literary Mgr. **Theatre:** professional **Works:** full-length plays, translations, adaptations **2nd productions:** yes **Maximum cast:** 8 **Stage:** proscenium, 500 seats **Casting:** Equity **Submission policy:** professional recommendation; agent submission **Response:** 6 months **Remuneration:** percentage

OMAHA MAGIC THEATRE　Omaha, NE　Mail addressed to this theatre has been returned as undeliverable; no phone number is listed.

OMAHA THEATER CO. FOR YOUNG PEOPLE　　**CY Ad 2d M**
2001 Farnam St., Omaha, NE 68102 (402) 345-4852 FAX (402) 345-7255 **Contact:** James Larson, Art. Director **Theatre:** professional **Works:** one-act children's plays, adaptations **2nd productions:** yes **Special interests:** multicultural issues; children's literature **Specifications:** maximum cast: 10; unit set preferred **Stages:** proscenium, 932 seats; black box, 175 seats **Submission policy:** professional recommendation; agent submission **Response:** 6 months **Your chances:** 48 new scripts read annually/usually 2 produced **Terms:** negotiable

THEATRES & PRODUCTION COMPANIES　　95

ONTOLOGICAL-HYSTERIC THEATER F-l x
131 E. 10th St., New York, NY 10003 (212) 420-1916 FAX (212) 529-2318 **Contact:** Damon Kiely, Production Mgr. **Theatre:** professional **Works:** full-length plays **Exclusive interest:** "Unconventional, experimental plays." **Stage:** proscenium, 70 seats **Submission policy:** query/synopsis, resume; professional recommendation **Best time:** Jan. **Response:** 3 months **Remuneration:** no **Programs:** readings, internships **Comment:** Theatre is located in St. Mark's Church.

THE OPEN EYE F-l 1- CY 2d ⊃
P.O. Box 959, Margaretville, NY 12455 (914) 586-1660 **Contact:** Amie Brockway, Producing Artistic Director **Theatre:** professional **Works:** full-length plays, one-acts, children's plays **2nd productions:** yes **Specifications:** small cast; single set **Tours:** yes **Casting:** professional **Audience:** "Age 8-adults of all ages; prefers universal themes." **Submission policy:** query/synopsis **Response:** "Only if interested." **Program:** script development

OPEN STAGE OF HARRISBURG F-l 2d
223 Walnut St., Harrisburg, PA 17101 (717) 232-6736 FAX (717) 232-1505 **Contact:** Mary Ann Fisher, Gen. Mgr. **Theatre:** professional **Works:** full-length plays **2nd productions:** "Occasionally." **Casting:** non-Equity **Comment:** This theatre has been closed to submissions; inquire for further information.

OREGON SHAKESPEARE FESTIVAL F-l Tr Ad 2d L
P.O. Box 158, Ashland, OR 97520 (541) 482-2111 FAX (541) 482-0446 **Contact:** Lue Douthit, Literary Mgr. **Theatre:** professional **Works:** full-length plays, translations, adaptations **2nd productions:** yes **Special interests:** "Interesting use of language; plays with ideas." **Stages:** thrust, 600 seats; outdoor Elizabethan, 1194 seats; black box, 140 seats **Submission policy:** professional recommendation; agent submission; commission **Best time:** fall **Your chances:** 200 new scripts read annually/possibly 1 produced, 2-3 receive readings **Terms:** negotiable **Program:** script development

PACE THEATRICAL GROUP, INC. F-l ♪
1515 Broadway 36th Floor, New York, NY 10036 (212) 704-7608 **Production company:** professional **Works:** full-length plays, musicals **Submission policy:** "Only from producers or agents with whom we have a longstanding working relationship."

PAN ASIAN REPERTORY THEATRE F-l Tr Ad ♪ 2d As ⊃
47 Great Jones St., New York, NY 10012 (212) 505-5655 FAX (212) 505-6014 **Contact:** Tisa Chang, Artistic/Producing Director **Theatre:** professional **Works:** full-length plays, translations, adaptations, musicals **2nd productions:** yes **Exclusive interest:** "Asian, Asian American writers/themes." **Maximum cast:** 8 preferred **Tours:** yes

Stage: open, 150 seats **Submission policy:** query/brief synopsis by fax **Best time:** summer **Response:** 9 months **Terms:** yes **Programs:** staged readings, workshops

PANDEMONIUM STAGE CO. New York Mail addressed to this theatre has been returned as undeliverable; no phone number is listed.

THE PASADENA PLAYHOUSE F-1 ♪ 2d
39 S. El Molino Ave., Pasadena, CA 91101 (626) 792-8672 FAX (626) 792-7343 e-mail dtucker@pasadenaplayhouse.com **Contact:** David A. Tucker II, Literary Mgr. **Theatre:** professional **Works:** full-length plays, small-cast musicals **2nd productions:** yes **Maximum cast:** 7-10 (no 1-person shows) **Stage:** proscenium, 686 seats **Casting:** Equity **Submission policy:** query/synopsis, 1st 15 pages of dialogue; no e-mail or fax submission **Response:** 6-9 months **Your chances:** 150-200 new scripts read annually/usually 0-1 produced **Remuneration:** negotiable

PASSAGE THEATRE COMPANY F-1 1- Rv 2d M
P.O. Box 967, Trenton, NJ 08605 (609) 392-0766 Contact: June Ballinger, Producing Art. Director **Theatre:** professional **Works:** full-length plays, related one-acts, cabarets **2nd productions:** if NJ premieres **Special interest:** "Multiethnic themes, common humanity of diverse peoples." **Specifications:** maximum cast: 8; unit set **Stage:** proscenium, 125 seats **Audience:** "Diverse: Italian American, African-American, middle class." **Submission policy:** unsolicited script, resume; professional recommendation; agent submission **Response:** 4 months **Your chances:** 50 new scripts read annually/usually 2 produced **Remuneration:** "6%." **Future commitment:** negotiable **Program:** WinterFest (see Special Programs) **Advice:** "Phone for our mission statement."

PAUL BUNYAN PLAYHOUSE F-1 ♪ CY 2d Lc cm Fm
314 Beltrami Ave., P.O. Box 752, Bemidji, MN 56619-0752 (218) 751-0752 FAX (218) 751-2838 e-mail pbphouse@northernnet.com **Contact:** Karen Millar Moe, Executive Director **Theatre:** professional **Works:** full-length plays, musicals, children's plays **2nd productions:** yes **Maximum cast:** 50 **Stage:** thrust, 316 seats **Casting:** non-Equity **Audience:** "Conservative; want to laugh; profanity is not tolerated." **Submission policy:** unsolicited script; query/synopsis, resume; videotape; agent submission **Best time:** fall-Dec. **Response:** 2-4 months **Your chances:** 40-50 new scripts read annually/usually none produced **Remuneration:** negotiable **Advice:** "No one-acts, please!"

PCPA F-1 ♪ 2d
P.O. Box 1700, Santa Maria, CA 93456 (805) 928-7731 FAX (805) 928-7506 Contact: Art. Director **Theatre:** professional **Works:** full-length plays, musicals **2nd productions:** yes **Casting:** students **Stages:** thrust, 450 seats; arena, 185 seats **Submission policy:** professional recommendation; agent submission; query/synopsis **Response:** 3 months

PCPA OUTREACH TOUR   CY 1- Tr Ad 2d H Hi C Esp ⌐⊐
P.O. Box 1700, Santa Maria, CA 93456 (805) 928-7731, Ext. 4117 FAX
(805) 928-7506 **Contact:** Leo Cortez, Outreach Director **Theatre:** professional **Works:** one-act and 30-minute children's plays, translations,
adaptations **2nd productions:** yes **Special interests:** "Historical,
Latino, social issues; bilingual children's plays." **Specifications:** cast
size: 3-5; shows tour **Submission policy:** unsolicited script; query/
synopsis; professional recommendation **Best time:** spring **Response:** 2
months **Future commitment:** yes **Program:** workshops

PEGASUS PLAYERS   F-l Tr Ad ♪ 2d
1145 W. Wilson Ave., Chicago, IL 60640 (773) 878-9761 FAX (773)
271-0857 **Contact:** Arlene Crewdson, Exec. Director **Theatre:** professional **Works:** full-length plays, translations, adaptations, musicals **2nd
productions:** yes **Casting:** non-Equity **Stage:** proscenium, 250 seats
Submission policy: query/synopsis, resume; professional recommendation **Response:** 1 month query; 4-6 months solicited script **Terms:**
negotiable **Program:** Chicago Young Playwrights Festival (see Contests)

PEGASUS THEATRE   F-l 2d C cm P
3916 Main St., Dallas, TX 75226 (214) 821-6005 FAX (214) 826-1671
Contact: Steve Erwin, Literary Mgr. **Theatre:** professional **Works:** full-
length plays **2nd productions:** yes **Special interest:** "Original satiric
comedies." **Specifications:** maximum cast: 10; single set; limited fly space;
"no mysteries, please" **Stage:** proscenium, 141 seats **Audience:** "Middle-
upper middle class, educated." **Submission policy:** query/synopsis, dialogue sample **Best time:** Mar.-Jun. **Response:** 6 weeks query; 3-6 months
solicited script **Your chances:** 200 new scripts read annually/usually 1
produced **Terms:** negotiable **Program:** staged readings

PENDRAGON THEATRE   F-l Tr Ad CY 2d cm dr ⌐⊐
148 River St., Saranac Lake, NY 12983-2031 (518) 891-1854 FAX
(805) 928-7506 **Contact:** Susan Neal, Artistic Director **Theatre:** professional **Works:** full-length plays, translations, adaptations, children's
plays **2nd productions:** yes **Special interests:** comedies, dramas,
children's plays **Specifications:** maximum cast: 8; simple set **Tours:** yes
Stage: black box, 132 seats **Casting:** non-Equity **Audience:** "Enjoys
variety--from classics to new work." **Submission policy:** query/syn-
opsis, brief dialogue sample, resume, script history, SASP; professional
recommendation; commission **Response:** 2 months query; 3 months
solicited script **Your chances:** 45 new scripts read annually/usually 1
produced **Terms:** negotiable **Program:** workshops

PENGUIN REPERTORY CO.   F-l Tr Ad Rv 2d cm dr Sp
P.O. Box 91, Stony Point, NY 10980 (914) 786-2873 FAX (914) 786-
3638 **Contact:** Joe Brancato, Art. Director **Theatre:** professional **Works:**
full-length plays, translations, adaptations, revues **2nd productions:**
yes **Special interests:** "New works, comedy, drama; the survival of the

human spirit." **Specifications:** cast size: 2-4; single, unit/suggestive set **Casting:** Equity **Stage:** proscenium, 108 seats **Submission policy:** unsolicited script, synopsis; commission **Best time:** May-Jun. **Response:** 2-3 months **Future commitment:** negotiable **Program:** staged readings

PENOBSCOT THEATRE CO./MAINE   F-l CY Am
SHAKESPEARE FESTIVAL   183 Main St., Bangor, ME 04401
(207) 942-3333   FAX (207) 947-6678   Contact: Mark Torres, Producing Artistic Director **Theatre:** professional **Works:** full-length plays, children's plays **Special interest:** new American plays **Specifications:** small cast; limited demands **Stages:** proscenium, 500 seats; proscenium, 132 seats; outdoor theatre **Submission policy:** query/synopsis **Best time:** late fall **Response:** 4 weeks query; 2 months solicited script

PENSACOLA JUNIOR COLLEGE THEATRE   F-l ♪ 2d cm dr
Dept. of Music & Theatre, 1000 College Blvd., Pensacola, FL 32504
(904) 484-1812   FAX (904) 484-1825   Contact: Stan Dean, Director **Works:** full-length plays, musicals **2nd productions:** yes **Special interests:** comedies, dramas **Casting:** students **Submission policy:** query/synopsis, SASP **Best time:** Jan. **Response:** 6-8 weeks **Your chances:** 30 new scripts read annually **Terms:** negotiable **Program:** workshop productions

THE PENUMBRA THEATRE CO.   F-l 1- Tr Ad ♪ CY 2d Af ⌂
270 N. Kent St., St. Paul, MN 55102   (612) 224-4601 FAX (612) 224-7074 Contact: Lou Bellamy, Art. Director **Theatre:** professional **Works:** full-length plays, one-acts, translations, adaptations, musicals, children's plays **2nd productions:** yes **Special interest:** African-American issues **Tours:** yes **Stage:** proscenium-thrust, 260 seats **Submission policy:** unsolicited script; query/synopsis; resume; available reviews **Response:** 6-9 months **Your chances:** 90 new scripts read annually/usually 1-2 produced **Terms:** negotiable **Program:** Cornerstone Dramaturgy and Development Project (see Contests)

PEOPLE'S LIGHT AND THEATRE COMPANY   F-l Tr Ad 2d
39 Conestoga Rd., Malvern, PA 19355-1798   (215) 647-1900 Contact: Alda Cortese, Literary Mgr. **Theatre:** professional **Works:** full-length plays, translations, adaptations **2nd productions:** yes **Specifications:** maximum cast: 12 preferred; single or unit set **Stages:** 2 flexible spaces, 99-150, 350 seats **Submission policy:** query/synopsis, 10-page dialogue sample; agent submission **Response:** 2 weeks query; 8-10 months solicited script **Your chances:** 350 new scripts read annually/usually 1-2 produced **Remuneration:** percentage **Future commitment:** yes

THE PERFORMANCE CIRCLE   F-l 1- Tr Ad ♪ CY
Gig Harbor, WA 98335   (253) 851-7529 Contact: Artistic Director **Theatre:** community **Works:** full-length plays, one-acts, translations, adaptations, musicals, children's plays **Specifications:** 9' ceiling; no fly

space; little wing space **Stages:** outdoor amphitheatre, 350 seats; proscenium, 96 seats **Casting:** non-Equity **Audience:** "Conservative, educated." **Submission policy:** unsolicited script **Remuneration:** "Possibly." **Program:** staged readings

PERIWINKLE NATIONAL THEATRE CY 12+ ▭
FOR YOUNG AUDIENCES 19 Clinton Ave., Monticello, NY 12701 (914) 794-1666, (800) 888-8271 FAX (914) 794-0304 **Contact:** Sunna Rasch, Exec. Director **Theatre:** professional, touring **Works:** plays for young audiences **2nd productions:** no **Special interests:** "Teen pregnancy; anti-violence themes." **Specifications:** maximum cast: 4-8; 45-60 minutes **Stage:** "We turn any area into theatre space." **Casting:** non-Equity **Audience:** "Educational theatre." **Submission policy:** query/synopsis **Best time:** spring **Response:** 2 weeks query; 6-8 months solicited script **Remuneration:** royalty **Advice:** "Contact us to see what theme interests us."

PERMIAN PLAYHOUSE OF ODESSA, INC. P.O. Box 13374,
Odessa, TX 79768 (915) 362-2329 Contact: Managing Director This theatre is closed to submissions in 1999; see *The Playwright's Companion 2000* or inquire for future plans.

PERRY PLAYERS, INC. - COMMUNITY F-l ♪ cm Lc
THEATRE OF PERRY, GEORGIA 909 Main St., P.O. Box 143, Perry, GA 31069 (912) 987-5354 **Contact:** Board of Governors **Theatre:** community **Works:** full-length plays, musicals **2nd productions:** no **Special interests:** comedies, musicals **Specifications:** maximum cast: 30; no more than 5 sets; minimum wing space; no fly space **Stage:** "30' width, 185 seats." **Audience:** "Local." **Submission policy:** query/synopsis **Best time:** spring **Response:** 2 weeks query; 4 weeks solicited script **Your chances:** 2 new scripts read annually/none produced to date **Remuneration:** "Standard royalties."

PERSEVERANCE THEATRE F-l 1- ♪
914 3rd St., Douglas, AK 99824 (907) 364-2421, -2151 FAX (907) 364-2603 e-mail persthr@ptialaska.net **Contact:** Peter DuBois, Art. Director **Theatre:** professional **Works:** full-length plays, one-acts, musicals **Submission policy:** query/brief synopsis, dialogue sample

THE PHILADELPHIA THEATRE CO. F-l ♪ 2d Am C M
The Belgravia, 1811 Chestnut St. Suite 300, Philadelphia, PA 19103 (215) 568-1920 FAX (215) 568-1944 **Contact:** John Rea, Literary Mgr. **Theatre:** professional **Works:** full-length plays, small-scale musicals **2nd productions:** yes **Special interests:** "Contemporary American plays; socio-political issues; minority writers." **Stage:** proscenium, 324 seats **Submission policy:** agent submission **Response:** 8 months **Future commitment:** yes **Program:** staged readings **Advice:** "No mysteries." **Comment:** Box office and performances are at 1714 Delancey St.

PHILIP ROSE PRODUCTIONS   F-l ♪ S

137 W. 78th St., New York, NY 10024 (212) 877-5538 Contact: Philip Rose, Producer **Production company:** professional **Works:** full-length plays, musicals **Exclusive interest:** works for adaptation to film **Submission policy:** unsolicited script

PHOENIX THEATRE   ♪ Rv CY

100 E. McDowell Rd., Phoenix, AZ 85004 (602) 258-1974 FAX (602) 253-3626 **Contact:** Michael Mitchell, Artistic Director **Theatre:** professional **Works:** musicals, revues, children's plays **Special interest:** "Works for a general audience." **Stages:** proscenium, 346 seats; arena, 175 seats **Submission policy:** query/synopsis, script history **Best time:** Jan., Aug. **Response:** 6 months query; 3 months solicited script

PHOENIX THEATRE, INC.

749 N. Park Ave., Indianapolis, IN 46202 (317) 635-7529 **Contact:** Bryan Fonseca, Artistic Director   This theatre currently accepts submissions through its Festival of Emerging American Theatre (see Contests) only; see *The Playwright's Companion 2000* for future plans.

PIER ONE THEATRE   F-l 1- Tr Ad ♪ CY 2d Rg ▭

P.O. Box 894, Homer, AK 99603 (907) 235-7333 **Contact:** Lance Petersen, Artistic Director **Theatre:** professional **Works:** full-length plays, one-acts, translations, adaptations, musicals, children's plays **2nd productions:** yes **Exclusive interest:** "AK playwrights and themes." **Tours:** yes **Stage:** proscenium, thrust, flexible--100 or 495 seats **Submission policy:** unsolicited script preferred; professional recommendation **Response:** 3 months **Your chances:** 400 new scripts read annually/usually 1-3 produced **Remuneration:** percentage **Programs:** readings, staged readings, workshop productions

PILLSBURY HOUSE   F-l 1- Tr Ad x C g/l M h/d W

THEATRE 3501 Chicago Ave. S, Minneapolis, MN 55407 (612) 825-0459 **Contact:** Brian Goranson, Dramaturg **Theatre:** professional **Works:** full-length plays, one-acts, translations, adaptations **Exclusive interest:** non-linear works promoting socio-political change: gay/lesbian, minority issues; disability; women's issues **Specifications:** maximum cast: 12; no fly space **Stage:** black box, 100 seats **Submission policy:** query/synopsis, dialogue sample **Response:** 10 weeks

PIONEER THEATRE COMPANY   F-l Tr Ad ♪ 2d

Univ. of Utah, Salt Lake City, UT 84112 (801) 581-6356 FAX (801) 581-5472 **Contact:** Charles Morey, Art. Director **Theatre:** professional **Works:** full-length plays, translations, adaptations, musicals **2nd productions:** yes **Stage:** proscenium, 1000 seats **Casting:** Equity **Submission policy:** query/synopsis, resume, dialogue sample; professional recommendation; agent submission **Best time:** fall **Response:** 1 month query; 6 months solicited script **Terms:** negotiable **Program:** workshops

PIRATE PLAYHOUSE–ISLAND   F-l 1- ♪ CY Rv
THEATRE   2200 Periwinkle Way, Sanibel Island, FL 33957 (941)
472-4109   FAX (941) 472-0055   e-mail pirateplay@aol.com   Contact:
Robert Kalfin, Producing Art. Director **Theatre:** professional **Works:**
full-length plays, one-acts, musicals **Stage:** flexible, 180 seats **Submission policy:** query/synopsis, 10-page dialogue sample, SASP **Response:**
1-3 months query; 3-5 months solicited script

PISGAH PLAYERS   F-l 1- Tr Ad ♪ 2d L Sp ▭
Literature Dept., UNCA, One University Hts., Asheville, NC 28804
(828) 254-6057 Contact: David Hopes, Director **Theatre:** community,
university **Works:** full-length plays, one-acts, translations, adaptations,
musicals **2nd productions:** yes **Special interests:** "Language, archetypes, spirituality." **Maximum cast:** 10 **Tours:** yes **Stages:** proscenium,
300 seats; flexible **Audience:** "Educated." **Submission policy:** unsolicited script **Best time:** fall-winter **Response:** "Quick." **Your chances:** 1
new play produced for each 20 read **Future commitment:** no **Program:** Pisgah Players Competition (see Contests)

PITTSBURGH PUBLIC THEATER   F-l Tr Ad ♪ 2d
Allegheny Sq., Pittsburgh, PA 15212-5349 (412) 323-8200 FAX (412)
323-8550 e-mail pittPublic@aol.com **Contact:** Todd Kreidler, Asst. to
Artistic Director **Theatre:** professional **Works:** full-length plays, translations, adaptations, musicals **2nd productions:** yes **Stage:** thrust or
arena, 457 seats **Submission policy:** query/synopsis, dialogue sample;
professional recommendation; agent submission **Response:** 1 month
query; 3 months solicited script **Terms:** negotiable

PLAYERS GUILD OF CANTON, INC.   F-l Ad 2d Lc
1001 Market Ave. N, Canton, OH 44702 (330) 453-7619 FAX (330)
452-4477 Contact: Ms. Kris Furlan, General Mgr. **Theatre:** community
Works: full-length plays, adaptations, musicals **2nd productions:** "Yes;
we are not currently producing new work." **Exclusive interest:** "Large-scale works." **Specifications:** "No sitcoms." **Stages:** proscenium, 480
seats; arena, 139 seats **Casting:** Equity, non-Equity **Submission policy:**
query/synopsis of previously produced work, resume

PLAYERS WORKSHOP OF THE   1- CY Rv 2d cm ▭
SECOND CITY   2936 N. Southport, Chicago, IL 60657 (773) 929-
6288 FAX (773) 477-8022 Contact: Linnea Forsberg, President **Theatre:**
semi-professional, theatre school **Works:** one-acts, children's plays, revues **2nd productions:** "If sent by agent or theatre professional." **Special interests:** "Interactive, educational shows that require some improvisation; satire, parody, complex comedy." **Specifications:** "Easy-touring,
low tech." **Stages:** thrust, 150 seats; flexible arena, 55 seats; proscenium,
40 seats **Casting:** non-Equity **Audience:** "Children for educational
shows; adults for revues." **Submission policy:** query/synopsis, SASP;

professional recommendation; agent submission **Best time:** Jan.-May **Response:** 1 month query; 2+ months solicited script **Your chances:** 2-10 new scripts read annually/"latest from outside our pool in 1991" **Remuneration:** royalty **Future commitment:** "Remount rights; credit for premiere." **Program:** The Improv School (see Special Programs)

PLAYHOUSE ON THE SQUARE F-l ♪ 2d
51 S. Cooper St., Memphis, TN 38104 (901) 725-0776 FAX (901) 272-7530 **Contact:** Jackie Nichols, Exec. Producer **Theatre:** professional **Works:** full-length plays, musicals **2nd productions:** yes **Stages:** 2 prosceniums, 250, 136 seats **Casting:** non-Equity **Audience:** "25-50, open-minded." **Submission policy:** unsolicited script **Response:** 6-9 months **Your chances:** 500 new scripts read annually/usually 1 produced **Remuneration:** $500 **Future commitment:** credit **Program:** Playhouse on the Square New Play Competition (see Contests)

PLAYMAKERS REPERTORY COMPANY F-l Tr Ad ♪ 2d Rs
Graham Memorial CB #3235, UNC, Chapel Hill, NC 27599 (919) 962-1122 FAX (919) 962-4069 **Contact:** Adam Versenyi, Dramaturg **Theatre:** professional **Works:** full-length plays, translations, adaptations, musicals **2nd productions:** yes **Specifications:** open staging **Stage:** thrust, 498 seats **Audience:** "University, community, professionals." **Submission policy:** professional recommendation; agent submission **Best time:** Sept.-Dec. **Response:** 3-5 months **Remuneration:** negotiable **Programs:** residencies, classes

PLAYS-IN-PROGRESS WORLD PREMIERE THEATRE F-l
615 4th St., Eureka, CA 95501 (707) 443-3724 **Contact:** Susan Bigelow-Marsh, Exec. Director **Theatre:** community **Works:** full-length plays **2nd productions:** no **Special interest:** "Plays that challenge an audience." **Specifications:** maximum cast: 8; single set or representational setting **Stage:** flexible, 99 seats **Casting:** non-Equity **Audience:** "Professionals looking for cutting edge theatre." **Submission policy:** unsolicited script, resume; query/synopsis, dialogue sample, resume **Best time:** winter **Response:** 3-5 weeks query; 6-8 months script **Your chances:** 300 new scripts read annually/6 produced, 8-10 receive staged readings; "we do a whole season based on submitted scripts" **Remuneration:** royalties **Future commitment:** credit **Programs:** workshop productions, script development; Plays-in-Progress Festival of New Works (see Special Programs)

PLAYS ON TAPE F-l 1- Rd
P.O. Box 5789, Bend, OR 97708-5789 (541) 923-5709 FAX (541) 923-9679 **e-mail** theatre@playsontape.com **Contact:** Silvia Gonzales, Literary Mgr. **Company:** audiotape producer **Works:** full-length plays, one-acts (75 minutes maximum), radio plays **Exclusive interests:** "Plays for recording; exciting plays that will hold the listener's attention." **Speci-

fications: cast size: 2-6; single setting **Submission policy:** unsolicited script; query/synopsis; flyers, notices, reviews **Remuneration:** negotiable fee; 10 copies **Advice:** "If your play is produced or receives a reading in New York City, Chicago, L.A. or Portland, OR, phone us about the possibility of having our representative attend."

PLAYWRIGHTS/ACTORS CONTEMPORARY THEATRE
105 W. 13th St. #5G, New York, NY 10011 (212) 242-5888 Contact: Juel Wiese, Mng. Director This theatre is closed to submissions in 1999; inquire, or see *The Playwright's Companion 2000* for future plans.

PLAYWRIGHTS HORIZONS F-l ♪ 2d Am
416 W. 42nd St., New York, NY 10036 (212) 564-1235 FAX (212) 594-0296 Contact: Lit. Mgr. **Theatre:** off Broadway, professional **Works:** full-length plays, musicals **2nd productions:** if NYC premieres **Exclusive interest:** "American authors." **Stages:** proscenium, 145 seats; black box, 74 seats **Audience:** "Urban, literate." **Submission policy:** unsolicited script, resume; query/synopsis, dialogue sample, resume; professional recommendation **Response:** 4 weeks query; 4-6 months script **Your chances:** 1200 new scripts read annually/usually 6 produced ("mostly from agents or writers we know") **Terms:** negotiable **Programs:** classes (call 212-529-8720); internships (contact Intern Coord.)

THE PLAYWRIGHTS' KITCHEN ENSEMBLE F-l S Tv Rs
Coronet Theatre, 368 N. La Cienega Blvd., Los Angeles, CA 90048 (310) 652-9602 FAX (310) 652-6401 Contact: Dan Lauria, Artistic Director **Production company:** professional **Works:** full-length plays **2nd productions:** no **Submission policy:** unsolicited script, SASP; professional recommendation; agent submission **Response:** 4-6 weeks **Your chances:** 1000 new scripts read annually/usually 40+ produced; "we produce a staged reading every week" **Remuneration:** possible travel for residency **Future commitment:** credit **Programs:** internships; PKE Playwrights Group (see Special Programs) **Comment:** "We introduce writers to TV and film professionals."

PLAYWRIGHTS THEATRE OF D F-l 1- ♪ Am cm dr C
NEW JERSEY 33 Green Village Rd., Madison, NJ 07940 (201) 514-1787 Contact: Peter Hays, Literary Mgr. **Theatre:** professional **Works:** full-length plays, one-acts, musicals **2nd productions:** no **Special interests:** "Works to be developed with the theatre; new American plays of substance and passion (comedies or dramas) that raise challenging questions about ourselves and our society; plays which work on stage in the most theatrical way possible." **Maximum cast:** 8 **Submission policy:** professional recommendation preferred; query/synopsis, 10-page dialogue sample **Best time:** Sept.-Apr. only **Response:** 6-7 months **Future commitment:** occasionally **Programs:** see listing in Special Programs

♫ PLOWSHARES THEATRE COMPANY   F-l ♪ Af
2870 E. Grand Blvd. Suite 600, Detroit, MI 48202-3146 (313) 872-0279 FAX (313) 872-0067 e-mail PlowshrThr@aol.com Contact: Gary Anderson, Producing Art. Director Theatre: professional Works: full-length plays, musicals Exclusive interest: African American writers and themes Submission policy: unsolicited script; cassette tape for musical Best time: fall-winter Response: 2 months Program: New Voices Play Development (see Special Programs)

PLYMOUTH PLAYHOUSE   F-l ♪ Rv 2d ⊐
Troupe America, Inc., 528 Hennepin Ave. Suite 206, Minneapolis, MN 55403 (612) 333-3302 FAX (612) 333-4337 Contact: Curt Wollan, Producer-Director Theatre: professional Works: full-length plays, musicals 2nd productions: yes Special interest: small musicals/musical revues Specifications: maximum cast: 6; unit set Tours: yes Stage: thrust, 211 seats Casting: non-Equity Audience: "White, educated." Submission policy: query/synopsis, dialogue sample, cassette tape of music Best time: spring Response: 6 months query; 1 year solicited script Your chances: 400 new scripts read annually/usually 0-1 produced Remuneration: royalty Future commitment: percentage, options

PONCA PLAYHOUSE   F-l Ad ♪ CY 2d Lc
P.O. Box 1414, Ponca City, OK 74602 (584) 765-7786 Contact: Brian Harpster, President Theatre: community Works: full-length plays, adaptations, musicals, children's plays 2nd productions: yes Special interest: 1-hour children's plays Maximum cast: 30 Stage: proscenium, 390 seats Audience: "Sophisticated, conservative." Submission policy: unsolicited script Best time: Aug.-Oct. Response: 3-4 weeks Your chances: 5 new scripts read annually/usually 0-1 produced

POPE THEATRE COMPANY   F-l ♪ CY 2d C Y Am
262 S. Ocean Blvd., Manalapan, FL 33462 (561) 585-3404 FAX (561) 588-4708 e-mail popetheatre@aol.com Contact: Louis Tyrrell, Producing Director Theatre: professional Works: full-length plays, musicals, children's plays 2nd productions: yes Special interests: "Issue-oriented, thought-provoking works; young American writers." Specifications: cast size: 2-8; single set Stage: thrust, 250 seats Casting: Equity Audience: "Likes new, innovative work." Submission policy: agent submission Response: 3-4 months Your chances: 250 new scripts read annually/usually 7 produced; 7 receive staged readings Remuneration: royalties Future commitment: varies Programs: readings, development

PORTLAND CENTER STAGE   Portland, OR This theatre is no longer open to submissions.

PORTLAND REPERTORY THEATER   Portland, OR Mail addressed to this theatre has been returned as undeliverable; the phone has been disconnected.

PORTLAND STAGE COMPANY   F-l Tr Ad 2d
P.O. Box 1458, Portland, ME 04104   (207) 774-1043 Contact: Peter
Still, Dramaturg/Lit. Mgr. **Theatre:** professional **Works:** full-length
plays, translations, adaptations **2nd productions:** yes **Stages:** proscenium, 290 seats; flexible, 90 seats **Casting:** Equity, non-Equity **Audience:** "Professionals." **Submission policy:** query/synopsis, first 10
pages; professional recommendation; agent submission **Best time:** Sept.-
May **Response:** 7-12 months **Your chances:** 200 new scripts read annually **Remuneration:** royalty **Program:** staged readings (Apr.-May)

POST THEATRE COMPANY   F-l 1- Tr ♪ Rv 2d W
**Dept. of Theatre & Film, LIU-C.W. Post Campus, 720 Northern
Blvd.**, Brookville, NY 11548-1300 (516) 299-2110 FAX (516) 299-3824
Contact: Director of Theatre **Theatre:** university **Works:** full-length
plays, one-acts, translations, musicals, revues **2nd productions:** yes
Special interest: "Strong roles for women." **Specifications:** medium-
sized cast (8-20) preferred; no fly space **Stages:** flexible black box, 40-
60 seats; flexible studio, 80-150 seats **Casting:** students **Audience:**
"Sophisticated." **Submission policy:** query/synopsis, resume **Best
time:** early fall **Response:** 3 weeks query; 4-6 months solicited script
Your chances: 20 new scripts read annually/usually none produced
Future commitment: no **Program:** American Theatre Festival (inquire)

POTLUCK PRODUCTIONS   F-l 1- ♪ 2d W
480 Lake Shore W, Kansas City, KS 66106 (913) 631-9406 **Contact:**
Glendora Davis, Co-Producer **Works:** full-length plays, one-acts, 10-
minute plays, musicals **2nd productions:** yes **Exclusive interest:**
women writers **Submission policy:** unsolicited script, cassette tape for
musical **Response:** 1 month **Comment:** Scripts are not returned.

POWERHOUSE THEATRE/ATOMIC   F-l 1- Tr Ad ♪ CY
THEATRE   3116 2nd St., Santa Monica, CA 90405 (310) 396-3680
Contact: Heath Corson, Lit. Mgr. **Works:** full-length plays, one-acts,
translations, adaptations, musicals, children's plays **Special interest:**
new works **Stage:** black box, 99 seats **Submission policy:** unsolicited
script **Response:** 6-8 weeks **Comment:** Scripts are not returned.

PRAIRIE PLAYERS CIVIC THEATRE   F-l ♪ 2d dr cm Fm Lc
60 S. Kellogg, Galesburg, IL 61401 (309) 342-2299 **Contact:** Candace
Dawson, Managing Director **Theatre:** community **Works:** full-length
plays, musicals **2nd productions:** yes **Special interests:** "Domestic
drama and comedy; adult themes, judged conservatively." **Specifications:**
maximum cast: 40; 2-4 sets **Stage:** proscenium, 966 seats **Casting:** non-
Equity **Audience:** "Rural, traditional, interested in popular if not current themes." **Submission policy:** unsolicited script, resume; professional recommendation **Best time:** fall **Response:** 3 months **Your chances:**
6-8 new scripts read annually/usually 0-1 produced **Remuneration:**
no **Future commitment:** credit for a world premiere

PRIMARY STAGES COMPANY　　F-l ♪ 1p 2d Am W M
584 Ninth Ave., New York, NY 10036 (212) 333-7471 FAX (212) 333-2025 Contact: Tricia McDermott, Literary Mgr. Theatre: off Broadway Works: full-length plays, small-cast musicals, 1-person shows 2nd productions: if NYC/American premieres Exclusive interests: "American writers only; women and minorities encouraged." Specifications: small-cast, 2-8 preferred, maximum 6 for musicals; unit set or simple changes Stages: 2 prosceniums, 99, 65 seats Submission policy: query/synopsis, structural description, 10-page dialogue sample, resume, cassette tape or CD for musical; agent submission Best time: Sept.-Jun. Response: 1-2 months query; 6 months solicited script Your chances: 2000+ new scripts read annually/usually 4-5 produced Remuneration: fee

PRIMAVERA PRODUCTIONS　　F-l ♪
387 1/2 Bleecker St., New York, NY 10014 (212) 242-3588 Production company: professional Works: full-length plays, musicals Submission policy: query/synopsis; professional recommendation; agent submission

PRINCETON REP COMPANY　　F-l Tr Ad 2d x ▭ $
44 Nassau St. #350, Princeton, NJ 08542 (609) 921-3682 e-mail prcarvl@aol.com Contact: Victoria Liberatori, Artistic Director Theatre: professional Works: full-length plays, translations, adaptations 2nd productions: yes Special interests: "Irreverent, experimental, innovative, site-specific works." Casting: Equity, non-Equity Audience: "20's-50's." Submission policy: unsolicited script, $10 reader's fee; query/synopsis, dialogue sample, resume; professional recommendation; agent submission Best time: late fall Response: 6 months query; 1-2 years script Your chances: 250+ new scripts read annually/usually 1 produced; 6 receive staged readings Remuneration: percentage Future commitment: no

THE PRODUCERS CLUB　　F-l 1- Tr Ad ♪ CY Rv 2d
THEATRES 358 W. 44th St., New York, NY 10036 (212) 315-4743 FAX (212) 220-4133 Contact: Ben Kolbert, Rita Espinosa Theatre: off off Broadway Works: full-length plays, one-acts, translations, adaptations, musicals, children's plays, revues 2nd productions: yes Stages: 5 prosceniums--30, 50, 70, 99 (2) seats Casting: Equity, non-Equity Audience: "Ethnic mix, all ages; likes new plays." Submission policy: phone for guidelines Terms: "Co-productions."

PUBLIC THEATRE　　F-l ♪ 2d cm dr
2301 NE 26th St., Ft. Lauderdale, FL 33305 (954) 564-6770 Contact: Vince Rhomberg, Exec. Director Theatre: professional Works: full-length plays, musicals 2nd productions: yes Special interests: comedy, drama Specifications: small cast Submission policy: unsolicited script Response: 18 months Program: workshops

THE PUBLICK THEATRE, INC.   F-l ♪ 2d Fm
11 Ridgemont St., Boston, MA 02134 (617) 782-5425 Contact:
Deborah Schoenberg, Exec. Director Theatre: professional Works: full-
length plays, musicals 2nd productions: yes Special interests: "Family-
oriented, commercial works; strong messages." Maximum cast: 15-20
Stage: outdoor, 200 seats Casting: Equity, non-Equity Submission
policy: professional recommendation; agent submission Best time: fall
Response: 1 month Your chances: "We have produced only 2 new plays
in 16 seasons." Future commitment: "Possibly."

PUERTO RICAN TRAVELING THEATRE   F-l Tr Ad ♪ Hi Esp
141 W. 94th St., New York, NY 10025 (212) 354-1293 FAX (212) 307-
6769 Contact: Miriam Colon, Artistic Director Theatre: professional
Works: full-length plays, translations, adaptations, musicals Special interests: contemporary Hispanic experience; 1-hour musicals Specifications: maximum cast: 8; single or unit set; no fly/wing space Stage: proscenium-thrust, 194 seats Submission policy: unsolicited script Best
time: Sept.-Jun. Response: 6 months Your chances: 15 new scripts
read annually Future commitment: negotiable Programs: Playwrights'
Workshop, Training Unit (see Puerto Rican Traveling Theatre in Special
Programs) Comment: "All productions are in English and in Spanish."

THE PURPLE ROSE THEATRE COMPANY   F-l 2d Rg
137 Park St., Chelsea, MI 48118 (313) 475-5817 FAX (313) 475-0802
e-mail purplerose@mail.earthlink.net Contact: Anthony Caselli, Literary Mgr. Theatre: professional Works: full-length plays 2nd productions: yes Special interest: "Plays for a middle-American audience."
Specifications: maximum cast: 10; no fly or wing space Stage: thrust,
119 seats Casting: Equity, non-Equity Audience: "Rural, small town,
young professionals." Submission policy: query/synopsis, dialogue
sample Response: 6-9 months Your chances: 150 new scripts read an-
nually/usually 3-4 produced Remuneration: negotiable

PUSHCART PLAYERS   CY ♪ 2d H Y ⊏⊐ Rs
197 Bloomfield Ave., Verona, NJ 07044 (973) 857-1115 FAX (973)
857-0980 Contact: Ruth Fost, Mng./Art. Director Theatre: professional
Works: children's plays/musicals 2nd productions: yes Special interest: "Curriculum-connected work: history, social studies, humanities."
Specifications: maximum cast: 4; single set Tours: yes Stages: 15'x10'
flexible; schools Casting: Equity Audience: "K-9." Submission policy:
send SASE for guidelines Programs: readings, classes for young playwrights, workshops, residencies, informances, summer programs, teacher
training, intern/apprenticeships

QUICK CENTER FOR THE ARTS   Fairfield Univ., Fairfield, CT
06430-7524 (203) 254-4242 Contact: Thomas Zingarelli, Art. Director
This theatre is closed to submissions.

RAINBOW CO. CHILDREN'S   F-l 1- Ad CY 2d
THEATRE **821 Las Vegas Blvd.** N, Las Vegas, NV 89101 (702) 229-6553 **Contact:** Karen McKenney, Artistic Director **Theatre:** community **Works:** full-length plays, one-acts, adaptations, children's plays **2nd productions:** yes **Stages:** 3 prosceniums, 90, 250, 360 seats **Audience:** children, adults **Submission policy:** query/synopsis; commission **Best time:** Feb.-Jun. **Response:** 1 year **Your chances:** 25 new scripts read annually/usually 1 produced **Remuneration:** royalty **Programs:** workshops, internships for playwrights

RALPH ROSEMAN, PRODUCER   F-l ♪
1501 Broadway Suite 1404, New York, NY 10036 (212) 840-4400 **FAX** (212) 764-3417 **Production company:** professional **Works:** full-length plays, musicals **Submission policy:** query/synopsis; agent submission; professional recommendation

RATTLESTICK PRODUCTIONS   F-l 2d Rg
224 Waverly Pl., New York, NY 10014 (212) 627-2556 **Contact:** Brian Adams, Literary Mgr. **Theatre:** professional **Works:** full-length plays **2nd productions:** "If NYC premieres." **Exclusive interest:** NYC-area writers **Maximum cast:** 8 **Submission policy:** unsolicited script, synopsis **Best time:** Jan.1-May 1 only **Response:** 6 months **Comment:** Playwright must work on other company season productions. **Program:** FARMworks (see Special Programs)

THE REALLY USEFUL CO.   New York, NY   This company is no longer open to submissions.

RED BARN ACTORS STUDIO   F-l 1- Ad ♪ CY Rv ▭
P.O. Box 707, Key West, FL 33040 (305) 296-9911 **FAX** (305) 293-3035 **Contact:** Mimi McDonald, Managing Director **Theatre:** professional **Works:** full-length plays, one-acts, adaptations, musicals, plays for young actors/audiences, revues **Specifications:** maximum cast: 8; no fly space **Tours:** children's plays **Stage:** proscenium, 88 seats **Submission policy:** query/synopsis, dialogue sample, resume **Best time:** Mar.-Aug. 1 **Response:** if interested **Your chances:** 150 new scripts read annually/ usually 0-1 produced, latest in Nov. 1997 **Remuneration:** negotiable

RED EYE THEATER   F-l mm 2d x Rg
15 W. 14th St., Minneapolis, MN 55403-2301 (612) 870-7531 **e-mail** redeye@mtn.org **Contact:** Steve Busa, Artistic Director **Theatre:** professional **Works:** full-length plays, multimedia works **2nd productions:** yes **Special interests:** new, non-naturalistic works; upper Midwest writers **Stage:** proscenium, 76-120 seats **Submission policy:** query/ synopsis, dialogue sample; commission **Response:** 6-9 months **Remuneration:** negotiable **Future commitment:** no **Program:** Isolated Acts: annual multidisciplinary festival (by invitation)

REP STAGE   F-l 1- Ad Rg
Howard Community College, 10901 Little Patuxent Pkwy., Columbia, MD 21044 (410) 772-4628 Contact: John Morogiello, Dramaturg
Theatre: professional Works: full-length plays, one-acts, adaptations
2nd productions: "Not if produced professionally." Exclusive interest:
"Local authors (MD, DC, DE, VA)." Specifications: maximum cast: 12;
no more than 2 sets Stages: proscenium, 350 seats; flexible, 100 seats
Casting: Equity, non-Equity Submission policy: unsolicited script, resume, script history, SASP; agent submission Best time: fall Response:
6 months Your chances: 50 new scripts read annually/usually 1-2 produced Remuneration: "$100-$300 for workshop production; negotiable
royalty for full production." Future commitment: credit

REPERTORIO ESPAÑOL   F-l Ad ♪ CY Hi Esp
138 E. 27th St., New York, NY 10016 (212) 889-2850 FAX (212) 686-
3732 Contact: Robert Weber Federico, Assoc. Artistic Director; Gilberto
Zaldívar, Producer Theatre: professional Works: full-length plays,
adaptations, musicals, operas, children's plays Exclusive interests:
"Hispanic themes; works in Spanish." Specifications: small cast Stage:
proscenium, 135 seats Submission policy: query/synopsis Best time:
Dec. Response: 1 month query; 6 months solicited script Program:
contests (inquire)

THE REPERTORY THEATRE OF ST. LOUIS   F-l ♪ 2d C
P.O. Box 191730, St. Louis, MO 63119 (314) 968-7340 Contact: Susan
Gregg, Assoc. Artistic Director Theatre: professional Works: full-length
plays, musicals 2nd productions: yes Special interest: contemporary
issues Specifications: maximum cast: 8, fewer preferred, 16 for musical;
single set; no naturalism Stages: thrust, 750 seats; flexible, 130 seats
Casting: Equity, non-Equity Audience: "Educated, conservative." Submission policy: query/synopsis, cassette tape of music; professional recommendation; agent submission Response: 1 month query; 2 years
solicited script Your chances: 750 new scripts read annually/none
produced to date Remuneration: "Travel, housing, stipend." Future
commitment: for premiere

THE RIANT THEATRE   F-l 1- Tr Ad ♪ Rv 2d
161 Hudson St., New York, NY 10013 (212) 925-8353 FAX (212)
925-8219 Contact: Van Dirk Fisher, Artistic Director Theatre: professional Works: full-length plays, one-acts, translations, adaptations,
musicals, revues 2nd productions: yes Maximum cast: 1-15 Submission policy: query/synopsis Best time: summer Response: 2-3 months
Program: workshops

RICHARD MARTINI, PRODUCER   F-l ♪
1501 Broadway Suite 1401, New York, NY 10036 (212) 730-9500
FAX (212) 764-5423 Production company: professional Works: full-
length plays, musicals Submission policy: query/brief synopsis

RICK HOBARD PRODUCTIONS   F-l my
234 W. 44th St., New York, NY 10036 (212) 354-8797 **Contact:** Rick
Hobard, Producer **Production company:** professional **Works:** full-
length plays **Special interests:** new murder mysteries, suspense thrillers
Submission policy: professional recommendation; agent submission

RIGHT COAST PROD. See Stone Productions, Inc. in this section.

RITES & REASON THEATRE   D F-l 1- 2d M ⌐⊐
P.O. Box 1148, Brown Univ., Providence, RI 02912 (401) 863-3558
FAX (401) 863-3559 (marked clearly for "Rites & Reason") **Contact:**
Elmo Terry-Morgan, Artistic Director **Theatre:** professional **Works:**
full-length plays, one-acts **2nd productions:** yes **Special interest:**
"Developing new multicultural plays." **Specifications:** small cast **Tours:**
yes **Stage:** black box, 150 seats **Audience:** "Diverse: community,
students." **Submission policy:** query/synopsis, resume, references
Response: 1 month query (if interested); 6 months solicited script
Program: George Houston Bass Play-Rites Festival (see Contests)

RIVERSIDE THEATRE   F-l Tr Ad Rv 2d ⌐⊐
P.O. Box 1651, Iowa City, IA 52244 (319) 338-7672 FAX (319) 354-
9941 **Contact:** Ron Clark, Artistic Director **Theatre:** professional
Works: full-length plays, translations, adaptations, revues **2nd productions:** yes **Specifications:** small cast; simple set **Tours:** yes **Stage:**
flexible, 118 seats **Audience:** "Educated; professionals, students, senior
citizens." **Submission policy:** query/synopsis; commission **Response:**
1 month query (if interested); 3-5 months solicited script **Your chances:**
200-300 queries received annually/usually no new plays produced
Remuneration: royalties

RIVERSIDE THEATRE, INC.   F-l Tr Ad ♪ CY C dr cm Sn
P.O. Box 3788, Vero Beach, FL 32964 (561) 231-5860 **Contact:** Sherrie
Dee Brewer, Production Mgr. **Theatre:** professional **Works:** full-length
plays, translations, adaptations, musicals, children's plays **2nd produc-
tions:** no **Exclusive interests:** "Important issues, serious or comic."
Maximum cast: 10 **Stages:** proscenium, 615 seats; flexible, 150+ seats
Casting: Equity **Submission policy:** query/synopsis **Best time:** fall
Response: 1 month (if interested) **Remuneration:** negotiable **Program:**
New Century Voices (see Special Programs)

THE ROAD CO. Johnson City, TN This theatre is permanently closed.

THE ROAD THEATRE COMPANY   F-l 1- Tr CY P
5108 Lankershim Blvd., North Hollywood, CA 91601 (818) 761-8838
FAX (818) 761-1378 **Contact:** Taylor Gilbert, Artistic Director
Theatre: professional **Works:** full-length plays, one-acts, translations,
children's plays **2nd productions:** "Usually world or L.A. premieres."
Specifications: maximum cast: 35; 4-5 sets **Stage:** black box, 49 seats

Casting: Equity, non-Equity, students **Audience:** "Likes a variety of new works." **Submission policy:** unsolicited script; query/synopsis; professional recommendation; agent submission; script history, resume, SASP with all material **Your chances:** 200 new scripts read annually/usually 5-6 produced; 40 receive staged readings **Remuneration:** "4%." **Programs:** workshop productions, development

ROADSIDE THEATER   D F-l Rg ⌂
91 Madison Ave., Whitesburg, KY 41858 (606) 633-0108 FAX (606) 633-1009 e-mail roadside@appalshop.org **Contact:** Dudley Cocke, Director **Theatre:** professional **Works:** full-length plays **2nd productions:** no **Exclusive interest:** Appalachia **Specifications:** small cast; set suitable for tours **Stage:** thrust, 150 seats **Casting:** ensemble **Audience:** "All ages, schooled, unschooled, working class." **Submission policy:** query/synopsis, dialogue sample **Response:** 2 weeks query; 1 month solicited script **Your chances:** "Usually no plays produced outside development process." **Remuneration:** negotiable

ROADWORKS PRODUCTIONS   F-l dr
1532 Milwaukee Ave., Chicago, IL 60622 (773) 489-7623 FAX (773) 489-7698 e-mail roadworksl@aol.com **Contact:** Shade Murray, Literary Mgr. **Theatre:** professional **Works:** full-length plays **Special interest:** "Drama for actors aged 20-30." **Submission policy:** query/synopsis, dialogue sample **Best time:** Sept.-Nov. **Response:** 1-3 months

ROBERT COLE PRODUCTIONS   F-l
165 W. 46th St. #512, New York, NY 10036 (212) 730-7280 **Production company:** professional **Works:** full-length plays **Submission policy:** agent submission

ROBERT L. YOUNG, PRODUCER   F-l 1- ♪
200 Medical Dr. Studio D, Carmel, IN 46032 (317) 818-3960 FAX (317) 818-3961 **Production company:** professional **Works:** full-length plays, one-acts, musicals **Submission policy:** query/brief synopsis; agent submission; professional recommendation

ROBERT V. STRAUS, PRODUCER   F-l ♪
19 W. 44th St. #1701, New York, NY 10036 (212) 398-2977 FAX (212) 398-7182 **Production company:** professional **Works:** full-length plays, musicals **Submission policy:** query/synopsis; agent submission; professional recommendation

RODGER HESS PRODUCTIONS   F-l ♪ cm
1501 Broadway, New York, NY 10036 (212) 719-2233 FAX (212) 719-2315 **Contact:** Rodger Hess, Producer **Production company:** Broadway **Works:** full-length plays, musicals **Special interests:** comedies, commercial polemics, musicals **Submission policy:** professional recommendation; agent submission

ROGER ALAN GINDI   See Gindi Theatrical Mgmt. in this section.

ROGER L. STEVENS   See Whitehead-Stevens Assoc. in this section.

ROUND HOUSE THEATRE   F-l Tr Ad ♪ CY 2d C x Cl cm
12210 Bushey Dr., Silver Spring, MD 20902 (301) 933-9530 FAX
(301) 933-2321 **Contact:** Jerry Whiddon, Producing Artistic Director;
Barbara Payne, Production Office Mgr. **Theatre:** professional **Works:**
full-length plays, translations, adaptations, small-scale musicals, children's plays **2nd productions:** yes **Special interests:** "Issues; experimentation; translations of lesser-known classics; comedies." **Specifications:** maximum cast: 6; single set preferred **Stage:** modified thrust, 216
seats **Submission policy:** query/synopsis, dialogue sample; agent submission **Response:** 2 months query (if interested); 1 year solicited script

ROY A. SOMLYO   240 W. 57th St., New York, NY 10107 (212) 765-
0606 FAX (212) 307-1910   Mr. Somlyo has closed his production
company and is now president of the American Theatre Wing.

THE RYAN REPERTORY CO.   F-l ♪ CY Rv 2d Fm cm dr Sn 1p
2445 Bath Ave., Brooklyn, NY 11214 (718) 996-4800 FAX (718) 646-
4029 **Contact:** Barbara Parisi, Exec. Director **Theatre:** professional
Works: full-length plays, musicals, children's plays, revues **2nd productions:** yes **Special interest:** musicals, comedies, dramas **Specifications:**
cast of 1-10; single set; "no nudity" **Stage:** flexible, 40 seats **Audience:**
"Seniors, families, children." **Submission policy:** unsolicited script, cassette tape and score for musical **Response:** 1 year **Your chances:** 20
new scripts read annually/usually 2 produced **Remuneration:** "Small."
Programs: staged readings, workshops, development **Advice:** "Call us."

SACRAMENTO THEATRE CO.   F-l Tr Ad Rv 2d C L Sp
1419 H St., Sacramento, CA 95814 (916) 446-7501 FAX (916) 446-
4066 **Contact:** Peggy Shannon, Artistic Director **Theatre:** professional
Works: full-length plays, translations, adaptations, revues **2nd productions:** yes **Special interests:** "Contemporary issues; vital language; life-affirming work; sympathetic characters." **Specifications:** cast size: 3-5;
1 unit set for realistic drama; no large-scale scripts **Stages:** proscenium,
300 seats; black box, 90 seats **Casting:** Equity, non-Equity **Audience:**
"Interested in literary merit." **Submission policy:** query/synopsis, resume **Best time:** Jun.-Dec. **Response:** 1 month query; 3 months solicited
script **Your chances:** 100-150 queries and new scripts read annually/
usually 1-3 produced **Terms:** negotiable

♫ **ST. CROIX FESTIVAL THEATRE**   F-l 1- Tr Ad
P.O. Box 801, St. Croix Falls, WI 54024-0801 (715) 294-2991 **e-mail**
festival@centuryinter.net **Contact:** Marilyn Mays, Literary Mgr.
Theatre: professional **Works:** full-length plays, one-acts, translations,

adaptations **Specifications:** maximum cast: 8; no more than 2 sets **Stage:** thrust, 200 seats **Submission policy:** query/synopsis, 1st 15 pages of script **Best time:** Mar.-May **Response:** 6 months

ST. LOUIS BLACK REPERTORY CO.   F-l ♪ CY Af M
634 N. Grand Blvd. Suite 10-F, St. Louis, MO 63103 (314) 534-3807 FAX (314) 533-3345 **Contact:** Ronald J. Himes, Producing Director **Theatre:** professional **Works:** full-length plays, musicals, children's plays **Exclusive interests:** "African-American, 3rd-World authors." **Stage:** thrust, 470 seats **Submission policy:** query/synopsis, 3-5 page dialogue sample, resume **Best time:** Jun.-Aug. **Response:** 2 months

SAK COMEDY LAB   F-l 1- ♪ cm Fm ▭
398 W. Amelia St., Orlando, FL 32801 (407) 648-0001 FAX (407) 648-1333 **e-mail** terry@sak.com **Contact:** Terry Olson, Mng. Director **Theatre:** professional **Works:** full-length plays, one-acts, musicals **2nd productions:** no **Exclusive interests:** "Wholesome, offbeat comedy; comedies with music." **Specifications:** maximum cast: 6; single set **Tours:** yes **Stage:** flexible, 150 seats **Casting:** "Ensemble, guests." **Audience:** "Young professionals, students." **Submission policy:** query/synopsis, dialogue sample **Response:** 60 days **Your chances:** usually 2 new scripts produced annually **Remuneration:** "3%." **Advice:** "Intimate works. Okay to break the fourth wall." **Comment:** Theater is located at 380 W. Amelia St.

THE SALT LAKE ACTING CO.   F-l Tr Ad ♪ 2d Am Rg
168 W. 500 N, Salt Lake City, UT 84103 (801) 363-0526 FAX (801) 532-8513 **Contact:** David Mong, Lit. Mgr. **Theatre:** professional **Works:** full-length plays, translations, adaptations, musicals **2nd productions:** yes **Special interest:** Western American writers **Stages:** thrusts, 90-130, 99 seats **Submission policy:** query/synopsis, 5-10 page dialogue sample, resume **Response:** 4-8 months **Remuneration:** yes **Program:** Salt Lake Acting Co. Reading Series (see Special Programs)

SALTWORKS PLAYERS SERIES   1- J † ▭
2553 Brandt School Rd., Wexford, PA 15090-7931 (724) 934-7820 FAX (724) 934-2815 **e-mail** stc@lm.com **Contact:** Scott W. Kirk, President/Artistic Director **Theatre:** professional, touring **Works:** one-acts (45 minutes) **Special interest:** "Judeo-Christian values/Biblical world view." **Stages:** churches **Casting:** amateur actors **Submission policy:** unsolicited script; query/synopsis, 4-page dialogue sample **Response:** 6-8 months **Remuneration:** yes

SALTWORKS THEATRE CO.   F-l 1- Tr Ad ♪ CY J † ▭
2553 Brandt School Rd., Wexford, PA 15090-7931 (724) 934-7820 FAX (724) 934-2815 **e-mail** stc@lm.com **Contact:** Scott W. Kirk, President **Theatre:** professional, touring **Works:** full-length plays, one-

acts, translations, adaptations, musicals, children's plays **Special interest:** "Judeo-Christian values/Biblical world view." **Stage:** proscenium, 150 seats **Casting:** non-Equity **Submission policy:** query/synopsis, 4-page dialogue sample, SASP; commission **Response:** 6 months **Your chances:** 30 new scripts read annually/usually 0-1 produced; 1-2 receive staged readings **Terms:** negotiable

SAN DIEGO F-l Tr Ad ♪ Rv mm 2d C M cm W Hi Esp
REPERTORY THEATRE 79 Horton Plaza, San Diego, CA 92101
(619) 231-3586 FAX (619) 235-0939 Contact: Nakissa Etemad, Resident Dramaturg **Theatre:** professional **Works:** full-length plays, translations, adaptations, musicals, literary cabaret, multimedia events **2nd productions:** yes **Special interests:** "Issues; multiethnic works; unusual incorporation of music; comedy with an edge; women writers; Hispanic plays for English and Spanish presentation." **Specifications:** no fly space in flexible space **Stages:** modified thrust, 550+ seats; flexible, 250 seats **Audience:** "Middle-upper middle class, white." **Submission policy:** query/synopsis **Response:** 3 months query; 1 year solicited script **Your chances:** 500 new scripts read annually **Programs:** readings, workshops

SAN JACINTO COLLEGE THEATRE Theatre Dept., San Jacinto College S, 13735 Beamer Rd., Houston, TX 77089 **(281) 484-1900 Ext. 3224 FAX (281) 922-3401 Contact:** Sheleigh Carmichael, Director This theatre is closed to submissions in 1999; see *The Playwright's Companion 2000* or inquire for future plans.

SAN JOSE REPERTORY CO. F-l Tr Ad ♪ 2d Af As Hi W
P.O. Box 2399, San Jose, CA 95109-2399 **(408) 291-2266 FAX (408) 995-0737 Contact:** J. R. Orlando, Asst. to Art. Director **Theatre:** professional **Works:** full-length plays, translations, adaptations, small-cast musicals **2nd productions:** yes **Special interests:** "African-American, Asian, Hispanic themes; women's issues." **Stage:** proscenium, 500+ seats **Submission policy:** agent submission **Best time:** Sept.-Nov. **Response:** 2-3 months **Program:** workshops

SAN JOSE STAGE F-l Tr Ad ♪ Rv 1p 2d
490 S. 1st St., San Jose, CA 95113 **(408) 283-7142 FAX (408) 283-7146 Contact:** Randall King, Artistic Director **Theatre:** professional **Works:** full-length plays, translations, adaptations, small-scale musicals, revues, 1-person shows **2nd productions:** "Possibly." **Specifications:** maximum cast: 9; unit set; minimal demands **Stage:** 3/4 thrust, 200 seats **Casting:** Equity, non-Equity **Audience:** "50+, moderate, well-read." **Submission policy:** professional recommendation preferred; unsolicited script, synopsis **Best time:** Jan.-Mar. **Response:** 8-10 weeks **Terms:** negotiable **Your chances:** 100 new scripts read annually/usually 1-2 produced **Program:** San Jose Downtown Art Series (see Special Programs)

SANTA FE STAGES   F-l Tr Ad

105 E. Marcy St. Suite 107, Santa Fe, NM 87501 (505) 982-6680 FAX (505) 982-6682 e-mail sfstages@ix.netcom.com **Contact:** Martin Platt, Art. Director **Theatre:** professional **Works:** full-length plays, translations, adaptations **Special interest:** "The cutting edge." **Stages:** proscenium, 525 seats; flexible, 100 seats **Submission policy:** agent submission **Best time:** Sept.-Apr. **Response:** 1 week-3 months

SANTA MONICA PLAYHOUSE   F-l 1- Tr Ad ♪ CY

1211 4th St., Santa Monica, CA 90401-1391 (310) 394-9779 FAX (310) 393-5573 **Contact:** Chris DeCarlo, Evelyn Rudie, Co-Artistic Directors **Theatre:** professional **Works:** full-length plays, one-acts, translations, adaptations, musicals, children's plays **Specifications:** maximum cast: 8; simple demands **Stages:** arena/thrust, 88 seats; flexible, 70 seats **Submission policy:** query/synopsis **Response:** 3-6 months

SEACOAST REPERTORY THEATRE   F-l ♪ CY 2d Am Fm

125 Bow St., Portsmouth, NH 03801 (603) 433-4793 FAX (603) 431-7818 **Contact:** Roy M. Rogosin, Artistic Director **Theatre:** professional **Works:** full-length plays, small-scale musicals, children's plays **2nd productions:** yes **Special interest:** "American plays for family audiences." **Stage:** thrust, 200+ seats **Casting:** Equity, non-Equity **Submission policy:** agent query/1-page synopsis, cassette tape for musical **Response:** 1 year **Terms:** negotiable **Comment:** Scripts are not returned.

SEASIDE MUSIC THEATER   ♪ CY Rv 2d

P.O. Box 2835, Daytona Beach, FL 32120 (904) 252-3394 FAX (904) 252-8991 **Contact:** Lester Malizia, General Mgr. **Theatre:** professional **Works:** musicals, children's musicals, revues **2nd productions:** yes **Specifications:** maximum cast: 8 for Winter Theater, 30 for Summer Repertory, 10 for children's plays; for winter theatre, small-scale works, minimal set requirements, no fly space **Stages:** winter: proscenium, 600 seats; summer: proscenium, 500 seats; children's theatre: modified thrust, 200 seats **Submission policy:** professional recommendation

SEATTLE CHILDREN'S THEATRE   CY ♪ 2d

P.O. Box 9640, Seattle, WA 98109-0640 (206) 443-0807 FAX (206) 443-0442 **Contact:** Deborah Frockt, Literary Mgr. **Theatre:** professional **Works:** children's full-length plays and musicals **2nd productions:** yes **Exclusive interest:** "Plays that respect children's intelligence." **Stages:** proscenium; thrust **Casting:** Equity **Audience:** "Enjoys thematic, stylistic variety." **Submission policy:** professional recommendation; agent submission **Response:** 6-8 months solicited script **Terms:** negotiable

SEATTLE REPERTORY THEATRE   F-l 1- Tr Ad ♪ Rv 2d

155 Mercer St., Seattle, WA 98109 (206) 443-2210 FAX (206) 443-2379 **Contact:** Kurt Beattie, Assoc. Art. Director **Theatre:** professional **Works:** full-length plays, one-acts, translations, adaptations, musicals,

revues **2nd productions:** yes **Stages:** 2 prosceniums, 856, 283 seats **Casting:** Equity, non-Equity **Audience:** "Eclectic." **Submission policy:** query/synopsis; professional recommendation; agent submission; commission **Response:** 2-3 weeks query; 4-6 months solicited script **Your chances:** 300 new scripts read annually/2+ produced, 2-4 receive staged readings **Terms:** negotiable **Programs:** workshops, internships

THE SECOND STAGE   F-l Ad ♪ 2d Am C W M
P.O. Box 1807 Ansonia Station, New York, NY 10023 (212) 787-8302
FAX (212) 877-9886 Contact: Christopher Burney, Literary Mgr.
Theatre: professional **Works:** full-length plays, adaptations, musicals **2nd productions:** yes **Special interests:** "American plays only; heightened realism; socio-political plays; women, minority writers." **Specifications:** "No fly space; keep it simple." **Stage:** endstage, 110 seats **Submission policy:** query/1-page synopsis, 5-10 page dialogue sample, cassette tape for musical, resume, any production history; agent submission **Response:** 1 month query; 4-6 months solicited script **Your chances:** 200-300 new scripts read annually/usually 4 produced **Remuneration:** varies **Future commitment:** no **Program:** The Second Stage Reading Series (see Special Programs)

SENIOR BARN PLAYERS   1- CY Rv 1p 2d Sn po cm Fm ⌐↘
P.O. Box 12767, Shawnee Mission, KS 66282-2767 (913) 381-4004
Contact: President **Theatre:** community **Works:** one-acts, dance, music, songs, poetry, revues, plays for Children's Hour (K-2nd grade) **2nd productions:** yes **Special interest:** "Comedy--upbeat material only." **Specifications:** maximum cast: 7, 3-5 preferred; performers over 55; no all-male casts; all shows tour; no scenery; 30 minutes maximum **Stages:** various spaces **Casting:** volunteers **Submission policy:** unsolicited script; query/synopsis **Response:** 1 month **Your chances:** 40 new plays read annually/usually 6 produced **Remuneration:** royalties **Programs:** staged readings; Senior Voices readings of poetry and prose **Advice:** "No political themes, messages or profanity."

SEVEN ANGELS THEATRE   F-l ♪ 2d
P.O. Box 3358, Waterbury, CT 06705 (203) 591-8223 FAX same
Contact: Semina DeLaurentis, Artistic Director **Theatre:** professional **Works:** full-length plays, musicals **2nd productions:** yes **Specifications:** maximum cast: 10; unit set preferred; no fly space **Stage:** proscenium, 350 seats **Casting:** Equity **Submission policy:** professional recommendation preferred; unsolicited script, SASP **Best time:** summer **Response:** only if interested

♫ **SHADOW LIGHT**   F-l 1- Tr Ad ♪ CY Rv V H
PRODUCTIONS   22 Chattanooga St., San Francisco, CA 94114
(415) 648-4461 FAX (415) 641-9734 e-mail shdw@sirius.com **Contact:** Kate Sheehan, Admin. Director **Theatre:** professional **Works:** full-length plays, one-acts, translations, adaptations, musicals, children's

plays, revues **Special interests:** plays for shadow theatre with both puppets and live actors only; mythological or historical figures; adaptations of stories or novels **Maximum cast:** 15 **Stage:** various spaces **Submission policy:** query/synopsis **Response:** 1 month

♫ SHADOW THEATRE COMPANY   F-l Af Rg M
1472 Josephine St. #308, Denver, CO 80206 e-mail shadowtheatre @uswest.net **Works:** full-length plays **Special interest:** African American writers in Colorado **Specifications:** multiracial casting **Submission policy:** query/synopsis

SHAKESPEARE & COMPANY   Ad 2d C ⊐
The Mount, P.O. Box 865, Lenox, MA 01240-0865 (413) 637-1199 **FAX** (413) 637-4237 e-mail training@shakespeare.org **Contact:** Artistic Associates **Theatre:** professional **Works:** adaptations **2nd productions:** yes **Exclusive interests:** "Socially relevant new works; adaptations of works by Edith Wharton and Henry James." **Specifications:** maximum cast: 8; minimal sets **Tours:** "Sometimes." **Stages:** 2 outdoor amphitheatres, 250, 500+ seats; thrust, 108 seats; endstage, 75-90 seats **Audience:** "NY audience, open to a broad range." **Submission policy:** query/ synopsis, 4-page dialogue sample preferred; unsolicited script; commission **Best time:** fall-winter **Response:** 6 months (if interested) **Your chances:** 30-40 new works read annually **Terms:** negotiable

SHAKESPEARE SANTA CRUZ   F-l 1- CY
PAC, UCSC, Santa Cruz, CA 95064 (408) 459-5109 FAX (408) 459-3552 e-mail karin_magaldi-unger@macmail.ucsc.edu **Contact:** Karin Magaldi-Unger, Literary Mgr. **Theatre:** professional **Works:** full-length plays, one-acts, children's plays **Special interest:** "Shakespeare spin-offs." **Specifications:** small cast; minimal set **Stages:** outdoor, 800 seats; thrust, 500 seats **Submission policy:** query/synopsis, resume; professional recommendation **Best time:** fall-winter **Response:** 1 month

THE SHAKESPEARE THEATRE   Tr Ad Cl
301 E. Capitol St. SE, Washington, DC 20003 (202) 547-3230 FAX (202) 547-0226 e-mail smazzola@shakespearedc.org **Contact:** Steven S. Mazzola, Asst. to Art. Director **Theatre:** professional **Works:** translations, adaptations **Exclusive interest:** "Classics." **Stage:** proscenium, 449 seats **Submission policy:** professional recommendation; agent submission **Best time:** summer **Response:** 2 months **Remuneration:** negotiable **Program:** The Rediscovery Series (see Special Programs)

SHEBOYGAN THEATRE COMPANY   F-l Ad ♪ 2d cm Fm
607 S. Water St., Sheboygan, WI 53081-4489 (414) 459-3779 FAX (414) 459-4021 **Contact:** Ralph Maffongelli, Director **Theatre:** community **Works:** full-length plays, adaptations, musicals **2nd productions:** yes **Special interests:** "Light comedy; comedies with sensitivity;

musicals." **Specifications:** maximum cast: 12 for play, more for musical; no more than 2 full sets or unit set for play **Stage:** thrust/proscenium, 500 seats **Casting:** non-Equity **Audience:** "Conservative." **Submission policy:** query/synopsis, dialogue sample, resume **Response:** 2 weeks query; 2 months solicited script **Your chances:** 10-12 new scripts read annually/1-2 produced, latest in Oct. 1998 **Remuneration:** "Small stipend." **Advice:** "No avant garde or ponderous pieces."

SHORENSTEIN HAYS/NEDERLANDER   F-l ♪
PRODUCTIONS 1182 Market St. Suite 320, St., San Francisco, CA 94102 (415) 551-2075 FAX (415) 431-5052 **Production company:** professional **Works:** full-length plays, musicals **Submission policy:** query/synopsis; agent submission; professional recommendation **Comment:** Formerly listed as Carole Shorenstein Hays, Producer.

SHORES PERFORMING ARTS   F-l Tr Ad ♪ CY 2d Lc
THEATRE 9806 NE 2nd Ave., Miami, FL 33138 (305) 751-0562 FAX (305) 751-9159 **Contact:** Pat Sapia, Mng. Director **Theatre:** professional **Works:** full-length plays, translations, adaptations, musicals, children's plays **2nd productions:** yes **Specifications:** maximum cast: 35; no more than 3 sets **Stage:** proscenium, 350 seats **Casting:** Equity, non-Equity **Submission policy:** query/synopsis, dialogue sample, resume; professional recommendation; agent submission **Best time:** summer **Response:** 1 month **Your chances:** 5 new scripts read annually/usually 1 produced **Remuneration:** no **Future commitment:** credit

SHOTGUN PRODUCTIONS, INC.   F-l 1- 2d W mm
165 E. 35th St. Suite 7J, New York, NY 10016 e-mail PRK4257@aol. com **Contact:** Linda S. Nelson, Producing Director **Production company:** off off Broadway **Works:** full-length plays, one-acts **2nd productions:** "If NYC premieres." **Special interests:** works by women; positive female roles; multimedia works **Submission policy:** unsolicited script, synopsis **Program:** annual New Playwrights Reading Series (inquire)

THE SHUBERT ORGANIZATION
234 W. 44th St., New York, NY 10036 (212) 944-3700 **Contact:** D. S. Moynihan, Creative Projects Director **Production company:** Broadway **Submission policy:** professional recommendation; agent submission

SIGNATURE THEATRE   F-l Ad 2d ♪ C cm
3806 S. Four Mile Run Dr., Arlington, VA 22206 (703) 820-9771 **Contact:** Marcia Gardner, Literary Mgr. **Theatre:** professional **Works:** full-length plays, adaptations, musicals **2nd productions:** if not professionally produced **Special interests:** issues, comedies **Specifications:** maximum cast: 10 preferred, no fly space **Stage:** black box, 126 seats **Submission policy:** agent submission **Best time:** Sept.-May **Response:** 4-6 months **Your chances:** 2 new plays produced each season; 1-2 receive workshop productions **Programs:** staged readings, development, classes

♫ **SIGNATURE THEATRE COMPANY, INC.**   **F-l 1-**
424 W. 42nd St. 2nd Floor, New York, NY 10036 (212) 967-1913 FAX
(212) 967-2957 **Contact:** James Houghton, Founding Art. Director
Theatre: professional **Works:** full-length plays, one-acts **Special interest:** "New plays by established playwrights." **Stage:** endstage, 160
seats **Submission policy:** professional recommendation; agent submission **Response:** only if interested

SINGULAR PROD. Culver City, CA Mail addressed to this theatre
has been returned as undeliverable; the phone has been disconnected.

SLIGHTLY ASKEW PLAYERS   **D F-l mm Sp**
P.O. Box 2335, Santa Barbara, CA 93101 (805) 965-3502 **Contact:** E.
Bonnie Lewis, Ken Gilbert **Theatre:** professional **Works:** full-length
plays **Exclusive interest:** "Development of new works which lift the
human spirit by means of characterization, acting styles, voice, movement
and music." **Submission policy:** unsolicited script; query/synopsis

SOARING EAGLE PROD. New York Mail addressed to this theatre
has been returned as undeliverable; the phone has been disconnected.

SOCIETY HILL PLAYHOUSE   **F-l Tr Ad ♪ 2d**
507 S. 8th St., Philadelphia, PA 19147 (215) 923-0210 FAX (215) 923-
1789 **e-mail** shpcerols.com **Contact:** Walter Vail, Literary Mgr. **Theatre:**
professional **Works:** full-length plays, translations, adaptations, musicals
2nd productions: if Philadelphia premieres **Specifications:** small cast
preferred **Stages:** proscenium, 223 seats; flexible, 90 seats **Casting:**
Equity, non-Equity **Submission policy:** query/synopsis; professional
recommendation; agent submission **Response:** 1 month query; 6 months
solicited script **Your chances:** 300+ new scripts read annually/usually
1-3 produced **Remuneration:** negotiable **Commitment:** credit

SOHO REPERTORY THEATRE 46 Walker St., New York 10013
(212) 941-8632 This theatre is now longer open to submissions.

SOMERSET COMMUNITY COLLEGE THEATRE   **1-**
808 Monticello Rd., Somerset, KY 41501 (606) 679-8501 **Contact:**
Steve Cleberg, Director **Works:** one-acts **Special interests:** 5-10 minute
plays; strong characterization **Specifications:** cast size: 4-12 preferred;
balance of male/female roles; limited demands; small budget **Stage:** proscenium, 107 seats **Casting:** students **Audience:** "Conservative, college
and community." **Submission policy:** unsolicited script

♫ **SONG CINEMA ENTERPRISES**   **C**
1380 First Ave. Suite 6D, New York, NY 10021 (212) 650-0566 FAX
same **e-mail** a.rosenbloom@mci2000.com **Contact:** Adam Rosenbloom,
Artistic Director **Production company:** cinema **Works:** plays to "provide the literary base for songs of major recording artists" **Special**

interests: "(A) a young girl longing to be in love, falling in love, and breaking up; (B) a story concerning rape, incest, or sexual abuse; (C) the spiritlessness of cynicism of modern society and the impact it has on sensitive and vulnerable youth; (D) a combination of A and C." **Specifications:** copyrighted works only **Submission policy:** unsolicited script **Remuneration:** royalties

SONOMA COUNTY REP THEATRE   F-l 1- Tr Ad CY Rg Rs
Main Street Theatre, 415 Humboldt St., Santa Rosa, CA 95404 (707) 544-7278   FAX (707) 522-5033   e-mail mstscr@mst-scr.com **Contact:** Doug Stout, Dramaturg **Theatre:** professional **Works:** full-length plays, one-acts, translations, adaptations; children's plays **2nd productions:** no **Specifications:** maximum cast: 12 for full-length, 5 for one-act; minimal set changes; translators/adaptors must secure permissions **Stage:** arena, 150 seats **Audience:** "More interested in themes than in relationships." **Submission policy:** CA writers only: unsolicited script; query/ synopsis **Response:** 2 weeks query; 3 months script **Your chances:** 50-60 new scripts read annually/usually 2 produced in Showcase; 8-10 receive readings **Remuneration:** fee **Future commitment:** credit **Programs:** Playwright in Residence, Monday Night Muse Readings (see Somoma County Rep Programs in Special Programs); MST-SCR Summer Showcase (see Contests) **Advice:** *"Professional Playscript Format only!"*

SOURCE THEATRE COMPANY   F-l 1- ♪ 2d
1835 14th St. NW, Washington, DC 20009 (202) 462-1073 Contact: Keith Parker, Literary Mgr. **Theatre:** professional **Works:** full-length plays, one-acts, musicals **2nd productions:** yes **Stage:** thrust, 100± seats **Casting:** Equity, non-Equity **Submission policy:** unsolicited script of play not professionally produced, resume; query/synopsis, review of professionally produced play **Best time:** by Jan. 15, 1999 only **Response:** Feb 15, 1999 query; May 15, 1999 script **Comment:** "600 new scripts are read annually; more than 50 receive workshop productions in our Washington Theatre Festival each Jul.; one receives Source Theatre Co. Literary Prize (see Contests). Scripts are not returned." **Advice:** "Please call or write for a detailed information letter."

SOUTH ARKANSAS ARTS CENTER   F-l 1- Ad ♪ CY 2d Fm
110 E. 5th, El Dorado, AR 71730 (870) 862-5474 Contact: Linda M. Boydston, Exec. Director **Theatre:** community **Works:** full-length plays, one-acts, adaptations, musicals, children's plays **2nd productions:** if AR premieres **Specifications:** small cast; unit or flexible set **Stages:** proscenium, 207 seats; flexible, 30-50 seats **Audience:** "Middle-upper class." **Submission policy:** query/synopsis, resume **Response:** 2 weeks query; 1 month solicited script **Your chances:** 10 new scripts read annually/ usually 1 produced **Remuneration:** "Usually $35 per performance." **Future commitment:** no **Program:** South Arkansas Arts Center Playwright's Competition (see Contests) **Advice:** "Stage 2 division does 'off the wall' performances, but anything too 'NC-17' will not work here."

SOUTH COAST REPERTORY   F-l 1- Tr Ad ♪ 2d ▭
P.O. Box 2197, Costa Mesa, CA 92628-2197 (714) 708-5500 Contact:
John Glore, Literary Mgr. **Theatre:** professional **Works:** full-length
plays, one-acts, translations, adaptations, musicals **2nd productions:**
yes **Maximum cast:** 15-20 **Tours:** yes **Stages:** proscenium, 507 seats;
thrust, 161 seats **Audience:** "Cosmopolitan." **Submission policy:**
query/synopsis; professional recommendation; agent submission **Response:** 2 weeks query; 3-6 months solicited script **Your chances:** 600-
700 new scripts read annually/usually 5-6 produced **Remuneration:**
negotiable **Future commitment:** participation in subsidiary rights
Programs: South Coast Repertory Hispanic Playwrights Project (see
Contests); Adult Conservatory, COLAB New Play Program, Pacific
Playwrights Festival (see South Coast Rep in Special Programs)

SOUTHERN APPALACHIAN REPERTORY F-l Ad ♪ Rv Rg
THEATRE SART, P.O. Box 1720, Mars Hill, NC 28754-1720 (828)
689-1384 **Contact:** Dianne J. Chapman, Mng. Director **Theatre:** professional **Works:** full-length plays, adaptations, musicals, cabarets **2nd
productions:** no **Special interests:** "Southern Appalachian playwrights
and themes." **Stage:** proscenium, 166 seats **Casting:** non-Equity **Audience:** "Educated, retired, summer residents." **Submission policy:** unsolicited script, resume; query/synopsis, resume; professional recommendation **Best time:** fall **Response:** 1 month query; 6 months script **Your
chances:** 80-120 new scripts read annually/usually 1-2 produced
Future commitment: no **Programs:** staged readings, script development; Southern Appalachian Playwrights Conference (see Contests)

SOUTHERN REP   F-l Tr Ad CY Rv Rg
7214 St. Charles Ave., Box 912 Broadway Campus, New Orleans,
LA 70118 (504) 861-8163 FAX (504) 861-5875 **Contact:** Rosary H.
O'Neill, Artistic Director **Theatre:** professional **Works:** full-length plays,
translations, adaptations, children's plays, revues **Special interest:**
"Southern writers/themes." **Stage:** proscenium, 150 seats **Submission
policy:** unsolicited script **Best time:** late summer **Response:** 6-12 months

SOUTH JERSEY REG. THEATRE 730 Bay Ave., Somers Point, NJ
08244 (609) 653-0553 **Contact:** Bill Marshall, Pres. This theatre, now
known as Gateway Playhouse, now produces commercial fare only and
is no longer interested in new plays.

SOUTH ORANGE COUNTY COMMUNITY THEATRE
See West Coast 10-Minute Playwrighting Festival in Contests.

SPOKANE INTERPLAYERS ENSEMBLE   F-l Tr Ad
P.O. Box 1961, Spokane, WA 99210 (509) 455-7529 FAX (509) 624-
9348 **e-mail** interplayers@interplayers.com **Contact:** Robert A. Welch,
Mng. Director **Theatre:** professional **Works:** full-length plays, translations, adaptations **Specifications:** maximum cast: 8 preferred; single set

Stage: thrust, 255 seats Casting: Equity, non-Equity Submission policy: query/synopsis, dialogue sample, resume, production history, reviews Response: 3 months query (if interested); 6 months solicited script Terms: negotiable Advice: "1-page faxes only."

STAGE LEFT THEATRE   F-l 1- 2d
3408 N. Sheffield, Chicago, IL 60657 (773) 883-8830 e-mail SLTCHICAGO@aol.com Contact: Drew Martin, Artistic Director Theatre: professional Works: full-length plays, one-acts 2nd productions: yes Stage: flexible, 50 seats Casting: non-Equity Submission policy: query/synopsis Your chances: 50 new scripts read annually/ usually 1 produced Remuneration: negotiable royalty Future commitment: percentage, credit Programs: workshop productions, festivals, Downstage Left Collaborative Play Development (phone for details)

STAGE ONE: LOUISVILLE   CY ♪ 2d Cl Fm Rs ⌑
CHILDREN'S THEATRE 5 Riverfront Plaza, Louisville, KY 40202 (502) 589-5946 FAX (502) 588-5910 e-mail kystageone@ aol.com Contact: Moses Goldberg, Producing Director Theatre: professional Works: children's plays and musicals 2nd productions: yes Special interests: "Stageworthy, respectful dramatizations of classic tales of childhood; relevance to young people, families, school curriculum." Maximum cast: 12 Casting: Equity, students Tours: yes Stages: thrust, 626 seats; arena, 350 seats Audience: "5-18; families." Submission policy: unsolicited script, resume; professional recommendation; agent submission; no synopsis or review; commission Best time: Aug.-Dec. Response: 4-6 months Your chances: 100-200 new scripts read annually/usually 1-2 produced Terms: vary Programs: readings, internships, residencies

STAGE TWO THEATRE   F-l 1- Tr Ad CY 2d
410 Sheridan Rd., Highwood, IL 60040 (847) 432-7469 Contact: Artistic Director Theatre: professional Works: full-length plays, one-acts, translations, adaptations, children's plays 2nd productions: yes Specifications: 1 unit set preferred; no fly/wing space Stage: shallow thrust, 93 seats Casting: non-Equity Submission policy: unsolicited script Best time: fall Response: "Several months." Your chances: 300 new scripts read annually/usually 7 produced, 12 receive staged readings Remuneration: royalties Future commitment: no Comment: Inquire for new address.

STAGE WEST   F-l Tr Ad 2d Hi C
3055 S. University Dr., Ft. Worth, TX 76109 (817) 924-9454 FAX (817) 926-8650 e-mail stgwest@ix.netcom.com Contact: Jim Covault, Artistic Director Theatre: professional Works: full-length plays, translations, adaptations 2nd productions: yes Special interest: hispanic and contemporary issues; universal themes Maximum cast: 9 preferred; single

or unit set **Stage:** arena, 200 seats **Casting:** Equity, non-Equity **Audience:** "Conventional in the style they prefer, fairly liberal in terms of subject matter." **Submission policy:** query/synopsis, resume, dialogue sample **Best time:** Jan.-Mar. **Response:** 1 month query; 3 months solicited script **Your chances:** 100 new scripts read annually/usually 1-2 produced, latest in Jun. 1998 **Remuneration:** 7%-8%

STAGES   **F-l 1- Tr Ad Fr Esp x**
1540 N. McCadden Pl., Hollywood, CA 90028 (323) 463-5356 FAX (323) 463-3904 **e-mail** ask@stageshollywood.com **Theatre:** professional **Works:** full-length plays, one-acts, translations, adaptations **Special interests:** "Foreign writers; plays in English, French, Spanish, and other languages; experimental works." **Maximum cast:** 5 preferred **Stages:** outdoor amphitheatre, 99 seats; proscenium, 49 seats; classroom, 25 seats **Submission policy:** query/synopsis **Response:** 3 months query; time varies for solicited script

STAGEWEST   Springfield, MA   Mail addressed to this theatre has been returned as undeliverable; the phone has been disconnected.

STAGEWORKS/SUMMIT INC.   **F-l Tr Ad ♪ CY 2d C**
Hyde & Watson Theatre, Kent Place School, 42 Norwood Ave., Summit, NJ 07901 (908) 273-9383 **FAX** (908) 273-9390 **Contact:** Robert Pridham, Artistic Director **Theatre:** professional **Works:** full-length plays, translations, adaptations, small-scale musicals, children's plays **2nd productions:** yes **Special interest:** political, topical issues **Maximum cast:** 8 **Submission policy:** unsolicited script **Response:** immediate if not interested **Remuneration:** royalties **Future commitment:** no **Program:** Hear & Now Series (see Special Programs)

STAMFORD THEATRE WORKS   **F-l ♪ 2d C**
95 Atlantic St., Stamford, CT 06901 (203) 359-4414 FAX (203) 356-1846 **Contact:** Jane Desy, Literary Mgr. **Theatre:** professional **Works:** full-length plays, musicals **2nd productions:** "Yes; we have moved plays to New York." **Special interest:** "Social relevance." **Specifications:** maximum cast: 7 preferred; single unit set preferred **Stage:** pit with raked audience, 150 seats **Casting:** Equity, non-Equity **Submission policy:** query/synopsis, 10-page dialogue sample; professional recommendation; agent submission; cassette tape of any music, script history, resume, SASP with all material **Response:** 3-6 months **Your chances:** 500 new scripts read annually/3 receive staged readings **Remuneration:** $500 fee **Future commitment:** no **Program:** Windows on the Works (see Special Programs)

STANLEY HOTEL THEATRE   **333 Wonderview Ave., P.O. Box 1767, Estes Park, CO 80517** (970) 586-3371 FAX (303) 586-3673 **Contact:** City of Estes Park   Renovation plans for this theatre continue; see *The Playwright's Companion 2000* or inquire for a progress report.

STARFISH THEATREWORKS (STW)   D Fl 1- Rg Rs C M
7 E. 14th St. Suite 1207, New York, NY 10003 (212) 741-9868 FAX
same **Contact:** Jeanette Horn, Literary Mgr., c/o Starfish Theatreworks
Theatre: off off Broadway **Works:** commissioned one-acts; "full-length
plays by artists we have already worked with in the one-act form" **2nd
productions:** "Works developed with STW only." **Special interests:**
"Character-driven work on serious, substantive themes that speak to a
diverse audience." **Specifications:** maximum cast: 4; simple sets; no comedies, farces, sketches **Stage:** black box, 100 seats **Casting:** Equity, non-
Equity **Audience:** "Culturally diverse, educated." **Submission policy:**
letter of introduction, reference, resume, 10-page sample **Response:** 6
months-1 year **Your chances:** "2 different productions of 4 commissioned
one-acts annually, developed in residence in thematically-linked clus-
ters." **Remuneration:** stipends, fees, royalties **Future commitment:**
"Credit; some subsidiary rights; use in rep; use in publication of commissioned works." **Programs:** script development, teaching opportunities
Advice: "Must enjoy rewriting; must live in commuting distance of NYC."

STARLIGHT MUSICAL THEATRE   ♪ 2d
P.O. Box 3519, San Diego, CA 92163-1519 (619) 544-7800 FAX (619)
544-0496 **Contact:** Brian Wells, Producing Art. Director **Theatre:** professional **Works:** musicals **2nd productions:** yes **Special interest:** "Broad
appeal." **Stage:** proscenium, 4200 seats **Casting:** "Equity, non-Equity;
volunteers for staged readings." **Audience:** "Mid-America." **Submission
policy:** query/synopsis **Best time:** fall **Response:** 3 months **Your
chances:** 10-15 new scripts read annually, none produced to date **Remuneration:** "Varies; none for staged reading." **Program:** workshops

♫ STATEMENT PRODUCTIONS   F-l
P.O. Box 496, Kittredge, CO 80457 (303) 670-8397 FAX (303) 670-
1897 **e-mail** FreeRobbie@aol.com **Contact:** Artistic Director **Theatre:**
professional **Works:** full-length plays **Maximum cast:** 5 **Submission
policy:** unsolicited script **Response:** 3 months

STEPPENWOLF THEATRE COMPANY   F-l Ad 2d
1650 N. Halsted St., Chicago, IL 60614 (312) 335-1888 FAX (312)
335-0808 **Contact:** Michele Volansky, Dramaturg **Theatre:** professional
Works: full-length plays, adaptations **2nd productions:** yes **Special interest:** new plays **Maximum cast:** 15-20 **Stages:** proscenium, 510 seats;
flexible, 300 seats **Casting:** Equity, non-Equity **Submission policy:** professional recommendation with query/synopsis and dialogue sample;
agent submission **Response:** 3-6 months **Your chances:** 850 new scripts
read annually/usually 0-2 produced **Future commitment:** percentage

STEPPIN' OUT PRODUCTIONS   F-l 1- ♪ 2d cm Lc
61 E. 8th St. #107, New York, NY 10003-1503 (212) 614-0089 FAX
(212) 353-2860 **Contact:** Steven Helgoth, Artistic Director **Theatre:** off
off Broadway **Works:** full-length plays, one-acts, musicals **2nd pro-**

ductions: yes **Special interests:** "Full-length plays, comedy, larger casts." **Specifications:** maximum cast: 25; no more than 1-2 sets **Stage:** flexible, 50-75 seats **Casting:** Equity, non-Equity **Audience:** "Likes farce, comedy, occasional evenings of one-acts." **Submission policy:** unsolicited script, SASP; query/synopsis, resume, script history, SASP; commission **Best time:** spring, fall **Response:** 1 month query; 6 months script **Your chances:** 30-40 new scripts read annually/usually 1-2 produced; 3-4 receive staged readings **Remuneration:** negotiable **Future commitment:** no **Program:** script development

STEVEN BARUCH, PRODUCER   F-l ♪
180 S. Broadway, White Plains, NY 10605 (914) 948-1300 FAX (914) 948-1327 **Production company:** professional **Works:** full-length plays, musicals **Submission policy:** query/brief synopsis; agent submission; professional recommendation

STEWART F. LANE PRODUCTIONS   F-l ♪ cm dr
Theatre Venture, Inc., 200 W. 57th St. #801, New York, NY 10019 (212) 315-0402 **Contact:** Stewart F. Lane, Producer **Production company:** off Broadway **Works:** full-length plays, musicals **Special interests:** comedies, musicals, dramas **Submission policy:** agent submission

STONE PRODUCTIONS, INC.   F-l ♪
260 W. 44th St. Suite 501, New York, NY 10036 (212) 768-8255 FAX (212) 768-4516 **Production company:** professional **Works:** full-length plays, musicals **Submission policy:** unsolicited script or query/synopsis, cassette tape for musical **Comment:** Formerly Right Coast Prods.

STRAND THEATRE   F-l 1- Ad
2317 Ship's Mechanic Row, Galveston, TX 77550 (409) 763-4591 FAX (409) 763-4879 **Contact:** William Burford, Exec. Director **Theatre:** semi-professional **Works:** full-length plays, one-acts, adaptations **Specifications:** small cast; single-story set, unit preferred **Submission policy:** send SASE for guidelines **Programs:** readings, workshops

STRAWDOG THEATRE   F-l 1- Ad x
3829 N. Broadway, Chicago, IL 60613 (773) 528-9889 FAX (773) 528-7238 e-mail StrawdogTC@aol.com **Contact:** David Warren, Literary Mgr. **Theatre:** professional **Works:** full-length plays, translations, adaptations **Special interests:** "Dark, edgy, urban, physical, unconventional plays that bend the rules, for ensemble aged 25-late 30s." **Specifications:** few sets; no wing or fly space; adaptors must secure rights **Stage:** black box, 74 seats **Casting:** non-Equity **Submission policy:** query/synopsis, 1st 10 pages of dialogue, script history, optional resume, SASP **Response:** 1-3 months **Your chances:** 250-300 new scripts read annually/ usually 1 produced, latest scheduled for fall 1999   **Remuneration:** percentage **Future commitment:** credit, percentage **Advice:** "Patience."

THE STREET THEATER **228 Fisher Ave., White Plains, NY 10606-2702 (914) 761-3307 Contact:** Gray Smith, Exec. Director This theatre is closed to submissions in 1999; see *The Playwright's Companion 2000* or inquire for future plans.

STUART OSTROW, PRODUCER ♪
Musical Theatre Lab, School of Theatre, Univ. of Houston, Houston, TX 77204-5071 (713) 743-3003 FAX (713) 749-1420 Contact: Stuart Ostrow **Production company:** professional **Works:** full-length musicals **Submission policy:** unsolicited script or score; videotape; cassette tape

STUDIO ARENA THEATRE **F-l Tr Ad 2d Rg Am H**
710 Main St., Buffalo, NY 14202-1990 (716) 856-8025 FAX (716) 856-3415 Contact: Gavin Cameron-Webb, Art. Director **Theatre:** professional **Works:** full-length plays, translations, adaptations **2nd productions:** yes **Special interests:** "Local and American history/culture." **Specifications:** maximum cast: 12; limited wing/fly space **Stage:** thrust, 637 seats **Casting:** Equity **Audience:** "Conservative." **Submission policy:** agent submission **Response:** 6 months **Your chances:** 60 new scripts read annually/usually none produced

THE STUDIO THEATRE **1333 P St. NW, Washington, DC 20005 (202) 232-7267** This theatre is no longer open to submissions.

𝕹 SU TEATRO **F-l Hi Esp**
4725 High St., Denver, CO 80216 (303) 296-0219 Contact: Anthony J. Garcia, Resident Playwright **Theatre:** professional **Works:** full-length plays **Exclusive interests:** Chicano/Latino themes; works in English, Spanish, or both **Tours:** yes **Submission policy:** unsolicited script

SUMMERNITE **F-l Tr Ad ♪ 2d C cm**
c/o Theatre Arts, NIU., DeKalb, IL 60115 (815) 753-8253 FAX (815) 753-8415 Contact: Chris Markle, Artistic Director **Theatre:** professional **Works:** full-length plays, translations, adaptations, small-scale musicals **2nd productions:** if Chicago premieres **Special interests:** "Political pieces; contemporary comedies." **Specifications:** maximum cast: 9; unit set **Tours:** yes **Stage:** flexible, 75-125 seats **Casting:** Equity, non-Equity **Audience:** "Enjoys issue plays, romances, farce." **Submission policy:** query/synopsis, resume, SASP **Best time:** Jan.-May **Response:** 1 month query; 6 months solicited script **Your chances:** 100+ new scripts read annually/usually 2 produced **Remuneration:** negotiable **Program:** NIU New Play Workshop (see Special Programs)

SUNSET PLAYHOUSE, INC. **F-l Ad ♪ CY 2d cm my Cl Fm**
800 Elm Grove Rd., Elm Grove, WI 53122 (414) 782-4431 FAX (414) 782-3150 Contact: Michael Duncan, Art. Director **Theatre:** community **Works:** full-length plays, musicals **2nd productions:** yes **Special interests:** "Comedy; mystery; family theatre; adaptations of classics."

Stage: proscenium, 297 seats **Casting:** non-Equity **Submission policy:** unsolicited script; videotape **Best time:** spring-summer **Response:** 3 months **Your chances:** 30 new scripts read annually/usually 1 produced **Remuneration:** yes **Future commitment:** credit

SUSAN GALLIN PRODUCTIONS   F-l C
250 W. 57th St. Suite 1818, New York, NY 10107 (212) 489-5333 FAX (212) 581-9373 **Production company:** Broadway **Works:** full-length plays **Special interest:** contemporary plays **Submission policy:** agent submission

SWINE PALACE PRODUCTIONS   F-l Ad ♪ 2d Rg Lc ⌒
P.O. Box 18699, Baton Rouge, LA 70893 (504) 388-3533 FAX (504) 388-4135 e-mail mehersey@aol.com **Contact:** Lucy Maycock, Dramaturg **Theatre:** professional **Works:** full-length plays, adaptations, musicals **2nd productions:** yes **Special interest:** "Louisiana." **Specifications:** maximum cast: 40; up to 10 sets **Tours:** yes **Stage:** proscenium, 400 seats **Casting:** Equity, non-Equity **Audience:** students, faculty, community **Submission policy:** unsolicited script; query/synopsis **Best time:** summer **Response:** 1-2 months **Your chances:** 25 new scripts read annually

SYNERGY THEATRE ARTS GROUP   F-l cm dr
P.O. Box 2625 Times Square Station, New York, NY 10108 (212) 502-8512 **Contact:** Tim Rhudy, Artistic Director **Theatre:** professional **Works:** full-length plays **Special interests:** "Dark comedies with an absurdist touch and dramas with non-naturalistic or absurdist elements." **Maximum cast:** 8 **Casting:** Equity **Submission policy:** unsolicited script with synopsis **Response:** "Slowly but surely." **Program:** workshops **Advice:** "We are not promising to return submissions presently; we are accepting new submissions."

SYRACUSE STAGE   F-l CY 2d 12+
820 E. Genesee St., Syracuse, NY 13210 (315) 443-4008 FAX (315) 443-9846 e-mail syrstage@sry.edu **Contact:** Robert Moss, Artistic Director **Theatre:** professional **Works:** full-length plays **2nd productions:** yes **Stage:** proscenium, 495 seats **Maximum cast:** 8 **Audience:** "Elementary schools to senior citizens." **Submission policy:** query/synopsis, dialogue sample, resume; agent submission **Response:** 2 months query; 9 months solicited script **Terms:** negotiable

TACOMA ACTORS GUILD   F-l Tr Ad ♪ 2d Fm
901 Broadway 6th Floor, Tacoma, WA 98402-4404 (206) 272-3107 FAX (206) 272-3358 **Contact:** Mr. Pat Patton, Producing Art. Director **Theatre:** professional **Works:** full-length plays, translations, adaptations, musicals **2nd productions:** yes **Specifications:** maximum cast: 10, simple unit set preferred; "no strong language or nudity" **Stage:** modified proscenium, 302 seats **Audience:** "Older, educated, moderate." **Submission policy:** query/synopsis, dialogue sample, SASP; agent submission

Best time: spring-summer **Response:** 1-2 months query; 1 year solicited script **Your chances:** 50 new scripts read annually/usually none produced **Terms:** negotiable

TADA!   ♪ CY 12+ Fm
120 W. 28th St., New York, NY 10001 (212) 627-1732 FAX (212) 243-6736 **Contact:** Janine Nina Trevens, Artistic Director **Theatre:** professional **Works:** "Musicals of and for children." **2nd productions:** no **Special interest:** "Ensemble pieces for performers aged 8-17." **Stage:** black box, 95 seats **Audience:** families **Submission policy:** unsolicited script (may lead to commission) **Best time:** Sept.-Jan. **Response:** 6 months **Your chances:** 100 new scripts read annually/usually 1 produced **Remuneration** "Contract upon commission." **Program:** TADA! Staged Reading Play Contest (see Contests) **Advice:** "Please consider the voice ranges of young children."

TAPROOT THEATRE   F-l 1- Ad ♪ CY 2d C Fm Sp 🐌 ▭
204 N. 85th St., Seattle, WA 98103 (206) 781-9705 FAX (206) 706-1502 **e-mail** taproot@taproot.org **Contact:** Scott L. Nolte, Producing Art. Director **Theatre:** professional **Works:** full-length plays, one-acts, adaptations, musicals, children's plays **2nd productions:** yes **Special interests:** "Values of hope/faith applied to issues; Christmas plays; one-acts (30-40 minutes) on issues for school tours." **Cast size:** 5-10 preferred, 12 maximum; tours: 3 men, 2 women, minimal demands **Stage:** thrust, 224 seats **Casting:** Equity, non-Equity **Audience:** "Tours: topical plays; mainstage: families." **Submission policy:** query/1-page synopsis, sample scene, music sample, resume; professional recommendation **Response:** 2 weeks query; 4 weeks solicited script **Your chances:** 50 new scripts read annually/usually 1-2 produced, latest in Dec. 1998 **Remuneration:** royalty

TARRAGON THEATRE   D F-l Tr Ad 2d Rg Rs ▭
30 Bridgman Ave., Toronto, Ontario, Canada M5R 1X3 (416) 536-5018 FAX (416) 533-6372 **e-mail** Tarragon@interlog.com **Contact:** Urjo Kareda, Art. Director **Theatre:** professional **Works:** full-length plays, translations, adaptations **2nd productions:** yes **Special interest:** "Developing the work of Canadian playwrights." **Tours:** yes **Stages:** 2 black boxes, 100, 215 seats **Casting:** Equity **Submission policy:** Canadian writer: unsolicited script; professional recommendation; agent submission; no U.S. submissions **Best time:** Sept.-May **Response:** immediate query; 1 month script **Your chances:** 400-500 new scripts read annually **Remuneration:** "10%." **Future commitment:** percentage, credit, options **Programs:** readings, workshops, script development, residencies, classes

TEATRO AVANTE   F-l Tr Ad 2d Hi C ▭
235 Alcazar Ave., Coral Gables, FL 33134-3005 (305) 445-8877 FAX (305) 445-1301 **Contact:** Mario Ernesto Sanchez, Producing Art. Director **Theatre:** professional **Works:** full-length plays, translations, adapta-

tions **2nd productions:** yes **Special interest:** Hispanic culture **Specifications:** maximum cast: 10, no more than 2 sets **Tours:** yes **Stage:** proscenium, 191 seats **Casting:** Equity, non-Equity **Audience:** "95% Hispanic; likes serious theatre." **Submission policy:** unsolicited script, resume; professional recommendation **Your chances:** 30 new scripts read annually/usually 1-2 produced **Remuneration:** $300-$500 **Future commitment:** negotiable **Programs:** staged readings, workshops

TEATRO DALLAS   F-l 1- Tr Ad CY 2d Hi ⌐
2204 Commerce St., Dallas, TX 75201 (214) 741-6833 FAX (214) 741-6735 **Contact:** Valerie Brogan, Exec. Director **Theatre:** professional **Works:** full-length plays, one-acts, translations, adaptations, children's plays **2nd productions:** yes **Exclusive interests:** "Hispanic playwrights, themes." **Specifications:** maximum cast: 8-10; simple set **Tours:** yes **Stage:** black box, 92 seats **Casting:** Equity, non-Equity **Audience:** "All ages." **Submission policy:** unsolicited script; query/synopsis, dialogue sample, resume; professional recommendation; agent submission; commission **Response:** 1 week-6 months **Your chances:** 25-50 new scripts read annually/usually 1 produced **Terms:** negotiable **Program:** workshops

TENNESSEE REPERTORY THEATRE   D ♪ 2d Am
427 Chestnut St., Nashville, TN 37203 (615) 244-4878 FAX (615) 244-1232 e-mail tnrep@isdn.net **Contact:** Don Jones, Assoc. Art. Director **Theatre:** professional **Works:** musicals **2nd productions:** yes **Special interests:** "New American musicals; works-in-progress." **Specifications:** maximum cast: 12; no more than 2 sets; minimal orchestration **Stage:** proscenium, 1050 seats **Casting:** Equity, non-Equity **Audience:** "Conservative." **Submission policy:** query/synopsis, dialogue sample, cassette tape or lead sheets; agent submission **Best time:** Jun.-Sept. **Response:** 4-6 weeks query; 1 year solicited script **Your chances:** 50 new scripts read annually/usually 1-2 produced **Terms:** negotiable

TEXAS WESLEYAN UNIV. THEATRE   Fort Worth, TX This theatre is no longer open to submissions.

THALIA SPANISH THEATRE   F-l Tr Ad Esp cm
P.O. Box 4368, Sunnyside, NY 11104 (718) 729-3880 **Contact:** Silvia Brito, Artistic/Exec. Director **Theatre:** professional **Works:** full-length plays, translations, adaptations **Exclusive interest:** "Plays in Spanish." **Specifications:** maximum cast: 6; single set **Stage:** proscenium, 74 seats **Casting:** non-Equity **Audience:** "Likes comedies." **Submission policy:** unsolicited script **Best time:** Dec.-Jan. **Response:** 3 months **Your chances:** 2 new plays read annually **Remuneration:** $50 per performance

THEATRE AMERICANA   F-l 2d Am H B
P.O. Box 245, Altadena, CA 91003-0245 (626) 683-1740 **Contact:** James Follett, Playreading Chair **Theatre:** community **Works:** full-length plays **2nd productions:** yes **Special interests:** "American authors,

background, history, the American experience." **Specifications:** unpublished works only; simple set, minimal changes preferred **Stage:** thrust/proscenium, 60-80 seats **Audience:** general **Submission policy:** unsolicited script; query/synopsis, resume **Best time:** before Feb. 1 **Response:** 3 weeks query; 2-4 months script **Your chances:** 200 new scripts read annually/usually 4 produced **Program:** David James Ellis Memorial Award (see Contests) **Advice:** "For biography: develop the play around a central conflict in the character's life."

THEATER ARTISTS OF MARIN   **P.O. Box 150473, San Rafael, CA 94915**   **(415) 453-6098**   **Contact:** Charles Brousse, Art. Director This theatre is not open to submissions in 1999; see *The Playwright's Companion 2000* or inquire for future plans.

THEATER AT LIME KILN   **P.O. Box 663, Lexington, VA 24450** **(540) 463-7088 FAX (540) 463-1082** e-mail limekiln@cfw.com **Contact:** Barry Mines, Art. Director   This theatre is not open to submissions in 1999; see *The Playwright's Companion 2000* for future plans.

THE THEATER AT MONMOUTH   CY 2d
P.O. Box 385, Monmouth, ME 04259-0385 (207) 933-2952 FAX same **Contact:** David Greenham, Mng. Director **Theatre:** professional **Works:** children's plays **2nd productions:** yes **Special interest:** "Traditional fare." **Specifications:** maximum cast: 9; simple set **Stage:** thrust, 275 seats **Casting:** Equity, non-Equity, no children **Submission policy:** unsolicited script; query/synopsis **Best time:** Nov. **Response:** 6 weeks query; 6 months script **Your chances:** 50 new scripts read annually/usually 0-1 produced **Remuneration:** royalty

THEATER BY THE BLIND   F-l 1- Tr Ad ♪ h/d
306 W. 18th St., New York, NY 10011 (212) 243-4337 FAX same **Contact:** Ike Schambelan, Artistic Director   **Theatre:** professional **Works:** full-length plays, one-acts, translations, adaptations, musicals **Exclusive interest:** "Plays by and about the blind." **Stages:** various spaces, 99 seats **Casting:** Equity, non-Equity **Submission policy:** unsolicited script **Response:** 2 months

♫ **THEATRE 808**   F-l 1-
311 N. Robertson Blvd. Suite 805, Beverly Hills, CA 90211 (310) 358-3808 Theatre: professional **Works:** full-length plays, one-acts **2nd productions:** no **Submission policy:** unsolicited script

THE THEATRE CO. UNIV. OF DETROIT MERCY   F-l 2d
4001 W. McNichols, Detroit, MI 48221 (313) 993-1130 e-mail thibaume@udmercy.edu **Contact:** David Regal, Artistic Director **Theatre:** university **Works:** full-length plays **2nd productions:** yes **Stages:** proscenium, 350 seats; black box, 170 seats **Submission policy:** unsolicited script **Best time:** Jan.-Mar. **Response:** varies

THEATRE DE LA JEUNE LUNE   **F-l Tr Ad 2d** ⌑
105 1st St. N, Minneapolis, MN 55401 (612) 332-3968 FAX (612) 332-0048 Contact: Barbra Berlovitz, Artistic Director **Theatre:** professional **Works:** full-length plays, translations, adaptations **2nd productions:** yes **Special interest:** "Universal themes." **Tours:** yes **Stage:** flexible, 500 seats **Casting:** non-Equity **Audience:** "Educated." **Submission policy:** query/synopsis, dialogue sample, resume **Response:** 10 weeks query; 4 months solicited script **Your chances:** 100 new scripts read annually/ usually none produced **Remuneration:** yes **Future commitment:** no

THEATRE: DRAMATIC WOMEN   **F-l 1- Rg W**
1070 Miramonte Dr. #7, Santa Barbara, CA 93109 (805) 965-5826 Contact: Bob Potter, Producer **Theatre:** professional **Works:** full-length plays, one-acts, 10-minute plays **2nd productions:** "Usually not." **Special interests:** "Local writers only; locally developed original scripts; participation of women in all aspects of theatre." **Submission policy:** local writers phone or write for information **Your chances:** 1-2 new scripts produced annually **Programs:** readings, workshops **Comment:** "Men are welcome in all activities."

THÈÂTRE DU GRAND-GUIGNOL ®   **1- F-l Tr Ad** ♪ ⌑
DE PARIS Embassy of Montmartre, 310 E. 70th St., New York, NY 10021 (212) 861-1813 Contact: Barry Alan Richmond, Directeur-Général **Theatre:** professional **Works:** primarily one-acts; also full-length plays, translations, adaptations, musicals **Exclusive interest:** "Our own trademarked Grand-Guignol style--shock, terror, horror, suspense, earthy laughter." **Specifications:** maximum cast: 10-12; no more than 3 sets **Tours:** yes **Stage:** proscenium **Audience:** "Sophisticated; no children." **Submission policy:** query/synopsis, resume, dialogue sample, reviews **Response:** 2+ months **Your chances:** "Of several hundred scripts submitted/5-6 have been produced." **Remuneration:** royalty **Future commitment:** no **Advice:** "Do some research before submitting."

THEATER EMORY   **F-l 1- Tr Ad Cl**
Emory Univ., Atlanta, GA 30322 (404) 727-3465 FAX (404) 727-6253 e-mail vmurphy@emory.edu **Contact:** Vincent Murphy, Artistic Director **Theatre:** professional **Works:** full-length plays, one-acts, translations, adaptations **Special interests:** translations/adaptations of literature/classics **Specifications:** maximum cast: 20; no wing or fly space **Stages:** 3 flexible, 120, 70, 60 seats **Audience:** "University, urban community." **Submission policy:** unsolicited script through members of Southeast Playwrights Project only (inquire for details) **Response:** 2-4 months **Programs:** Theatre Emory Programs (see Special Programs)

THEATER FOR THE NEW CITY   **F-l x Am C mm po**
155-57 First Ave., New York, NY 10003-2906 (212) 254-1109 Contact: Crystal Field, Artistic Director **Theatre:** off off Broadway **Works:** full-length plays **2nd productions:** no **Special interests:** "Experimental

American works; issues; plays integrating music, dance, poetry." **Stages:** 3 flexible spaces, 200, 100, 75 seats; cabaret **Submission policy:** unsolicited script; professional recommendation; commission **Best time:** summer **Response:** 9-12 months **Your chances:** 780 new scripts read annually/usually 40 produced **Remuneration:** "For a commissioned play and when the playwright attends every performance." **Advice:** "New American theatre, new artists, lesser known writers."

THEATRE IV CY Tr Ad 2d ⊂▶
114 W. Broad St., Richmond, VA 23220 (804) 783-1688 FAX (804) 775-2325 e-mail millertiv@aol.com **Contact:** Bruce Miller, Art. Director **Theatre:** professional **Works:** full-length children's plays, translations, adaptations **2nd productions:** yes **Cast size:** 3-5 for touring **Stages:** proscenium, 604 seats; flexible, 84 seats **Submission policy:** query/synopsis; professional recommendation **Response:** 2 months query (if interested); 2 years solicited script **Terms:** negotiable

THEATRE GAEL F-l Tr Ad CY ℭ ⊂▶
P.O. Box 77156, Atlanta, GA 30357 (404) 876-1138 FAX (404) 876-1141 e-mail theatregael@mindspring.com **Contact:** John Stephens, Art. Director **Theatre:** professional **Works:** full-length plays, translations, adaptations, children's plays **Special interests:** "Ireland, Scotland, Wales; America's Celtic heritage." **Tours:** all shows **Stages:** flexible, 90-180 seats; churches, schools, 80-330 seats **Submission policy:** query/synopsis **Response:** 1 month query; 3 months solicited script **Program:** Worldsong Children's Theatre: tours to schools, libraries

THEATRE GUILD PRODUCTIONS 135 Central Park West Suite 4 South, New York, NY 10023 (212) 873-0676 FAX (212) 873-5972 This production company is closed to submissions in 1999; see *The Playwright's Companion 2000* for future plans.

THE THEATRE IN OLD TOWN ♪ 2d
4040 Twiggs St., San Diego, CA 92110 (619) 688-2494 FAX (619) 688-0960 **Contact:** Paula Kalustian, Art. Director **Theatre:** professional **Works:** musicals **2nd productions:** yes **Specifications:** maximum cast: 8; unit set **Stage:** thrust, 244 seats **Casting:** Equity, non-Equity **Audience:** "High-energy entertainment." **Submission policy:** unsolicited script; query/synopsis, resume; professional recommendation; agent submission **Response:** 1-3 weeks query, 1-3 months script **Your chances:** 10 new scripts read annually/usually 0-1 produced **Terms:** negotiable

THEATRE IN THE PARK F-l 1- Tr Ad ♪ CY 2d Sn Rs ⊂▶
107 Pullen Rd., Raleigh, NC 27607 (919) 831-6936 FAX (919) 831-9475 e-mail raleightip@pol.com **Contact:** Ira David Wood, Exec. Director **Theatre:** community **Works:** full-length plays, one-acts, translations, adaptations, musicals, children's plays **2nd productions:** yes **Tours:** yes **Stages:** flexible, 200 seats; proscenium, 40 seats **Audience:** "Seniors,

professionals, students." **Submission policy:** unsolicited script; query/synopsis, 8-12 page dialogue sample; script history, resume, SASP; commission **Best time:** early winter **Response:** 4 weeks query; 3 months script **Your chances:** 50 new scripts read annually/usually 1-2 produced; 8-10 receive staged readings **Remuneration:** negotiable **Future commitment:** credit **Programs:** development, residencies, classes

THEATRE IN THE SQUARE   F-l 1- Tr ♪
11 Whitlock Ave., Marietta, GA 30064 (770) 422-8369 FAX (770) 424-2637 **Contact:** Literary Mgr. **Theatre:** professional **Works:** full-length plays, one-acts, translations, musicals **Special interests:** "Southeastern and world premieres." **Specifications:** maximum cast: 9; unit set; no fly space **Stages:** proscenium, 225 seats; flexible, 80 seats **Submission policy:** query/synopsis **Best time:** Dec.-Feb. **Response:** 1 month query (if interested); 6 months solicited script

THEATRE KEY WEST   F-l 1- Tr Ad ♪
P.O. Box 992, Key West, FL 33041-0092 (305) 292-3725 **e-mail** theatrekw@aol.com **Contact:** Joan McGillis, Artistic Director **Theatre:** professional **Works:** full-length plays, one-acts, translations, adaptations, musicals **2nd productions:** no **Maximum cast:** 8 **Submission policy:** 2 professional recommendations; agent submission **Program:** Key West Theatre Festival (see Contests)

THEATER OF THE FIRST AMENDMENT   F-l 1- Tr Ad 2d H
MS 3E6, George Mason Univ., Fairfax, VA 22030 (703) 993-2195 FAX (703) 993-2191 **e-mail** rdavi4@gmu.edu **Contact:** Rick Davis, Artistic Director **Theatre:** professional **Works:** full-length plays, one-acts, translations, adaptations **2nd productions:** yes **Special interests:** "A sense of history rather than history dramatized; psychological issues; translations, adaptations." **Specifications:** simple demands; no fly space; roles for student actors **Stage:** flexible, 150-200 seats **Audience:** university, community **Submission policy:** query/synopsis, resume, dialogue sample; agent submission **Best time:** Aug.-Jan. **Response:** 2 weeks query; 6 months solicited script **Your chances:** 200 new scripts read annually/usually 3-4 produced **Remuneration:** royalty, per diem **Programs:** readings, workshops, development

♫ THEATRE WITH YOUR COFFEE?   F-l ♪
P.O. Box 81, Hollywood, FL 33081 **Contact:** Roberto Presigiacomo, Artistic Director **Theatre:** professional **Works:** full-length plays, musicals **2nd productions:** no **Submission policy:** unsolicited script; query/synopsis **Response:** 6 months **Program:** staged readings

THEATRE OF NOTE   F-l 1- 2d x Lc
1517 N. Cahuenga Blvd., Hollywood, CA 90028 (323) 856-8611 **Contact:** David Conner, Selection Chair **Theatre:** professional **Works:** full-length plays, one-acts **2nd productions:** if L.A. premieres **Special**

interests: "New experimental works; large casts." **Stage:** flexible, 50 seats **Casting:** Equity, non-Equity **Audience:** "Loyal, serious theatre-goers." **Submission policy:** unsolicited script, script history **Your chances:** 100 new scripts read annually/usually 5-10 produced **Remuneration/commitment:** no **Programs:** readings, writers' workshops **Advice:** "Take risks."

THEATRE OF YALE DRAMA ALUMNI (TYDA)   1- Rg 2d

100 W. 92nd St. #28F, New York, NY 10025 (212) 496-7452 **Contact:** Howard Pflanzer, Chair, Reading Committee **Theatre:** professional, alumni **Works:** one-acts **2nd productions:** yes **Exclusive interests:** works by Yale Drama School alumni **Submission policy:** unsolicited script **Response:** 3-6 months

THEATRE OF YOUTH CO.   F-l Tr Ad CY 2d C Fm ⌂

282 Franklin St., Buffalo, NY 14202 (until Jul. 1999) (716) 856-4410 **Contact:** Meg Quinn, Artistic Director **Theatre:** professional **Works:** children's plays, adaptations **2nd productions:** yes **Special interest:** issues **Specifications:** maximum cast: 10; small set for school tours **Stages:** proscenium-thrust, 480 seats **Audience:** "Pre-K, K-12; adults." **Submission policy:** unsolicited script; query/synopsis, dialogue sample; commission **Best time:** May-Jul. **Response:** 3 months **Your chances:** 15 new scripts read annually/usually none produced; latest in fall 1998 **Remuneration:** fee; royalty **Comment:** Address after Jul. 1, 1999: 207 Allen St., Buffalo, NY 14201.

THEATRE ON THE SQUARE   F-l ♪ 2d ⌂

450 Post St., San Francisco, CA 94102 (415) 433-6461 **FAX** (415) 433-2910 **e-mail** tots@wenet.net **Contact:** Jonathan Reinis, Artistic Director **Theatre:** professional **Works:** full-length plays, musicals **2nd productions:** yes **Specifications:** maximum cast: 16; no fly space **Tours:** yes **Stage:** proscenium/thrust, 750 seats **Casting:** Equity **Submission policy:** query/synopsis, video or cassette tape of music, reviews; professional recommendation; agent submission **Response:** 6 months query; 1 year solicited script **Your chances:** 150 new scripts read annually/usually 1-2 produced **Remuneration:** percentage **Future commitment:** yes

THE THEATRE OUTLET   F-l 1- Tr Ad ₵ H Rg

29 N. 9th St., Allentown, PA 18101 (610) 820-9270 **FAX** (610) 820-9130 **e-mail** theaterout@aol.com **Contact:** George Miller, Artistic Director **Theatre:** professional **Works:** full-length plays, one-acts, translations, adaptations **Special interests:** "The Irish/Scotch/Welsh experience; history/culture of eastern PA." **Specifications:** limited wing/fly space **Stage:** black box, 100 seats **Submission policy:** query/synopsis **Best time:** summer **Response:** 1 month query; 2 months script **Program:** The Counter-Culture Mon. Cafe Series (see Special Programs)

THEATRE RHINOCEROS   F-l 1- Tr Ad ♪ 2d g/l

2926 16th St., San Francisco, CA 94103 (415) 552-4100 FAX (415) 558-9044 **Contact:** Doug Holsclaw, Literary Mgr. **Theatre:** professional **Works:** full length plays, one-acts, translations, adaptations, musicals **2nd productions:** yes **Exclusive interest:** "Gay, lesbian themes." **Maximum cast:** 8-10 **Stages:** proscenium, 112 seats; studio, 60 seats **Casting:** non-Equity **Submission policy:** unsolicited script; query/synopsis, dialogue sample; professional recommendation **Response:** 4-6 months **Remuneration:** royalty **Future commitment:** for premiere

THE THEATRE-STUDIO,   F-l 1- Tr Ad Rv S Tv Fr Esp 2d
INC.   750 8th Ave. Suite 200, New York, NY 10036 (212) 719-0500
Contact: A. M. Raychel, Producing/Artistic Director **Theatre:** resident, off off Broadway **Works:** full-length plays, one-acts, translations, adaptations, cabarets, screenplays, teleplays, foreign-language plays **2nd productions:** "Encouraged." **Specifications:** minimal demands **Stage:** flexible, 60 seats **Casting:** Equity, non-Equity **Submission policy:** unsolicited script or videotape, synopsis, resume; query/synopsis, dialogue sample; professional recommendation; agent submission **Response:** 1-6 months **Your chances:** 1200-1500 new scripts read annually/400 one-acts produced; 200 full-length plays receive cold or staged readings **Remuneration:** no **Future commitment:** credit, percentage **Programs:** workshops, script development, internships, classes; PLAYTIME Series, New York City Playwrights' Festival (see The Theatre-Studio Programs in Special Programs) **Advice:** "Be willing to rewrite and rework with different directors."

THEATRE THREE, INC.   F-l ♪ 2d C cm

2800 Routh St., Dallas, TX 75201 (214) 871-2933 FAX (214) 871-3139 **Contact:** Jac Alder, Exec. Producer **Theatre:** professional **Works:** full-length plays, musicals **2nd productions:** yes **Special interests:** "Sophisticated comedies on socially relevant topics." **Specifications:** cast size: 6-15; no large-scale works **Stage:** modified arena, 242 seats **Casting:** Equity **Submission policy:** query/synopsis preferred; unsolicited script; cassette tape for musical; professional recommendation; agent submission; **Best time:** fall **Response:** 1 week query; 2 months script **Your chances:** 100 new scripts read annually/usually 1 produced **Remuneration:** "6%." **Future commitment:** yes **Programs:** readings, internships

THEATRE THREE PRODUCTIONS   1-

P.O. Box 512, Pt. Jefferson, NY 11777-0512 (516) 928-9100 **Contact:** Jeffrey E. Sanzel, Artistic Director **Theatre:** professional **Works:** one-acts **2nd productions:** no **Specifications:** maximum cast: 6 preferred; unit set preferred **Stage:** thrust, 100 seats **Casting:** non-Equity **Submission policy:** unsolicited script; query/synopsis **Response:** 2 months **Your chances:** 250+ new scripts read annually **Program:** Theatre Three One-Act Play Festival (see Contests)

THEATRE WEST VIRGINIA   F-l 1- Tr Ad ♪ CY 2d H 12+ ▭
P.O. Box 1205, Beckley, WV 25802 (304) 256-6800 FAX (304) 256-6807 **Contact:** Marina Dolinger, Artistic Director **Theatre:** professional, touring **Works:** full-length plays, one-acts, translations, adaptations, musicals, children's plays **2nd productions:** yes **Special interests:** "Adaptations of well known works; historical outdoor dramas; educational plays--grades K-12." **Specifications:** maximum cast: 6; no more than 2 sets **Tours:** "Educational touring--winter." **Stage:** summer: outdoor 50'x50' stage, 1385 seats **Casting:** non-Equity **Audience:** "Family-oriented." **Submission policy:** query/synopsis **Best time:** Nov. **Response:** 2 months **Your chances:** 10 new scripts read annually **Remuneration:** "Royalties and flat fee."

THEATRE X   D F-l 2d x ▭
P.O. Box 92206, Milwaukee, WI 53202 (414) 278-0555 **Contact:** Michael Ramach, Producing Director **Theatre:** professional **Works:** full-length plays **2nd productions:** yes **Special interests:** "Plays written with or for the company; avant garde." **Tours:** yes **Stage:** flexible, 99 seats **Casting:** non-Equity **Submission policy:** unsolicited script, resume; professional recommendation; commission **Response:** 6 months **Your chances:** 20 new scripts read annually/usually 1-2 produced **Remuneration:** royalty **Future commitment:** no

THEATREFEST   D F-l ♪ x
Dept. of Theatre, Montclair State Univ., Upper Montclair, NJ 07043 (201) 655-7496 FAX (201) 655-5366 **Contact:** John Wooten, Artistic Director **Theatre:** professional **Works:** full-length plays, musicals **2nd productions:** if play has not received Equity production **Special interest:** "Innovative contemporary plays; plays may be experimental and expand the boundaries of the traditional box set." **Specifications:** maximum cast: 8; single set; simple demands **Stage:** flexible, 125 seats **Casting:** Equity, non-Equity **Audience:** "Likes new plays and standard fare." **Submission policy:** 1-5 page synopsis **Best time:** Oct 1-Jan. 1 **Notification:** 1-3 months **Future commitment:** percentage, credit, options **Programs:** workshops, internships; TheatreFest National Playwriting Contest (see Contests) **Advice:** "No phone calls, please." **Comment:** Theatre may not be accepting submissions other than through contest in 1999; send SASE for policy.

THEATREVIRGINIA   F-l ♪ 2d
2800 Grove Ave., Richmond, VA 23221-2466 (804) 353-6100 FAX (804) 353-8799 **Contact:** George Black, Producing Artistic Director **Theatre:** professional **Works:** full-length plays, musicals **2nd productions:** yes **Maximum cast:** 20 **Stage:** proscenium, 500 seats **Casting:** Equity, non-Equity **Audience:** "Conservative, 'theatre savvy.'" **Submission policy:** query/synopsis, dialogue sample, resume; agent submission **Response:** 2-4 weeks if interested in query; 6-8 months solicited script **Your chances:** 20-30 new scripts read annually **Terms:** negotiable

THEATREWORKS   F-1 2d Am
1 Gold St., Hartford, CT 06103 (860) 727-4027 FAX (860) 525-0758
Contact: Steve Campo, Art. **Director Theatre:** professional **Works:** full-length plays **2nd productions:** yes **Special interest:** new American plays **Specifications:** maximum cast: 6; single or simple set; limited demands **Casting:** Equity **Stage:** thrust, 200 seats **Submission policy:** query/synopsis, dialogue sample **Response:** 3 months **Future commitment:** no

THEATREWORKS   F-l Tr Ad ♪ 2d Sp M
1100 Hamilton Ct., Menlo Park, CA 94025 (650) 463-7126, -1950 FAX (650) 463-1963 **e-mail** mail@theatreworks.org **Contact:** Jeannie Barroga, Literary Mgr. **Theatre:** semi-professional **Works:** full-length plays, translations, adaptations, musicals **2nd productions:** yes **Special interest:** "Plays that celebrate the human spirit; multiethnic casting." **Stages:** proscenium, 625 seats; thrust, 117 seats **Casting:** Equity, non-Equity **Audience:** "Wealthy, educated." **Submission policy:** full-length play or musical: unsolicited script; query/synopsis; dialogue sample; cassette tape of music (indicate whether orchestrations exist), SASP; translation/adaptation: query letter with SASP; professional recommendation; agent submission **Best time:** Jan.-Nov. **Response:** 1 month query; 4 months or longer script **Your chances:** 200 new scripts read annually/usually 1 produced **Terms:** negotiable **Advice:** "Indicate on submission if multiethnic casting is possible."

THEATREWORKS/USA   CY ♪ 2d H Cl C ⌂
151 W. 26th St. 7th Floor, New York, NY 10001 (212) 647-1100 FAX (212) 924-5377 **e-mail** Info@Theatreworksusa.org **Contact:** Barbara Pasternack, Assoc. Artistic Director **Theatre:** professional **Works:** children's plays/musicals **2nd productions:** yes **Special interests:** "History, fairy tales, classics, contemporary literature." **Specifications:** maximum cast: 5 (with doubling); set tours **Stage:** proscenium, 398 seats **Casting:** Equity; non-Equity **Audience:** 6-14 **Submission policy:** query/synopsis, dialogue sample, cassette tape, lyric sheet preferred; unsolicited script **Best time:** summer **Response:** 1 month query; 6 months script **Your chances:** 100 new scripts read annually/usually 3 produced **Remuneration:** "$1500 commission advance; 6% divided among collaborators." **Future commitment:** yes **Program:** Theatreworks/USA Commissioning Program (see Special Programs)

THEATRICAL OUTFIT   F-l Ad 2d Cl
P.O. Box 1555, Atlanta, GA 30301 (404) 577-5257 FAX (404) 577-5259 **e-mail** katewarner@theatricaloutfit.org **Contact:** Kate Warner, Mng. Dir. **Theatre:** professional **Works:** full-length plays, adaptations **2nd productions:** if work is to be reevaluated **Special interests:** new plays; classics **Stage:** proscenium, 400 seats **Casting:** Equity, non-Equity **Audience:** "All ages/interests." **Submission policy:** query/synopsis, 1st 10 pages of script, bio, SASP **Best time:** spring-summer **Response:** 2 months **Terms:** negotiable **Program:** New Play Festival (see Contests)

TIMOTHY CHILDS THEATRICAL ♪

1560 Broadway Suite 1100, New York, NY 10036 (212) 840-3900 FAX (212) 840-1973 e-mail childstim@aol.com **Contact:** Timothy Childs, President **Production company:** Broadway **Works:** "Musicals and plays with emotion and sweep." **Submission policy:** agent submission

ℜ TINFISH PRODUCTIONS F-l 1-

4223 N. Lincoln Ave., Chicago, IL 60618 (773) 549-1888 FAX same **Contact:** Dejan Avramovich, Artistic Director **Theatre:** professional **Works:** full-length plays, one-acts **Submission policy:** query/synopsis **Response:** 2 months

TODO CON NADA AKA NADA F-l 1- Ad ♪ Rv 2d

167 Ludlow St., New York, NY 10002-1520 (212) 420-1466 FAX (212) 420-1679 Contact: Aaron Beall, Exec. Director **Theatre:** professional co-producer **Works:** full-length plays, one-acts, adaptations, musicals, revues **2nd productions:** yes **Exclusive interest:** "Artists who can assemble a production." **Stages:** 4 theatres, 50-75 seats **Submission policy:** unsolicited script; videotape; query/synopsis, dialogue sample, script history, resume, SASP; professional recommendations; agent submission **Your chances:** 500+ new scripts read annually/usually 5-10 co-produced; 2-3 receive readings **Remuneration:** percentage **Future commitment:** credit **Programs:** readings, workshops, development

TOLEDO REPERTORY THEATRE F-l ♪ CY ⇨

406 Adams St., Toledo, OH 43604 (419) 243-9277 Contact: Brian Bethune, Artistic Director **Theatre:** semi-professional **Works:** full-length plays, musicals, children's plays **Special interest:** full-length plays **Tours:** children's plays **Stages:** 2 prosceniums, 250, 872 seats **Submission policy:** query/synopsis, dialogue sample; "scripts through Midwestern Playwrights Festival (see Contests)--IL, IN, MI, OH playwrights only" **Response:** 1-4 months **Remuneration:** yes **Program:** readings

TORSO THEATRE F-l 1- Tr Ad 2d cm Cl Lc

2641 N. Clyborn Ave., Chicago, IL 60614 (773) 404-5501 Contact: B. Bermingham, Producing Director **Theatre:** professional **Works:** full-length plays, one-acts, translations, adaptations **2nd productions:** "If not produced in Chicago in 10 years." **Special interests:** "Black comedies, satire, radical adaptations of classics." **Specifications:** maximum cast: 25; 1 elaborate set or multiple minimal sets **Stages:** proscenium, 200 seats; flexible studio, 100 seats **Submission policy:** unsolicited script or videotape, resume; professional recommendation; agent submission; no query/synopsis **Response:** 1-2 years **Your chances:** 175 new scripts read annually/usually 3-4 produced **Remuneration:** yes **Future commitment:** for world premiere **Advice:** "Be fearless--try to shock us!"

TOTEM POLE PLAYHOUSE/   F-l 1- ♪ 2d Fm cm
THUNDERBIRD LTD., INC.   P.O. Box 603, Fayetteville, PA
17222-0603 (717) 352-2164 FAX (717) 352-8870 **Contact:** Carl Schurr,
Producing Artistic Director **Theatre:** professional **Works:** full-length
plays, one-acts, musicals **2nd productions:** yes **Special interests:**
"Musicals and light comedies for a general audience." **Specifications:**
"No vulgarity or nudity." **Submission policy:** unsolicited script; query/
synopsis, dialogue sample; cassette tape for musical **Best time:** fall
Response: 1-2 months query; 6 months script

TOUCHSTONE THEATRE   D
321 E. 4th St., Bethlehem, PA 18105 (610) 867-1689 FAX (610) 867-
0561 **e-mail** ttheatre@aol.com **Contact:** Mark McKenna, Artistic
Director **Theatre:** professional **Exclusive interest:** ensemble pieces
created in collaboration with resident company **Stage:** 18'x20' black
box, 74 seats **Submission policy:** query/proposal **Response:** 1 month

♫ **TRACER PRODUCTIONS**   F-l
P.O. Box 13861, Denver, CO 80201 (303) 430-2907 **Theatre:** professional **Works:** full-length plays **2nd productions:** no **Stages:** 3 spaces,
120, 85, 70 seats **Submission policy:** query/synopsis, dialogue sample

TRIANGLE THEATRE COMPANY   F-l Ad ♪ Rv 2d C Sp
316 E. 88th St., New York, NY 10128 (212) 860-7244 FAX (212) 289-
4155 **Contact:** John Margulis, Artistic Director **Theatre:** off off Broadway **Works:** full-length plays, adaptations, musicals, revues **2nd productions:** if not previously produced in NYC **Special interests:** "Social,
moral, spiritual issues." **Stage:** proscenium, 72-99 seats **Casting:** Equity
Submission policy: unsolicited script or query/synopsis, resume **Response:** 1 year **Your chances:** 20 new scripts read annually/usually
none produced **Remuneration:** $500 **Future commitment:** "Varies."
Programs: readings, workshops **Advice:** "Keep it small. Be patient."

♫ **TRIARTS**
P.O. Box 2273, New York, NY 10108 (212) 802-9115 FAX (212) 924-
4177 **Contact:** Thomas Morrissey, Artistic Director **Theatre:** professional **Works:** inquire **Casting:** Equity **Submission policy:** send SASE
for guidelines/interests **Comment:** Summer address is Tri-State Center
for the Arts, P.O. Box 712, Pine Plains, NY 12567; (518) 398-SHOW.

TRINITY HOUSE THEATRE   D F-l 1- Tr Ad ♪ CY 2d C † ⌂
38840 W. Six Mile Rd., Livonia, MI 48152-2605 (734) 464-6302
Contact: Jim Leach, Exec. Director **Theatre:** community **Works:** full-
length plays, one-acts, translations, adaptations, musicals, children's
plays **2nd productions:** yes **Special interests:** "Developing playwrights; issues; Biblical prespectives." **Specifications:** maximum cast:
14, fewer preferred; no more than 3 small sets; many plays tour **Stage:**

flexible proscenium, 100 seats **Audience:** "Mostly Christian, middle class." **Submission policy:** unsolicited script **Best time:** summer-fall **Response:** 90 days **Your chances:** 100 new scripts read annually/ usually 1 produced **Remuneration:** "Royalty; more if playwright is part of the process." **Programs:** readings, workshops, development

TRINITY REPERTORY COMPANY F-l Tr Ad 2d
201 Washington St., Providence, RI 02903 (401) 521-1100 e-mail info @trinityrep.com **Contact:** Craig Watson, Literary Mgr. **Theatre:** professional **Works:** full-length plays, translations, adaptations **2nd productions:** yes **Stages:** 2 thrusts, 440 and 297 seats **Submission policy:** query/synopsis, dialogue sample, resume (addressed to Literary Mgr.); agent submission **Response:** 3 months **Future commitment:** negotiable

THE TROIKA ORGANIZATION ♪
1700 Rockville Pike Suite 280, Rockville, MD 20852 (301) 468-6800 FAX (301) 468-0125 Production company: professional **Works:** musicals **Submission policy:** unsolicited script, query/synopsis; cassette tape of music; agent submission; professional recommendation

TRUSTUS THEATRE COMPANY F-l 1- 2d C cm dr
P.O. Box 11721, Columbia, SC 29211-1721 (803) 254-9732 FAX (803) 771-9153 e-mail Trustus88@aol.com **Contact:** Tim Gardner, Literary Mgr. **Theatre:** professional **Works:** full-length plays, one-acts **2nd productions:** yes **Special interests:** "Contemporary and alternative comedy and drama; issues." **Specifications:** maximum cast: 8; no more than 2 sets **Stage:** flexible, 100 seats **Casting:** Equity, non-Equity, students **Submission policy:** request guidelines **Best time:** Jan. 1-Mar. 1 only **Response:** 3-6 months **Remuneration:** negotiable **Future commitment:** no **Programs:** staged readings, Late Night Series; South Carolina Playwrights' Festival (see Contests)

TURNIP THEATRE COMPANY F-l Rg
145 W. 46th St., New York, NY 10036 (212) 768-4016 Contact: Literary Committee **Theatre:** professional **Works:** full-length plays **2nd productions:** no **Exclusive interest:** "NYC-area writers." **Specifications:** cast size: 4-10; simple set **Stage:** black box, 74-90 seats **Submission policy:** query/synopsis, dialogue sample; professional recommendation **Best time:** Aug.-Nov. **Response:** 2-4 months **Program:** New York City 15 Minute Play Festival (see Contests)

TWO ROADS THEATRE/ F-l 1- Tr ♪ Cy Rv 2d ⌐ cm
WEST END ARTISTS THEATRE CO. **18034 Ventura Blvd. #291, Encino, CA 91316 (818) 766-9318 FAX (818) 762-9840 Contact:** Edmund Gaynes, Producing Art. Director **Theatre:** professional **Works:** full-length plays, one-acts, translations, musicals, children's plays, revues **2nd productions:** yes **Specifications:** maximum cast: 15; "we pro-

duce at many venues, of all sizes, in Los Angeles, New York and throughout the country" **Stage:** Two Roads Theatre, 48 seats **Casting:** Equity, non-Equity **Audience:** "Emphasis on entertainment industry professionals; comedies and musicals are most popular." **Submission policy:** unsolicited script; videotape; query/synopsis, dialogue sample, resume; agent submission **Your chances:** 100 new scripts read annually/usually 2 produced **Remuneration:** 6% of gross **Future commitment:** percentage, credit, options **Programs:** staged readings, workshop productions, script development **Advice:** "Be willing to cooperate with a director regarding rewrites during the course of production."

UBU REPERTORY THEATER   F-l Tr Ad 2d Fr Cl C Rs
15 W. 28th St., New York, NY 10001 (212) 679-7540 FAX (212) 679-2033 **e-mail** uburep@spacelab.net **Contact:** Françoise Kourilsky, Artistic Director **Theatre:** professional **Works:** full-length plays, one-acts, translations, adaptations **2nd productions:** yes **Exclusive interests:** "French-speaking writers; translations of contemporary French-language works; French 'modern classics' in French and English." **Specifications:** maximum cast: 6; single set; no 'commercial' theatre; "works must have originally been written in French" **Stage:** proscenium, 99 seats **Casting:** Equity **Audience:** "Interested in francophone culture, social issues, new works." **Submission policy:** unsolicited script; query/synopsis; professional recommendation; agent submission; "translations may be submitted with the original" **Best time:** summer **Response:** 1 month query; 3 months script **Your chances:** 200 new scripts read annually/usually 4 produced **Remuneration:** royalty **Future commitment:** no **Programs:** staged readings, referrals, residencies, library, publishing (see listing in Publishers)

UKIAH PLAYERS THEATRE   F-l 1- ♪ Rv 2d ▭
1041 Low Gap Rd., Ukiah, CA 95482 (707) 462-9226 FAX (707) 462-1790 **Contact:** Michael Ducharme, Exec. Director **Theatre:** semi-professional **Works:** full-length plays, one-acts, musicals, revues **2nd productions:** yes **Specifications:** small cast, simple set preferred **Tours:** yes **Stage:** proscenium, 138 seats **Submission policy:** query/synopsis **Response:** 2 weeks **Programs:** staged readings, workshops; New American Comedy Festival (see Contests)

UNICORN THEATRE   F-l 2d C
3828 Main St., Kansas City, MO 64111 (816) 531-7529 Ext. 18 FAX (816) 531-0421 **Contact:** Herman Wilson, Literary Asst. **Theatre:** professional **Works:** full-length plays **2nd productions:** if not previously produced by Equity theatres **Special interest:** "Issues." **Specifications:** maximum cast: 10; settings after 1950; small cast; simple sets **Stage:** thrust, 150 seats **Casting:** Equity, non-Equity **Audience:** "Inquisitive; like provocative, disturbing plays on contemporary issues." **Submission policy:** query/synopsis, resume, dialogue sample **Best time:** before

Apr. 15 **Response:** 2-4 weeks **Your chances:** 400 new scripts read annually/usually 1 produced, latest in Apr. 1998 **Remuneration:** royalty **Future commitment:** percentage, credit **Program:** Unicorn Theatre National Playwright's Award (see Contests)

UNIVERSITY OF ALABAMA NEW PLAY- D F-l Tr Ad ♪ Rs
WRIGHTS PROGRAM Theatre & Dance, Univ. of Alabama, P.O. Box 870239, Tuscaloosa, AL 35487-0239 (205) 348-9032 FAX (205) 348-9048 e-mail pcastagn@woodsquad.as.ua.edu **Contact:** Paul Castagno, Director/Dramaturg **Theatre:** university **Works:** full-length plays, translations, adaptations, musicals **2nd productions:** yes **Special interests:** "Development; experienced writers; challenges for graduate actors." **Stages:** mainstage, 338 seats; studio lab, 100 seats **Submission policy:** unsolicited script; query/synopsis; proposal for workshop **Best time:** Sept.-Apr. **Response:** 6 months **Your chances:** 200 new scripts read annually/usually 2 produced **Remuneration:** stipend, travel, expenses **Future commitment:** writer may be required to offer workshops **Comment:** Production is considered for entry in Kennedy Center American College Theatre Festival (see Contests).

UNIVERSITY OF MICHIGAN THEATRE F-l 1-
Theatre Dept., Univ. of Michigan, Flint, MI 48502 (810) 762-3349 FAX (810) 762-3687 e-mail friesen_l@crob.flint.umich.edu **Contact:** Lauren Friesen, Director of Playwriting **Works:** full-length plays, one-acts **Specifications:** maximum cast: 20; single set **Stages:** thrust, 410 seats; black box, 70 seats **Casting:** students **Audience:** university, community **Submission policy:** unsolicited script **Best time:** Sept.-Jan. **Response:** 1-6 months **Advice:** *"Professional Playscript Format only!"*

UNIVERSITY OF MINNESOTA THEATRE F-l ♪
Dept. of Theatre, 141 MPAC/10 University Dr., Duluth, MN 55812 (218) 726-6313 FAX (218) 726-6798 **Contact:** Script Selection **Theatre:** university **Works:** full-length plays, musicals **Specifications:** "Balance of male and female roles." **Casting:** students **Audience:** university, community **Submission policy:** unsolicited script **Best time:** fall **Response:** 2-4 months **Future commitment:** no

UNIVERSITY OF MOBILE THEATRE F-l 1- ♪
P.O. Box 13220, Mobile, AL 36633 (334) 675-5990 Ext. 383 **Contact:** Diane Murphree, Chair, Theatre Dept. **Works:** full-length plays, one-acts, musicals **Maximum cast:** 12 **Audience:** university, community **Submission policy:** unsolicited script, cassette tape for musical

UNIVERSITY OF NEBRASKA F-l 1- Ad ♪ 2d Rg
AT KEARNEY THEATRE Speech Communication & Theatre Arts, UNK, 905 W. 25th St., Kearney, NE 68849-3230 (308) 865-8406 e-mail greenj@platte.unk. edu **Contact:** Artistic Director **Theatre:** university **Works:** full-length plays, one-acts, adaptations, musicals **2nd**

productions: yes **Special interest:** "Great Plains/Midwest subjects."
Specifications: maximum cast: 15; single set **Stages:** proscenium, 350
seats; flexible amphitheatre, 200 seats; black box, 200 seats **Casting:**
non-Equity **Audience:** students, community **Submission policy:** unsolicited script or query/synopsis, **Best time:** Dec.-Mar. **Your chances:**
200 new scripts read annually/usually 7 produced **Remuneration:**
"$75/$50." **Programs:** staged readings, workshops, internships, resi-
encies, Great Platte River Playwrights Festival (see Contests)

UNIVERSITY OF TEXAS AT TYLER THEATRE   F-l 1- ♪
Theatre Prog., 3900 University Blvd., Tyler, TX 75701 (903) 566-7425
Contact: James Hatfield, Chairman **Works:** full-length plays, one-acts,
musicals **Special interests:** "Unproduced plays less than 3 years old."
Specifications: limited demands and orchestration **Casting:** non-Equity,
students **Submission policy:** unsolicited script **Best time:** summer-
early fall **Response:** 6 months **Future commitment:** credit

UNIVERSITY OF TOLEDO THEATRE   F-l 1- ♪
Dept. of Theatre, Film & Dance, Univ. of Toledo, Toledo, OH 43606
(419) 530-2202 FAX (419) 530-8439 **Contact:** Chairman **Works:** full-
length plays, one-acts, musicals **Specifications:** no fly system **Stages:**
black box, proscenium **Casting:** students, community **Audience:** university, urban community **Submission policy:** unsolicited script **Best time:**
fall **Response:** 6 months **Future commitment:** no

UTAH SHAKESPEAREAN FESTIVAL   See Special Programs.

VALENCIA CHARACTER CO.   F-l Rg
Valencia Comm. College, P.O. Box 3028, Orlando, FL 32802 (407)
299-5000 Ext. 2296 FAX (407) 277-0621 e-mail jgagne@valencia.
cc.fl.us **Contact:** Julie Gagne, Artistic Director **Theatre:** college **Works:**
full-length plays **2nd productions:** "No, except if produced in staged
readings only." **Exclusive interest:** Florida playwrights **Specifications:** works suitable for college actors and audience **Stage:** black box
Submission policy: unsolicited script **Best time:** Jun.-Sept. **Response:**
3 months **Program:** workshops

VENTURE THEATRE   1p 2d C M
18 S. 7th St., Philadelphia, PA 19106 (215) 923-2766 FAX (215) 923-
5927 **Contact:** Betty P. Lindley, Exec. Director **Theatre:** professional
Works: 1-5 person shows **2nd productions:** yes **Exclusive interest:**
"Cultural/ethnic characters, themes." **Casting:** Equity **Submission
policy:** query/synopsis, 1st 26 pages of dialogue **Response:** 6 months
Future commitment: varies

VERMONT STAGE COMPANY   F-l
P.O. Box 874, Burlington, VT 05402 (802) 656-4351 FAX (802) 656-

0349 **Contact:** Blake Robison, Producing Art. Director **Theatre:** professional **Works:** full-length plays **Stage:** thrust, 300 seats **Submission policy:** query/synopsis **Response:** 1 month query; varies for solicited script **Program:** VT Young Playwrights Project (see Special Programs)

VERONICA'S VEIL THEATRE   F-l Tr Ad 2d CY † Sn Fm W ⌐
St. Joseph and St. Michael's Rectory, 1314 Central Ave., Union City,
NJ 07085 (201) 864-7825 **Contact:** Deacon Barrett **Theatre:** community
Works: full-length plays, translations, adaptations **2nd productions:**
yes **Special interest:** "Religious themes; nothing controversial." **Specifications:** "Mostly women's roles; limited set changes." **Tours:** yes **Stage:**
proscenium, 1000 seats **Audience:** "Church groups, seniors, school children." **Submission policy:** unsolicited script, synopsis; videotape; query/
synopsis, dialogue sample, resume; professional recommendation; agent
submission **Response:** 1 year **Remuneration:** negotiable

VICTORY GARDENS THEATER   F-l Ad ♪ 2d Rg ⌐
2257 N. Lincoln Ave., Chicago, IL 60614 (312) 549-5788 **Contact:**
Sandy Shinner, Assoc. Artistic Director **Theatre:** professional **Works:**
full-length plays, adaptations, small-cast musicals **2nd productions:** yes
Special interest: "Chicago playwrights." **Specifications:** maximum cast:
10 preferred; simple set **Tours:** yes **Stages:** 2 mainstages, 220 seats each;
2 studios, 60 seats each **Submission policy:** unsolicited script from
Chicago-area writer; query/synopsis, 10-page dialogue sample from
other writer; professional recommendation; agent submission **Best time:**
Mar.-Jun. **Response:** 1 month query; 6 months script **Your chances:** 800
new scripts read annually/3-4 produced **Remuneration:** "Standard
royalty." **Programs:** staged readings, workshops; Victory Gardens Playwrights Ensemble (see Special Programs)

VILLAR-HAUSER THEATRE CO.   F-l 1- 2d dr Rg
11 Charlton St., New York, NY 10014 (212) 255-3940 FAX (212) 255-
3729 **Contact:** Ludovica Villar-Hauser, Artistic Director **Theatre:** professional **Works:** full-length plays, one-acts **2nd productions:** yes **2nd
productions:** yes **Exclusive interest:** "Dramas by New York City-area
playwrights." **Submission policy:** unsolicited script **Response:** 3
months **Program:** workshops

♫ **VINEYARD PLAYHOUSE**   F-l Tr Ad CY M C Am
P.O. Box 2452, 24 Church St., Vineyard Haven, MA 02568 (508) 693-
6450 **Contact:** Ms. M. J. Munafo, Artistic Director **Theatre:** professional **Works:** full-length plays, translations, adaptations, children's
plays **Special interests:** "Cultural diversity; contemporary social
issues; American works." **Specifications:** maximum cast: 10; simple sets
Stage: black box, 120 seats **Submission policy:** query/brief synopsis;
professional recommendation; agent submission **Response:** only if interested **Advice:** Most scripts are solicited directly from writer or agent.

VINEYARD THEATRE   F-l ♪ 2d po C cm x
108 E. 15th St., New York, NY 10003 (212) 353-3366 FAX (212) 353-3803 **Contact:** Douglas Aibel, Artistic Director **Theatre:** professional **Works:** full-length plays, musicals **2nd productions:** yes **Special interests:** "Poetic quality; unique incorporation of music; musicals with strong narrative quality; political themes; dark comedy; eccentric forms." **Maximum cast:** 10-12 **Stages:** flexible, 120-130 seats; thrust, 70± seats **Submission policy:** query/synopsis, dialogue sample, cassette tape for musical, resume **Response:** 6 months **Future commitment:** negotiable **Program:** Vineyard Theatre Lab Program (see Special Programs)

VINNETTE CARROLL REPERTORY CO.   F-l 1- ♪ 2d M
P.O. Box 030473, 503 SE 6th St., Ft. Lauderdale, FL 33303 (954) 462-2424 **Contact:** Vinnette Carroll, Artistic Director **Theatre:** professional **Works:** full-length plays, one-acts, musicals **2nd productions:** yes **Special interest:** multiracial casting **Specifications:** maximum cast: 8; minimal set **Submission policy:** query/synopsis **Response:** 4 months **Future commitment:** "Possibly."

THE VIRGINIA AVENUE PROJECT   1- CY 12+ Mb Y
1653 18th St. #2, Santa Monica, CA 90404 (310) 828-7443 **Contact:** Leigh Curran **Works:** one-act children's plays **Exclusive interest:** works for young actors (6-18) **Submission policy:** unsolicited script; query/synopsis, dialogue sample **Program:** membership program for adult playwrights interested in working with young writers (inquire)

VIRGINIA STAGE COMPANY F-l 1- Tr Ad ♪ CY 2d Rg ▭
P.O. Box 3770, Norfolk, VA 23514 (757) 627-6988 FAX (757) 628-5958 **Contact:** Kenton Yeager, Assoc. Art. Director **Theatre:** professional **Works:** full-length plays, one-acts, translations, adaptations, musicals, children's plays **2nd productions:** yes **Special interest:** VA writers **Maximum cast:** 8 **Tours:** yes **Stages:** proscenium, 700 seats; flexible, 99 seats **Casting:** Equity, non-Equity **Submission policy:** query/synopsis, dialogue sample, videotape, resume; agent submission **Best time:** May-Sept. **Response:** 2 weeks query; 6 months solicited script **Terms:** negotiable

VIV ENTERPRISES   F-l ♪ my
1650 Broadway #601, New York, NY 10019 (212) 586-1616 FAX (212) 765-0207 **Contact:** Nan Pearlman, Producer **Production company:** professional **Works:** full-length plays, musicals **Special interests:** musicals, mysteries **Submission policy:** unsolicited script; query/synopsis; agent submission; professional recommendation

VOICE & VISION THEATRE   F-l 1- Tr Ad ♪ CY W mm
220 E. 4th St., New York, NY 10009 (212) 502-1151 **Contact:** Marya Mazor, Artistic Director **Theatre:** professional **Works:** full-length plays, one-acts, translations, adaptations, musicals, children's plays

Special interests: women writers only; young casts; multidisciplinary works **Stage:** proscenium, 99-250 seats **Submission policy:** unsolicited script **Response:** 1 year **Program:** see listing in Special Programs

VORTEX REPERTORY COMPANY   F-l 1- Tr Ad 2d
2307 Manor Rd., Austin, TX 78722-2135 (512) 478-LAVA FAX (512) 472-8644 Contact: Patricia Wappner, Literary Mgr. **Theatre:** professional **Works:** full-length plays, one-acts, translations, adaptations **2nd productions:** yes **Special interest:** "New territory." **Specifications:** minimal demands **Stages:** thrust, 90 seats; outdoor, 130 seats **Casting:** non-Equity **Submission policy:** unsolicited script, resume, script history; videotape; query/synopsis, 15-page dialogue sample; professional recommendation **Best time:** spring, fall **Response:** 3 months query; 6 months script **Your chances:** 35 new scripts read annually/usually 5 produced, 2-3 receive staged readings **Remuneration:** negotiable

WALNUT STREET THEATRE   F-l Tr Ad ♪ Rv 2d Sp Fm
9th & Walnut Sts., Philadelphia, PA 19107 (215) 574-3550 Ext. 515 FAX (215) 574-3598 Contact: Beverly Elliott, Literary Mgr. **Theatre:** professional **Works:** full-length plays, translations, adaptations, musicals, revues **2nd productions:** yes **Special interest:** uplifting material **Specifications:** maximum cast: 14 mainstage; 4 studio; single set preferred **Stages:** proscenium, 1052 seats; black box, 80 seats **Casting:** Equity **Audience:** "Conservative; popular appeal." **Submission policy:** query/synopsis, 10-14 page dialogue sample, SASP **Best time:** winter **Response:** 4-6 months **Your chances:** 450 new scripts read annually/5 receive staged readings **Remuneration:** negotiable

WASHINGTON STAGE GUILD   F-l Tr Ad 2d
4048 7th St. NE #4, Washington, DC 20017-1939 (202) 529-2084 FAX (202) 529-2740 Contact: William Largess, Dramaturg **Theatre:** professional **Works:** full-length plays, translations, adaptations **2nd productions:** yes **Special interests:** "Literary quality; neglected works; new translations." **Specifications:** maximum cast: 10; no more than 2 sets **Casting:** Equity, non-Equity **Stage:** flexible, 150 seats **Submission policy:** query/synopsis, resume **Response:** 6 months **Remuneration:** royalty **Future commitment:** credit **Program:** staged readings

WATERLOO COMMUNITY F-l 1- Tr Ad CY 2d Lc cm ♥ Rs
PLAYHOUSE/BLACK HAWK CHILDREN'S THEATRE
P.O. Box 433, Waterloo, IA 50704 (319) 235-0367 FAX (319) 235-7489 Contact: Charles Stilwill, Mng. Artistic Director **Theatre:** community **Works:** full-length plays, one-acts, translations, adaptations, children's plays **2nd productions:** yes **Specifications:** maximum cast: 50 preferred; no fly space **Stage:** proscenium **Audience:** "32% seniors; prefers comedy." **Submission policy:** unsolicited script **Response:** 6-10 months turndown; 1-4 years production **Your chances:** 400 new scripts read an-

nually/usually 1-3 produced, latest in Oct. 1998 **Remuneration:** royalty; travel, housing; possible honorarium **Future commitment:** credit **Programs:** readings, development, residencies **Advice:** "Good adaptations of well-known books and stories for our Children's Theatre and our holiday show, and good plays for our adult theatre."

WATERTOWER THEATRE, INC. F-l 1- ♪ CY
15650 Addison Rd., Addison, TX 75248 (972) 450-6220 FAX (972) 450-6244 **Contact:** Gayle Pearson, Producing Director **Theatre:** professional **Works:** full-length plays, one-acts, musicals, children's plays **Special interest:** "Creative, theatrical use of our space." **Stage:** flexible, 100-300 seats **Audience:** "Mixed, urban and suburban." **Submission policy:** unsolicited script **Response:** 2 months

WAVECREST PRODUCTIONS F-l ♪ cm dr
377 W. 11th St., #4A, New York, NY 10014 (212) 633-6159 FAX same **Contact:** Pamela Koslow **Production company:** professional **Works:** full-length plays, musicals **Special interests:** "Comedies and dramas." **Submission policy:** agent submission

WEST COAST ENSEMBLE F-l 1- ♪ 2d D
P.O. Box 38728, Los Angeles, CA 90038 (310) 449-1447 FAX (310) 453-2254 **Contact:** Les Hanson, Artistic Director **Theatre:** professional **Works:** full-length plays, one-acts, musicals **2nd productions:** "If reworked." **Specifications:** maximum cast: 12; single set **Stage:** proscenium, 80 seats **Casting:** Equity, non-Equity **Submission policy:** unsolicited script; query/synopsis **Best time:** full-length: Jan.-Jun.; one-act: Sept.-Dec. **Response:** 2 weeks query; 6 months script **Your chances:** one-act: 700 new scripts read annually/usually 6-9 produced; full-length: 600 new scripts read annually/usually 2 produced **Remuneration:** "$500 for full-length, or negotiable royalty." **Future commitment:** credit **Programs:** workshop productions, script development; West Coast Ensemble Competitions (see Contests); West Coast Ensemble Playwrights Unit (see Special Programs)

WESTBETH THEATRE CENTER F-l 1- ♪ 2d D
151 Bank St., New York, NY 10014 (212) 691-2272 FAX (212) 924-7185 **Contact:** Director, Playwright Program **Theatre:** off and off off Broadway **Works:** full-length plays, one-acts, 10-minute plays, musicals **2nd productions:** "If not produced in New York and playwright seeks further development." **Specifications:** maximum cast: 10; 1-2 simple sets; simple costumes **Stage:** black box, 60-99 seats **Audience:** "Downtown NYC, Greenwich Village." **Submission policy:** query/synopsis, resume, cassette tape for musical **Response:** 3 months query; 4 months solicited script **Future commitment:** credit, possible percentage **Program:** Westbeth Playwright Program (see Special Programs)

THE WESTERN STAGE   F-l Ad ♪ CY Rv Lc ▭
156 Homestead Ave., Salinas, CA 93901 (831) 755-6990 FAX (831) 755-6954 **Contact:** Joyce L. Sherry, Assoc. Art. Director **Theatre:** professional **Works:** full-length plays, adaptations, musicals, children's plays, revues **2nd productions:** yes **Special interests:** "Adaptations of works of literary significance; large casts." **Tours:** yes **Stages:** proscenium, 500 seats; thrust, 101 seats; cabaret, 250 seats **Casting:** Equity, non-Equity, students **Audience:** "Sophisticated, eclectic tastes." **Submission policy:** query/synopsis, resume, cassette tape for musical, permission for adaptation; commission **Best time:** fall-spring **Response:** 1 week query; 2-3 months script **Your chances:** 300 new scripts read annually/usually 1-6 produced **Terms:** negotiable

W.H.A.T. WELLFLEET HARBOR ACTORS' THEATRE
P.O. Box 797, Wellfleet, MA 02667 (508) 349-6835 **e-mail** jz@c4.net **Contact:** Jeff Zinn, Co-Artistic Director **Theatre:** professional This theatre is not open to submissions in 1999; see *The Playwright's Companion 2000* or inquire for future plans.

WHITEHEAD-STEVENS ASSOCIATES   F-l ♪
1501 Broadway, New York, NY 10036 (212) 354-8350 FAX (212) 768-4614 **Production company:** professional **Works:** full-length plays, musicals **Submission policy:** query/synopsis; agent submission; professional recommendation

THE WILL GEER THEATRICUM   F-l Tr Ad ♪ 2d
BOTANICUM   P.O. Box 1222, Topanga, CA 90290 (310) 455-2322 FAX (310) 455-3724 **Contact:** Ellen Geer, Artistic Director **Theatre:** professional **Works:** full-length plays, translations, adaptations, musicals **2nd productions:** yes **Cast size:** 4-10 **Stage:** outdoor arena, 350 seats **Submission policy:** query/synopsis, dialogue sample, cassette tape for musical **Best time:** Sept. **Response:** 3-4 weeks query; 6 months solicited script **Your chances:** 150 new scripts read annually/usually 1 produced **Remuneration:** negotiable **Future commitment:** no

WILLIAMSTOWN THEATRE FESTIVAL   F-l Ad ♪ 2d
Sept.-May 100 E. 17th St. 3rd Floor, New York, NY 10003 (212) 228-2286 FAX (212) 228-9091; **Jun.-Aug. P.O. Box 517, Williamstown, MA 01267-0517** (413) 458-3200 FAX (413) 458-3147 **Contact:** Elizabeth Whitaker, Literary Mgr. **Theatre:** professional **Works:** full-length plays, adaptations, musicals **2nd productions:** yes **Specifications:** maximum cast: 14, 10 for musical; simple set for 2nd stage **Stages:** proscenium, 521 seats; thrust, 96 seats **Submission policy:** agent submission **Best time:** Sept. 1-Feb. 15 **Response:** several months **Your chances:** 300-400 new scripts read annually/usually 4 produced **Remuneration:** "Small fee." **Future commitment:** yes **Program:** Williamstown Theatre Festival Staged Readings (see Special Programs)

WILLOWS THEATRE CO.   F-l Tr Ad ♪ 2d cm C Fm
1975 Diamond Blvd. #A-20, Concord, CA 94520 (925) 798-1300 FAX
(925) 676-5276 e-mail willowsth@aol.com **Contact:** Richard H. Elliott,
Artistic Director **Theatre:** professional **Works:** full-length plays, translations, adaptations, musicals **2nd productions:** yes **Special interests:**
"Commercially viable, small-medium musicals; witty comedies; contemporary edge; no dramas in 1999." **Specifications:** maximum cast: 15, 9
musicians; unit or simple set; no fly, limited wing space **Stage:** proscenium, 203 seats **Casting:** Equity, non-Equity **Audience:** "Suburban;
'safe' fare." **Submission policy:** query/synopsis; professional recommendation; agent submission **Best time:** Apr.-May only **Response** 2-3
months **Your chances:** 400 new scripts read annually/usually 1 produced **Terms:** negotiable **Program:** workshops

THE WILMA THEATRE   F-l Tr Ad ♪ 2d po mm ⤸
265 Broad St., Philadelphia, PA 19107 (215) 893-9456 FAX (215) 893-
0895 e-mail wilma@libertynet.org **Contact:** Michael Hollinger, Literary
Mgr. **Theatre:** professional **Works:** full-length plays, translations, adaptations, musicals **2nd productions:** yes **Special interests:** "Poetic dimensions; multimedia." **Specifications:** maximum cast: 12 preferred; simple
sets **Tours:** yes **Stage:** proscenium, 300 seats **Casting:** Equity **Audience:** "Sophisticated adults." **Submission policy:** professional recommendation; agent submission **Response:** 2-4 months query; 9-12 months
solicited script **Your chances:** 250 new scripts read annually/usually 1
produced **Terms:** negotiable **Programs:** readings, classes

WINGS THEATRE COMPANY   F-l ♪ 2d g/l
154 Christopher St., New York, NY 10014 (212) 627-2960 FAX (212)
462-0024 **Contact:** Jeffrey Corrick, Artistic Director **Theatre:** off off
Broadway **Works:** full-length plays, musicals **2nd productions:** yes
Exclusive interests: "Plays must be appropriate for either (1) New
Musicals Series--full-length musicals on any subject or theme, or (2) Gay
Plays Series--plays or musicals with major gay characters or themes."
Stage: small flexible, 75 seats **Submission policy:** unsolicited script,
cassette tape for musical; agent submission **Response:** Jul.-Aug. **Your
chances:** 500 new scripts read annually/usually 8-10 produced
Remuneration: "$100 advance; 5%."

WOMAN THEATRE INC.   F-l 1- 2d W ⤸ $
948 N. 8th St., Philadelphia, PA 19123 (215) 413-1950 FAX **Contact:**
Artistic Director **Theatre:** professional **Works:** full-length plays, one-
acts **2nd productions:** yes **Exclusive interests:** "Women playwrights,
women's issues." **Maximum cast:** 6 **Tours:** yes **Casting:** non-Equity
Submission policy: unsolicited script, $10 reading fee **Best time:**
summer **Response:** 6 months **Your chances:** 50 new scripts read
annually/usually 1 produced, latest in Sept. 1997 **Remuneration:**
negotiable **Future commitment:** credit, options **Programs:** readings,
staged readings, workshop productions, script development, internships

THE WOMEN'S PROJECT AND   Mb F-l ♪ Rv W
PRODUCTIONS   55 West End Ave., New York, NY 10023 (212)
765-1706 FAX (212) 765-2024 **Contact:** Lisa McNulty, Literary Mgr.
Theatre: professional, membership **Works:** full-length plays, musicals,
revues **Exclusive interest:** "Plays by women." **Stage:** 199 seats
Casting: Equity **Submission policy:** query/synopsis, dialogue sample,
resume; agent submission **Response:** 2-4 weeks query; 3-6 months
solicited script **Your chances:** 500 new scripts read annually/usually 3
produced **Remuneration:** yes **Programs:** staged readings, workshops,
Playwrights Lab; New American Theater School (see Special Programs)

WOMEN'S REPERTORY PROJECT   See Stages Repertory Theatre
Festivals in Contests.

THE WOODEN O DRAMA STUDIO   Los Angeles   Mail
addressed to this theatre has been returned as undeliverable; no phone
number is listed.

WOOLLY MAMMOTH THEATRE CO.   F-l Tr Ad 2d x
1401 Church St. NW, Washington, DC 20005 (202) 234-6130 FAX
(202) 667-0904 **e-mail** gaowoolly@aol.com **Contact:** Gary Oiler, Literary Mgr. **Theatre:** professional **Works:** full-length plays, translations,
adaptations **2nd productions:** yes **Special interest:** "Off-beat, non-
realistic works." **Specifications:** maximum cast: 8; minimal set **Stage:**
thrust, 132 seats **Submission policy:** unsolicited script **Response:** 6-12
months **Remuneration:** negotiable **Future commitment:** no

THE WOOSTER GROUP   P.O. Box 654 Canal St. Station, New
York, NY 10013 (212) 966-9797 FAX (212) 226-6576 **Contact:** Kim
Whitener, Mng. Director   This theatre develops its own work and is no
longer open to submissions.

WORCESTER FOOTHILLS   F-l Tr Ad ♪ 2d Fm
THEATRE CO. 100 Front St. Suite 137, Worcester, MA 01608 (508)
754-3314 FAX (508) 767-0676 **Contact:** Marc P. Smith, Artistic Director
Theatre: professional **Works:** full-length plays, translations, adaptations, small-scale musicals **2nd productions:** yes **Special interest:**
"Plays for a multigenerational audience." **Specifications:** maximum cast:
10 preferred; single or simple set; "no strong language or gratuitous
violence" **Stage:** proscenium, 349 seats **Submission policy:** query/
synopsis **Response:** 3 months query; 4 months solicited script

WPA THEATRE   F-l ♪ C Am
519 W. 23rd St., New York, NY 10011 (212) 206-0523 **Contact:** Kyle
Renick, Artistic Director **Theatre:** professional **Works:** full-length
plays, musicals **Special interest:** "Contemporary American realism;
issues." **Specifications:** maximum cast: 8; unit set **Stage:** proscenium,

122 seats **Submission policy:** agent submission; alumni referral **Response:** 6-12 months **Your chances:** 100 new scripts read annually/ usually 4 produced **Remuneration:** $2600 **Future commitment:** yes

YALE REPERTORY THEATRE   F-l Tr Ad 2d Cl
P.O. Box 208244, New Haven, CT 06520-8244 (203) 432-1560 FAX (203) 432-1550 e-mail catherine.sheehy@yale.edu **Contact:** Resident Dramaturg **Theatre:** professional **Works:** full-length plays, translations, adaptations **2nd productions:** yes **Special interest:** "New translations of classics and foreign plays." **Stages:** proscenium, 654 seats; modified thrust, 487 seats **Submission policy:** query/synopsis, resume, 10-page dialogue sample; agent submission **Response:** 6 weeks query; 3 months solicited script **Terms:** negotiable

THE YORK THEATRE COMPANY   ♪ Rv 2d D
Theatre at St. Peter's Church, 619 Lexington Ave, New York, NY 10022-4610 (212) 935-5820 **Contact:** Literary Dept. **Theatre:** off Broadway **Works:** small-cast musicals/musical revues **2nd productions:** for collaborative development **Special interests:** small-cast musicals; plays with music **Stage:** flexible, 148 seats **Submission policy:** send SASE for guidelines **Response:** 6-8 months **Remuneration/commitment:** no

ZACHARY SCOTT THEATRE CENTER   Austin, TX
This theatre is no longer open to submissions.

ZEITGEIST THEATRE CO.   F-l 2d
8201 Encino Ave., Northridge, CA 91325 (818) 343-6967 **Contact:** John and Linda Martin **Theatre:** professional **Works:** full-length plays **2nd productions:** no **Submission policy:** phone or send SASE for guidelines **Program:** Writers Workshop

ZOLLO PRODUCTIONS, INC.   C
257 W. 52nd St. 2nd Floor, New York, NY 10019 (212) 957-1300 FAX (212) 957-1315 **Contact:** Frederick M. Zollo, Producer **Production company:** Broadway **Special interest:** "Social problems." **Submission policy:** query/synopsis; agent submission

The following companies and producers have recently issued calls for scripts for specific projects. As interests, policies, and deadlines may change, we advise writers to inquire before submitting scripts.

ARTEMIS ASSOCIATES 545 Eighth Ave. Suite 401, New York, NY 10018 New full-length plays not produced in NYC; modern settings and themes preferred; cast of 2 women, 1 man minimum; maximum cast: 8

BARKING LEGS THEATER 1307 Dodds Ave., Chattanooga, TN 37404 (423) 624-5347 **Contact:** Koren Gaines, Development Coord. Unproduced one-acts by women playwrights living in the Southeast

THE BAUM HOUSE   24-45 N. Lincoln, Chicago, IL 60614   New plays not produced in Chicago, screenplays, and films (on standard VHS tape, 16mm compatible) for productions, readings, and showings by multimedia production company; works of all lengths welcome; some remuneration; plays in *Professional Playscript Format* only.

COLLEAGUES THEATER CO.   2124 Broadway #202, New York, NY 10023 Contact: Len Stanger, Dramaturg   Unproduced full-length plays for competition; major roles for actors aged 50 and older, "works that embrace the richness of the mature experience; possible reading fee

EULIPIONS THEATRE CO.   1770 Sherman St., Denver, CO 80203 (303) 863-0026   Full-length plays, one-acts, musicals, children's plays dealing with "the African diaspora"; accepts query/synopses; sponsors Women's Ways (see Special Programs)

FL THEATRE   P.O. Box 683 Times Sq. Sta., New York, NY 10108 Small-cast plays (5 actors; doubling accepted); scripts are not returned

GENOA'S MOTHER PRESENTS   1616 S. Grant, Denver, CO 80210 (303) 733-1571   Works by female playwrights; plays with strong roles for women; must be suitable for 49-seat shop space

HARD HAT CO.   10061 Riverside Dr. Suite 166, Toluca Lake, CA 91602 Contact: J. D. Roberto, Art. Dir.   Original works for staged readings/productions; comedy, political satire; send synopsis, dialogue sample

INFERNAL BRIDEGROOM PROD.   P.O. Box 131644, Houston, TX 77219 Contact: Jason Nodler, Art. Dir.   Avant-garde, alternative works

INFINI PRODUCTIONS   1709 1/2 E. 87th St #225, Chicago, IL 60617 Writers to create monologues for "Screen Test" cable tv show

KUUMBA HOUSE   811 Westheimer #110B, Houston, TX 77006 Contact: Lindi Yeni, Art. Director   African-American writers and themes

THE LIDA PROJECT   P.O. Box 13553, Denver, CO 80201 (888) 293-9193 e-mail lida@denver.net   Experimental, cutting-edge plays

LOVI PRODUCTIONS   540 Boston Post Rd., Mamaroneck, NY 10543 Comic sketches, monologues, songs for off Broadway revue

STUDIO 44   2865 W. 44th Ave., Denver, CO 80211 (303) 458-5071 **Contact:** Greg Ward, Director   New works suitable for a 72-seat black box; accepts query/synopsis with dialogue sample

SUSAN PATCH-EAM   8723 57th Rd., Elmhurst, NY 11373   One-acts for production in New Plays Festival; small cast preferred

TALENTO BILINGUE DE HOUSTON   P.O. Box 230326, Houston, TX 77223 Hispanic playwrights, issues, themes

THEATER LAB HOUSTON   1760 Alamo St., Houston, TX 77223 **Contact:** Jerry LaBita   Off and off off Broadway style fare; also alternative theatre works

For playwrights who are interested in producing, here is a short list of rental theatres.

ACTORS' CENTER   3047 N. Lincoln Ave., Chicago, IL 60657 (773) 549-1888 Rehearsal space, days and evenings. Inquire for details, terms.

BAILIWICK REPERTORY   1229 W. Belmont, Chicago, IL 60657 (312) 883-1090   100-seat flexible space; fully equipped **Rates:** inquire

INTERNATIONAL TALENT NETWORK 873 Broadway Suite 303, New York, NY 10003   (212) 387-0651 **Contact:** Adam Zoblotsky **Theatre:** Union Sq. location, 99-seat house **Extras:** lighting, sound, casting provided; actors may also be provided; playwright/producer provides director and has full creative control **Rates:** negotiable; inquire

JOHN HOUSEMAN THEATER CENTER   450 W. 42nd St., New York, NY 10036 (212) 967-7079 **Theatre:** 2 studio theatres, 74 and 50 seats, on Theatre Row **Rates:** inquire

THE LAMB'S THEATRE CO. 130 W. 44th St., New York, NY 10036 (212) 575-0300 **Contact:** Bob Rizzo **Theatre:** off Broadway theatre in heart of Theatre District; stages: proscenium, 350 seats; flexible, 116 seats **Rates:** inquire

PLAYERS REHEARSAL LOFT 115 McDougal St., New York, NY 10012 (212) 982-4434 **Theatre:** 3 rehearsal spaces of various sizes **Rates:** $15, $18 per hour

PRODUCERS CLUB THEATRES   358 W. 44th St., New York, NY 10036 (212) 315-4743 **Contact:** Ben Kolbert 5 Theatre District theatres and studio spaces: 15'x12' stage, 30 seats; 15'x20' stage, 50 seats; 16'x16' stage, 70 seats; 20'x20' stage, 99 seats; 23'x19' stage, 99 seats; lounge/full-service bar; discount pricing; advice on free listings, agents **Rates:** inquire

SHORES PERFORMING ARTS THEATRE   9806 NE 2nd Ave., Miami, FL 33138 (305) 751-0562 FAX (305) 751-9159 **Contact:** Pat Sapia **Theatre:** proscenium, 400 seats **Rates:** inquire

STRAWDOG THEATRE   3829 N. Broadway, Chicago, IL 60613 (773) 528-9889 **Contact:** Mike Dailey 75-seat uptown theatre available off and late nights; fully equipped. **Rates:** inquire

THEATRE EAST   12655 Ventura Blvd., Studio City, CA 91601 (818) 760-4160 **Contact:** Susan O'Sullivan   Inquire for details, terms.

TINFISH THEATRE   4223 N. Lincoln Ave., Chicago, IL 60618 (773) 549-1888   70-seat theatre available for rehearsals and performances **Rates:** inquire

Contests

Mini-Checklist

What to Send to Contests

With a script:
- ☐ A cover letter.
- ☐ As many copies of the script as required by the contest (Comply with each contest's guidelines concerning the placement of your name, address, and phone number--on the title page or on a separate sheet .
- ☐ A cassette tape of any original music used in the play.
- ☐ Completed entry forms, written statements, letters of recommendation, fees, and other materials required by the contest.
- ☐ Your SASP or #10 SASE for notification of receipt.
- ☐ Your #10 SASE for notification of status.
- ☐ Your SASE for return of the script.

With a request for guidelines and entry forms:
- ☐ A letter requesting the desired materials.
- ☐ Your #10 SASE.
- ☐ Any additional materials requested.

Tip: Because contests sometimes change their guidelines, regulations, and deadlines, it's a good idea to request information well before the deadlines stated in the listings.

With a query/synopsis:
- ☐ A cover letter.
- ☐ A play synopsis, including character and technical breakdowns and a summary of the play's action.
- ☐ A script history: previous productions, workshops, readings, publications, awards. Include favorable reviews.
- ☐ Other materials required by the contest (bio, dialogue sample, letters of recommendation, etc.).
- ☐ Your SASP or #10 SASE for response.

Tip: If you're interested in a contest which charges an entry fee, send the fee with your entry materials--not with your request for guidelines and entry forms!

Contests

AATE PLAYWRITING AWARDS CY 12+
c/o AATE, Theatre Dept., Arizona State Univ., Box 872002, Tempe, AZ 85287-2002 (602) 965-6064 Contact: Christy Taylor, Admin. Director Frequency: annual Awards: plaque, staged reading for plays in 3 categories Works: plays for young audiences, books relating to children's theatre Regulations: entries must have been published in 1998; caterories: upper and secondary age audiences, elementary and middle school age audiences, adaptations from existing childrens literature for either age audience Procedure: nomination by publisher only; send SASE for guidelines, or contact Joe Lauderdale, Laguna Playhouse, P.O. Box 1747, Laguna Beach, CA 92652-1747, (714) 494-8022 FAX (714) 497-6948 Deadline: TBA (mid-Mar.)

ACT OUT F Rg x
Actor's Theatre of Washington, c/o 1625 Q St. NW #106, Washington, DC 20009 e-mail safford@aol.com Contact: Paul MacWhorter, Literary Director Award: staged reading in festival (Oct.-Nov.), possible production Exclusive interest: local writers Regulations: entries must be unpublished, unproduced Procedure: inquire Deadline: TBA Future commitment: no Advice: "The offbeat, the eccentric, the different, the non-traditional."

ALASKA NATIVE PLAYS COMP. Dept. of Theatre, Univ. of AK,
3211 Providence Dr., Anchorage, AK 99508 (907) 786-1792 FAX (907) 786-1799 Contact: David Edgecombe, Coord. This contest is inactive in 1999; see *The Playwright's Companion 2000* for future plans.

AMERICAN RENAISSANCE THEATRE
FREE PLAYREADING SERIES See listing in Special Programs.

AMERICAN THEATER AND LITERATURE F-l 1- Tr $
PROGRAM CONTEST Sun & Moon Press, 6026 Wilshire Blvd., Los Angeles, CA 90036 (213) 857-1115 e-mail djmess@sunmoon.com Frequency: annual Awards: publication of 2 winning plays, royalty, 10 complimentary copies Works: full-length plays, one-acts, translations Guidelines: entries must be unpublished Procedure: send script, $25 fee Response: 2-6 months

AMERICAN TRANSLATORS ASSOCIATION AWARDS Tr
ATA Honors & Awards Committee, 1800 Diagonal Rd. Suite 220, Alexandria, VA 22314-2840 (703) 683-6100 FAX (703) 683-6122 e-mail ata@atanet.org Contact: Eric McMillan, Chair Regulations: entries must have been published in U.S. by an American publisher during the 2 years before deadline and must conform to PEN guidelines (see PEN American Center in Special Programs) Procedure: nominations submitted by publisher; 2 copies of book, 10 consecutive pages of original, extra jacket, available advertising copy, brief vita of translator

AMERICAN TRANSLATORS ASSN. AWARDS (Cont.)

GERMAN LITERARY TRANSLATION PRIZE   Tr
Frequency: biennial odd years **Award:** $1000, expenses to attend conference (up to $500) **Works:** full-length and one-act translations into English from original German **Regulations:** entries must have been published as 1 volume or in a collection **Deadline:** May 15, 1999 postmark **Notification:** fall 1999

LEWIS GALANTIÈRE LITERARY TRANSLATION   Tr
PRIZE **Frequency:** biennial even years **Award:** $1000, expenses to attend conference (up to $500) **Exclusive interest:** literary translations from any language (except German) into English **Deadline:** May 15, 2000 **Notification:** fall 2000

ANNA ZORNIO MEMORIAL CHILDREN'S   CY ♪
THEATER PLAYWRITING AWARD   Theatre & Dance, UNH,
30 College Rd., **Durham, NH 03824** **(603) 862-3046** **FAX (603) 862-0298** **Contact:** Carol Julie Brinker, Director of Theatre Ed. **Frequency:** every 4 years **Award:** $1000, production **Guidelines:** entries must be unpublished children's plays, not professionally produced; 1-hour maximum; authors must be U.S. or Canadian residents; single or unit set preferred; no more than 2 entries per author **Procedure:** send SASE for guidelines **Deadline:** Sept. 1, 2001 **Notification:** May 2002

♫ ARIZONA PLAYWRIGHTS CONTEST   F-l Rg
Dept. of Theatre, Box 872002, Arizona State Univ., Tempe, AZ 85287-2002 **(602) 965-0519, -5359** **FAX (602) 965-5351** **Contact:** Prof. Guillermo Reyes **Frequency:** biennial even years **Award:** $500, staged reading **Works:** full-length plays **Regulations:** authors must be AZ residents (not associated with AZ State Univ.); entries must be unpublished, unproduced; minimal set changes; no musicals **Procedure:** send script **Deadline:** TBA (Aug.)

ARLENE R. AND WILLIAM P. LEWIS   F-l ♪ W $
PLAYWRITING CONTEST FOR WOMEN   Dept. of Theatre &
Media Arts, P.O. Box 26405, Brigham Young Univ., Provo, UT 84602 **(801) 378-7768** **FAX (801) 378-5988** **e-mail** sdfriel@byugatebyu.edu **Contact:** Danae Friel, Coord. **Frequency:** annual **Award:** $1000, possible travel, staged reading, possible production **Works:** full-length plays, musicals **Regulations:** entries must be unpublished, unproduced, uncommitted; authors must be women; collaborations welcome **Procedure:** send 2 copies of script, bio, $10 fee **Deadline:** Mar. 22, 1999 **Comment:** Scripts are not returned. **Advice:** *"Professional Playscript Format only."*

THE ARTS AND LETTERS PRIZE   1- $
P.O. Box 44, Dept. of English, Speech & Journalism, Georgia College & State Univ., Milledgeville, GA 31061 **Contact:** David Muschell, Assoc. Editor **Frequency:** annual **Award:** $1000, publication

in *Arts & Letters Journal of Contemporary Culture*, possible production **Works:** one-acts **Regulations:** entries must be unpublished **Procedure:** send script, $15 fee **Deadline:** Apr. 30, 1999; no submission before Jan. 1 **Notification:** Aug. 1999 **Your chances:** 100 entries/8 judges/2+ readings per entry/1 prominent playwright to choose winner **Comment:** Formerly Dogwood National One-Act Play Competition.

ASF TRANSLATION PRIZE   Tr po
American-Scandinavian Foundation, 725 Park Ave., New York, NY 10021 (212) 879-9779 FAX (212) 249-3444 e-mail agyongy@amscan.org **Contact:** Publishing Office **Frequency:** annual **Works:** translations from Scandinavian languages into English **Awards:** $2000, publication of excerpt in *Scandinavian Review*; $500 for runner-up **Regulations:** entries must be unpublished; original work must be by a Scandinavian author after 1800; entries must be at least 50 pages long if prose, 25 pages if poetry, and conceived as part of a book **Procedure:** send SASE for guidelines; upon entry: 4 copies of translation, 1 copy of original and permission **Deadline:** Jun. 1, 1999 **Notification:** fall 1999

ASHLAND NEW PLAYS FESTIVAL   F F-l Tr Ad ♪ CY Rg
ArtWork Enterprises, Inc., P.O. Box 453, Ashland, OR 97520 Contact: Marianne Wunch, Producer **Frequency:** annual **Awards:** $250 stipend/royalty, rehearsed reading in festival, travel, housing **Works:** full-length plays, translations, adaptations, musicals, children's plays and musicals **Regulations:** authors must reside in CA, OR, WA, ID, MT, NV; entries must be unproduced; translators/adaptors must secure permissions; 1 entry per author; winners must attend festival rehearsals, reading **Procedure:** send script, 1-page synopsis **Deadline:** TBA (fall)

ATTIC THEATRE CENTRE ONE-ACT MARATHON   F 1- $
6562 1/2 Santa Monica Blvd., Hollywood, CA 90038 (213) 469-3786 FAX (213) 463-9571 Contact: James Carey, Producing Art. Director **Frequency:** annual **Awards:** $250 1st prize, $100 2nd prize, $50 3rd prize; production of 9 finalists in festival **Works:** one-acts (45 minutes maximum) **Regulations:** entries must be unproduced; authors must hold copyrights **Procedure:** send script, synopsis, character breakdown, cover letter, resume, $10 fee **Deadline:** TBA (Oct.) **Notification:** late 1999

AUSTIN HEART OF FILM FESTIVAL   F S CY Fm $
SCREENPLAY COMPETITION 1600 Nueces, Austin, TX 78701 (800) 310-FEST FAX (512) 478-6205 Frequency: annual **Awards:** 1st prize $3000, long-term work with industry professional; all finalists receive passes to festival (Oct. 1999) **Works:** full-length screenplays (100-130 pages) **Regulations:** 2 categories: Children/Family themes, Adult/Mature themes; entries must not be optioned or sold at time of submission **Procedure:** send SASE for guidelines and application form; upon entry: $35 fee **Deadline:** TBA (May) **Comment:** Scripts are not returned. Activities include classes, seminars, writing roundtables.

AWP AWARDS   po $

The Associated Writing Programs, Tallwood House, Mail Stop 1E3, George Mason Univ., Fairfax, VA 22030 (703) 933-4301 FAX (703) 993-4302 **e-mail** awp@gmu.edu **Contact:** David Sherwin, Publications Mgr. **Frequency:** annual **Award:** $2,000, publication by a major university press **Works:** fiction, poetry, creative nonfiction **Procedure:** send SASE for guidelines in Nov. 1999; upon entry: fee (reduced for AWP members; see The Associated Writing Programs in Special Programs)

BAKER'S PLAYS HIGH SCHOOL PLAY-   F-l 1- ♪ 12+ Y

WRITING CONTEST Baker's Plays, 100 Chauncy St., Boston, MA 02111 (617) 482-1280 FAX (617) 482-7613 **Contact:** Ray Pape, Assoc. Editor **Frequency:** annual **Awards:** $500, publication; $250 2nd prize; $100 3rd prize **Works:** full-length plays, one-acts, musicals **Exclusive interest:** "The high school stage." **Regulations:** authors must be high school students; entries must be unpublished; collaborations accepted **Procedure:** write for guidelines **Deadline:** Jan. 30, 1999 postmark; no submission before Sept. 1, 1999 for 2000 deadline **Notification:** May 1999 **Your chances:** 100 entries **Advice:** "Play should have a staged reading or production prior to submission." **Comment:** The judge reserves the right to withhold awards.

BALTIMORE PLAYWRIGHTS FESTIVAL   F Rg

c/o Fells Point/Corner Theatre, 251 S. Ann St., Baltimore, MD 21231 (410) 276-2153 **Contact:** John Bruce Johnson, Librarian **Frequency:** annual **Awards:** production with stipend in festival; possible public readings of other entries **Regulations:** authors must have resided (presently or in the past) in Maryland for a significant period of time; entries must be unproduced; small casts, simple sets encouraged **Procedure:** send SASE for guidelines; upon entry: 3 copies of script **Deadline:** Sept. 30 every year **Your chances:** 80 entries/7-10 plays selected **Advice:** "5-10 area theatres participate. *Professional Playscript Format* only!"

BEVERLY HILLS THEATRE GUILD-JULIE HARRIS   F-l

PLAYWRIGHT AWARD COMPETITION 2815 N. Beachwood Dr., Los Angeles, CA 90068-1923 (213) 465-2703 **Contact:** Marcella Meharg, Competition Coordinator **Frequency:** annual **Awards:** 1st prize $5000; 2nd prize $2000; 3rd prize $1000; possible rehearsed reading **Works:** full-length plays, 90-minutes minimum **Regulations:** authors must be U.S. citizens; entries must be unpublished, unproduced (i.e., no production for which actors or authors were paid and/or admission was charged), unoptioned; collaborations accepted; 1 entry per author; previous entries and winners of other contests ineligible **Procedure:** send SASE for quidelines and application form **Deadline:** Nov. 1, 1999 postmark; no submission before Aug. 1 **Notification:** Jun. 2000 **Your chances:** 600 entries/10-12 readers/2 semi-final judges/celebrity panel of 5 judges/2+ readings per entry **Future commitment:** promotions, credit **Advice:** "No first drafts." **Comment:** Scripts are not returned.

♫ BEVERLY HILLS THEATRE GUILD PLAY   CY Tr Ad
COMPETITION FOR CHILDREN'S THEATRE
2815 N. Beachwood Dr., Los Angeles, CA 90068-1923 (213) 465-2703
Contact: Marcella Meharg, Coord. **Frequency:** annual **Awards:** 1st prize $750; Runner-Up $250; possible rehearsed readings **Works:** children's plays, 40-50 minutes **Regulations:** authors must be U.S. citizens; entries must be unpublished, unproduced (i.e., no production for which actors or authors were paid and/or admission was charged), unoptioned; collaborations accepted; translators and adaptors must secure permissions; 1 entry per author **Procedure:** send SASE for guidelines **Deadline:** Feb. 28, 1999 postmark; no postmark before Jan. 15 **Notification:** Jun. 1999 **Future commitment:** promotions, credit **Advice:** "Plays that not only entertain but also foster an appreciation of and an interest in live theatre." **Comment:** Scripts are not returned.

BIENNIAL PROMISING PLAYWRIGHT   F-l 1- Ad Rg
AWARD   Colonial Players Inc., 108 East St., Annapolis, MD 21401
Contact: Coord. **Frequency:** biennial even years **Award:** $750, production **Works:** full-length plays, 2 related one-acts, adaptations **Regulations:** authors must reside in MD, DE, VA, WV, PA or DC; entries must not have been produced professionally, must be free of restrictions; adaptations must be of works in public domain; collaborations accepted; maximum cast: 10; no more than 2 sets; 90-120 minutes; winner must attend rehearsals **Stage:** arena, 180 seats **Casting:** non-Equity **Procedure:** send SASE for guidelines **Deadline:** Dec. 31, 2000; no submission before Sept. 1, 2000 **Notification:** Jun. 2001 **Your chances:** 75 entries/ 6-12 judges/2-3 readings per entry **Future commitment:** credit; 2-year option **Comment:** The judges reserve the right to withhold the award.

THE BLANK THEATRE CO. YOUNG   F F-l 1- ♪ CY Y
PLAYWRIGHTS FESTIVAL   1301 Lucile Ave., Los Angeles, CA
90026-1519 (323) 662-7734 FAX (323) 661-3903 e-mail btc@primenet. com **Contact:** Ginnie Held, Producer **Frequency:** annual **Awards:** workshop productions for 9± winners **Works:** full-length plays, one-acts, musicals, operas, children's plays **Regulations:** authors must be 19 years of age or younger as of deadline **Procedure:** send SASE for guidelines in late Feb. 1999 **Deadline:** TBA (Apr.) **Notification:** May 1999 **Comment:** Scripts are not returned.

BORDER PLAYWRIGHTS PROJECT   D F-l M Rg Esp
Borderlands Theater, P.O. Box 2791, Tucson, AZ 85702 (520) 882-8607 FAX (520) 882-7406, call first **e-mail** bltheater@aol.com **Contact:** Barclay Goldsmith, Producing Director **Frequency:** annual **Awards:** development/production for 1-2 plays; negotiated stipends, travel, room, board **Works:** full-length plays **Exclusive interests:** "Cultural diversity of the border; the border as metaphor." **Regulations:** entries must be unpublished, unproduced, may be in English, Spanish or both **Procedure:** send synopsis **Deadline:** Jan. 1, 1999 **Notification:** Mar. 1, 1999

CALIFORNIA YOUNG PLAYWRIGHTS   D F-l 1- ♪ Y
CONTEST **Playwrights Project, 450 B St. Suite 1020, San Diego, CA 92101-8002 (619) 239-8222 FAX (619) 239-8255 e-mail youth@ playwright.com Contact:** Deborah Salzer, Exec. Director **Frequency:** annual **Awards:** $100, production, development, variable travel **Works:** full-length plays, one-acts, musicals **Regulations:** authors must be CA residents under age 19 as of deadline; entries must be unpublished, not professionally produced; collaborations accepted; suggested maximum cast: 6; suggested set limit: 2-3; 10-page minimum; small budget **Stage:** arena, 225 seats **Casting:** non-Equity **Procedure:** send SASE for guidelines **Deadline:** Apr. 1, 1999 **Your chances:** 150 entries/10-15 initial readers/2-3 readings per entry; 4 scripts produced annually **Future commitment:** credit **Comment:** Scripts are not returned. The judges reserve the right to withhold the awards.

CANADIAN JEWISH PLAYWRITING CONTEST   F-l J Rg
Jewish Theatre Committee, c/o The Bloor JCC, 750 Spadina Ave., Toronto, Ontario, Canada M5S-2J2 (416) 924-6211 FAX (416) 924-0442 e-mail bloorjcc@lglobal.com **Frequency:** annual **Award:** staged readings **Works:** full-length plays **Regulations:** Canadian writers only; entries must have Jewish content and must not have been produced professionally **Procedure:** request guidelines **Deadline:** TBA

CENTER THEATER INTERNATIONAL PLAY-   F-l $
WRIGHTING CONTEST **1346 W. Devon Ave., Chicago, IL 60660 (773) 508-0200 Contact:** Jay Skelton, Producing Artistic Director **Frequency:** annual **Award:** $300, possible production **Works:** full-length plays **Regulations:** entries must not be published, produced. or optioned; maximum cast: 8 (doubling possible); minimal demands for black box theatre **Procedure:** send SASE for guidelines; upon entry: $15 fee **Deadline:** TBA **Comment:** Scripts are not returned.

CHARLOTTE FESTIVAL/NEW PLAYS IN   F F-l Tr Ad
AMERICA **Charlotte Rep., 129 W. Trade St., Charlotte, NC 28203 (704) 333-8587 Contact:** Claudia Carter Covington, Literary Mgr. **Frequency:** annual **Awards:** staged reading, travel, housing for 4 winners; cash award, possible production; travel, housing **Works:** full-length plays, translations, adaptations **Regulations:** entries must not have been professionally produced; no children's plays; authors must participate; "emphasis on text/actors' contributions to character development" **Procedure:** send script, resume **Deadline:** ongoing program **Notification:** 3-4 months **Your chances:** 500 entries/5 judges/2 readings per entry **Comment:** The judges reserve the right to withhold the awards.

CHICAGO YOUNG PLAYWRIGHTS   F 1- Y Rg ⊐
FESTIVAL **Pegasus Players, 1145 W. Wilson Ave., Chicago, IL 60640 (773) 878-9761 FAX (773) 271-8057 Contact:** Arlene Crewdson, Artistic Director **Frequency:** annual **Awards:** winners $250, runners-

up $50; certificates for all **Works:** short plays (30 minutes maximum) **Special interest:** "Teenage voices." **Regulations:** authors must be Chicago private/public school students, aged 11-19 **Procedure:** send SASE for guidelines and application form **Deadline:** TBA **Your chances:** 400 entries/7 final judges/3 readings per entry **Advice:** "We value every single script. Teachers are encouraged to call."

CHICANO/LATINO LITERARY CONTEST   F-l Esp dr po
Dept. of Spanish and Portuguese, UC-Irvine, Irvine, CA 92697-5275 (714) 824-5443 Contact: Ruby Trejo, Coordinator **Awards:** $1000, publication, travel; $500 2nd prize, $250 3rd prize **Regulations:** authors must be citizens or residents of U.S.A.; entries must be unpublished full-length plays (at least 100 double-spaced pages) written in English and/or Spanish; 1 entry per author; award rotates among 4 genres (novel, short story, poetry, drama) **Procedure:** send SASE for Guidelines: upon entry: 2 copies of script **Deadline:** drama: TBA (Apr.)

CHRISTOPHER COLUMBUS SCREENPLAY   S $
DISCOVERY AWARDS 433 N. Camden Dr. #600, Beverly Hills, CA 90210 (310) 288-1881 FAX (310) 288-0257 e-mail writing@screen writers.com **Contact:** Janice Pennington, Co-Founder **Frequency:** annual **Awards:** Discovery of the Month: development, possible referral to industry professions for up to 3 scripts per month; Discovery of the Year: option (up to $10,000) for up to 3 scripts per year **Regulations:** entries must be unproduced, unoptioned screenplays **Procedure:** send SASE for guidelines; upon entry: $45 fee **Deadline:** annual cycle: Dec. 1, 1999; monthly selection: last day of each month **Comment:** The judges reserve the right to withhold the awards. Scripts are not returned.

CIRCLE THEATRE PLAY SEARCH   Omaha, NE   This contest has been discontinued.

CITY PLAYHOUSE SHORT PLAY FESTIVAL   F 1-
L.A. City College Theatre Academy, 855 N. Vermont Ave., Los Angeles, CA 90029 (213) 953-4336 FAX (213) 953-4500 Contact: Cliff O'Connell, Theatre Mgr. **Frequency:** annual **Award:** production in festival (May); possible development into full-length, consideration for season production, entry into Kennedy Center ACTF **Works:** 10-15 minute plays **Special interest:** "Younger characters." **Maximum cast:** 5, 2-4 preferred **Stage:** black box, 99 seats **Casting:** students, alumni **Procedure:** send script **Deadline:** Jan. 31, 1999 **Your chances:** 750 entries/ usually 14 plays selected **Advice:** "Plot twists: what appears is not necessarily so. Strong characters." **Comment:** Scripts are not returned.

CLAUDER COMPETITION FOR EXCELLENCE   F-l Rg
IN PLAYWRITING P.O. Box 383259, Cambridge, MA 02238-3259 (617) 322-3187 Contact: Betsy Carpenter, Director **Frequency:** biennial odd years **Awards:** 1st prize $2500, production; $500, staged

reading for runners-up **Works:** full-length plays   **Regulations:** authors must be residents of CT, MA, ME, NH, RI. or VT or students in those states; entries must be unpublished and must not have been professionally produced; 45 minutes minimum; maximum cast: 8; unit set; no more than 1 entry per author **Casting:** Equity **Procedure:** send SASE for guidelines **Deadline:** TBA (Oct.) **Your chances:** 350 entries/2 readings per entry **Advice:** *"Professional Playscript Format only!"*

CLEVELAND PUBLIC THEATRE FESTIVAL   F $
OF NEW PLAYS   6415 Detroit Ave., Cleveland, OH 44102   (216)
631-2727   FAX   (216) 631-2575   e-mail cpt@en.com **Contact:** Terence Cranendonk, Festival Director **Frequency:** annual **Procedure:** send SASE for guidelines; upon entry: script, script history, tape/score, $10 waivable fee **Deadline:** Sept. 1, 1999; no submission before Feb. 1 **Notification:** Dec. 1, 1999 **Your chances:** 250 entries/3-5 judges/2 readings per entry **Future commitment:** credit **Advice:** "The stage, not TV. Be daring--do not try only to 'entertain' and pacify." **Comment:** The judges reserve the right to withhold the awards.

FESTIVAL OF STAGED READINGS   F F-l 1- ♪ x Rg
Awards: staged readings (winter) of up to 12 plays, housing, some travel for out-of-town playwrights **Works:** full-length plays, one-acts, musicals **Special interest:** "Alternative works; no commercial fare." **Regulations:** entries must be unproduced except in workshops or significantly revised; OH authors preferred

KATHERINE AND LEE CHILCOTE AWARD   F Rg
Award: $2000 for 2 plays, 1 of which receives production **Guidelines:** plays selected from Festival; 1 award goes to an OH playwright

COE COLLEGE NEW WORKS FOR THE STAGE   F F-l Rs
Theatre Arts Dept., Coe College, 1220 1st Ave. NE, Cedar Rapids, IA 52402 (319) 399-8689 FAX (319) 399-8557 e-mail swolvert@coe.edu **Contact:** Susan Wolverton, Festival Chair **Frequency:** biennial even years **Award:** $325, staged reading (Jan. 2001); airfare, housing for 1-week residency **Regulations:** entries must be unpublished, unproduced full-length plays on a specific theme (TBA) **Procedure:** send SASE for guidelines **Deadline:** May 1, 2000 **Notification:** Sept. 1, 2000 **Your chances:** 100+ entries/3 judges/1-3 readings per entry **Future commitment:** credit, percentage **Comment:** The judges reserve the right to withhold the award.

COLORADO CHRISTIAN UNIV./ENSEMBLE THEATRE CO. NEW CHRISTIAN PLAYS COMPETITION **Dept. of Theatre, 180 S. Garrison St., Lakewood, CO 80226 (303) 238-5386 Ext. 131 e-mail** prdorn@aol.com **Contact:** Patrick Rainville Dorn, Literary Mgr. This competition is inactive in 1999; see *The Playwright's Companion 2000* or inquire for future plans.

CONNECTIONS   Delaware Theatre Co., 200 Water St., Wilmington, DE 19801-5030   (302) 594-1104   FAX (302) 594-1107   Contact: Fontaine Syer, Art. Dir.   This program, inactive in 1999, will resume in spring 2000; see *The Playwright's Companion 2000* or inquire for plans.

CORNERSTONE DRAMATURGY AND   D F-l 1- Af Rs
DEVELOPMENT PROJECT   Penumbra Theatre Co., 270 N. Kent St., St. Paul, MN 55102 (612) 224-4601 FAX (612) 224-7074 Contact: Lou Bellamy, Artistic Director **Frequency:** annual **Awards:** 3-4 week residency, production for 1 writer; 4-week residency, staged reading for 1 writer; staged readings for 3 other writers **Works:** full-length plays, one-acts **Exclusive interest:** "Pan African/African-American experience." **Regulations:** entries must not have been produced professionally **Procedure:** send SASE for guidelines **Deadline:** ongoing program

THE CUNNINGHAM PRIZE   F-l 1- ♪ CY Rg Sp
DePaul Univ. Theatre School, 2135 N. Kenmore, Chicago, IL 60614-4111 (773) 325-7938 **Contact:** Selection Committee **Frequency:** annual **Award:** $5000 **Works:** full-length plays, one-acts, musicals, children's plays **Guidelines:** entrants must live or work within 100 miles of downtown Chicago; works must affirm "the centrality of religion and the human quest for meaning, truth, and community" **Procedure:** write for guidelines **Deadline:** Dec. 1, 1999 **Notification:** Mar. 1, 2000 **Comment:** The judges reserve the right to withhold the award.

DALE WASSERMAN AWARD   Madison, WI   Mail addressed to this contest has been returned as undeliverable; the phone has been disconnected.

DAVID JAMES ELLIS MEMORIAL AWARD   F-l Am H B
Theatre Americana, P.O. Box 245, Altadena, CA 91003-0245 (626) 683-1740 **Contact:** James Follett, Playreading Chair **Frequency:** annual **Award:** $500 to the best of 4 plays produced, videotape **Works:** full-length plays **Special interests:** "American authors; American background, history, the American experience." **Regulations:** entries must be unpublished; simple sets, minimal changes preferred; 2-hour maximum; no more than 2 entries per author **Procedure:** send script with synopsis, resume, bio **Deadline:** Feb. 1, 1999 postmark **Notification:** Jul.-Aug. 1999 **Advice:** "For biography: develop the play around a central conflict in the character's life, rather than presenting a full lifetime on stage."

DAYTON PLAYHOUSE FUTUREFEST   F F-l Ad
1301 E. Siebenthaler Ave., Dayton, OH 45414-5357 (937) 277-0144 FAX (937) 277-9539 **Contact:** Mng. Director **Frequency:** annual **Awards:** full production (Jul.) for 3 winners; staged readings for 3 more; 1st prize $1000, $100 each to other 5 participants; travel and hotel provided for all 6 playwrights **Works:** full-length plays, adaptations **Regulations:** entries must be unpublished, unproduced except in work-

shops **Stage:** flexible, 200 seats **Casting:** non-Equity **Audience:** "Ages 30-75." **Procedure:** send SASE for guidelines **Deadline:** Oct. 31, 1999; no submission before Aug. 1 **Notification:** May 2000 **Your chances:** 200-300 entries/25 readers/5 professional judges/3 readings per entry **Advice:** "New ideas; old ideas told in a new way."

DEEP SOUTH WRITERS CONFERENCE AWARDS   F $
English Dept., Box 44691, Univ. of Southwestern LA, Lafayette, LA 70504 (313) 482-6918 FAX (318) 482-6195 Contact: Willard Fox, Director **Frequency:** annual **Works:** plays, 1-person shows **Procedure:** send SASE for guidelines **Deadline:** Jul. 15, 1999 **Notification:** Sept. 1999 **Comment:** The judges reserve the right to withhold the awards.

JAMES H. WILSON FULL-LENGTH PLAY   F-l 1p $
AWARD   **Awards:** 1st prize $300; 2nd prize $100 **Regulations:** entries must be unpublished full-length plays or 1-person shows, not commercially produced; upon entry: $15 fee **Your chances:** 50-60 entries/10 judges

PAUL T. NOLAN ONE-ACT PLAY AWARD   1- 1p $
Awards: 1st prize $200, 2nd prize $100; possible publication **Regulations:** entries must be unpublished one-act plays or 1-person shows (50 pages maximum), not produced commercially; plays for adult audiences preferred; upon entry: $10 fee **Your chances:** 80 entries

DGP NEW PLAYWRIGHT AWARD   F-l 1-
359 W. 54th St. Suite 4FS, New York, NY 10019 Contact: Joseph C. Koenenn, Award Chair **Frequency:** annual **Award:** $500, off Broadway production **Works:** full-length plays, full evenings of one-acts **Regulations:** authors must never have had a professional NYC production under paid Equity contract; 1 full-length play or evening of 1-acts per author; no musicals, translations, adaptations, collaborations, or foreign-language works **Procedure:** send script, bio **Deadline:** Dec. 1, 1999; no submission before Sept. 1

DOBAMA THEATRE CONTESTS 1846 Coventry Rd., Cleveland Heights, OH 44118 (216) 932-6838 FAX (216) 932-3259 Contact: Literary Mgr. **Frequency:** annual

MARILYN BIANCHI KIDS' PLAYWRITING   1- Y Rg
FESTIVAL   **Awards:** savings bonds, publication and/or production for several winners **Works:** short plays **Guidelines:** authors must be students in Cuyahoga County schools, grades 1-12 **Procedure:** write for application form **Deadline:** TBA (Feb. 1999)

ONE WORLD PREMIERE   F-l M C Rg
Award: mainstage season production **Guidelines:** new plays; diverse casts; contemporary themes **Procedure:** request details **Deadline:** Feb. 1, 1999 **Notification:** May 15, 1999 **Comment:** "Preference given to Cleveland Play House playwrights [see Theatres]."

DOGWOOD NATIONAL ONE-ACT PLAY COMPETITION
See the Arts and Letters Prize in this section.

DRAMA WEST PRODUCTIONS ONE-ACT PLAY CONTEST   1- dr cm Rg
P.O. Box 5022-127, Lake Forest, CA 92630 (949) 770-7405 Contact: Catherine Stanley, Artistic Director **Award:** professional staged reading **Works:** one-acts **Special interests:** drama, comedy; "creative insight to the ongoing human dilemma; plays that encourage intelligent debate" **Regulations:** authors must reside in the Southern CA area **Procedure:** send SASE for guidelines **Deadline:** ongoing program

DRAMAFEST 2000   F F-l ♪ CY
Lodi Arts Commission, 125 S. Hutchins St. Suite D, Lodi, CA 95240 (209) 367-5442 FAX (209) 367-5461 Contact: Cyndi Olagaray, Arts Coord. **Frequency:** biennial odd years **Awards:** $1000 for full-length play or musical; $1000 for children's play; production; expenses for rehearsals **Guidelines:** entries must be unpublished, unproduced except in workshops **Procedure:** send SASE for guidelines **Deadline:** Apr. 1, 1999 postmark; no submission before Jan. 1, 1999 **Notification:** fall 1999 **Your chances:** 250 entries/40 judges/3 readings per entry **Advice:** "Come for final rehearsals and festival." **Comment:** The judges reserve the right to withhold the awards.

DRAMARAMA   1- F-l $
Playwrights' Center of San Francisco, P.O. Box 460466, San Francisco, CA 94146-0466 (415) 626-4603 FAX (415) 863-0901 e-mail play ctrsf@aol.com **Contact:** Sheppard Kominars, Chairman **Frequency:** annual **Awards:** $500 for best one-act (60 minutes maximum); $500 for best full-length play (60 minutes minimum); staged readings in festival (Oct. 1999) **Regulations:** entries must be unpublished, unproduced except in workshops **Procedure:** send SASE for guidelines; upon entry: $25 fee **Deadline:** Mar. 15, 1999 postmark; no entries before Jan. 1, 1999 **Your chances:** 125-150+ entries/8 judges/2-4 readings per entry **Future commitment:** credit **Comment:** The judges reserve the right to withhold the awards. **Advice:** *"Professional Playscript Format only!"*

DREAMBUILDER SESH INC. CELEBRATION SCRIBE AWARD
Cleveland, OH   This contest has been discontinued.

DRURY COLLEGE 1-ACT PLAYWRITING CONTEST   1-
900 N. Benton Ave., Springfield, MO 65802 (417) 873-7430 e-mail sasher@lib.drury.edu **Contact:** Sandy Asher, Writer-in-Residence **Frequency:** biennial even years **Awards:** 1 prize of $300, 2 prizes of $150 each; possible production; "recommendation to The Open Eye" (see Theatres) **Regulations:** entries must not be committed, published or professionally produced except in workshops; no more than 1 entry per author; small cast, single set, 20-45 minutes preferred; no musicals, adap-

tations, children's plays, or monologues **Procedure:** send SASE for guidelines **Deadline:** Dec. 1, 2000 postmark, Dec. 8, 2000 receipt, no submission before May 1, 2000 **Notification:** Apr. 1, 2001 **Your chances:** 250 entries/14 judges/1-3 readings per entry **Future commitment:** "Royalty-free production--2 years." **Comment:** The judges reserve the right to withhold the awards or divide the prize money differently.

DUBUQUE FINE ARTS PLAYERS (DFAP)   **1- Ad Fm $**
NATIONAL ONE-ACT PLAYWRITING CONTEST
1321 Tomahawk Dr., Dubuque, IA 52003 (319) 583-6748 Contact: Jennie G. Stabenow, Coord. **Frequency:** annual **Awards:** 1st prize $600, 2nd prize $300, 3rd prize $200; possible production **Works:** one-acts: plays, adaptations **Regulations:** entries must be unpublished, unproduced except in workshops; adaptators must secure permission; maximum cast: 5 preferred; simple set and props preferred; 35 pages, 40 minutes maximum; no musicals or children's plays **Stage:** proscenium, 700 seats **Casting:** non-Equity **Procedure:** send SASE for guidelines; upon entry: 2 copies of script, $10 fee **Deadline:** Jan. 31, 1999 postmark **Notification:** Jun. 30, 1999 **Your chances:** 150-200 entries/3-7 readings per entry/10 finalists read by 5 judges **Future commitment:** option, promotions **Advice:** "Avoid unnecessary obscenities." **Comment:** Review sheets available. The judges reserve the right to withhold the awards.

EDGAR ALLAN POE AWARD   **my**
Mystery Writers of America, 17 E. 47th St. 6th Floor, New York, NY 10017 Frequency: annual **Regulations:** entries must be professionally produced or published mysteries by U.S. authors **Procedure:** send SASE for guidelines and entry forms **Deadline:** Dec. 31, 1999

♫ **ENCHANTED PLAYERS ONE-ACT COMPETITION 1- Rg**
105A Taylortown Rd., Boonton, NJ 07005 Contact: Beth Eden **Frequency:** annual **Awards:** $100 1st prize; production of 3 winners **Works:** one-acts (30-35 minutes) **Regulations:**NY or NJ writers only; 1 entry per author **Procedure:** send script **Deadline:** TBA (Oct.)

EWP NEW VOICES PLAYWRITING   **F-1 ♪ CY As $**
CONTEST   **East West Players, 244 S. San Pedro St. Suite 301, Los Angeles, CA 90012 (213) 625-7000 FAX (213) 625-7111 Contact:** Ken Narasaki, Literary Mgr. **Frequency:** annual **Award:** 1st prize $1000; 2nd prize $500; reading; possible workshop or production **Works:** full-length plays, musicals, children's plays **Special interest:** "Asian Pacific writers, casts, or themes preferred." **Regulations:** entries must be in English, unpublished, unproduced except in workshops; no translations or adaptations **Procedure:** send SASE for guidelines; upon entry: 2 copies of script, $15 fee **Deadline:** Apr. 1, 1999 postmark **Notification:** Jul. 1, 1999 **Your chances:** 50 entries/6-9 judges/2-6 readings per entry **Future commitment:** percentage, credit **Comment:** The judges reserve the right to withhold the award.

FESTIVAL OF EMERGING   F F-l 1- Tr Ad ♪ CY Rv C $
AMERICAN THEATRE (FEAT) COMPETITION P h o e n i x
Theatre, 749 N. Park Ave., **Indianapolis, IN 46202** (317) 635-PLAY
FAX (317) 635-0010 Contact: Bryan Fonseca, Art. Director **Frequency:**
annual **Awards:** $1000 for full-length play, $350 for one-act; production
of 2 works (full-length plays or bills of one-acts), housing **Works:** full-
length plays, single or related one-acts, translations, adaptations, musicals, children's plays, revues **Exclusive interest:** contemporary issues
Regulations: entries must be unpublished, not professionally produced,
suitable for 150-seat proscenium or 75-seat black box; moderate cast size
and demands; 1 entry per author **Procedure:** send script, 1-2 page synopsis, resume, $5 fee **Deadline:** Feb. 28 **Notification:** usually Aug. **Your
chances:** 400 entries/15-20 judges/1+ readings per entry **Future commitment:** 1st refusal, 6 months **Advice:** "Be available for rehearsals."

FESTIVAL OF FIRSTS PLAYWRITING   F F-l $
COMPETITION **Sunset Center, P.O. Box 1950, Carmel, CA 93921**
(831) 624-3996 FAX (831) 624-0147 Contact: Director **Frequency:**
annual **Awards:** possibly up to $1000, possible production; runners-up
may receive staged readings **Works:** full-length plays **Regulations:**
entries must be unpublished, unproduced **Procedure:** send SASE for
guidelines and application form; upon entry: $15 fee **Deadline:** Aug. 31,
1999; no submission before Jun. 15 **Advice:** "Stage plays only. No musicals." **Comment:** The judges reserve the right to withhold the awards.

FIRSTSTAGE PLAYWRIGHTING CONTEST   1- $
**P.O. Box 38280, Los Angeles, CA 90038 (213) 850-6271 FAX (213)
850-6295 Contact:** Dennis Safren, Literary Mgr. **Frequency:** annual
Awards: 1st prize $100; 2nd prize $50; 3rd prize $50; staged reading for
3 winners **Works:** one-acts (45 minutes maximum) **Regulations:** entries
must be unpublished, unproduced except in workshops **Procedure:** send
script, $10 fee **Deadline:** May 1, 1999 postmark **Notification:** Nov. 1,
1999 **Comment:** The judges reserve the right to withhold the award.

FLORIDA STUDIO THEATRE CONTESTS   1241 N. Palm Ave.,
Sarasota, FL 34236 (813) 366-9017 FAX (813) 955-4137 Contact: Chris
Angermann, Assoc. Director **Frequency:** annual **Regulations:** entries
must be unproduced except in workshops **Procedure:** send SASE for
guidelines by Jan. 1 annually **Your chances:** 250 entries/15 judges/4
readings per entry **Comment:** Scripts are not returned.

> **AMERICAN SHORTS**   F 1-
> **Award:** $500, production **Works:** shorts (5 page maximum) **Special
> interest:** theme TBA

> **SARASOTA FESTIVAL OF NEW PLAYS**   F Y
> **Awards:** TBA **Guidelines:** 3-tier festival including Young Play-
> wrights Festival: workshop productions of works by playwrights
> grades K-6 (May); 7-12 (Oct.)

FMCT NATIONAL PLAYWRIGHTS' COMPETITION 1-
Fargo-Moorhead Community Theatre, 333 4th St. S, Fargo, ND 58103-1913 (701) 235-1901 FAX (701) 235-2685 Contact: Cindy Snelling, NPC Administrator Frequency: biennial odd years Award: $1000; or $500, production, travel, housing Works: one-acts (less than 1 hour) Regulations: entries must be unpublished, unproduced except in workshops; small cast, simple demands preferred; plays of 35-45 minutes encouraged; 1 entry per author Stage: thrust, 372 seats Procedure: send SASE for guidelines Deadline: Jul. 1, 1999; no submission before May 1, 1999 Notification: Dec. 1999 Comment: The judges reserve the right to extend the competition and to withhold the award. Winning one-act may be entered in the National AACT Festival.

FRANCESCA PRIMUS PRIZE F-l W Rs
Denver Center Theatre Co., 1050 13th St., Denver, CO 80204 (303) 893-4000 FAX (303) 825-2117 e-mail bsevy@star.dcpa.org Contact: Bruce Sevy, Assoc. Art. Director Frequency: annual Award: $2000-$3000, workshop, rehearsed reading with expenses for residency Works: full-length plays Regulations: authors must be women; entries must be unproduced and unencumbered Procedure: send script Deadline: Jan. 1, 1999 postmark Notification: Mar.-Apr. 1999

FRANK McCLURE ONE-ACT PLAY AWARD 1- Tr Ad CY $
Amelia Magazine, 329 E St., Bakersfield, CA 93304 (805) 323-4064 e-mail amelia@lightspeed.net Contact: Frederick A. Raborg, Editor Frequency: annual Award: $150, publication, 10 free copies Works: one-act plays, translations, adaptations, children's plays Regulations: entries must be unpublished; adaptors must secure permission; 45 minutes maximum Procedure: send script, resume, script history, $15 fee Deadline: May 15, 1999 Notification: Sept. 15, 1999 Your chances: 90-100 entries/3 judges/3-4 readings per entry Comment: "The judges will not withhold the award; publication may be debated."

GEORGE HAWKINS PLAYWRITING 1- ♪ CY 12+ Af
CONTEST The Ensemble Theatre, 3535 Main St., Houston, TX 77002 (713) 520-0055 FAX (713) 520-1269 Contact: Eileen Morris, Artistic Director Awards: cash award, production (summer); staged readings for 2nd, 3rd place winners Regulations: "Entries must be original work, not professionally produced, that illuminates the African-American experience for young people aged 6-18"; maximum cast: 7, simple sets and props, 45 minutes maximum preferred Procedure: write for guidelines Deadline: Apr. 20, 2000 Notification: Jun. 20, 2000

GEORGE HOUSTON BASS PLAY-RITES D F 1- C M
FESTIVAL Rites & Reason, Box 1148, Brown Univ., Providence, RI 02912 (401) 863-3558 FAX (401) 863-3559 (marked "Rites & Reason") Contact: Elmo Terry-Morgan, Artistic Director Frequency: annual

Awards: "Up to 4 winners receive $250, staged reading, expenses to attend rehearsals and festival; $1000 Memorial Award; workshop production in subsequent season." **Works:** one-acts **Special interests:** "Issue-oriented plays which deal with the diverse cultural experiences of the Americas." **Regulations:** writer must attend 1-week rehearsal workshop and must be willing to develop work **Procedure:** send script, 1-page cover letter, synopsis, statement ("why play fits the mission of the festival"), cassette tape of music **Deadline:** Mar. 1, 1999

GEORGE R. KERNODLE PLAYWRITING COMPETITION — 1- $

Dept. of Drama, Kimpel Hall 619, Univ. of Arkansas, Fayetteville, AR 72701 (501) 575-2953 FAX (501) 575-7602 **Contact:** Director **Frequency:** annual **Awards:** 1st prize $300, 2nd prize $200, 3rd prize $100; possible production or staged reading **Regulations:** authors must be residents of U.S. or Canada; entries must be unpublished one-acts (1-hour maximum), unproduced except in workshops; no more than 3 entries per author; no adaptations, musicals or children's plays; maximum cast: 8 **Procedure:** send SASE for guidelines; upon entry: $3 fee **Deadline:** Jun. 1, 1999; no submission before Jan. 1 **Notification:** Nov. 1, 1999

GILMAN AND GONZALEZ-FALLA THEATRE FOUNDATION ANNUAL MUSICAL THEATRE AWARD — ♪ Am

109 E. 64th St., New York, NY 10021 (212) 734-8011 FAX (212) 734-9606 **e-mail** soncel@msn.com **Contact:** Peggy Alvarez, Coord. **Frequency:** annual **Award:** $25,000 **Works:** musicals **Regulations:** "Writers (or teams) must have had at least 1 musical professionally produced; emphasis on American musical theatre works." **Procedure:** send SASE for guidelines **Deadline:** TBA (fall)

GILMORE CREEK PLAYWRITING COMPETITION

Winona, MN   This competition has been discontinued.

THE GREAT PLAINS PLAY CONTEST — F-l Ad ♪ CY H C Rg

University Theatre, 317 Murphy Hall, Univ. of Kansas, Lawrence, KS 66045 (913) 864-3381 FAX (913) 864-5251 **e-mail** dunruh@falcon.cc.ukans.edu **Contact:** Delbert Unruh, Director **Frequency:** annual **Awards:** "Production Award": $2000, production, $500 in expenses; Development Award: $500, to encourage further development of a promising work; possible publication **Works:** full-length plays, adaptations, musicals, operas, children's plays **Special interest:** "Historical or contemporary aspects of the human story on the Great Plains; Kansas themes preferred." **Regulations:** entries must not have been produced professionally **Procedure:** send script and/or score; or, send SASE for guidelines **Deadline:** ongoing (scripts received before Sept. 1, 1999 will be considered for 2000-2001 season)

GREAT PLATTE RIVER PLAYWRIGHTS   D F F-l 1- ♪ CY
FESTIVAL Univ. of Nebraska-Kearney Theatre, Kearney, NE
68849-5260 (308) 865-8406 FAX (308) 865-8806 e-mail garrisonj@
platte.unk.edu **Contact:** Artistic Director **Frequency:** annual **Awards:**
1st prize $500, 2nd prize $300, 3rd prize $200; production, travel,
housing **Works:** full-length plays, one-acts, musicals, children's plays
Special interest: "Works-in-progress for development." **Guidelines:** entries must be unpublished and unproduced **Procedure:** send script, cassette tape of music **Deadline:** Apr. 1, 1999 **Notification:** Jul. 1999
Comment: The judges reserve the right to withhold the awards.

HAROLD MORTON LANDON TRANSLATION   Tr po
AWARD The Academy of American Poets, 584 Broadway Suite
1208, New York, NY 10012 (212) 274-0343 Ext. 14 FAX (212) 274-
9427 e-mail poets@artswire.org **Contact:** India Amos, Program Director
Frequency: annual **Award:** $1000 **Works:** translations: book-length
poems or collections of poems **Regulations:** translators must be living
U.S. citizens; play entries must be verse drama translated into English
verse, published in 1999; collaborations eligible; no anthologies of work
by a number of translators **Procedure:** send 3 copies of book (no manuscripts) **Deadline:** Dec. 31, 1999 **Comment:** Books are not returned.

HENRICO THEATRE CO. ONE-ACT   1- ♪ Fm
PLAYWRITING COMPETITION County of Henrico, Division of
Recreation & Parks, P.O. Box 27032, Richmond, VA 23273 (804)
501-5100 FAX (804) 501-5284 **Contact:** Amy Perdue, Cultural Arts Coordinator **Frequency:** annual **Awards:** 1st prize $250, production; 2
runners-up $125 **Works:** one-act plays and musicals **Regulations:**
entries must be unpublished, unproduced; small cast, simple set preferred;
no controversial material **Procedure:** send SASE for guidelines; upon
entry: 2 copies of script **Deadline:** Jul. 1, 1999 **Notification:** mid-Nov.
1999 **Your chances:** 150 entries/5 judges/5 readings per entry
Comment: The judges reserve the right to withhold the award.

HRC'S ANNUAL PLAYWRITING CONTEST   F-l 1- Rg $
Hudson River Classics, Inc., P.O. Box 940, Hudson, NY 12534 (518)
828-1329 **Contact:** W. Keith Hedrick, President **Frequency:** annual
Award: $500; staged reading; travel, housing, board to attend performance **Works:** full-length plays, one-acts **Guidelines:** authors must be
residents of Northeastern U.S.A.; works must be unpublished; 60-90
minutes **Procedure:** send script, $5 fee **Deadline:** Jun. 1, 1999; no submission before Mar. 1 **Notification:** Nov. 15, 1999

HUMBOLDT STATE UNIV. NEW PLAY SEASON   F-l
Theatre Arts Dept., Humboldt State Univ., Arcata, CA 95521 (707)
826-3566 FAX (707) 826-5494 e-mail mcelrath@laurel.humboldt.edu
Contact: Margaret Thomas Kelso, Head, Dramatic Writing Program **Frequency:** triennial **Awards:** production, expenses for 2 winners **Works:**

full-length plays **Regulations:** entries must be unpublished, unproduced except in small workshops; inquire for theme **Casting:** non-Equity **Procedure:** send SASE for guidelines **Deadline:** TBA (Spring 1999)

JACKIE WHITE MEMORIAL NATIONAL   CY ♪ Lc $
CHILDREN'S THEATRE COMPETITION 1999 Columbia
Entertainment Co., 309 Parkade Blvd., Columbia, MO 65202 (314)
874-5628 Contact: Betsy Phillips, Director **Frequency:** annual **Award:**
$250, possible production, travel **Works:** children's full-length plays,
musicals **Exclusive interest:** "Large-cast plays with characters of all
ages to be presented by our pupils, aged 10-15." **Regulations:** entries
must be unpublished; maximum cast: 50+; "children move set pieces; stock
costumes preferred" **Procedure:** send SASE for guidelines; upon entry:
$10 fee **Deadline:** Jun. 1, 1999 postmark; no submission before Feb. 1
Notification: Aug. 30, 1999 **Your chances:** 45 entries/12 judges/3-12
readings per entry **Advice:** "Ideal play has a message without moralizing,
does not talk down to the audience and is challenging for our students."

JAMES D. PHELAN LITERARY AWARD   F-l 1- CY po Rg Y
San Francisco Foundation/Intersection for the Arts, 446 Valencia
St., San Francisco, CA 94103 Contact: Awards Coord. **Frequency:** annual **Award:** $2000 **Works:** fiction, non-fiction, poetry, drama **Regula-
tions:** authors must be CA natives aged 20-35; entries must be unpublished; 1 entry per author; previous entries ineligible **Procedure:** send
SASE for guidelines; after Oct. 1 for 2000 guidelines **Deadline:** Jan. 31,
1999 **Notification:** Jun. 15, 1999 **Your chances:** 200 entries/6 judges/3
readings per entry **Future commitment:** no **Comment:** The judges
reserve the right to withhold the award.

JANE CHAMBERS PLAYWRITING AWARD   W x
ATTN: Mary A. Donahoe, Dept. of Theatre Arts, Wright State Univ.,
Dayton, OH 45435-0001 Frequency: annual **Awards:** $1000, re-
hearsed reading at conference (late Jul.); Student Award: $250 **Regula-
tions:** women authors only; "feminist perspective, majority of roles for
women"; experimental works encouraged; 1 entry per author; winner
must attend conference **Procedure:** send SASE for guidelines and application form **Deadline:** Feb. 15 **Notification:** Jun. 30 **Comment:** The
judges reserve the right to withhold the awards. Scripts are not returned.

JCC HALLE THEATRE OF CLEVELAND DOROTHY   F-l J Rs
SILVER PLAYWRITING COMPETITION   3505 Mayfield Rd.,
Cleveland Heights, OH 44118 (216) 382-4000 Ext. 275 FAX (216)
382-5401 Contact: Elaine Rembrandt, Director, Cultural Arts **Frequency:** annual **Award:** $500, $500 residency expenses, staged reading, possible production **Works:** full-length plays **Exclusive interest:** "Fresh
perspective on the Jewish experience." **Regulations:** entries must be unproduced except in workshops **Procedure:** send script **Deadline:** Dec.
15, 1999 **Comment:** The judges reserve the right to withhold the award.

JEFFERSON STREET THEATRE CHILDREN'S   CY ♪
MUSICAL CONTEST 8919 Shady Pine Rd., Klamath Falls, OR
97601 (541) 882-3300 FAX same, call first e-mail warshauerp@aol.com
Contact: Paul Warshauer, President **Frequency:** annual **Award:** production, cash award **Works:** children's musicals **Procedure:** send SASE
for guidelines **Deadline:** Mar. 31, 1999 **Notification:** Apr. 15, 1999
Your chances: 25 entries/4 judges/4 readings per entry **Comment:** The
judges reserve the right to withhold the award.

JEWEL BOX THEATRE PLAYWRITING AWARD   F-l $
3700 N. Walker, Oklahoma City, OK 73118 (405) 521-1786 **Contact:**
Charles Tweed, Production Director **Frequency:** annual **Award:** $500,
possible production **Works:** full-length plays **Special interest:**
"Characterization." **Regulations:** entries must be unpublished, unproduced except in workshops; 1 entry per author **Procedure:** send SASE
for guidelines (send SASE in Oct. 1999 for 2000 guidelines); upon entry:
2 copies of script and $10 fee **Deadline:** Jan. 15, 1999 **Notification:**
May 1999 **Your chances:** 100 entries/10 judges/10 readings per finalist
Comment: The judges reserve the right to withhold the award.

JOHN GASSNER AWARD   See NETC Awards in this section.

KENNEDY CENTER AMERICAN COLLEGE THEATER   F Y
FESTIVAL AWARDS **Kennedy Center Education Dept.,** Washington, DC 20566 (202) 416-8850 FAX (202) 416-8802 **Contact:** John
Lion, Producing Dir. **Frequency:** annual **Regulations:** authors must be
full-time college students; works must be produced by schools **Procedure:** application form completed by school **Deadline:** Dec. 1, 1999

ANCHORAGE PRESS THEATRE FOR YOUTH   CY 12+ ♪
PLAYWRITING AWARD **Award:** $1000, publication with
royalties, $1250 fellowship to attend New Visions/New Voices Festival or National Youth Theatre Symposium **Guidelines:** entries must
appeal to ages K-grade 12

THE FOURTH FREEDOM FORUM PLAY-   F-l C Y Rs
WRITING AWARD **Awards:** 1st prize $5000, publication by
Palmetto Play Service; residency at Sundance Theatre Lab; 2nd prize
$2500; grants ($1500, $1000) to schools **Guidelines:** entries must be
full-length plays on world peace/international disarmament

♫ **JEAN KENNEDY SMITH PLAYWRITING**   F-l Ad ♪ h/d
AWARD **Award:** $2500, Dramatists Guild membership; fellowship
to a playwriting program **Works:** full-length plays, adaptations,
musicals **Regulations:** plays must explore living with disability

KC/ACTF COLLEGE MUSICAL THEATER AWARD   ♪ Y
Awards: $1000 each for lyrics, music, book, producing school **Works:**
full-length musicals, related one-act musicals, musical adaptations
Regulations: 50% of writing team must meet ACTF requirements

LORRAINE HANSBERRY PLAYWRITING   F-l Af Y
AWARD   **Awards:** 1st prize $2500, internship at National Playwrights Conference, publication by Dramatic Publishing Co.; 2nd prize $1000; grants ($750, $500) to producing schools **Regulations:** full-length plays dealing with the black experience **Your chances:** 15 entries/2 judges/2 readings per entry

NATIONAL AIDS FUND CFDA-VOGUE   F-l Ad ♪ h/d Y
INITIATIVE AWARD FOR PLAYWRITING **Award:** $2500, fellowship to Bay Area Playwrights Festival **Regulations:** full-length plays, adaptations, musicals concerning personal-social implications of HIV/AIDS

NATIONAL STUDENT PLAYWRITING   F-l Ad ♪ Y
AWARD   **Awards:** $2500, production in Kennedy Center festival (Apr.-May 2000), Dramatists Guild membership, publication by Samuel French, fellowship to attend Sundance Theatre Lab; $1000 to producing school **Works:** full-length plays, adaptations, musicals **Your chances:** 30 entries/3 judges/2 readings per entry

THE SHORT PLAY AWARDS PROGRAM   1- Ad Y
Awards: $1000, publication by Samuel French, Dramatists Guild membership for up to 3 winners **Works:** one-acts and adaptations

KEY WEST THEATRE FESTIVAL   F
Theatre Key West, P.O. Box 992, Key West, FL 33041-0992 (305) 2923725 FAX (305) 293-0845 Contact: Joan McGillis, Art. Director **Frequency:** annual **Awards:** production of up to 5 plays during Oct. festival; travel, housing **Works:** stage plays, musicals (all genres) **Guidelines:** entries must be unproduced except in workshops; maximum cast: 8; single set; simple demands **Procedure:** request guidelines **Deadline:** Mar. 31, 1999 **Notification:** 6-12 months **Your chances:** 200 entries/3 judges **Comment:** The judges reserve the right to withhold the awards.

THE KINDNESS OF STRANGERS CONTESTS
4378 Lankershim Blvd., North Hollywood, CA 91602 (818) 752-9566 FAX (818) 985-9227 e-mail MarlynMan@aol.com **Contact:** Jan Marlyn Reesman, Artistic Director **Deadline:** ongoing program

MINUTE MUSICALS   ♪ $
Awards: $100 1st prize; $50 runners-up; readings, workshops, possible productions **Works:** short musicals (1-30 minutes) of all genres **Regulations:** entries must be unpublished; small cast and minimal sets, appropriate for a 50-seat initmate theatre **Procedure:** send script, score; availble cassette tapes; $10 fee for 1-3 submissions per author

SHORT-ACT FESTIVAL   F 1- $
Awards: $100, production or staged reading; $50 each for 3 runners-up **Works:** one-acts (1-30 minutes) **Regulations:** entries must be unproduced except in workshops; no more than 3 entries per author; "no restrictions, but if the play is unproducible in our limited space it will

receive only a reading" **Stage:** flexible, 50 seats **Casting:** Equity, non-Equity **Procedure:** send script, resume, $10 fee **Your chances:** 200 entries/3 judges/3 readings per entry **Future commitment:** credit **Advice:** "Get our interest on the opening page."

THE KLEBAN AWARD ♪ Am

Kleban Foundation Inc., 270 Madison Ave. Suite 1410, New York, NY 10016 (212) 683-5320 FAX (212) 686-2182 **Contact:** Alan J. Stein, Secretary **Frequency:** annual **Awards:** TBA ($100,000 each to lyricist and librettist in 1997) **Regulations:** authors must work in American musical theatre and must have had a work produced or have been a member of a professional musical theatre workshop; authors whose work has been performed on Broadway for a cumulative period of 2 years ineligible **Procedure:** request guidelines and application form **Deadline:** TBA

KUMU KAHUA PLAYWRITING CONTEST F-l 1- Rg

Dept. of Theatre & Dance, Univ. of Hawaii-Manoa, 1770 East-West Rd., Honolulu, HI 96822 (808) 956-2588 FAX (808) 956-4234 **Contact:** Dennis Carroll, Chair **Frequency:** annual **Regulations:** entries must be unproduced; previous entries ineligible **Procedure:** send SASE for guidelines **Deadline:** Jan. 1, 1999 **Notification:** May 1, 1999 **Your chances:** 30 entries/3 judges/5 readings per entry **Advice:** "No purely commercial work." **Comment:** The judges reserve the right to withhold the awards.

HAWAII PRIZE F-l Rg

Award: $500 **Regulations:** entries must be full-length plays set in Hawaii or dealing with Hawaiian subject matter

PACIFIC RIM PRIZE F-l Rg

Award: $400 **Regulations:** entries must be full-length plays set in or deal with Pacific Islands or Pacific-Asian American experience

RESIDENT PRIZE F-l 1- Rg

Award: $200, reading and/or production if playwright is present **Regulations:** authors must be HI residents; entries must be full-length or one-act plays; no restrictions on subject matter

L.A.D.T. PLAY COMMISSIONING F-l 1- Tr Ad ♪ cm C Sp

PROJECT P.O. Box 1883, Studio City, CA 91614-0883 (323) 650-9600, (323) 654-2700 TDD and ISDN FAX (323) 654-3260 e-mail ladesigners@juno.com **Contact:** Richard Niederberg, Artistic Director **Award:** production with royalty, possible publication **Works:** full-length plays, related one-acts, translations, adaptations, musicals **Special interest:** "Cutting-edge; nudity, street language okay but not required." **Regulations:** entries must be unpublished, unoptioned, unproduced except in workshops; 80-second set change; no orchestra pit **Procedure:** "Send proposal with non-returnable material that best represents your writing." **Deadline:** Feb. 15, 1999 comedy with socially unpopular theme; May 15, 1999 political theme; Aug. 15, 1999 religious (not sentimental) theme; Nov. 15, 1999 satire on classic **Your chances:** 1200 entries/1-5 readings per entry **Future commitment:** 2%, 1st refusal, credit **Advice:** "Commercial, easy to promote. State your proposed involvement beyond the traditional role. We commission plays, written to our specifications, guaranteed production after rewrites."

L. ARNOLD WEISSBERGER COMPETITION   New York
This competition has been discontinued.

LAMIA INK! INTERNATIONAL ONE-PAGE PLAY   1-
COMPETITION   P.O. Box 202 Prince Street Station, New York, NY 10012 **Contact:** Cortland Jessup, Editor **Frequency:** annual **Awards:** 1st prize $200; reading in NYC, publication in *Lamia Ink!* (see Publishers) for winner and 11 finalists **Works:** one-page plays **Regulations:** no more than 3 entries per author **Procedure:** send SASE for guidelines; upon entry: $1 fee per play **Deadline:** Mar. 15, 1999 **Notification:** May 15, 1999 **Your chances:** 10/judges/4-6 readings per entry

THE LEE KORF PLAYWRITING   F-l 1- Ad ♪ M $
AWARD   Cerritos College Theatre Dept., 11110 Alondra Blvd., Norwalk, CA 90650   (562) 860-2451 Ext. 2638 FAX (562) 467-5097 **Contact:** Gloria Manriquez, Theatre Production Specialist **Frequency:** annual **Awards:** $750, production; $250, staged reading **Works:** full-length plays, musicals, theatre pieces, "extravaganzas" **Special interests:** "Diverse cultures." **Procedure:** send SASE for guidelines and application form; upon entry: 2 copies of script, $5 fee **Deadline:** Sept. 1, 1999 postmark **Notification:** Apr. 1, 2000 **Your chances:** 100 entries/3 judges/3 readings per entry **Future commitment:** credit **Advice:** "Prefer unproduced pieces by authors who can attend rehearsals and preproduction festivities." **Comment:** Judges reserve the right to withhold the awards.

LETRAS DE ORO   This contest has been discontinued.

LIVE OAK THEATRE CONTEST   F-l Tr Ad Rg
& LARRY L. KING AWARD 719 Congress Ave., Austin, TX 78701   (512) 472-5143 FAX (512) 472-7199 **Contact:** Literary Mgr. **Frequency:** annual **Awards:** Live Oak Theatre Contest $1000; Larry L. King Award $500 for best play by a Texas resident; 1-week workshop, staged reading in annual Harvest Festival; possible production; runners-up may receive workshops **Works:** full-length plays, translations, adaptations **Regulations** authors must be U.S. citizens or residents; entries must be unproduced professionally; no musicals; 1 entry per author; previous entries ineligible **Casting:** Equity, non-Equity **Audience:** "Mainstream." **Procedure:** send script with $15 fee **Deadline:** Apr. 1, 1999; no submission before Feb. 1 **Notification:** fall 1999 **Your chances:** 500 entries/5 judges/3 readings per entry **Comment:** This contest, recently suspended, has been reactivated.

LOFT FEST Tampa, FL   Mail sent to this festival has been returned as undeliverable; no phone number is listed.

LOIS & RICHARD ROSENTHAL NEW PLAY PRIZE   F-1 ♪
Cincinnati Playhouse in the Park, P.O. Box 6537, Cincinnati, OH 45206 (513) 345-3342 FAX: (513) 345-2254 **Frequency**: annual **Awards**: $10,000, production, travel, housing **Works**: full-length plays, musicals **Regulations**: entries must be unpublished, not produced professionally; 1 entry per author **Stages**: 2 modified thrusts, 225, 629 seats **Casting**: Equity **Procedure**: send 2-page abstract (synopsis, character breakdown, bio,), 5-page dialogue sample, cassette tape for musical; agent submission **Deadline**: TBA **Notification**: 2 months synopsis; 6 months if script is requested **Your chances**: 600 entries/3 judges/1-2 readings per entry **Future commitment**: negotiable

LOVE CREEK FESTIVALS   F 1- W
c/o Granville, 162 Nesbit St., Weehawken, NJ 07087 e-mail Creek read@aol.com **Contact**: Cynthia Granville-Callahan, Literary Mgr. **Awards**: New York mini-showcase productions in festival for at least 40 finalists **Regulations**: entries must be unpublished, not produced in NYC area within past year; major roles for women preferred; minimum cast: 2, larger preferred; simple sets, costumes; 40 minutes maximum; no more than 2 entries per author per festival **Procedure**: send SASE for guidelines; "entry must include letter of permission to produce; statement as to whether Equity showcase is acceptable" **Future commitment**: credit **Comment**: The judges reserve the right to withhold the awards.

ANNUAL SHORT PLAY FESTIVAL   F 1- W
Frequency: annual **Awards**: winner $300 **Special interests**: open to all subjects **Deadline**: ongoing program

MINI-FESTIVALS   F 1- g/l Sp W
Frequency: at least twice yearly **Awards**: awards vary **Works**: one-acts **Special interests**: Themes TBA; Gay and Lesbian Festival: positive depictions of gay/lesbian life; 'Fear of God'; Religion in the 90's." **Deadline**: TBA

MARC A. KLEIN PLAYWRITING AWARD   F-l 1- Y Rs
Theater Arts, Case Western Reserve Univ., 10900 Euclid Ave., Cleveland, OH 44106-7077 (216) 368-4868 FAX (216) 368-5184 e-mail ksg@po.cwru.edu **Contact**: John Orlock, Chair, Reading Committee **Frequency**: annual **Awards**: $500, $500 for residency expenses, production **Works**: full-length plays, related one-acts **Regulations**: authors must be enrolled in U.S. colleges-universities; entries must be unpublished in tradebook, unproduced except in workshops, endorsed by a drama teacher **Procedure**: send SASE for guidelines **Deadline**: May 15, 1999 **Notification**: Aug. 1, 1999 **Your chances**: 40 entries/4 judges/2 readings per entry **Comment**: The judges reserve the right to withhold the awards; director may work with author on rewrites before production."

MARGARET BARTLE   CY Ad ♪ W ⊑ Fm H B Cl
ANNUAL PLAYWRITING CONTEST   Community Children's
Theatre, 8021 E. 129th Terrace, Grandview, MO 64030 (816) 761-
5775 **Contact:** Mrs. Blanche Sellens, Chair **Frequency:** annual **Award:**
$500, possible production **Works:** children's plays, adaptations, and
musicals **Regulations:** entries must be unpublished; maximum cast: 8; all
roles suitable for adult women ("male roles should not be overly virile");
shows tour elementary schools; 60 minutes maximum; no seasonal plays
Procedure: send script (double-spaced; author's name and address on
title page); or, send SASE for guidelines **Deadline:** Jan. 31, 1999 **Notification:** Apr.-May 1999 **Your chances:** 40-60 entries/5 judges/45
readings per entry **Future commitment:** right to perform for 2 years
royalty free **Advice:** "Original ideas, legends, folklore, history, biographies, adaptations of classics. No violence, mature love stories, slang
or cursing." **Comment:** "The judges reserve the right to withhold the
award, or, in the event that 2 or more scripts are selected, to apportion
the cash award at the discretion of the Reading Committee."

MARKET HOUSE THEATRE BI-ANNUAL   F 1-
NATIONAL ONE-ACT PLAYWRITING COMPETITION
141 Kentucky Ave., Paducah, KY 42003 (502) 444-6828 **Contact:**
Michael Cochran, Exec. Director **Frequency:** biennial even years
Awards: $100, workshop production in festival (spring 2001), video-
taping for 1-2 winners **Works:** one-acts **Regulations:** entries must have
been written within the past 3 years; must be unpublished, unproduced
except in workshops; 60 pages maximum; maximum cast: 10; single or sec-
tional set **Procedure:** send script (author's name, address, phone number
on title page only), brief synopsis/bio (separate from script); or, send
SASE for guidelines **Deadline:** Oct. 31, 2000; no submissions before Jun.
2000 **Comment:** The judges reserve the right to withhold the award.

MARVIN TAYLOR PLAYWRITING AWARD   F-l Ad ♪
Sierra Repertory Theatre, P.O. Box 3030, Sonora, CA 95370 (209)
532-3120 FAX (209) 532-7270 e-mail srt@mlode.com **Contact:** Dennis
Jones, Producing Director **Frequency:** annual **Award:** $500, possible
production **Works:** full-length plays, adaptations, musicals **Regulations:** entries must be unpublished, no more than 2 productions/staged
readings; 1 entry per author; maximum cast: 8 preferred; no more than 2
sets **Procedure:** send script, #10 SASE **Deadline:** Aug. 31, 1999 postmark **Notification:** Mar. 2000 **Your chances:** 350 entries/3 judges
Comment: The judges reserve the right to withhold the award.

MAXIM MAZUMDAR NEW PLAY   F-l 1- ♪ CY x $
COMPETITION   Alleyway Theatre, One Curtain Up Alley,
Buffalo, NY 14202-1911 (716) 852-2600 FAX (716) 852-2266 e-mail
alleywayth@aol.com **Contact:** Kevin Stevens, Lit. Mgr. **Frequency:** annual **Awards:** $400, production, royalty, travel, lodging for full-length;

$100, production for one-act **Works:** full-length plays, one-acts, musicals, children's plays **Special interest:** "Boundaries of theatricality." **Regulations:** entries must be unproduced except in workshops; 1 entry per author per category (full-length, one-act, children's play); maximum cast: 10 for full-length, 6 for one-act, 5 for children's play; unit or simple set; minimum 90 minutes full-length; maximum 60 minutes one-act and children's play **Procedure:** send SASE for guidelines; upon entry: $5 fee **Deadline:** Jul. 1, 1999 **Notification:** Nov. 1, 1999 **Your chances:** 400 entries/5 judges/2-3 readings per entry **Future commitment:** credit

McLAREN MEMORIAL COMEDY F-l 1- Tr Ad ♪ CY cm $
PLAYWRITING COMPETITION Midland Community Theatre,
2000 W. Wadley, Midland, TX 79705 (915) 682-2544 FAX (915) 682-6136 Contact: Mary Lou Cassidy, Coord. **Frequency:** annual **Awards:** $400, production, travel, housing; 4 finalists receive staged readings **Works:** full-length plays, one-acts, translations, adaptations, musicals, children's plays **Exclusive interest:** comedies **Regulations:** entries not professionally produced preferred, plays with 1 production by a nonprofit theatre eligible **Procedure:** send script, $5 fee **Deadline:** Jan. 31, 1999; no submission before Dec. 1 for 2000 deadline **Notification:** May 16, 1999 **Your chances:** 150 entries/10 judges/3 readings per entry **Future commitment:** no

♫ MESA STATE COLLEGE THEATRE ONE-ACT 1- $
PLAYWRITING COMPETITION P.O. Box 2647, Grand Junction,
CO 81502 (970) 248-1233 FAX (970) 248-1159 Contact: Nancy Gore, Competition Coord. **Frequency:** annual **Awards:** $100 1st prize, $75 2nd prize, $50 3rd prize; possible production **Regulations:** entries must be unpublished, unproduced; maximum cast: 6; 45 minutes running time **Procedure:** send SASE for bulletin; upon entry: 4 copies of script, $10 fee **Deadline:** Jan. 1, 1999 postmark (inquire for 2000 deadline) **Notification:** after mid-Feb. **Advice:** *"Professional Playscript Format only!"*

MIDWESTERN PLAYWRIGHTS F F-l Tr Ad ♪ Rg Rs
FESTIVAL Dept. of Theatre, Film & Dance; Univ. of Toledo,
Toledo, OH 43606-3390 (419) 537-2207 FAX (419) 530-8439 Contact: John S. Kuhn, Festival Director **Frequency:** annual **Awards:** 1st prize $1000, staged reading (fall), production (spring 2000 at Toledo Rep), expenses and per diem for 2-week residency; 2nd prize $350; 3rd prize $150; staged reading **Works:** full-length (2-act) plays, translations, adaptations, musicals **Regulations:** entries must be unpublished, unproduced except in workshops; authors must be residents of IL, IN, MI, OH; maximum cast: 10, simple set; 1 entry per author **Procedure:** send SASE for guidelines; upon entry: 2 copies of script **Deadline:** May 1, 1999 **Notification:** Sept. 1, 1999 **Your chances:** 100-150 entries/12-15 judges/2 readings per entry **Future commitment:** no **Comment:** The judges reserve the right to withhold the awards.

MILDRED AND ALBERT PANOWSKI   F-l Ad Rs
PLAYWRITING AWARD Forest Roberts Theatre, Northern
Michigan Univ., 1401 Presque Isle, Marquette, MI 49855 (906) 227-
2553 **Contact**: Erica A. Milkovich, Award Coord. **Frequency**: annual
Award: $2000, production, expenses for residency **Works**: full-length
plays, adaptations **Regulations**: entries must be unpublished, unproduced except in workshops; no more than 1 entry per author **Procedure**: send SASE for guidelines **Deadline**: TBA (Nov.) **Your chances**:
400-500 entries/3 judges/2 or more readings per entry **Future commitment**: "1-week summer workshop with professional dramaturg; 1-week
residency with classroom, media, seminar, and workshop appearances."
Comment: The judges reserve the right to withhold the award.

MILL MOUNTAIN THEATRE NEW PLAY   F-l 1- ♪ Rs
**COMPETITION: NORFOLK SOUTHERN FESTIVAL OF NEW
WORKS** Market Sq. SE 2nd Floor, Roanoke, VA 24011 (540) 342-
5730 FAX (540) 342-5745 e-mail mmtmail@intrlink.com **Contact**: Jack
Parrish, Lit. Mgr. **Frequency**: annual **Award**: 1st prize $1000 staged
reading, possible full production with travel, stipend, housing for limited
residency **Works**: full-length plays, one-acts (at least 25 minutes), musicals (with demo tape) **Regulations**: authors must reside in U.S.; entries
must be written in English, unpublished, unproduced except in workshops; 1 entry per author; no resubmission except for finalists after substantial changes; maximum cast: 10; no translations, adaptations, 10-min-
ute plays, TV or screenplays **Procedure**: submission by agent or recommendation by a director, literary mgr,, or dramaturg; send script (contact
information on title page), synopsis, script history, bio, SASP **Deadline**:
Jan. 1, 1999 postmark; no submission before Oct. 1, 1999 for 2000 deadline **Notification**: Aug. 1, 1999 **Your chances**: 500+ entries/5 judges/2-
3 readings per entry **Comment**: The judges reserve the right to withhold
the award. **Advice**: *"Professional Playscript Format only!"*

THE MORTON R. SARETT MEMORIAL AWARD   F-l ♪
Theatre Arts Office, UNLV, 4505 Maryland Pkwy., Box 455036, Las
Vegas, NV 89154-5036 (702) 895-3666 **Contact**: Corrine A. Bonate,
Coord. **Frequency**: biennial odd years **Award**: $3000, production,
travel, housing **Works**: full-length plays, musicals **Regulations**: entries
must be unpublished, unproduced except in workshops; no adaptations
Procedure: send SASE for guidelines, available mid-summer; upon entry:
2 copies of script **Deadline**: Dec. 15, 1999; no submission before Sept. 1
Notification: Jun. 2000 **Advice**: "Producible scripts to be evaluated by
25 judges/3 final round judges/1-2 readings per entry." **Comment**: The
judges reserve the right to withhold the award.

MRTW SCRIPT CONTEST   Rd $
KOPN Radio, 915 E. Broadway, Columbia, MO 65201 (573) 874-
5676 FAX (573) 499-1662 e-mail mrtw@mrtw.org **Contact**: Sue
Zizza, Exec. Director **Frequency**: annual **Awards**: $800 divided among

2-4 winners; possible radio production, distribution, possible publication in scriptbook, scholarship to Midwest Radio Theatre Workshop (see Special Programs); 10-12 honorable mentions **Works:** short radio plays (15-30 minutes) **Regulations:** entries must be in radioscript format; 1 entry per author; no adaptations; scripts may be revised/adapted by directors for timing **Casting:** non-Equity, students **Procedure:** send SASE for guidelines; upon entry: 3 copies of script, $10 fee **Deadline:** Nov. 15, 1999; no submission before Aug 1 **Notification:** Mar. 2000 **Your chances:** 100-150 entries/3 judges/4 readings per entry **Comment:** The judges reserve the right to withhold the awards.

♫ MST-SCR SUMMER SHOWCASE   F-l 1- Tr Ad CY Rg D
415 Humboldt St., Santa Rosa, CA 95404 (707) 544-7278 FAX (707) 522-5033 **e-mail** mstscr@mst-scr.com **Contact:** Script Director **Frequency:** annual **Awards:** cash award; showcase production (Jun.) **Works:** 1- and 2-act plays, translations, adaptations, children's plays **Guidelines:** CA playwrights only; works must be unpublished, unproduced; maximum cast: 12 for 2-act play, 5 for one-act; simple sets; translators/adaptors must secure permissions; playwright must attend rehearsals or workshop performances **Procedure:** request guidelines and application form **Deadline:** May 1, 1999 **Notification:** Jun. 1999 **Advice:** *"Professional Playscript Format only!"*

♫ MYRIAD ARTS FESTIVAL   F 1- ♪ Pl S
P.O. Box 631, New York, NY 10185 (212) 344-1727 FAX (212) 459-9201 **e-mail** jjb6772@is.nyu.edu **Contact:** Jonathan Betchler, Producer **Award:** production/showing in festival **Works:** one-acts, musicals, short films **Procedure:** request guidelines and application form; upon entry: $5 fee **Deadline:** Jun. 30, 1999 **Notification:** 6 months

NANTUCKET SHORT PLAY COMPETITION   1- CY $
Nantucket Theatrical Productions, P.O. Box 2177, Nantucket, MA 02584-2177 (508) 228-5002 **Contact:** Jim Patrick, Literary Mgr. **Award:** $200, staged reading (Jul.) **Works:** one-acts, children's plays **Special interest:** "Compelling characters." **Regulations:** entries must not be published by a major publisher nor produced by an Equity theatre; minimal sets and props suggested; 40-page maximum; finalists selected at staged readings; final winner and finalists for calendar year will then be selected **Stages:** various small spaces **Casting:** non-Equity **Procedure:** send SASE for guidelines; upon entry: $7 fee **Deadline:** ongoing competition **Your chances:** 250 entries/5 judges/2 or more readings per entry **Future commitment:** credit for 1st public reading

NATIONAL CHILDREN'S THEATRE   F CY Ad ♪ ⊐ Esp $
FESTIVAL   Actors' Playhouse, 280 Miracle Mile, Coral Gables, FL 33134 (305) 444-9293 FAX (305) 444-4181 **Contact:** Earl Maulding, Director, Children's Theatre **Frequency:** annual **Awards:** 1st place musical $1000, production; 1st place play $100, staged reading **Works:**

children's plays, adaptations, and musicals **Regulations:** entries must be unpublished; 45-60 minute musicals with flexible act break, for audiences aged 5-12; 40-50 minute plays with no intermission, for audiences aged 12-17; maximum cast: 8 for musical; 6 for play; doubling encouraged; simple set; plays may be in English or English/Spanish; adaptors must secure permission **Procedure:** request guidelines (unusual format); upon entry: $10 fee **Deadline:** Jul. 1, 1999 **Commitment:** yes **Comment:** The judges reserve the right to withhold the awards.

NATIONAL HISPANIC PLAYWRITING AWARD   F-l 1- ♪ Hi Esp

Arizona Theatre Co., P.O. Box 1631, Tucson, AZ 85702 (520) 884-8210 FAX (520) 628-9129 **Contact:** Samantha Wyer, Asst. Artistic Director **Frequency:** annual **Award:** $1000, possible inclusion in reading series **Works:** full-length plays, one-acts, musicals **Regulations:** authors must be Hispanic residents of U.S., its territories or Mexico; entries must be unpublished, unproduced except in workshops, written in English (works in Spanish must be accompanied by translation); 1 entry per author **Procedure:** send script (title and author's name on front cover), 1-page cover letter (including script history), available cassette tape of music **Deadline:** Oct. 31, 1999

NATIONAL MUSIC THEATER CONFERENCE   F D Rs ♪ $

O'Neill Theater Center, 234 W. 44th St. Suite 901, New York, NY 10036 (212) 382-2790 FAX (212) 921-5538 **Contact:** Michael Nassar, Assoc. Director **Frequency:** annual **Award:** developmental residency at O'Neill Center (Waterford, CT) for new musical theatre works **Regulations:** 1 entry per author **Procedure:** send SASE for guidelines and application form; upon entry: $15 fee **Deadline:** Mar. 1, 1999 postmark; Mar. 8, 1999 receipt **Notification:** early Jul. 1999 **Comment:** Scripts are not returned.

NATIONAL ONE-ACT PLAYWRITING COMPETITION   1- $

Little Theatre of Alexandria, 600 Wolfe St., Alexandria, VA 22314 (703) 683-5778 FAX (703) 683-1378 **Contact:** Chairman, Playreading Committee **Frequency:** annual **Awards:** 1st prize $350, 2nd prize $250, 3rd prize $150; production of top 2-3 plays **Works:** one-acts (20-60 minutes) **Regulations:** entries must be unpublished, unproduced except in workshops; no more than 2 entries per author; single set preferred; few scene changes **Procedure:** send SASE for guidelines; upon entry: $5 fee **Deadline:** Mar. 31, 1999 **Notification:** Sept. 1, 1999 **Your chances:** 130-200 entries/12 judges/2-5+ readings per entry **Advice:** "Precis should precede abstract work." **Comment:** The theatre reserves the right to withhold the awards.

NATIONAL PLAY AWARD   F-l $

P.O. Box 286, Hollywood, CA 90078 (213) 465-9517 FAX (310) 652-2543 **e-mail** nrtf@nrtf. org **Contact:** Raul Espinoza, Chair **Frequency:** annual **Awards:** 1st prize $5000, staged reading; 4 runners-up receive

$500 each   **Regulations:** entries must be unpublished full-length plays
which have not been produced with a paid Equity cast or won a major
award; previous entries ineligible **Procedure:** send script, $25 fee (pay-
able to National Repertory Theatre Foundation) **Deadline:** Mar. 31,
1999; no submission before Jan. 1 **Notification:** Dec. 31, 1999

NATIONAL PLAYWRIGHTS CONFERENCE

F D Rs F-l 1- Tv S $

O'Neill Theater Center, 234 W. 44th St. #902,
New York, NY 10036 (212) 382-2790 FAX (212) 921-5538 Contact:
Mary F. McCabe, Mng. Director **Frequency:** annual **Awards:** development, staged reading, stipend, expenses for conference in Waterford, CT
(Jul. 2000) for 9-12 plays, 1-3 screenplays/teleplays **Works:** full-length
plays, teleplays, screenplays; related one-acts **Regulations:** authors
must be U.S. citizens or residents; entries must be unproduced,
unoptioned; no translations or adaptations **Procedure:** send SASE for
guidelines after Sept, 15, 1999; upon entry: $15 fee **Deadline:** Dec. 1,
1999; no submission before Sept. 1 **Notification:** early May 2000

NATIONAL TEN-MINUTE PLAY CONTEST

1-

Actors Theatre of Louisville, 316 W. Main St., Louisville, KY 40402-
4218 (502) 584-1265 **Contact:** Michael Bigelow Dixon, Literary Mgr.
Frequency: annual **Awards:** $1000, possible production with royalty
Works: short plays (10-minute, 10-page maximum) **Regulations:** authors
must be U.S. citizens or residents; entries must not have received Equity
productions; no more than 2 entries per author; 1 set **Procedure:** send
SASE for guidelines **Deadline:** Dec. 1, 1999 postmark **Your chances:**
2100 entries/6 judges **Comment:** "Plays that meet the following criteria
will also be considered for biannual showcase: cast of 3 or more;
characters aged 18-28; minimal sets, props, costumes."

NETC AWARDS

Rg $

c/o Dept. of Theatre, Northeastern Univ., 360 Huntington Ave.,
Boston, MA 02115 (617) 424-9275 FAX (617) 424-1057 **Contact:** Corey
Boniface, Mgr. of Operations **Frequency:** annual **Awards:** 1st prize
$1000, 2nd prize $500; staged reading, possible publication **Regulations:** authors must be New England residents or NETC members (see
New England Theatre Conf. in Special Programs); entries must be unpublished, not professionally produced, optioned or under consideration
elsewhere; 1 entry per author per award **Procedure:** send SASE for
guidelines; upon entry: $10 non-member fee **Deadline:** Apr. 15, 1999
postmark **Notification:** Sept. 1, 1999 **Advice:** "No phone calls, please."

♫ **AURAND HARRIS MEMORIAL PLAYWRITING   CY
AWARD**   **Works:** children's plays **Comment:** New award in
honor of the revered author of plays for young audiences.

JOHN GASSNER MEMORIAL PLAYWRITING AWARD F-l
Works: full-length plays **Your chances:** 90 entries/8 judges/3
readings per entry

NEW AMERICAN COMEDY (NAC) FESTIVAL   F D F-l cm
Ukiah Players Theatre, 1041 Low Gap Rd., Ukiah, CA 95482 (707)
462-1210 FAX (707) 462-1790 Contact: Michael Ducharme, Exec. Director Frequency: biennial odd years Awards: 2000: $50, staged readings for 2 finalists; 2001: $300, production, $400 travel/housing, per diem for winner Regulations: entries must be unpublished, unproduced full-length comedies Casting: non-Equity Procedure: send SASE for guidelines and entry form Deadline: Nov. 30, 1999 Your chances: 150 entries/5 judges/3 readings per entry Future commitment: credit Comment: The judges reserve the right to withhold the awards.

NEW DIRECTIONS THEATRE PLAY   F-l 1- Tr Ad ♪ $
CONTEST   IRT Group Theatre, 154 Christopher St. #3B, New
York, NY 10014 (212) 206-6875 Contact: Luane Davis, Art. Director Frequency: annual Awards: Grand prize: NYC showcase production; 1st Prize: Greenwich Village production; 2nd Prize: staged reading Works: all genres Procedure: send script, $10 fee Deadline: TBA

NEW ENGLAND NEW PLAY COMPETITION & SHOWCASE
Vineyard Haven, MA   This contest has been discontinued.

NEW LINE THEATRE   See listing in Theatres.

NEW PLAY FESTIVAL OF THEATRICAL   F F-1 1- Tr Ad
OUTFIT   P.O. Box 1555, Atlanta, GA 30301 (404) 577-5257 Ext. 14
FAX (404) 577-5259 e-mail katewarner@theatricaloutfit.org Contact:
Tom Key, Producing Art. Director Frequency: annual Awards: reading in Monday Night Series (winter 2000); possible cash awards, possible full production Works: full-length plays, one-acts, translations, adaptations Procedure: send query, first 10 pages of script, bio Deadline: Mar. 1, 1999 Notification: 6 months

NEW PLAYS FOR DOG DAYS FESTIVAL   F F-l 1- Tr Ad
Generic Theater, P.O. Box 11071, Norfolk, VA 23517 (804) 441-2160
e-mail generic@generictheater.org Contact: Steven Harders, Artistic Director Frequency: annual Awards: production, stipend for 4 winners Works: full-length plays, full evening of one-acts, translations, adaptations Regulations: entries must be unpublished, unproduced except in workshops; maximum cast: 7; simple sets Stage: flexible, 80 seats Casting: non-Equity Audience: "Adventurous." Procedure: send script, SASP Deadline: Mar. 1, 1999 postmark Notification: Apr. 1999 Your chances: 90+ entries/7-9 judges/3 readings per entry

NEW PROFESSIONAL THEATRE   F F-l ♪ Af W cm dr $
WRITERS FESTIVAL   424 W. 42nd St. 3rd Floor, New York, NY
10036 (212) 290-8150 FAX (212) 290-8202 e-mail newprof@aol.com
Contact: Sheila Davis, Artistic Director; Kenneth Johnson, Literary Mgr. Frequency: annual Awards: $2000, performances for each of 3

winners **Regulations:** entries must be full-length dramas, comedies, or musicals by African-American women **Procedure:** send script, resume, $15 fee, SASP **Deadline:** Jun 1, 1999 **Notification:** Sept. 1999

NEW VILLAGE GAY/LESBIAN SHORT PLAY CONTEST
New York   This contest has been discontinued.

NEW VOICES PLAYWRIGHTS WORKSHOP   F F-l
Univ. of West Florida, Dept. of Theatre, 11000 University Pkwy., Pensacola, FL 32514 Contact: Ron Roston, Director, New Voices **Awards:** participation in summer workshop, rehearsed public reading; travel, lodging, per diem; 1-2 entries receive full production (summer 1999) **Regulations:** entries must be unproduced full-length plays; 1 entry per author **Procedure:** send script, 1-page bio **Deadline:** Feb. 1, 1999

NEW WOMEN PLAYWRIGHTS FESTIVAL   F F-l cm W $
Off Center Theater, Tampa Bay Performing Arts Center, P.O. Box 518, Tampa, FL 33601-0518   (813) 222-1000 FAX (813) 222-1057 Contact: Karla Hartley, Artistic Assoc. **Award:** production, travel, housing **Regulations:** entries must be unproduced full-length comedies about women and women's issues; small cast aged 20s-40s, at least 50% women **Procedure:** send script, synopsis, $15 fee **Deadline:** ongoing program **Advice:** "Be willing to rewrite."

NEW YORK CITY 15 MINUTE PLAY FESTIVAL   F 1-
Turnip Theatre Co., 145 W. 46th St., New York, NY 10036 (212) 768-4016 Contact: Gino Dilorio, Festival Director **Frequency:** annual **Awards:** cash prizes in 4 categories, production in 4-week festival (Jan.-Feb. 2000) **Works:** short plays (maximum 15 pages) **Regulations:** playwrights are responsible for producing their plays; limited sets and lighting provided **Procedure:** send SASE for guidelines by Oct. 1 **Deadline:** Nov. 1, 1999 **Advice:** *"Professional Playscript Format only!"*

NORTH CAROLINA   F-l 1- Tr Ad ♪ CY Rv Rg
NEW PLAY PROJECT Greensboro Playwrights' Forum, City Arts-Greensboro Cultural Center, 200 N. Davie St. Box #2, Greensboro, NC 27401 (336) 335-6426 FAX (336) 373-2659 e-mail gsoplaywrights @juno.com **Contact:** Stephen D. Hyers, Director **Frequency:** annual **Award:** $100, workshop production (Memorial Day weekend) in conjunction with Livestock Players 2nd Stage **Regulations:** authors must be NC playwrights; new plays only **Procedure:** request guidelines **Deadline:** Jan. 13, 1999 **Advice:** "All themes/genres are accepted; plays with small casts and minimal sets may be given preference."

OFF-OFF BROADWAY ORIGINAL SHORT PLAY   F F-l 1-
FESTIVAL c/o Samuel French, Inc., 45 W. 25th St., New York, NY 10010 (212) 206-8990 FAX (212) 206-1429 Contact: William Talbot, Festival Coordinator **Frequency:** annual **Award:** production in festival

(late spring 1999) hosted by Love Creek Productions (see Theatres); possible publication by Samuel French **Works:** one-acts, segments of full-length plays **Regulations:** entries must be unpublished products of theatres, professional schools, or colleges that have playwriting programs; 40 minutes maximum **Procedure:** nomination by producing organization only; send SASE for guidelines and application form **Deadline:** TBA (Jan.-Mar. 1999) **Notification:** 2 weeks **Your chances:** 175 entries/3 judges/1-3 readings per entry **Future commitment:** no **Advice:** "No elaborate sets; monologues are less welcome."

OGLEBAY INSTITUTE TOWNGATE THEATRE   **F-l dr**
PLAYWRITING CONTEST   **Oglebay Institute, Stifel Fine Arts Ctr., 1330 National Rd., Wheeling, WV 26003 (304) 242-7700 FAX (304) 242-7747 Contact:** Kate Crosbie, Director of Performing Arts **Frequency:** annual **Award:** $300, production, partial travel **Regulations:** entries must be unpublished full-length dramas, not professionally produced; simple set **Procedure:** send script, resume **Deadline:** Dec. 31, 1999 **Your chances:** 80-150 entries/8-10 judges **Future commitment:** no **Comment:** The judges reserve the right to withhold the award.

THE OHIOANA AWARDS   **Rg ♪**
Ohioana Library Assn., 65 S. Front St. #1105, Columbus, OH 43215 (614) 466-3831 FAX (614) 728-6974 e-mail ohioana@winslo.ohio.gov **Contact:** Linda Hengst, Director **Frequency:** annual **Awards:** awards to "Ohioans who have made outstanding contributions to the arts and humanities as authors, poets, musicians, artists, or performers" **Regulations:** nominees must be OH natives or must have lived in OH for at least 5 years **Procedure:** send SASE for guidelines **Deadline:** Dec. 31, 1999

THE OHIOANA CAREER AWARD   Rg
Guidelines: nominee must be a native Ohioan; recipient must be present to receive the award at Ohioana Day (fall 1999)

OHIOANA CITATIONS   Rg Pl ♪
Guidelines: 4 awards generally presented in 4 different fields, including theatre, dance; awards include the Ohioana Music Citation

OHIOANA PEGASUS AWARD   Rg
Guidelines: nominee must have made unique or outstanding contributions or achievements in the arts and humanities

THE ONE-MINUTE PLAY CONTEST   **1-**
c/o Joel Selmeier, 310 State St., New York, NY 11201 (212) 714-9875 e-mail joelselm@ix.netcom.com **Award:** cash prize, presentation with other 1-minute plays in ongoing series **Regulations:** entries must be less than 60 seconds; 2 or more characters; carry-on props only; no light or sound other than self-generated; unlimited costumes **Procedure:** send script or prepare audition: playwrights must perform their own work or arrange for performance; send synopsis, resume; or, inquire for details

PACIFIC NORTHWEST WRITERS CONFERENCE   F 1- $
LITERARY CONTEST   2033 6th Ave. Suite 804, Seattle, WA 98121 (206) 443-3807 FAX (206) 441-8262 e-mail pnwriterscons@halcyon.com **Contact:** Shirley Bishop, Exec. Director **Frequency:** annual **Awards:** 1st prize $300, 2nd $200, 3rd $150; reading at summer conference; all finalists receive critique **Works:** one-acts; works in 12 other genres **Regulations:** entries must be unpublished, unproduced; 40 pages maximum; maximum cast: 4; 1 entry per author **Procedure:** send SASE for guidelines and registration form; upon entry: 2 copies of script, fee ($25 members, $35 non-members) **Deadline:** Feb. 15, 1999

♬ PAGE TO STAGE CONTEST   1- Rg
Orange County Playwrights Alliance, P.O. Box 6927, Fullerton, CA 92834 (714) 738-3841 FAX (714) 714-7833 e-mail elbro@earthline.net **Contact:** Contest Coord. **Frequency:** annual **Awards:** 1st prize $100, 2nd prize $50, 3rd prize $25; staged reading **Works:** short one-acts (15 minutes maximum) **Regulations:** writers must make their primary residence in CA; no more than 2 entries per author **Procedure:** send script with cast/character list, $5 fee payable to "OCPA" per script **Deadline:** Jul. 1, 1999 postmark **Notification:** Feb. 2000 **Advice:** *"Professional Playscript Format only!"*

PATHWAY PRODUCTIONS   F-l 1- ♪ 12+ W Lc
NATIONAL PLAYWRITING CONTEST   9561 E. Daines Dr., Temple City, CA 91780 (818) 287-4771 e-mail PathWayPro@aol.com **Contact:** R. Brent Beerman, Art. Director **Frequency:** annual **Award:** $200, workshop production **Works:** full-length plays, one-acts, musicals **Exclusive interest:** "Plays for and about teenagers; mature themes, large female casts preferred." **Casting:** "As few adults as possible." **Audience:** "High schools; youth programs." **Procedure:** send SASE for guidelines **Deadline:** May 1, 1999 **Your chances:** 100 entries/10 judges/4 readings per entry **Advice:** "Honest, cutting-edge plays."

PAUL GREEN PLAYWRIGHTS PRIZE   F-l 1- $
North Carolina Writers' Network, P.O. Box 954, Carrboro, NC 27510 (919) 967-9540 FAX (919) 929-0535 e-mail ncwn@sunsite.unc.edu **Contact:** Frances Dowell, Coordinator **Frequency:** annual **Award:** $500, possible production **Works:** full-length plays, one-acts **Regulations:** entries must be unpublished, unproduced **Procedure:** send 2 copies of script, separate cover sheet (with title, author's name, contact information), synopsis, fee ($10 non-members, $7.50 members), SASE for winners list; or, send SASE for guidelines, spring 1999 **Deadline:** Sept. 30, 1999

PEACE PLAY CONTEST   1- C
Goshen College Theatre Office, 1700 S. Main St., Goshen, IN 46526 (219) 535-7393 **Contact:** Doug Caskey, Director of Theatre **Frequency:** biennial odd years **Award:** $500, production, room, board **Works:** one-

acts **Regulations:** entries must be unpublished, on contemporary peace themes; no more than 2 entries per author **Procedure:** send 1-paragraph description of play and SASE for guidelines **Deadline:** Dec. 31, 1999 **Your chances:** 100 entries/3 judges/4 readings per entry

PEN AMERICAN CENTER AWARDS
568 Broadway, New York, NY 10012 (212) 334-1660 FAX (212) 334-2181 Contact: John Morrone, Literary Awards Mgr.

THE GREGORY KOLOVAKOS AWARD   Tr Hi
Frequency: biennial odd years **Award:** $2000 **Regulations:** recipient must demonstrate lifetime achievement in translation of Hispanic literature, not specifically translation of plays **Procedure:** nomination only; inquire for guidelines **Deadline:** Dec. 15, 1999

PEN BOOK-OF-THE-MONTH CLUB TRANSLATION   Tr
PRIZE Frequency: annual **Award:** $3000 **Works:** translations **Regulations:** entries must be book-length translations from any language into English published in U.S. during current calendar year **Procedure:** send SASE for guidelines; upon entry: 3 copies of book **Deadline:** Dec. 15, 1999

PEN/LAURA PELS AWARD FOR DRAMA   F-l Am L
Frequency: annual **Award:** $5000 **Regulations:** author must be a mid-career American playwright, writing in English, whose achievements are "vividly apparent in the rich and striking language of his or her work," and who has had a "professional production of at least 2 full-length works in a theatre of at least 299 seats and contracted specifically for limited or open runs" **Procedure:** nomination by peers (producers, agents, critics, playwrights) who should write a letter of support, "describing in some detail the literary character of the candidate's work, accompanied by a list of candidate's produced work"; script, supporting materials only upon request **Deadline:** Jan. 1, 1999 **Comment:** A medal will also be presented to a master American dramatist to be chosen by the judges--nominations not accepted.

RENATO POGGIOLI TRANSLATION AWARD   Tr Y
Frequency: annual **Award:** $3000 **Works:** translations (of plays and other genres) **Regulations:** entries must be book-length translations (or translations-in-progress) from Italian into English by young translators **Procedure:** send sample of translation, original text, curriculum vitae, statement of purpose **Deadline:** Jan. 1, 1999

PEN CENTER USA WEST LITERARY AWARD   F-l S Tv Rg
FOR DRAMA 672 S. Lafayette Park Pl. #41, Los Angeles, CA 90057 (213) 365-8500 FAX (213) 365-9616 e-mail rit2writ@netcom.com **Contact:** Christina Apels, Coordinator **Frequency:** annual **Award:** $1000 **Works:** full-length plays, screenplays, teleplays **Regulations:** writers must reside west of Mississippi River; entries must have been

produced during 1999 season **Procedure:** request guidelines and entry form; author, agent, or publicist may submit; upon entry: 4 copies of script **Deadline:** Jun. 31, 2000 **Future commitment:** recipient must attend awards banquet **Comment:** Entries are not returned.

PENDRAGON THEATRE YOUNG PLAYWRIGHTS
Saranac Lake, NY This contest has been discontinued.

♫ PETERSON EMERGING PLAYWRIGHT   F-l
COMPETITION Theatre Arts, Catawba College, 2300 W. Innes St., Salisbury, NC 28144 (704) 637-4440 e-mail jepperso@catawba.edu **Contact:** Jim Epperson, Chair **Frequency:** annual **Award:** $2000, mainstage or workshop production, travel, lodging, meals **Works:** full-length plays **Guidelines:** works must be unproduced plays by emerging playwrights; winner must attend rehearsals and performances **Procedure:** send SASE for guidelines **Deadline:** Dec. 1 each year

PISGAH PLAYERS SEARCH FOR THEATER OF   F-l 1-
RITUAL COMPETITION Literature Dept., UNCA, One University Hts., Asheville, NC 28804 (828) 251-6411 FAX (828) 251-6603 e-mail dhopes@unca.edu **Contact:** David Hopes, Director **Award:** reading, possible production **Works:** full-length plays, one-acts **Exclusive interest:** "The ritualistic and mythological powers of the theatre." **Procedure:** send SASE for guidelines **Deadline:** ongoing program

PITTSBURGH NEW WORKS FESTIVAL   F 1- CY
P.O. Box 42419, Pittsburgh, PA 15203 (412) 881-6888 Contact: Tracey Perles **Frequency:** annual **Awards:** $25 (or more), full productions in Sept. festival; staged readings for 6 runners-up **Works:** one-acts, children's plays **Regulations:** entries must be unproduced; 30 minutes maximum; maximum cast: 8; simple demands; no music **Stage:** arena, 100 seats **Casting:** non-Equity **Procedure:** request guidelines **Deadline:** TBA (Apr.) **Your chances:** 135 entries **Future commitment:** no **Comment:** "12 theatres do 12 one-acts at 1 theatre; 2 theatres do 2 children's plays at 1 theatre; some will remount plays at their own theatres."

PLAYHOUSE ON THE SQUARE NEW PLAY   F-l ♪ Rg
COMPETITION 51 S. Cooper, Memphis, TN 38104 (901) 725-0776 FAX (901) 272-7530 Contact: Jackie Nichols, Exec. Director **Frequency:** annual **Award:** $500, production **Works:** full-length plays, musicals **Special interest:** Southern authors **Regulations:** entries must be unproduced; small cast; full arrangement for piano required for musical **Procedure:** send script **Deadline:** Apr. 1, 1999

PLAYWRIGHTS FIRST PLAYS-IN-PROGRESS AWARD   F-l
National Arts Club, 15 Gramercy Park S, New York, NY 10003 (212) 249-6299, 677-1966 Contact: Michèle Hovde, President **Frequency:** annual **Award:** best play $1000; possible staged readings of selected

plays **Works:** full-length plays **Regulations:** entries must be unproduced; no translations or adaptations; 1 entry per author **Procedure:** send script, resume **Deadline:** Oct. 15, 1999 **Your chances:** 200 entries/ 20 judges/2-20 readings per entry **Future commitment:** no **Advice:** *"Professional Playscript Format* only!" **Comment:** The judges reserve the right to withhold the award. Scripts are not returned.

PLAYWRIGHTS PREVIEW PRODUCTIONS AWARDS   See Urban Stages/Playwrights Preview Productions Awards in this section.

PLAYWRIGHTS STUDIO THEATER FESTIVAL   F 1- Fm $ **OF TEN-MINUTE PLAYS**   5222 W. Wisconsin Ave., Milwaukee, **WI 53208-3059 (414) 476-8984 Contact:** Michael Neville, Artistic Director **Frequency:** annual **Award:** $150, production in festival (late Feb.-early Mar.) **Works:** 10-minute plays; 10-page maximum **Regulations:** cast size: 2-4; single, minimal set; minimal costumes; no more than 2 entries per author **Stage:** flexible, 200± seats **Casting:** non-Equity **Audience:** "Prefers 'PG' rather than 'R' language." **Procedure:** send script, $3 fee **Deadline:** TBA (Sept.)

PLAYWRIGHTS WEEK   F F-l 1- Tr Ad ♪ $ **The Lark Theatre Co., 939 8th Ave. Suite 400, New York, NY 10019 (212) 246-2676 FAX (212) 246-2609 e-mail** LARKCO@aol.com **Contact:** Miles Lott, Literary Mgr. **Frequency:** annual **Awards:** staged readings (spring) for selected scripts; Barebones Productions for 3-5 scripts **Works:** full-length plays, one-acts, translations, adaptations, musicals **Regulations:** entries must be unproduced except in workshops or showcases; 1 entry per author **Stage:** large studio space **Casting:** Equity, non-Equity **Procedure:** send script, $15 fee **Deadline:** Nov. 30, 1999; no submission before Jul. 1 **Notification:** Mar. 1, 2000 **Your chances:** 400 entries/8 judges/2 readings per entry/8 scripts selected **Future commitment:** not for staged readings **Comment:** "Playwrights selected are requested to participate in rehearsals and to attend readings during Playwrights Week; possible travel assistance."

PREMIERE ONE-ACT COMPETITION   1- $ **Moving Arts, 1822 Hyperion Ave., Los Angeles, CA 90027 (213) 665-8961 FAX (213) 665-1816 e-mail** rrasmussen@movingarts.org **Contact:** Rebecca Rasmussen, One-Act Coord. **Frequency:** annual **Award:** $200, production **Regulations:** 1-acts only, not produced in Southern CA **Procedure:** send script, $8 fee **Deadline:** Feb. 28, 1999 **Notification:** Jul. 31, 1999 **Comment:** The judges reserve the right to withhold the award.

PRINCESS GRACE AWARDS: PLAYWRIGHT   Rs Y **FELLOWSHIP**   Princess Grace Foundation--USA, 150 E. 58th St. **21st Floor, New York, NY 10155 (212) 317-1470 FAX (212) 317-1473 e-mail** pgfusa@pgfusa.com **Contact:** Ms. Toby Boshak, Exec. Director **Frequency:** annual **Award:** $7500 grant, 10-week residency at New

Dramatists, travel; inclusion of script in New Dramatists' library and ScriptShare; possible publication by Dramatists Play Service **Regulations:** authors must be U.S. citizens or permanent residents, not more than 30 years of age at upon application; works must be unpublished, unproduced except in workshops; no adaptations; 1 entry per author **Procedure:** send SASE for guidelines **Deadline:** Mar. 31, 1999 **Advice:** "The award is based primarily on the artistic quality of the submitted play and the potential of the fellowship to assist the writer's growth."

♫ PROGRESSIVE VOICES SHORT PLAY COMPETITION 1- Rg

Vox Theater Co., 51 Dell St., Sleepy Hollow, NY 10591 **Contact:** Tom Berdick, Literary Div. **Frequency:** annual **Award:** Best in Show award, prize TBA **Works:** one-acts (20 minutes maximum) **Regulations:** Manhattan writers only; minimal set/lighting **Procedure:** send script **Deadline:** TBA (Sept.) **Comment:** Scripts are not returned.

PUTTIN' ON THE RITZ NEW PLAY FESTIVAL F 1-

Ritz Theatre, 915 White Horse Pike, Oaklyn, NJ 08107 (609) 858-5230 **e-mail** Forrest37@aol.com **Contact:** Alex Wilkie, Development **Award:** production in Jun. festival **Works:** one-acts **Guidelines:** entries must be new plays, unproduced except in workshops, 10-40 minutes; 1 entry per author **Procedure:** send script **Deadline:** Jan. 15, 1999

QRL POETRY SERIES AWARDS F-l 1- Tr po $

Quarterly Review of Literature, Poetry Series, Princeton Univ., 26 Haslet Ave., Princeton, NJ 08540 (609) 921-6976 **Contact:** Renée Weiss, Co-Editor **Frequency:** annual **Awards:** $1000, publication, 100 complimentary copies; as many as 6 awards per year **Works:** full-length plays, one-acts, translations **Exclusive interest:** "Poetry/poetic drama; 50-100 pages." **Procedure:** send SASE for guidelines; upon entry: $20 fee for subscription to series **Deadline:** "Submit in May and Nov. only."

REP STAGE PLAYREADING SERIES See Rep Stage in Theatres.

REVA SHINER PLAY CONTEST F-l ♪ $

308 S. Washington, Bloomington, IN 47401 (812) 334-1188 **Contact:** John Edward Kinzer, Art. Director **Frequency:** annual **Award:** $500, staged reading; production **Works:** full-length plays, musicals **Regulations:** entries must be unpublished, unproduced, 75-150 minutes; minimal set **Stage:** small, 65 seats **Casting:** amateur **Audience:** middle class **Procedure:** send SASE for guidelines; upon entry: $5 fee **Deadline:** Jan. 15, 1999 **Comment:** The judges reserve the right to withhold the award.

THE RICHARD RODGERS AWARDS ♪

American Academy of Arts and Letters, 633 W. 155th St., New York, NY 10032 (212) 368-5900 FAX (212) 491-4615 **Contact:** Virginia Dajani, Exec. Director **Frequency:** annual **Award:** production, staged reading or studio production by NYC theatre **Works:** musicals **Regula-**

tions: authors must be U.S. citizens or permanent residents, not established in musical theatre; works must be unproduced; 1 entry per author or team; previous entries ineligible **Procedure:** send SASE for guidelines and application form **Deadline:** Nov. 2, 1999; no submission before Jun. 1 **Notification:** Mar. 2000 **Your chances:** 150 entries/9 judges **Comment:** The judges reserve the right to withhold the award.

♫ RIVERSIDE STAGE CO. FOUNDER'S   F-l ♪ Am $
AWARDS   c/o Riverside Stage Co., P.O. Box 253, Wilton, CT 06897 (203) 762-8130 **Contact:** Awards Coord. **Award:** $500, possible production **Works:** full-length plays, musicals **Regulations:** authors must be American playwrights; entries must be unproduced **Procedure:** send script, synopsis, $10 fee **Deadline:** Jan. 15, 1999

ROADSIDE ATTRACTIONS   F 1- W M
12 Miles West Theatre Co., P.O. Box 849, Montclair, NJ 07042 (973) 746-7181 Contact: Brian Shnipper, Literary Mgr. **Frequency:** annual **Award:** production in festival (Jan.) **Works:** one-acts (10-30 minutes) **Special interest:** "Women and minority writers." **Regulations:** authors must be NJ residents at least 18 years of age; no more than 2 entries per author **Procedure:** send script (with contact information and brief bio on separate cover sheet) **Deadline:** TBA (Nov.)

ROBERT BONE MEMORIAL AWARD   F-l ♪ Rg $
Playwrights' Project, Sammons Ctr. #12, 3630 Harry Hines Blvd., Dallas, TX 75219 (214) 497-1752 Contact: Priscilla Sample, Art. Dir. **Frequency:** annual **Award:** $500; all entries critiqued **Works:** full-length plays, musicals **Regulations:** residents of AZ, AR, CO, NM, OK, TX only; entries must be unproduced except in workshops; 1 entry per author **Procedure:** send script, synopsis, cassette tape for musical, bio, $15 fee, SASE for critique **Deadline:** May 1, 1999 **Notification:** Aug. 1999

ROBERT J. PICKERING AWARD FOR PLAYWRITING F-l Rg
EXCELLENCE Coldwater Comm. Theater, 89 S. Division, Coldwater, MI 49036 (517) 279-7963 Contact: J. Richard Colbeck, Play Selection Chair **Frequency:** annual **Award:** $300, production, housing **Works:** full-length plays **Exclusive interest:** "Works for a Midwest audience." **Regulations:** entries must be unproduced **Procedure:** send script **Deadline:** Jan. 1, 1999 **Notification:** Jan. 15, 1999 **Your chances:** 150 entries/8 judges/2+ readings per entry **Future commitment:** credit

ROCHESTER PLAYWRIGHT FESTIVAL 2000 F F-l 1- ♪ CY
Midwest Theatre Network, 5031 Tongen Ave. NW, Rochester, MN 55901 (507) 281-1472 Contact: Joan Sween, Exec. Director, MTN **Frequency:** biennial odd years **Awards:** production, possible cash awards and expenses for 4-8 winners **Works:** full-length plays, grouped one-acts, musicals, children's plays **Regulations:** entries must be unpublished, not produced professionally except in workshops; 4-8 theatres will produce

winning scripts **Procedure:** send SASE for guidelines; "1 submission per author free; each additional submission--$10 fee." **Deadline:** Nov. 30, 1999 **Notification:** Mar. 31, 2000 **Your chances:** 850 entries/20 judges/3 or more readings per entry **Future commitment:** no **Advice:** "Send submissions early to guarantee slower, more thoughtful readings."

ROY BARKER PLAYWRIGHTING F F-l 1- Tr Ad ♪ CY Y $
PRIZE **Rocky Mountain Student Theater Project, P.O. Box 1626, Telluride, CO 81435 (970) 728-4052 e-mail** playfest@aol.com **Contact:** Owen Perkins, Exec. Director **Frequency:** annual **Awards:** 1st prize $500, travel, lodging; 2nd prize $250; 3rd prize $100; production of 3 winners in festival **Works:** full-length plays, one-acts, translations, adaptations, musicals, children's plays **Regulations:** authors must be high school students; entries must be unpublished; one-acts (30-45 minutes) preferred **Procedure:** send script, author's contact information on separate sheet (not on script), $5 fee **Deadline:** May 1, 1999 **Notification:** Jun. 1, 1999 **Your chances:** 100 entries/3 judges/3 readings per entry **Comment:** Formerly Rocky Mtn. Student Playwrighting Festival.

SAM EDWARDS DEAF PLAYWRIGHTS F-l 1- h/d $
COMPETITION **New York Deaf Theater, 305 7th Ave. 11th Floor, New York, NY 10001-6008 (212) 924-9535** (teletypewriter) **e-mail** nydt@juno.com **Contact:** Robert De Mayo, Art. Director **Frequency:** annual **Awards:** $400 full-length plays, $200 one-act, possible staged reading or production **Works:** full-length plays (odd years), one-acts (even years) **Special interests:** "Deaf culture; advancing sign language theatre for a deaf and hearing audience." **Regulations:** deaf authors only; entries must be unproduced except in workshops **Casting:** Equity, non-Equity **Procedure:** send SASE for guidelines; upon entry: $10 fee ($15 outside U.S.) **Deadline:** Dec. 31, 1999 **Notification:** Aug. 2000 **Your chances:** 5-6 entries/7± judges **Future commitment:** "If we produce." **Advice:** "Be willing to rewrite." **Comment:** The judges reserve the right to withhold the awards.

THE SCHOLASTIC ART & WRITING Y Pl po S Tv Rd
AWARDS **555 Broadway, New York, NY 10012 (212) 343-6892 FAX (212) 343-4885 Contact:** Sarah Fewster, Writing Awards Coord. **Frequency:** annual **Awards:** $5000 scholarship for 5 best portfolios; $1000 merit award toward tuition to Tisch School of the Arts Dramatic Writing Program; cash prizes to other entrants **Works:** high school seniors: portfolios of 3-8 pieces (fiction, poetry, drama, etc); grades 7-12: individual pieces in various categories (including stage, film, TV, radio plays) **Regulations:** authors must be in grades 7-12; portfolio (50 pages maximum); script must be unpublished, 30 mintues maximum **Procedure:** write for guidelines and entry form by Oct. 1, 1999 **Deadline:** TBA (Jan. 2000) **Notification:** May 2000 **Comment:** Materials are not returned.

SETC NEW PLAY PROJECT   F-l 1- Rg
P.O. Box 9868, Greensboro, NC 27429 (336) 272-3645 Contact: Elizabeth Spicer, Coord. **Frequency**: annual **Award**: $1000, staged reading
at Southeastern Theatre Conf. convention, travel, room, board; submission to National Playwrights Conf. **Works**: full-length plays, full evening
of one-acts **Regulations**: residents of AL, FL, GA, KY, MS, NC, SC, TN,
VA, WV only; entries must be unproduced except in workshops; 1 entry
per author **Procedure**: send script (1-acts in 1 folder) **Deadline**: Jun. 1,
1999; no submission before Mar. 15 **Notification**: Nov. 1999 **Your
chances:** 60+ entries/16+ judges/2-4 readings per entry **Comment**: The
judges reserve the right to withhold the award.

SHORT GRAIN CONTEST   1p $
Grain Magazine, P.O. Box 1154, Regina, Saskatchewan S4P 3B4,
Canada (306) 244-2828 FAX (306) 244-0255 e-mail grainmag@sk.
sympatico.ca **Contact**: Steven Ross Smith, Bus. Mgr. **Frequency**: annual
Awards: $500 1st prize, $300 2nd prize, $200 3rd prize (Canadian $);
publication for winners and honorable mentions **Regulations**: entries
must be unpublished, unproduced monologues not submitted elsewhere,
500 words maximum **Procedure**: write for guidelines; upon entry: $24
fee for 1st 2 entries (includes subscription), $5 each additional entry
Deadline: Jan. 31, 1999 **Notification**: Apr. 30, 1999 **Comment**: Scripts
are not returned. **Advice**: "Canadian stamps or IRCs on SASE!"

SHUBERT FENDRICH MEMORIAL   F-l 1- CY C 12+ Fm
PLAYWRITING CONTEST Pioneer Drama Service, Inc., P.O.
Box 4267, Englewood, CO 80155 (303) 779-4035 FAX (303) 779-4315
e-mail piodrama@aol.com **Frequency**: annual **Award**: $1000 royalty
advance, publication; all entries considered for publication **Works:**
plays up to 90 minutes **Special interests**: "Children's theatre; social
issues for teens." **Regulations**: entries must be unpublished, previously
produced, appropriate for schools and community theatres; cast balance
favoring female roles, minimal sets preferred; authors currently published by Pioneer Drama Service ineligible **Procedure**: send script.
proof of production **Deadline**: Mar. 1, 1999 **Notification**: 12+ weeks

SIENA COLLEGE INTERNATIONAL PLAYWRIGHTS' F-l Rs
COMP. Theatre Prog., Dept. of Creative Arts, Siena College, 515
Loudon Rd., Loudonville, NY 12211 (518) 783-2381 FAX (518) 783-
4293 e-mail maciag@siena.edu **Contact**: Gary Maciag, Dir. of Theatre
Frequency: biennial even years **Award**: $2000, production, up to $1000
for expenses **Works**: full-length plays **Regulations**: entries must be unpublished, unproduced except in workshops; no musicals; small cast preferred; college-age actors/audience; 4-6 week residency (spring 2001) required **Procedure**: send SASE for guidelines **Deadline**: Jun. 30, 2000
postmark; no submission before Feb. 1 **Notification**: Sept. 30, 2000 **Your
chances:** 300+ entries/12 judges/1-3 readings per entry **Comment**:
The judges reserve the right to withhold the award.

SOURCE THEATRE CO. LITERARY PRIZE 1999   F-l 1- ♪

1835 14th St. NW, Washington, DC 20009 (202) 462-1073 Contact: Keith Parker, Literary Mgr. **Frequency:** annual **Award:** $250, workshop production in Washington Theatre Festival (Jul. 8-Aug. 8, 1999) **Works:** full-length plays, one-acts, musicals **Regulations:** entries must not have been professionally produced **Procedure:** send script, synopsis, resume **Deadline:** Jan. 15, 1999 **Notification:** May 15, 1999 **Comment:** Scripts are not returned.

SOUTH ARKANSAS ARTS CENTER   F-l 1- Rg Fm
ANNUAL ARKANSAS PLAYWRIGHT'S COMPETITION

110 E. 5th St., El Dorado, AR 71730 (870) 862-5474 **Contact:** Linda M. Boydston, Exec. Director **Frequency:** annual **Award:** honorarium, $200 or more, production **Works:** full-length plays, one-acts **Specifications:** small stage; no fly space; limited wing space **Regulations:** AR residents only; entries must be unpublished, unproduced except in workshops; no more than 2 entries per author **Procedure:** send 6 copies of script; or, phone for guidelines **Deadline:** TBA (Oct.) **Your chances:** 10± entries/ 6-8 judges/6-8 readings per entry **Future commitment:** 1st production **Advice:** "Bad language or poking seriously at religion won't fly here." **Comment:** The judges reserve the right to withhold the award.

SOUTH CAROLINA PLAYWRIGHTS'   F F-l 1- C cm $
FESTIVAL   Trustus Theatre, P.O. Box 11721-1721, Columbia, SC

29211 (803) 254-9732 FAX (803) 771-9153 e-mail Trustus88@aol.com **Contact:** Tim Gardner, Literary Mgr. **Frequency:** annual **Awards:** full-length play: 1st prize $500, production, travel, housing; 2nd prize $250, staged reading; one-act: $50, reading in Late Night Series **Works:** full-length plays (80 minutes minimum); one-acts **Special interests:** "Hard-hitting issues; comedies." **Regulations:** entries must be unpublished, not professionally produced; maximum cast: 8; single set preferred; 1 entry per author **Procedure:** request guidelines and application packet; upon entry: $15 fee **Deadline:** Mar. 1; no submission before Jan. 1 **Notification:** Jul. 1 **Your chances:** 100-200 entries/5-7 judges/1-3 readings per entry **Future commitment:** no **Comment:** The judges reserve the right to withhold the awards.

SOUTH COAST REP. CALIFORNIA PLAYWRIGHTS
COMPETITION   This competition has been discontinued.

SOUTH COAST REPERTORY HISPANIC   D F-l 1- Hi Rs
PLAYWRIGHTS PROJECT   P.O. Box 2197, Costa Mesa, CA

92628-2197 (714) 708-5500 Ext. 5405 **Contact:** Juliette Cayrillo, Project Director **Frequency:** annual **Awards:** participation in workshop (Jun. 7-27, 1999); expenses, honorarium; possible commission; 2-3 plays selected for 6-day workshop culminating in public reading/discussion; plays receive dramaturgical development, professional cast **Regula-**

tions: authors must be Hispanic Americans; entries may be full-length plays or one-acts, written essentially in English; unproduced works preferred; pre-workshop meeting May 1999 **Procedure:** send script, synopsis, bio **Deadline:** Jan. 15, 1999 **Notification:** Apr. 1999 **Your chances:** 100 entries/3 judges/2 readings per entry

SOUTH FLORIDA CHAPTER   F-l 1- cm dr $
NATIONAL WRITERS ASSOCIATION 1999 COMPETITION
SFCNWA, P.O. Box 570415, Miami, FL 33257-0415 (305) 235-2867, 275-8666 **Contact:** Charles Aye, Contest Chairman **Awards:** 1st prize $300; 2nd prize $100 **Works:** full-length plays and one-act comedies and dramas **Regulations:** entries must be unpublished and not professionally produced; no musicals or children's plays **Procedure:** send SASE for brochure; or, send script, cover letter with author's contact information and play title, and $10 fee **Deadline:** Jan. 15, 1999 **Notification:** Apr. 1999 **Advice:** *"Professional Playscript Format* only!"

SOUTHERN APPALACHIAN PLAY-   F F-l Ad ♪ Rg
WRIGHTS CONFERENCE SART, P.O. Box 1720, Mars Hill, NC
28754-1720 (828) 689-1384 **e-mail** sart@mhc.edu **Contact:** Dianne J. Chapman, Mng. Director **Frequency:** annual **Awards:** readings (Apr. 1999), room and board for 5 winners; possible production (summer), housing, $500 honorarium **Works:** full-length plays, adaptations, musicals **Special interest:** "Southern Appalachian authors, themes." **Regulations:** entries must be unpublished, unproduced except in workshops **Procedure:** send script, synopsis, resume **Deadline:** TBA (Oct. in previous years) **Your chances:** 80-120 entries/8 judges/4-8 readings per entry **Future commitment:** no

SOUTHERN PLAYWRIGHTS COMPETITION   F-l Rg
210 Stone Center, Jacksonville State Univ., Jacksonville, AL 36265 (205) 782-5411 **FAX** (205) 782-5441 **Contact:** Steven J. Whitton, Coordinator **Frequency:** annual **Award:** $1000, production, housing **Works:** full-length plays **Exclusive interest:** "The Southern experience." **Regulations:** authors must be natives or residents of AL, AR, FL, GA, KY, LA, MS, NC, SC, TN, TX, VA, WV; entries must be unpublished; 1 entry per author **Procedure:** write or phone for guidelines and entry form **Deadline:** Feb. 15, 1999 postmark **Notification:** May 1, 1999 **Your chances:** 50-75 entries/15 judges/2 readings per entry **Future commitment:** credit **Comment:** The judges reserve the right to withhold the award.

♫ STAGES: A NEW PLAY FESTIVAL   F-l 1- Tr Ad ♪ CY
S.T.A.G.E., P.O. Box 214820, Dallas, TX 75221 (214) 630-7722 **FAX** (214) 630-4468 **Awards:** $15,000 **Regulations:** writers must be U.S. citizens; open to all styles, themes, genres **Procedure:** send SASE for guidelines **Deadline:** May 31, 1999 **Notification:** Apr. 1, 2000

STAGES REPERTORY THEATRE ANNUAL FESTIVALS   F
3201 Allen Pkwy. **Suite 101, Houston, TX 77019** (713) 527-0240 **Contact:** Rob Bundy, Artistic Director **Award:** staged reading in festival (Jun.) **Regulations:** 1 entry per author per festival **Procedure:** send script (typed, bound, double-spaced) with author's name and contact information on title page only **Your chances:** 3 judges

♫ CHILDREN'S THEATRE PLAY- F CY Ad ♪ Esp
WRIGHT FESTIVAL **Regulations:** entries must be children's plays, adaptations, or musicals, addressed primarily but not exclusively to ages 4-10 and performed by adults; maximum cast: 8; 50 minutes maximum; bilingual works accepted **Deadline:** Feb. 14, 1999; no submission before Oct. 1, 1999 for 2000 deadline **Notification:** May 1999

♫ HISPANIC PLAYWRIGHTS' FESTIVAL F Hi Esp
Regulations: authors must be of Hispanic/Latino heritage; complete English translations must accompany all plays written in Spanish; excerpts from 2 finalists will also receive readings **Deadline:** Dec. 31, 1999; no submission before Oct. 1

TEXAS PLAYWRIGHTS FESTIVAL F Rg
Regulations: writers must be native Texans or current or previous TX residents, or plays must have TX settings or themes; entries must be unproduced professionally; small cast preferred **Deadline:** Feb. 14, 1999; no submission before Oct. 1, 1999 for 2000 deadline **Notification:** May 1999

WOMEN'S REPERTORY PROJECT F W
Regulations: women writers only **Deadline:** Dec. 31, 1999; no submission before Oct. 1 **Notification:** May 2000

STANLEY DRAMA AWARD F-l 1- ♪
Theatre Dept., Wagner College, One Campus Rd., Staten Island, NY 10301 (718) 390-3325 **FAX** (718) 390-3323 **Frequency:** annual **Award:** $2000 **Works:** full-length plays, thematically related one-acts, musicals **Regulations:** entries must not have received tradebook publication or professional production; previous entries and former winners ineligible; 1 entry per author **Procedure:** send SASE for guidelines and application form **Deadline:** TBA

SUMMER SHORTS FESTIVAL F 1- x Esp
City Theatre, P.O. Box 248268, Coral Gables, FL 33124 (305) 284-3605 **FAX** (305) 365-9623 **Contact:** Stephanie Norman, Producer **Frequency:** annual **Award:** production (with royalties) in festival (Jun. 2000) **Works:** one-acts (2-12 minutes) **Regulations:** entries may be experimental or naturalistic; bilingual (English/Spanish) works accepted; simple sets; 1 entry per author **Procedure:** send script (with contact information and bio on title page) **Deadline:** Nov. 20, 1999 **Your chances:** 500 entries/3 readings per entry **Comment:** Scripts are not returned.

SUMMERFIELD G. ROBERTS AWARD F-l po B Rg
The Sons of the Republic of Texas, 1717 8th St., Bay City, TX 77414
(409) 245-6644 FAX same e-mail srttexas@tgn.net Contact: Melinda
Williams, Admin. Asst. Frequency: annual Award: $2500, to be presented at spring meeting Works: full-length plays, poetry, fiction, nonfiction Exclusive interest: "Life in the Republic of Texas." Regulations:
entries must have been written or published during calendar year preceding the deadline; previous entries ineligible Procedure: send 5 copies of
script Deadline: Jan. 15, 1999 postmark Notification: Apr. 1999 Your
chances: 15-20 entries/3 judges/1 reading per entry Future commitment: credit Advice: "The purpose is to encourage literary effort and
research into events and personalities during the days of the Republic of
Texas, 1836-1846." Comment: "Winners of the award in the last 3 years
serve as judges." Scripts are not returned.

THE SUSAN SMITH BLACKBURN PRIZE F-l W
3239 Avalon Pl., Houston, TX 77019 (713) 308-2842 FAX (713) 654-
8184 Contact: Emilie S. Kilgore, Board of Directors Frequency: annual
Awards: 1st prize $5000, signed print by Willem de Kooning; 2nd prize
$2000; 8-10 other finalists receive $500 Works: full-length plays Regulations: authors must be women writing in English; entries must be unproduced or produced within 1 year of deadline Procedure: "Theatres
are asked to submit plays; send SASE for brochure." Deadline: Sept. 20,
1999 Notification: Jan.-Feb. 2000 Your chances: 90-95 entries/15
readers/6 final judges/3+ readings per entry Future commitment: no
Advice: "Bring your work to the attention of one of our source theatres
(send SASE [2 oz. postage] for list)." Comment: The judges reserve the
right to withhold the 1st prize.

SWTA ANNUAL NEW PLAY CONTEST F F-l 1- Ad $
**Southwest Theatre Assn., Theatre Arts, Univ. of Texas at Arlington,
Box 19103, Arlington, TX 76019-0103** (817) 272-3141 e-mail acg@
utarlg.uta.edu Contact: Andrew Gaupp, Dennis Maher, Co-Chairs Frequency: annual Award: $200, staged reading at convention (Nov. 1999),
publication in journal Works: full-length plays, one-acts, adaptations
Regulations: writers must reside in U.S.; entries must be unpublished,
unproduced except in workshops, previous entries ineligible; no musicals
or children's plays Procedure: send SASE for guidelines; or, send script,
synopsis, $10 fee (payable to SWTA); "a letter of professional recommendation is appreciated" Deadline: Mar. 16, 1999 postmark Notification:
fall 1999 Your chances: 100 entries/5 judges/3 readings per entry

TADA! STAGED READING PLAY CONTEST CY 1- 12+
120 W. 28th St., New York, NY 10001 (212) 627-1732 FAX (212) 243-
6736 Contact: Janine Nina Trevens, Artistic Director Frequency: annual Awards: cash prize, staged reading for 5 winners Works: one-act
children's plays Special interests: "Child casts, 8-18; teen topics." Regulations: entries must be unpublished, unproduced; "no children in adult

roles; may cast 2-3 adults; plays may be for a specific age" **Procedure:** send SASE for guidelines; or, send 2 copies of script, character and technical breakdowns **Deadline:** Jul. 1, 1999 **Notification:** Sept. 15, 1999 **Your chances:** 150 entries/5 judges/2 readings per entry **Comment:** The judges reserve the right to withhold the awards.

TALENT FEST   F 1- Tr Ad ♪ CY $

Inner City Cultural Center, P.O. Box 272, Los Angeles, CA 90028 (213) 627-7670 FAX (213) 622-5881 Contact: Coordinator **Frequency:** annual **Awards:** $1000 1st prize or paid professional internship to film studio, $500 2nd prize, $250 3rd prize **Works:** one-acts, translations, adaptations, musicals, operas, children's plays **Regulations:** entries must be fully mounted productions of unpublished plays (center provides basic tech support, promotions); translations and adaptations must be of unpublished works; small cast; minimal set; 40 minutes maximum; 1 entry per author; productions Mar.-May 1999 **Procedure:** send SASE for guidelines; upon entry: $45 fee **Deadline:** Mar. 21, 1999 **Your chances:** 40 entries/4-6 judges/4-6 viewings per entry

THE TEN-MINUTE MUSICALS PROJECT   ♪ 1-

P.O. Box 461194, West Hollywood, CA 90046 Contact: Michael Koppy, Producer **Frequency:** annual **Award:** $250, development toward professional production in show comprised of short works; equal share of licensing royalties **Works:** complete short musicals **Special interest:** "Strong story: beginning, middle, end." **Regulations:** maximum cast: 10, 6 preferred; playing time: 8-14 minutes, over 50% sung material; excerpts must be self-contained; adaptors must secure permission **Procedure:** write or phone for guidelines **Deadline:** Aug. 31, 1999 **Notification:** Oct. 31, 1999 **Your chances:** 75-125 entries/3 judges/3 readings per entry **Advice:** "Possibly start from an extant short story; avoid children's material. Create plot twists and a real climax; one or more full-cast 'production numbers.'" **Comment:** The judges reserve the right to withhold the award.

TENNESSEE CHAPBOOK PRIZE   1- $

Poems & Plays, English Dept., Middle Tennessee State Univ., Murfreesboro, TN 37132 **(615) 898-2712 FAX (615) 898-5098 Contact:** Dr. Gaylord Brewer, Editor **Frequency:** annual **Award:** publication in magazine, 50 copies **Works:** one-acts, combinations of short one-acts **Regulations:** 24-30 pages maximum **Procedure:** send script, $10 fee (for 1 copy of issue) **Deadline:** Jan 15, 1999; no submission before Oct. 1, 1999 for 2000 deadline

TENNESSEE WILLIAMS/NEW ORLEANS   F 1- $
LITERARY FESTIVAL ONE-ACT PLAY CONTEST

5500 Prytania St. Suite 217, New Orleans, LA 70115 **(504) 581-1144 FAX (504) 529-2430 e-mail** twfest@gnofn.org **Contact:** Lou Ann Morehouse, Festival Mgr. **Frequency:** annual **Award:** $1000, production at festival, staged reading **Works:** one-acts **Regulations**: entries must be unpublished, not professionally or semi-professionally produced except in workshops; 1 hour± **Stage:** flexible, 75 or 50 seats **Casting:** non-Equity, students **Audience:** "Festival: educated, aged 30-50, 60% white; university: aged 20-30, 50-50 black/white." **Procedure:** send script, $15 fee; or, request guidelines **Deadline:** Dec. 1, 1999 **Notification:** Mar. 2000 **Your chances:** 250-300 entries/12 judges/3+ readings per entry **Future commitment:** no **Comment:** Scripts are not returned. The judges reserve the right to withhold the award.

TENNESSEE WILLIAMS THEATRE FESTIVAL F 1- Rg **Rhodes College and Playwright's Forum, 2000 N. Parkway, Memphis, TN 38107-1690 (901) 843-3937 FAX (901) 843-3406 e-mail** ewing @rhodes.edu **Contact:** Julia Cookie Ewing, Chair, Theatre Dept. **Frequency:** annual **Awards:** $50, possible production at summer festival, possible publication in anthology for 5 winners **Works:** 10-minute plays (10 pages maximum) **Regulations:** entries must not have had Equity productions; Southern themes, settings, or subject matter; no more than 2 entries per author **Procedure:** send script, 1/2-page synopsis, resume **Deadline:** TBA **Your chances:** 7 judges/2 readings per entry **Advice:** "Small cast, simple set, few properties." **Comment:** The judges reserve the right to withhold the award.

TEXAS PLAYWRIGHTS FESTIVAL   See Stages Repertory Theatre Annual Festivals in this section.

THEATER AT LIME KILN PLAYWRITING CONTEST **14 S. Randolph St., Lexington, VA 24450 (540) 463-7088 FAX (540) 463-1082 e-mail** limekiln@cfw.com **Contact:** Eleanor Connor, Dramaturg This contest is inactive in 1999; see *The Playwright's Companion 2000* for future plans.

THEATRE CONSPIRACY NEW PLAY CONTEST F F-1 $ **10091 McGregor Blvd., Fort Myers, FL 33919 (941) 936-3239 Contact:** Contest Coordinator **Frequency:** annual **Award:** $500, production in New Arts Festival **Works:** full-length plays **Regulations:** entries must be unproduced; maximum cast: 6; simple demands; no musicals **Procedure:** send script, 1-page synopsis, bio, $10 fee **Deadline:** Jan. 10, 1999 **Notification:** Apr. 1999

THEATRE MEMPHIS NEW PLAY COMP. P.O. Box 240117, **Memphis, TN 38124 (901) 682-8601** This contest is being reevaluated; see *The Playwright's Companion 2000* or send SASE for new guidelines.

THEATREFEST NATIONAL PLAYWRITING D F-1 C x **CONTEST Dept. of Theatre, Montclair State Univ., Upper Montclair, NJ 07043 (201) 655-7496 FAX (201) 655-5366 Contact:** John Wooten, Art. Director **Awards:** $500, script development, production

(Jun.-Jul. 1999), certificate, housing for out-of-state playwright; readings for 3 finalists **Works:** full-length plays **Exclusive interest:** "Contemporary plays that explore the human condition in a unique and innovative way." **Regulations:** entries must be unpublished, unproduced; maximum cast: 8; suitable for flexible black box, 125 seats **Casting:** Equity, students, alumni **Procedure:** send 1-5 page synopsis **Deadline:** Jan. 1, 1999 **Notification:** Feb. 1, 1999 for 1st finalists **Your chances:** "After evaluation of synopses, 10 applicants will be invited to submit scripts; 3 will be chosen for a reading judged by TheatreFest staff and a celebrity director." **Future commitment:** percentage, options, credit **Advice:** "Plays may be experimental in nature and expand the boundaries of the traditional box set. Please follow guidelines. Do not phone." **Comment:** "For the year 2000, TheatreFest will hold an international contest for a new play that promises to be truly a 'world premiere.'"

♫ THEATRE THREE ONE-ACT PLAY FESTIVAL 1-
P.O. Box 512, Pt. Jefferson, NY 11777-0512 (516) 928-9100 Contact: Jeffrey E. Sanzel, Art. Director **Frequency:** annual **Award:** production in festival (Feb.-Mar.) **Works:** one-acts **Guidelines:** maximum cast: 6; simple/suggested set preferred **Procedure:** send query/synopsis **Deadline:** TBA (Sept)

♫ THEATRIX ANNUAL "DROP YOUR SHORTS" 1- $
SHORT PLAY COMPETITION
P.O. Box 9 Cooper Station, New York, NY 10276 Contact: Competition Coord. **Frequency:** annual **Awards:** cash awards, production for 20 winners **Works:** 15-minute plays **Regulations:** authors must reside in NYC Metro area **Procedure:** send script, $1 fee **Deadline:** inquire

THEODORE WARD PRIZE FOR AFRICAN- F-l Tr Ad Af
AMERICAN PLAYWRIGHTS
Columbia College Chicago, Theatre/Music Ctr., 72 E. 11th St., Chicago, IL 60605 (312) 663-1600 Ext. 6136 FAX (312) 663-9591 e-mail chigochuck@aol.com **Contact:** Chuck Smith, Facilitator **Frequency:** annual **Awards:** 1st prize $2000, production, travel, housing; 2nd prize $500, staged reading; 3rd prize staged reading at Goodman Theatre **Works:** full-length plays, translations, adaptations **Exclusive interest:** African-American writers, themes **Regulations:** authors must be U.S. residents; entries must be unpublished, not professionally produced; adaptations must be of works in public domain; 1 entry per author **Stage:** black box, 70 seats **Procedure:** send SASE for guidelines **Deadline:** Jul. 1, 1999; no submission before Apr. 1 **Notification:** Nov. 1999 **Future commitment:** percentage, options **Comment:** The judges reserve the right to withhold the awards.

TOWSON STATE UNIV. PRIZE FOR LITERATURE Rg
Towson State Univ., Towson, MD 21252-7097 (410) 830-2128 **Contact:** Dean, College of Liberal Arts **Frequency:** annual **Award:** $1000 **Works:** single plays, collections **Regulations:** authors must have been

MD residents for at least 3 years, not over age 40; entries must have been published within 3 years or be scheduled for publication within 1 year **Procedure**: send SASE for guidelines; upon entry: 5 copies of script **Deadline**: May 15, 1999 **Notification**: Dec. 1, 1999 **Your chances**: 10-15 entries/5 judges **Comment**: Scripts are not returned.

UNICORN THEATRE NATIONAL PLAYWRIGHT'S AWARD F-1 C Rs

3828 Main St., Kansas City, MO 64111 (816) 531-7529 Ext. 18 **FAX** (816) 531-0421 **Contact**: Herman Wilson, Literary Asst. **Frequency**: annual **Award**: $1000, production, staged reading, possible residency **Works**: full-length plays **Special interest**: "Contemporary, issue-oriented works." **Regulations**: entries must be unpublished, unproduced except in workshops; maximum cast: 10; no musicals or historical plays; no more than 2 entries per author **Stage**: thrust, 150 seats **Casting**: Equity **Audience**: "Prefers cutting-edge, contemporary, off Broadway plays." **Procedure**: send SASE for guidelines; script upon request only **Deadline**: Apr. 30, 1999 postmark; no submission before Sept. 1, 1999 for 2000 deadline **Notification**: Sept. 30, 1999 **Your chances**: 400 entries/10 judges/2 readings per entry **Future commitment**: percentage **Advice**: "No dot matrix printouts; entry materials must be firmly bound." **Comment**: The judges reserve the right to withhold the award.

UNIVERSITY OF LOUISVILLE GRAWEMEYER AWARD ♪ $

FOR MUSIC COMPOSITION School of Music, Univ. of Louisville, Louisville, KY 40292 (502) 8526907 **Contact**: Paul Brink, Exec. Secretary **Frequency**: annual **Award**: $150,000 in 5 annual installments **Works**: operas, musicals, other musical genres **Special interest**: "Serious works, substantial content." **Regulations**: entries must have premiered Jan. 1, 1994-Dec. 31, 1998, must be sponsored by professional musical organizations or individuals **Procedure**: request application form; upon entry: score, cassette tape of professional-level performance, documentation of premiere, supporting letter from sponsor, composer's photo and bio, $30 fee **Deadline**: Jan. 25, 1999 **Notification**: late spring 2000 **Your chances**: 180 submissions/3 judges **Comment**: Materials are not returned. The judges reserve the right to withhold the award.

URBAN STAGES/PLAYWRIGHTS PREVIEW PRODUCTIONS

17 E. 47th St., New York, NY 10017 (212) 289-2168 **FAX** same **Contact**: Charlie Schoeder, Project Director **Frequency**: annual

EMERGING PLAYWRIGHT AWARD F-1 1- M

Award: $500, production, travel **Works**: full-length plays, one-acts **Special interest**: minority writers, racially diverse casts, related one-acts **Regulations**: entries must be unpublished, not previously produced in NYC **Procedure**: send script, bio, any script history **Deadline**: ongoing program; best time: Jul.-Aug., Dec. **Your chances**: 500 entries/10 judges/3 readings per entry **Future commitment**: 1-year option **Comment**: The judges reserve the right to withhold the award.

URBAN STAGES AWARD   1- M

Award: $200, 4-6 staged readings in New York City libraries **Works:** short plays (1 hour maximum) **Special interests:** minority writers, multiracial casts **Regulations:** entries must not have been produced in New York City; maximum cast: 5 **Procedure:** send SASE for guidelines **Deadline:** Jun. 15, 1999

UTAH PLAYFEST   Theatre Arts Dept., Utah State Univ., Logan, UT 84322 (801) 797-3046 FAX (801) 797-0086 Contact: PlayFest Director

This contest is under review; inquire, or see *The Playwright's Companion 2000* for future plans.

VAN LIER FELLOWSHIPS   F-l 1- Tr Ad M Rg Y

New York Theatre Workshop, 79 E. 4th St., New York, NY 10003 (212) 780-9037 FAX (212) 460-8996 Contact: Chiori Miyagawa **Frequency:** annual **Award:** fellowship **Works:** full-length plays, one-acts, translations, adaptations **Guidelines:** authors must be playwrights of color, under 30 years of age, who reside in New York City area; 1 entry per author **Procedure:** send script, letter of intent, resume **Deadline:** TBA (phone Feb. 1999 for date) **Your chances:** 45 entries/3-5 judges/2-3 readings per entry

VENTANA PUBLICATIONS PLAY AWARD   P.O. Box 191973, San Francisco, CA 94119 (415) 522-8989 Contact: J. P. Allen, Director

This contest is inactive in 1999; see *The Playwright's Companion 2000* or inquire for future plans.

VERMONT PLAYWRIGHTS AWARD   F-l CY Rg

The Valley Players, P.O. Box 441, Waitsfield, VT 05673-0441 (802) 496-3751 e-mail mitchnjen@madriver.com **Contact:** Jennifer Howard, Chair **Frequency:** annual **Award:** $1000, possible production **Works:** full-length plays, children's plays **Regulations:** authors must be residents of Northern New England (ME, NH, VT); entries must be unpublished, unproduced; works that have received staged readings or workshops encouraged; no grid or fly space; no special lighting; works suitable for a community theatre; no musicals **Procedure:** send SASE for guidelines; upon entry: 2 copies of script **Deadline:** Feb. 1, 1999 **Notification:** spring 1999 **Your chances:** 12 entries/5 judges/5 readings per entry **Comment:** The judges reserve the right to withhold the award.

VSA PLAYWRIGHT DISCOVERY PROGRAM   h/d

1300 Connecticut Ave. NW Suite 700, Washington, DC 20036 (202) 628-2800, (800) 933-8721, TTY (202) 737-0645 FAX (202) 737-0725 e-mail playwright@vsarts.org **Contact:** Elena Widder, Program Mgr. **Frequency:** annual **Award:** monetary award, production at Kennedy Ctr., travel, expenses **Works:** full-length plays, single and related one-acts, musicals, children's plays **Exclusive interest**: "Scripts must document the experience of living with a disability." **Regulations**: authors must be people with disabilities who reside in the U.S.A.; entries must be unpublished, unproduced **Stage**: flexible, 350 seats **Casting**: non-Equity, students **Procedure**: request guidelines and application form by mail or e-mail; upon entry: 2 copies of script, synopsis, bio **Deadline**: TBA (early May 1999) **Notification**: summer 1999 **Your chances**: 3-8 judges/ 1 reading per entry **Comment**: Scripts are not returned.

WALDO M. AND GRACE C. BONDERMAN F Rs CY Ad L
**IUPUI NATIONAL YOUTH THEATRE PLAYWRITING
DEVELOPMENT WORKSHOP** 425 University Blvd. Rm. 309,
Indianapolis, IN 46202 (317) 274-2095 FAX (317) 278-1025 e-mail
dwebb@iupui.edu **Contact**: Priscilla Jackson, Literary Mgr. **Frequency**: biennial even years **Awards**: $1000 for each of 4 winners; production or staged reading at symposium (Apr.-May), travel and housing for 1-week residency **Works**: children's plays, including adaptations **Special interests**: "Strong story lines, compelling characters, attention to language." **Regulations**: entries must be unpublished, uncommitted to publication; 45-90 minutes; adaptors must secure permission; winners must attend workshop and symposium; 1 entry per author **Procedure**: send SASE for guidelines and application form; upon entry: 3 copies of script **Deadline**: Sept. 1, 2000 postmark; Sept. 7, 2000 receipt; no submission before May 1, 2000 **Notification**: Jan. 2001 **Your chances**: 125-150 entries/25-32 judges/2+ readings per entry **Future commitment**: credit **Comment**: The judges reserve the right to withhold the awards.

WAREHOUSE THEATRE CO. ONE-ACT 1- W Y $
COMPETITION Box 2077, Stephens College, Columbia, MO
65215 (314) 876-7194 **Contact**: Artistic Director **Frequency**: annual
Award: $200, production **Works**: one-acts **Special interest**: "Works by, for or about women." **Regulations**: authors must be high school, undergraduate or graduate students; entries must be unpublished, unproduced except in workshops **Casting**: women students **Procedure**: send script (with contact information on title page), $10 fee **Deadline**: Jan. 1, 1999 postmark **Notification**: Feb. 1, 1999 **Your chances**: 40 entries/9 judges/9 readings per script **Comment**: The judges reserve the right to withhold the award. **Advice**: "*Professional Playscript Format* only!"

WARNER THEATER CENTER FOR THE ARTS 1- Rg $
CONNECTICUT ONE-ACT PLAY CONTEST P.O. Box 1012,
Torrington, CT 06790 (860) 489-7180 **Contact**: Coord. **Frequency**: annual **Award**: production **Works**: one-acts **Regulations**: CT playwrights only; entries must unproduced, simple set and technical demands; winning writers must attend some rehearsals **Procedure**: send SASE for guidelines and application form ; upon entry: $5 fee **Deadline**: Oct. 15, 1999 postmark

"WE DON'T NEED NO STINKIN' DRAMAS" F-l ♪ C cm M
PLAYWRITING CONTEST Mixed Blood Theatre Co., 1501 S. 4th
St., Minneapolis, MN 55454 (612) 338-0937 Contact: David Kunz,
Script Czar Frequency: annual Award: $1000, possible production +
$1000 Works: full-length comedies, musical comedies Special interests:
"Contemporary issues; race, sports, politics." Regulations: authors must
be U.S. citizens who have had at least 1 work produced or work-
shopped; entries must be original works which not have had productions
to which tickets were sold; 65-page minimum; no more than 2 entries per
author; previous entries ineligible; no translations, adaptations, his-
tories, or children's plays Procedure: send SASE for guidelines Deadline: Feb. 1, 1999 Advice: "Mixed Blood is a multiracial theatre dedicated to promoting cultural pluralism and individual equality."

WEST COAST ENSEMBLE COMPETITIONS
P.O. Box 38728, Los Angeles, CA 90038 (310) 449-1447 FAX (310)
453-2254 Contact: Les Hanson, Artistic Director Frequency: annual
Regulations: entries must not have been produced in Southern CA
Future commitment: credit Advice: "If submitting to more than 1 competition, please use separate envelopes." Comment: The judges reserve
the right to withhold the awards.

MUSICAL STAIRS ♪
Awards: $500, production; staged readings for 5 finalists Works:
musicals Regulations: 1 entry per creative team; 2nd productions
welcome if not produced in Southern CA Specifications: maximum
cast: 12; simple sets; "simple orchestrations (2 pianos, synthesizer,
etc.)" Procedure: send script, cassette, available score or lead sheets
Deadline: Jun. 30, 1999 postmark; Jul. 15, 1999 receipt; no submission
before Jul. 1, 1999 for 2000 deadline Notification: Dec. 1999 Your
chances: 100 entries/8 judges/3 readings per entry Advice: "No restrictions on style."

WEST COAST ENSEMBLE COMPETITION FOR F-l
FULL-LENGTH PLAYS Award: $500, production Regulations:
1 entry per author; maximum cast: 12 Procedure: send script Deadline: Dec. 31, 1999 postmark; Jan. 15, 2000 receipt Notification: Jun.
30, 2000 Your chances: 600 entries/15 judges/3 readings per entry

♫ WEST COAST 10-MINUTE PLAYWRITING FESTIVAL F 1-
"SIX AT EIGHT" P.O. Box 18438, Irvine, CA 92623-8438 e-mail
jillkat@employees.org Contact: Jill Forbath-Roden, Art. Director Frequency: annual Awards: 1st prize $100, 2nd prize $75, 3rd prize $50;
8 performances each in festival (Jun.); 4th place staged reading Works:
10-minute plays, 10 pages maximum Guidelines: entries must not have
received Equity performances; no more than 2 entries per author; no
musicals, children's plays, or "macabre" Stage: flexible, 70 seats Casting: non-Equity Procedure: send script Deadline: Nov. 1 every year

WESTERN GREAT LAKES PLAY COMP. South Bend Civic Theatre, P.O. Box 11375, South Bend, IN 46634 (219) 234-1112 This contest is inactive in 1999; see *The Playwright's Companion 2000* or inquire for future plans.

WHITE BIRD PLAYWRITING CONTEST F-1 C
White Bird Productions, 27 Prospect Park SW, Brooklyn, NY 11215 (718) 788-5984 **Contact:** Kathryn Dickinson, Art. Director **Frequency:** annual **Award:** $200, staged reading, possible travel **Works:** full-length plays **Exclusive interest:** the environment **Regulations:** no more than 2 entries per author; no musicals **Procedure:** send script, resume **Deadline:** Feb. 15, 1999 **Notification:** Oct. 1999 **Your chances:** 50-75 entries/6-8 judges/2 readings per script **Comment:** The judges reserve the right to withhold the award.

WHITE-WILLIS THEATRE COMP. 5266 Gate Lake Rd., Ft. Lauderdale, FL 33319 (954) 721-9411 **Contact:** Dorothy Willis This contest will be in effect in 1999; see *The Playwright's Companion 2000* or send SASE for guidelines.

WICHITA STATE UNIVERSITY PLAYWRITING F-1 1- Y **CONTEST** Univ. Theatre, 1845 Fairmount, Wichita, KS 67260-0153 (316) 689-3368 **FAX** (316) 689-3951 **Contact:** Leroy Clark, Contest Director **Frequency:** annual **Award:** production, travel, housing **Works:** full-length plays, related one-acts **Regulations:** authors must be students in U.S. colleges; entries must be unpublished, unproduced except in workshops; 90 minutes minimum; no children's plays; previous entries eligible if revised **Stages:** proscenium, 630 seats; 2nd stage **Procedure:** send SASE for guidelines **Deadline:** Feb. 15, 1999 postmark **Notification:** after Apr. 15, 1999 **Your chances:** 65+ entries/3 judges/3 readings per entry **Future commitment:** no **Comment:** The judges reserve the right to withhold the award.

WOMEN AT THE DOOR F D F-1 W
Famous Door Theatre, P.O. Box 57029, Chicago, IL 60657 (773) 404-8283 **FAX** (773) 404-8292 **Contact:** Producer **Frequency:** annual **Award:** cash award, production or staged reading in festival **Works:** full-length plays **Regulations:** women writers only; works must be unproduced except in workshops **Procedure:** send 1-page synopsis, 1st scene or 1st 10 pages of play, resume **Deadline:** TBA (fall)

WOMEN PLAYWRIGHTS PROJECT D F-1 W Rs
Centenary Stage Co., 400 Jefferson St., Hackettstown, NJ 07840 (908) 979-0900 **FAX** (908) 813-1984 **Contact:** Catherine Rust, Project Director **Frequency:** annual **Award:** $200, staged reading, expenses for 1-week residency **Works:** full-length plays **Regulations:** authors must be women **Procedure:** send script **Deadline:** TBA (Nov.)

WOMENKIND FESTIVAL F 1p W $

Cosmic Leopard Productions, P.O. Box 2668 Times Square Station, New York, NY 10108 (212) 769-6814 **Contact:** Emma Palzere, Exec. Producer **Frequency:** semi-annual **Award:** production in festival **Works:** 1-woman pieces **Special interests:** "Any style, any subject, any genre." **Regulations:** "Production is the responsibility of the submitter, with technical assistance from Cosmic Leopard." **Procedure:** send query/synopsis **Deadline:** TBA **Response:** TBA **Your chances:** 100 entries/6+ judges **Future commitment:** credit

WOMEN'S PLAYWRITING FESTIVAL F 1- W $

The Perishable Theatre, P.O. Box 23132, Providence, RI 02903 (401) 331-2695 FAX (401) 331-7811 **Contact:** Vanessa Gilbert, Festival Director **Frequency:** annual **Awards:** $250, production for each of 3 winners, publication **Works:** one-acts **Regulations:** women writers only; entries must be unpublished, unproduced except in workshops; 1 hour maximum; no more than 2 entries per author **Procedure:** send script, $5 fee **Deadline:** Dec. 31, 1999 **Notification:** Mar. 2000 **Your chances:** 350 entries/ 4 judges/2 readings per entry **Future commitment:** credit **Comment:** Judges reserve the right to withhold the awards.

WRITER'S DIGEST WRITING COMPETITION F-l 1- CY $

1507 Dana Ave., Cincinnati, OH 45207-1005 (513) 531-2690 Ext. 580 FAX (513) 531-1843 **Contact:** Competition Coord. **Frequency:** annual **Awards:** Grand Prize: $1000, trip to NYC to meet with editors and agents; other cash prizes for 5 other winners **Works:** 1st 15 pages of full-length plays, one-acts, children's plays **Regulations:** entries must be unpublished, unproduced except in workshops, not accepted elsewhere **Procedure:** send SASE for guidelines; upon entry: $10 fee **Deadline:** May 30, 1999 postmark **Notification:** fall 1999 **Advice:** "*Professional Playscript Format* only!"

WRITERS' VISION PLAYSEARCH F-1 1- $

P.O. Box 11126, Glendale, CA 91226 **e-mail** writerviz4@aol.com **Contact:** Christopher Case, Managing Director **Frequency:** annual **Award:** $500 **Works:** full-length plays, one-acts **Regulations:** entries must be unpublished; maximum cast: 10; simple set **Procedure:** request information; upon entry: $10 fee **Deadline:** Jun. 15, 1999

YEAR-END SERIES (Y.E.S.) NEW PLAY F F-l Ad ♪

FESTIVAL Dept. of Theatre, Northern Kentucky Univ., Highland Heights, KY 41099 (606) 572-6362 FAX (606) 572-6057 **e-mail** forman @nku.edu**Contact:** Sandra Forman, Project Director **Frequency:** biennial even years **Awards:** $400, production, travel, and housing for 3 winners to attend festival **Works:** full-length plays, adaptations, musicals **Regulations:** entries must be unproduced except in workshops; adaptations must be of works in the public domain; small orchestra for musical; 1

entry per author; winners must be present for festival's opening weekend (Apr. 2001) **Stages:** proscenium, 346 seats; flexible black box, 120 seats **Casting:** "Students, occasional guest artist." **Procedure:** send SASE for guidelines and application form; "musicals should have complete orchestrations; tape of score is helpful" **Deadline:** Oct. 31, 2000 postmark; no submission before May 1, 2000 **Notification:** Jan. 2001 **Your chances:** 500 entries/10-12 judges/2-3 readings per entry **Advice:** "Plays requiring many mature characters are less likely to be selected." **Comment:** The judges reserve the right to withhold the awards.

♫ **YOUNG CONNECTICUT**   **Y F-l 1- Tr Ad ♪ CY**
PLAYWRIGHTS FESTIVAL   **Maxwell Anderson Playwrights Series, P.O. Box 671, West Redding, CT 06896**   **(203) 938-2770**
Contact: Bruce Post, Dramaturg **Frequency:** annual **Awards:** staged reading in festival (May); certificate **Works:** full-length plays, one-acts, translations, adaptations, musicals, children's plays **Regulations:** CT residents aged 12-19 only; 60-page maximum **Procedure:** send SASE for guidelines **Deadline:** Apr. 3, 1999 **Notification:** May 1999

YOUNG PLAYWRIGHTS INC.   **F-l 1- Y**
321 W. 44th St. Suite 906, New York, NY 10036 (212) 307-1140 FAX (212) 307-1454 Contact: Sheri M. Goldhirsch, Artistic Director **Frequency:** annual **Works:** full-length plays, one-acts **Procedure:** send SASE for guidelines **Comment:** Scripts are not returned.

YOUNG PLAYWRIGHTS FESTIVAL   **F F-l 1- Y Rs**
Award: production with royalty or staged reading; travel, residency **Regulations:** authors must be 18 years of age or younger as of deadline **Deadline:** TBA **Your chances:** 1600 entries

NEW YORK CITY HIGH SCHOOL   **F-l 1- Y**
PLAYWRITING CONTEST Award: $500 **Regulations:** authors must be students in New York City high schools; writers under age 18 are automatically entered in Young Playwrights Festival **Deadline:** TBA

Information on the following contest reached us too late to be included in our alphabetical listing, Cross Reference, Deadline Calendar, or Index:

♫ **EMPIRE SCREENPLAY CONTEST**   **Pl S**
Empire Productions, 12358 Ventura Blvd. #602, Studio City, CA 91604-2508 (818) 375-7827 FAX (818) 506-1207 e-mail empireprod@ aol.com **Contact:** Michael J. Ferrand, Admin. **Frequency:** annual **Award:** $2000 **Guidelines:** 3 categories: "Hollywood or Bust"(expensive to produce), "High Value" (inexpensive), "Cinematic Plays" (stage plays for adaptation to film) **Procedure:** request guidelines and application form; upon entry: $30-$40 fee **Deadline:** Oct. 1, Nov. 1, Dec. 1, 1999 **Notification:** Apr. 1, 2000 **Your chances:** 600 entries/2 judges/2 works selected **Comment:** Scripts are not returned.

-- Notes --

Special Programs

Mini-Checklist

What to Send to Special Programs

With a request for guidelines and entry forms:
- ☐ A letter requesting the desired materials.
- ☐ Your #10 SASE.
- ☐ Any additional materials requested.

Tip: Because programs sometimes change their guidelines, it's a good idea to request information well before the deadlines stated in the listings.

Tip: It's also a good idea to send that #10 SASE even if the listing doesn't mention it in "Procedure"--a program's policy may change during the year. If in doubt, call the program and ask what they require.

With a script:
- ☐ A cover letter.
- ☐ As many copies of the script as required by the program.
- ☐ A cassette tape of any original music used in the play.
- ☐ Completed application forms, written statements, project proposals or descriptions, work samples, letters of recommendation, fees, and all other required materials.
- ☐ Your SASP or #10 SASE for notification of receipt.
- ☐ Your SASE for return of the script.

With a query/synopsis:
- ☐ A cover letter.
- ☐ A play synopsis, including character and technical breakdowns and a summary of the play's action.
- ☐ A script history: previous productions, workshops, readings, publications, award. Include favorable reviews.
- ☐ Completed application forms, written statements, project proposals or descriptions, work samples, letters of recommendation, and all other required materials.
- ☐ Your SASP or #10 SASE for response.

Tip: If you're interested in a program which charges an application fee, send the fee with your completed application materials--not with your request for guidelines!

Special Programs

ABINGDON THEATRE CO. BI-WEEKLY   **D F-l 1- cm dr**
READINGS & STAGED READINGS   **P.O.** Box 110 Radio City
Station, New York, NY 10101-0110   **(212) 802-8383**   **Contact:** Ray
Atherton, Literary Mgr.   **Program:** 2-step development program for full-
length plays and works-in-progress; Step 1: bi-weekly precast readings
with audience discussion; Step 2: directed, rehearsed staged readings for
core members and public, supportive critiques by members; occasional
one-act or short play readings; 2 plays per season selected for mainstage
production **Special interest:** "Structurally cohesive, thematically developed plays." **Procedure:** send script; professional recommendation; agent
submission **Response:** 6 months

THE ACADEMY OF AMERICAN POETS   **Mb Am po**
584 Broadway #1208, New York, NY 10012 (212) 274-0343 FAX (212)
274-9427 e-mail poets@artswire.org **Program:** membership organization for American poets, including writers of verse drama, at all career
levels; sponsors Harold Morton Landon Award (see Contests)

ACTORS ALLEY READING SERIES   **D Rg**
5269 Lankershim Blvd., N. Hollywood, CA 91601   **(818) 508-4200**
FAX (818) 508-5113 Contact: Jeremiah Morris, Art. Director   **Program:**
ongoing reading series for new plays; emphasis on Southern CA playwrights **Procedure:** request information; or, send script

ACTORS FORUM THEATRE WORKSHOP   **D**
10655 Magnolia Blvd., North Hollywood, CA 91601   **(818) 506-0600**
FAX (213) 465-6898 e-mail audsin@aol.com   **Contact:** Audrey Marlyn
Singer, Artistic Director   **Program:** workshop meeting weekly (Tues.
7:30-10:30 p.m.) in which playwrights and actors work together
Procedure: call for information   **Deadline:** ongoing program

ACTORS' PLAYHOUSE PLAYREADING SERIES   **D F-l ♪**
280 Miracle Mile, Coral Gables, FL 33134 (305) 444-9293 FAX (305)
444-4181 Contact: George Contini, Literary Mgr. **Program:** new year-
round series of informal readings of new full-length plays and musicals
Guidelines: works must be unproduced except in workshops   **Procedure:** write or call for application information

ACTORS THEATRE OF LOUISVILLE PROGRAMS
316 W. Main St., Louisville, KY 40402-4218 (502) 584-1265

FLYING SOLO AND FRIENDS   **F 1p**
Program: annual festival (fall) of solo performances **Guidelines:**
previously produced works; performers may present their own work
or that of another playwright; works receive only technical rehearsals
Procedure: send videotape, reviews **Deadline:** Dec. 31, 1999 **Notification:** Jun. 2000 **Your chances:** 200 entries/4 or more pieces selected

ACTORS THEATRE OF LOUISVILLE PROGRAMS (Cont.)

HUMANA FESTIVAL OF NEW AMERICAN PLAYS
F Am 1-

Program: annual festival (Mar. 2000) of full productions of 10-15 new works and works-in-progress **Procedure:** professional recommendation; agent submission **Best time:** "Plays are read mostly in Mar.-Oct." **Notification:** late summer-early fall 1999

ACTS INSTITUTE, INC.
i

P.O. Box 30854, Palm Beach Gardens, FL 33420 (561) 625-2273 e-mail p009259b@pb.seflin.org **Contact:** Charlotte Plotsky, Director **Program:** organization presenting educational talks on "creativity and on writers' colonies, retreats, residencies and other programs of interest to creative people." **Procedure:** send SASE for information

¡AHA! ASSOCIATION OF HISPANIC ARTS
Mb Hi i

250 W. 26th St. 4th Floor, New York, NY 10001 (212) 727-7227 FAX (212) 727-0549 e-mail aha96@ad.com **Contact:** Sandra Garcia, Director of Programs & Services **Program:** organization for Hispanic artists and organizations; services include technical assistance to Hispanic writers, newletter, information services **Procedure:** request guidelines

ALCAZAR STAGED READINGS SCRIPTS IN PROGRESS
D

650 Geary St., San Francisco, CA 94102 (415) 441-6655 FAX (415) 441-9567 **Contact:** Kim Parolari **Program:** 3-month development program (Jun.-Sept. 2000) for unproduced plays; 2 staged readings; possible full production with 4 weeks of rehearsal **Remuneration:** royalties, room and board for full production **Procedure:** send SASE for guidelines; or, send script with resume **Deadline:** TBA (Sept. 1999) **Your chances:** 150 applications/4 playwrights selected

THE ALFRED HODDER FELLOWSHIP
g/f Rs

Humanities Council, Princeton Univ., 122 E. Pyne, Princeton, NJ 08544-5264 (609) 258-4717 FAX (609) 258-2783 e-mail humcounc@princeton.edu **Contact:** Marjorie Asbury, Administrator **Program:** annual fellowship ($44,500 in 1999-2000) for a humanist in the early stages of his/her career; office provided, library available **Guidelines:** fellow must spend academic year (Sept.-Jun. 2000) at Princeton Univ. **Procedure:** send SASE for brochure **Deadline:** TBA (Nov.) **Your chances:** 250-300 applications/1 fellow selected

ALLIANCE OF LOS ANGELES PLAYWRIGHTS
Mb Sv i Rg

(ALAP) 7510 Sunset Blvd., Suite 1050, Los Angeles, CA 90046-3418 (323) 957-4752 e-mail ALAPNews@aol.com **Contact:** Dick Dotterer, Co-Chair **Program:** membership/service organization for playwrights in L.A. area; activities include symposia, panel discussions, networking, social events, C. Bernard Jackson Award to individuals and organizations which nurture and support L.A. playwrights; publications include membership directory, *The Hotline*, and bi-monthly *News-Flash* **Dues:** $29.95 **Procedure:** request membership application form

♫ IN OUR OWN VOICES D
Program: member playwrights read their own work **Procedure:** inquire for details

♫ PLAYWRIGHTS EXPO F
Program: gathering of L.A. playwrights and many representatives of L.A. and national theatres **Procedure:** inquire for dates and details

THE ALLIANCE OF RESIDENT THEATRES/ Mb Sv i
NEW YORK **131 Varick St. Room 904, New York, NY 10013-1410**
(212) 989-5257 FAX (212) 989-4880 Contact: Virginia Louloudes, Exec. Director **Program:** service organization for non-profit theatres in NYC; publications include *Art/New York Rehearsal and Performance Space Guide* ($20), *Directory* ($10), *Hot Seats* listings of members' productions

THE ALLIANCE WRITER'S PROJECT D C
3204 W. Magnolia Blvd., Burbank, CA 91505 (818) 566-7935 FAX (213) 876-4673 Contact: Steve Liska, Dramaturge **Program:** script development program meeting monthly (1st Tues.) for readings, workshops, collaborative projects **Special interest:** contemporary social/political issues **Fee:** $15 per month **Procedure:** request guidelines

ALTERNATE ROOTS Mb Rg C
1083 Austin Ave., Atlanta, GA 30307 (404) 577-1079 FAX (404) 577-7991 Contact: Greg Carraway, Mng. Director **Program:** organization for Southeastern theatre artists and presenting organizations, committed to "social/economic justice and the preservation of the natural world" **Guidelines:** for residents of the 13 Southeastern states; members are accepted after 1-year's provisional status **Fee:** $50 per year **Procedure:** send SASE for information; or, attend a meeting or workshop

ALTOS DE CHAVON ARTIST-IN-RESIDENCE Rs Esp Hi
PROGRAM c/o **Parsons School of Design, 2 W. 13th St. Room 707, New York, NY 10011 (212) 229-5370, -5370 FAX** same **e-mail** altos@ spacelab.net **Contact:** Stephen D. Kaplan, Arts/Ed. Director **Program:** residencies of 3 1/2 months (starting Feb. 1, Jun. 1, Sept. 1, 2000) in Dominican Republic; efficiency studios or apartments, small studios, visual-arts library; no meals provided **Guidelines:** published or produced writers only; preference: Spanish-speaking applicants whose work relates to Latin American themes **Fee:** $350 per month **Procedure:** request guidelines; upon acceptance: supporting materials, $100 advance fee **Deadline:** Jul. 1, 1999 **Notification:** Aug. 15, 1999 **Your chances:** 40 proposals/usually 3 dramatic writers selected

AMERICAN ALLIANCE FOR THEATRE   **Mb CY**
& EDUCATION   Theatre Dept., Arizona State Univ., Box 872002
Tempe, AZ 85287-2002 (602) 965-6064   Contact: Christy Taylor,
Admin. Director **Program:** membership organization for teachers (pre-K
through university); students, publishers. and artists presenting young
people's theatre; sponsors AATE Playwriting Awards (see Contests)
Dues: individual $90, retiree $65, student $55, organization $120

AMERICAN ANTIQUARIAN SOCIETY   **Rs g/f S H**
VISITING FELLOWSHIPS FOR HISTORICAL RESEARCH
**185 Salisbury St. Room 301, Worcester, MA 01609-1634 (508) 752-
5813 e-mail** jdm@mwa.org **Contact:** James David Moran **Program:** 4-6
week residential fellowships of $1200 per month and travel expense
allowance, for historical research by creative and performing artists,
writers, film makers and others whose goals are to produce works
dealing with American history and culture before 1877 **Procedure:**
request guidelines and application form **Deadline:** TBA (Oct.) **Your
chances:** 3 fellowships awarded

AMERICAN FILM INSTITUTE   **Mb i S Tv**
**2021 N. Western Ave., P.O. Box 27999, Los Angeles, CA 90027 (213)
856-7600 FAX (213) 461-4013 Contact:** Jean Picker Firstenberg, Director
East Coast offices: Kennedy Center, Washington, DC 20566 (202) 828-
4000; 1180 Ave. of the Americas 10th Fl., New York, NY 10036 (212)
398-6890 **Program:** organization established to advance and preserve
film /TV arts; Center for Advanced Film & Television Studies; National
Center for Film & Video Preservation; National Theatre at Kennedy Ctr.

TELEVISION WRITERS SUMMER WORKSHOP   **D Tv**
Program: annual 2-4 week advanced teleplay training program for
10-12 new writers with media or theatre backgrounds, who have no
major commercial TV writing credits **Fee:** $475; 3 scholarships
available **Procedure:** phone 213-856-7721 for application form

AMERICAN MUSIC CENTER   **Mb Sv i Am ♪**
**30 W. 26th St. #1001, New York, NY 10010-2011 (212) 366-5260 FAX
(212) 366-5265 e-mail** center@amc.net **Contact:** Richard Kessler, Exec.
Director **Program:** national organization fostering the creation, performance, publication, and recognition of contemporary American music;
copying assistance; library; information services; publishes *Opportunities in New Music* **Dues:** individual $55, student/senior $35

AMERICAN RENAISSANCE THEATRE FREE   **D F F-l 1- Rg**
PLAYREADING SERIES & PLAYWRIGHT DEVELOPMENT
WORKSHOP   **10 W. 15th St. Suite 325, New York, NY 10011 (212)
924-6862 Contact:** Rich Stone, Artistic Director **Program:** rehearsed
public readings (May-Jun. 1998) with audience critique for up to 5
plays-in-progress; possible production; participants attend workshop on

"the business of playwriting" **Regulations:** authors must be NYC-area residents; entries must be full-length or one-act plays, unproduced except in workshops **Procedure:** send synopsis, 10-page dialogue sample; SASE for response **Deadline:** Jan. 15, 1999 **Notification:** Jan.. 30, 1999 **Your chances:** 200 entries/3 judges **Future commitment:** credit

♫ AMERICAN PLAYWRIGHTS THEATRE **D 1- Am**
P.O. Box 604167, Bayside, NY 11360 Contact: Frances Galton, Artistic Director **Program:** workshop productions of unpublished, previously unproduced one-acts in fall festival **Special interest:** "American cultural experiences." **Procedure:** send script, SASE for reply **Comment:** Scripts are not returned.

AMERICAN-SCANDINAVIAN FOUNDATION **g/f**
725 Park Ave., New York, NY 10021 (212) 879-9779 FAX (212) 249-3444 e-mail grants@amscan.org **Contact:** Exchange Division **Program:** grants and fellowships for study and research in Scandinavia for U.S. citizens and permanent residents with undergraduate degree; $3000 grants for short visits; $15,000 academic year fellowships; ASF Translation Prize (see Contests) **Procedure:** request guidelines and application form **Deadline:** Nov. 1, 1999

AMERICAN TRANSLATORS ASSOCIATION (ATA) **Mb Tr**
1800 Diagonal Rd. Suite 220, Alexandria, VA 22314-2840 (703) 683-6100 FAX (703) 683-6122 e-mail ata@atanet.org **Contact:** Walter W. Bacak, Exec. Director **Program:** membership association seeking to promote recognition of the translating profession **Guidelines:** active membership open to U.S. citizens or permanent residents who have passed ATA accreditation examination or demonstrated professional attainment; associate membership open to others **Dues:** individual $95, student $50 **Procedure:** request application form or information

AMERICAN VOICES See GeVa Theatre Programs in this section.

APOSTLE ISLANDS NATIONAL LAKESHORE **Rs**
Rte. 1, Box 4, Bayfield, WI 54814 (715) 779-3397 FAX (715) 779-3049 Contact: Myra Dec, Chief, Resources Ed. **Program:** free 2-3 week residency (Jun.-Sept.) for accomplished writer in cabin on island in national park; no electricity/water; resident donates 1 work to park, presents 1 program **Procedure:** request guidelines **Deadline:** Jan. 15, 1999; no submission before Oct. 1 for 2000 deadline **Notification:** Mar. 1, 1999

ARENAFEST **F M Af**
Karamu House for the Performing Arts, 2355 E. 89th St., Cleveland, OH 44106 (216) 795-7070 Contact: Gerry McClamy, Interim Exec. Director **Program:** annual festival (Apr.-May) of fully produced plays **Special interest:** multiethnic, African-American themes **Procedure:** phone or write for guidelines **Deadline:** TBA (Apr. 1999 for 2000 Fest)

♫ ARIZONA ROSE THEATRE DEVELOPMENT   D ♪
P.O. Box 77335, Tucson, AZ 85703 (520) 888-0509 **Program:** developmental program for new musicals **Procedure:** inquire for details

♫ ARIZONA YOUTH THEATRE   D Y
5671 E. **Speedway, Tucson, AZ 85712 (520) 546-9805 Program:** small storefront theatre offering classes in all aspects of theatre (writing, performance, technical work) for young people up to age 18 **Procedure:** call or write for information

ARKANSAS REP NEW PLAY READING   D Rg Am M C
SERIES   P.O. Box 110, Little Rock, AR 72203-0110 (501) 378-0445
FAX (501) 378-0012 Contact: Brad Mooy, Literary Mgr. **Program:** series of readings of new plays; emphasis on small casts and Southern, regional, national, and multiracial issues **Procedure:** inquire for information

ARTISTIC & LITERARY RESOURCES   D Sv my $
824 N. **Juanita Ave.**, Redondo Beach, CA 90277-2229 **Contact:** Sally Atman, Program Director **Program:** script doctor service offering agent and co-playwright referrals; audio- and videotaped productions of works-in-progress **Special interests:** "Suspense, mystery, psychodrama; tight plots; no fantasy or sci fi." **Procedure:** write for script doctor price list; send script, bio, $5 reader's fee; "material on disk or as e-mail attachment will be read first (MS Word 6 or less or Word-Perfect 6.0 or less)" **Advice:** "If you send a rough draft for critique and plan to send a finished draft for production, attach a note describing intended changes."

ARTIST TRUST   Mb Sv Rg i
1402 3rd Ave. #404, Seattle, WA 98101-2118 (206) 467-8734 FAX (206) 467-9633 **e-mail** arttrust@drizzle.com **Contact:** Heather Dwyer, Program Director **Program:** membership/service organization for WA State artists

FELLOWSHIPS   g/f ♪ S Tv Rd
Program: annual fellowships of $5000 to practicing professional creative artists **Guidelines:** recipients must be WA residents **Procedure:** send SASE for guidelines in Apr. 1999 **Deadline:** TBA (Jun.) **Notification:** Nov. 2000 **Your chances:** 430 total applications/65-75 theatre applicants/4 fellowships awarded **Advice:** "Strong, professional supporting materials."

GAP (GRANTS FOR ARTIST PROJECTS)   g/f
Program annual grants of up to $1200 to individual artists for initiation, development or completion of specific projects **Procedure:** send SASE for guidelines and application form **Deadline:** Feb. 26, 1999 postmark **Notification:** late May 1999 **Your chances:** 633 total applications/30 theatre applicants/3-5 grants awarded **Advice:** "Strong, professional supporting materials."

ARTISTS-IN-BERLIN PROGRAMME g/f Rs Y

German Academic Exchange Service (DAAD), 950 Third Ave. 19th **Floor, New York, NY 10022 (212) 758-3223 FAX (212) 755-5780 e-mail** daadny@daad.org **Contact:** Antje Wiessmann, Program Officer **Program:** monthly grants to cover expenses for residency in Berlin (beginning Jan.-Jun. 2000); for internationally known artists in fields of literature, music, and film **Procedure:** request guidelines and application form **Deadline:** Jan. 1, 1999 **Your chances:** 15-20 participants

ARTS INTERNATIONAL PROGRAMS g/f

Institute of International Education, 809 United Nations Plaza, New York, NY 10017-3580 (212) 984-5370 FAX (212) 984-5574 e-mail thefund@iie.org/ai **Procedure:** request guidelines

℞ CINTAS g/f Hi

Contact: Linda Walton, Program Officer **Program:** fellowships for Cuban citizens and descendants living in exile; award rotates among disciplines, 1999-2000 genre TBA **Procedure:** call for information

FUND FOR U.S. ARTISTS AT INTERNATIONAL g/f

FESTIVALS & EXHIBITIONS e-mail thefund@iie.org **Contact:** Linda Walton, Program Officer **Program:** triannual grants (usually $500-$10,000) to performing artists and groups for foreign travel, housing, per diem, production costs for U.S. citizens or permanent residents who have been invited to participate in festivals abroad **Procedure:** request guidelines **Deadline:** Jan. 15, May 1, Sept. 1, 1999

INROADS g/f Af As Hi M

e-mail ainternational@iie.org **Contact:** Cheryl Katz, Program Officer **Program:** annual grants of $20,000-$30,000 for performing artists and U.S. host organizations for short-term planning residencies for collaborations between artists in different disciplines **Guidelines:** 1 artist must be U.S. resident, 1 must be resident of Africa, Asia, Caribbean, Latin America, Middle East, or Pacific Islands **Procedure:** request guidelines **Deadline:** TBA (Jun.)

ARTSLINK Mb ₢

CEC International Partners, 12 W. 31st St., New York, NY 10001 (212) 643-1985 Ext. 21 FAX (212) 643-1996 e-mail artslink@cecip.org **Contact:** Fritzie Brown, Artslink Program Mgr. **Program:** programs "to encourage artistic exchange with Central and East Europe, and Newly Independent States"

♫ COLLABORATIVE PROJECTS g/f ₢

Program: grants of $2500-$10,000 to support projects by U.S. artists and arts organizations working in Eastern and Central Europe **Guidelines:** projects should offer "demonstrable benefits" to participants from both countries **Deadline:** Mar. 15, 1999 **Procedure:** request information

ARTSLINK (Cont.)

♫ RESIDENCIES   g/f Rs ℰ
Program: grants to U.S. non-profit arts organizations to support 5-week residencies for fellows (artists or arts managers) from Central and Eastern Europe **Procedure:** request brochure and application information in Apr.-Jun. 1999

ASCAP (AMERICAN SOCIETY OF COMPOSERS,   Mb Sv ♪
AUTHORS AND PUBLISHERS) 1 Lincoln Plaza, New York, NY
10023 (212) 621-6234 FAX (212) 724-9064 Contact: Michael A. Kerker, Director, Musical Theatre **Program:** organization for publishers of musical works and composers and lyricists whose works have been commercially recorded or regularly published; services include clearinghouse for performing rights, licensing, license fee collection **Dues:** $10

ASCAP MUSICAL THEATRE WORKSHOP   D ♪
Program: 10 evening sessions during which participating composers and lyricists present selections from works-in-progress to panels of professionals; Bernice Cohen Musical Theatre Fund Award: $500 to most promising participating individual or team **Procedure:** send cassette tape including 4 theatre songs (not pop), resume **Deadline:** Mar. 15, 1999 **Notification:** Jan. 2000

ASIAN AMERICAN ARTS ALLIANCE   Mb i As Sv g/f
74 Varick St. Suite 302, New York, NY 10013-1914 (212) 941-9208 FAX (212) 941-7978 e-mail artsalliance@earthlink.net **Contact:** Lillian Cho, Exec. Director **Program:** service organization dedicated to promoting Asian American arts and artists; information, networking, advocacy, professional assistance, public forums, roundtables, referrals, resource library, Technical Assistance and Regrant Initiative, Chase Smarts regrant program for NYC Asian American arts groups; publications include *Resource Directory of Asian American Arts Organizations and Touring Artists,* bi-monthly *Asian American Arts Calendar,* and *Dialogue* biannual magazine **Dues:** $20-$1000 depending upon level

ASIAN AMERICAN THEATER CO. NEW PLAYS   D F-l 1- As
& PLAYWRIGHTS DEVELOPMENT PROGRAM 1840 Sutter St.
#207, San Francisco, CA 94115 (415) 440-5545 FAX (415) 440-5597 e-mail aatc@wenet.net **Contact:** Pamela A. Wu, Prod. Director **Program:** workshop for 2-4 full-length or one-act scripts, leading to staged readings or productions **Guidelines:** for American, Canadian, or U.K. writers of Asian-Pacific descent; plays in English; Asian-Pacific American themes preferred **Procedure:** send script, cover letter, resume

ASIAN CULTURAL COUNCIL GRANTS   g/f As
437 Madison Ave., New York, NY 10022-7001 (212) 412-4300 FAX (212) 412-4299 Contact: Ralph Samuelson, Director **Program:** annual grants to support residencies in Japan for American artists in creative

(non-performance) activities and research/training projects and to support collaborative projects for artists in East and Southeast Asia **Procedure:** send project description and request guidelines, application form **Deadline:** Feb. 1, 1999

A.S.K. THEATER PROJECTS PROGRAMS   D
11845 W. Olympic Blvd. Suite 1250 West, Los Angeles, CA 90064 (310) 478-3200 FAX (310) 478-5300 e-mail askplay@primenet.com **Contact:** Mead Hunter, Director of Literary Programs **Program:** nonprofit theatre sponsoring workshop productions and readings; publishes annual playwrights' journal *Parabasis* (free to playwrights); programs include Mark Taper Forum's New Work Festival (in this section) **Procedure:** inquire for guidelines

L.A. PUBLIC LIBRARY UNPUBLISHED PLAY PROJECT Rg
Program: collection of unpublished plays which have had premiere productions in southern California; see Audrey Skirball-Kenis Unpublished Play Collection in Publishers

LINCOLN CENTER THEATER'S   D Am F-l ♪
AUDREY SKIRBALL-KENIS PLAYWRIGHTS PROGRAM
Program: series for new works by American writers; reading series, new play and musical development workshop, workshop productions, Directors' Lab

♫ PLAYWRIGHT-COMPOSER STUDIO   ♪ D
Program: 2-week intensive workshop in which 5 playwrights, 5 composers, and 5 performers collaborate on original music-theatre pieces

PLAYWRIGHT PRACTICAL LABS   D Rs
Program: playwrights' laboratories including conferences, symposiums; lectures followed by discussions; exchange programs with the Playwright's Center (MN), the Royal Court Theatre in London and New Dramatists (see listing in this section)

♫ PLAYWRIGHTS-IN-THE-SCHOOLS   Rs
Program: professional playwrights teach Los Angeles high school students the fundamentals of dramatic writing, culminating in public readings of students' works

ASSITEJ/USA (INTERNATIONAL ASSOCIATION   Mb CY
OF THEATRE FOR CHILDREN & YOUNG PEOPLE) P.O. Box
22365, Seattle, WA 98122 (425) 392-2147 FAX (425) 443-0442 Contact: Dana Childs, Membership Coord. **Program:** membership organization for individuals and theatres interested in theatre for young audiences **Dues:** $50, student/retiree $25 **Procedure:** send SASE for membership application

THE ASSOCIATED WRITING PROGRAMS   Mb Sv i
Tallwood House, Mail Stop 1E3, George Mason Univ., Fairfax, VA 22030 (703) 933-4301 FAX (703) 993-4302 e-mail awp@gmu.edu **Contact:** Membership Services **Program:** organization for writers, university writing programs, students; activities and services include annual conference, job list, placement service, advocacy, publications; AWP Awards (see Contests) **Procedure:** request membership information

ASSOCIATION FOR THEATRE IN HIGHER   Mb i
EDUCATION   **Program in Theatre, Graduate School & Univ. Center, CUNY, 33 W. 42nd St., New York, NY 10036 (212) 342-2231 e-mail** jdolan@email.gc.cuny.edu **Contact:** Association Mgr. **Program:** organization for college-level teachers of theatre; Playwrights' Program provides support to authors for development of new plays, sponsors annual ATHE Student Playwriting Awards (inquire for guidelines) and readings and hosts annual conference on play development and playwrights' issues **Dues:** $105, $50 student, $80 retiree

ASSOCIATION OF INDEPENDENT VIDEO &   Mb S
FILMMAKERS   **304 Hudson St. 6th Floor, New York, NY 10013 (212) 807-1400 FAX (212) 463-8519 e-mail** info@aivf.org **Contact:** Ruby Lerner, Exec. Director **Program:** membership/advocacy organization for independent video/filmmakers; publishes *The Independent Film & Video Monthly* **Procedure:** request membership information

ATLANTA BUREAU OF CULTURAL AFFAIRS
675 Ponce de Leon Ave., Atlanta, GA 30308 (404) 817-6815 FAX (404) 817-6827 Contact: Nikki Tucker, Project Coordinator

ARTISTS PROJECT   g/f Rg
Program: annual grant of up to $3000 **Guidelines:** applicants must be practicing professional artists who have been Atlanta residents for at least 1 year prior to deadline **Procedure:** send SASE for guidelines **Deadline:** Dec. 17, 1999 **Notification:** 3 months

MAYOR'S FELLOWSHIPS IN THE ARTS   g/f Rg
Program: award of $5000 rotating among disciplines **Guidelines:** applicants must be professional artists who have been Atlanta residents for at least 3 consecutive years prior to deadline **Procedure:** send SASE for guidelines (playwrights apply under Literary Arts or Theatre Arts; composers, librettists, and lyricists apply under Music) **Deadline:** Feb. 16, 1999 **Notification:** 3 months

ATLANTIC CENTER FOR THE ARTS MASTER ARTIST-   Rs
IN-RESIDENCE PROGRAM   **1414 Art Center Ave., New Smyrna Beach, FL 32168 (904) 427-6975 FAX (904) 427-5669 e-mail** program@ atlantic-centerarts.org **Contact:** Nicholas Conroy, Program Director **Program:** interdisciplinary artist-in-residence community, "providing

opportunities for talented artists from all over the world to work with internationally acclaimed Master Artists in a variety of disciplines"; private room and bath, kitchen privileges, common dining room, resource library, black box theatre **Fee:** housing $25 per day, tuition $100 per week; scholarships available **Procedure:** phone 800-393-6975 for guidelines **Deadline:** TBA **Your chances:** 35 applications per Master Artist position/up to 10 Master Artists accepted

THE AUTHORS LEAGUE FUND AND Mb g/f
THE DRAMATISTS GUILD FUND 330 W. 42nd St., New York, NY 10036 (212) 268-1208 FAX (212) 564-8363 Contact: Susan Drury, Administrator **Program:** interest-free loans for professional writers and playwrights in time of personal emergency **Procedure:** request guidelines and application form; supporting materials required upon application **Response:** 2-4 weeks **Your chances:** 150 applications/30 loans approved **Comment:** "No grants-in-aid for career purposes."

BAILIWICK REPERTORY PROGRAMS 1229 W. Belmont, Chicago, IL 60657 (312) 883-1090 FAX (312) 525-3245 Contact: David Zak, Art. Director **Procedure:** send SASE for Submission Guidelines

BAILIWICK REPERTORY ANNUAL F 1- Ad ♪ cm dr **DIRECTORS' FESTIVAL Program:** production in black box theatre of 48 new one-act plays: musicals, comedies, dramas, adaptations; 10-50 minutes **Deadline:** ongoing program

♫ **DBA (DEAF BAILIWICK ARTISTS)** D h/d **Program:** developmental program for works by deaf writers for acting troupe of deaf and hearing artists **Deadline:** ongoing program

PRIDE PERFORMANCE SERIES F F-l 1- Tr Ad ♪ g/l **Program:** series of performances (summer festival) of "special interest to Chicago's gay/lesbian community" **Works:** full-length plays, one-acts, translations, adaptations, musicals **Deadline:** ongoing program

BALTIMORE THEATRE PROJECT, INC. Mb Rg x **45 W. Preston St., Baltimore, MD 21201 (410) 539-3091 FAX (410) 539-2137 Contact:** Bobby Mrozek, Art. Director **Program:** membership/organization/theatre for previously unproduced works; roundtables, seminars, workshops, auditions, database of affiliated Baltimore-area artists, newsletter **Special interest:** experimental works **Dues:** inquire **Remuneration:** possible housing **Procedure:** send script, resume, project proposal, budget **Advice:** "Proposals are given first priority."

BANFF CENTRE PROGRAMS Rs ♪ Tv **Banff Ctr. for the Arts, P.O. Box 1020 Sta. 28, 107 Tunnel Mountain Dr., Banff, Alberta, Canada T0L 0C0 (403) 762-6180, (800) 565-9989 FAX (403) 762-6345 e-mail** arts_info@banffcentre.ab.ca **Contact:** Office of the Registrar **Program:** arts center/complex in the mountains of Banff

National Park; programs vary from year to year but may include residencies and activities in theatre arts, music, writing, TV, media, visual, and literary arts; Thematic Residencies (fall), Special Focus Residencies (Jan.-Mar.), Self-Directed Residencies (May-Sept.), and Summer Drama Program (every other year) are also available **Guidelines:** non-Canadians may require authorization from Immigration; information provided on acceptance **Procedure:** request brochure

LEIGHTON STUDIOS FOR INDEPENDENT Rs ♪
RESIDENCIES
Program: year-round residencies of 1 week-3 months for writers, composers, musicians, and visual artists working individually **Fee:** studio $315 Canadian per week; single room $245 Canadian per week; flex meal plan $98 per week; discount available on studio fee for those with demonstrated need **Procedure:** request guidelines and application form **Deadline:** 6 months before desired residency **Your chances:** 8 studios; usually 9-10 applicants selected

PLAYWRIGHTS' COLONY Rg Rs F-l 1- CY
Program: 1-4 week residency (mid-Aug.--mid-Sept.); Canadian playwrights at all levels work on revisions of full-length plays, one-acts, translations, or children's plays in preparation for rehearsal or production **Procedure:** phone for guidelines **Your chances:** 60-100 applicants/10-12 playwrights selected **Deadline:** TBA (Feb.)

BAY STREET THEATRE READING SERIES F-l ♪ 2d Sp
P.O. Box 810, Sag Harbor, NY 11963 (516) 725-0818 FAX (516) 725-0906 **Contact:** Mia Emlen Grosjean, Literary Mgr. **Program:** 2 new plays receive readings (fall, spring) **Guidelines:** emphasis on uplifting, challenging works; maximum cast: 8-9 **Remuneration:** $50 honorarium, travel from NYC **Procedure:** agent submission to theatre (see Theatres) **Deadline:** ongoing program **Notification:** 3-6 months

BIG D FESTIVAL Dallas, TX This program has been discontinued.

BLACK THEATRE ARTISTS WORKSHOP D F-l 1- Af
P.O. Box 2518, Venice, CA 90294 (310) 399-9193, (213) 934-7023 **Contact:** Sabaka Barry Henley, Tarabu Betserai **Program:** developmental workshop for full-length plays and one-acts on African-American themes **Procedure:** send SASE for guidelines

BLACK THEATRE NETWORK Mb Sv i Af
2603 NW 13th St. #312, Gainesville, FL 32609 (352) 495-2116 FAX (352) 495-2051 e-mail manicho@aol.com **Contact:** Mikell Pinkney, President **Program:** national membership/service organization for professionals and academics working in or studying black theatre; activities include annual forum; conferences, workshops; *BTN News* quarterly, *Black Theatre Directory, Black Theatre Connections* jobs bulletin; *Black Voices* play catalog ($20) **Dues:** $85, retiree/student $25

BLACKJACKS FESTIVAL See CAP 21 Programs in this section.

BLUE MOUNTAIN CENTER   Rs C $
P.O. Box 109, Blue Mountain Lake, New York 12812 (518) 352-7391
Contact: Harriet Barlow, Director **Program:** 4-week residencies (Jun.-
Oct.) in Adirondacks, for writers whose work is for a general audience
and reflects social concerns; room, board provided **Fee:** voluntary **Pro-
cedure:** send SASE for guidelines; upon application: $20 fee **Deadline:**
Feb. 1, 1999 **Notification:** Apr. 1999 **Your chances:** 14 residents selected

BMI (BROADCAST MUSIC INCORPORATED)   Mb Sv ♪
320 W. 57th St., New York, NY 10019-3790 (212) 586-2000 FAX (212)
262-2824 **Contact:** Jean Banks, Senior Director, Musical Theater and
Jazz **Program:** performing rights organization acting as steward for
public performance of music of members; open to published songwriters;
BMI Foundation provides support for individuals in furthering their
music education and for organizations in providing training programs

BMI/LEHMAN ENGEL MUSICAL THEATRE   D ♪
WORKSHOP (212) 830-2515 FAX (212) 262-2824 **Contact:** Jean
Banks, Senior Director, Musical Theater **Programs:** Composer-Lyri-
cist Workshop (Sept.-May); Librettists Workshop: all genres **Fee:** none
Procedure: send SASE for guidelines **Deadline:** librettists: May 1,
1999; composers, lyricists: Aug. 1, 1999 **Notification:** Aug. 1999

BOARSHEAD STAGED READINGS   D F-l x C cm
425 S. Grand Ave., Lansing, MI 48933 (517) 484-7800 FAX (517) 484-
2564 **Contact:** John Peakes, Founding Art. Director **Program:** staged
readings of 5 full-length plays per season; emphasis on new conventions,
social issues, comedies **Remuneration:** travel, housing, per diem **Procedure:** send query/synopsis with 5-10 page dialogue sample, SASP; no
SASE necessary **Deadline:** ongoing program **Notification:** 1-6 months

BRANYON PLAYWRITING WORKSHOP   D F-l 1-
142 West End Ave. #30-P, New York, NY 10023 (212) 799-3868
Contact: Alexandra Branyon, Director **Program:** 6-session workshop
meeting bi-monthly (Sept.-May) **Guidelines:** for unpublished, unproduced full-length plays or one-acts **Fee:** $300; 1 scholarship available
per series **Procedure:** send letter of inquiry (with phone number), synopsis, 10-page dialogue sample, bio **Deadline:** ongoing program

BRITISH AMERICAN ARTS ASSOCIATION   See Center for
Creative Communities in this section.

BROADWAY ON SUNSET   D ♪ Rg
10800 Hesby St., North Hollywood, CA 91601 (818) 508-9270 FAX
(818) 508-1806 **e-mail** brdwysunst@aol.com **Contact:** Kevin Kaufman,
Exe. Director **Program:** development program for L.A.-area writers of
musicals in any style and at all career levels; readings, workshops,

classes, possible weekend workshops for out-of-town writers **Procedure:** send book, 4-song maximum cassette tape of stage musical **Fee:** determined by level of development; partial scholarships available **Deadline:** ongoing program

BROADWAY TOMORROW   D ♪ Rg
191 Claremont Ave. Suite 53, New York, NY 10027 (212) 864-4736 **FAX** same **Contact:** Elyse Curtis, Artistic Director **Program:** concert reading series with writer participation for new musicals by New York City-area writers **Fee:** $50 **Procedure:** recommendation by former participant **Deadline:** Aug. 31, 1999

BRODY ARTS FUND   g/f Rg
California Community Foundation, 606 S. Olive Suite 2400, Los Angeles, CA 90014-1526 (213) 242-7489 **FAX** (213) 629-4782 **Contact:** Cindy DiGiampaolo, Senior Program Secretary **Program:** $5000 fellowship for residents of Los Angeles County, awarded triennially to emerging artists in literary and media arts **Procedure:** request guidelines and application form **Your chances:** 100-150 applications received/usually 5 fellowships awarded **Deadline:** TBA (Feb.-Mar. 1999 for 2000 playwrights' cycle)

BUSH ARTIST FELLOWSHIP   g/f Pl S Rg
The Bush Foundation, E-900 1st Natl. Bank Bldg., 332 Minnesota St., St. Paul, MN 55101-1387 (651) 227-5222, (800) 605-7315 **FAX** (651) 297-6485 **Contact:** Kathi Polley, Program Asst. **Program:** annual grants of $40,000 each; applications accepted in various disciplines **Guidelines:** applicants must be at least 25 years of age and residents of MN, ND, SD or the 26 counties of Western WI which lie in the 9th Federal Reserve District, and must have had at least 1 professional production or workshop or screenplay option or sale; students ineligible **Procedure:** request guidelines and application form (available Aug. 1, 2000) for ScriptWorks (playwriting/screenwriting), Music Composition or Film/Video **Deadline:** TBA (Oct. 2000) **Notification:** Feb. 2001 **Your chances:** 450+ applications/up to 15 fellowships awarded

BYRDCLIFFE ART COLONY   Rs $
The Woodstock Guild, 34 Tinker St., Woodstock, NY 12498 (914) 679-2079 **FAX** (914) 679-4529 **e-mail** wguild@ulster.net **Contact:** Arts Residency Program **Program:** 1-month residencies (Jun.-Sept.) at 600-acre historic colony in Catskills, for serious writers and visual artists **Fee:** $500 per session **Procedure:** send SASE for guidelines; upon application: supporting materials, $5 fee **Deadline:** Apr. 1, 1999

CAC PLAYWRIGHT'S FORUM   D Pl Tr ♪ Rg
Contemporary Arts Ctr., P.O. Box 30498, New Orleans, LA 70190 (504) 523-1216 **e-mail** cacno.aol.com **Contact:** Michael Callender, Performance Coord. **Program:** 9-month workshop (Sept.-May) providing

opportunities for development and staged readings **Guidelines:** for playwrights, translators, lyricists, and librettists in New Orleans area only **Fee:** none **Procedure:** send script **Deadline:** ongoing program

CALIFORNIA LAWYERS FOR THE ARTS Sv i
1641 18th St., Santa Monica,CA 90404 (310) 998-5590 FAX (310) 998-5594 e-mail UserCLA@aol.com **Program:** organization providing lawyer referrals, educational programs, publications, dispute resolution services, and a resource library **Procedure:** request information

CAP 21 PROGRAMS
Collaborative Arts Project 21, Inc., 18 W. 18th St., New York, NY 10011 (212) 807-0202 FAX (212) 807-0166 Contact: Jennifer Camp, Literary Mgr. **Procedure:** send unsolicited full script, cassette tape for musical **Deadline:** ongoing programs **Response:** 4-6 months

BLACKJACKS FESTIVAL D F-l ♪
Program: biennial developmental program (usually Nov., Mar.) for new, unproduced works or works that have been developed with CAP 21 (see Collaborative Arts Project 21 Inc. in Theatres), Monday Night Reading Series (below), or other organizations and are almost ready to be produced

♫ MONDAY NIGHT READING SERIES D F-l ♪
Program: developmental program (presented 2 Mondays each month) for new, unproduced works and works in progress **Works:** full-length plays, musicals

CAMARGO FOUNDATION g/f Rs Fr
Park Sq. Ct., 400 Sibley St. Suite 125, St. Paul, MN 55101-1928 (612) 290-2237 Contact: William Reichard **Program:** grants for residence (Sept.-Dec., Jan.-May) in Cassis, France, for writers, artists, scholars, and graduate students who wish to pursue specific creative projects or projects in the humanities relative to French and francophone cultures **Procedure:** write for brochure and application form **Deadline:** Feb. 1, 1999 for 1999-2000 academic year **Notification:** Apr. 1, 1999 **Your chances:** 100+ applications received

CAPITAL REPERTORY THEATRE D F-l Tr Ad ♪ 2d
AUTHOR'S THEATRE 111 N. Pearl St., Albany, NY 12207 (518) 462-4531 FAX (518) 465-4531 Ext. 293 e-mail submissions@capitalrep.org **Contact:** Maggie Mancinelli-Cahill, Producing Art. Director **Program:** new play development for full-length plays, translations, adaptations, small-scale musicals **Guidelines:** "Adaptations of work from other media, or work by authors of other media working in theatre for the first time." **Maximum cast:** 10 **Procedure:** query/synopsis with 1st 10 pages of dialogue, production history **Best time:** May-Aug. **Response:** 6 months **Your chances:** 200 applications/1-3 plays selected **Remuneration:** stipend, travel **Future commitment:** negotiable

CARNEGIE FUND FOR AUTHORS   g/f
1 Old Country Rd. Suite 113, Carle Place, NY 11514 **Program:** emergency grants for playwrights who have had at least 1 play or collection of plays published commercially in book form (not in anthologies); emergency must have placed recipient in substantial, verifiable financial need **Procedure:** request guidelines

CAROLINA PLAYWRIGHTS CENTER   D Mb Sv i Rg W Af
P.O. Box 1705, Pinehurst, NC 28374 (910) 295-6896 FAX (910) 295-1203 **Contact:** Carolyn Cole Montgomery, Director **Program:** membership/service organization for playwrights in need; research and support services; especially interested in women and black writers **Procedure:** call or write for information

CASTILLO THEATRE PLAYWRITING WORKSHOP   D F
500 Greenwich St. Suite 201, New York, NY 10013 (212) 941-5800 FAX (212) 941-8340 e-mail castilloth@aol.com **Contact:** Dan Friedman, Dramaturg **Program:** 10-week developmental workshop (held 3 times a year) for new playwrights and those with works-in-progress **Procedure:** phone or write for guidelines

CENTER FOR CREATIVE COMMUNITIES   ₡ i
118 Commercial St., London E1 6NF, UK 44-171-247-5385 FAX 44-171-247-5256 **Contact:** Jennifer Williams, Exec. Director **Program:** organization for research in arts, education, and community development; services include quarterly newsletter and library providing information on the arts and community development **Comment:** Formerly British American Arts Association.

CENTRUM   P.O. Box 158, Port Townsend, WA 98368 (360) 385-3102 FAX (360) 385-2470 This residency program is undergoing a restructuring in 1999; interested writers should inquire for new guidelines.

♫ CHAMELEON STAGE   Mb D Rg
P.O. Box 22420, Denver, CO 80222 **Program:** playwrights' company meeting weekly with visiting professional actors to read new work; members must reside in Denver area; activities include workshop readings and 1-2 full productions per year **Procedure:** send work samples, production history, bio, SASE

CHATEAU DE LESVAULT   This program has been discontinued.

CHESTERFIELD FILM CO./WRITER'S FILM   D Rs S $
PROJECT   1158 26th St., Box 544, Santa Monica, CA 90403 (213) 683-3977 FAX (310) 260-6116 **Contact:** Douglas Rosen, Director of Development **Program:** 1-year screenwriting workshop meeting 3-5 times a week; participant writes 2 feature screenplays; possible production **Remuneration:** $20,000 stipend **Procedure:** request guidelines

and application form; upon application: writing samples, $39.50 fee **Deadline:** TBA **Your chances:** 3500 applications/up to 5 writers selected **Comment:** Materials are not returned.

CHICAGO ALLIANCE FOR PLAYWRIGHTS   Mb Sv i Rg
(CAP) 1225 W. Belmont, Chicago, IL 60657-3205 (773) 929-7367 Ext. 60 FAX (773) 338-3060 Contact: Allan Chambers **Program:** organization providing services to assist playwrights and encouraging production of new plays; seminars, workshops, newsletter, directory **Guidelines:** playwrights must be current or former residents of the Midwest **Procedure:** request membership information **Dues:** $25

CHICAGO DRAMATISTS   Mb D Pl S
1105 W. Chicago Ave., Chicago, IL 60622-5702 (312) 633-0630 FAX (312) 633-0610 e-mail NewPlays@aol.com **Contact:** Russ Tutterow, Artistic Director **Program:** developmental theatre for playwrights at all career stages; classes in beginning and advanced playwriting, screenwriting; selected programs open to all playwrights **Fee:** classes/workshops: TBA ($75-$240 in 1998) **Procedure:** write or phone for application procedure **Advice:** "English language only; limited resources for musicals." **Comment:** Formerly Chicago Dramatists Workshop.

PLAYWRIGHTS' NETWORK   Mb D Sv F
Contact: Carson Becker, Director **Program:** service providing written critiques, annual New Voices Festival of readings, class discounts, and consideration for productions and all developmental programs **Fee:** $95 per year **Procedure:** write or phone for registration materials **Deadline:** ongoing program

RESIDENT PLAYWRIGHT PROGRAM   D Rs Rg
Program: 3-year (renewable) residency which seeks to nurture and promote the work of accomplished or promising Chicago-area dramatists **Procedure:** write or phone for application procedure **Deadline:** Apr. 1, 1999; no submission before Mar. 1 **Notification:** Sept. 1, 1999

THE 10-MINUTE WORKSHOP   D 1-
Contact: Robin Stanton, Producing Director **Program:** quarterly staged readings of 6-8 10-minute plays and scenes (12-page maximum) with discussions moderated by guest judges from local theatres **Guidelines:** open to playwrights able to attend workshops; maximum cast: 6 **Procedure:** call for full information and deadlines

♫ CHILDREN'S THEATRE FOUNDATION   g/f CY
OF AMERICA P.O. Box 8067, New Orleans, LA 70182 Contact: Orlin Corey, President **Program:** endowed charitable foundation for advancing children's theatre in America; activities include scholarships in playwriting, festivals, international exchanges, conferences/symposiums, publications, awards, performances, lectures

CHILDREN'S THEATRE FOUNDATION (Cont.)

♫ **THE ALVIN COHEN MEMORIAL FUND**　　**g/f CY**
Program: fund reserved until maturity to assist special projects of national significance which are sponsored by national associations dedicated to theatre for young people **Procedure:** request guidelines

♫ **THE AURAND HARRIS CHILDREN'S**　　**g/f CY**
THEATRE FELLOWSHIPS　**Program:** fellowships of up to $2500 for a calendar year for playwrights and other artists working on specific projects "particularly sensitive to the needs of children's theatre" **Guidelines:** U.S. residents only **Procedure:** send artistic statement (500 words maximum), 3 letters of recommendation, resume, calendar for proposed project **Deadline:** May 1, 1999 **Notification:** Sept. 1, 1999 **Future commitment:** summary report; credit

♫ **THE AURAND HARRIS CHiLDREN'S**　　**g/f CY**
THEATRE GRANTS　**Program:** grants of up to $3000 to assist in costs of premiere productions of "important and promising" children's plays **Procedure:** request guidelines; supporting materials required **Future commitment:** summary report, credit

♫ **THE AURAND HARRIS MEMORIAL FUND**　　**g/f CY**
Program: fund to assist special proposals of non-profit children's theatres and to support the Aurand Harris Playwriting Fellowships

COLORADO DRAMATISTS　　**Mb D**
P.O. Box 101405, Denver, CO 80250-1405 (303) 595-5600 **Contact:** Bob Woolsey, President **Program:** development for playwrights at all levels; public readings, workshops, showcase, mentoring program, festival **Procedure:** send name, address, phone number, $30 annual dues

♫ **COLORADO WOMEN PLAYWRIGHTS**　　**F F-l 1- Rg W**
FESTIVAL　**c/o Industrial Arts Theatre, P.O. Box 40066, Denver, CO 80204** (303) 595-3800 **Program:** annual festival producing new works by Colorado women writers **Procedure:** send script

COMMONWEAL NEW PLAYS WORKSHOP　　**D Rs**
P.O. Box 15, Lanesboro, MN 55949 (507) 467-2525 FAX (507) 467-2468 **e-mail** cmmnweal@means.net **Contact:** Hal Cropp, Core Artist **Program:** annual 2-week developmental workshop for 1 play; culminating in rehearsed reading for an invited audience **Remuneration:** housing **Procedure:** professional recommendation **Best time:** Oct.-Dec.

THE COUNTER-CULTURE MONDAY CAFE　　**D ₵ H Rg**
SERIES　**The Theatre Outlet, 29 N. 9th St., Allentown, PA 18102** (610) 820-9270 FAX (610) 820-9130 **e-mail** theaterout@aol.com **Contact:** George Miller, Art. Dir. **Program:** 3 10-week series of readings of new plays (all genres); emphasis on Irish/Scotch/Welsh experience, eastern PA history/culture **Procedure:** inquire for guidelines, dates

THE COYOTE THEATRE FESTIVAL   F 1- Rg C x
OF TEN-MINUTE PLAYS   P.O. Box 403 Back Bay Annex, Boston, MA 02117 (617) 695-0659 FAX (617) 695-6775 call first **Contact:** Joshua White, Literary Mgr. **Program:** festival of 10-minute plays by New England writers (CT, ME, MA, NH, RI, VT) **Guidelines:** works with "social relevance; innovative works"; maximum cast: 5 **Procedure:** send SASE for guidelines; or, call for details

CPAF READING SERIES   D
Carmel Performing Arts Festival, P.O. Box 221473, Carmel, CA 93922 (831) 644-8383 FAX (831) 622-7631 **Contact:** Barbara Bishop **Program:** annual staged reading-workshop series (Oct. 1999) **Remuneration:** small honorarium **Procedure:** send query/synopsis **Deadline:** Apr. 15, 1999 **Notification:** May 30, 1999

CURTAINUP   i
http://www.curtainup.com **Contact:** Elyse Sommer, Editor-Publisher, esommer@pipeline.com   **Program:** an online theater magazine updated several times a week; coverage includes reviews of shows in NYC and the Berkshires, monthly reports from DC; reviews of theater-related books, interviews, quotes, news column

DANA SINGER, SEMINARS   D i
The Business of Writing for the Theater, 2275 Amigo Dr., Missoula, MT 59808-5035 (406) 728-5248 FAX (406) 728-2729 e-mail Stage write@aol.com **Contact:** Dana Singer **Program:** full- and half-day seminars, lectures, graduate- and undergraduate-level classroom instruction, panel discussions across the U.S.A.; program encompasses entire range of topics relevant to stage writing **Fee:** varies **Procedure:** request information **Comment:** Dana Singer is author of *Stage Writers Handbook: A Complete Business Guide for Playwrights, Composers, Lyricists and Librettists* (see The Playwright's Library) and former Exec. Director of the Dramatists Guild. She also presents workshops with Jeffrey Sweet, addressing both the business and the craft of playwriting.

DAVID HENRY HWANG WRITERS INSTITUTE   D
244 S. San Pedro St. Suite 301, Los Angeles, CA 90012 (213) 625-7000 FAX (213) 625-7111 **Contact:** Ken Narasaki, Literary Mgr. **Program:** 20-week development program meeting weekly; opportunity for semi-public readings in which playwrights read from their own work; beginning and advanced classes; program culminates in staged readings by professional actors **Fee:** $350 tuition; 1 scholarship awarded per session **Procedure:** phone or write for guidelines

DEEP SOUTH WRITERS CONFERENCE   D F
English Dept., Univ. of Southwestern Louisiana, Box 44691, Lafayette, LA 70504-4691 (318) 482-6918 FAX (318) 482-6195 (with cover sheet addressed to "Deep South Writers Conf.") e-mail wxf8424@

usl.edu **Contact:** Willard Fox, Director **Program:** annual conference; workshops, lectures, readings, awards (see listing in Contests) **Procedure:** send SASE for guidelines **Comment:** Materials are not returned.

DISCOVERY SERIES   D
Eureka Theatre Co., 330 Townsend St. #210, San Francisco, CA 94107 (415) 243-9899 FAX (415) 243-0789 Contact: Joe DeGuglielmo, Art. Director **Program:** ongoing series of rehearsed public readings of new plays **Procedure:** send query/synopsis, resume, dialogue sample, SASP

THE DISCOVERY SERIES   F CY Fm Y 12+ H M
Indiana Rep. Theatre, 140 W. Washington, Indianapolis, IN 46204 (317) 635-5277 FAX (317) 236-0767 e-mail irt@iquest.net **Contact:** Lit. Mgr. **Program:** new play series (fall-winter) for family audiences; "focus on youth, history, literature, ethnic diversity" **Procedure:** send query/synopsis, dialogue sample to theatre **Response:** 3-6 months

DJERASSI RESIDENT ARTISTS PROGRAM   Rs M $
2325 Bear Gulch Rd., Woodside, CA 94062-4405 (650) 747-1250 FAX (650) 747-0105 e-mail drap@djerassi.org **Contact:** Dennis O'Leary, Exec. Director **Program:** residencies of 1 month (Jul., Aug., Sept.) or 6 weeks (Apr.-May, May-Jun., Oct.-Nov.) at 600-acre ranch in Santa Cruz Mountains **Guidelines:** for artists at all career levels; Oshita Fellowship for composer of color **Fee:** none **Procedure:** send SASE for brochure and application forms; upon application: $25 fee **Deadline:** Feb. 15, 1999 for 2000 fellowships

DOBIE-PAISANO PROJECT   Rs g/f Rg
Dobie House, 702 E. Dean Keeton St., Austin, TX 78705 Contact: Audrey N. Slate, Director **Program:** 2 annual fellowships with $1200 monthly living allowance; 6-month residency at Paisano Ranch; families welcome; for TX natives or residents of at least 2 years, or those whose published work is on a TX subject **Procedure:** request guidelines and application form **Deadline:** Jan. 22, 1999 **Notification:** May 1999

♫ DOLGIAN HOUSE ARTISTS' COLONY   Rs $
Heighington, R.R. 4, Meaford, Ontario, Canada N4L 1W7 (416) 968-1228 Program: residencies (Jul.-Aug) of 1 week or more for writers and photographers on a private lake in a nature preserve near lake Huron; studio available **Fee:** $15 per day **Procedure:** send SASE for guidelines and application form; upon application: $7 fee

THE DON AND GEE NICHOLL FELLOWSHIPS   g/f S Tv $
IN SCREENWRITING   **Academy of Motion Picture Arts and Sciences, 8949 Wilshire Blvd., Los Angeles, CA 90211-1972 (310) 247-3059 Contact:** Greg Beal, Coord. **Program:** annual fellowships of $25,000 for writers who have not worked as professional screen or TV writers or sold screen or TV rights **Guidelines:** entries must be original

screenplays or screen adaptations of writer's work, originally written in English, 100-130± pages **Procedure:** send SASE for guidelines after Jan. 1, 1999; upon application: $30 fee **Deadline:** May 1, 1999 **Notification:** after Oct. 15, 1999 **Your chances:** 4000+ applications/up to 5 screenwriters selected

DORLAND MOUNTAIN ARTS COLONY Rs $
P.O. Box 6, Temecula, CA 92593 (909) 676-5039 e-mail dorland@ ez2.net **Contact:** Admissions **Program:** residencies of 1-2 months for writers, composers, and visual artists on a 300-acre nature preserve; 6 rustic cottages, private baths and kitchens, propane cooking, kerosene lamps, woodstoves, no electricity **Fee:** $300 per month (meals, travel not included) **Procedure:** send SASE for guidelines; upon acceptance: $50 processing fee **Deadline:** Mar. 1, 1999; Sept. 1, 1999 **Notification:** 10 weeks **Your chances:** 70-100 applications/usually several playwrights selected **Advice:** "Playwrights, apply!"

DORSET COLONY HOUSE FOR WRITERS Rs
P.O. Box 519, Dorset, VT 05251 (802) 867-2223 FAX (802) 867-0144 Contact: John Nassivera, Director **Program:** 1 week-2 month residencies (fall, spring) for writers of serious purpose and professional achievement **Fee:** voluntary $125 per week **Procedure:** send resume and project description indicating desired dates; work sample may be required **Deadline:** ongoing program **Notification:** 1-3 weeks

DRAMA LEAGUE OF NEW YORK NEW WORKS D Rs F-l ♪
PROGRAM 165 W. 46th St., #601, New York, NY 10036 (212) 302-2100 FAX (212) 302-2254 e-mail dlny@echonyc.com **Program:** 4-weeks' development (summer) for playwright-director teams; rehearsal space provided **Works:** full-length plays, musicals **Remuneration:** $1000 per team **Procedure:** send SASE for guidelines **Deadline:** Feb. 15, 1999 postmark **Notification:** Apr. 1999 **Your chances:** 3 projects selected

DRAMA WEST PRODUCTIONS 1- S dr cm Rg
P.O. Box 5022-127, Lake Forest, CA 92630 Contact: Catherine Stanley, Art. Director **Program:** developmental workshop for one-act plays and screenplays by accomplished Southern CA writers; outreach program provides professional actors/directors to perform staged readings; sponsors Drama West Productions One-Act Play Contest (see Contests) **Special interests:** dramas, comedies; "creative insight to the ongoing human dilemma; plays that encourage intelligent debate" **Procedure:** send query/synopsis with dialogue sample **Deadline:** ongoing program

THE DRAMATISTS GUILD, INC. Mb Sv i
1501 Broadway Suite 701, New York, NY 10036 (212) 398-9366 FAX (212) 944-0420 Contact: Membership Dept. **Program:** professional association of playwrights, composers and lyricists; services include standard contracts, contract business advice, advice on relationships

with producers and agents, script retrieval, royalty collection, symposia, emergency funds (See Authors League Fund in this section), quarterly journal, monthly newsletter, annual *Resource Directory* **Dues:** active member $125 per year, associate $75, student $35, outside U.S.A. $10 additional **Procedure:** request application form

EARLY STAGES   D F-l ♪ CY Fm
American Stage Festival, 14 Court St., Nashua, NH 03060 (603) 889-2336 FAX same, call first **Contact:** Artistic Director **Program:** staged readings (summer) of new full-length plays and musicals **Guidelines:** works for young audiences and families **Procedure:** send SASE for guidelines **Deadline:** ongoing program

THE EDWARD F. ALBEE FOUNDATION, INC.   Rs
14 Harrison St., New York, NY 10013 (212) 226-2020 **Contact:** David Briggs, Foundation Secretary **Program:** 1-month residencies (Jun.-Sept.) at the William Flanagan Memorial Creative Persons Center, Montauk, NY, for writers and visual artists **Procedure:** request guidelines **Deadline:** Apr. 1, 1999 **Notification:** May 15, 1999 **Your chances:** 150-250 applications/usually 12 playwrights accepted

EUDORA WELTY NEW PLAYS SERIES   F F-l Rs
New Stage Theatre, P.O. Box 4792, Jackson, MS 39296-4792 (601) 948-0143 FAX (601) 948-3538 **Contact:** John Maxwell, Artistic Director **Program:** readings (fall, spring) of full-length plays for an invited audience; possible full production **Procedure:** send query/synopsis **Deadline:** TBA **Remuneration:** possible expenses for weekend residency

♫ **EXPANDED ARTS 94 PLAYS IN 94 DAYS**   F
85 Ludlow St., New York, NY 10002 **Contact:** Coord. **Program:** annual new play series; playwright may select director; plays 45-90 minutes in length **Procedure:** send script with cover letter "indicating if you have a director with whom you wish to work" **Deadline:** inquire

EXPERIMENTAL PUPPETRY THEATRE (XPT)   D V x
Center for Puppetry Arts, 1404 Spring St. NW, Atlanta, GA 30309 (404) 873-3089 FAX (404) 873-9907 e-mail puppet@mindspring.com **Contact:** Bobby Box, Producer **Program:** annual program (dates TBA) in which a Center for Puppetry Arts staff member works with participating playwright on a work-in-progress; program culminates in workshop production **Guidelines:** works must be for puppets or actor/puppet combinations **Procedure:** submit proposal for work-in-progress **Deadline:** TBA (inquire) **Remuneration:** no

♫ **FACE TO FACE WORKSHOP**   D F-l 1- Tr Ad 2d g/l
SERIES About Face Theatre, 3212 N. Broadway, Chicago, IL 60657 (773) 549-7943 FAX (773) 935-4483 e-mail faceline1@aol.com **Contact:** Carl Hippensteel, Lit. Mgr. **Program:** readings/"rough staging," with

audience response, of full-length plays, one-acts, shorts, translations, adaptations, musicals; gay/lesbian writers and themes only **Procedure:** send query/synopsis, 1st 10 pages of dialogue, resume; agent submission encouraged **Response:** 1 month query; 3 months solicited script

♫ FARMWORKS   D
c/o Theatre Off Park, 224 Waverly Pl., New York, NY 10014 (212) 627-2556 Contact: Brian Adams **Program:** workshop productions of new plays using minimal production elements in black box theatre **Procedure:** write or call for information and application **Deadline:** ongoing program **Comment:** Sponsored by Rattlestick Productions.

THE FIELD   D Sv
161 Sixth Ave., New York, NY 10013 (212) 691-6969 FAX (212) 255-2053 e-mail thefield@aol.com. **Contact:** Katherine Longstreth, Exec. Director **Program:** organization assisting performing artists and groups; Fieldwork: 10-week developmental workshops culminating in readings or performances; activities and services include management, training, video access **Dues:** membership $75, individual programs $25-$75

FINE ARTS WORK CENTER IN PROVINCETOWN   Rs $
24 Pearl St., Provincetown, MA 02657 (508) 487-9960 FAX (508) 487-8873 Contact: Hunter O'Hanian, Exec. Director **Program:** 7-month residency (Oct. 1, 1999-May 1, 2000) for emerging writers, poets, and visual artists in complex in Cape Cod, MA; $600 monthly stipend **Procedure:** request guidelines and application form; upon application: $35 fee **Deadline:** Dec. 1, 1999 **Your chances:** 1 playwright selected

FIRST ACT   D F-l Rg
A Contemporary Theatre, 700 Union St., Seattle, WA 98101-2330 (206) 292-7660 FAX (206) 292-7670 Contact: Liz Engelman, Literary Mgr. **Program:** commissions and developmental workshops for full-length works by Seattle-area playwrights **Procedure:** request guidelines; or, send query/1-page synopsis with resume

FIRST LOOK   D Pl ♪
Sol Goldman YM-YWHA of The Education Alliance, 344 E. 14th St., New York, NY 10003 (212) 780-0800 Ext. 267 Contact: Mark Weiser, Producer, First Look **Program:** new reading series (Mon. nights) of new plays and musicals **Stage:** 14th St. Y, 200 seats **Procedure:** write for information

FIRSTSTAGE   Mb Sv D
P.O. Box 38280, Los Angeles, CA 90038 (213) 850-6271 FAX (213) 850-6295 Contact: Dennis Safren, Literary Mgr. **Program:** service/membership organization; programs include development of new works; Firststage Playwrighting Contest (see Contests) **Dues:** $120 per year,

$35 per quarter; non-local $58 yearly; no fee for staged reading **Procedure:** send script, resume; membership not required for submission **Deadline:** ongoing program **Notification:** 6 months **Your chances:** 300-600 applications/"all are welcome"

FLEETWOOD STAGE PLAYWRIGHTS Mb D F-l 1- Rg
FORUM 44 Wildcliff Dr., New Rochelle, NY 10802 (914) 654-8533 Contact: Bruce Post, Literary Mgr. **Program:** membership/development program for New Rochelle-area playwrights with full-length plays or one-acts; 10-week sessions of weekly meetings in which members work with directors and actors, public readings, possible productions **Fee:** $250 per session **Procedure:** send script, resume to Playwrights Forum **Deadline:** ongoing program **Your chances:** 20 members per session

FLORIDA PLAYWRIGHTS' PROCESS D Rg
PACT Institute, Ruth Eckerd Hall, 1111 McMullen-Booth Rd., Clearwater, FL 33759 (727) 791-7060 Contact: Elizabeth Brincklow, Program Director **Program:** annual project to encourage development of original plays by playwrights who are legal residents of FL; activities include workshops and full productions **Procedure:** request guidelines **Deadline:** TBA (Dec.1 in 1998) **Comment:** Formerly West Central Florida Playwrights Process

THE FOREPLAY READING SERIES D F-l Tr Ad x
Woolly Mammoth Theatre Co., 1401 Church St. NW, Washington, DC 20005 (202) 234-6130 Ext. 513 FAX (202) 667-0904 e-mail gao woolly@aol.com **Contact:** Gary Oiler, Literary Mgr. **Program:** 4 series each year of rehearsed readings before public audiences; open to full-length plays, translations, adaptations; emphasis on "off-beat, non-realistic works" **Procedure:** send script **Deadline:** ongoing program **Your chances:** 4 plays read in each series

THE 42ND STREET WORKSHOP Mb D Pl Tr Ad
432 W. 42nd St. 5th Floor, New York, NY 10036 (212) 695-4173 FAX (212) 695-3384 Contact: Michelle Bouchard, James DeMarse, Artistic Director **Program:** membership/developmental theatre; programs include Mon. night writing labs in which new plays, translations, and adaptations, or excerpts, receive cold readings with critiques **Dues:** $25 per month **Procedure:** send SASE for guidelines **Deadline:** Sept. 1, 1999 **Notification:** Dec. 1, 1999

THE FOUNDATION CENTER Sv i
79 Fifth Ave. 2nd Floor, New York, NY 10003-3076 (212) 620-4230 FAX (212) 807-3677 Contact: Judith Margolin, Director of Public Services, New York Library **Program:** service organization providing information on foundation philanthropy; publishes directories, *Foundation Grants to Individuals* and monographs for grant seekers **Procedure:** for nearest field office call toll-free 800-424-9836

FRANK SILVERA WRITERS' WORKSHOP   D M

P.O. Box 1791 Manhattanville Station, New York, NY 10027 (212) 281-8832 FAX (212) 281-8839, call first e-mail playrite@artswire.org Contact: Garland Lee Thompson, Founding Exec. Director Program: annual writers' lab for new plays by playwrights of all backgrounds and colors; Mon. readings with critiques; Wed. seminars; staged readings; Equity showcases Dues: $35 per year, $10 per Wed. seminar Procedure: phone for information; or, attend a Mon. night reading or Sept. open house Advice: "Interested writers are encouraged to attend."

FREDERICK DOUGLASS CREATIVE ARTS   D Pl S Tv
CENTER WRITING WORKSHOPS 270 W. 96th St.,

New York, NY 10025 (212) 864-3375 FAX (212) 864-3474, call first Contact: Fred Hudson, Artistic Director Program: 8-week writing workshops in 4 cycles per year; weekly sessions in beginning and advanced playwriting (advanced session includes readings, possible production), sessions in TV and film Remuneration $500 produced play; $50 staged reading Fee: workshop $150 Procedure: send SASE for guidelines Deadline: Jan., May, Jul., Sept. 1999 (exact dates TBA) Advice: "Attend the workshops, and read!"

FRESH INK SERIES   D F-l 1- Tr Ad ♪ W g/l M

Illusion Theater, 528 Hennepin Ave. Suite 704, Minneapolis, MN 55403 (612) 339-4944 FAX (612) 337-8042 Contact: Michael Robins, Exec. Producing Director Program: 1-weekend production with minimal staging and costumes; audience discussion Procedure: send script or query/synopsis, cassette tape for musical Best time: Jul.-Nov. Response: 6 months query; 6 months-1 year script Your chances: 5-6 plays selected

FULBRIGHT SCHOLAR AWARDS FOR U.S. FACULTY   g/f
AND PROFESSONALS USIA, Fulbright Senior Scholar Program,

Council for International Exchange of Scholars, 3007 Tilden St. NW Suite 5M, Washington, DC 20008 (202) 686-7877 FAX (202) 362-3442 e-mail apprequest@cies.iie.org Contact: Program Officer (for country of interest) Program: grants in research and university lecturing for periods of 3 months to a full academic year in foreign countries Procedure: request guidelines and application form Deadline: Aug. 1, 1999 Notification: 11 months

THE GELL WRITERS CENTER   Rs

c/o Writers & Books, 740 University Ave., Rochester, NY 14607 (716) 473-2590 FAX (716) 729-0982 Contact: Joseph Flaherty, Exec. Director Program: residency in private house in wooded setting; bedroom provided; residents provide meals; creative writing workshop may be available for additional fee Fee: $35 per day Procedure: request brochure Deadline: ongoing program Notification: 1 week

THE GENESIS FESTIVAL: A CELEBRATION   D F Af
OF NEW VOICES IN AFRICAN-AMERICAN THEATRE
Crossroads Theatre Co., 7 Livingston Ave., New Brunswick, NJ
08901 (732) 249-5581 FAX (732) 249-1861 Contact: Lenora Inez Brown,
Literary Mgr.   Program: script development program offering spring
series of public readings Procedure: participants selected from theatre
submissions; send query/synopsis, dialogue sample

THE GENESIUS GUILD DEVELOPMENTAL   Mb D F-l ♪
WORKSHOP   P.O. Box 2273, New York, NY 10108 (212) 946-5625
Contact: Thomas Morrissey, Artistic Director Program: professional
membership/developmental organization for the creation of new full-
length plays plays and musicals Procedure: send query/synopsis, bio
Deadline: ongoing program

GEORGE BENNETT FELLOWSHIP   Rs g/f $
Phillips Exeter Academy, 20 Main St., Exeter, NH 03833-2460 Contact: Charles Pratt, Coord., Selection Committee Program: annual fellowship (Sept.-Jun.) providing $6000 stipend, housing for academic year for
Fellow and family Guidelines: "Writer must need time, freedom from
material considerations, to complete a work-in-progress." Procedure:
send SASE for guidelines; upon application: $5 fee Deadline: Dec. 1
1999 Notification: Mar. 2000 Your chances: 150 applications Advice:
"Beginning writers, i.e., without major credits, preferred."

GEVA THEATRE PROGRAMS   Rochester, NY 14607 (716) 232-
1366 FAX (716) 232-4031 Contact: Jean Ryon, New Plays Coord. Procedure: send query/synopsis, brief dialogue sample, script history, resume to theatre

   AMERICAN VOICES NEW PLAY READING SERIES D Am
   Program: 5 new plays by American writers receive readings each
   year

   ♫ REGIONAL PLAYWRIGHTS AND YOUNG   F Rg Y
   WRITERS' FESTIVAL Program: annual festival for playwrights
   and other young writers from 5-county area of Genesee Valley

   ♫ HIBERNATUS INTERRUPTUS   F D
   Program: annual winter festival (Jan.) of new plays; 2-week workshops

GOLDEN WEST PLAYWRIGHTS   Mb D F-l 1- Rg W M
P.O. Box 2149, Hollywood, CA 90078-2149 e-mail jonbastian@earth
link.net Contact: Jon Bastian, Co-Director Program: development work-
shop/professional support group meeting biweekly Guidelines:
members must be residents of Southern CA; women and minority playwrights encouraged Procedure: send sample full-length play or related
one-acts, resume

THE GREENSBORO PLAYWRIGHTS' FORUM   Mb Rg
City Arts-Greensboro Cultural Center, 200 N. Davie St., Box #2, Greensboro, NC 27401 (336) 335-6426 FAX (336) 373-2659 e-mail gsoplaywrights@juno.com **Contact:** Director **Program:** membership organization serving playwrights in the NC Piedmont; monthly meetings, Dramatist Playground workshop, Evening of Short Plays, Reader's Theatre, new play catalog, newsletter; North Carolina New Play Project (see Contests) **Dues:** $25 per year **Procedure:** phone, write, or e-mail for guidelines **Your chances:** all accepted

HAMBIDGE CENTER FOR CREATIVE ARTS   Rs $
& SCIENCES   P.O. Box 339, Rabun Gap, GA 30568 (706) 746-5718 FAX (706) 746-9933 e-mail hambidge@acme-brain.com **Contact:** Exec. Director **Program:** 2 week-2 month residencies on 600 acres in the mountains of northeast GA; private cottage/studio; dinner provided Mon.-Fri. May-Oct. only **Fee:** $125 per week minimum **Procedure:** send SASE for guidelines; upon application: $20 fee **Deadline:** May 1 for Sept.-Dec.; Nov. 1 for Mar.-Aug. **Notification:** 2-3 months

THE HARBOR THEATRE LAB   Mb D F-l ♪ Rg
160 W. 71st St. PHA, New York, NY 10023 (212) 787-1945 FAX (212) 712-2378 **Contact:** Stuart Warmflash, Art. Director/Founder **Program:** non-profit membership/support organization and play development program (Sept. 1999-May 2000) in which members cast actors for specific roles in a play or musical they have committed to develop; weekly readings followed by moderated discussion; annual public readings; annual scene showcase of playwrights' work and full productions mounted by the Harbor Theatre **Guidelines:** participants must reside in NYC metropolitan area **Fee:** $350 (covers costs) **Procedure:** phone or send query; no script until requested **Deadline:** ongoing program **Your chances:** 50-75 applications/group limited to 10 playwrights **Advice:** "Experienced, committed writers."

THE HAROLD PRINCE MUSICAL THEATRE   D ♪
PROGRAM   The Directors Co., 311 W. 43rd St. #307, New York, NY 10036 (212) 246-5877 **Contact:** Michael Parva, Art. Dirctor **Program:** monthly meetings (fall-Jun.) of writers, composers, directors for development of new full-length musicals or operettas; production in NYC **Guidelines:** works must not have been professionally produced in NYC **Remuneration:** fee for option on 1st production **Procedure:** send script (at least 1 act completed), cassette tape of score, synopsis, resume, letter of interest, 3 letters of recommendation **Deadline:** ongoing program

HAWTHORNDEN CASTLE INTERNATIONAL   Rs ℭ
RETREAT   Lasswade, Midlothian, Scotland EH18 1EG 44-131-440-2180 **Contact:** Administrator **Program:** 4-week residencies (Feb.-Jul., Sept.-Dec.) in medieval castle outside Edinburgh **Guidelines:** for creative writers who have published at least 1 book or have had a play profes-

sionally produced **Fee:** none **Procedure:** write or phone for guidelines and application form **Deadline:** Sept. 30, 1999 for 2000 sessions **Notification:** Jan. 2000 **Your chances:** 5 residents per session

HEADLANDS CENTER FOR THE ARTS   Rs Rg
944 Ft. Barry, Sausalito, CA 94965 (415) 331-2787 FAX (415) 331-3857 Contact: Kathryn Reasoner, Exec. Dir. **Program:** 1-3 month residencies (Feb.-Dec. 2000) for CA, NC, OH artists in all disciplines; 11-month "live-out residencies" for Bay Area artists **Remuneration:** $500 monthly stipend, travel for CA, NC, OH artist; $2500 stipend for Bay Area artist; no students **Procedure:** request guidelines **Deadline:** Jun. 4, 1999

HEAR & NOW SERIES   F-l Tr Ad CY C
Stageworks/Summit Inc., Hyde & Watson Theatre, Kent Place School, 42 Norwood Ave., Summit, NJ 07901 (908) 273-9383 FAX (908) 273-9390 Contact: Robert Pridham, Artistic Director **Program:** staged readings of full-length plays, translations, adaptations, children's plays; emphasis on political issues **Procedure:** inquire for guidelines

HEDGEBROOK   Rs W M $
2197 E. Millman Rd., Langley, WA 98260 (360) 321-4786 Contact: Linda Bowers, Director **Program:** 1 week-2 month residencies on Whidbey Island, for women writers of diverse cultural backgrounds, all genres **Fee:** none **Procedure:** send SASE for quidelines; upon application: $15 fee **Deadline:** Apr. 1, 1999 for summer/fall 1999; Oct. 1, 1999 for winter/spring 2000 **Notification:** 2 months

HEDGEROW HORIZONS PLAYREADING PROGRAM   D
Hedgerow Theatre, 146 Rose Valley Rd., Rose Valley, PA 19086 (610) 565-4211 Contact: Walt Vail, Lit. Mgr. **Program:** staged readings (May 30, 1999), development **Procedure:** send script or query/synopsis, SASP **Deadline:** Feb. 28, 1999 **Notification:** Apr. 30, 1999 **Your chances:** 50 submissions/6-10 staged readings **Advice:** "No phone calls."

HELENE WURLITZER FOUNDATION OF NEW MEXICO   Rs
P.O. Box 545, Taos, NM 87571 (505) 758-2413 FAX (505) 758-2559 Program: 3-6 month residencies (Apr.-Sept., on limited basis Oct.-Mar.) for creative (not interpretive) artists in all media **Fee:** none **Procedure:** send SASE or fax for guidelines **Deadline:** ongoing program **Your chances:** 500 applications each year/program is booked into 2001

♫ HORSECHART THEATRE/DENVER   F D F-l 1- Ad CY Rg
FESTIVAL   3317 Wyandot, Denver, CO 80211 (303) 458-0755 e-mail horsechart@prodigy.net **Program:** festival of workshop productions of 8 new plays in cooperation with several venues in Denver **Works:** full-length plays, one-acts, adaptations, children's plays **Guidelines:** authors must reside in the Rocky Mountain area or the western Midwest **Procedure:** send script **Deadline:** inquire

♫ **THE HUMOR HATCHERY** D H Am
The American Place Theatre, 111 W. 46th St., New York, NY 10036
(212) 840-2960 Contact: Literary Dept. Program: development of
humorous plays by American writers; works not previously produced in
NYC; small cast, moderate demands Procedure: inquire for guidelines

IMMIGRANTS' THEATRE PROJECT, INC. 1- M ⊐
Immigrants' Theatre Project, Inc., 44 Douglas St., Brooklyn, NY
11231-4714 (718) 237-4545 FAX (718) same Contact: Marcy Arlin,
Artistic Director Program: American Dreams: readings in NYC libraries
of short plays about immigrant experiences Guidelines: works must be
mobile; minimal set; plays with music welcome Procedure: send script,
include cassette tape of music Comment: "Play listed on ITP Play List
prepared for library--play is selected by library."

NEW IMMIGRANT PLAY FESTIVAL F Pl ♪ M W C
Program: festival (fall 1999) of full productions and staged readings
Guidelines: plays and musicals about the immigrant experience; "in
1999 emphasis will be on women playwrights and immigrant issues"
Remuneration: fee, percentage of box office Fee: "$250 and up."
Procedure: send script, include cassette tape for musical Deadline:
Feb. 1, 1999 Notification: Jun. 1999

THE IMPROV SCHOOL D
Players Workshop, 2936 N. Southport, Chicago, IL 60657 (773) 929-
6288 FAX (773) 477-8022 Contact: Stephen Roath, Gen. Mgr. Program:
6 terms of 24-hours each in improvisational training for writers, actors,
and other creative professionals Fee: $200 per term Procedure: phone
for information and current class schedule Deadline: ongoing program

INDEPENDENT FEATURE PROJECT Mb S
104 W. 29th St. 12th Floor, New York, NY 10001 (212) 465-8200 FAX
(212) 465-8525 e-mail ifpny@ifp.org Contact: Michelle Byrd, Exec. Dir.
Program: organization encouraging creativity-diversity in films produced outside established system; seminars, showcases, Independent
Feature Film Market; *Filmmaker* quarterly Dues: $100 or more per year

INSTITUTE OF INTERNATIONAL EDUCATION g/f
U.S.I.A. FULBRIGHT GRANTS USIA, 809 United Nations Plaza,
New York, NY 10017-3580 (212) 984-5330 Contact: U.S. Student Pro-
grams Div. Program: annual fellowships or grants for study abroad
Procedure: request guidelines Deadline: Oct. 23 every year

INSTITUTE OF OUTDOOR DRAMA i
CB 3240, Nations Bank Plaza, UNC, Chapel Hill, NC 27599-3240
(919) 962-1328 FAX (919) 962-4212 e-mail outdoor@unc.edu Contact:
Scott J. Parker, Director Program: advisory/research agency encouraging creation of new outdoor dramas; network for producers and
resource for writers

INTAR NEW WORKS LAB   D F-l 1- ♪ Hi Esp
P.O. Box 788 Times Square Station, New York, NY 10108 (212) 695-
6134, -6135 Ext. 17 FAX (212) 268-0102 Contact: Lorenzo Mans, Literary
Mgr. Program: developmental workshops for new full-length plays,
one-acts, and musicals by Hispanic-American writers; also Reading
Series Procedure: send script Notification: 3-6 months

INTERACT THEATRE CO. PLAY DEVELOPMENT LAB   D
Theatre Exchange, 11855 Hart St., N. Hollywood, CA 91605 (818)
773-7862 Contact: Anita Khanzadian, Director of Play Development
Program: weekly lab (Tues. 7:30 p.m.), culminating in public presentations Fee: none, contributions welcome Procedure: call for information

♫ INTERACTIVE THEATRICS   Mb D Rg
P.O. Box 65004, West Newton, MA 02165 (617) 527-3222 Contact:
Paulette Idelson Program: monthly readings of works-in-progress by
Boston-area playwrights Procedure: send script Advice: "Serious play-
wrights able to work in a supportive atmosphere."

INTERNATIONAL THEATRE INSTITUTE OF THE   Sv i
UNITED STATES (ITI/US) 47 Great Jones St., New York, NY
10012-1114 (212) 254-4141 FAX (212) 254-6814 e-mail info@iti-usa.
org Contact: Louis A. Rachow, Library Director Program: organization
with centers in 92 countries, founded by UNESCO "to promote international exchange of knowledge and practice in the theatre arts"; services include assistance for theatre artists traveling abroad, library docu-
menting theatre activities in 146 countries and housing 13,000 plays from
97 countries, information/consultation service, Music Theatre Committee, Theatre of Nations festival, quarterly newsletter

THE INTERNATIONAL WOMEN'S WRITING GUILD Mb W
P.O. Box 810 Gracie Station, New York, NY 10028-0082 (212) 737-
7536 FAX (212) 737-9469 e-mail iwwg@iwwg.com Contact: Hannelore
Hahn, Exec. Director Program: "network for the personal and professional empowerment of women through writing"; annual conference/
retreat at Skidmore College Dues: $35, foreign member $45

THE ISIDORA AGUIRRE PLAYWRIGHTING   D F-l Hi Esp
LAB El Teatro de la Esperanza, P.O. Box 40578, San Francisco, CA
94140-0578 (415) 255-2320 FAX (415) 255-8031 Contact: Prog. Mgr.
Program: 6-week course (Jun.-Jul. 1999) culminating in staged reading,
possible production Guidelines: Latino writers; full-length plays-in-
progress reflecting Chicano experience; bilingual plays preferred; maximum cast: 6 (with doubling) Remuneration: stipend for housing, meals
Procedure: send SASE for guidelines; upon application: 3 copies of
script Deadline: Mar. 15, 1999 Notification: May 1999 Your chances:
30+ applications/1-3 plays selected Comment: Scripts are not returned.

ISLE ROYALE NATL. PARK ARTIST-IN-RESIDENCE   Rs
800 E. Lakeshore Dr., Houghton, MI 49931 (906) 482-0984, 487-7152 FAX (906) 482-8753 Contact: Greg Blust, Coord. **Program:** free residencies (Jun.-Sept.) of 2-3 weeks for 1 writer at a time in a cabin on an island in a national park; no electricity or water **Procedure:** request guidelines **Deadline:** Feb. 16, 1999 postmark **Notification:** Apr. 15, 1999

THE JAMES THURBER PLAYWRIGHT-IN-RESIDENCE   Rs
The Thurber House, 77 Jefferson Ave., Columbus, OH 43215 (614) 464-1032 FAX (614) 228-7445 Contact: Trish Houston, Director, Education & Outreach **Program:** 1-quarter (winter or spring) residency for playwright who has had at least 1 play published and/or produced by a major theatre; resident teaches a course at OSU **Remuneration:** $6000 stipend, furnished 3rd-floor apartment in James Thurber's home **Procedure:** nominator or nominee may send letter of interest and curriculum vita **Deadline:** Dec. 15, 1999 **Notification:** 2 months

THE JAPAN FOUNDATION ARTIST FELLOWSHIPS   g/f As
152 W. 57th St. 39th Floor, New York, NY 10019 (212) 489-0299 FAX (212) 489-0409 Contact: Chris Watanabe, Program Asst. **Program:** annual fellowships of 2-6 months for accredited professional artists to pursue creative projects in Japan **Guidelines:** for U.S. citizen or permanent resident affiliated with a Japanese artist or institution **Remuneration:** monthly stipend of 370,000 yen or 430,000 yen; travel, insurance, dependent allowances **Procedure:** request guidelines and application form in mid-Sept. 1999, stating citizenship, position, theme of project; references required upon application **Deadline:** Dec. 1, 1999 (tentative)

JEFFREY SWEET WRITING WORKSHOPS   D
Artistic New Directions, 250 W. 90th St. #15G, New York, NY 10024 (212) 875-1857 FAX (212) 724-7512 e-mail dgsweet@aol.com **Contact:** Kristine Niven, Coord. **Program:** weekly classes in New York; weekend intensives in NYC and around the country, alone or in conjunction with Dana Singer (see listing in this section); focus is on the use of improvisation in developing new work; private consultation also available **Fee:** varies by program **Procedure:** phone or e-mail for information

JENNY McKEAN MOORE WRITER IN WASHINGTON   Rs
Dept. of English, The George Washington Univ., Washington, DC 20052 (202) 994-6180 Contact: Faye Moskowitz, Chair **Program:** 1-year fellowship; writer gives public reading and teaches workshop and 1 class each semester **Guidelines:** genres rotate; 1999 genre: fiction; fellow must reside in the DC area Sept. 1999-Apr. 2000 **Remuneration:** $48,000, benefits **Procedure:** request guidelines in spring 1999 **Deadline:** Nov. 15, 1999 **Your chances:** 150 applications

JEROME FOUNDATION TRAVEL AND STUDY GRANTS
See Travel and Study Grants in this section.

JET THEATRE FESTIVAL OF NEW PLAYS   D F F-11- ♪ CY J
IN STAGED READINGS 6600 W. Maple Rd. #102, W. Bloomfield,
MI 48322 (810) 788-2900 FAX (810) 661-3680 Contact: Literary Desk
Frequency: annual Program: staged readings (Mar.-Apr.) possible production of full-length plays, musicals, children's plays Special interest: Jewish writers/themes--not exclusive Regulations: works must be unproduced; simple set; no fly space Procedure: send script, synopsis, cassette tape of music Best time: May-Dec. Notification: 6 months

JOHN F. KENNEDY CENTER FOR THE PERFORMING ARTS
2700 F St. NW, Washington, DC 20566   Program: U.S. national
theatre; produces plays, musicals, operas; sponsors Kennedy Center
ACTF Awards and VSA Playwright Discovery Program (see Contests)

FUND FOR NEW AMERICAN PLAYS   g/f dr cm
(202) 416-8024 FAX (202) 416-8205 e-mail mawoodward@mail.
kennedy-center.org Contact: Max Woodward, Director Program:
funds to provide a better premiere production than a theatre could normally afford: $10,000 grant to U.S. citizen whose work is being premiered by a professional non-profit theatre; up to $100,000 awarded
to theatre; $5000 award to most promising comedy writer; possible
Roger L. Stevens Award: $2500 to promising playwright Procedure:
theatre may request guidelines Deadline: Apr. 30, 1999 Notification:
fall 1999 Your chances: 100 applications/5± grants

NEW VISIONS/NEW VOICES   F D CY ♪
(202) 416-8880 FAX (212) 416-2897 Contact: Kim Peter Kovac, Mgr,
Youth & Family Programs Program: biennial 5-day developmental
forum (May, even years) in which professional playwrights, composers, directors, and performers rewrite, revise, rehearse new children's
plays- and musicals-in-progress; program culminates in staged readings during 3-day national conference Audience: theater professionals, educators, publishers Procedure: request guidelines for forum
and conference Deadline: Oct. 1, 1999 Notification: Jan. 15, 2000

JOHN SIMON GUGGENHEIM MEMORIAL   g/f
FOUNDATION FELLOWSHIPS 90 Park Ave., New York, NY
10016 (212) 687-4470 e-mail fellowships@gf.org Program: 1 year
fellowships to further the development of scholars and artists Procedure: write for guidelines and application form Deadline: Oct. 1, 1999
Your chances: 3000+ applicants/usually 0-4 playwrights selected

THE JOHN STEINBECK WRITER'S ROOM   ws
LIU-Southampton Campus Library, Southampton, NY 11968 (516)
287-8382 FAX (516) 287-4049 e-mail sclibrary@sunburn.liunet.edu
Contact: Robert Gerbereux, Library Director Program: small room
with space for 4 writers working under contract or with specific commitment Fee: none Procedure: request guidelines and application form

KALANI OCEANSIDE RETREAT Rs $
Institute for Cultural Awareness, RR 2, Box 4800, Pahoa-Beach Road., Pahoa, HI 96778 (808) 965-7828, -9613 FAX (800) 800-6886 e-mail kalani@kalani.com **Program:** 2 week-2 month residencies in lodge or private cottages in coastal forest location **Procedure:** request guidelines: upon application: $10 fee **Comment:** Formerly Kalani Eco-Resort.

THE KINDNESS OF STRANGERS D Mb
4378 Lankershim Blvd., N. Hollywood, CA 91602 (818) 752-9566 FAX (818) 985-9227 e-mail MarlynMan@aol.com **Contact:** Dennis Clontz, Dramaturge-Mentor **Program:** 3-month developmental program for playwrights; material receives workshop and/or production; workshops; sponsors The Kindness of Strangers Contests: Minute Musicals and Short-Act Festival (see Contests) **Fee:** $60 per month **Procedure:** send query, resume **Your chances:** 8-10 members/new members invited to join every 12 sessions as openings become available

L. A. BLACK PLAYWRIGHTS Mb D Rg Af
5926 5th Ave., Los Angeles, CA 90043 (213) 292-9438 **Contact:** James Graham Bronson, President **Program:** membership development program for L.A. playwrights; members mainly but not exclusively black **Procedure:** request guidelines **Deadline:** ongoing program

L. A. THEATRE WORKS RADIO THEATRE Rd F-l 1- Ad
SERIES FOR NEW PLAYS 681 Venice Blvd., Venice, CA 90291 (310) 827-0808 FAX (310) 827-4949 e-mail Latwokrs@aol.com **Contact:** Kirsten Dahl, Literary Mgr. **Program:** bimonthly radio performances of new works **Guidelines:** full-length plays, one-acts, adaptations; maximum cast: 7-10 **Procedure:** agent submission **Notification:** 6-12 months

LA MAMA EXPERIMENTAL THEATER PROGRAMS D
74A E. 4th St., New York, NY 10003 (212) 254-6468 FAX (212) 254-7597 **Contact:** Beverly Petty, Assoc. Director **Program:** development/performance programs including New Voices/New Plays: weekly readings with audience response **Procedure:** send SASE for guidelines

CROSS CULTURAL INSTITUTE OF THEATER D M
ART STUDIES **Program:** creation/development of texts promoting intercultural artistic exchange; workshops, premieres

ONE NIGHT STAND SERIES F mm
Program: weekly series of performances by emerging multidisciplinary performers; stage manager, lighting, sound provided

THE LAST WORD: A PLAYWRIGHTS' COLLECTIVE Mb D
c/o Erwin Pond, 11328 Erwin St., N. Hollywood, CA 91606 (818) 980-0287 FAX (818) 753-9390 e-mail cbcshick@ix.netcom.com **Contact:** Catherine Coke, Director **Program:** membership/development organiza-

tion meeting weekly for in-house readings, public staged readings, on-book workshop presentations; for professional playwrights who have had works produced or published **Fee:** $35 per month **Procedure:** send work sample, resume **Advice:** "All types of playwriting are accepted. We hope to create a new paradigm in script development, replacing 'Workshop Hell' with 'Helpful Work.'"

LEAGUE OF CHICAGO THEATRES/LEAGUE OF Sv i
CHICAGO THEATRES FOUNDATION 67 E. Madison Ave.
Suite 2116, Chicago, IL 60603-3013 (312) 977-1730 FAX (312) 977-1661 **Program:** trade/service organization for Chicago artists, theatres, theatre personnel; services include marketing, advocacy, resource files, information clearinghouse, newsletter

LEAGUE OF PROFESSIONAL THEATRE WOMEN/NY Mb W
c/o Shari Upbin Productions, 300 E. 56th St. #2A, New York, NY 10022 (212) 583-0177 FAX (212) 583-0549 **Contact:** Shari Upbin, President **Program:** membership organization serving and promoting women in all areas of professional theatre **Guidelines:** writers must have had a 1st Class or NYC-theatre production, or 2 productions by resident theatres **Dues:** $75 **Procedure:** request Membership Information brochure

LEDIG HOUSE INTERNATIONAL WRITERS' Rs
COLONY 59 Letter S Rd., Ghent, NY 12075 (518) 392-7656, -4568 FAX (518) 392-2848 **Contact:** Exec. Director **Program:** residencies (Apr. 1-Jun. 26, Aug. 15-Oct. 31) of 2 weeks-2 months for professional writers in all fields; private or combined work/living space, meals provided; no families, no transportation **Procedure:** send latest published work, 1-page description of work to be done in residence, bio, professional recommendation **Future commitment:** endorsement **Comment:** Residencies are awarded in Oct. and Jan. for the following year.

LEE GUBER PLAYWRIGHTS' LAB D Pl ♪ J
Jewish Rep. Theatre, c/o 92nd Street Y, 1395 Lexington Ave., New York, NY 10128 (212) 415-5550 FAX (212) 415-5575 e-mail jrep@ echonyc.com **Contact:** Ran Avni, Art. Director **Program:** workshop (Oct.-Jun.) for playwrights, composers, lyricists, librettists **Exclusive interest:** "Plays in English relating to Jewish experience; maximum cast: 7." **Procedure:** send script , Sept.-May; no queries **Notification:** 4-6 weeks

THE LEHMAN ENGEL MUSICAL THEATRE D ♪ $
WORKSHOP 33 N. Brand Blvd., Glendale, CA 91203 (818) 502-3309 FAX (818) 502-3365 e-mail jsparksco@aol.com **Contact:** John Sparks, Artistic Director **Program:** workshop for composers, lyricists, librettists meeting every 5th week (Mon.-Thurs. evenings, Sept.-Jun.); after 1st year, participant may be invited to continue **Dues:** $500 1st year (includes non-refundable $25 application fee), $300 subsequent

years; limited scholarships available **Procedure:** request guidelines and application form **Deadline:** Aug. 15, 1999 **Notification:** Sept. 1999 **Your chances:** 50 applications/usually 20+ participants accepted

LITERARY MANAGERS AND DRAMATURGS   Mb i
OF THE AMERICAS (LMDA)   CASTA, CUNY Grad. Ctr., 33 W.
42nd St. Rm. 1206A, New York, NY 10036   (212) 642-2657 **Program:** organization for literary managers/dramaturgs in U.S. and Canada; script exchange; conference; associate membership open to playwrights

♫ LIVE THEATRE WORKSHOP   D
5317 E. Speedway, Tucson, AZ 85712 (520) 882-9721 **Program:** workshops, classes, camps, children's series; season of 6 productions (inquire)

LOS ANGELES CULTURAL AFFAIRS DEPT.   g/f Rg
433 S. Spring St. 10th Floor, Los Angeles, CA 90013   (213) 620-8635 **FAX (213) 485-6835 Contact:** Roella Hsieh Louie, Director of Grants **Program:** grants of up to $10,000 for Artists-in-the-Community and/or emerging arts organizations **Procedure:** send SASE for guidelines and application form **Deadline:** Jul. 1, 1999 **Notification:** Nov. 1999

LOTTA THEATRICAL FUND   g/f W
11 Beacon St. #1005, Boston, MA 02108   (617) 742-5920 **Contact:** Claire M. McCarthy, Trust Mgr.   **Program:** $100-$1000 scholarships for young women in the theatre and women theatre professionals with emergency need **Procedure:** send letter, resume **Notification:** 1 month

LUMINOUS VISIONS   Mb D M S Tv
267 W. 89th St., New York, NY 10024   (212) 581-7455 FAX (212) 581-3964 **Contact:** Carla Pinza, Co-Founder **Program:** multicultural organization for writers seeking employment in English-speaking TV-film; workshop, forum, staged readings **Procedure:** send SASE for guidelines

THE MacDOWELL COLONY   Rs Pl ♪ S mm
100 High St., Peterborough, NH 03458   (603) 924-3886   FAX (603) 924-9142 **Contact:** Admissions Coord. **Program:** residencies of up to 8 weeks for writers, composers, video/filmmakers, multidisciplinary artists, and others; room, board, studio provided **Fee:** voluntary contribution **Procedure:** request guidelines and application form **Deadline:** Jan. 15 for May-Aug.; Apr. 15 for Sept.-Dec.; Sept. 15 for Jan.-Apr.

MADISON REPERTORY READING SERIES   D Rg
122 State St. Suite 201, Madison, WI 53703-2500   (608) 256-0029 FAX (608) 256-7433 **e-mail** madisonrep@aol.com   **Contact:** D. Scott Glasser, Artistic Director **Program:** special reading series for plays in development at Madison Repertory Theatre; special interest: maximum cast: 8 **Procedure:** send query/synopsis, dialogue sample, SASP; professional recommendation, agent submission **Response:** 3-4 months

MAIN STREET ARTS   94 Main St., Nyack, NY 10960 (914) 358-7701 FAX same **e-mail** msapaul@juno.com

♫ A MIDSUMMER NIGHT'S ONE-ACT FESTIVAL   F 1-
Contact: Literary Mgr. **Works:** one-acts, 30 minutes maximum **Guidelines:** maximum cast: 3; minimal sets **Procedure:** send synopsis, writing sample **Deadline:** Mar. 1, 1999 **Notification:** Mar. 31, 1999 **Your chances:** 6-9 plays produced

♫ PLAYREADING SERIES   D
Contact: Don Monaco, Director, Playreading Series **Program:** rehearsed reading of 1 new play per month with actors and director, audience discussion **Procedure:** send script **Notification:** 3 weeks

MANHATTAN PLAYWRIGHTS UNIT   Mb Rg
338 W. 19th St. #6B, New York, NY 10011 (212) 989-0948 **Contact:** Saul Zachary, Artistic Director **Program:** organization of produced or published playwrights in NYC area; meetings; discussions **Procedure:** send query letter, resume **Your chances:** 100+ applications/2-5 playwrights accepted

MANHATTAN THEATRE CLUB FELLOWSHIP   Rs Rg Y M
311 W. 43rd St. 8th Floor, New York, NY 10036 (212) 399-3000 FAX (212) 399-4329 **Contact:** Alyse Rothman, Literary Asst. **Program:** fellowship consisting of 1-year residency for New York-based minority playwrights with demonstrated financial need **Remuneration:** $10,000, including commission, paid assistantship on MTC production **Procedure:** send SASE for guidelines **Deadline:** TBA **Your chances:** 100+ applications/2 fellowships awarded

MARIN INDIVIDUAL ARTIST GRANT   g/f Rg
251 N. San Pedro, San Rafael, CA 94903 (415) 499-8350 **Program:** biennial grant (usually $2000-$5000) for playwrights residing in Marin County, CA **Procedure:** request guidelines and application form **Deadline:** Feb. 4, 1999

MARK TAPER FORUM PROGRAMS   D
135 N. Grand Ave., Los Angeles, CA 90012 (213) 972-7574 **Contact:** Pier Carlo Talenti, Literary Assoc. **Procedure:** send query/description (not synopsis) of play with 5-10 page dialogue sample; agent submission

ASIAN THEATER WORKSHOP   D As
Program: script development for Asian-Pacific artists **Remuneration:** honorarium

BLACKSMYTHS   D Af
Program: year-long developmental program for black playwrights; activities include symposium (Jun.) with staged readings and workshop productions **Guidelines:** stage plays only

THE LATINO THEATRE INITIATIVE   g/f D Hi
Contact: Luis Alfaro **Program:** fellowships, commissions, readings, workshops and mainstage productions for works by Latino Artists and for Latino audiences

NEW WORK FESTIVAL   F D
Program: festival in which 16-18 new plays receive rehearsed readings or workshops including 2-weeks of rehearsal and 2 public presentations **Guidelines:** plays must be unpublished, unproduced **Deadline:** Apr. 30, 1999 for queries

OTHER VOICES SUMMER CHATAUQUA   D h/d
WORKSHOP   **Contact:** Victoria Ann Lewis **Program:** summer workshop (late Jun.) for disabled writers, 18 and older; individual mentoring, cultural dialogue, group exercises, attendance at L.A. theatre productions; per diem; travel, housing provided for out-of-town participants **Guidelines:** for previously unproduced plays-in-progress **Deadline:** TBA

MARY ANDERSON CENTER FOR THE ARTS   Rs $
101 St. Francis Dr., Mount St. Francis, IN 47146 (812) 923-8602 FAX (812) 923-3200 e-mail sry847@aol.com **Contact:** Sarah Robertson Yates, Exec. Director **Program:** 2 week-2 month residencies for writers, composers, visual artists; housing, meals provided; fellowships available **Fee:** suggested--$210 per week **Procedure:** send SASE for guidelines; upon application: 2 copies of script, supporting materials, possible fee **Deadline:** 1 month prior to desired residency **Notification:** 4 weeks

MARY FLAGLER CARY CHARITABLE TRUST   g/f ♪ Rg
COMMISSION   122 E. 42nd St. Rm. 3505, New York, NY 10168 **(212) 953-7705 Contact:** Gayle Morgan, Music Program Director **Program:** grants to assist NYC non-profit companies in commissioning new musicals **Procedure:** inquire for guidelines, policies

MARY INGRAHAM BUNTING INSTITUTE OF   g/f mm W $
RADCLIFFE COLLEGE/BUNTING FELLOWSHIP PROGRAM
34 Concord Ave., Cambridge, MA 02138 (617) 495-8212 FAX (617) 495-8136 Contact: Paula Soares, Fellowships Coord. **Program:** Multidisciplinary Program for women of demonstrated accomplishment; Bunting Fellowship Program: $36,500 for appointment (Sept. 15, 2000-Aug. 15, 2001) for professional woman **Procedure:** request details; upon application: $45 fee **Deadline:** Oct. 15, 1999 **Your chances:** 500 applicants

MARY ROBERTS RINEHART AWARDS   g/f
Mail Stop #3E4, English Dept., George Mason Univ., Fairfax, VA 22030 (703) 993-1185 Contact: Director, Writing Prog. **Program:** 2 biennial grants ($1000±, Mar. odd years) to dramatists who have not had

work professionally produced/published **Procedure:** nomination by professor of writing, established writer, agent, or editor; request guidelines **Deadline:** Nov. 30, 1999 **Notification:** Mar. 2000

THE MAXWELL ANDERSON PLAYWRIGHTS D F
SERIES

P.O. Box 671, West Redding, CT 06896 (203) 938-2770 **Contact:** Bruce Post, Dramaturg **Program:** staged readings with professional director and actors, audience discussion; sponsors Young CT Playwrights Festival (see Contests) **Guidelines:** unproduced plays; small casts preferred **Remuneration:** stipend **Procedure:** send script **Deadline:** ongoing program **Your chances:** 10 scripts selected each year

MEDICINE WHEEL ARTISTS' RETREAT Rs

P.O. Box 1088, Groton, MA 01450-3088 (978) 448-3717 FAX same e-mail medwheel@tiac.net **Program:** 1-3 week residency (Sept.) at Camp Collier, Gardner, MA **Fee:** $150-$250 for room and meals; some scholarships **Procedure:** send #10 SASE for guidelines **Notification:** 1 week

MEET THE COMPOSER GRANT PROGRAMS Mb Sv ♪ g/f

2112 Broadway Suite 505, New York, NY 10023 (212) 787-3601 **Program:** national composers' service organization; programs include support for all styles of music; Affiliate Network

ARTS ENDOWMENT COMMISSIONING MUSIC/ g/f ♪
USA

Contact: Kelly Rauch, Program Mgr. **Program:** annual commissioning grants (up to $30,000) to cover composer, librettist, and writers' fees for music-theatre work or opera, for musical and presenting organizations which have been presenting for at least 3 years **Procedure:** organizations may request guidelines **Deadline:** TBA (Jun.) **Notification:** Aug.

♫ MEET THE COMPOSER FUND g/f ♪

Contact: Diane Girer, Program Mgr. **Program:** awards and grants (up to $250) to support composer participation in a performance of his/her work **Procedure:** request guidelines

♫ NEW MUSIC FOR SCHOOLS g/f Rs ♪

Contact: Diane Girer, Program Mgr. **Program:** awards, grants (up to $5000) to support 2-week to 6-month residencies for professional composers in primary/secondary schools in the Midwest, NY, CT; commissions of new works; composers work with teachers, students, families **Deadline:** TBA (Oct.) **Notification:** 6 weeks after deadline

NEW RESIDENCIES Rs ♪

Contact: Pablo Martinez, Vice Pres. for Programs **Program:** annual grants (up to $100,000) to support 3-year composer's salary/residency, for organizations which form Residency Partnership (2 performing arts organizations, 1 community-based organization) **Procedure:** performing organizations may request guidelines **Deadline:** TBA

MERCANTILE LIBRARY ASSN. WRITERS STUDIO   ws
17 E. 47th St., New York, NY 10017 (212) 755-6710 FAX (212) 758-1387 **e-mail** mercantile_library@msn.com **Contact:** Harold Augenbraum, Director of Library **Program:** private lending library of 175,000 volumes, offering 17 carrel spaces for playwrights and librettists; access to library resources **Fee:** $200 for 3 months, renewable up to 1 year **Procedure:** request application form **Deadline:** ongoing program

MERELY PLAYERS   Mb D
49 Murray St. #1, New York, NY 10007 (212) 349-0369 FAX (212) 349-1335 **e-mail** hayesmon@aol.com **Contact:** Monica M. Hayes, Artistic Director **Program:** membership organization of professional actors, directors and writers; script development **Fee:** $80 per year; initial participation free **Procedure:** send script to reading committee **Your chances:** 200 submissions/6 members, up to 20 associates chosen **Advice:** "You must have at least 1 full-length script developed through our process before being asked to join."

MIDWEST RADIO THEATRE WORKSHOP   Sv i D Rd
KOPN Radio, 915 E. Broadway, Columbia, MO 65201 (573) 874-5676 FAX (573) 499-1662 **e-mail** mrtw@mrtw.org **Contact:** Sue Zizza, Exec. Director **Program:** resource/service organization for radio-theatre artists, teachers, and organizations; sponsors MRTW Script Contest (see Contests) **Fee:** $320 per workshop **Procedure:** request guidelines and application form; non-refundable deposit ($100 in previous years) required upon application

MRTW LIVE PERFORMANCE SPRING   D Rd F-l
WORKSHOP **Program:** annual 6-day workshop (late May 1999); "hands-on experience producing radio theatre under the direction of seasoned professionals" **Guidelines:** full-length plays, radio theatre format; radio plays commissioned or selected through MRTW Script Contest **Fee:** $320 **Procedure:** request guideline; possible non-refundable deposit required upon application **Deadline:** Apr. 1, 1999 for workshop scholarships **Your chances:** 55 participants

MILLAY COLONY FOR THE ARTS   Rs
P.O. Box 3, Austerlitz, NY 12017-0003 (518) 392-3103 **e-mail** application@millaycolony.org **Contact:** Gail Giles, Asst. Director **Program:** free 1-month residency for artists on estate in upstate NY; studio space, private bedroom, meals provided **Procedure:** send SASE for guidelines **Deadline:** Feb. 1, 1999 for Jun.-Sept. 1999; May 1, 1999 for Oct. 1999-Jan. 2000; Sept. 1, 1999 for Feb.-May 2000 **Notification:** 2 months after deadline **Your chances:** 500-600 applications/72 residents per year

MINT THEATRE CO. MUSICAL THEATRE LAB   D ♪
311 W. 43rd St. 5th Floor, New York, NY 10036 (212) 315-9434 This program is inactive in 1999; see *The Playwright's Companion 2000* for future plans.

THE MISSOURI ASSOCIATION   **Mb D Rg**
OF PLAYWRIGHTS (MAP)   830 N. Spoede Rd., St. Louis, MO
63141-7748 (314) 567-6341 FAX (314) 647-0945 e-mail lovinsload@
aol.com **Contact:** Jo Lovins, President **Program:** membership/develop-
mental organization for playwrights in Missouri, Illinois, and out-state
areas; monthly staged readings (Sept.-May) of plays by members only;
seminars on various aspects of theatre; periodic full productions of one-
acts **Dues:** $20 per year **Procedure:** send SASE for guidelines

MONTALVO ARTIST RESIDENCY PROGRAM   **Rs Pl S $**
Villa Montalvo-California's Historic Estate for the Arts, P.O. Box
158, Saratoga, CA 95071-0158 (408) 961-5818 FAX (408) 961-5850 e-
mail kfunk@villamontalvo.org **Contact:** Kathryn Funk, Program Director **Program:** 1-3 month residencies in the Santa Cruz Mountains south
of San Francisco; for playwrights, composers, other writers **Fee:** $100
refundable deposit if accepted; "4 fellowships available per year to high-
est ranking applicants" **Procedure:** send SASE (2 oz. postage) for application form; upon application: 4 copies of script, supporting materials,
$20 fee **Deadline:** Mar. 1, 1999 postmark; Sept. 1, 1999 postmark **Noti-**
fication: 4 months **Your chances:** 160 applications/6 writers selected/
chances 1 in 8 for playwrights and filmmakers

MONTANA ARTISTS REFUGE   **Rs**
P.O. Box 8, Basin, MT 59631 (406) 225-3532, -3500 Contact: M. J.
Williams, Residency Coord. **Program:** residencies of 3 months-1 year in
rural community near mountains **Fee:** funds raised by residents **Proce-**
dure: send SASE for guidelines and application form

MONTANA PERFORMING ARTISTS' SHOWCASE   **F**
c/o Montana Arts, 321 E. Main St. Room 212, Bozeman, MT 59715
(406) 585-9551 Contact: John C. Barsness **Program:** annual weekend
juried showcase (late Jan.) held in conjunction with Block-booking Conference **Guidelines:** promotional booths required of artists accepted for
showcasing **Fee:** inquire **Procedure:** request guidelines and application
form **Deadline:** TBA (Oct.) **Your chances:** 17 time-slots available

MOUNT SEQUOYAH NEW PLAY RETREAT Dept. of Drama,
Kimpel Hall 619, Univ. of AR, Fayetteville, AR 72701 (501) 575-2953
FAX (501) 575-7602 e-mail rdgross@comp. uark.edu **Contact:** Roger
Gross, Director This program is inactive in 1999; see *The Playwright's*
Companion 2000 for future plans.

MUSIC THEATRE INTERNATIONAL   ♪
421 W. 54th St., New York, NY 10019 (212) 541-4684 FAX (212) 397-
4684 e-mail mtishows@aol.com **Contact:** Nicholas Brown, Acquisitions
Program: licensing agency for unproduced musicals **Procedure:** inquire
for services and policies

MUSIC THEATRE OF CONNECTICUT   ♪ Ad
STAGED READING PROGRAM   P.O. Box 344, Westport, CT
06881-0344 (203) 454-3883   FAX (203) 227-8818 Contact: Kevin
Connors, Producing Art. Director   Program: staged readings of new
musical theatre works and musical adaptations; also developmental
musical theatre workshops Special interest: "Premieres!" Procedure:
request guidelines

NANTUCKET PLAYWRIGHTS RETREAT   Nantucket, MA
This program has been discontinued.

NATIONAL ALLIANCE FOR MUSICAL   Mb Sv ♪ F
THEATRE 330 W. 45th St. Lobby B, New York, NY 10036-3854
(212) 265-5376 FAX (212) 582-8730 e-mail namtheatre@aol.com
Contact: Helen Sneed, Exec. Director   Program: service organization
for professional companies producing or presenting musical theatre;
publishes Alliance News newsletter; programs include annual Festival of
New Musicals in NYC Procedure: festival entries must be submitted to
and sponsored by member theatres (inquire)

NATIONAL BLACK THEATRE FESTIVAL   F Af
N.C. Black Repertory Co., 610 Coliseum Dr., Winston-Salem, NC
27106 (910) 723-7907 FAX (910) 723-2223 Contact: Larry Leon
Hamlin, Exec. Director Program: biennial festival (Aug. 2-7, 1999) of
plays on the black experience Guidelines: inquire Procedure: send
script Deadline: Feb. 28, 1999 Notification: 3-6 months

NATIONAL ENDOWMENT FOR THE ARTS   g/f
1100 Pennsylvania Ave. NW, Washington, DC 20506

   ♫ NEA INTERNATIONAL PROGRAMS   g/f
   Room 618 (202) 682-5429 Contact: Pennie Ojeda, Acting Director
   Program: United States/Japan Creative Artists' Fellowships--monthly
   stipend to cover housing, expenses, support for 6 consecutive months,
   round-trip travel for artists and family members; stipend to study
   Japanese language (in U.S. if necessary) Guidelines: U.S. citizens or
   permanent residents who have not spent more than 3 months in Japan
   Procedure: request guidelines: Japan/U.S. Friendship Commission,
   1120 Vermont Ave. NW, #925, Washington, D.C. 20005 (202) 275-7712
   Deadline: TBA (Jun. 1999) Comment: For other NEA International
   Programs see Artslink and Fund for U.S. Artists at International
   Festivals & Exhibitions in this section.

   NEA LITERATURE PROGRAM 1999   g/f Tr po
   Room 720 (202) 682-5428 Contact: Cliff Becker, Acting Director
   Program: fellowships of $20,000 for previously published transla-
   tors of verse drama Procedure: write for deadlines and application
   form Deadline: TBA (Mar. 1999)

SPECIAL PROGRAMS   253

NATIONAL ENDOWMENT FOR THE   g/f Rd Tv
HUMANITIES PROJECTS IN MEDIA Div. of Public Programs
1100 Pennsylvania Ave. NW, Washington, DC 20506 (202) 606-8280
FAX (202) 606-8557 Contact: James J. Dougherty, Asst. Dir. Program: annual grants to support radio/TV projects Procedure: request guidelines
Deadline: Feb. 1, 1999 for planning, research, scripting, production;
Nov. 1, 1999 for planning grants Notification: Jul. 1999; Mar. 2000

NATIONAL FOUNDATION FOR JEWISH CULTURE   i J
330 7th Ave. 21st Floor, New York, NY 10001 (212) 629-0500 FAX
(212) 629-0508 e-mail NFJC@jewishculture.org Contact: Richard A.
Siegel, Exec. Director Program: cultural organization for the American
Jewish community Procedure: request information on programs

NEW PLAY COMMISSIONS IN JEWISH THEATRE   g/f J
Ext. 205 Contact: Grants Administrator   Program: annual grant of
$1000-$5000 to a non-profit theatre in North America which has presented at least 2 seasons of public performances and is commissioning a
new work which deals with issues of Jewish life, values, history,
tradition Procedure: theatre may request guidelines Deadline: TBA

NATIONAL LEAGUE OF AMERICAN PEN WOMEN   Mb W
1300 17th St. NW, Washington, DC 20036-1973 (202) 785-1997
Contact: Judith LaFourest, Natl. President Program: organization of
professional women writers, composers, visual artists Dues: $40 initial
membership, $30 per year plus branch and state dues Procedure:
contact local branch

NLAPW SCHOLARSHIPS FOR MATURE   g/f Am W $
WOMEN   Contact: S. Helberg, Natl. Scholarship Chairman
Program: biennial scholarships for American women over age 35; 3
awards: $1000 each in letters, music, art Procedure: send SASE for
guidelines after Aug. 1, 1999 to R.D. #4, Box 4245, Spring Grove, PA
17362; upon application: $8 fee Deadline: Jan. 15, 2000 postmark
Notification: Jun. 2000 Your chances: 280 applications/2 judges

THE NATIONAL MUSIC THEATER NETWORK   Sv Mb i ♪
1697 Broadway #902, New York, NY 10019 (212) 664-0979 FAX (212)
664-0978 Contact: Tim Jerome, Art. Director Program: service organization for the discovery, evaluation, promotion of new music theatre
Works: completed musicals and operas which have not had major productions Fee: $45 for evaluation Procedure: send SASE for guidelines

NATIONAL THEATRE WORKSHOP   Sv Mb h/d D F Rs
FOR THE HANDICAPPED 354 Broome St. Loft 5-F, New York,
NY 10013 (212) 941-9511 FAX (212) 941-9486 Contact: Rick Curry,
Founder/Artistic Director Program: service/advocacy organization
for physically disabled adults; programs include professional training in
playwriting, annual festival of short works, professional theatre com-

pany to showcase members' work **Procedure:** send SASE for festival guidelines; request information on training programs **Your chances:** 100 applications/usually 8 playwrights accepted for training program **Advice:** "Plays should not try to explain or 'solve' disability." **Comment:** National Theatre Workshop now has a Residential School in Belfast, ME, for the training of actors and Playwrights (inquire for guidelines)

NAUTILUS MUSIC-THEATER COMPOSER/ D ♪ Rg
LIBRETTIST STUDIO   308 Prince St. #250, St. Paul, MN 55101 (651) 298-9913 FAX (651) 298-9924 Contact: Ben Krywosz, Art. Dir. **Program:** annual 2-week lab for MN composers, librettists **Guidelines:** emphasis on developing writers' skills rather than on finished work **Remuneration:** $400 **Procedure:** send SASP for guidelines

NEBRASKA REP. THEATRE NEW THEATRE FESTIVAL
215 Temple Bldg., 12th & R Sts., Lincoln, NE 68588-0201 (402) 472-2072 FAX (402) 472-9055 e-mail: jeh@unlgrad1.unl.edu **Contact:** Julie Hagemeier, Mng. Director This festival has been undergoing a reevaluation; see *The Playwright's Companion 2000* or inquire for future plans.

NEW AMERICAN THEATER SCHOOL OF THE D Pl S
WOMEN'S PROJECT AND PRODUCTIONS 55 West End Ave., New York, NY 10023 (212) 765-1706 FAX (212) 765-2024 e-mail WPP@earthlink.net **Contact:** Milan Stitt, Director **Program:** classes in playwriting and screenwriting; cold and staged readings **Fee:** varies **Procedure:** request guidelines

NEW ARTS THEATRE NEW PLAY D F-l 1- Tr Ad 2d C
READINGS P.O. Box 81, Bristol, TN 37621 Contact: William Ratcliffe, Literary Mgr. **Program:** staged readings of full-length plays, one-acts, translations, adaptations dealing with current issues; previously produced plays eligible **Procedure:** write for information, or send script

NEW CENTURY VOICES D F-l Rg C
Riverside Theatre, P.O. Box 3788, Vero Beach, FL 32964 (407) 231-5860 Contact: Sherrie Dee Brewer, Production Mgr. **Program:** reading series for new full-length plays by FL playwrights; "important issues, serious or comic"; maximum cast: 10 **Procedure:** request guidelines

NEW DRAMATISTS Mb D Rg
424 W. 44th St., New York, NY 10036 (212) 757-6960 FAX (212) 265-4738 e-mail newdram@aol.com **Contact:** Todd London, Artistic Director **Program:** membership organization for emerging playwrights with access to New York City; programs include readings and workshops, musical theatre development and training, ScriptShare distribution program, national and international playwright exchanges **Guidelines:** members admitted for 7-year terms; teams eligible **Procedure:** request guidelines **Your chances:** 300 applications/usually 5-7 new members accepted

NEW ENGLAND THEATRE CONFERENCE (NETC)   Mb Rg
**Dept. of Theatre, Northeastern Univ., 360 Huntington Ave., Boston,
MA 02115 (617) 424-9275 FAX (617) 424-1057 Contact:** Corey Boniface, Mgr. of Operations **Program:** organization for theatre artists, teachers, and students in New England; sponsors John Gassner Memorial Playwriting Award and Aurand Harris Memorial Playwriting Award (see NETC Awards in Contests) **Procedure:** send SASE for membership information

THE NEW GROUP PLAYWRIGHTS UNIT   D F-l
**85 Fifth Ave. 5th Floor, New York, NY 10003 (212) 647-0752
Contact:** Kevin Scott, Literary Mgr. **Program:** 3-month developmental program for full-length plays, meeting weekly (Mon., 7-10 p.m., Sept.-Jul.) **Fee:** none **Procedure:** send script **Notification:** 6 months

NEW HARMONY PROJECT   F D F-l Ad ♪ CY S Tv Sp
**613 N. East St., Indianapolis, IN 46202 (317) 464-9405 FAX (317)
635-4201 Contact:** Jim Houghton, Artistic Director **Program:** annual 2 $1/2$-week developmental conference/lab (May-Jun. 1999) for unproduced full-length plays, adaptations, musicals, children's plays, screenplays and teleplays; activities include rehearsals with directors and actors, readings, critiques, discussions; small stipend, travel, housing, meals provided **Guidelines:** "Our primary objective is to identify and nurture writers whose scripts emphasize the dignity of the human spirit and celebrate the worth of the human experience." **Procedure:** send 10-page writing sample, project proposal, statement of artistic purpose **Deadline:** TBA **Your chances:** 200 applications/6-10 playwrights selected

NEW JERSEY PLAYWRIGHTS WKSP. 45 Ocean Ave. #7L, Monmouth Beach, NJ 07750 (732) 229-5491   This program is inactive in 1999; see *The Playwright's Companion 2000* or inquire for future plans.

NEW JERSEY THEATRE GROUP   Sv Mb Rg i
**P.O. Box 21, Florham Park, NJ 07932 (201) 593-0189 FAX (201) 377-
4842 e-mail** njtg@nj.com **Program:** alliance of non-profit professional theatres in NJ; programs and services include Job Bank referrals, annual Job Fair (Mar.), symposia, actor search, audio description for visually impaired audience members, Family Week at the Theatre (Feb. 27-Mar. 7, 1999); publications: *Professional Theatre Directory, Theatre Season Calendar & Sampler Series*, annual *Toward Knowing by Art* (on members' outreach programs), free *Guide to New Jersey's Professional Theatres*

NEW PLAYWRIGHTS Mb D Rg i Sv F-l 1- Tr Ad ♪ CY S Tv
**FOUNDATION WRITERS' WORKSHOP c/o 608 San Vicente
Blvd. #18, Santa Monica, CA 90402 (310) 393-3682 e-mail** phyllis@ dbc.cms.com **Contact:** Jeffrey Lee Bergquist, Artistic Director **Program:** membership/service organization for playwrights, screenwriters, TV, and video writers **Guidelines:** "We develop and sometimes help produce

members' plays, video projects, and short and feature-length film projects; members must be able to attend workshops in Santa Moncica." **Fee:** optional $25 per year dues **Procedure:** submit work after attending at least 3 meetings **Your chances:** 50-60 applicants/15 playwrights selected **Advice:** "Be open to suggestions for making your script tighter."

NEW TUNERS WORKSHOP   D ♪
New Tuners Theatre, 1225 W. Belmont Ave., Chicago, IL 60657 (312) 929-7367 Ext. 22   FAX (312) 327-1404   e-mail JUDYTUNE@ aol.com **Contact:** Judy Myers, Workshop Co-Director **Program:** a 3-step musical theatre writing workshop meeting every 6th weekend (Fri.-Sun.) **Fee:** $300 per level; $200 per year after 3rd level **Procedure:** send SASE for guidelines **Deadline:** Aug. 31, 1999 **Notification:** Sept.7, 1999 **Your chances:** 45 applications/usually 12 participants selected

NEW VILLAGE PRODUCTIONS PLAYWRIGHTS WING   D
145 E. 27th St. Suite 1A, New York, NY 10016   (212) 779-3051 Contact: China Clark, Artistic Director **Program:** script workshop meeting 1 evening each month (Sept.-Jun.) **Fee:** $200 per 6 weeks **Procedure:** send script, resume; professional recommendation **Notification:** 4-6 weeks **Your chances:** 13-14 applications/3-6 playwrights selected

NEW VOICES FOR A NEW AMERICA
Arena Stage, 1101 6th St. SW, Washington, DC 20024 (202) 554-9066 Contact: Cathy Madison, Literary Mgr.   This program is inactive in 1999; see *The Playwright's Companion 2000* for future plans.

NEW VOICES PLAY DEVELOPMENT   D F F-l 1- CY Af
Plowshares Theatre Co., 2870 E. Grand Blvd. Suite 600, Detroit, MI 48202 (313) 872-0279 FAX (313) 274-3671 e-mail PlowshrThr@aol. com **Contact:** Gary Anderson, Producing Art. Director **Program:** annual 8-week festival; African-American playwrights collaborate with director, dramaturg, actors **Guidelines:** permanent U.S. residents only; plays must be unproduced, unoptioned full-length plays, one-acts, or children's plays about African-American life **Remuneration:** $200 stipend for travel; $1000 "Best of Festival" award **Procedure:** request guidelines; upon application: 3 copies of script **Deadline:** Jan. 5, 1999 **Notification:** Mar. 1999 **Your chances:** 75 applications/90% accepted **Future commitment:** credit; 1st refusal for production

NEW WORKS FOR A NEW WORLD   Rs D Af M
SUMMER PLAY LAB   c/o Dept. of Theater, Univ. of MA, 112 Fine Arts Ctr. Amherst, MA 01003-2620 (413) 545-1972 Contact: Lucy Burns, Literary Mgr.   **Program:** 2-week residency (Jul.); plays are developed with director, actors, dramaturg; culminates in staged reading **Special interests:** "Black writers; multicultural issues." **Remuneration:** $1500 stipend, travel, housing **Procedure:** send SASE for guidelines **Deadline:** TBA (Jul. 31 in 1998) **Your chances:** 4 writers selected

NEW YORK FOUNDATION FOR THE ARTS g/f
**155 Avenue of the Americas 14th Floor, New York, NY 10013-1507
(212) 366-6900 FAX (212) 366-1778 e-mail** nyfaafp@artswire.

org

ARTISTS' FELLOWSHIPS g/f F-l 1- Ad ♪ CY S Rg
Contact: Penelope Dannenberg, Director of Programs **Program:** biennial fellowship of $7000 **Guidelines:** applicants must have resided in NY State for 2 years prior to deadline; students ineligible **Procedure:** request guidelines, available Jul. 2000; upon application: 6 copies of script **Deadline:** TBA **Your chances:** 4000 applications/usually 12-15 dramatic writers selected

ARTISTS IN RESIDENCE PROGRAM Rs g/f Rg
(212) 366-6900 Ext. 222 Contact: Alyson Holonbek, Program Officer **Program:** matching grants for sponsoring schools and cultural organizations to help support residencies of 12 days-10 months (Sept. 1999-Jun. 2000) for NY State residents in various art fields; resident holds workshops, lecture-demonstrations, readings, performances **Remuneration:** at least $250 per day suggested **Procedure:** sponsor may request Sponsor Guidelines; individual artist may contact program for assistance in locating a sponsor **Deadline:** Feb. 15, Apr. 2, Jun. 15, Oct. 15, Nov. 5, 1999

SPONSORSHIP PROGRAM g/f D Sv i
e-mail sponsor@artswire.org **Contact:** Sarah Jarkow, Program Officer **Program:** fiscal sponsorship for the development, production, and distribution of new projects **Procedure:** write for guidelines and application form **Deadline:** TBA **Your chances:** 100+ applicants each year **Advice:** "After receiving guidelines, please call to make sure your project is appropriate for fiscal sponsorship or a fellowship."

INDIVIDUAL ARTISTS g/f
Guidelines: for emerging and established artists (in New York and nationwide) with solid proposals and realistic budgets **Fee:** $50 contract fee; 8% of grants and contributions received **Advice:** "Artists should attend a free orientation seminar held on the 1st Monday of each month (call for times)."

EMERGING ORGANIZATIONS g/f
Guidelines: for emerging arts organizations nationwide **Fee:** $100 contract fee; 7% of all income, earned and unearned, plus banking charges of $35 per quarter

NEW YORK MILLS ARTS RETREAT Rs
24 N. Main Ave., P.O. Box 246, New York Mills, MN 56567 (218) 385-3339 FAX (218) 385-3366 e-mail nymills@uslink.net **Contact:** Kent Scheer, Coordinator **Program:** 2-4 week residency for 1 artist at a time in a small farming community; housing ranging from bed & breakfast to the retreat house; some meals provided; $750 stipend for 2 weeks, $1500 for 4 weeks **Guidelines:** for emerging artists of demonstrated ability;

resident must donate 8 hours each week to community outreach **Procedure:** request guidelines and application form **Deadline:** Apr. 1, Oct. 1, 1999 **Notification:** 8 weeks after deadline

NEWGATE THEATRE'S INFORMAL　　　F-l 1- Tr Ad D Rg
READING SERIES/NEW PLAY DEVELOPMENT 134 Mathewson St., Providence, RI 02906 (401) 921-9680 **Contact:** New Works Coord. **Program:** readings leading to possible workshop or full productions of full-length plays, one-acts, translations, adaptations; essentially for residents of southern New England, but all playwrights are welcome **Stage:** black box **Procedure:** send synopsis **Deadline:** Feb. 1, 1999 **Your chances:** 30 applicants/4-5 playwrights accepted

THE NEXT STAGE　　　　　　　　　　D F F-l Rg
The Cleveland Play House, P.O. Box 1989, Cleveland, OH 44106-0189 (216) 795-7010 FAX (216) 795-7005 Contact: Scott Kanoff, Lit. Mgr. **Program:** development of unproduced full-length plays Stage One: The Playwrights Unit, ongoing workshop for full-length plays by northern OH residents, participants receive access to administrative resources, reimbursement for professional expenses; Stage Two: Next Stage Festival (Jan. 2000) rehearsed readings, participants receive stipend, travel, housing; Premiere Series: mainstage production. negotiable terms **Remuneration:** varies **Procedure:** send query letter, script, resume **Submission Period:** Stage One: Apr. 1-30, 1999; Stage Two: May 15-Jun. 30, 1999 **Your chances:** 250 applicants/4-8 playwrights selected

NIU NEW PLAY WORKSHOP　　　　　F-l Tr Ad C cm
c/o Theatre Arts, Northern IL Univ., DeKalb, IL 60115 (815) 753-8253 FAX (815) 753-8415 **Contact:** Chris Markle, Artistic Director **Program:** spring productions of new plays **Special interests:** political issues; contemporary comedies **Guidelines:** full-length plays, translations, adaptations suitable for student actors; maximum cast: 9; unit set **Procedure:** request submission information

NORCROFT: A WRITING RETREAT FOR WOMEN　　Rs W
32 E. 1st St. #330, Duluth, MN 55802 (218) 727-5199, (800) 770-0058 FAX (218) 727-3119 **Contact:** Administrator **Program:** 1-4 week residencies (May-Oct. 1999), free to women writers in an isolated location on Lake Superior **Guidelines:** for writers 21 or older whose work "demonstrates commitment to feminism;" all genres/levels of experience **Procedure:** write or phone for information **Deadline:** Oct. 1, 1999

NORTH CAROLINA ARTS COUNCIL FELLOWSHIPS g/f Rg
Dept. of Cultural Resources, Raleigh, NC 27601 (919) 733-2821 FAX (919) 733-4834 e-mail ncartscl@tmn.com **Program:** biennial grants of $8000 for NC playwrights; students ineligible **Procedure:** request guidelines **Deadline:** Nov. 1, 1999

NORTH CAROLINA WRITERS' NETWORK Mb Sv Rg i Pl S
P.O. Box 954, Carboro, NC 27510 (919) 967-9540 FAX (919) 929-0535
e-mail ncwn@sunsite.unc.edu **Contact:** Linda Whitney Hobson, Exec.
Director **Program:** membership/service organization for NC writers of
all genres; services and activities include NCWN Library (3501 Hwy. 54
W., Studio C, Chapel Hill), critiques, newsletter, scholarships, work-
shops, conferences, playwrights' and screenwriters' groups; Paul Green
Playwrights Prize (see Contests)

♫ **NORTH SHORE MUSIC THEATRE NEW WORKS** D Rs ♪
DEVELOPMENT PROGRAM **P.O. Box 62, Dunham Rd., Beverly,**
MA 01915 (978) 922-8500 FAX (978) 921-0793 e-mail nsmt@aol
Contact: Kevin P. Hale, Asst. to Producer **Program:** workshop produc-
tions (spring, fall) of new musical works with authors in residence;
stipend, housing provided **Procedure:** request guidelines

NORTHWEST PLAYWRIGHTS GUILD Mb Sv i D Rg
P.O. Box 95259, Seattle, WA 98145-2259 (206) 298-9361; P.O. Box
1728, Portland, OR 97207 (503) 244-1606 Contact: Barbara Callander
(WA); Michael Whelan (OR) **Program:** membership/service organization
providing in-house and public readings, workshops, newsletters **Fee:**
$25 per year **Procedure:** send fee for 1 year **Advice:** "Anyone may join;
we focus on playwrights residing in the Northwest."

NORTHWOOD UNIV. ALDEN B. DOW CREATIVITY Rs $
CENTER FELLOWSHIP PROGRAM **3225 Cook Rd., Midland,**
MI 48640-2398 (517) 837-4478 FAX (517) 837-4468 Contact: Ron
Koenig, Exec. Director **Program:** 10-week residency (Jun.-Aug. 1999)
for an artist in any discipline; culminates in presentation **Remunera-**
tion: $750 stipend, travel **Procedure:** request brochure/application in-
formation; upon application: $10 fee **Deadline:** Dec. 31 each year **Your**
chances: 150 applications **Advice:** "Creative aspect of the project must
be done during the residency; rewrites, editing are not valid proposals."

OAK RIDGE COMMUNITY PLAYHOUSE PROGRAMS D
P.O. Box 5705, Oak Ridge, TN 37831-5705 (423) 482-9999 FAX (423)
482-0945 Contact: Beverly Broyles, Gen. Mgr. **Procedure:** send script

FOOTLIGHT SERIES F D Rs
Program: script development series for new plays of all genres; playwrights participate at their own expense in a 5-week rehearsal
process culminating in production **Your chances:** 4-5 plays selected

JUNIOR PLAYHOUSE D CY 12+ Y C Rg
Program: theatre of young people (grades 1-12) in Anderson, Knox
Counties, TN; projects in acting, technical theatre, productions in year-
round project; 2-days of 3 shows per day (summer) for young audiences,
1 evening public performance **Special interests:** "Contemporary plays;
young playwrights encouraged." **Your chances:** 4 plays selected

OLD PUEBLO PLAYWRIGHTS   **Mb D F**
P.O. Box 767, Tucson, AZ 85702 (520) 297-0940 FAX (520) 887-6741
e-mail 4stern@92starnet.com **Contact:** Chris Stern, Member **Program:**
membership/development organization meeting weekly (Mon. 7:30 p.m.),
for playwrights at all stages of their careers; staged readings at annual
New Play Festival (Jan.) **Dues:** $24 per year **Procedure:** "Attend at
least 3 meetings." **Deadline:** ongoing program **Advice:** "Facilitators
introduce new members to actors and directors and receive feedback on
behalf of members whose work has received a reading."

OLLANTAY CENTER FOR THE ARTS   **Hi Esp ⌐**
P.O. Box 720449, Jackson Heights, NY 11372-0449 (718) 565-6499
FAX (718) 446-7806 Contact: Pedro R. Monge-Rafuls, Exec. Director
Program: multidisciplinary Hispanic arts center; Traveling Theatre
tours plays by local playwrights; publishes *Ollantay Theater Magazine*
(see Publishers) **Dues:** $20 individual, $35 organization

OLLANTAY UNIQUE PLAYWRITING   **D Esp Hi**
WORKSHOP Program: annual 3-6 week intensive course for playwrights writing in Spanish; participants work under direction of
major Latin American playwrights residing outside U.S.A. **Procedure:**
send SASE for guidelines

ONE-ACTS IN PERFORMANCE PROJECT   **F 1-**
AT POLARIS NORTH 1265 Broadway Rm. 803, New York, NY
10001 (212) 684-1985 Contact: Diane Martella **Program:** series of 3-
night workshop productions of one-act plays **Guidelines:** previously
unproduced works, 30 minutes maximum; maximum cast: 4; single set; no
musicals, monologues, children's plays **Procedure:** send script **Deadline:** ongoing program **Notification:** 1 month

OPERA AMERICA   **Sv i ♪**
1156 15th St. NW Suite 810, Washington, DC 20005 (202) 293-4466
FAX (202) 393-0735 e-mail frontdesk@operaam.org **Contact:** Jamie
Driver, Diana Hossack, Co-Mgrs. The Next Stage **Program:** service organization for professional opera; resource for media, funders, govern-
ment agencies, and the public

♫ THE NEXT STAGE   **g/f ♪**
Program: 3-year program providing financial, technical, information-
al assistance for the production of neglected operas by American composers; grants for member companies **Procedure:** request information

ORANGE COUNTY PLAYWRIGHTS' ALLIANCE   **Mb D i**
P.O. Box 6154, Fullerton, CA 92834 (714) 738-3841 FAX (714) 714-
7833 e-mail elbro@earthline.net **Contact:** Eric Eberwein, Eleanor
Brook, Directors **Program:** developmental membership workshop and
resource/information service for advanced writers; activities include

monthly meetings, informal cold readings, staged readings before an audience; sponsors Page to Stage (see Contests) **Fee:** $20 per quarter **Procedure:** write for information

ORIGINALS PLAYWRIGHTS WORKSHOP D
Diamond Head Theatre, 520 Makapuu Ave., Honolulu, HI 96816 **(808) 734-8763 FAX (808) 735-1250 Contact:** John Rampage, Artistic Director **Program:** monthly public readings, discussions of works-in-progress **Fee:** $5 per session **Procedure:** inquire for session dates and times, attend a workshop session **Deadline:** ongoing program

OWEN KELLY ADOPT-A-PLAYWRIGHT D F-l Rg Rs
PROGRAM Dobama Theatre, 1846 Coventry Rd., Cleveland Hts., OH 44118 (216) 932-6838 FAX (216) 932-3259 Program: 2-week developmental program (Jul. 1999); playwrights work with director, actors, dramaturg; program culminates in workshop production **Guidelines:** full-length plays by OH writers; writers must participate **Procedure:** send script program **Deadline:** Feb. 1, 1999 **Notification:** May 15, 1999 **Your chances:** 2 plays selected

♫ PARIS WRITERS' WORKSHOP D F-l ₵ Fr
20 Boulevard Montparnasse, Paris, France 75015 011/45-667-550 FAX 011/45-659-653 Contact: Ellen Hinsley, Director **Program:** 5-day morning workshop sessions with writers in residence, afternoon lectures with visiting writers, evening readings **Fee:** $350 **Procedure:** send full-length script **Deadline:** Jun. 19, 1999 (See Wice Paris Writers' Wksp.)

PEN AMERICAN CENTER Mb i
568 Broadway, New York, NY 10012 (212) 334-1660 FAX (212) 334-3181 e-mail pen@echonyc.com **Contact:** Michael Robert, Exec. Director **Program:** International PEN organization; publishes *Grants and Awards Available to American Writers* ($15); sponsors PEN American Center Awards (see Contests) **Guidelines:** playwrights with 2 or more full-length plays produced by established theatres **Procedure:** "Apply to Membership Committee."

PEN WRITERS' FUND g/f
Contact: Joan Dalin, Program Coordinator **Program:** up to $1000 in emergency assistance for published or produced writers **Procedure:** request guidelines **Notification:** 6 weeks

PEW FELLOWSHIPS IN THE ARTS g/f Pl ♪ S Rg
University of the Arts, 250 S. Broad St. Suite 400, Philadelphia, PA 19102 (215) 875-2285 FAX (215) 875-2276 Contact: Melissa Franklin, Director **Program:** annual fellowships of $50,000 for playwrights, composers, screenwriters, and other artists at least 25 years of age who are residents of southeastern PA; award rotates among disciplines **Procedure:** call for guidelines and application form **Deadline:** Dec. 1999 (call for exact date) **Your chances:** up to 12 fellowships awarded

PHILADELPHIA ART ALLIANCE   Mb i mm
251 S. 18th St., Philadelphia, PA 19103 (215) 545-4302 FAX (215-545-0767 e-mail PAA@libertynet.org Contact: James McClelland, **Exec. Director Program:** multidisciplinary arts organization founded in 1915; "all the arts under one roof"

FILMS IN THE PARLOUR   Rg S
Contact: David Borden, Flim Curator **Program:** readings by professional actors of unproduced full-length screenplays by Philadelphia-area writers **Procedure:** request guidelines **Deadline:** TBA **Your chances:** 8-10 screenplays selected

PHILADELPHIA DRAMATISTS CENTER   Mb Sv i D
1516 South St., Philadelphia, PA 19146 (215) 735-1441 Contact: Ed Shockley, President **Program:** membership/service organization for playwrights who have completed at least 1 script; programs and services include readings, annual conference, library, copyright forms, newsletter **Procedure:** request application form **Dues:** $25 per year

PILGRIM PROJECT   g/f F-l 1- ♪ CY C 2d
156 Fifth Ave. Suite 400, New York, NY 10010 (212) 627-2288 FAX (212) 627-2184 Contact: Davida Goldman, Secretary **Program:** grant of $1000-$7000 for reading, workshop, or full production of a new play dealing with questions of moral significance **Guidelines:** for full-length plays, one-acts, musicals, children's plays; plays may have been previously produced **Procedure:** send SASE for guidelines **Deadline:** ongoing program **Your chances:** 300 applications/7-10 playwrights selected

PKE PLAYWRIGHTS GROUP   D F-l 1-
The Playwrights' Kitchen Ensemble, Coronet Theatre, 368 N. La Cienega Blvd., Los Angeles, CA 90048 (818) 980-3641 FAX (818) 766-5288 e-mail jbunzel@aol.com **Contact:** John Bunzel, Director **Program:** workshop offering readings/discussions of full-length plays, one-acts **Fee:** $300 per year **Procedure:** send SASE for guidelines **Deadline:** ongoing program **Your chances:** 300 applicants/20 participants selected

PLAY LAB   D F-l Tr Ad
Artists Rep., 1516 SW Alder St., Portland, OR 97205 (503) 241-9807 FAX (503) 241-8268 e-mail allen@artistsrep.org **Contact:** Allen Nause, Art. Director **Program:** developmental staged readings of full-length plays, translations, adaptations **Procedure:** send SASE for guidelines

PLAYFEST   F CY ♪
823 Congress Ave. #5, Austin, TX 78701 (512) 499-8388 FAX (512) 499-8026 Contact: Celia Hughes, PlayFest Coord. **Program:** 10-week festival (spring-summer 1999) of children's plays and musicals **Guidelines:** entries must be performance-ready fully-mounted productions; 50 minutes maximum **Fee:** $150 **Procedure:** request guidelines and application packet **Deadline:** TBA (Sept.) **Notification:** 1-2 months

PLAYFORMERS
Mb D

51 Essex Dr., Little Silver, NJ 07739 (212) 213-9835 Contact: John Fritz, Exec. Director Program: membership group meeting Sept.-Jun. for readings, staged readings of works-in-progress Dues: $15 initiation, $75 per year Procedure: "Call Sue Kistler at above number for details."

PLAYMARKET
Mb Sv i D Rs g/f ws Rg

P.O. Box 9767, Wellington, New Zealand 64-4-382-8462 FAX 64-4-382-8461 e-mail plymkt@clear.net.nz Contact: Greg Wikström, Administrator Program: membership/service agency for playwrights in New Zealand; programs include script advisory/assessment, agent service, workshops, work space, libraries in NZ and Australia, grants Fee: $50 NZ for membership Procedure: request guidelines

PLAYQUEST
Arena Stage, 1101 6th St. SW, Washington, DC 20024 (202) 554-9066 This program is inactive in 1999; see *The Playwright's Companion 2000* or inquire for future plans.

PLAYS FOR LIVING READING SERIES
505 8th Ave. #2209, New York, NY 10018 This series has been suspended in 1999; see *The Playwright's Companion 2000* for future plans.

PLAYS-IN-PROGRESS FESTIVAL OF NEW WORKS
F D F-l Rg

Plays-in-Progress World Premiere Theatre, 615 4th St., Eureka, CA 95501 (707) 443-3724 Contact: Susan Bigelow-Marsh, Exec. Dir. Program: May, Oct. festivals of new full-length plays; 8-10 scripts receive 3-4 weeks of development culminating in staged readings; housing, meals provided Guidelines: mainly for CA writers; plays must be unpublished, unproduced Procedure: send SASE for guidelines Deadline: Mar. 1, 1999 for spring festival; Aug. 1, 1999 for fall festival

♫ PLAYSCAPE FESTIVAL
F F-l Rg

Heartlande Theatre, P.O. Box 2014, Birmingham, MI 48012 Program: annual festival of unproduced full-length plays by Midwest playwrights Guidelines: small cast, single or unit set Procedure: send query, 1-page synopsis, 15-page dialogue sample, resume Deadline: Nov. 15, 1999

THE PLAYWORKS FESTIVAL
UTEP, El Paso, TX 79968 (915) 747-7854 FAX (915) 747-5438 This festival in inactive in 1999; see *The Playwright's Companion 2000* for guidelines for Playworks 2000.

THE PLAYWRIGHT/DIRECTOR WORKSHOP
D Pl S

c/o Charles Maryan, Director, 777 West End Ave. Apt. 6C, New York, NY 10025-5551 (212) 864-0542 Program: 20-week workshop (Oct.-May) for developing directors, playwrights and screenwriters Fee: $440 Procedure: send script Notification: 2 weeks Your chances: 20-30 applications/usually 1-2 participants accepted

THE PLAYWRIGHTS' CENTER   Mb D
2301 Franklin Ave. E, Minneapolis, MN 55406-1099 (612) 332-7481
FAX (612) 332-6037 e-mail pwcenter@mtn.org Contact: Carlo Cuesta,
Exec. Director Program: membership organization; readings, workshops, other services Guidelines: general membership provides discounts on classes, eligibility for readings and Jones One-Act Commissions, newsletter; membership not necessary for fellowships or PlayLabs
Dues: $40 per year Procedure: send SASEs for membership application
and for particular programs

JEROME PLAYWRIGHT-IN-RESIDENCE   Rs g/f
FELLOWSHIPS Program: annual fellowships of $7200 for U.S
citizens or permanent residents who have not had more than 2 plays
produced professionally; fellows must spend Jul. 2000-Jun. 2001 in residence Deadline: TBA (Sept.)

MANY VOICES COLLABORATION GRANTS   g/f M Rg
Program: annual grants ($200-$2000) to ethnically diverse teams
Guidelines: lead artist must be MN playwright of color; team must
have production commitment from a MN theatre Deadline: Jul. 1, 1999

MANY VOICES PLAYWRITING RESIDENCY Rs g/f M Rg
AWARDS Program: annual awards of $750 stipend (contingent
on funding); 1-year Center membership; scholarship for playwriting
class Guidelines: for MN residents of color Deadline: Jul. 1, 1999

McKNIGHT ADVANCEMENT GRANTS   g/f Rg
Program: 3 annual grants of $8500, additional funds of up to $1500
for workshops, staged readings Guidelines: for U.S. citizens, residents of MN since Aug. 1, 1997, who have had at least 1 work professionally produced Deadline: Feb. 1, 1999 postmark

McKNIGHT FELLOWSHIPS   g/f Rs
Program: 2 annual fellowships of $10,000 for 1-month residency at
Center, funds of up to $2000 for workshops, staged readings, for play-
wrights whose work has made a "significant impact on contemporary
theatre" Guidelines: for U.S. citizens who have had at least 2 works
professonally produced Deadline: Jan. 15, 1999 postmark

PLAYLABS   D
Contact: Elissa Adams, Art. Director Program: 2-week conference
(summer 2000); 4-6 new works developed with professional actors,
director, dramaturg playwright's choice; culminates in public readings
Guidelines: for U.S. citizens or permanent residents Deadline: TBA

YOUNG PLAYWRIGHTS SUMMER CONFERENCE   F Y
Program: annual 2-week conference (daily sessions, Jul.) for young
playwrights (grades 8-12); students receive college credit Fee: TBA,
financial aid available Procedure: call 612-332-4481 Ext. 18 Deadline: Apr. 22, 1999 Your chances: 40 students accepted

THE PLAYWRIGHTS' CENTER OF SAN FRANCISO D Mb Rg
P.O. Box 460466, San Francisco, CA 94146-0466 (415) 626-4603 FAX (415) 863-0901 e-mail playctrsf@aol.com **Contact:** Sheppard Kominars, Chairman **Program:** membership organization for Bay Area playwrights; weekly staged readings, discussions; sponsors DramaRama (see Contests) **Dues:** $45 per year; some scholarships available **Procedure:** send SASE for information **Deadline:** ongoing program **Your chances:** all applicants accepted

PLAYWRIGHTS FORUM   Mb D i Rg
P.O. Box 5322, Rockville, MD 20848 (301) 816-0569 e-mail pforum@erols.com **Contact:** Ernest Joselovitz, President **Program:** membership/development/resource organization for Washington DC-area playwrights; programs and services include workshops, readings, production observerships, newsletter, handbook, special classes, informal gatherings, guest professionals, free theatre tickets, annual conference, Musical Theatre Wing, publishing program **Guidelines:** 3-tier range of memberships: Forum 2 for professional playwrights (by invitation), Forum 1 for apprentices (Jan., May, Sept.), Associate Membership; participants must reside within commuting distance **Fee:** $90 Forum 2 (1/3 year) and Forum 1 (each 6-meeting session); Associate Membership $25 per year; most special classes $75; "fees adjusted in cases of financial need" **Procedure:** Forum 2: send script and bio (prior Forum 1 membership preferred); Forum 1: register Jan., May, Sept.; Associate: request application form **Your chances:** "Forum 2: 50/50 chance if coming in 'cold'; Forum 1: we try to accommodate all applicants without overcrowding."

THE PLAYWRIGHTS FOUNDATION   Mb D Rg
P.O. Box 460357, San Francisco, CA 94146 (415) 263-3986 **Contact:** Belinda Taylor, President **Program:** membership/developmental program for U.S. playwrights; 10-minute play contest for members; readings **Special interest:** Northern CA playwrights

BAY AREA PLAYWRIGHTS FESTIVAL   D F
Contact: Jayne Wenger, Art. Director **Program:** dramaturgical work, rehearsals, 6-days for rewrites during 2-week festival (Sept. 1999; prefestival weekend retreat in Aug.) at the Magic Theatre **Remuneration:** small stipend, travel **Procedure:** send script, resume **Deadline:** Feb. 1, 1999 **Notification:** May 1999

PLAYWRIGHTS GALLERY   Mb D
2124 Broadway Suite 2700, New York, NY 10023 e-mail savadge@juno.com **Contact:** Deborah Savadge, Coordinator **Program:** membership organization meeting every 2 weeks (Sept.-Jun.) for readings of draft scenes by professional actors and occasional script-in-hand performances **Fee:** share of rental space **Procedure:** send query, 10-page dialogue sample **Deadline:** Jan. 2, 1999 for winter; Sept. 1, 1999 for fall

THE PLAYWRIGHTS GROUP   D
2062 N. Vine St. #5, Los Angeles, CA 90068 (310) 394-9818 FAX
(310) 394-9612 e-mail MBRANDPRO **Contact:** Joanna Miles, Artistic
Director **Program:** workshop meeting weekly (Thurs., 7:30 p.m.) for
readings, occasional mounted performances; member playwrights are
assisted by directors and actors **Fee:** $20 per month **Procedure:** attend
meetings before submitting **Comment:** Workshop meets at 1261 N.
Fairfax Ave. in West Hollywood.

PLAYWRIGHTS' INK   Sv
414 W. 121st St. **Suite 55, New York, NY 10027 (212) 666-4470 e-**
mail playink@aol.com **Contact:** Jonathan J. Samarro, Vice President
Program: organization "dedicated to providing goods and services
helpful to the playwright"; activities include sales of books on playwriting, bulk-binding, proofreading **Procedure:** request free catalog

PLAYWRIGHTS' PLATFORM   Mb D F Rg
164 Brayton Rd., Boston, MA 02135 (617) 254-4482 **Contact:** Beverly
Creasey, President **Program:** membership/development organization
for MA residents with unpublished, unproduced plays; summer festival
of full productions **Remuneration:** percentage for festival production
Dues: $35 **Procedure:** send #10 SASE for information **Deadline:** on-
going program

PLAYWRIGHTS PREVIEW PRODUCTIONS   See Urban Stages/
Playwrights Preview Productions in this section.

PLAYWRIGHTS PROJECT   D Rs Pl S Tv
1620A E. 4th St. #106, Charlotte, NC 28204 (704) 342-4142 FAX
(704) 342-4145 **Contact:** Mark Woods, Founder **Program:** 12-week
residency (Jun. 1999) for serious writers for stage, film, TV; laboratory
space and development resources (including directors, actors, designers),
travel, stipend, housing, meals provided **Guidelines:** applicant must
have a specific project and must spend 12-week period in residence **Pro-**
cedure: request guidelines **Deadline:** ongoing program **Advice:** "Selection will be made on the basis of the applicant's body of work--pub-
lished, unpublished, produced, unproduced." **Comment:** "The object is
to provide opportunities for serious writers to complete projects and be
made aware of resources."

PLAYWRIGHTS PROJECT   i Sn
450 B St. Suite 1020, San Diego, CA 92101-8002 (619) 239-8222 FAX
(619) 239-8255 e-mail youth@playwright.com **Contact:** Deborah
Salzer, Exec. Director **Program:** a not-for-profit arts education
organization which brings playwriting courses to southern CA schools
and seniors' residences **Fee:** none **Procedure:** "Phone Deborah Salzer
at above number or Kathryn Johnson Schwartz at (818) 242-3984 in
L.A." **Program:** California Young Playwrights Contest (see Contests)

THE PLAYWRIGHTS' PROJECT   Sv Mb D Rg $ Rs
Sammons Center #12, 3630 Harry Hines Blvd., Dallas, TX 75219
(972) 497-1752 Contact: Priscilla Sample, Director **Program:** service organization for Dallas-Ft. Worth area playwrights; bi-weekly labs, readings, workshops, newsletter **Dues:** $50 (waivable); sponsors Robert Bone Memorial Award (see Contests) **Procedure:** send 1 full-length play or 2 one-acts (1 hour minimum), bio, cover letter/brief synopsis, $5 fee **Deadline:** Jun. 1, 1999 for residencies beginning in fall 1999

PLAYWRIGHT'S STAGE   Kansas City, MO   This program has been discontinued.

PLAYWRIGHT'S THEATRE   D F-l 1- CY Sv Rg
1121 N. 1st St., Phoenix, AZ 85004 **(602) 253-5151 Program:** script service/development program for unpublished, unproduced plays by AZ writers, maximum cast: 8-10; programs include awards, acting classes for adults and children; outreach; newsletter **Fee:** $90-$700 **Procedure:** request guidelines **Comment:** Formerly Playwright's Workshop Theatre.

ADVANCED PLAYWRITING WORKSHOP   D
Program: weekly workshop (Sun. 2:00-4:00 p.m., mid-Sept.--early May) for experienced playwrights; readings, critiques **Fee:** TBA

ARTIST RESIDENCIES/SCHOOLS & COMMUNITIES   Rs
Program: residencies for AZ artists in schools and other organizations **Remuneration:** awards/fees **Procedure:** request guidelines and application form **Deadline:** ongoing program **Notification:** 2 months **Your chances:** 80 applications/10+ residents selected

INTRODUCTION TO PLAYWRITING WORKSHOP   D
Program: 8-week script development session (Sun. 4:30-6:00 p.m., mid-Sept.--early Nov.) for beginning playwrights; workshop culminates in staged readings **Fee:** TBA

THE EDGE PROJECT & FESTIVAL   D F F-l 1-
Program: annual 9-month collaborative forum for unproduced full-length plays and one-acts; writers work with actors and guest playwrights; culminates in staged reading or production **Deadline:** TBA

♫ STAGE KIDS SATURDAYS   D Y 12+
Program: workshop for young people (aged 7-17) meeting 1st and 3rd Sat. each month; participants write plays, create roles, design for theatre

PLAYWRIGHTS THEATRE OF NEW JERSEY   Mb D Sv F Y
33 Green Village Rd., Madison, NJ 07940 **(201) 514-1787 Contact:** Peter Hays, Literary Mgr. **Program:** membership/developmental/service organization; programs include playwriting and creative dramatics classes, playwriting-in-the-schools, playwriting-for-teachers, Writers-in-the-Schools, special needs projects, young playwrights' festivals and symposiums **Procedure:** send SASE for information

PLAYWRIGHTS THEATRE OF NEW JERSEY (Cont.)

NEW PLAY DEVELOPMENT PROGRAM   D F-l 1- ♪ Am
Program: development of unproduced full-length plays, one-acts, small-scale musicals by American writers **Remuneration:** royalty **Procedure:** send SASE for brochure **Best time:** Sept.-Apr. only **Your chances:** 300+ applications/10-15 playwrights accepted

PLAYWRIGHTS UNION OF CANADA   Mb Sv i
54 Wolseley St., Toronto, Ontario, Canada M5T 1A5 (416) 703-0201 FAX (416) 703-0059 e-mail cdplays@interlog.com **Contact:** Angela Rebeiro, Exec. Director **Program:** membership/information/service organization open to Canadian citizens and landed immigrants who have had at least 1 Canadian Equity production or are members of Professional Association of Canadian Theatres or equivalent; script services; contract negotiations; *CanPlay* bi-monthly newsletter **Dues:** $130 per year + 7% tax **Procedure:** request information

PLAZA DE LA RAZA   Mb i Hi Rg
3540 N. Mission Rd., Los Angeles, CA 90031 (213) 223-2475 FAX (213) 223-1804 e-mail admin@plazaraza.org **Contact:** Rose Cano, Exec. Director **Program:** educational-cultural center serving the Chicano community of East L.A.; classes in drama, dance, music; teachers' resources; performances; Nuevo L.A. Chicano Art Series **Advice:** "Open to all."

NUEVO L.A. CHICANO THEATREWORKS   D 1- Hi Esp Rg
Program: 2-week workshop held approximately every 4th year, for development of new one-acts by Chicano playwrights, culminating in public readings, possible production **Guidelines:** authors must be Latino residents of CA **Procedure:** request guidelines

PROFESSIONAL ASSN. OF CANADIAN THEATRES/ Mb Sv
PACT COMMUNICATIONS CENTRE   30 St. Patrick St. 2nd Fl., Toronto, Ontario, Canada M5T 3A3 (416) 595-6455 Ext. 12 FAX (416) 595-6450 e-mail pact@idirect.com **Contact:** Rich Sherman, Membership Communications Coord. **Program:** national service/trade association of professional English-language theatres in Canada; services include advocacy, labor relations, professional development, communications; publications: *Impact* quarterly newsletter, *The Theatre Listing* annual directory, *Artsboard* monthly jobs bulletin **Procedure:** request guidelines for "Supporting Membership"; membership open to all interested parties

PUERTO RICAN TRAVELING THEATRE PROGRAMS   D Hi
141 W. 94th St., New York, NY 10025 (212) 354-1293 FAX 307-6769

PLAYWRIGHTS' WORKSHOP   D M Rg
Contact: Allen Davis III, Director **Program:** workshops (Oct. 1999-Jun. 2000); units for professional and beginning playwrights; showcase productions **Guidelines:** for New York City minority writers

and others interested in multicultural theatre **Fee:** $100 registration **Procedure:** professional playwrights send full-length script; beginners phone for details **Deadline:** TBA (Oct..)

TRAINING UNIT FOR YOUNG PEOPLE   D Esp Y
Contact: Virginia Rambal, Director **Program:** bilingual (English and Spanish) training program in theatre (Jan.-Jul.) for ages 14-23 **Fee:** $75 registration **Procedure:** phone for information **Your chances:** 250± participants accepted

PULSE ENSEMBLE THEATRE STUDIO SEASON   D F-l C Rg
432 W. 42nd St., New York, NY 10036 (212) 695-1596 **Contact:** Alexa Kelly, Artistic Director **Program:** development of unpublished full-length plays by NY playwrights **Special interests:** "Meaningful plays which challenge the audience emotionally or intellectually; social/ political issues." **Guidelines:** "We perform the play for 1 week, then allow the playwright to rewrite for 1 month; then we rehearse and present the play for 1 week." **Procedure:** send synopsis, 15-page dialogue sample **Your chances:** 200 applicants/5 playwrights selected **Advice:** "Play must have a response to the 'so what?' factor."

♫ PULSE ENSEMBLE PLAYWRIGHTS CIRCLE   Mb D F-l 1-
Contact: Lezley Steele, Writer in Residence **Program:** 15-member group meeting weekly with company actors for readings of members' works-in-progress; 2 levels of readings; possible full production **Fee:** $50 per month **Procedure:** call (212) l736-1255 for details **Deadline:** ongoing program **Your chances:** 60 applications/10 new members selected **Advice:** "Must have a work-in-progress."

♫ RABBIT HILL WRITERS' STUDIO   Rs D Pl S po
1015 Clay Rd., Lititz PA 17543 (717) 626-8481 FAX same **Contact:** Duncan Weymouth, Director **Program:** 10-week workshops in various genres: fiction, poetry, writing for children, creative non-fiction, screenwriting (Sept.-Nov.); also weekend and summer workshops; future plans include playwriting workshops and online workshops (inquire for webpage) **Fee:** $199 for 10-week workshop, housing not included; $499 for weekend workshops, housing in nearby B&B included **Procedure:** write of call for brochure **Deadline:** 1 week prior to workshop; inquire for dates **Response:** 1 week **Comment:** "Rabbit Hill is located in Amish Country and offers Amish-related activities."

RAGDALE FOUNDATION   Rs $
1260 N. Green Bay Rd., Lake Forest, IL 60045-1106 (847) 234-1063 FAX (847) 234-1075 **Contact:** Sonja Carlborg, Exec. Director **Program:** 2 week-2 month residencies **Fee:** $105 per week; possible waiver **Procedure:** send SASE for guidelines and application form; upon application: $20 fee **Deadline:** Jan. 15, 1999 for Jun-Dec. 1999; Jun. 1, 1999 for Jan.-May 2000 **Notification:** 90 days after deadline **Your chances:** 600 applications overall/usually 6-10 playwrights accepted

RAINBOW ARTIST WORKSHOPS   D Pl ♪ g/l C
112 S. College, Santa Maria, CA 93454 e-mail rawtheatre@aol.com
Contact: Leo Cortez, Dir., New Works Program: workshops for plays
and small-cast musicals Guidelines: gay/lesbian writers/themes; social
issues; maximum cast: 4-7 Procedure: send script, synopsis, cassette tape
for musical Best time: fall Response: 4 months

THE REDISCOVERY SERIES   F Tr Ad Cl
The Shakespeare Theatre, 516 8th St. SE, Washington, DC 20003
(202) 547-3230 FAX (202) 547-0226 e-mail smazzola@shakespearedc.
org Contact: Michael Kahn, Artistic Director Program: staged readings
(2 in fall, 2 in spring) of new translations or adaptations of classical
material Procedure: send query/synopsis, 10-page dialogue sample;
professional recommendation Best time: summer Remuneration: no

REMEMBRANCE THROUGH THE   D Rs F-l Rg
PERFORMING ARTS NEW PLAY DEVELOPMENT   3300 Bee
Caves Rd. Suite 650, Austin, TX 78746 (512) 329-9118 Contact: Marla
Macdonald, Director, New Play Dev. Program: 18-month developmental
workshops (Jun.-Sept.) in 3 phases: 1) 6-week workshops for 8 full-
length plays, culminating in staged readings; 2) 4 plays progress to works-
in-progress series with playwrights in residence for 3 weeks; (3) 2 plays
progress to full productions Guidelines: authors must be residents of
central TX; works must not have had Equity productions Procedure:
send script, resume Deadline: Feb. 1, 1999 Notification: Apr. 1, 1999

THE ROCKEFELLER FOUNDATION'S BELLAGIO   Rs ¢
STUDY AND CONFERENCE CENTER Bellagio Center Office,
420 Fifth Ave., New York, NY 10018 (212) 869-8500 e-mail bellagio@
rockfound.org Program: 4-week residencies at Villa Serbelloni on Lake
Como, Italy, for mid-career scholars and artists with substantial publications; teams accepted; spouses welcome Procedure: write for guidelines Deadline: TBA (Jan. for fall-winter; May for spring) Notification: 3-4 months Your chances: 800 applicants/140± residents accepted

ROCKY MOUNTAIN STUDENT THEATER PROJECT   D Y
P.O. Box 1626, Telluride, CO 81435 (970) 728-4052 e-mail playfest@
aol.com Contact: Owen Perkins, Exec. Director Program: organization
for young playwrights; activities include readings, possible productions;
Roy Barker Prize (see Contests) Procedure: request guidelines

ROGER HENDRICKS SIMON STUDIO   D Rs Pl ♪ Rd Tv S
1501 Broadway #1303, New York, NY 10036 (212) 704-0488 FAX
(212) 543-0286 Contact: Roger Hendricks Simon, Producing Art. Director Program: Professional Lab for Writers: off Broadway development/
production center for plays, musicals, radio/TV plays, screenplays; residencies of up to 6 weeks, consulting service, staged readings, possible
presentations Fee: $95-$325 Procedure: request guidelines

♫ RWM PLAYWRIGHTS LAB D h/d
19 Commerce St. #12A, New York, NY 10014 Contact: Dr. Larry Meyers **Program:** biweekly workshops dealing with issues of life-threatening diseases **Procedure:** send script or query/synopsis, $15 fee **Deadline:** ongoing program **Comment:** Materials are not returned.

THE SALT LAKE ACTING CO. READING D F-l Am Rg
SERIES 168 W. 500 N, Salt Lake City, UT 84103 (801) 363-0526
FAX (801) 532-8513 Contact: David Mong, Literary Mgr. **Program:** readings (winter, spring, fall) of full-length plays; emphasis on Western American writers **Procedure:** send query/synopsis, 5-10 page dialogue sample **Deadline:** ongoing program **Notification:** 4-8 months

SAN JOSE DOWNTOWN ART SERIES F M
490 S. 1st St., San Jose, CA 95113 (408) 283-7142 FAX (408) 283-7146 Contact: Mary Smith, Dev. Director **Program:** semi-annual series (6 weeks in Jan.-Feb., 4 weeks in Jun.-Jul.) of plays produced by local multi-cultural companies **Procedure:** professional recommendation preferred; or, send script, synopsis **Best time:** Jan.-Mar.

THE SCHOOLHOUSE D Rg
Owens Rd., Croton Falls, NY 10519 (914) 234-7232 FAX (914) 234-4196 Contact: Douglas Michael, Lit. Mgr. **Program:** development program culminating in public reading or full production **Guidelines:** for residents of Westchester or Putnam Cty., NY, Fairfield Cty., CT **Fee:** nominal **Procedure:** send script or 10-page excerpt **Notification:** 1 month

THE SCRIPTEASERS Mb
3404 Hawk St., San Diego, CA 92103-3862 (619) 295-4040 FAX (619) 299-2084 Contact: Jonathan Dunn-Rankin, Corresponding Secretary **Program:** membership/support organization sponsoring cold readings of new scripts **Fee:** none **Procedure:** send script to Rick Briggs, The Scripteasers, 2905 Clarissa Ct., Lemon Grove, CA 91945 (619) 287-0552 **Advice:** "Attend readings. Request a copy of our 'Guideline for Writers.'"

♫ SCRIPTWRITERS/HOUSTON Mb D 1-
P.O. Box 981106, Houston, TX 77019 Contact: Director **Program:** twice monthly meetings with guest speakers and play readings; workshops; newsletter; Ten by Ten: annual presentation of members' 10-minute plays; annual bill of one-acts **Procedure:** request information

THE SCRIPTWRITERS NETWORK Mb D Pl S Tv $
11684 Ventura Blvd. #508, Studio City, CA 91604 (323) 848-9477 Contact: Bill Lundy, Chair **Program:** affiliation of film, TV, and corporate/industrial writers (playwrights welcome); programs include guest speakers, developmental feedback on scripts, possible staged readings, contests for members; newsletter **Dues:** $60 per year **Procedure:** send SASE for application form; $15 initiation fee

THE SECOND STAGE READING   D F-l Ad ♪ 2d Am C W M
SERIES   P.O. Box 1807 Ansonia Station, New York, NY 10023 (212) 787-8302 FAX (212) 877-9886 **Contact:** Christopher Burney, Literary Mgr. **Program:** annual series of readings of new and previously produced American plays, adaptations, musicals; emphasis on "heightened realism, socio-political plays, women and minority writers" **Procedure:** send query/1-page synopsis, 5-10 page dialogue sample, cassette tape for musical, resume, script history

SEWANEE WRITERS' CONFERENCE   F D
Univ. of the South, 310-0 St. Luke's Hall, 735 University Ave., Sewanee, TN 37383-1000 (931) 598-1141 **Contact:** Cheri Peters, Conf. Coord. **Program:** annual conference (Jul. 20-Aug. 1, 1999) featuring workshops, readings, and lectures in playwriting, fiction and poetry; other literary and social events **Fee:** $1200 includes room and board; fellowship and scholarships available **Procedure:** request guidelines, available Feb. 1999; upon application: 2 copies of script

SHENANDOAH INTERNATIONAL PLAY-   D Rs Pl S
WRIGHTS RETREAT   Shenanarts, Pennyroyal Farm, Rte. 5, Box 167-F, Staunton, VA 24401 (540) 248-1868 FAX (540) 248-7728 e-mail shenarts@cfw.com **Contact:** Robert Graham Small, Director **Program:** 1-month workshop/retreat/residency (Jul.-Aug.) at Pennyroyal Farm for playwrights and screenwriters **Remuneration:** full fellowship **Procedure:** request guidelines; upon application: 2 copies of script **Deadline:** Feb. 1, 1999 **Notification:** after Jun. 10, 1999 **Your chances:** 300+ applications/usually 10-12 participants accepted

THE SIX O'CLOCK MUSICAL THEATRE LAB   D ♪
AMAS Musical Theatre, 450 W. 42nd St.Suite 2J, New York, NY 10036 (212) 563-2565 FAX (212) 268-5501 **Contact:** Donna Trinkoff, Producing Director **Program:** reading series for new musicals; writer (composer, lyricist, librettist) provides musical director and cast; AMAS provides theatre and promotions **Procedure:** request information

SNUG HARBOR CULTURAL CENTER   ws
1000 Richmond Terrace, Staten Island, NY 10301-9926 (718) 448-2500 FAX (718) 442-8534 **Contact:** Rental Coord. **Program:** studio workshop at performing arts center in historic park, for professional artists **Fee:** $11± per square foot per month for 1-year; tenant provides insurance **Procedure:** send work sample, resume

SOFER JEWISH WRITER'S WORKSHOP   D J
Olin-Sang-Ruby Union Institute, 555 Skokie Blvd. Suite 225, Northbrook, IL 60062 (847) 509-0990 FAX (847) 509-0970 e-mail dunnfried@aol.com **Contact:** Deanne Dunn Friedman **Program:** annual 4-day workshop for professional and non-professional Jewish writers and teachers **Procedure:** request guidelines

THE SONGWRITERS GUILD OF AMERICA   Mb ♪
1560 Broadway #1306, New York, NY 10036 (212) 768-7902 FAX
(212) 768-9048 e-mail songnews@aol.com Contact: Claudia Koal, Natl.
Projects Director Program: association for songwriters; Pro Shop, Song
Critique, Urban Music Workshop, Ask-A-Pro Q & A Procedure: request
application form for Full (published songwriters) or Associate Membership Dues: full member $70-$400; associate $55

♫ SONOMA COUNTY REP PROGRAMS   Rg D
415 Humboldt St., Santa Rosa, CA 95404 (707) 544-7278 FAX (707)
522-5033 e-mail mstscr@mst-scr.com Contact: Doug Stout, Dramaturg
Guidelines: CA playwrights only

PLAYWRIGHT IN RESIDENCE PROGRAM   D Rs
Program: a new script development program for playwrights at all
levels; staged readings, possible full productions Special interests:
"Strong characterization, crisp dialogue, driving story, substantial
theme." Procedure: request guidelines

MONDAY NIGHT MUSE READINGS   D F-l 1-
Program: staged readings (Sept.-Apr.) at Main St. Theatre in Sebasto-
pol; possible production (Jun.) in Summer Showcase (see MST-SCR
Summer Showcase in Contests) Works: 1- or 2-act plays Specifications: maximum cast: 12 for full-length, 5 for one-act; simple sets
preferred; no musicals Procedure: request guidelines Your chances:
50-60 new scripts read annually/usually 8-10 receive readings

SOUTH COAST REP PROGRAMS   P.O. Box 2197, Costa Mesa,
CA 92628 (714) 708-5509

ADULT CONSERVATORY   D i
Contact: Sheila Hillinger Program: evening classes for adults in
beginning and advanced playwriting and acting Procedure: phone for
information and schedule

COLAB NEW PLAY PROGRAM   D
Program: script development: readings, staged readings, workshop
and full productions Remuneration: varies by project (grant,
commission, royalties) Procedure: "See main listing for South Coast
Repertory [in Theatres]."

♫ PACIFIC PLAYWRIGHTS FESTIVAL   F D Hi
(714) 708-5500 Ext. 5406 Contact: Shannon Flynn Program:
development (Jun. 7-27, 1999) for 6-8 new plays with readings and
workshop productions presented to public audiences and representatives of visiting theatres Guidelines: works are chosen from plays
developed in South Coast Repertory Hispanic Playwrights Project (see
Contests), regular submissions to South Coast Repertory (see Theatres), and nominations offered by other theatres

SOUTHERN WRITERS' PROJECT   D F-l Tr Ad ♪ CY Rg
Alabama Shakespeare Festival, 1 Festival Dr., Montgomery, AL
36117 (334) 271-5300 FAX (334) 271-5348 e-mail Pr4bard@wsnet.
com **Contact:** Jennifer Hebblethwaite, Lit. Assoc.
Program: commissioning/
development project; activities include readings, workshops; at least 1
production from project is included in theatre's mainstage season
Procedure: send SASE for guidelines **Comment:** "Project seeks to provide for the growth of a 'new' voice for Southern writers and to
encourage new works on Southern issues."

S.T.A.G.E.   Mb D I Sv Rg
P.O. Box 214820, Dallas, TX 75221 (214) 630-7722 Contact: Mark E.
Hawkins, Exec. Director **Program:** organization for theatres and
theatre artists in north TX; monthly playwrights' forum, development,
possible showcase production of new one-acts (30 minutes maximum);
sponsors Stages: A New Play Festival (see Contests) **Procedure:** send
SASE for application form **Dues:** $45 or more; $25 student

STAGE II WORKSHOPS   Long Wharf Theatre, 222 Sargent Dr.,
New Haven, CT 06511 (203) 787-4284   This program is inactive
in 1999; see *The Playwright's Companion 2000* for future plans.

STAGEWRIGHTS, INC.   D F F-l 1- Rg
P.O. Box 4745 Rockefeller Center Station, New York, NY 10185
(212) 642-6611 Contact: John Albanese **Program:** a craft workshop
(10 weeks in fall, 10 weeks in spring) meeting Mon. evenings (6:30-9:30)
for playwrights in NYC area; One-Act Festivals, staged readings of full-
length plays **Procedure:** phone for information Sept.-early Dec., Jan.-Feb.

STANISLAVSKI SEMINARS   P.O. Box 162, Leonia, NJ 07605
(793) 763-6110 Contact: Isaac Dostis, Co-Director   This program is inactive in 1999; see *The Playwright's Companion 2000* for future plans.

STUDIO FOR CREATIVE INQUIRY   Rs mm
Carnegie Mellon Univ., College of Fine Arts, Pittsburgh, PA 15213-
3890 (412) 268-3454 FAX (412) 268-2829 e-mail mmbm@andrew.cmu.
edu **Contact:** Marge Myers, Assoc. Director **Program:** residencies of 2
weeks-3 months or 6 months-3 years for artists in all disciplines; interdisciplinary collaborative projects preferred **Procedure:** send letter of
application, resume, work sample **Advice:** "Our mission: to support cross-
disciplinary work and infuse the arts with contemporary technology."

SUMMERPLAY   F 1- Rg
The Changing Scene, 1527 1/2 Champa St., Denver, CO 80202
(303) 893-5775 Contact: Alfred Brooks, President **Program:** annual
festival of one-acts to be presented late Jul.-late Aug. **Guidelines:** for
residents of CO, KS, NE, WY **Procedure:** send SASE for guidelines
Deadline: Mar. 31, 1999

THE SUNDANCE INSTITUTE FEATURE FILM   D S $
PROGRAM   225 Santa Monica Blvd. 8th Floor, Santa Monica, CA
90401 (310) 394-4662   FAX (310) 394-8353   e-mail sundance@deltanet.
com **Program:** developmental program for screen-writers and filmmakers
working on original scripts or adaptations   **Remuneration:** travel,
room, board for at least 1 participant   **Procedure:** send SASE for
guidelines; upon application: $25 fee   **Deadline:** May 3, 1999   **Your
chances:** 2000 applicants/20 writers selected

THE SUNDANCE THEATRE LABORATORY   Rs D
P.O. Box 16450, Salt Lake City, UT 84116   (801) 328-3456   FAX (801)
575-5175 **Contact:** Managing Director   **Program:** 3-week developmental
residency (Jul. 1999) providing workshops and readings of unproduced
plays   **Fee:** none   **Procedure:** nomination by director; send SASE for
application form in Oct. 1999 **Deadline:** TBA (Dec.)   **Your chances:** 200
nominations/10 playwrights selected

SUNDAY EVENING READERS THEATRE   D Sn M
Centre Stage--South Carolina!, P.O. Box 8451, Greenville, SC
29604-8451 (864) 233-6733   FAX (864) 233-3901   e-mail cbla@info
ave.net **Contact:** Claude W. Blakely, Admin. Director   **Program:** ongoing
series of rehearsed readings before public audiences; audience discussion
follows reading; emphasis on issues of interest to senior citizens and
minorities   **Procedure:** request information

T C G GRANT PROGRAMS   g/f
Theatre Communications Group, 355 Lexington Ave., New York,
NY 10017-0217 (212) 697-5230 FAX (212) 983-4847 e-mail grants@tcg.
org **Contact:** Emilya Cachapero, Director of Grant Programs   **Frequency:** annual (contingent on funding)   **Deadline:** TBA

EXTENDED COLLABORATION GRANTS $5000 for a TCG
Constituent theatre to augment its normal development resources by
enabling a playwright/collaborating artist(s) to develop work over a
longer period than the theatre would normally support   **Procedure:**
artistic director may request guidelines

NATIONAL THEATRE ARTIST RESIDENCY CATEGORY I:
$50,000 or $100,000 for residencies for experienced theatre artists at
non-profit theatres **Guidelines:** proposals developed jointly by artists
and institutions **Procedure:** artists or theatres may request guidelines
CATEGORY II: up to $50,000 to continue Category I residencies

NEA/TCG THEATRE RESIDENCY PROGRAM FOR PLAY-
WRIGHTS $25,000 for U.S. citizens or permanent residents who
have had plays published or produced in the past 5 years; playwrights
work in association with non-profit theatres with established script
development programs   **Procedure:** playwrights may request guidelines and application materials

T. SCHREIBER STUDIO   D F-l 1- Ad S Tv
**151 W. 26th St. 7th Floor, New York 10001 (212) 741-0209 FAX (212)
741-0948 Contact:** Mary Boyer, General Mgr.   **Program:** professional
school producing full-length plays, one-acts, adaptations, screenplays
and teleplays developed in classes **Procedure:** send script, phone number

TEXAS YOUNG PLAYWRIGHTS FESTIVAL   D F 1- Rg Y
**Dougherty Arts Center, 1110 Barton Springs Rd., Austin, TX 78704
(512) 397-1457 FAX (512) 397-1451 Program:** 1-week workshop (Jun.
1999); possible full production **Guidelines:** for TX residents under age
18 on Jan. 1, 1999; original one-acts; collaborations eligible **Procedure:**
author must send script (typed 12-point, pages numbered, all margins 1";
on title page: author's name, birth date, permanent address, phone number,
parents' phone number; on 1st page: character names/gender, synopsis
Deadline: Jan. 30, 1999 postmark **Comment:** Scripts are not returned.

♫ THE THANKS BE TO GRANDMOTHER   g/f W
WINIFRED FOUNDATION   P.O. Box 1449, Wainscott, NY
11975-1449 (516) 725-0323 Program: awards ($500-$5000) for
women dramatists aged 54 and older; for projects dealing with women's
issues **Procedure:** send SASE for guidelines and application form
Deadline: Mar. 21, 1999; inquire for Sept. deadline

THEATRE ASSN. OF PENNSYLVANIA (TAP)   Mb Sv i
**P.O. Box 148, Mt. Gretna, PA 17064 (717) 964-1944 FAX (717) 964-
1945 Contact:** Lisa Myers Sweeney, Exec. Director **Program:** service
organization for theatres, training programs, and artists; competitions,
festivals, workshops, conferences **Dues:** $30 individual; $15 student

THEATRE EAST   D
12655 Ventura Blvd., Studio City, CA 91601 (818) 760-4160 Contact:
Susan O'Sullivan **Program:** workshop/lab; staged readings, inter-
action with directors and actors, possible workshop productions
Procedure: send script, resume

THEATER EMORY PROGRAMS   F D Rs
**Annex C, Emory Univ., Atlanta, GA 30322 (404) 727-3465 FAX (404)
727-6253 e-mail** vmurphy@emory.edu **Contact:** Vincent Murphy, Art.
Producing Director

BRAVE NEW WORKS   F
Program: biennial spring staged reading series for new plays **Proce-
dure:** recommendation by artistic director or Southeast Playwrights
Project **Deadline:** TBA (spring, fall) **Response:** 4 months

THE PLAYWRITING CENTER RESIDENCY   D Rs
Program: biennial 5-13 week residency (1999-2000) for established
playwright to teach student workshop and develop new work **Remuneration:** $25,000 **Procedure:** recommendation by artistic director

THEATRE ARTISTS WORKSHOP OF WESTPORT
Mail addressed to this workshop has been returned as undeliverable; the phone is not in service.

THEATRE BAY AREA
Mb i Rg

657 Mission St. Suite 402, San Francisco, CA 94105 (415) 957-1557 FAX (415) 957-1556 e-mail tba@best.com **Contact:** Sabrina Klein, Exec. Director **Program:** membership/resource organization for Bay Area theatre artists and theatres; publications include *Callboard Magazine* and *Theater Directory of the San Francisco Bay Area* **Dues:** individual $37 per year, plus $14 postage **Procedure:** request information

THEATRE COMMUNICATIONS GROUP (TCG)
Mb i

355 Lexington Ave., New York, NY 10017-0217 (212) 697-5230 FAX (212) 983-4847 e-mail tcg@tcg.org **Contact:** John Sullivan, Exec. Director **Program:** national organization of non-profit theatres; publications include *ArtSearch* jobs bulletin and *Dramatists Sourcebook* (see The Playwright's Library); catalog available **Procedure:** subscribe to *American Theatre* ($30 1 year, $55 2 years; $20 student) for membership

THEATRE JOBS
i

www.theatrejobs.com, **1730 E. Republic Rd. Suite A186, Springfield, MO 65804 (417) 882-1336 FAX (417) 882-6609 Contact:** Jane Childs, Sales Mgr. **Program:** online job placement service for theatre and related areas; listings include summer stock and festivals, internships, assistantships, apprenticeships and fellowships

THEATRE L A
Mb Sv Rg

644 S. Figueroa St., Los Angeles, CA 90017 (212) 614-0556 FAX (212) 614-0561 Contact: Alisa Fishbach, Exec. Director **Program:** membership/service organization for theatres and producers in L.A. area; activities include workshops and seminars **Fee:** Full membership (producers) $220, Associate (individuals) $35

THE THEATER PROJECT AT HOUSING WORKS
♪ D h/d

594 Broadway #700, New York, NY 10012 (212) 966-0466 Ext. 100 Contact: Victoria McElwaine, Artistic Director **Program:** organization serving clients of Housing Works, Inc.: homeless and formerly homeless people with AIDS/HIV; volunteer playwrights, composers and lyricists work with The Theater Project to create original musical pieces; 6-month development/rehearsal period culminates in production **Procedure:** to volunteer, send query letter with work samples, or phone for information

THE THEATRE-STUDIO, INC.
D 1- Tr Ad Rv S Tv Esp Fr

PROGRAMS 750 Eighth Ave. Suite 200, New York, NY 10036 (212) 719-0500 Contact: A. M. Raychel, Producing/Artistic Director **Works:** full-length plays, one-acts, translations, adaptations, cabarets, screenplays, teleplays, foreign-language plays **Submission policy:** unsolicited script or videotape with synopsis and resume, query/synopsis and/or professional recommendation with dialogue sample; agent submission **Response:** 1-6 months **Your chances:** 9-12 new plays produced every week **Remuneration:** no **Future commitment:** credit, percentage **Advice:** "Be willing to rewrite and rework with different directors."

PLAYTIME SERIES D
Program: support organization and year-round developmental program for playwrights; 9-12 plays produced each week

NEW YORK CITY PLAYWRIGHTS' FESTIVAL F Rg
Program: full productions of 72± plays in annual festival (Aug-Sept.); for playwrights residing in NYC **Deadline:** May 30, 1999

THEATRE WEST WRITERS WORKSHOP Mb D Rg F-l
3333 Cahuenga Blvd. W, Los Angeles, CA 90068 (213) 851-4839 FAX (213) 851-5286 Contact: Ms. Chris DiGiovanni, Doug Haverty, Workshop Co-Moderators **Program:** membership/workshop for L.A.-area playwrights with full-length plays **Dues:** $40 per month **Procedure:** send script and resume to apply for membership **Response:** 4 months **Your chances:** usually 4-5 playwrights accepted each year **Comment:** Formerly Theatre West Playwrights Lab.

THEATREWORKS/USA D 1- Ad ♪ CY H B Cl C ▭
COMMISSIONING PROGRAM 151 W. 26th St. 7th Floor, New
York, NY 10001 (212) 647-1100 FAX (212) 924-5377 e-mail Info@ Theatreworksusa.org Contact: Barbara Pasternack, Literary Mgr. **Program:** step commissioning process: 2-week developmental workshop resulting in production of 1-hour plays with music and children's musicals **Special interests:** historical and biographical topics and adaptations of fairy tales, classics, and contemporary literature **Regulations:** maximum cast: 5, doubling acceptable; set suitable for touring **Procedure:** send treatment with sample scenes, lyric sheets, cassette tape of music (preferred method); or, send script **Deadline:** ongoing program

THE TUESDAY GROUP Mb D
c/o William Gadea, 78 Eighth Ave. #6E, Brooklyn, NY 11215 (212) 462-9135 Program: playwrights' collective meeting every 2 weeks in midtown Manhattan to read and respond to members' work; possible workshops with resident directors and ensemble; yearly one-act series for members' work **Fee:** $60 every 3 months **Procedure:** send query with writing sample

TRAVEL AND STUDY GRANTS g/f Rg
125 Park Square Ct.., St. Paul, MN 55101-1928 (612) 224-9431 (MN, NYC 800-995-3766) FAX (612) 224-3439 Contact: Cynthia Gehrig, President, Jerome Foundation **Program:** annual grant of up to $4000 for travel in U.S., up to $5000 for travel abroad, for MN residents **Procedure:** request guidelines and application form **Deadline:** TBA (spring)

THE TYRONE GUTHRIE CENTER   Rs ₢
Annaghmakerrig, Newbliss, County Monaghan, Ireland 011/353-
47-54003   FAX 011/353-47-54380   e-mail thetgc@indigo.ie   Contact:
Bernard Loughlin, Resident Director   Program: 3 week-3 month residencies for produced or published artists   Fee: £2000 Irish per month;
self-catering houses in old farmyard available at £300 per week
Procedure: request application form   Notification: 3 months

UCROSS FOUNDATION RESIDENCIES   Rs
2836 US Hwy. 14-16 E, Clearmont, WY 82835   (307) 737-2291 FAX
(307) 737-2322 e-mail ucrossfdn@aol.com   Contact: Sharon Dynak,
Exec. Director Program: 2-8 week residencies for 8 concurrent residents
(writers, composers, visual artists) at restored historic site in the foothills of the Big Horn Mountains   Fee: no Procedure: send SASE for
guidelines and application form Deadline: Mar. 1, 1999 for Aug.-Dec.
1999; Oct. 1, 1999 for Feb.-Jun. 2000   Notification: 8 weeks   Your
chances: 300 applications/usually 8 dramatic writers accepted

URBAN STAGES/PLAYWRIGHTS PREVIEW   D
PRODUCTIONS   17 E. 47th St., New York, NY 10017 (212) 421-
1380 FAX same Contact: David Sheppard, Lit. Mgr. Program: development program (Oct.-Nov., Feb.-Mar.) for plays not previously produced
in NYC area; sponsors Playwright's Preview Productions Awards (see
Contests) Procedure: send script with cast breakdown, bio, script
history Deadline: ongoing program; best time: Jul.-Aug., Dec.

U.S.--MEXICO FUND FOR CULTURE GRANTS g/f M Hi Esp
Londres 16 P.B., Col. Juárez México, DF, Mexico 06600 52-5-592-
5386 FAX 52-5-208-8943 Contact: Beatriz Nava, Prog. Officer Program: annual grants ($2000-$25,000) to U.S. and Mexican artists and
institutions Procedure: send 8.5"x11" SASE ($1.01 postage) to US--
Mexico Fund for Culture, Benjamin Franklin Library, Laredo, TX 78044;
supporting materials (some in Spanish) required Deadline: Mar. 31,
1999; no application before Jan. 15 Notification: Aug. 1999

U S WEST THEATRE FEST   D F-l Rs
Denver Center Theatre Co., 1050 13th St., Denver, CO 80204 (303)
893-4000 FAX (303) 825-2117 e-mail bsevy@star.dcpa.org Contact:
Bruce Sevy, Assoc. Art. Director   Program: workshops and rehearsed
readings (late May-early Jun. 1999) for unproduced full-length plays;
culminates in public presentation Remuneration: stipend, travel, housing Procedure: send SASE for guidelines Deadline: Jan. 1, 1999

UTAH SHAKESPEAREAN FESTIVAL   D F Rs F-l Rg C NA
"NEW PLAYS-IN-PROGRESS READINGS," 351 W. Center St.,
Cedar City, UT 84720-2498 (801) 586-7880 FAX (801) 865-8003
Contact: Douglas N. Cook, Producing Art. Director Program: staged
reading series (Aug.) for full-length plays by western authors on western

themes: historical, contemporary, Native American **Guidelines:** maximum cast: 12; no sets; minimal demands; playwright must spend week with festival to work on play **Procedure:** request information; professional recommendations accepted Sept.-Dec. **Notification:** 6 months

VERMONT STUDIO CENTER WRITING PROGRAM   Rs po $
P.O. Box 613, Johnson, VT 05656 (802) 635-2727 FAX (802) 635-2730 Contact: Gary Clark, Director **Program:** 2-12 week residencies for writers of all genres at center in Green Mountains; 12 1-month residencies featuring 2 visiting writers of 1 of 3 genres: fiction, non-fiction, poetry **Fee:** $2800 for 4-week residency, 12 full fellowships awarded on basis of merit, grants on basis of merit and need **Procedure:** write for application form; upon application: $25 fee **Notification:** 4-6 weeks

VERMONT YOUNG PLAYWRIGHTS PROJECT   Rs Rg
Vermont Stage Co., P.O. Box 874, Burlington, VT 05402 (802) 656-4351 FAX (802) 656-0349 Contact: Blake Robison, Producing Art. Director **Program:** educational program in which VT playwrights teach playwriting in secondary schools **Procedure:** request guidelines

VICTORIA SCHOOL OF WRITING 1999   D
Box 8152, Victoria, B.C., Canada V8W 3R8 (250) 598-5300 FAX (250) 598-0066 e-mail writeawy@islandnet.com **Contact:** Margaret Dyment, Director **Program:** workshops (Jul. 20-23, 1999) in playwriting and other genres **Fee:** $470 Canadian **Procedure:** request guidelines; upon application: 2 copies of script **Your chances:** most applications accepted

VICTORY GARDENS PLAYWRIGHTS ENSEMBLE   Mb
2257 N. Lincoln Ave., Chicago, IL 60614 (312) 549-5788 Contact: Sandy Shinner, Assoc. Artistic Director **Program:** ensemble of 12 playwrights who have been resident playwrights at Victory Gardens **Procedure:** membership by invitation

THE VICTORY THEATRE STAGED READINGS   F D Am
3326 W. Victory Blvd., Burbank, CA 91505 (818) 841-4404 FAX (818) 841-6328 Contact: Maria Gobetti, Tom Ormeny, Art. Co-Directors **Program:** bi-monthly series; 12 members work with Victory Acting School students to present staged readings **Procedure:** send script **Comment:** "The Victory is chartered to do original plays by American dramatists."

VINEYARD THEATRE LAB PROGRAM   D F-l ♪ po C cm x
& NEW WORKS AT THE VINEYARD   108 E. 15th St., New York, NY 10003-9689 (212) 353-3366 FAX (212) 353-3803 Contact: Douglas Aibel, Art. Director **Program:** workshop for new plays and musicals; emphasis on "unique incorporation of music; musicals with strong narrative quality; political themes, dark comedy, eccentric forms" **Procedure:** inquire for guidelines; or, send query/synopsis, 10-page dialogue sample, cassette tape of music; resume **Deadline:** ongoing program

VIRGINIA CENTER FOR THE CREATIVE ARTS   Rs Pl ♪
P.O. Box VCCA, Mt. San Angelo, Sweet Briar, VA 24595 (804) 946-7236 FAX (804) 946-7239 e-mail vcca@vcca.com **Contact:** Director **Program:** writers' colony offering 2-8 week residential fellowships at 450-acre estate in the Blue Ridge Mountains; for writers, composers, performance and visual artists; bedroom, studio, meals provided **Fee:** minimum $30 per day, "as means allow" **Procedure:** request guidelines **Deadline:** Jan. 15, 1999 for May-Aug. 1999; May 15, 1999 for Sept.-Dec. 1999; Sept. 15, 1999 for Jan.-Apr. 2000 **Notification:** 2 months **Your chances:** 1200 applications/20± playwrights accepted

VOICE & VISION/PLAY WITH YOUR FOOD   D W
220 E. 4th St., New York, NY 10009 (212) 502-1151 **Contact:** Marya Mazor, Artistic Director **Program:** dinner/play reading series: workshop for women writers; readings, possible full productions of works-in-progress; Dramatic Action educational program for young women **Procedure:** send script **Deadline:** ongoing program

VOLUNTEER LAWYERS FOR THE ARTS (VLA)   Mb
1 E. 53rd St. 6th Fl., New York, NY 10022 (212) 319-2787 FAX (212) 752-6575 **Contact:** Amy Schwartzman, Exec. Director **Program:** national organization arranging free legal representation and counseling for low-income artists and organizations with arts-related legal problems; seminars include "Copyright Basics"; publications include *Model Contracts for Independent Contractors* **Referral Fee:** $50-$150

WALDEN RESIDENCY PROGRAM   Rs Rg
Extended Campus Programs, Southern OR Univ., 1250 Siskiyou Blvd., Ashland, OR 97520 (541) 552-6901 FAX (541) 552-6047 e-mail friendly@sou.edu **Contact:** Brooke Friendly, Arts Coord. **Program:** free 6-week residencies (Mar.-Jul. 2000) for OR writers **Procedure:** send SASE for guidelines in Sept. 1999 **Deadline:** Nov. 30, 1999 **Notification:** Dec. 1999 **Your chances:** 30 applications/3 residencies

WALT DISNEY STUDIOS FELLOWSHIP   Rs g/f S Tv
500 S. Buena Vista St., Burbank, CA 91521 (818) 560-6894 **Contact:** Troy Nethercott, Prog. Admin. **Program:** 1-year fellowship (beginning Oct. 1999) for writers to work full-time in Disney Studios features or TV division **Guidelines:** no previous film/TV experience required **Remuneration:** $33,000, travel, 1-month's housing for writers from outside L.A. area **Procedure:** call for guidelines; members of Writers Guild call Employment Access (213) 782-4646 **Deadline:** TBA (spring) **Notification:** Aug. 1999 **Your chances:** up to 10 writers selected

WATERFRONT ENSEMBLE PLAY DEVELOPMENT   D Rg
P.O. Box 1486, Hoboken, NJ 07030 **Contact:** Pete Ernst, Art. Director **Program:** development program for NJ and NY residents with unproduced works; 5-10 public staged readings, 4 full productions each year

Fee: $75 per year, or $30 for 10 weeks; scholarships available **Procedure:** send SASE for information; or, send script, resume **Notification:** 2 months **Future commitment:** credit

WEST CENTRAL FLORIDA PLAYWRIGHTS PROCESS
See Florida Playwrights' Process in this section.

WEST COAST ENSEMBLE PLAYWRIGHTS UNIT   D F-l 1-
P.O. Box 38728, Los Angeles, CA 90038 (310) 449-1447 FAX (310) 453-2254 **Contact:** Les Hanson, Art. Dir. **Program:** development process for invited playwrights; meetings with literary manager, artistic director; performances of short plays; staged readings, productions of full-length plays **Procedure:** send script **Your chances:** 6-8 playwrights selected

WESTBETH PLAYWRIGHT PROGRAM   D F-l
Westbeth Theatre Center, 151 Bank St., New York, NY 10014 (212) 691-2272 **Contact:** Director, Playwright Program **Program:** staged readings, development and showcase productions for full-length modern plays with small casts, simple sets **Procedure:** send SASE for guidelines **Your chances:** 300 applications/5-10 playwrights chosen **Deadline:** ongoing program **Notification:** 3-6 months

♫ WICE PARIS WRITER'S WORKSHOP   D po ₵
PPW/WICE, 20 bd. du Montparnasse, 75015 Paris, France **Program:** annual workshop (late Jun.-early Jul.) in fiction, non-fiction, poetry, creativity; offering morning sessions with writers in residence, afternoon lectures, evening readings, other events **Fee:** $350, housing not included **Procedure:** send SASE for guidelines **Deadline:** TBA (Jun.) **Your chances:** 12 writers accepted per class (See Paris Writers' Workshop.)

WILLIAMSTOWN THEATRE FESTIVAL   D F F-l Ad
NEW PLAY STAGED READINGS   Sept.-May: 100 E. 17th St. 3rd
Fl., New York, NY 10003 (212) 228-2286 FAX (212) 224-9091; Jun.-Aug.: P.O. Box 517, Williamstown, MA 01267 (413) 458-3200 **Contact:** Michael Ritchie, Producer **Program:** development for full-length plays, adaptations; bi-weekly staged readings (Jun.-Aug.) **Remuneration:** stipend, travel, housing **Procedure:** send query/synopsis, dialogue sample, resume **Deadline:** Feb. 28, 1999

WINDOWS ON THE WORKS   D F-l
Stamford Theatre Works, 95 Atlantic St., Stamford, CT 06901 (203) 359-4414 FAX (203) 356-1846 **Contact:** Jane Desy, Literary Mgr. **Program:** workshops and staged readings for new plays which have not had full productions **Procedure:** inquire for guidelines and policies

WINTERFEST   F F-l 1- M Sp
Passage Theatre Co., P.O. Box 967, Trenton, NJ 08605 (609) 392-0766 **Contact:** June Ballinger, Producing Art. Director **Program:** festival of staged readings (Feb. 2000) of 10-minute and full-length plays **Guide-**

lines: "Multiethnic themes, works celebrating the common humanity of diverse peoples"; maximum cast: 8; unit set **Procedure:** send script, resume to WinterFest; professional recommendation; agent submission **Deadline:** TBA (Dec.); no submission before Sept. **Your chances:** 6-8 shorts and 2 full-length plays accepted **Advice:** "Phone for mission statement."

WOMEN AT THE DOOR   See listing in Contests.

WOMEN'S THEATRE ALLIANCE   Mb D F i W 1p Rg
P.O. Box 64446, Chicago, IL 60664-0446 (312) 408-9910 FAX (312) 408-0095 **Contact:** Jennifer Yeo, President **Program:** membership/resource and development organization for Chicago-area women theatre artists; programs include actors' scene showcase, monthly salons, staged readings, developmental workshops, annual New Plays Festival, and annual festival of 1-woman shows **Guidelines:** open to projects in all stages of development **Dues:** $30 **Procedure:** request Membership/Information form **Your chances:** "All theatre lovers are accepted."

♫ **WOMEN'S WAYS**   F W F-l 1- ♪ CY Af
Eulipions Theatre Co., 1770 Sherman St., Denver, CO 80203 (303) 863-0026 **Program:** annual festival of plays by women writers "of every ethnicity" **Stages:** auditorium, 500 seats; cabaret, 150 seats **Procedure:** send query/synopsis **Comment:** Eulipions Theatre Co. produces work dealing with "the African diaspora."

WOODSTOCK GUILD RESIDENCIES   Rs
34 Tinker St., Woodstock, NY 12498 (914) 679-2079 FAX (914) 679-4529 **Program:** 1-month residencies (Jun.-Sept. 1999) in historic turn-of-the-century inn on a mountain; open to writers, visual artists, composers **Fee:** $500 per month **Procedure:** send SASE for application form **Deadline:** Apr. 1, 1999 **Your chances:** 10 residents chosen per session

WORDS THAT SPEAK   D
Moving Arts, 1822 Hyperion Ave., Los Angeles, CA 90027 (213) 665-8961 FAX (213) 665-1816 e-mail leewochner@movingarts.org **Contact:** Lee Wochner, Artistic Director **Program:** 8-session workshop (Sat. 10 a.m.-1 p.m. or Tues. 7:00-10:00 p.m.) led by a professional playwright/director, for beginning and "blocked" intermediate level playwrights, emphasis on a finished play **Fee:** $175 **Procedure:** request guidelines; writing sample required

WRITERS GUILD OF AMERICA, EAST   Mb Sv S Tv Rd Rg
(WGAE) 555 W. 57th St., New York, NY 10019-2967 (212) 767-7800 FAX (212) 582-1909 **Contact:** Mona Mangan, Exec. Director **Program:** union for freelance writers in motion pictures, TV, and radio who reside east of the Mississippi River; collective bargaining; credit determinations; annual awards; newsletter **Procedure:** request guidelines

WRITERS GUILD OF AMERICA, WEST   Mb Sv S Tv Rd Rg
(WGAW)   7000 W. 3rd St., Los Angeles, CA 90048-4329   (213) 951-4000 FAX (213) 782-4800 Contact: Brian Walton, Exec. Director **Program:** labor union representing writers in the motion picture, broadcast, cable, and new technologies industries who reside west of the Mississippi River **Procedure:** request guidelines

THE WRITERS ROOM   ws
10 Astor Place 6th Floor, New York, NY 10003 (212) 254-6995 Contact: Donna Brodie, Exec. Director **Program:** urban writers' colony open 24 hours, 7 days a week; subsidized private work space for writers; monthly readings **Fee:** $175 per quarter **Procedure:** request application form **Notification:** 1 month

THE WRITER'S VOICE   5 West Side YMCA, New York, NY 10023 Contact: Glenda K. Pleasants, Director   This program offers workshops in other genres but no longer in dramatic writing.

YADDO   Rs Pl ♪ S $
P.O. Box 395, Saratoga Springs, NY 12866-0395   (518) 584-0746 FAX (518) 584-1312 e-mail chwait@aol.com **Contact:** Candace Wait, Program Coord. **Program:** free 2-8 week residencies for writers, composers, choreographers, film/video artists **Procedure:** send SASE (2 oz. postage) for guidelines; upon application: $20 fee **Deadline:** Jan. 15, 1999 postmark for May 1999-Feb. 2000; Aug. 1, 1999 postmark for late Oct. 1999-May 2000 **Notification:** Apr. 1, 1999, Sept. 30, 1999 **Your chances:** 1000 applicants/200 residents accepted/7.5% playwrights

YOUNG PLAYWRIGHTS INC.   D F Y
321 W. 44th St. #906, New York, NY 10036 (212) 307-1140 FAX (212) 307-1454 e-mail Writeaplay@aol.com **Contact:** Sheri M. Goldhirsch, Art. Director **Program:** production/development of plays by writers 18 or younger in annual festival and NYC High School Contest (see Young Playwrights Inc. in Contests); participants' plays receive off-Broadway productions; professional staged readings of Festival plays; Writing on Your Feet: in-school playwriting workshops; Teacher Training Institute ($225 tuition); "Wordplay" newsletter **Procedure:** request guidelines

♫ YPI URBAN RETREAT   D Rs Y
Program: annual retreat for writers aged 16-21; participants study playwriting with professionals, attend 3-daily intensive sessions, and write a short play to be performed in cabaret with professional actors and directors; activities include guest lectures; individual sessions with teachers; performances of Broadway and off Broadway plays; meals, supervised housing, tickets provided **Fee:** $1100; assistance available **Procedure:** send 2-3 page sample in any genre of creative writing; name, address, phone, date of birth, school, grade level, $50 deposit; essay on assigned theme required **Deadline:** TBA (Jun.)

Information on the following programs reached us too late to be included in our alphabetical listing of Special Programs:

𝄞 **BREADLINE THEATRE GROUP**   D x
6829 N. Lincoln Ave. #138, Lincolnwood, IL 60646 (773-275-4342 **FAX** same, call first **e-mail** BREADTHGRP@aol.com **Contact:** Paul Kampf, Artistic Director **Program:** developmental theatre ensemble; playwrights, directors, actors collaborate on projects resulting in "a coming together of ideas from all members of the group." **Special interests:** "New work, bold, innovative style." **Procedure:** call or e-mail for information **Advice:** "Become familiar with our work before contacting us."

𝄞 **TRAINING CENTER FOR ACTORS, DIRECTORS,**   i
PLAYWRIGHTS & SINGERS   1346 W. Devon, Chicago, IL 60660 (773) 508-0200 FAX (773) 508-9584 **Program:** classes in various theatre-related areas, including dramatic writing **Procedure:** request guidelines, dates, fees

Publishers

Mini-Checklist

What to Send to Publishers

With a query/synopsis:
- A cover letter, including a description of your intended audience.
- A play synopsis, including the play's length in pages, character and technical breakdowns, and a summary of the action.
- A script history: previous productions, workshops, readings, publications, awards. Include favorable reviews.
- A dialogue sample.
- Your resume or bio.
- Your SASP or #10 SASE for response.

With an unsolicited script:
- A cover letter, including a description of your intended audience.
- A new copy of the script, typed in *Professional Playscript Format* . (Some publishers prefer scripts bound in folders; others want only unbound scripts; see each listing.)
- A succinct play synopsis, including character and technical breakdowns, and a summary of the action.
- A script history: previous productions, workshops, readings, publications, awards. Include favorable reviews.
- Your resume or bio.
- Your SASP or #10 SASE for response.
- Your SASE for all materials you want returned.
- Any additional materials requested by the publisher.

With a solicited script:
- A cover letter (politely reminding the editor that he or she requested the play).
- A new copy of the script, typed in *Professional Playscript Format* , bound or unbound according to the publisher's preference.
- A succinct play synopsis including character and technical breakdowns, and a summary of the action.
- A script history: previous productions, workshops, readings, publications, awards. Include favorable reviews.
- Your resume or bio.
- Your SASP or #10 SASE for response.
- Your SASE for all materials you want returned.
- Any additional materials requested by the publisher.

Publishers

ALABAMA LITERARY REVIEW   **F-l 1- Tr Ad**
253 Smith Hall, Troy State Univ., **Troy, AL 36082**   (334) 670-3307
FAX (334) 670-3519 **Contact:** Theron Montgomery, Chief Editor **Publication:** annual journal for contemporary, literary publications **Works:** full-length plays, one-acts, translations, adaptations **Guidelines:** 50 pages maximum, 30 preferred; unpublished works preferred **Submission policy:** unsolicited script, unbound; query/synopsis; professional recommendation; simultaneous submissions accepted **Response:** 2 weeks query; 3 months script **Your chances:** 15 scripts submitted/usually 1 published **Remuneration:** "Small honorarium ($5-$10 per page), when available; 3 copies (more if requested)." **Future commitment:** credit

ALR ONLINE PUBLICATIONS   **Sv F-l 1-**
Artistic & Literary Resources, 824 N. Juanita Ave., Redondo Beach, CA 90277-2229 e-mail murderus@mindspring.com **Contact:** Sally Atman, Page Editor **Publication:** writers' service publishing scripts on the Internet (1-month online with by-line) **Works:** full-length plays (broken into acts, published in "series" form), one-acts, vignettes, skits **Remuneration:** brief critique, comments from readers **Procedure:** send SASE for guidelines **Future commitment:** no **Advice:** "New playwrights have a better chance of acceptance."

AMERICAN WRITING: A MAGAZINE-NIERIKA   **1- Tr x**
EDITIONS 4343 Manayunk Ave., Philadelphia, PA 19128 Contact: Alexandra Grilikhes, Editor **Publication:** biennial literary/arts journal **Works:** one-acts **Guidelines:** 5000 words maximum **Submission policy:** unsolicited script; query/synopsis; agent submission; simultaneous submissions accepted **Best time:** "Anytime except Dec. and Jun." **Response:** 1 month query; 6 weeks-6 months script **Your chances:** 25-30 scripts submitted/usually 1-2 published **Remuneration:** 2 copies **Future commitment:** "Our permission to republish."

THE AMERICAS REVIEW   **1- Hi Esp**
Univ. of Washington, Romance Languages, Box 35, Seattle, WA 98195-4360 (206) 543-4343 FAX (206) 685-7054 e-mail lflores@u. washington.edu **Contact:** Lauro Flores, Editor **Publication:** tri-quarterly magazine **Works:** one-acts **Special interests:** U.S. Hispanic Literature only; works in Spanish **Readership:** college teachers **Procedure:** inquire for procedure and policy

ANCHORAGE PRESS, INC.   **CY F-l 1- Tr Ad ♪ Fm**
P.O. Box 8067, New Orleans, LA 70182 (504) 283-8868 FAX (504) 866-0502 Contact: Orlin Corey, Editor **Works:** children's plays: full-length plays, one-acts, translations, adaptations, musicals **Exclusive interest:** "Universal appeal to young people and families." **Guidelines:** "Unpublished works with at least 3 productions; works for trained actors; no lesson plans, theses or advocacy plays." **Readership:** "12,000

producers of elementary, middle and high school plays; community, college, semi-professional/professional theatres." **Submission policy:** unsolicited script, bound or unbound; query/synopsis; professional recommendation; agent submission; proof of productions; simultaneous submissions accepted **Response**: 30 days query; 120 days script **Your chances**: 1000+ scripts submitted/usually 10 published **Remuneration**: negotiable royalty; 6 copies **Future commitment**: no **Advice**: "Read literature in the field; see our catalogue." **Comment**: Anchorage Press holds the copyright.

ARAN PRESS   F-l 1- Tr Ad ♪ cm dr
1320 S. Third St., Louisville, KY 40208-2306 (502) 636-0115 FAX (502) 634-8001 e-mail aranpres@aye.net **Contact:** Tom Eagan, Editor/Publisher **Works**: full-length plays, one-acts, translations, adaptations, musicals **Special interests**: "High quality comedies, dramas." **Guidelines**: unpublished works **Readership**: "Theatres of all types." **Submission policy**: query/synopsis, SASP; simultaneous submissions accepted **Response**: 1 week query; 2 weeks solicited script **Your chances**: 200-300 scripts submitted/40± published **Remuneration**: royalties: 10% book sales, 50% production; 1 copy **Future commitment**: no **Comment**: Writers subsidize publication: $300 full-length, $150 one-act. **Advice**: "Look at our Catalogue. Try to get a production first. *Professional Playscript Format* only!"

ART CRAFT PUBLISHING See Heuer Publishing Co. in this section.

ARTE PUBLICO PRESS   F-l 1- Tr Ad ♪ CY Hi Esp
Univ. of Houston, 4800 Calhoun, Houston, TX 77204-2090 (713) 743-2841 FAX (713) 743-2847 **Contact:** Nicholas Kanellos, Publisher **Works**: full-length plays, one-acts, translations, adaptations, musicals, children's plays **Guidelines**: U.S. Hispanic authors only; unpublished works in English or Spanish **Submission policy**: query/synopsis, SASP; no simultaneous submissions **Response**: 2-4 weeks query; 3-6 months solicited script **Remuneration**: royalties or fee; copies

ASIAN PACIFIC AMERICAN JOURNAL   1- As
37 St. Marks Pl. #B, New York, NY 10003 (212) 228-6718 FAX (212) 228-7718 e-mail aaww@panix.com **Contact:** Editors **Publication:** semi-annual literary journal **Guidelines:** one-act plays by new and emerging Asian-American writers; 20-page maximum, double-spaced; themes TBA (inquire) **Submission policy:** 2 copies of script **Deadline:** Feb. 15, Aug. 15, 1999 **Response:** 6 months **Remuneration:** 2 copies

♫ **AUDREY SKIRBALL-KENIS**   F-l 1- Tr Ad ♪ CY
UNPUBLISHED PLAY COLLECTION   630 Fifth Ave., Los **Angeles, CA 90071** (213) 228-7327 **Contact:** Tom Harris, Project Director **Guidelines:** works must be unpublished; all genres considered for publication **Submission policy:** unsolicited script; score for musical

BAKER'S PLAYS   F-l 1- Ad ♪ CY 12+ Sp
**100 Chauncy St., Boston, MA 02111-1783 (617) 482-1280 FAX (617)
482-7613 Contact:** Ray Pape, Assoc. Ed. **Works:** full-length plays, one-acts, adaptations, musicals, children's plays **Special interests:** "Roles for/plays by high school students; plays for religious organizations." **Readership:** theatres of all types **Submission policy:** unsolicited script, bound; query/synopsis; professional recommendation; agent submission; "script history, resume, tape of music are helpful"; simultaneous submissions accepted **Best time:** Sept.-May **Response:** 1 month query; 3-4 months script **Your chances:** 700 scripts submitted/usually 15-25 published **Remuneration:** book and production royalties; 10 copies **Program:** Baker's Plays High School Playwriting Contest (see Contests)

THE BELLINGHAM REVIEW   1-
**The Signpost Press, MS 9053 Western WA Univ., Bellingham, WA
98225 Contact:** Robin Hemley, Editor **Publication:** semi-annual literary periodical **Works:** one-acts, short plays **Guidelines:** unpublished works, 10,000 words maximum **Submission policy:** unsolicited script, SASP; simultaneous submissions accepted **Best time:** Oct. 1-May 1 only **Response:** 3 months **Remuneration:** 1-year subscription; 1 copy

BLIZZARD PUBLISHING   F-l 1- Tr Ad CY C
**73 Furby St., Winnipeg, Manitoba, Canada R3C 2A2   (204) 775-
2923, (800) 694-9256 FAX (204) 775-2947 e-mail** atwood@blizzard.
mb.ca **Contact:** Peter Atwood, Mng. Editor **Publication:** "Contemporary drama." **Works:** full-length plays, one-acts, translations, adaptations, children's plays, academic anthologies, theatre related textbooks **Special interest:** "Relevant, contemporary material." **Guidelines:** unpublished works **Submission policy:** query/synopsis, script history, reviews, resume; professional recommendation; agent submission; no simultaneous submissions **Best time:** Mar.-Nov. only **Response:** 4+ months **Your chances:** 100+ scripts submitted/usually 11 published **Remuneration:** 10% royalties; copies." **Future commitment:** "1st refusal on new work."

BROADWAY PLAY PUBLISHING INC.   F-l Am
**56 E. 81st St., New York, NY 10028-0202 (212) 772-8334 FAX (212)
772-8358   e-mail** broadwaypl@aol.com **Works:** full-length plays **Special interest:** new American playwrights **Guidelines:** unpublished, produced plays; no historical works **Readership:** "Producers." **Submission policy:** query/synopsis **Response:** immediate query; 3 months solicited script **Your chances:** 100 scripts submitted/15± published **Remuneration:** royalties: 10% book, 80% amateur, 90% stock; 10 copies

CALLALOO   1- Tr Af
**Dept. of English, Univ. of VA, 322 Bryan Hall, Charlottesville, VA
22903 (804) 924-6637 FAX (804) 924-6472 e-mail** callaloo@virginia.
edu **Contact:** Charles H. Rowell, Editor **Publication:** journal of Afro-American/African arts **Works:** one-act plays and translations **Guide-**

lines: unpublished works; produced plays preferred; 50 pages **Submission policy:** in triplicate: unsolicited script, unbound, resume; agent submission; prior notice of simultaneous submissions **Response:** 6 months **Your chances:** 15 scripts submitted/usually 1 published **Remuneration:** possible payment; copies, offprints **Future commitment:** yes

CHILDREN'S STORY SCRIPTS   CY Ad
Baymax Productions, 2219 W. Olive Ave. #130, Burbank, CA 91506- (818) 563-6105 FAX (818) 563-2968 e-mail baymax@earthlink.net **Contact:** Deedra Bebout, Editor **Publication:** readers theatre-style stories **Works:** "Stories in script form." **Special interest:** "Stories that dovetail with classroom subjects." **Guidelines:** "Works may be published and/or produced; cast size: 5-20; 20 minutes; we don't publish plays, per se; we mix dialogue/prose narration." **Audience:** teachers, children (K-8th grade) **Submission policy:** unsolicited script, unbound; simultaneous submissions accepted **Response:** 2 weeks **Your chances:** 500 new scripts read annually/1-3 published **Remuneration:** royalties: 10%-15%, 10 copies **Future commitment:** by contract **Advice:** Send #10 SASE with 2 stamps for our guidelines."

COLLAGES AND BRICOLAGES   1- Tr x
P.O. Box 360, Shippenville, PA 16254 (814) 226-5799 e-mail mfortis @mail.penn.com **Contact:** Marie-José Fortis, Editor **Publication:** annual journal of international writing **Works:** one-act plays and translations **Guidelines:** unpublished works, 20 pages maximum **Special interests:** "Literary, innovative writing." **Readership:** "Writers; theatre, literature, arts enthusiasts." **Submission policy:** unsolicited script, unbound; query/synopsis; cover letter, 2-3 sentence bio; no simultaneous submissions **Deadline:** Nov. 15, 1999; no submission before Aug. 1 **Notification:** 2 weeks-3 months **Your chances:** 20 scripts submitted/1-4 published **Remuneration:** 2 copies **Advice:** "Send work you are proud of."

CONFRONTATION   1-
English Dept., C.W. Post College of LIU, Brookville, NY 11548 (516) 299-2391 FAX (516) 299-2735 e-mail mtucker@liu.edu **Contact:** Martin Tucker, Editor-in-Chief **Publication:** semi-annual journal **Guidelines:** unpublished one-acts, 40 pages maximum **Readership:** "College teachers, students." **Submission policy:** unsolicited script, unbound; query/synopsis; professional recommendation; agent submission; simultaneous submissions accepted **Best time:** Sept.-May only **Response:** 2 weeks query; 8 weeks script **Your chances:** 60 scripts submitted/usually 3 published **Remuneration:** $40±; copies **Future commitment:** credit **Comment:** Copyright will be transferred to author on request.

CONTEMPORARY DRAMA SERVICE   F-l 1- Ad ♪ 12+ cm V C
Meriwether Publishing, Ltd., 885 Elkton Dr., Colorado Springs, CO 80907 (719) 594-4422 FAX (719) 594-9916 **Contact:** Ted Zapel, Editor **Publisher:** "Non-professional plays for middle grades to college

market." **Works**: full-length plays, one-acts, adaptations, musicals **Special interests**: "Musical comedies based on public domain; comedy sketches; variety shows; social commentary." **Specifications**: unpublished plays; 75 pages maximum; "no serious, adult plays" **Readership**: "Teens, church groups, theatres." **Submission policy**: unsolicited script; query/synopsis; professional recommendation; agent submission **Best time**: Jun.-Aug. **Response**: 30 days query; 60 days script **Your chances**: 500 scripts submitted/30-40 published **Remuneration**: fee; possible royalty; 10-20 copies or 2 playkits **Future commitment**: no **Advice**: "Our catalog and guidelines ($2) show what we sell."

CRAZY QUILT QUARTERLY 1-
P.O. Box 632729, San Diego, CA 92163-2729 (619) 688-1023 FAX (619) 688-1753 Contact: Marsh Cassady, Drama Editor **Publication**: quarterly literary journal **Works**: one-acts **Special interest**: "Anything except pornography." **Specifications**: unpublished works; 20 pages maximum **Readership**: "Libraries, writers, agents." **Submission policy**: unsolicited script; simultaneous submissions accepted **Response**: 3 weeks **Your chances**: 20-30 scripts submitted/usually 8-10 published **Remuneration**: 2 copies **Future commitment**: no

DESCANT F-l 1-
P.O. Box 314 Station P, Toronto, Ontario, Canada M5S 2S8 (416) 593-2557 Contact: Mary Myers, Mng. Editor **Publication**: quarterly literary magazine **Guidelines**: unpublished full-length plays, one-acts, performance art **Submission policy**: unsolicited script **Response**: 6 months **Your chances**: usually 2 plays published each year **Remuneration**: $100 honorarium; 1 copy, 40% discount on additional copies **Comment**: Publisher holds 1st North American rights only.

DRAMATIC PUBLISHING COMPANY F-l 1- Tr Ad ♪ CY
311 Washington St., P.O. Box 129, Woodstock, IL 60098 (815) 338-7170 FAX (815) 338-8981 e-mail plays@dramaticpublishing.com **Contact**: Linda Habjan, Acquisitions Ed. **Works**: full-length plays, one-acts, translations, adaptations, musicals, children's plays **Guidelines**: produced plays preferred; works for stock, amateur market; 30 minutes minimum **Readership**: theatres of all types **Submission policy**: unsolicited script, reviews, photos; professional recommendation; agent submission **Response**: 4-6 months **Remuneration**: "Standard royalty; 10 copies, 30% discount on extra copies."

DRAMATICS MAGAZINE F-l 1- Tr Ad C 12+
3368 Central Pkwy., Cincinnati, OH 45225-2392 (513) 559-1996 e-mail pubs@one.net **Contact**: Don Corathers, Editor **Publication**: monthly educational magazine **Works**: full-length plays, one-acts, translations, adaptations **Special interest**: "Roles for and concerns of high school students." **Guidelines**: produced plays **Readership**: "Teens, young adults, theatre directors." **Submission policy**: unsolicited script; query/

synopsis; professional recommendation; agent submission **Response**: 2 weeks query; 2-3 months script **Your chances**: 500 scripts submitted/ usually 7 published **Remuneration**: negotiable: $100-$400; 5 copies **Future commitment**: "1st serial rights only."

DRAMATISTS PLAY SERVICE   F-l 1- Tr Ad ♪ CY
440 Park Ave. S., New York, NY 10016 (212) 683-8960 FAX (212) 213-1539 e-mail postmaster@dramatists.com **Contact**: Stephen Sultan, President **Works**: full-length plays, one-acts, translations, adaptations, musicals, children's plays **Exclusive interest**: "Plays for stock and amateur markets." **Guidelines**: "Professionally produced works--in NYC preferred." **Readership**: "Producers." **Submission policy**: query/synopsis; professional recommendation; agent submission; simultaneous submissions accepted **Response**: 4 months **Remuneration**: advance against royalties; 10% book royalty, 80% amateur, 90% stock; 10 copies **Future commitment**: performance rights **Advice**: "We seldom find a market for a play that has not had a commercially successful production"

EARTH'S DAUGHTERS   F-l 1- Tr Ad W
P.O. Box 41 Central Park Station, Buffalo, NY 14215 (716) 837-7778 Publication: feminist literary/art periodical **Guidelines**: unpublished full-length plays, one-acts, translations, adaptations, excerpts **Special interest**: women authors; theme issues--themes available in Mar. **Submission policy**: unsolicited script, unbound; query/synopsis; simultaneous submissions accepted **Best time**: spring **Response**: 3 weeks query; 2 months script **Remuneration**: 2 copies **Comment**: "Occasionally an issue will be devoted to 1 play text." Publisher holds the copyright.

ELDRIDGE PUBLISHING CO., INC.   F-l 1- Ad ♪ CY Fm
P.O. Box 1595, Venice, FL 34284 (800) 800) 447-8243 e-mail info@hi stage.com **Contact**: Nancy Vorhis, Editor **Works**: full-length plays, one-acts, adaptations, musicals, children's plays **Special interests**: produced works preferred; content acceptable for community theatre, churches, schools; minimum cast: 6 for full-length **Submission policy**: unsolicited script; query/synopsis; cassette tape and score for musical **Response**: 3 weeks query; 2 months script **Your chances**: 350 scripts submitted/ usually 50-75 published **Remuneration**: 50% royalties, 10% copy sales for full-length; outright purchase of material for church market; 12 copies

ENCORE PERFORMANCE   F-l 1- Tr Ad ♪ CY Fm C 12+ J †
PUBLISHING P.O. Box 692, Orem, UT 84059 (801) 225-0605 FAX (801) 765-0489 e-mail encoreplay@aol.com **Contact**: Michael C. Perry, President **Works**: full-length plays, one-acts, translations, adaptations, musicals, children's plays **Special interests**: "Family themes, teen and child issues, musicals for girls, Judeo-Christian subjects." **Guidelines**: works with at least 2 productions **Specifications**: "Balance of male/female roles; up to 120 minutes." **Readership**: "Elementary school-college; community/professional theatres." **Submission policy**: query/synop-

sis, script history, resume, tape of music, reviews, proof of production, 2 letters of recommendation, SASP; agent submission; commission; no simultaneous submissions; bound solicited script **Best time:** Sept.-May **Response:** 2 weeks query; 2 months solicited script **Your chances:** 250 scripts submitted/45± published **Remuneration:** 10% book, 50% performance royalties; 10 copies **Future commitment:** credit; lifetime contract: 10% **Advice:** "No profanity or misuse of names of Deity. Controversial topics if tastefully handled."

THE FOUR DIRECTIONS - AMERICAN INDIAN LITERARY QUARTERLY   P.O. Box 729, Tellico Plains, TN 37385 (423) 253-3680 **Contact:** William Meyer, Publisher This publication is currently inactive; see *The Playwright's Companion 2000* for future plans.

FREELANCE PRESS   CY Ad ♪ C Cl
P.O. Box 548, Dover, MA 02030 (508) 785-8250 FAX (508) 785-8291 **Contact:** Narcissa Campion, Mng. Editor **Works:** children's musicals **Guidelines:** unpublished musicals on issues or musical adaptations of classics for actors aged 8-17; 1 hour **Readership:** "Drama teachers, art programs, arts camps." **Submission policy:** unsolicited script, bound or unbound; query/synopsis **Response:** 3 months **Remuneration:** royalty: book, score, and performance royalties; 1 copy

HEUER PUBLISHING COMPANY   F-l 1- ♪ cm 12+ Fm
P.O. Box 248, Cedar Rapids, IA 52406 (319) 364-6311 FAX (319) 364-1771 **e-mail** editor@hitplays.com **Contact:** C. E. McMullen, Editor **Works:** full-length plays, one-acts, musicals **Guidelines:** "Unpublished works, melodramas, spoofs, farces--within scope of high school students no offensive language." **Readership:** "Middle-high schools, church groups." **Submission policy:** unsolicited script; simultaneous submissions accepted **Response:** 1-2 months **Remuneration:** "Royalty or purchase; copies." **Comment:** "Heuer or playwright holds copyright."

I. E. CLARK PUBLICATIONS   F-l 1- Tr Ad ♪ CY
P.O. Box 246, Schulenburg, TX 78956 (409) 743-3232 **Contact:** Donna Cozzaglio, Ed. Dept. **Publication:** plays, theatre books **Guidelines:** produced full-length plays, one-acts, translations, adaptations, musicals, children's plays **Readership:** theatres of all types **Submission policy:** unsolicited script, bound; videotape; cassette tape-sample score sheets for musical; simultaneous submissions accepted **Response:** 2-6 months **Your chances:** 1000 scripts submitted/5-7 published **Remuneration:** royalties; 10 copies **Comment:** I.E. Clark holds copyright in author's name.

KALLIOPE, A JOURNAL OF WOMEN'S ART   1- x Fm W
Florida Community College, 3939 Roosevelt Blvd., Jacksonville, FL 32205 904) 381-3511 Contact: Mary Sue Koeppel, Editor **Publication:** journal published 3 times a year **Works:** one-acts, 25 minutes maximum **Special interest:** "Innovation; no erotica." **Guidelines:** women authors;

unpublished works **Readership:** "Writers, artists, professionals, libraries." **Submission policy:** unsolicited script, bound or unbound; no simultaneous submissions **Best time:** fall **Response:** 1-3 months **Your chances:** 3 scripts submitted/usually 0-1 published **Remuneration:** 1 copy or 1-year subscription **Future commitment:** "*Kalliope* holds copyright until asked to return it; credit." **Advice:** "No traditional pieces."

KENYON REVIEW   1-
Kenyon College, Gambier, OH 43022   **(740) 427-5208**   **FAX (740) 427-5117**   **e-mail** kenyonreview@kenyon.edu   **Contact:** David H. Lynn, Editor **Publication:** literary journal   **Guidelines:** unpublished one-acts, excerpts, 30 pages maximum **Readership:** "Young adults, college students, teachers." **Submission policy:** unsolicited script, unbound; query/synopsis; agent submission; no simultaneous submissions **Best time:** Feb.-Mar, Sept.-Nov. only **Response:** 2 weeks query; 3 months script **Your chances:** 15 scripts submitted/2 published **Remuneration:** fee; 2 copies **Future commitment:** no **Comment:** "E-mail queries only--no scripts!"

KIMBALL & MORASKE LTD./K & M MUSICALS   ♪ CY
88 Sherwood Pl., Greenwich, CT 06830 (203) 661-4325   **FAX** same **Contact:** Dan Moraske, Co-Mng. Dir. **Special interest:** "Musicals for all ages." **Guidelines:** unpublished musicals, children's plays **Readership:** theatres, teachers (K-12), professionals, church groups, general public **Submission policy:** query/synopsis, cassette tape, SASP **Response:** 2-3 weeks query; 2-3 months solicited script **Terms:** negotiable

LAMIA INK!   1- 1p   x NA As po
P.O. Box 202 Prince St. Station, New York, NY 10012   **Contact:** Cortland Jessup, Ed. **Publication:** magazine **Works:** monologues, 1-page plays **Special interests:** "Native American, Japanese, Pacific Rim writers; manifestos, essays, poets' theatre." **Guidelines:** experimental pieces; 5 pages maximum, 2-3 preferred **Submission policy:** unsolicited script **Deadline:** Mar. 30 for May issue; Sept. 30 for Dec. issue; Dec. 30 for Feb. issue **Response:** 2-3 weeks after deadline **Remuneration:** 4 copies

LILLENAS DRAMA   F-l 1- Ad ♪ CY Fm † ✹
RESOURCES/LILLENAS PUBLISHING CO. P.O. Box 419527, **Kansas City, MO 64141**   **(816) 931-1900, (800) 877-0700**   **FAX (816) 753-4071**   **e-mail** drama@lillenas.com   **Contact:** Paul M. Miller, Editor **Works:** full-length plays (90 minutes-2 hours), one-acts (30-45 minutes), adaptations, musicals, children's plays, sketches, skits **Special interest:** "Wholesome entertainment for dinner theatres, schools." **Guidelines:** unproduced plays, outlines **Readership:** "Christians, all ages." **Submission policy:** send SASE for "Contributor's Guidelines" and list of current needs **Best time:** "Christmas plays: fall for the following year." **Response:** 3 months **Your chances:** 200 scripts submitted/usually 12-15 published **Remuneration:** flat payment or royalty

MUSIC THEATRE INTERNATIONAL   See Special Programs.

NEW PLAYS INCORPORATED   CY Tr Ad ♪ 12+
P.O. Box 5074, Charlottesville, VA 22905 (804) 979-2777 FAX (804) 984-2230 e-mail patwhitton@aol.com Contact: Patricia Whitton, Publisher Works: children's plays, translations, adaptations and musicals Special interest: "Plays for adult and teenage performers." Guidelines: produced plays; 40-90 minutes Submission policy: unsolicited script, preferably bound; query/synopsis; professional recommendation; simultaneous submissions of solicited script accepted Response: 1 month or longer Your chances: 300-500 scripts submitted/usually 2-4 published Remuneration: 50% production royalties, 10% script sales; 6 copies Advice: "Read our catalogue to get an idea of the plays we publish."

OLLANTAY THEATER MAGAZINE   Rg Hi Esp
P.O. Box 720449, Jackson Heights, NY 11372-0449 (718) 565-6499 FAX (718) 446-7806 Contact: Pedro R. Monge-Rafuls, Editor Publication: semi-annual journal on Hispanic theatre, in English and Spanish Guidelines: open to all U.S. Latino writers; all dramatic genres except adaptations Submission policy: unsolicited script, bound; agent submission; simultaneous submissions accepted Your chances: 20+ scripts submitted/usually 4 published Remuneration: fee; 3-5 copies

PACIFIC REVIEW   1- C
English Dept., Cal State Univ., 5500 University Pkwy., San Bernardino, CA 92407-2397 (909) 880-5894 Contact: James Brown, Juan Delgado, Faculty Eds. Publication: annual literary journal Works: one-acts, 25 pages maximum Special interest: "Realistic, contemporary works." Submission policy: unsolicited script Best time: Sept. 1-Feb. 1 only Response: 2 months Remuneration: 2 copies

PAJ PUBLICATIONS   F-l 1- Tr
P.O. Box 260 Village Station, New York, NY 10014-0260 (212) 243-3885 FAX same e-mail pajpub@aol.com Contact: Bonnie Marranca, Gautam Dasgupta, Co-Publishers Works: full-length plays, one-acts, translations, critical literature on performing arts Special interest: translations Readership: "Academic, literary." Submission policy: query/synopsis; professional recommendation; agent submission; simultaneous submissions accepted Response: 2 months Remuneration: royalty and/or fee Future commitment: no

PERFORMING ARTS JOURNAL   F-l 1- Tr C Am x
Works: full-length plays, one-acts, translations Special interests: "20th-century performance and drama; American avant-garde; full-length plays under 40 pages." Submission policy: query/synopsis; professional recommendation; agent submission; simultaneous submissions accepted Response: 2 months Your chances: 20+ scripts submitted/4-6 published Remuneration: fee Future commitment: no

PALMETTO PLAY SERVICE   **F-l 1- Rg**
P.O. Box 123, Pendleton, SC 29670-0123 (864) 225-1725 e-mail pal
play@concentric.net **Contact:** Lew Holton, Mng Ed. **Guidelines:** produced full-length plays, one-acts; Southeastern themes **Submission
policy:** query/synopsis <u>with</u> professional recommendation **Response:** 1
month **Remuneration:** 75%-80% production royalties, 10% script sales

℞ PASSAIC REVIEW/MILLENNIUM EDITIONS   1- CY
P.O. Box 732, Spring Lake, NJ 07762 **Contact:** Richard Quatrone,
Publisher/Ed. **Publication:** semi-annual literary review **Works:** 5-page
one-acts and children's plays **Submission policy:** unsolicited script,
bound; simultaneous submissions accepted **Response:** 1 year **Your
chances:** usually 1 play published per year **Remuneration:** 1 copy

PIONEER DRAMA SERVICE, INC. F-l 1- Ad ♪ CY C 12+ Lc
P.O. Box 4267, Englewood, CO 80155 (800) 33DRAMA, (303) 779-
4035 **FAX** (303) 779-4315 e-mail piodrama@aol.com **Contact:** Steven
Fendrich, Publisher **Works:** full-length plays, one-acts, adaptations,
musicals, children's plays **Special interests:** "Children's theatre; teen
issues." **Guidelines:** unpublished, produced works; large casts; minimal
sets preferred; 30-90 minutes **Submission policy:** query/synopsis, resume, proof of production **Best time:** Nov.-Mar. **Response:** 2-3 weeks
query; 3 months solicited script **Your chances:** 500 scripts submitted/
usually 15 published **Remuneration:** 10% copy sales, 50% royalties;
10 copies **Program:** Shubert Fendrich Memorial Contest (see Contests)

PLAYERS PRESS, INC.   F-l 1- Tr Ad ♪ CY
P.O. Box 1132, Studio City, CA 91614-0132 (818) 789-4980 **Contact:**
Robert W. Gordon, Vice President, Editorials **Publisher:** "Specialists in
performing arts books, plays, musicals, video/audio recordings." **Works:**
full-length plays, one-acts, translations, adaptations, musicals, children's
plays; books on theatre, TV, dance **Guidelines:** plays must be unpublished, produced (1 professional or 2 amateur productions) **Readership:** "Worldwide." **Submission policy:** query/synopsis preferred; unsolicited script, unbound; videotape; reviews, proof of production, cassette tape of music, resume; no simultaneous submissions **Response:** 1
week query; 3-12 months script **Your chances:** 350 scripts submitted/
usually 60 published **Remuneration:** "Book and performance royalties;
2 copies." **Future commitment:** percentage, credit, options

PLAYS ON TAPE   See listing in Theatres.

**PLAYS, THE DRAMA MAGAZINE   1- CY ✹ B 12+ Fm Lc
FOR YOUNG PEOPLE   120 Boylston St., Boston, MA 02116 (617)**
423-3157 **Contact:** Elizabeth Preston, Mng. Ed. **Publication:** monthly
journal (Oct.-May) **Works:** one-acts for young audiences **Special interests:** "Holiday plays; biographies of achievers; thoughtful plays for
junior high level that <u>do not</u> deal with drugs, alcohol, or sex." **Guide-**

lines: unpublished works; adaptations of works in public domain; 20-30 minutes for junior-senior high, 15-20 minutes for middle grades, 8-15 minutes for lower grades **Specifications:** maximum cast: 30; no more than 3 sets **Submission policy:** unsolicited script, unbound; query/synopsis for adaptation; no simultaneous submissions **Best time:** spring-summer **Response:** 1-2 weeks query; 3 weeks script **Your chances:** 200 scripts submitted/25-30 published **Remuneration:** fee; 1 copy **Future commitment:** "We buy all rights; if we use a play in a collection, we pay a fee." **Advice:** "Message should take a back seat to entertainment value."

POEMS & PLAYS   1- po
English Dept., Middle TN State Univ., Murfreesboro, TN 37132 (615) 898-2712 FAX (615) 898-5098 Contact: Dr. Gaylord Brewer, Ed. **Publication:** annual magazine **Works:** one-acts **Guidelines:** unpublished plays; short one-acts preferred **Submission policy:** unsolicited script **Best time:** Oct.1-Jan. 15 only **Response:** 1-2 months **Your chances:** 2-3 plays published in each issue **Remuneration:** 1 copy **Program:** Tennessee Chapbook Prize (see Contests)

PRISM INTERNATIONAL   1- Tr
Creative Writing Prog., UBC, Buch E462 1866 Main Mall, Vancouver, BC, Canada V6T 1Z1 (604) 822-2514 e-mail prism@unixg.ubc.ca **Contact:** Emily Snyder, Exec. Ed. **Publication:** quarterly literary magazine **Works:** one-acts, translations, excerpts **Guidelines:** unpublished works; 30 pages maximum **Submission policy:** unsolicited script, unbound; agent submission; no simultaneous submissions **Response:** 2-6 months **Your chances:** 20-30 scripts submitted/usually 1-2 published **Remuneration:** $20 per printed page; selected authors published on web site earn additional $10 per page **Program:** upcoming contest (send SASE guidelines) **Advice:** "Short work; it <u>must</u> read well on the page."

PROVINCETOWN ARTS   1- Tr Rg
Provincetown Arts Press, 650 Commercial St., Provincetown, MA 02657 (508) 487-3167 FAX (508) 487-8634 e-mail press@capecod access.com **Contact:** Christopher Busa, Ed. **Publication:** annual magazine **Works:** one-acts, translations **Special interest:** "Artists and writers on the tip of Cape Cod." **Guidelines:** unpublished work, 39 pages maximum **Readership:** "Affluent, estimated at 34,000." **Submission policy:** unsolicited script **Best time:** Sept.-Mar. **Response:** 2 months **Your chances:** 1 play published in each issue; also 1 play or collection of plays published each year **Remuneration:** $50-$300; 2 copies

RAG MAG   F-l 1- x
Black Hat Press, P.O. Box 12, Goodhue, MN 55027 (612) 923-4590 Contact: Beverly Voldseth, Ed./Publisher **Publication:** semi-annual literary magazine **Works:** full-length plays, excerpts, one-acts, 4-5 pages **Special interests:** innovation, character plays, short one-acts; 1999 themes TBA **Readership:** "General." **Submission policy:** one-act: un-

solicited script, unbound, brief summary; full-length play: query/synopsis, 10-page dialogue sample, 2-3 line bio; simultaneous submissions accepted **Best time:** "No submissions until Oct. 1999; then Oct.-Apr. only." **Response:** 2 months **Your chances:** 10 scripts submitted/usually 2 published **Remuneration:** 1 copy **Future commitment:** no

RESOURCE PUBLICATIONS 1- h/d Sp
160 E. Virginia St. #290, San Jose CA 95112 (408) 286-8505 Contact : Ken Guentert, Ed. **Special interests:** "Education, prevention resources." **Guidelines:** skits (7-15 minutes) "for discussion starters" **Submission policy:** unsolicited script **Response:** 2 months **Remuneration:** royalty

ROCKFORD REVIEW 1- cm
P.O. Box 858, Rockford, IL 61105 Contact: David Ross, Ed. **Publication:** tri-quarterly journal **Special interest:** satire **Guidelines:** unpublished one-acts, 10 pages maximum **Submission policy:** unsolicited script, bound or unbound; query/synopsis; simultaneous submissions accepted **Response:** 2 months **Remuneration:** 1 copy; possible $25 prize **Your chances:** 50 scripts submitted/4-5 published **Future commitment:** credit **Advice:** "Send $5, request a copy containing a play." **Comment:** Rockford Review holds 1st North American Serial Rights only.

SAMUEL FRENCH, INC. F-l 1- Tr Ad ♪ CY cm my W
45 W. 25th St., New York, NY 10010 (212) 206-8990 Contact: Lawrence Harbison, Ed. **Works:** full-length plays, one-acts, translations, adaptations, musicals, children's plays **Special interests:** "Light comedy, mystery, on and off Broadway hits." **Guidelines:** Samuel French format ($4.03) **Submission policy:** unsolicited script, bound; query/synopsis; professional recommendation; agent submission; simultaneous submissions accepted **Response:** 1 week query; 2-12 months script **Your chances:** 1500 scripts submitted/usually 10-50 published **Remuneration:** 10% book royalty, varying stock and amateur commissions; 10 copies, 40% off additional copies **Future commitment:** "Usually 1st dibs on next 3 plays." **Advice:** "As many female roles as possible."

SCRIPTS AND SCRIBBLES F-l 1- x
141 Wooster St., New York, NY 10012 (212) 473-6695 FAX (212) same Contact: Daryl Chin, Consulting Ed. **Works:** full-length plays, one-acts, performance art **Exclusive interest:** non-traditional work produced outside NYC **Submission policy:** query/synopsis; no unsolicited script **Response:** 6 months **Remuneration:** 25 copies

UNITED ARTS 1- Tr x
Publication: periodic journal **Works:** one-acts, translations, manifestos **Exclusive interest:** avant garde work **Submission policy:** query/synopsis preferred; unsolicited script **Response:** 6 months **Remuneration:** copies

SINISTER WISDOM 1- g/l
P.O. **Box 3252, Berkeley, CA 94703 Contact:** Margo Mercedes Rivera-
Weiss, Ed. **Publication:** literary/arts quarterly **Works:** one-acts, excerpts, 3000 words maximum **Guidelines:** lesbian writers/themes; unpublished works preferred **Submission policy:** send SASE for themes;
unsolicited script, unbound; query/synopsis; simultaneous submissions
accepted **Deadline:** Feb. 1, Jun. 1, Oct. 1 **Response:** 1 month query; 9
months script **Your chances:** 4+ new scripts read annually/1-2 published

SMITH AND KRAUS, INC. F-l 1- Tr Ad CY 1p W
THE ACTOR'S PUBLISHER P.O. **Box 127, Lyme, NH 03768**
(603) 643-6431 FAX (603) 643-1831 e-mail sandk@sover.net **Contact:**
Marisa Smith, Pres. **Publication:** scene and monologue books, women's
plays, contemporary plays **Works:** full-length plays, one-acts, translations, adaptations, children's plays **Special interests:** "Books for actors;
produced plays only." **Readership:** "Actors, schools, theatres." **Submission policy:** unsolicited script, bound preferred; query/synopsis; agent
submission; cassette tape of music, proof of production, SASP; no simultaneous submissions **Best time:** before mid-Aug. **Response:** 4 months
Remuneration: fee or royalty; 10 copies **Future commitment:** varies

SUN & MOON PRESS F-l 1- Tr
6026 Wilshire Blvd., Los Angeles, CA 90036 (213) 857-1115 e-mail
djmess@sunmoon.com **Contact:** American Theater & Literature Program
Publication: 1-play volumes **Works:** full-length plays, one-acts, translations **Guidelines:** unpublished works **Submission policy:** unsolicited
script for contest (see American Theater & Literature Prog. in Contests);
inquire for other policies **Response:** 2-6 months **Your chances:** 10±
plays published each year **Remuneration:** royalty; 10 copies

THEATER MAGAZINE F-l 1- Tr Ad x C
**222 York St., New Haven, CT 06520 (203) 432-1568 FAX (203)
4328336 e-mail** theater.magazine@yale.edu **Contact:** Erika Munk, Ed.
Publication: theatre journal **Works:** full-length plays, one-acts, translations, adaptations **Special interest:** "Experimental, innovative works;
American and international works; political/cultural debates." **Readership:** "Theatre professionals, teachers, critics, scholars." **Submission
policy:** unsolicited script, bound or unbound, resume **Your chances:** 100
scripts submitted/5± published **Remuneration:** negotiable, copies

THEATREFORUM F-l Tr Ad x
**Theatre Dept., UCSD, 9500 Gilman Dr., La Jolla, CA 92093 (619)
534-6598 FAX (619) 534-1080 e-mail** theatreforum@ucsd.edu **Contact:**
Jim Carmody, Ed. **Publication:** semi-annual journal **Works:** full-length
plays, translations, adaptations **Exclusive interest:** "Innovative work."
Guidelines: unpublished, produced works **Submission policy:** professional recommendation **Response:** 3 months **Remuneration:** varies; 10
copies **Future commitment:** "First-time rights only."

THIS MONTH ON STAGE   F-l 1- Ad
P.O. Box 62, Hewlett, NY 11557 (800) 536-0099 **e-mail** tmosmais@
aol.com **Contact:** Play Submissions **Publication:** journal published 8
times per year **Works:** full-length plays, one-acts, adaptations **Special
interest:** "Scripts that read well on paper; one-acts preferred." **Readership:** "Casual theatregoers; theatre professionals." **Submission policy:**
unsolicited script; agent submission; simultaneous submissions accepted
Best time: Jun.-Aug., Nov.-Feb. **Response:** 1 year **Your chances:** 6-8
plays published annually **Remuneration:** $1.00; 2 copies **Comment:**
"Send a separate SASE for each manuscript, please!"

TOMORROW MAGAZINE   1- ♪ 1p cm
P.O. Box 148486, Chicago, IL 60614 (312) 904-8524 **e-mail** audrelv@
xsite.net **Contact:** Tim W. Brown, Ed. **Publication:** semi-annual magazine **Works:** one-acts, musicals, monologues; 10 pages maximum **Special
interest:** "Comedy." **Submission policy:** unsolicited script **Response:** 3
weeks-3 months **Your chances:** usually 1-2 plays published each year
Remuneration: 1 copy **Advice:** "Send $5 for sample copy."

UBU REPERTORY THEATER   Tr Fr M C Cl
15 W. 28th St., New York, NY 10001 (212) 679-7540 **FAX** (212) 679-
2033 **e-mail** uburep@spacelab.net **Contact:** Françoise Kourilsky, Art.
Director **Publication:** "Multicultural, themed anthologies and single
plays" **Guidelines:** "Translations: contemporary works from around
the French-speaking world in translation, and French 'modern classics'
in French and English." **Audience:** "Interested in francophone culture,
social issues, new works." **Submission policy:** unsolicited script;
query/synopsis; professional recommendation; agent submission; simultaneous submissions accepted; "translations may be submitted along with
the French-language original" **Best time:** summer **Your chances:** 200+
scripts submitted/usually 1-2 published **Remuneration:** 3 copies
Future commitment: credit **Advice:** "Request our catalog."

VENTANA PRODUCTIONS/PUBLICATIONS
P.O. Box 191973, San Francisco, CA 94119 (415) 522-8989 **Contact:** J.
P. Allen, Director   This publisher is not open to submissions in 1999;
see *The Playwright's Companion 2000* for future plans.

Agents

Mini-Checklist

What to Send to an Agent

With a query/synopsis:
- A cover letter.
- A play synopsis.
- A script history: previous productions, workshops, readings, publications, awards. Include favorable reviews.
- A dialogue sample, if requested.
- Your resume or bio.

With an unsolicited script:
- A cover letter.
- A new copy of the script, typed in *Professional Playscript Format* and bound in a new folder.
- A script history: previous productions, workshops, readings, publications, awards. Include favorable reviews.
- Your resume or bio.
- Your SASE if you want the script returned.

Tip: Don't send unsolicited scripts to an agent who does not indicate a willingness to read them.

- **With a solicited script:**
- A cover letter (politely reminding the agent that he or she requested the play).
- A new copy of the script, typed in *Professional Playscript Format* and bound in a new folder.
- A script history: previous productions, workshops, readings, publications, awards. Include favorable reviews.
- Your resume or bio.
- Your SASE if you want the script returned.

Agents

AGENCY FOR THE PERFORMING ARTS
888 Seventh Ave. Suite 602, New York, NY 10106 (212) 582-1500
Contact: Leo Bookman Special interests: "Broad interests, all genres."
Submission policy: query, resume

ALLIANCE TALENT AGENCY   S
1501 Broadway Suite 404, New York, NY 10036 (212) 840-6868 FAX
(212) 840-7235 Contact: Carole Davis Exclusive interest: "Filmscripts
only." Submission policy: query/synopsis, resume

ANN ELMO AGENCY   G dr
60 E. 42nd St., New York, NY 10165 (212) 661-2880 FAX (212) 661-
2883 Contact: Mari Cronin Special interests: "All types of drama."
Submission policy: query, resume

ANN WRIGHT REPRESENTATIVES   Pl
165 W. 46th St. Suite 1105, New York, NY 10036-2501 (212) 764-6770
FAX (212) 764-5125 Contact: Dan Wright Special interest: "Plays; no
musicals." Submission policy: query, resume

ℛ AUSTIN WAHL AGENCY   G
1820 N. 76th Ct., Elmwood, IL 60070 (708) 456-2301 Submission
policy: query/synopsis, dialogue sample, script history

BAKER'S PLAYS   12+ Fm
100 Chauncy St., Boston, MA 02111-1783 (617) 482-1280 FAX (617)
482-7613 Special interests: "Plays for high school and community
theatre." Submission policy: unsolicited script, resume

BARBARA HOGENSON AGENCY   F-l
165 West End Ave. Suite 19C, New York, NY 10023 (212) 874-8084
Contact: Barbara Hogenson Special interest: "Full-length plays." Submission policy: professional recommendation

BEN F. KAMSLER, LTD.   Pl S Tv
5501 Noble Ave, Sherman Oaks, CA 91411 (818) 785-4167 FAX
(818) 988-8304 Contact: Ben F. Kamsler Special interests:"Plays,
screenplays, TV scripts." Submission policy: query/synopsis, resume

BERMAN, BOALS AND FLYNN   F-l
208 W. 30th St. #401, New York, NY 10001 (212) 868-1068 Contact:
Judy Boals, Jim Flynn Special interest:"Full-length plays." Submission policy: query, bio

THE BETHEL AGENCY   G
360 W. 53rd St. #BA, New York, NY 10019 (212) 664-0455 Contact:
Lewis Chambers Special interest: broad interests Submission policy:
query/synopsis, bio Best time: "Any time except holiday seasons."

B. K. NELSON, INC.   F-l ♪
84 Woodlawn Rd., Pleasantville, NY 10570 (914) 741-1322 FAX same
Contact: Bonita K. Nelson Special interests:"Full-length plays, musicals." Submission policy: query/synopsis, cassette tape of music, bio

BRETT ADAMS, LTD.   G
448 W. 44th St., New York, NY 10036 (212) 765-5630 FAX (212) 265-
2212 Contact: Brett Adams, Bruce Ostler Special interests:"Open to all
types of material." Submission policy: query/synopsis, resume

CONTEMPORARY ARTISTS, LTD.   G
1317 5th St. #200, Santa Monica, CA 90401 (310) 395-1800 FAX (310)
394-3308 Contact: Gary Fuchs Special interests: "All dramatic
genres." Submission policy: query/synopsis, resume

DON BUCHWALD AND ASSOCIATES   G
10 E. 44th St., New York, NY 10017 (212) 867-1200 (FAX) (212) 972-
3209 Contact: Tina Freedman, Literary Agent Special interest: "Open
interests." Submission policy: query/synopsis, bio

DRAMATIC PUBLISHING COMPANY   G
311 Washington St., P.O. Box 129, Woodstock, IL 60098 (815) 338-
7170 FAX (815) 338-8981 Contact: Linda Habjan Special interests:
"Plays for all audiences." Submission policy: unsolicited script with
cover letter and production history

DUVA-FLACK ASSOCIATES, INC.   G
200 W. 57th St. Suite 1008, New York, NY 10019 (212) 957-9600
FAX (212) 957-9606 Special interests: "All dramatic genres." Submission policy: query/synopsis

ELAINE MARKSON AGENCY   44 Greenwich Ave., New York,
NY 10011 (212) 243-8480 This agency is not open to playwrights in
1999; see *The Playwright's Companion 2000* or future plans.

ELLEN HYMAN   F-l ♪ S Tv
90 Lexington Ave., New York, NY 10016 (212) 689-0727 Special
interests: "Full-length plays, musicals, screenplays, teleplays." Submission policy: query, resume

ELISABETH MARTON AGENCY   Pl Am
1 Union Sq. W., Rm. 612, New York, NY 10003-3303 (212) 255-1908
Contact: Tonda Marton Special interest: "Established American playwrights who are produced abroad." Submission policy: query, resume

EPSTEIN-WYCKOFF AND ASSOCIATES   Pl S Tv
380 S. Beverly Dr. #400, Beverly Hills, CA 90212 (310) 278-7222
Contact: Karin Wakefield Special interests: "Playwrights, screenwriters, sit-com writers." Submission policy: inquire

FARBER LITERARY AGENCY G
14 E. 75th St., New York, NY 10021 (212) 861-7075 FAX (212) 861-7076 **Contact:** Ann Farber **Special interests:** "All dramatic genres." **Submission policy:** "Query with resume or phone call."

FIFI OSCARD AGENCY, INC. F-l
24 W. 40th St. 17th Floor, New York, NY 10018 (212) 764-1100 **Contact:** Fifi Oscard, Carmen LaVia, Kevin McShane, Peter Sawyer **Special interests:** "No one-acts." **Submission policy:** query, resume

FLORA ROBERTS, INC. ♪ Pl
157 W. 57th St., New York, NY 10019 (212) 355-4165 FAX (212) 246-7136 **Contact:** Flora Roberts, Sarah Douglas **Special interests:** "Librettists, lyricists, composers for musical theatre; some playwrights with outstanding credentials." **Submission policy:** query, resume

FREIDA FISHBEIN ASSOCIATES F-l
P.O. Box 723, Bedford, NY 10506 (914) 234-7232 FAX (914) 234-9146 **Contact:** Douglas Michael, Heidi Carlson **Exclusive interest:** "Full-length plays." **Submission policy:** "Query, resume, genre of play."

GAGE GROUP S Tv
9255 Sunset Blvd. Suite 515, Los Angeles, CA 90069 (310) 859-8777 (310) 859-8166 **Contact:** Martin Gage **Special interests:** "Primarily filmscripts, TV scripts." **Submission policy:** query/synopsis, resume

THE GERSH AGENCY Pl S Tv
130 W. 42nd St. Suite 2400, New York, NY 10036 (212) 997-1818 **Contact:** Peter Hagen, John Buzzetti **Special interests:** "All dramatic genres, including film and TV." **Submission policy:** query, resume

GOLD MARSHAK ASSOCIATES Pl S Tv
3500 W. Olive Ave., Burbank, CA 91505 (818) 972-4333 **Contact:** Evan Corday, Jeff Melnick **Special interests:** "Screenplays, teleplays, stage plays." **Submission policy:** professional recommendation

GRAHAM AGENCY F-l ♪
311 W. 43rd St., New York, NY 10036 (212) 489-7730 **Contact:** Earl Graham **Special interests:** "Full-length plays; some musicals." **Submission policy:** query/synopsis

HARDEN-CURTIS ASSOCIATES G
850 Seventh Ave. #405, New York, NY 10019 (212) 977-8502 **Contact:** Mary Harden **Special interests:** "All dramatic genres." **Submission policy:** query, resume

HELEN MERRILL AGENCY G
425 W. 23rd St. Suite 1F, New York, NY 10011 (212) 691-5326 **Contact:** Patrick Herold **Special interests:** "All dramatic genres; serious, entertaining writing." **Submission policy:** query, resume

I. E. CLARK G
P.O. Box 246, Schulenburg, TX 78956 (409) 743-3232 (409) 743-4765
Comment: "We act as agents for the works we publish"; see Publishers.

IMPULSE PLAYWRIGHTS AGENCY G cm my dr
3131 S.W. Sherwood Pl., Portland, OR 97201 (503) 228-8877
Contact: Ed Udovic **Special interests:** all genres, mysteries, dramas
Submission policy: unsolicited script, cassette tape for musical, resume

INTERNATIONAL CREATIVE MANAGEMENT Pl S Tv
40 W. 57th St., New York, NY 10019 (212) 556-5600 **Contact:** Bridget
Aschenberg, Sam Cohn, Arlene Donovan, Mitch Douglas **Special interests:** all genres, TV, film **Submission policy:** query/2-page synopsis

℘ **INTERNATIONAL LEONARDS CORPORATION** S Tv
3612 N. Washington Blvd., Indianapolis, IN 46205 (317) 926-7566
Special interests: screenplays, teleplays **Submission policy:** query/
synopsis, SASE

THE JOYCE KETAY AGENCY Pl S
1501 Broadway Suite 1908, New York, NY 10036 (212) 354-6825
FAX (212) 354-6732 **Contact:** Joyce Ketay, Carl Mulert, Wendy Streeter
Special interests: "Playwrights, screenwriters." **Submission policy:**
professional recommendation

KAPLAN/STAHLER AGENCY Pl S Tv
8383 Wilshire Blvd., Beverly Hills, CA 90211 (213) 653-4483 **FAX**
(213) 653-4506 **Contact:** Mitch Kaplan **Special interests:** "Playwrights, screen and TV writers." **Submission policy:** query, resume

KERIN-GOLDBERG ASSOCIATES G
155 E. 55th St. Suite 5D, New York, NY 10022 (212) 838-7373 **FAX**
(212) 838-0774 **Contact:** Charles Kerin, Allison Goldberg **Special interests:** "All dramatic genres." **Submission policy:** query, resume

THE LANTZ OFFICE G
888 Seventh Ave. #3001, New York, NY 10106 (212) 586-0200
Contact: Robert Lantz, Dennis Aspland **Special interests:** "Broad
interests; all dramatic genres." **Submission policy:** "Letter, resume."

LITERARY ARTISTS REPRESENTATIVES G
575 West End Ave., New York, NY 10024 (212) 787-3808 FAX (212)
595-2098 **Contact:** Madeline Perrone **Special interests:** "All genres."
Submission policy: query/synopsis, resume; phone call

MARTIN HURWITZ ASSOCIATES Pl S Tv
427 N. Cannon Dr. #215, Beverly Hills, CA 90210 (310) 274-0240
FAX (310) 274-2070 **Contact:** Scott Cooke **Special interests:** "Plays,
screenplays, teleplays." **Submission policy:** "Query with professional
recommendation <u>only</u>."

MCINTOSH & OTIS   **G**
310 Madison Ave., New York, NY 10017 (212) 687-7400 Special
interests: "Open." Submission policy: query/synopsis, resume

MICHAEL IMISON PLAYWRIGHTS, LTD.   **G**
28 Almeida St., London N1 1TD, England 011-44-171-354-3174 FAX
011-44-171-359-6273 Special interests: "Open." Submission policy:
professional referral, resume

MICHELINE STEINBERG PLAYWRIGHTS   **G**
409 Triumph House, 187-191 Regent St., London, W1P 7WF England 011-44-171-287-4383 FAX 011-44-171-287-4384 Special interests: "All dramatic genres." Submission policy: query, resume

MUSIC THEATRE INTERNATIONAL   ♪
421 W. 54th St. 2nd Floor, New York, NY 10019 (212) 541-4684
Special interests: "Musicals only." Submission policy: "Query/syn-
opsis of musical produced in New York."

♫ OTITIS MEDIA LITERARY AGENCY   **G**
1926 Dupont Ave. S, Minneapolis, MN 55403 (612) 377-4918 Special interests: "Any material except 'new age'." Submission policy:
query/1-paragraph synopsis, 1st 20 pages, resume, SASE

THE PALMER & DODGE AGENCY   **G**
1 Beacon St., Boston, MA 02108 (617) 573-0118 FAX (617) 227-4420
Contact: Elaine Rogers, Director of Subsidiary Rights Special interests:
"All genres." Submission policy: query, resume

PEREGRINE WHITTLESEY   **G**
345 E. 80th St. #31F, New York, NY 10021 (212) 737-0153 FAX (212)
734-5176 Contact: Peregrine Whittlesey Special interests: "Truly
original writing; all genres." Submission policy: query, resume

RAY L'DERA AGENCY   **Pl ♪ CY W**
P.O. Box 6365, New York, NY 10128 (212) 229-7533 e-mail RayLDera
@aol.com Contact: Ray L'Dera Special interests: "Plays, musicals,
children's plays, women's roles; emerging authors; primary focus: community and regional theatres." Submission policy: synopses, 1st 10
pages of dialogue of 3 different scripts

ROBERT A. FREEDMAN DRAMATIC AGENCY   **Pl S**
1501 Broadway Suite 2310, New York, NY 10036 (212) 840-5760
FAX (212) 840-5776 Contact: Robert A. Freedman Special interests:
"Playwrights and screenwriters." Submission policy: query, resume

ROSENSTONE/WENDER   **G**
3 E. 48th St. 4th Floor, New York, NY 10017 (212) 832-8330 FAX
(212) 759-4524 Contact: Howard Rosenstone, Phyllis Wender Special
interests: "All dramatic genres." Submission policy: query, resume

SAMUEL FRENCH, INC. 45 W. 25th St., New York, NY 10010
See listing in Publishers.

SHUKAT COMPANY, LTD. G
340 W. 55th St. #1A, New York, NY 10019 (212) 582-7614 Contact:
Scott Shukat, Pat McLaughlin **Special interests:** "Open." **Submission
policy:** "Query/brief precis, resume, 10-12 page dialogue sample."

SOIREE FAIR, INC. G
133 Midland Ave. Suite 10, Montclair, NJ 07042-2959 (973) 783-
9051 FAX (973) 746-5980 Contact: Karen L. Gunn, President **Special
interests:** "All dramatic genres." **Submission policy:** query, resume;
professional recommendation

♫ STEWART TALENT G
58 W. Huron, Chicago, IL 60610 (312) 943-0892 Contact: Literary
Div. **Submission policy:** query/2-page synopsis, SASE

SUSAN GURMAN AGENCY Pl
865 West End Ave. #15A, New York, NY 10025 (212) 749-4618 Contact: Susan Gurman **Special interests:** "Playwrights, all types of plays."
Submission policy: "Query/resume from produced playwright only."

SUSAN SCHULMAN LITERARY AGENCY Pl W M
454 W. 44th St., New York, NY 10036 (212) 713-1633 FAX (212) 581-
8830 Contact: Susan Schulman **Special interests:** "Emerging playwrights; women, minorities." **Submission policy:** query, resume, SASE

THE TANTLEFF OFFICE G
375 Greenwich St. #700, New York, NY 10013 (212) 941-3939 FAX
(212) 941-3948 Contact: Jack Tantleff, Charmaine Ferenczi **Special
interests:** "All dramatic genres." **Submission policy:** query, resume

WILLIAM MORRIS AGENCY, INC. G Tv S
1325 Ave. of the Americas 15th & 16th Fl., New York, NY 10019
(212) 586-5100 FAX (212) 246-3583; 151 El Camino Dr., Beverly
Hills, CA 90212 (310) 274-7451 Contact: Peter Franklin, George Lane,
Owen Laster, Bill Liff, Mary Meagher, Gilbert Parker **Special interests:** "Open: stage plays, teleplays, screenplays." **Submission policy:**
query, resume

WRITERS & ARTISTS AGENCY Pl S Tv
19 W. 44th St. #1000, New York, NY 10036 (212) 391-1112; 924
Westwood Blvd. #900, Los Angeles, CA 90024 Contact: Jeff Berger,
William Craver, Greg Wagner **Special interests:** "Playwrights, screen,
TV writers; all types of material." **Submission policy:** query, resume

College
and
University
Playwriting Programs

About Playwriting Programs . . .

Many colleges and universities across the United States offer courses in dramatic writing (playwriting, musical theatre, screenwriting, teleplay writing) through departments of Theatre, English, Communication, or Film Studies.

Most courses are intended to contribute to an undergraduate Liberal Arts degree (Bachelor of Arts) or a graduate degree (Master of Arts in Theatre, Master of Fine Arts in Playwriting, or Doctor of Philosophy). These courses are also offered as "electives" for students in all areas of study who are interested in dramatic writing.

For all writers of all ages who want to learn new skills or "brush up" their techniques without investing the time and energy necessary to pursue a college degree, however, other options are available. A number of playwriting courses are open to "auditors," students who attend lectures and may be allowed to participate in class discussions and to complete class assignments but do not receive a grade or credit. Auditors pay a fee rather than regular tuition, and they are not entitled to the same share of the teacher's attention as fully enrolled students. "Special students" are also welcome in a number of the courses we list. These are fully enrolled students who take a course for a grade and receive official credit but are not at present applying the course toward a degree.

Many of the teachers listed in this section also teach students through "independent study," in which the student meets individually with the professor to receive instruction and completes specific assignments for a grade and course credit.

In this section, we provide general information on more than 100 playwriting programs--information which we have received directly from the professors themselves. For more detailed information and advice, we suggest contacting the professor whose name appears in the listing, or the "Director of Playwriting."

College and University Playwriting Programs

AMHERST COLLEGE - DEPT. OF THEATRE & DRAMA
Amherst, MA 01002 (413) 542-2411 Contact: Prof. Constance Congdon **Program:** undergraduate courses and playwriting studio with possible production and advanced independent study

APPALACHIAN STATE UNIV. -THEATRE & DANCE DEPT.
Boone, NC 28608 (704) 262-3028 Contact: Prof. Ed Pilkington **Program:** 1 undergraduate course with in-class readings

ARIZONA STATE UNIVERSITY - THEATRE DEPT.
Box 872002, Tempe, AZ 85287 (602) 965-5359 FAX (602) 965-5351 Contact: Prof. Guillermo Reyes **Program:** undergraduate/graduate courses: in-class/staged readings, workshop productions, possible full productions; 3-year MFA: screenwriting, literary management courses; possible ACTF entry; graduate students work with actors

BATES COLLEGE - DEPT. OF THEATRE & RHETORIC
Lewiston, ME 04240 (207) 786-6257 Contact: Prof. L. Pope **Program:** undergraduate course with workshop productions and public readings

BOSTON UNIVERSITY - ENGLISH DEPT.
Boston, MA 02215 (617) 353-5899 Contact: Prof. Derek Walcott **Program:** MA: 4 workshops, staged readings, possible productions

BOSTON UNIVERSITY - SCHOOL OF THEATRE ARTS
Boston, MA 02215 (617) 353-3390 Contact: Prof. Jonathan Lipsky **Program:** 1 undergraduate course

BRANDEIS UNIVERSITY - THEATRE ARTS DEPT.
Waltham, MA 02154 (781) 736-3340 Contact: Prof. Arthur Holmberg **Program:** MFA: 2-year program with possible full productions

BRIDGEWATER STATE COLLEGE - THEATRE ARTS
Bridgewater, MA 02325 (508) 697-1348 Contact: Prof. Stephen Levine **Program:** 2 undergraduate courses; independent study, staged readings

BRIGHAM YOUNG UNIVERSITY - THEATRE DEPT.
D581 HFAC, Provo, UT 84602 (801) 378-6645 Contact: Prof. Tim Slover **Program:** undergraduate beginning and advanced courses with staged readings; Playwrights Workshop: seminar, possible production

BRISTOL COMMUNITY COLLEGE - THEATRE DEPT.
777 Elsbree St., Fall River, MA 02720 (508) 678-2811 Ext. 2440 Contact: Prof. Rylan Brenner **Program:** 1 undergraduate course; script development in studio theatre encouraged

BROWN UNIVERSITY - ENGLISH DEPT.
Providence, RI 02912 (401) 863-3260 Contact: Prof. Charles Mee **Program:** 11 courses with in-class/staged readings; BA in Creative Writing; MFA: workshop production of thesis; Great American Play Bake-Off

CARNEGIE MELLON UNIVERSITY - SCHOOL OF DRAMA
Pittsburgh, PA 15213 (412) 268-2392 Contact: Prof. Milan Stitt **Program:** MFA: 2-year program with possible production

CASE WESTERN RESERVE UNIV. - THEATRE ARTS DEPT.
10900 Euclid Ave., Cleveland, OH 44106 (216) 368-2858 Contact: Prof. John Orlock **Program:** undergraduate/graduate course; independent study leading to staged readings of full-length plays

CATHOLIC UNIVERSITY OF AMERICA - DEPT. OF DRAMA
Washington, DC 20064 (202) 319-5358 e-mail cua_drama@cua.edu **Contact:** Prof. William Foeller **Program:** 3-year MFA: workshop production; company-based program includes actors, directors, dramaturgs

CLEMSON UNIVERSITY - PERFORMING ARTS DEPT.
221 Brooks Ctr., Clemson, SC 29634 (864) 656-3043 FAX (864) 656-1013 e-mail sraymon@clemson.edu **Contact:** Prof. Raymond Sawyer **Program:** undergraduate/graduate courses; workshops with staged readings; possible production; New Plays Premiere: readings of plays from advanced workshop; MA in English with production of thesis play

COLGATE UNIVERSITY - THEATRE PROGRAM
13 Oak Dr., Hamilton, NY 13346 (315) 228-7639 FAX (315) 228-7002 e-mail jlevy@center.colgate.edu **Contact:** Prof. Jacques Levy, Director, Theatre Program **Program:** 1 undergraduate course with in-class readings and studio productions; independent study courses

COLLEGE OF CHARLESTON - DEPT. OF THEATRE
Charleston, SC 29424 (803) 953-8149 FAX (803) 953-8210 e-mail ashleyf.@cofc.com **Contact:** Dr. Franklin Ashley **Program:** undergraduate intro course with staged readings, workshop, emphasis on short plays, possible ACTF entry; Playwriting II and III courses emphasize longer plays, entry in ATHE New Play Competition; "several students have published and won 1st prize in ATHE and ACTF competitions"

COLLEGE OF WILLIAM & MARY - THEATRE & SPEECH
Williamsburg, VA 23187-8795 (757) 221-2656 Contact: Prof. Louis E. Catron **Program:** 4 undergraduate courses with in-class readings, possible workshop and studio productions; advanced writers may write TV scripts; playwriting is taught every semester

COLLEGE OF WOOSTER - THEATRE DEPT.
Wooster, OH 44691 (330) 263-2028 Contact: Prof. Dale Shield **Program:** 1 undergraduate course with possible workshop production; advanced independent study with staged readings

COLUMBIA UNIVERSITY - THEATRE ARTS DEPT.
605 Dodge Hall, New York, NY 10027 (212) 854-3408 FAX (212) 854-3344 e-mail DKS13@Columbia.edu **Contact:** Prof. Eduardo Machado **Program:** many undergraduate and 4 graduate courses with in-class and

staged readings, workshop and full productions; MFA: 3-year program which includes participation in New Works Program (fully staged productions) and internships with New York theatres

CORNELL UNIVERSITY - THEATRE DEPT.
430 College Ave., Ithaca, NY 14850 (607) 254-2700 FAX (607) 254-2733 e-mail rgw6@postoffice3.mail.cornell.edu **Contact:** Prof. Ronald Wilson **Program:** 2 undergraduate courses with in-class and staged readings; advanced independent study

DARTMOUTH COLLEGE - DRAMA DEPT.
Hanover, NH 03755 (603) 646-3104 Contact: Prof. Peter Parnell **Program:** undergraduate intro and advanced courses; possible independent study and staged readings; spring playwriting contest

DEPAUL UNIVERSITY - THE THEATRE SCHOOL
2135 N. Kenmore, Chicago, IL 60614 (773) 325-7999 FAX (773) 325-7920 e-mail mmeltzer@wppost.depaul.edu **Contact:** Prof. Dean Corrin **Program:** BFA in playwriting: 3 undergraduate courses; in-class readings, workshop productions, staged readings at Chicago Dramatists, new play festivals, possible mainstage productions; independent study

DUKE UNIVERSITY - DRAMA PROGRAM
Durham, NC 27708 (919) 660-3343 Contact: Prof. Erin Wilson **Program:** undergraduate intro and advanced playwriting with possible workshops; New Works for Stage: campus-wide spring festival

EASTERN MICHIGAN UNIVERSITY - THEATRE DEPT.
Ypsilanti, MI 48197 (734) 487-1220 Contact: Prof. Annette Martin **Program:** 2 undergraduate (one-acts) and 2 graduate (full-length plays) courses: intro and advanced playwriting workshop; in-class and staged readings; 3 student plays selected in annual contest

EMERSON COLLEGE - THEATRE DEPT.
100 Beacon St., Boston, MA 02116 (617) 824-8500 Contact: Prof. Miles Coiner **Program:** undergraduate intro course; graduate advanced course; possible workshop and Festival of New Plays

FLORIDA ATLANTIC UNIVERSITY - DEPT. OF THEATRE
Boca Raton, FL 33431 (561) 297-3000 Contact: Prof. Thomas Atkins **Program:** 1 undergraduate course with in-class readings

FLORIDA STATE UNIVERSITY - SCHOOL OF THEATRE
Tallahassee, FL 32306-1160 (850) 644-6795 Contact: Dr. Frank Trezza, Academic Dean **Program:** 1 undergraduate course; play and screenwriting also taught in English Dept., screenwriting in Film Dept.

GODDARD COLLEGE - THEATRE DEPT.
Box 98, Plainfield, VT 05667 (800) 468-4888 Contact: Admissions **Program:** undergraduate/graduate courses in playwriting and screenwriting; MFA in writing

GOUCHER COLLEGE - THEATRE DEPT.
1021 Dulaney Valley Rd., Towson, MD 21204 (410) 337-6275 FAX (410) 336-6411 e-mail msimoncu@goucher.edu **Contact:** Prof. Michael Curry **Program:** 2-courses with in-class and staged readings, workshop productions, possible full productions; emphasis on short plays; possible entry in ACTF and other contests; courses in screenwriting with possible video production; independent study; auditors, special students welcome

GRAMBLING STATE UNIV. - DEPT. OF SPEECH & THEATRE
Grambling, LA 71245 (318) 274-2732 Contact: Prof. A. Williams **Program:** undergraduate course with in-class and staged readings

HOPE COLLEGE - DEPT. OF THEATRE
Holland, MI 49422-9000 (616) 395-7600 FAX (616) 395-7922 e-mail tammi@hope.edu **Contact:** Prof. John K. Tammi **Program:** 3 undergraduate courses with possible readings, staged readings, workshops and full productions; offered jointly with Dept. of English

HUMBOLDT STATE UNIV. - THEATRE ARTS DEPT.
Arcata, CA 95521 (707) 826-3566 FAX (707) 826-5494 e-mail mcelrath @laurel.humboldt.edu **Contact:** Prof. Margaret Thomas Kelso, Head, Dramatic Writing Program **Program:** MFA: 3-year program with guaranteed production; 7 courses with readings, staged readings, workshop productions; possible ACTF entry

INDIANA UNIVERSITY - DEPT. OF THEATRE & DRAMA
Bloomington, IN 47405 (812) 855-4503 Contact: Prof. Dennis J. Reardon **Program:** 2 courses with in-class readings; MFA with possible minimal-budget production; emphasis on acting/directing students

INDIANA UNIV. OF PENNSYLVANIA - THEATRE DEPT.
104 Waller Hall, Indiana, PA 15705 (724) 357-2965 FAX (724) 357-7899 Contact: Prof. Ed Simpson **Program:** 1 undergraduate course with readings, staged readings, possible workshop and full productions

ITHACA COLLEGE - THEATRE ARTS DEPT.
Ithaca, NY 14850 (607) 274-3345 Contact: Chair **Program:** 2 undergraduate courses with in-class/staged readings, workshop productions

KANSAS STATE UNIVERSITY - THEATRE PROGRAM
Nichols Hall 129, Manhattan, KS 66506 (913) 532-6875 Contact: Prof. Carl Hinrichs **Program:** 1 undergraduate course; advanced undergraduate/graduate course; possible staged reading in Sunday series

KENT STATE UNIV. - SCHOOL OF THEATRE & DANCE
Kent, OH 44242 (330) 672-2082 Contact: Prof. Marya Bednerik **Program:** undergraduate and graduate courses with in-class and staged readings and workshop and full productions; possible entry in competitions; independent study in playwriting and other genres

LOUISIANA STATE UNIVERSITY - DEPT. OF THEATRE
217 Music & Dramatic Arts, Baton Rouge, LA 70803 (504) 388-4174, -3537 FAX (504) 388-4135 e-mail theuba@lsuvm.snec.lsu.ed **Contact:** Dr. Femi Euba **Program:** 3-year MFA; 1 graduate and 2 undergraduate courses: readings, staged readings; possible entry in competitions; Intro to Writing Plays, Advanced Writing Plays; independent study; auditors, special students welcome; Theatre and English Depts. offer courses

LOYOLA UNIVERSITY - DRAMA & SPEECH DEPT.
New Orleans, LA 70118 (504) 865-3840 FAX (504) 865-2284 e-mail ferlita@beta.loyno.edu **Contact:** Prof. Ernest Ferlita **Program:** undergraduate course with in-class readings; emphasis on playwright's journal and short plays

MARS HILL COLLEGE - DEPT. OF THEATRE ARTS
Mars Hill, NC 28754 (704) 689-1203 Contact: Prof. C. Robert Jones **Program:** undergraduate course with emphasis on one-acts; advanced course with possible production

MARYMOUNT MANHATTAN COLLEGE - THEATRE DEPT.
221 E. 71st St., New York, NY 10021 (212) 517-0475 Contact: Playwriting Program **Program:** 1 course with staged readings

MASSACHUSETTS INSTITUTE OF TECHNOLOGY - MUSIC & THEATER ARTS DEPT.
14N-307 Cambridge, MA 02142 (617) 253-3210 Contact: Prof. Janet Sonenberg **Program:** 2 undergraduate courses (intro to playwriting; workshop) with in-class and staged readings, possible studio production; emphasis on one-acts; independent study; auditors and special students welcome

McMURRAY UNIVERSITY - THEATRE DEPT.
Abilene, TX 79697 (915) 691-6302, -6200 Contact: Prof. Charles Hukill **Program:** 2 undergraduate courses with in-class readings, possible workshop and full productions

MIAMI UNIVERSITY - THEATRE DEPT.
131 CPA, Oxford, OH 45056 (513) 529-3053 Contact: Prof. Howard Blanning **Program:** BA and MA with focus in playwriting; workshop production of thesis play

MICHIGAN STATE UNIVERSITY - DEPT. OF ENGLISH
East Lansing, MI 48824 (517) 355-7570 FAX (517) 353-3755 Contact: Prof. Arthur Athanason **Program:** 1 undergraduate course and 1 graduate course (one-acts) with weekly scenes receiving occasional in-class readings and staged readings; possible tutorial/independent study

MIDDLEBURY COLLEGE - THEATRE & DANCE DEPT.
Middlebury, VT 05753 (802) 443-5600 Contact: Prof. Douglas Sprigg **Program:** undergraduate intro to playwriting with class readings; possible independent study and workshop productions

MINOT STATE UNIVERSITY - DRAMA DEPT.
Minot, ND 58707 (701) 858-3171 FAX (701) 858-3894 e-mail davidsoc @warple.cs.misu.nodak.edu **Contact:** Prof. Conrad Davidson **Program:** 1 undergraduate course with in-class readings, possible workshop production, possible ACTF entry; emphasis on short plays; independent study; auditors and special students welcome

MONTCLAIR STATE UNIV. - DEPT. OF THEATRE & DANCE
Upper Montclair, NJ 07043 (973) 655-4217 Contact: Dr. Ramon Delgado **Program:** 1 undergraduate course (one-acts): in-class readings

NEW MEXICO STATE UNIVERSITY - ENGLISH DEPT.
Box 30001, Dept. 3E, Las Cruces, NM 88003 (505) 646-3931 Contact: Prof. Denise Chávez **Program:** 1 undergraduate and 1 graduate course with in-class readings and possible staged readings; auditors and special students welcome

NEW YORK UNIVERSITY - TISCH SCHOOL OF THE ARTS
719 Broadway 8th Fl. New York, NY 10003 (212) 998-1940 FAX (212) 995-4069 Contact: Prof. Gary Garrison, Assoc. Chair **Program:** degrees in dramatic writing; BFA: 15 undergraduate courses, Thesis Readings; MFA: 22 graduate courses, Graduate Reading Series, Marathon Festival of New Work (1st year), Thesis Readings; also 2 festivals of Equity-Approved Showcases; Ten-Minute Play Festival, Screenplay Festival, Festival of New Works, Provincetown Playhouse Festival

NEW YORK UNIVERSITY - TISCH SCHOOL OF THE ARTS
MUSICAL THEATRE 111 Second Ave. #5M, New York, NY 10003 (212) 998-1830 FAX (212) 533-0299 e-mail musical.theatre@nyu.edu **Contact:** Marie Costanza, Admin. Director 2-year course for lyricists, composers, and librettists, leading to an MFA degree

NORTH CAROLINA A & T STATE UNIVERSITY -
THEATRE DIVISION Greensboro, NC 27411 (336) 334-7852 Contact: Prof. Samuel Hay **Program:** undergraduate intro course with in-house readings; possible staged readings

NORTHEASTERN UNIVERSITY - DEPT. OF THEATRE
360 Huntington Ave., Boston, MA 02115 (617) 373-2244 Contact: Prof. Ed Bullins **Program:** 1 undergraduate course

NORTHERN KENTUCKY UNIVERSITY - THEATRE DEPT.
Highland Heights, KY 41099 (606) 572-5560 Contact: Prof. Joe Conger **Program:** undergraduate course with possible staged reading

THE OHIO STATE UNIVERSITY - THEATRE DEPT.
Columbus, OH 43210 (614) 292-5821 Contact: Guest Playwright, Thurber House **Program:** undergraduate/graduate course without production

OREGON STATE UNIVERSITY - THEATRE ARTS DEPT.

Corvallis, OR 97331-3505 (541) 737-4920 Contact: Prof. Harry Mac-Cormack **Program:** 1 undergraduate course, 1 graduate course with in-class readings, studio productions; possible full production; possible entry in ACTF and other contests; MA: emphasis on playwriting; 1 screenwriting course; independent study; auditors, special students welcome

PENNSYLVANIA STATE UNIVERSITY - THEATRE DEPT.

103 Arts Bldg., University Park, PA 16802 (814) 865-7586 Contact: Prof. Charles Dumas **Program:** undergraduate/graduate beginning course with emphasis on one-act plays

PURCHASE COLLEGE, STATE UNIV. OF NEW YORK DRAMA STUDIES DEPT. **Purchase, NY 10577-1400 (914) 251-6570 Contact:** Prof. Julius Novick **Program:** 2 courses with in-class readings, possible productions; independent study

PURCHASE COLLEGE, STATE UNIV. OF NEW YORK - DRAMATIC WRITING DEPT. **735 Anderson Hill Rd., Purchase, NY 10577 (914) 251-6500 FAX (914) 251-6559 Contact:** Prof. Julius Novick **Program:** 4-year BA: courses in all dramatic writing genres; in-class/staged readings, workshop/studio productions; independent study

QUEENS COLLEGE, CITY UNIV. OF NEW YORK - THEATRE DEPT. **65-30 Kissena Blvd., Flushing, NY 11367 (718) 997-3090 Contact:** Prof. Ralph G. Allen **Program:** 1 undergraduate course with in-class readings

RADFORD UNIVERSITY - THEATRE DEPT.

Radford, VA 24142 (540) 831-5207 Contact: Prof. Jerry McGlon **Program:** undergraduate beginning and advanced courses with possible staged readings and workshop productions

RUTGERS UNIVERSITY - THEATRE ARTS DEPT.

Mason Gross School, New Brunswick, NJ 08903 (732) 932-8225 Contact: Prof. Roger Cornish **Program:** 2 undergraduate courses; 3-year MFA: 13 playwriting courses, full production (with 1-week run) of at least 1 one-act (1st & 2nd year) and of full-length thesis play (3rd year)

SMITH COLLEGE - DEPT. OF THEATRE

Northampton, MA 01063 (413) 585-3206 e-mail lberkman@smith. smith.edu **Contact:** Prof. Leonard Berkman **Program:** 2 undergraduate and 4 graduate courses and independent studies with in-class and staged readings and possible workshop and full productions; BA including playwriting emphasis; MFA in playwriting; for admission forms: Smith College Graduate Studies Office, Northampton, MA 01063

SOUTHERN ILLINOIS UNIVERSITY - THEATRE DEPT.

Carbondale, IL 62901 (618) 453-5747 Contact: Dr. David Rush **Program:** 2 undergraduate and 4 graduate courses (including musical theatre, TV- and screenwriting) with in-class and staged readings, workshop and studio productions; possible ACTF entry; 3-year MFA with full production in Summer New Plays Series; PhD with creative dissertation; independent study; correspondence courses

SOUTHERN METHODIST UNIVERSITY - THEATRE DEPT.
Meadows School of the Arts, Dallas, TX 75275 (214) 768-2937 FAX (214) 768-1136 e-mail gesmith@mail.smu.edu **Contact:** Dr. Gretchen Smith **Program:** BFA in theatre arts with playwriting focus; 4 courses with in-class and staged readings and possible workshop and mainstage productions; also Spring Festival of New Plays

SOUTHWEST STATE UNIV. - THEATRE ARTS PROGRAM
Marshall, MN 56258 (507) 537-7103 Contact: Dr. William Hezlep **Program:** 2 undergraduate courses with in-class readings and workshop productions

SOUTHWEST TEXAS STATE UNIV. - THEATRE DEPT.
San Marcos, TX 78666 (512) 245-2147 Contact: Prof. Charles Pascoe **Program:** undergraduate/graduate course; independent study; possible staged readings

STATE UNIV. OF NEW YORK - ALBANY - THEATRE DEPT.
PAC 262, Albany, NY 12222 (518) 442-4200 Contact: Prof. James Farrell **Program:** 1 undergraduate/graduate course with in-class readings; space for student-initiated productions

STATE UNIV. OF NEW YORK AT STONY BROOK -
DEPT. OF THEATRE Stony Brook, NY 11794 (516) 632-7300 Contact: Prof. Jonathan Levy **Program:** undergraduate course in play analysis; graduate course in playwriting

STEPHEN F. AUSTIN STATE UNIV. - THEATRE DEPT.
P.O. Box 9090 SFA Sta., Nacogdoches, TX 75962-9090 (409) 468-4003, (888) 722-3396 FAX (409) 468-7601 e-mail anielsen@sfasu.edu **Contact:** Prof. Alan Nielsen **Program:** 3 undergraduate/graduate courses (playwriting, screenwriting) with in-class and staged readings; possible workshop, studio, and full productions; emphasis on one-acts; independent study; special students welcome

TEXAS A & M UNIVERSITY - THEATRE PROGRAM
College Station, TX 77843 (409) 845-2588 Contact: Prof. Steven DeKorne **Program:** 1 undergraduate course with in-class readings and possible production

TEXAS A & M UNIVERSITY AT COMMERCE -
COMMUNICATION & THEATRE Performing Arts Ctr., Commerce, TX 75429-3011 (903) 886-5346 FAX (903) 458-3280 e-mail John_Hanners@tamu-Commerce.edu **Contact:** Prof. John Hanners **Program:** 1 undergraduate/graduate course with in-class/staged readings,

possible workshop, studio, and mainstage productions; possible ACTF entry; play development; independent study; auditors, special students welcome; opportunities through Texas A&M System Theatre Institute

UNIVERSITY OF ARIZONA - DEPT. OF THEATRE ARTS
Tucson, AZ 85721 (602) 621-7008 Contact: Prof. William Lang **Program:** 1 undergraduate/graduate course without production

UNIVERSITY OF ARKANSAS - DEPT. OF DRAMA
Fayetteville, AR 72701 (501) 575-2953, 521-0123 FAX (501) 575-7602 Contact: Prof. Roger Gross **Program:** 3 undergraduate courses with staged readings; 3-year MFA with staged readings and guaranteed production of thesis play; possible ACTF entry

UNIVERSITY OF CALIFORNIA L.A. - THEATRE DIVISION
405 Hilgard Ave., Los Angeles, CA 90024 (310) 206-6874 Contact: Profs. Edit Villareal, Gary Gardner, Carol Sorgenfrei **Program:** 4 undergraduate courses; MFA: 7-quarter core program with staged reading, "rehearsal condition production"; guest playwrights and screenwriters

UNIVERSITY OF CALIFORNIA AT SAN DIEGO -
DEPT OF THEATRE La Jolla, CA 92093 (619) 534-3791 Contact: Prof. Adele Shank **Program:** undergraduate courses, 2 advanced workshops, possible production; 3-year MFA with guaranteed productions

UNIVERSITY OF CALIFORNIA, SANTA BARBARA -
DEPT. OF DRAMATIC ART Santa Barbara, CA 93106 (805) 893-8303 FAX (805) 893-3242 e-mail potter@humanitas.ucsb.edu **Contact:** Prof. Robert Potter **Program:** BA in Dramatic Art with playwriting emphasis: 1-year course (intro, advanced playwriting, workshop) with in-class/staged readings, mini-productions; possible production in festival; screenwriting available through Dept. of Film Studies; MA in Dramatic Art, Playwriting, Dramaturgy; submit script with application

UNIVERSITY OF EVANSVILLE - THEATRE DEPT.
Evansville, IN 47722 (812) 479-2937 e-mail sl29@evansville.edu **Contact:** Prof. Scott Lank **Program:** 1 undergraduate course with in-class and staged readings, possible workshop and studio productions; possible entry in ACTF and other competitions; screenwriting; independent study; auditors and special students welcome

UNIVERSITY OF FLORIDA - DEPT. OF THEATRE
Gainesville, FL 32611 (352) 392-2038 FAX (352) 392-5114 e-mail rer @nervm.nerdc.ufl.edu **Contact:** Prof. Ralf Remshardt **Program:** 1 undergraduate course with in-class/staged readings; student showcases; Dept. offers Judi Ann Mason Playwriting Prize: $500

UNIVERSITY OF GEORGIA - THEATRE DEPT.
Athens, GA 30602 (706) 542-2836 Contact: Prof. Stanley Longman **Program:** MFA in dramatic writing with thesis production

UNIVERSITY OF HOUSTON - SCHOOL OF THEATRE

Houston, TX 77204 (713) 743-3003 FAX (713) 749-1420 e-mail sju dice@uh.edu Contact: Prof. Sidney Berger Program: 3-tier program taught by Edward Albee: basic-advanced playwriting, possible production with inclusion in festival; possible production by Houston theatres

UNIVERSITY OF IOWA - DEPT. OF THEATRE ARTS

Iowa City, IA 52242 (319) 353-2401 Contact: Prof. Art Burreca Program: 3-year MFA with production workshops and festival

UNIVERSITY OF KANSAS - DEPT. OF THEATRE & FILM

Lawrence, KS 66045 (913) 864-3381 FAX (913) 864-5251 e-mail rwillis@kuhub.cc.unans,edu Contact: Prof. Ronald A. Willis Program: undergraduate intro; undergraduate/graduate advanced course with in-class readings; possible staged readings, workshop and full productions

UNIVERSITY OF KENTUCKY - THEATRE DEPT.

114 Fine Arts Bldg., Lexington, KY 40506 (606) 257-3297 Contact: Prof. James W. Rodgers Program: undergraduate/graduate course with possible studio production and ACTF entry

UNIVERSITY OF MAINE - THEATRE/DANCE DIVISION

School of Performing Arts, 1944 Hall, Orono, ME 04469 (207) 581-4700 FAX (207) 581-4701 e-mail miko@maine.maine.edu Contact: Prof. Thomas J. Mikotowicz Program: undergraduate/graduate course, in-class readings

UNIVERSITY OF MARYLAND-BALTIMORE -

THEATRE DEPT. Baltimore, MD 21228 (410) 455-2917 Contact: Prof. Wendy Salkind Program: undergraduate courses, staged readings

UNIVERSITY OF MASSACHUSETTS - DEPT. OF THEATRE

Amherst, MA 01003 (413) 545-3490 Contact: Prof. Virginia Scott Program: extensive undergraduate coursework leading to Dramatic Discovery: spring festival of student plays

UNIVERSITY OF MEMPHIS - THEATRE & DANCE DEPT.

Memphis, TN 38152 (901) 678-2523 FAX (901) 678-4331 e-mail theatrelib@tcc.memphis.edu Contact: Prof. Stephen Hancock Program: 1 repeatable undergraduate course with possible staged readings; 3 graduate courses and workshop with possible production

UNIVERSITY OF MICHIGAN - FLINT - THEATRE DEPT.

CROB 238, Flint, MI 48502-2186 (810) 762-3230 e-mail friesen_l@crob.flint.umich.edu Contact: Prof. Lauren D. Friesen Program: 1 repeatable undergraduate course, staged reading, possible black box production, possible ACTF entry; possible expansion of theatre courses

UNIVERSITY OF MISSOURI - THEATRE ARTS DEPT.

Columbia, MO 65211 (573) 882-2021 Contact: Prof. David Crespy Program: 2 undergraduate courses with possible production

UNIVERSITY OF MISSOURI-KANSAS CITY -
PROFESSIONAL WRITING PROGRAM   University House/
UMKC, 5101 Rockhill Rd., Kansas City, MO 64110-2499 Contact:
Prof. James McKinley **Program:** professional writing program; MA in
stage and screenwriting (33-hour program); limited graduate teaching
assistantships available

UNIVERSITY OF MISSOURI-KANSAS CITY -
DEPT. OF THEATRE **4949 Cherry, Kansas City, MO 64110 (816)
235-2781 FAX (816) 235-5367 e-mail** LondreF@umkc.edu **Contact:** Prof.
Felicia Londré **Program:** undergraduate/graduate courses; possible
independent study; staged readings; MA with possible thesis production

UNIVERSITY OF NEBRASKA - DEPT. OF THEATRE ARTS
Lincoln, NE 68588   (402) 472-2072   Contact: Prof. Tice Miller
Program: undergraduate courses: intro and advanced playwriting

UNIVERSITY OF NEVADA LAS VEGAS -
DEPT. OF THEATRE ARTS **Las Vegas, NV 89154 (702) 895-4340**
Contact: Prof. Julie Jensen **Program:** 3-year MFA including seminar
workshop; staged readings, possible full production of full-length plays

UNIVERSITY OF NEW HAMPSHIRE - DEPT. OF THEATRE
Paul CAC, 30 College Rd., Durham, NH 03824 Contact: Prof. Gay
Nordene **Program:** undergraduate courses, possible productions

UNIVERSITY OF NEW MEXICO - DEPT. OF THEATRE
Albuquerque, NM 87131 (505) 277-4332 e-mail digby@unm.edu
Contact: Prof. Digby Wolfe **Program:** 2 undergraduate/graduate
courses (including other genres) with in-class and staged readings; MFA
with possible mainstage production; possible entry in competitions;
independent study; auditors and special students welcome

UNIVERSITY OF NORTH CAROLINA - DRAMATIC ART
Chapel Hill, NC 27599   (919) 962-1132   Contact: Prof. Tom Huey
Program: 2 undergraduate courses with possible staged readings

UNIVERSITY OF NORTH CAROLINA GREENSBORO -
THEATRE DIV.   **Greensboro, NC 27412 (336) 334-5191 Contact:**
Prof. Alan Cook **Program:** 1 undergraduate course with in-class and
staged readings, possible workshops; emphasis on one-acts; possible
ACTF entry; independent study

UNIVERSITY OF NORTH DAKOTA - THEATRE ARTS
Grand Forks, ND 58202 (701) 777-2888 Contact: Prof. Ronald Engle
Program: beginning-advanced undergraduate course

UNIVERSITY OF OKLAHOMA - SCHOOL OF DRAMA
Norman, OK 73019 (405) 325-4021 Contact: Prof. Steven Wallace
Program: 1 graduate course without production

UNIVERSITY OF SOUTH DAKOTA - THEATRE DEPT.

Vermillion, SD 57069 (605) 677-5418 FAX (605) 677-5988 Contact: Prof. Kenneth Robbins **Program:** 3 undergraduate, 4 graduate courses: in-class/staged readings, possible workshop productions; graduate seminar; MA: playwriting emphasis, possible ACTF entry; Beer & Cheerios Playwriting Society; Wayne S. Knutson Award: $500 to student writers

UNIVERSITY OF SOUTHERN CALIFORNIA - SCHOOL OF THEATRE Los Angeles, CA 90089 (213) 740-1285

Contact: Prof. Velina Houston **Program:** MFA: 2-year program with workshop production of full-length play

UNIVERSITY OF SOUTHERN INDIANA - THEATRE DEPT.

Evansville, IN 47712 (812) 465-1668 Contact: Prof. Elliot Wasserman **Program:** intro and advanced courses; possible staged reading

UNIVERSITY OF SOUTHERN MAINE - THEATRE DEPT.

Gorham, ME 04038 (207) 780-5480 Contact: Prof. Walter Stump **Program:** 2 undergraduate courses; staged readings, possible production

UNIVERSITY OF TEXAS - DEPT. OF THEATRE & DANCE

Austin, TX 78712 (512) 471-5793 FAX (512) 471-0824 e-mail mklut ringer@mail.utexas.edu **Contact:** Prof. David Mark Cohen **Program:** 6 undergraduate, 7 graduate courses: in-class/staged readings, possible workshop, studio, mainstage productions; 3-year MFA: production; possible entry in ACTF; independent study; TV and screenwriting available

UNIVERSITY OF TEXAS AT EL PASO - THEATRE DEPT.

Fox FAC, El Paso, TX 79968 (915) 747-7854 FAX (915) 747-5438 Contact: Dept. Chair **Program:** beginning and advanced courses with in-class and public readings, annual productions

UNIVERSITY OF TOLEDO - THEATRE PROGRAM

Center for Performing Arts, Toledo, OH 43606 (419) 537-2202 Contact: Prof. Christine Child **Program:** 3 undergraduate courses with daily in-class readings, staged readings, possible workshop productions

UNIVERSITY OF VIRGINIA - DEPT. OF DRAMA

Charlottesville, VA 22903 (804) 924-8971 Contact: Prof. L. Douglas Grissom **Program:** undergraduate intro and workshop, possible production; 3-year MFA with possible full production of thesis play

UNIVERSITY OF WYOMING - THEATRE & DANCE DEPT.

Laramie, WY 82071 (307) 766-2198 e-mail downs@uwyo.edu **Contact:** Prof. Bill Downs **Program:** BFA in playwriting/directing; readings, workshop and full productions; possible ACTF entry

VASSAR COLLEGE - DEPT. OF DRAMA

Poughkeepsie, NY 12601 (914) 437-5594 Contact: Prof. James B. Steerman **Program:** undergraduate course in dramatic writing; independent study with staged readings and workshop productions

VILLANOVA UNIVERSITY - THEATRE DEPT.

Villanova, PA 19085 (610) 519-4760 Contact: Prof. Michael Hollinger **Program:** graduate course, independent study with possibility of produced play which may be substituted for MA thesis

WABASH COLLEGE - DEPT. OF THEATRE

Crawfordsville, IN 47933 (765) 361-6342 e-mail WatsonD@Wabash. edu **Contact:** Prof. Dwight E. Watson **Program:** undergraduate intro course (one-acts) with in-class readings, possible public readings and workshop productions

WAKE FOREST UNIVERSITY - THEATRE ARTS DEPT.

Winston-Salem, NC 27109 (336) 758-5294 Contact: Prof. John E. R. Friedenberg **Program:** 1 undergraduate workshop; possible staged reading and/or full production

WARREN WILSON COLLEGE - THEATRE DEPT.

Asheville, NC 28815 (704) 298-3325 Ext. 349 Contact: Prof. Edward G. Bierhaus **Program:** undergraduate intro course with in-class and staged readings, possible workshop production

WASHINGTON UNIVERSITY - PERFORMING ARTS DEPT.

St. Louis, MO 63130 (314) 935-5858 Contact: Prof. Patricia Cobey **Program** 1 undergraduate course, 1 graduate workshop: in-class/staged readings; possible full production, possible "Best Play Award"

WAYNE STATE UNIVERSITY - THEATRE DEPT.

95 W. Hancock, Detroit, MI 48202 (313) 577-3508 Contact: Prof. David Magidson **Program:** 1 undergraduate and 2 graduate courses with in-class and staged readings, workshop and studio productions; possible ACTF entry; screenplay and teleplay courses; independent study; auditors and special students welcome

♫ WESTERN MICHIGAN UNIV.-ENGLISH DEPT.

Kalamazoo, MI 49008 (616) 387-2572 FAX (616) 387-2562 e-mail arniejohnston@wmich.edu **Contact:** Prof. Arnie Johnston, Chair **Program:** 2+ undergraduate courses (one-acts), 2+ graduate courses (one-acts, full-lengths); courses are repeatable; seminars in musicals, screenplays, teleplays; in-class readings; possible staged readings, workshop, studio, mainstage productions; auditors, special students welcome; 2-3 year MFA, BA with playwriting emphasis, Ph.D. with creative dissertation; thesis plays receive staged reading, possible studio production, possible contest entry; opportunities at local theatres

WESTERN WASHINGTON UNIV. - THEATRE ARTS DEPT.

Bellingham, WA 98225 (360) 650-3876 Contact: Prof. Thomas E. Ward **Program:** 5 undergraduate courses and graduate courses with in-class readings and possible workshop and full productions; 10± new plays by students receive staged readings each year in New Playwright Theatre series

WICHITA STATE UNIVERSITY - DIVISION OF THEATRE
Wichita, KS 67208 (316) 978-3368 Contact: Prof. Leroy Clark
Program: undergraduate courses: intro and advanced playwriting with
staged readings; 1 graduate course with workshop production

WILLIAMS COLLEGE - THEATRE DEPT.
1000 Main St., Williamstown, MA 01267 (413) 597-2342 Contact:
Prof. Jean-Bernard Bucky **Program:** 1 undergraduate course with in-
class readings

YALE UNIVERSITY - SCHOOL OF DRAMA
222 York St., New Haven, CT 06520 (203) 432-1505 Contact: Prof.
Mark Bly **Program:** MFA: 3-year program with in-class and staged
readings and guaranteed workshop production each year; possible full
production at Yale School of Drama or Yale Repertory Theatre (see
Theatres); 3rd-year students receive Equity staged reading at Yale Rep

State Arts Councils
and
Commissions

- Notes -

State Arts Councils

State arts councils welcome mail and phone inquiries and will send information on request. Programs offered by the councils (including the grants and fellowships listed below) are exclusively for residents of each particular state. Guidelines and deadlines vary from state to state.

ALABAMA STATE COUNCIL ON THE ARTS
201 Monroe St. (RSA Tower) #110, Montgomery, AL 36104 (334) 242-4076 FAX (334) 240-3269 **Contact:** Bill Bates, Becky Mullen **Program:** $5000 grants **Procedure:** request details **Deadline:** May 1, 1999

ALASKA STATE COUNCIL ON THE ARTS
411 W. 4th Ave. Suite 1E, Anchorage, AK 99501 (907) 269-6610 FAX (907) 269-6601 **Contact:** Shannon Planchon, Grants Officer **Procedure:** phone for information

ARIZONA COMMISSION ON THE ARTS
417 W. Roosevelt St., Phoenix, AZ 85003 (602) 255-5882 FAX (602) 256-0282 **Contact:** Claire West, Performing Arts Director **Program:** $5000-$7000 grants, rotating among disciplines **Procedure:** inquire for guidelines **Deadline:** TBA (Sept. in 1998)

ARKANSAS ARTS COUNCIL
1500 Tower Bldg., 323 Center St., Little Rock, AR 72201 (501) 324-9766 FAX (501) 324-9154 **Contact:** Jess Anthony, Grants Program Mgr. **Program:** grants of up to $10,000 for institutions; $1000 grants for individuals **Procedure:** contact "Artists Information" for details

CALIFORNIA ARTS COUNCIL
1300 I Street Suite 930, Sacramento, CA 95814 (916) 322-6555 FAX (916) 322-6575 **Contact:** Ray Tatar, Program Officer **Program:** fellowships and residencies for playwrights **Procedure:** phone (916) 322-6395 for information on programs

COLORADO COUNCIL ON THE ARTS
750 Pennsylvania St., Denver, CO 80203 (303) 894-2617 FAX (303) 894-2615 **Contact:** Fran Holden, Exec. Director **Program:** Governor's Awards for Excellence in the Arts and individual grants **Procedure:** phone for General Guidelines: (800) 294-2787

CONNECTICUT COMMISSION ON THE ARTS
One Financial Plaza, Hartford, CT 06103 (860) 566-4770 Ext. 307 **Contact:** Linda Dente, Senior Program Mgr. **Program:** grants **Procedure:** request guidelines

DELAWARE DIVISION OF THE ARTS
820 N. French St., Wilmington, DE 19801 (302) 577-8278 **Contact:** Public Information Officer **Program:** Individual Artist Grants ($2000 for emerging artist; $5000 for established artist) **Deadline:** Aug. 1, 1999

DISTRICT OF COLUMBIA COMMISSION ON THE ARTS &
HUMANITIES   410 8th St. NW 5th Fl., Washington, DC 20004
(202) 724-5613 Contact: Carlos Arrien, Program Coord.   Program:
grants of varying amounts Deadline: TBA

FLORIDA DEPT. OF STATE - DIVISION OF CULTURAL
AFFAIRS The Capitol, Tallahassee, FL 32399-0250 (850) 487-2980
FAX (850) 922-5259 Contact: Fellowship Program   Program: annual
fellowships of $5000 Procedure: request application form Deadline:
Jan. 15, 1999

GEORGIA COUNCIL FOR THE ARTS
260 14th St. NW, Atlanta, GA 30318-5360 (404) 651-7920   FAX (404)
685-2787 Contact: Rick George, Program Director Program: grants for
theatres; no individual artist grants in 1999 Deadline: Jan. 15, 1999

HAWAII STATE FOUNDATION ON CULTURE & THE ARTS
44 Merchant St., Honolulu, HI 96813 (808) 586-0300   FAX (808) 586-
0308 Contact: Holly Richards, Exec. Director   Procedure: inquire for
programs supporting theatre

IDAHO COMMISSION ON THE ARTS
P.O. 83720, Boise, ID 83720 (208) 334-2119   FAX (208) 334-2488
Contact: Frederick J. Hebert, Exec. Director; Cort Conley, Literature Pro-
grams Program: grants, fellowships Procedure: inquire for guidelines

ILLINOIS ARTS COUNCIL
James R. Thompson Ctr., 100 W. Randolph St. #10-500, Chicago, IL
60601 (312) 814-6750   FAX (312) 814-1471 Contact: Kassie Davis,
Exec. Director; Alan Leder, Director, Media Arts Program (312) 814-
4990 Program: annual playwriting fellowships   Deadline: Sept. 1,
1999 Procedure: request guidelines; inquire for other programs

INDIANA ARTS COMMISSION
402 W. Washington St. Room 072, Indianapolis, IN 46204-2741
(317) 232-1268   FAX (317) 232-5595   Contact: Dorothy Ilgen, Exec.
Director Program: no individual artist grants available in 1999

IOWA ARTS COUNCIL
600 E. Locust, Capitol Complex, Des Moines, IA 50319-0290 (515)
281-4451   FAX (515) 242-6498   Contact: William H. Jackson, Exec.
Director   Program: Access to Arts Programs for organizations and
individuals   Procedure: call (515) 242-6500

KANSAS ARTS COMMISSION
Jayhawk Tower, 700 SW Jackson Suite 1004, Topeka, KS 66603
(785) 296-3335   FAX (785) 296-4989 Contact: Tom Klocke, Arts
Program Coordinator   Program: mini-fellowships of $500, fellowships
of $5000 Deadline: TBA (Oct.)

KENTUCKY ARTS COUNCIL
31 Fountain Pl., Frankfort, KY 40601 (502) 564-3757 FAX (502) 564-2839 Contact: John Benjamin, Director, Arts and Theatre Program Program: grants and fellowships Procedure: inquire for guidelines

LOUISIANA DIVISION OF THE ARTS
1051 N. 3rd St., P.O. Box 44247, Baton Rouge, LA 70804 (504) 342-8180 FAX (504) 342-8173 Contact: Dee Hamilton, Director, Performing Arts Program Program: grants of $5000; fellowships Deadline: Mar. 2, 1999 for grants; Sept. 1, 1999 for fellowships

MAINE ARTS COMMISSION
State House, Station 25, Augusta, ME 04333 (207) 287-2724 FAX (207) 287-2335 Contact: Kathy Ann Jones, Assoc. for Contemporary Arts Program: biennial (odd years) fellowships of $3000 for playwrights and screenwriters Deadline: Feb. 2, 1999

MARYLAND STATE ARTS COUNCIL
601 N. Howard St. 1st Floor, Baltimore, MD 21201 (410) 767-6555 FAX (410) 333-1062 Contact: Ann Hood, Dance/Theatre Program Director Program: biennial Individual Artist Awards ($1000, $3000, $6000); operating grants for organizations Deadline: TBA (Jul. 1999 for individual artists; Dec. 1999 for organizations)

MASSACHUSETTS CULTURAL COUNCIL
120 Boylston St. 2nd Floor, Boston, MA 02116 (617) 727-3668 Ext. 354 Contact: Michael Brady, Individual Artist Fellowships Program: biennial grants of $7500 Deadline: TBA (Jan. 1999)

MICHIGAN COUNCIL FOR THE ARTS & CULTURAL AFFAIRS
1200 6th St. #1180, Executive Plaza, Detroit, MI 48226 (313) 256-3731 FAX (313) 256-3781 Contact: Betty Boone, Exec. Dir. Program: annual Creative Artists Grants, administered with Arts Found. of MI Procedure: call Kim Adams, ArtServe MI (348) 557-8288

MINNESOTA STATE ARTS BOARD
Park Square Court, 400 Sibley St. Suite 200, St. Paul, MN 55101 (612) 215-1600 FAX (612) 215-1602 Contact: Robert Booker, Exec. Director, Individual Artists Program Program: Playwriting Fellowship of $8000 Deadline: Oct. 1, 1999

MISSISSIPPI ARTS COMMISSION
239 N. Lamar St. #207, Jackson, MS 39201 (601) 359-6030 FAX (601) 359-6008 Contact: Tim Hedgepeth, Program Admin. Program: fellowships of $5000 for individual artists Deadline: Mar. 1, 1999

MISSOURI ARTS COUNCIL
111 N. 7th St. Suite 105, St. Louis, MO 63101 (314) 340-6845 FAX (314) 340-7215 Contact: Michael Hunt, Program Admin., Dance, Music & Lit.erature Procedure: write for "Guide to Programs"

MONTANA ARTS COUNCIL

316 N. Park Ave. Suite 252, Helena, MT 59620 (406) 444-6430 FAX (406) 444-6545 **Contact:** Arlynn Fishbaugh, Exec. Director **Program:** grants and fellowships **Deadline:** TBA

NEBRASKA ARTS COUNCIL

3838 Davenport, Omaha, NE 68131-2329 (402) 595-2122 (402) 595-2334 **Contact:** Jennifer Severin Clark, Exec. Director **Program:** grant and fellowships for artists **Procedure:** request "Grant Book"

NEVADA ARTS COUNCIL

602 N. Curry St., Carson City, NV 89703 (702) 687-6680 **Contact:** Susan Boskoff, Exec. Director **Program:** fellowships of $5000 **Procedure:** inquire for guidelines

NEW HAMPSHIRE STATE COUNCIL ON THE ARTS

40 N. Main St., Phenix Hall, Concord, NH 03301 (603) 271-2789 (603) 271-3584 **Contact:** Audrey Sylvester, Artist Services Coord. **Program:** annual artists' fellowships **Deadline:** Jul. 1, 1999

NEW JERSEY STATE COUNCIL ON THE ARTS

20 W. State St., P.O. Box 306, Trenton, NJ 08625 (609) 292-6130 FAX (609) 989-1440 **Contact:** Barbara Russo, Exec. Director **Program:** residencies **Procedure:** request "Guide to Programs & Services"

NEW MEXICO ARTS DIVISION

228 E. Palace Ave., Santa Fe, NM 87501 (505) 827-6490 FAX (505) 827-6043 **Contact:** Randy Forrester, Arts Coord. **Program:** funds for organizations or individuals through organizations

NEW YORK STATE COUNCIL ON THE ARTS

915 Broadway, New York, NY 10010 (212) 387-7000 FAX (212) 387-7164 **Contact:** Kathleen Masterson, Director of Literature **Program:** annual grants **Deadline:** Mar. 1, 1999

NORTH CAROLINA ARTS COUNCIL

Dept. of Cultural Resources, Raleigh, NC 27601-2807 (919) 733-2821 FAX (919) 733-4834 **Contact:** Nancy Trovillion, Asst. Director **Program:** playwrights' grants of $8000 **Deadline:** Nov. 1, 1999

NORTH DAKOTA COUNCIL ON THE ARTS

418 E. Broadway Ave. Suite 70, Bismarck, ND 58501-4086 (701) 328-3954 FAX (701) 328-3963 **Contact:** Patsy Thompson, Exec. Director **Program:** grants for professional development

OHIO ARTS COUNCIL

727 E. Main St., Columbus, OH 43205 (614) 466-2613 FAX (614) 466-4494 **Contact:** Jamie Goldstein, Public Information Officer **Program:** grants for individual artists **Procedure:** request guidelines

OKLAHOMA STATE ARTS COUNCIL
2101 N. Lincoln Blvd. #640, P.O. Box 52001-2001, Oklahoma City, OK 73152-2001 (405) 521-2931 FAX (405) 521-6418 Contact: Betty Price, Exec. Director Program: performance space and other support for playwrights Procedure: Shirley Blaske at Individual Artists of OK (405) 232-6060

OREGON ARTS COMMISSION
775 Summer St. NE, Salem, OR 97310 (503) 986-0082 FAX (503) 986-0260 Contact: Michael Faison, Admin. Director Program: biennial grants, fellowships Deadline: TBA for 2000

PENNSYLVANIA COUNCIL ON THE ARTS
Room 216 Finance Bldg., Harrisburg, PA 17120 (717) 787-6883 FAX (717) 783-2538 Contact: Philip Horn, Exec. Director Program: grants of $5000 for playwrights Deadline: Aug. 1, 1999

RHODE ISLAND STATE COUNCIL ON THE ARTS
95 Cedar St. Suite 103, Providence, RI 02903-1062 (401) 222-3880 FAX (401) 521-1351 Contact: Randall Rosenbaum, Exec. Director Program: Fellowships in Literature ($5000, $1000); Requests for Proposals grants Deadline: Apr. 1, 1999 for fellowships; Apr. 1, Oct. 1, 1999 for grants

SOUTH CAROLINA ARTS COMMISSION
1800 Gervais St., Columbia, SC 29201 (803) 734-8696 FAX (803) 734-8526 Contact: Sara June Goldstein Program: Artists Project Support Grants of $1000-$5000; fellowships of $7500 Deadline: Feb. 15, 1999 for fellowships; Apr. 1, 1999 for grants

SOUTH DAKOTA ARTS COUNCIL
State Library, 800 Governor's Dr., Pierre, SD 57501-2294 (605) 773-3131 FAX (605) 773-6962 Contact: Dennis Holub, Exec. Director Program: artist project grants (up to $3000) Deadline: Mar. 1, 1999

TENNESSEE ARTS COMMISSION
401 Charlotte Ave., Nashville, TN 37243-0780 (615) 741-1701 FAX (615) 741-8559 Contact: Rod Reiner, Director, Perf. Arts Program: grants and fellowships Procedure: request "Grants Guidelines Book"

TEXAS COMMISSION ON THE ARTS
P.O. Box 13406 , Austin, TX 78711-3406 (512) 463-5535 Ext. 42334 FAX (512) 475-4887 Contact: Brenda Tharp, Admin. for Performing Arts Program: Artists-in-Schools Program with training provided

UTAH ARTS COUNCIL
617 E. South Temple, Salt Lake City, UT 84102 (801) 236-7555 FAX (801) 236-7556 Contact: Tay Haines, Individual Artists Coord; or ATTN: Funding Resource Coordinator Program: grants of $1000 Deadline: postmarks: Feb. 1, 1999; Jun. 1, 1999; Oct. 1, 1999

VERMONT COUNCIL ON THE ARTS
136 State St. Drawer 33, Montpelier, VT 05633-6001 (802) 828-3291
FAX (802) 828-3363 Contact: Alexander Aldredge, Exec. Director
Program: Artist Development Grants ($250-$500) for individual artists
Deadline: Mar. 15, 1999

VIRGINIA COMMISSION FOR THE ARTS
223 Governor St., Richmond, VA 23219-2010 (804) 225-3132   FAX
(804) 225-4327 Contact: Peggy Baggett, Exec. Director Procedure: request "Program Guidelines"

WASHINGTON STATE ARTS COMMISSION
P.O. Box 42675, Olympia, WA 98504-2675 (360) 753-3860 FAX (360)
586-5351 Contact: Bitsy Bidwell, Program Mgr. for Community Development Program: $5000 fellowships for writers Procedure: contact
Artist Trust in Seattle (206) 467-8734

WEST VIRGINIA DIVISION OF CULTURE & HISTORY
ARTS & HUMANITIES SECTION 1900 Kanawha Blvd. E,
Cultural Center, Charleston, WV 25305-0300 (304) 558-0240 FAX
(304) 558-2779 Contact: Ms. Lakin Ray Cook, Director of Arts &
Humanities; or phone General Information: (304) 558-0220 Program:
various programs, including grants, fellowships, residencies, showcases
Procedure: request "Grants Programs" booklet

WISCONSIN ARTS BOARD
101 E. Wilson St. 1st Floor, Madison, WI 53702 (608) 266-0190 FAX
(608) 267-0380 Contact: George Tzougros, Exec. Director Individual
Artist Program Program: grants and fellowships Procedure: inquire
early in 1999 for amounts and deadlines

WYOMING COUNCIL ON THE ARTS
2320 Capitol Ave., Cheyenne, WY 82002 (307) 777-7742 FAX (307)
777-5499 Contact: Michael Shay, Mgr., Literature Program Program:
fellowships of $2000 Deadline TBA (summer 1999) Procedure:
request guidelines

The Playwright's
Submission Record

*

Cross Reference
to Special Interests

*

The Playwright's Calendar

*

The Playwright's Library

*

Index to Listings

The Playwright's Submission Record

Play title: _____ Draft: _____

Query submitted:_____
           (date)

    Accompanying materials: _____
    _____
    _____
    _____

Script submitted:_____
           (date)

    Accompanying materials: _____
    _____
    _____
    _____

Fee paid: $_____ Check deposited:_____
                                             (date)

To: Contact: _____

Organization: _____

Address: _____
            _____

Phone: (___)_____ FAX: (___)_____

E-mail: _____

SASP/SASE returned:_____
               (date)

Response expected:_____ Response received: _____
             (date)   (date)

Result: _____
        _____

Follow-up: _____
            _____

Cross Reference to Special Interests

Biblical/Christian/Religious Themes

A.D. Players 3
Baker's Plays 291
The Cunningham Prize 165
Encore Performance Publishing 294
Freed-Hardeman University Theatre 51
L.A.D.T. Play Commissioning Project 176
Lillenas Drama Resources/Lillenas Publishing Co. 296
Los Angeles Designers' Theatre 74
Love Creek Mini-Festivals 178
Master Arts Company 79
Saltworks Players Series 114
Saltworks Theatre Co. 114
Taproot Theatre Company 129
Trinity House Theatre 140
Veronica's Veil Theatre 145

Biographical & Historical Works

Abraham Lincoln Cabin Theatre 4
American Antiquarian Society Visiting Fellowships 216
American Living History Theater 11
Artreach Touring Theatre 18
California Theatre Center 28
Counter-Culture Monday Cafe Series 230
Creede Repertory Theatre 39
Cumberland County Playhouse 40
David James Ellis Memorial Award 165
Discovery Series (IN) 232
Drama Committee Repertory Theatre 44
Great American History Theatre 55
The Great Plains Play Contest 171
Margaret Bartle Annual Playwriting Contest 178
Metropolitan Playhouse 81
New Play Commissions in Jewish Theatre 254
PCPA Outreach Tour 98
Plays, The Drama Magazine for Young People 298
Pushcart Players 108
Shadow Light Productions 117
Studio Arena Theatre 127
Summerfield G. Roberts Award 199
Theatre Americana 130
Theater of the First Amendment 134
Theatre Outlet 135

Biographical & Historical Works (Continued)

Theatre West Virginia 137
TheatreWorks/USA 138, 279
Utah Shakespearean Festival 280

French-Language Plays

Camargo Foundation 227
Paris Writers' Workshop 262
Stages 124
The Theatre-Studio, Inc. 136, 278
Ubu Repertory Theatre 142, 302
Wice Paris Writers' Workshop 283

Gay & Lesbian Themes & Characters

About Face Theatre & Face to Face Workshop Series 4, 234
Bailiwick Pride Performance Series 223
Celebration Theatre 30
The Glines 54
Illusion Theater 61
Interborough Repertory Theatre 63
Love Creek Productions 74, 178
New Conservatory Theatre Center 87
Pillsbury House Theatre 101
Rainbow Artist Workshops 271
Sinister Wisdom 301
Theatre Rhinoceros 136
Wings Theatre Company 150

Health & Disability

Cleveland Signstage 35
Creative Productions 39
DBA (Deaf Bailiwick Artists) 223
Deaf West Theatre Company 41
Free Street Programs 51
Interborough Repertory Theatre 63
Jean Kennedy Smith Playwriting Award 174
Milwaukee Public Theatre 82
National AIDS Fund CFDA-Vogue Initiative Award 175
National Theatre of the Deaf 85
National Theatre Workshop for the Handicapped 254
Other Voices Summer Chatauqua Workshop 249
Pillsbury House Theatre 101
Resource Publications 300

Seniors' Issues, Older Actors, Older Audiences

The Playwright's Calendar 1999

Included in this calendar are specific deadlines for the 1999 calendar year. For dates yet to be announced or falling after December 31, 1999, request information from contacts indicated in the alphabetical listings. Also keep in mind that deadlines may be changed without notice--submit materials as far in advance of these dates as each organization allows.

January

March

March (Continued)

April

May

July

August

September

September (Continued)

15 The MacDowell Colony 247
    Virginia Center for the Creative Arts 282
20 Susan Smith Blackburn Prize 199
30 Baltimore Playwrights Festival 160
    Christopher Columbus Screenplay Discovery Awards 163
    Hawthornden Castle International Retreat 239
    Lama Ink! 296
    Paul Green Playwrights Prize 188

October

1 Hedgebrook 240
    John Simon Guggenheim Memorial Foundation Fellowship 244
    Minnesota State Arts Board 331
    New York Mills Arts Retreat 258
    New Visions/New Voices 244
    Norcroft, a Writing Retreat for Woman 259
    Rhode Island State Council on the Arts 333
    Sinister Wisdom 301
    Ucross Foundation Residencies 280
    Utah Arts Council 333
15 Mary Ingraham Bunting Fellowships 249
    New York Foundation Artists in Residence 258
    Playwrights First Plays-in-Progress Award 190
    Warner Center for the Arts CT One-Act Play Contest 205
23 USIA Fulbright Grants 241
31 Christopher Columbus Screenplay Discovery Awards 163
    Dayton Playhouse FutureFest 165
    National Hispanic Playwriting Award 183
    New York Stage and Film 90

November

1 American-Scandinavian Foundation 217
    Beverly Hills Theatre Guild-Julie Harris Competition 160
    Hambidge Center for Creative Arts 239
    National Endowment for the Humanities Projects in Media 254
    New York City 15 Minute Play Festival 186
    North Carolina Arts Council Fellowship 259, 332
    West Coast 10-Minute Playwriting Festival "Six at Eight" 206
2 The Richard Rodgers Awards 192
5 New York Foundation Artists in Residence 258
15 Collages and Bricolages 292
    Jenny McKean Moore Writer in Washington 243
    Playscape Festival 264
    L.A.D.T. Play Commissioning Project (satire) 176
    MRTW Script Contest 181

The Playwright's Library

Magazines, Trade Papers, and Newsletters

American Theatre

TCG, 355 Lexington Ave., New York, NY 10017-0217 (212) 697-5230 FAX (212) 557-5817 e-mail custserv@ tcg.org Monthly magazine dealing with the activities of not-for-profit theatres in the U.S. Includes articles, editorials, reviews. $4.95 per issue; $35 for 1 year (10 issues).

Back Stage

1515 Broadway, 14th Floor, New York, NY 10036-8986 (212) 764-7300 FAX (212) 536-5318 e-mail bstage96@aol.com Theatre weekly focusing on casting. Issues include "Playwrights' Corner" column, reviews, regional reports. $3.50 per issue (mail); $79 for 1 year/ $129 for 2 years.

Hollywood Scriptwriter

P.O. Box 10277, Burbank, CA 91510 (818) 845-5525 e-mail lgrantt@primenet.com Monthly newsletter essentially for screenwriters. Includes essays, interviews, advice, "Plays Wanted" section. Back issues available. $44 for 1 year (11 issues), $25 for 6 months.

Market Insight . . . for Playwrights

P.O. Box 1758, Champaign, IL 61824-1758 (800) 895-4720 e-mail minsight@aol.com Monthly newsletter for playswrights, providing submission policies and guidelines for theatres, contests, publishers, residencies, other programs. $40 for 1 year (12 issues; $25 for 6 months; free sample available on request.

Ollantay Theater Magazine

P.O. Box 720636, Jackson Heights, NY 11372-0636 (718) 565-6499 FAX (718) 446-7806 Semi-annual journal in English and Spanish featuring plays by Hispanic playwrights and articles by Hispanic critics and scholars. $18 per year for individual; $25 per year for organization.

PerformINK: Chicago's Entertainment Trade Paper

3223 N. Sheffield, Chicago, IL 60657 (773) 296-4600 FAX (773) 296-4621 e-mail performink@aol. com Bi-weekly publication featuring news items; reports (including "NY State of Mind" by Jeffrey Sweet), Theatre Listings (current shows), Production Listings, and "Film Scene"; Hotlines ads with a section on opportunities for writers. $32.95 for 1 year, $59.95 for 2 years, $84.95 for 3 years.

Show Music

Box 466, Goodspeed Landing, East Haddam, CT 06423-0466 (203) 873-8664 FAX (203) 873-2329 Quarterly magazine on the musical theatre, published by Goodspeed Opera House Foundation. Includes articles, reviews, new releases, "Composers' and Lyricists' Corner," film and video news. $5.95 per issue; $19 per year (U.S.A.).

Stage Directions

P.O. Box 41202, Raleigh, NC 27629 (919) 872-7888 FAX (919) 872-6888 e-mail stagedir@aol.com Monthly magazine for and about regional, community, academic theatre. Includes articles, letters, book reviews, Q & A. $3.50 per issue, $26 for 1 year (10 issues), $48 for 2 years.

Theater Magazine

222 York St., New Haven, CT 06520 (203) 432-1568 FAX (203) 432-8336 e-mail theatre.magazine@quickmail.yale.edu Academically oriented magazine. Includes essays, interviews, new scripts. $22 for 1 year, $40 for 2 years.

The Writer

120 Boylston St., Boston, MA 02116-4615 (617) 423-3157 FAX (617) 423-2168 Monthly magazine for aspiring and professional writers of all genres; each September issue focuses on play markets. $28 for 1 year (12 issues), $52 for 2 years, $75 for 3 years.

Books and Booklets

The Art of Dramatic Writing

Lajos Egri. 1942. Simon & Schuster, 1230 Ave. of the Americas, New York, NY 10020 (212) 698-7000 This 305-page hardback book presents the techniques of playwriting in four comprehensive chapters: "Premise," "Character," "Conflict," and "General." $10.95.

The Book: An Actor's Guide to Chicago

Edited by Kevin Heckman, Ghristine Gatto, Carrie L. Kaufman. 1998. PerformINK Books, 3223 N. Sheffield, Chicago, IL 60657 Essentially for actors, this 200-page paperback provides lists of Chicago theatres, literary agents, and writing programs. $15.00 + $3.00 shipping.

Characters in Action: Playwriting the Easy Way

Marsh Cassady. 1995. Meriwether Publishing. 885 Elkton Dr., Colorado Springs, CO 80907 (719) 594-4422 FAX (719) 594-9916 This paper-back comprises 12 chapters, providing an overview of the process. Topics include characters in conflict, plots and subplots, structure and dialogue, revision, and winning an audience. $14.95.

Copyright Basics

Register of Copyrights, Library of Congress, Washington, DC 20559 (202) 707-9100 (forms), (202) 707-3000 (information) This free brochure explains copyright in general terms. This and other materials are also available through the Internet: <www.loc.gov>.

Dramatists Sourcebook 1998-99

Edited by Kathy Sova and Wendy Weiner. TCG, 355 Lexington Ave., New York, NY 10017-0217 (212) 697-5230 FAX (212) 557-5817 e-mail custserv@tcg.org. This annual 340-page paperback, published each September, provides information on more than 1000 markets and opportunities for dramatic writers. Listings include non-profit theatres, contests, publishers, agents, grants, and more. $18.95 + $3.00 shipping.

The Dramatist's Toolkit
The Craft of the Working Playwright
Jeffrey Sweet. 1993. **Heinemann, 361 Hanover St., Portsmouth, NH 03801 (603) 431-7894 FAX (603) 431-7840.** This paperback describes the building blocks of playwriting, character relationships, and exposition and explores the similarities and differences in plays and musicals and in stage plays and screenplays. $13.95.

The Elements of Playwriting
Louis E. Catron. 1993. **Macmillan, 866 Third Ave., New York, NY 10022.** This 220-page hardback book begins with chapters devoted to inspiring creativity and then discusses characterization, plot, and dialogue in terms of creating a producible and marketable play. $18.00.

A Handbook for Literary Translators
1995. **PEN, 568 Broadway, New York, NY 10012 (212) 334-1660** This 35-page handbook contains "A Translator's Model Contract," discusses "Negotiating a Contract" and "The Responsibilities of Translation," and includes selected resources. $2.50 shipping included.

How Plays are Made
Stuart Griffiths. 1982. **Prentice Hall, Gloucester, NJ (800) 643-5506.** This 158-page paperback explores the techniques of dramatic construction in 14 brief chapters including discussions of such basics as thought, character, dialogue, and theme. $17.00.

Literary Agents: A Writer's Guide
Adam Begley. 1993. **Poets & Writers, 72 Spring St., New York, NY 10012 (212) 226-3586 FAX (212) 226-3963** e-mail pwsubs@aol.com. This 196-page paperback explains the services provided by literary agents and lists more than 200 agents. $10 + $3.90 shipping + tax.

The Playwright's Process
Buzz McLaughlin. 1997. **Back Stage Books, 1515 Broadway, New York, NY 10036 (212) 764-7300 FAX (212) 536-5318** e-mail bstage96@aol. com. This 288-page paperback culls ideas from interviews with some 16 contemporary American dramatists to support an exploration of the process of playwriting. $18.95.

The Playwright's Workbook
Jean-Claude van Itallie. 1997. **Applause, 211 W. 71st St., New York, NY 10023 (212) 496-7511 FAX (212) 721-2856.** This 142-page paperback uses a workshop/assignment approach; 13 chapters include dialogue, building blocks, plot, alienation, dreams, and production. $16.95.

Playwriting from Formula to Form
William Missouri Downs and Lou Anne Wright. 1998. **Harcourt Brace, 6277 Sea Harbor Dr., Orlando, FL 32887 (800) 782-4479** This 335-page paperback discusses readings, productions, screenplays, teleplays, and the playwriting process. The book concludes with a chapter on "Becoming a Playwright." $17.00.

Playwriting in Process
Michael Wright. 1997. Heinemann, 361 Hanover St., Portsmouth, NH 03801 (603) 431-7894 FAX (603) 431-7840. This 203-page paperback presents the playwriting process through an analysis of "etudes," defined as "the tools of theatre games,"developed in discussions of technique, character, plot, and structure. $17.95.

Playwriting: Writing, Producing, and Selling Your Play
Louis E. Catron. 1984. Waveland Press. This 272-page paperback emphasizes the writer's credo as well as the six Aristotelian elements of drama: plot, character, thought, diction, music, and spectacle. $15.95.

Professional Playscript Format Guidelines & Sample
Feedback Theatrebooks, 305 Madison Ave. #1146, New York, NY 10165 (800) 800-8671 FAX (207) 359-5532 e-mail feedback@hyper net.com This booklet explains all aspects of professional set-up: including title page, pagination, acts, scenes, dialogue, character titles, directions. Samples, "Margin & Tab Guide, included. $4.95 + $1.75 shipping.

Senior Theatre Connections
Edited by Bonnie L. Vorenberg, 1236 N.E. Siskiyou St., Portland, OR 97212 (503) 249-1137 FAX same e-mail bonnie@teleport.com This directory of senior theatre in the U.S.A. lists performance groups, practitioners, and others, both professional and amateur, working in the field and includes a bibliography and lists of organizations and resources. Mission: "Connecting senior arts to the information age." $15.

Stage Writers Handbook
Dana Singer. 1997. TCG 355 Lexington Ave., New York, NY 10017 (212) 697-5230 FAX (212) 557-5817 e-mail custserv@tcg.org. This 302-page paperbook, provides "a complete business guide for playwrights, composers, lyricists and librettists" through a discussion of copyright, collaboration, underlying rights, marketing and self-promotion, production contracts, representation by agents and lawyers, and publishing. $16.95 + $3.00 shipping.

Three Genres: The Writing of Poetry, Fiction, and Drama
By Stephen Minot. 1998. Prentice Hall, Gloucester, NJ (800) 643-5506 Inquire for a 30-day examination copy of this new paperback. $30.60.

Working on a New Play
Edward M. Cohen. 1988. Prentice Hall, Gloucester, NJ (800) 643-5506 This 216-page hardback book explores and explains the process of collaboration among writer, director, actors, and designers in the developmental process and discusses the elements involved in production.

A Writer's Guide to Copyright
Poets & Writers, 72 Spring St., New York, NY 10012 (212) 226-3586 FAX (212) 226-3963 e-mail pwsubs@aol.com. This 63 page-guide explains the functions of the Copyright Office, copyright law, and writer's rights and provides sample forms. $10 + $3.90 shipping + applicable tax.

Index to Listings

INDEX 357

INDEX 361

Feedback Theatrebooks
"All-American Plays Series"

Plays from *On Stage, America!*
(Now available individually.)

The Contrast (1787) by Royall Tyler, a biting and hilarious social commentary on conflicting English and American cultures, attitudes, and manners. Col. Manly, a stalwart American hero, finds romance in New York, while Jonathan, his unworldly servant, gets an education. $3.95.

Metamora (1829) by John Augustus Stone, a heart-rending social drama on the conflict between the "noble savage" and the white man, still relevant today. Metamora, chieftan and the last of his tribe, demands only fair treatment but resorts to bitter revenge when his trust is betrayed. $3.95.

The Stage-Struck Yankee (1840) by Oliver E. Durivage, a rollicking farce and spoof on the theatre. When a traveling company brings *Richard III* to town, Zachariah Hotspear, an impressionable young "bumpkin," fancies himself in love with the leading lady. Chaos reigns until common sense and true love save the day. $2.95.

Fashion (1845) by Anna Cora Mowatt, a good-natured comic satire on hypocrisy and pretension. A phony French count, a scheming villain, a meddlesome spinster, and a housemaid with a "past" are sure to delight every reader. $3.95.

Glance at New York (1848) by Benjamin A. Baker, a hilarious romp through mid-19th century Manhattan, introducing Mose the fire b'hoy whose antics kept him popular for years. $2.95.

Rip Van Winkle (1865) by Joseph Jefferson (with some dramaturgical assistance from Dion Boucicault), a touching rendition of Washington Irving's classic tale which kept Joe Jefferson on the stage for decades. $3.95.

Under the Gaslight (1867) by Augustin Daly, the quintessential "hiss-the-villain" melodrama of the 19th century American stage, tempered with a keen social insight. Crisp dialogue, exciting action, and a breath-taking rescue keep this play on the boards today. $3.95.

Young Mrs. Winthrop (1882) by the "Dean of American Drama," Bronson Howard, a perceptive comedy-drama on American life. Home and business find themselves at odds, and a good marriage is threatened--until an old friend applies humor and common sense. A blind girl, her ardent beau, and a plain-spoken "lady of society" round out a delightful cast. $3.95.

The Old Homestead (1886) by Denman Thompson, local color and down-home wisdom combined in a folksy work of Americana still performed every season at the Potash Bowl in West Swanzey, N.H. Uncle Josh Whitcomb goes to New York to find his errant son, soothes his weepy sister, patches up a long-standing feud, and steals the show! $4.95.

Margaret Fleming (1890) by James A. Herne, later called "epoch marking," but a failure in its own time (audiences rejected the "details of unpleasant and unhealthy forms of unruly life" which the play was seen to present). An unfaithful husband brings tragedy upon his family and others, but his strong and tenacious wife prevails. $3.95.

A Trip to Chinatown (1891) by Charles H. Hoyt, the longest running play in New York to that date, in which generational warfare, the battle of the sexes, and a lovable hypochondriac-- of the variety found only in America--create a racy farce. $2.95.

The Girl of the Golden West (1905) by David Belasco, dramatizing the traditions of the American West: a rowdy saloon; a colorful collection of miners; a spirited if ingenuous heroine; a pair of uniquely American anti-heroes; and a hair-raising, winner-take-all poker game. Here are all the features of fine drama--suspense, action, romance, pathos, humor! $4.95.

Et Cetera, Et Cetera, Et Cetera!

Cross-Referencing *The Playwright's Companion*

You don't have to make your way through *The Playwright's Companion* listing-by-listing to find the right markets and opportunities! *Et Cetera, Et Cetera, Et Cetera!* does it for you! Locate everyone who produces One-Acts, Musicals, Comedies, Experimental Plays, Children's Plays, Issue Plays, Works by Local Writers, and many more! You can even locate every theatre in your home state--just by turning a page! $2.95.

✉ Mail this Order Form to:

Feedback Theatrebooks, Order Dept.
P.O. Box 220, Brooklin, ME 04616

or FAX: 1-207-359-5532

or E-mail: feedback@hypernet.com

Name _____ Phone (____)_____

Address _____

City, State, Zip _____

Qty.	Book Title	Amt. Due
____	_____	_____
____	_____	_____
____	_____	_____
____	_____	_____
____	_____	_____
____	_____	_____
____	_____	_____
____	_____	_____

Subtotal: _____

SALES TAX -- ME residents add 5.5%, NY residents add 8.25%.: _____

SHIPPING: $3.00 for 1st book, $1.75 <u>each</u> for the next 2 books, 60¢ each additional book: _____

Total: $ _____

METHOD OF PAYMENT (Payment must accompany order.)

Check or money order enclosed__ Amt. Enclosed: $_____

Visa __ or MasterCard __ #: __ __ __ __-__ __ __ __-__ __ __ __-__ __ __ __

Exp. date: ____/____ Name on credit card: _____

Signature _____

*** Free catalog available on request. ***